The Routledge Companion
to Medieval Warfare

This comprehensive volume provides easily accessible factual material on all major areas of warfare in the medieval west. The whole geographical area of medieval Europe, including eastern Europe, is covered, together with essential elements from outside Europe such as Byzantine warfare, nomadic horde invasions and the Crusades.

The Routledge Companion to Medieval Warfare is presented in themed, illustrated sections, each preceded by a narrative outline offering a brief introduction. Within each section, Jim Bradbury presents clear information on battles and sieges, and generals and leaders. Readable and engaging, this detailed work makes use of archaeological information and includes clear discussions of controversial issues. The author examines practical topics including castle architecture, with descriptions of specific castles, shipbuilding techniques, improvements in armour, specific weapons, and developments in areas such as arms and armour, fortifications, tactics and supply.

Jim Bradbury taught at a secondary school for ten years before becoming a senior lecturer and head of section for history at Borough Road College, now part of Brunel University. He has written widely on medieval history, with an emphasis on military history.

The Routledge Companion
to Medieval Warfare

JIM BRADBURY

Routledge
Taylor & Francis Group

LONDON AND NEW YORK

First published 2004 by Routledge
11 New Fetter Lane, London EC4P 4EE

Simultaneously published in the USA and Canada by Routledge
29 West 35th Street, New York, NY 10001

Routledge is an imprint of the Taylor & Francis Group

Typeset in Trump Mediaeval by The Running Head Limited, Cambridge
Printed and bound in Great Britain by TJ International Ltd, Padstow, Cornwall

British Library Cataloguing in Publication Data
A catalogue record for this book is available from the British Library

Library of Congress Cataloging in Publication Data
Bradbury, Jim
The Routledge companion to medieval warfare / Jim Bradbury
p. cm.
Includes bibliographical reference and index.
1. Military art and science— Europe—History—To 1500.
2. Military history, Medieval. 3. Middle Ages. I Title.

U37.B63 2004
355'.0094'0902—DC 22   2003020094

ISBN 0–415–22126–9 (Hardcover)

To Will and Maisie who have joined us since my last book

Contents

CONTENTS

Preface

This book has been nearly five years in the making. The idea was first put to me by the publisher and agreed with Heather McCallum, who has since moved on. Vicky Peters has taken over the unenviable task of keeping an eye on the project. It has been my intention to make the work enjoyable rather than a chore. I should also like to thank Carole Drummond and the people at The Running Head for their work in preparing the manuscript for publication. They have been extremely careful and accurate in their suggested corrections. I can honestly say that of the eight or so books I have so far had published they have done the best work of this nature that I have encountered. The length may be deceptive but certainly does not imply comprehensive cover. Firstly the book only attempts to look at warfare in medieval Europe, with the Crusades included as a western venture. Then, early on, it became clear that one must be selective in every area if the material was to be contained within one volume. It is therefore obvious that there must be omissions. My thanks for help go to my many friends in the field of medieval warfare who have talked over some areas included in the book, including Matt Bennett, Nick Hooper, John Gillingham, Cyril Edwards and many others. I hope that the book will be of use to students of the subject at various levels who can use it as a starting point. Probably the most useful part is the (very select) bibliography, from which the works mentioned will undoubtedly lead on the interested reader to many other contributors to this subject. I can only say that history has been a lifelong friend to me and I hope it may be to others.

Jim Bradbury
Selsey November 2003

PART I

Generals and leaders, A–Z

Generals and leaders, A–Z

ABD-AL-RĀHMAN III, AL-NĀSIR (THE VICTORIOUS), CALIPH OF CÓRDOBA (889–961)

Umayyad Emir of Córdoba from 912, Caliph from 929. This was the start of an independent Iberian Muslim state – al-Andalus. From a reduced territory around Córdoba he expanded his power over much of Iberia, uniting the Muslims and taking tribute from Christian powers. His rule is seen as the golden age of the caliphate. His successes included the taking of Seville, Beja and Toledo. He defeated León at Pamplona in 920. He suffered defeat by Ramiro II of León at Simancas and Alhandega in 939, and at Talavera in 951, but lost little territory. His interests moved to North Africa where he captured Ceuta in 931 and Tangier in 951. He developed a Mediterranean navy. He was succeeded by his son al-Hakim II.

ABŪ YŪSUF YA'QŪB, AL-MANSŪR, ALMOHAD CALIPH (d.1199)

Caliph from 1184. He assumed al-Mansūr (the victorious) as a title. His reign in North Africa began with a six-year civil war, which allowed the Christian *Reconquista* in Iberia to advance. Abū Yūsuf took an army to Iberia in 1190. In 1191 he recovered Silves from Portugal. In 1195 he defeated Alfonso VIII of Castile at Alarcos. He besieged Madrid in 1197 but failed to take it. On his return to Marakesh in 1198 he fell ill and died in January 1199. He was succeeded by his son al-Nāsir.

ADHÉMAR (OF MONTEIL) OF LE PUY (d.1098)

Adhémar of Monteil, bishop of Le Puy, was the religious leader of the First Crusade. His ancestors were the Counts of Valentinois. In 1086 he made a pilgrimage to Jerusalem. He was the first to take the crusading vow at Clermont-Ferrand in 1095 and was appointed by Urban II to lead the crusaders. Le Puy was the assembly point for the Crusade. Although the People's Crusade ignored this and went ahead, most knightly leaders brought their men to Le Puy. Adhémar travelled with Raymond of Toulouse and helped give unity to the Crusade. Before reaching Constantinople Adhémar was wounded and captured by Pechenegs, though released when found to be a bishop. He died on 1 August of disease (probably typhoid) at Antioch, a loss to the Crusade's unity.

AEGIDIUS (d.464)

Roman general for Emperor Majorian, a member of the Syagrii family, Gallo-Roman aristocrats near Lyons. At Soissons he established a Roman enclave, which Gregory of Tours called a kingdom. He defeated Odoacer at Angers, and the Visigoths at Orléans, 463. He favoured an alliance with the Vandals, possibly the reason for his death by poisoning. He was succeeded by his son Syagrius. Through Aegidius the region became the land of the Franks rather than the Goths.

AELLE, KING OF SUSSEX

According to the *Anglo-Saxon Chronicle* he led the south coast invasion in 477 with his sons, Cymen, Wlencing and Cissa. They landed at *Cymenes ora* (Cymen's landing place), probably Selsey Bill. In 485 Aelle defeated the British at Mearcredesburna on an unidentified river frontier. They were driven into the forest of the Weald. Aelle captured the stronghold of Anderida (Pevensey) in 491 and slaughtered all within. He established the kingdom of the South Saxons (Sussex) and was named first *Bretwalda* (wide ruler), showing his prominent position in the early invasion period. He may have ruled an area greater than Sussex. Several Sussex names derive from his sons, including Chichester from Cissa – renaming the old Roman town – and Lancing from Wlencing.

AETHELRED II, UNRAED (THE UNREADY) (c.966–1016)

King of England from 978, son of Edgar. He became king at the age of about 12 when his half-brother, Edward (the Martyr), was murdered at Corfe possibly with the connivance of Aethelred's mother. Aethelred's second marriage in 1002 was to Emma, daughter of Richard I duke of Normandy, a continental alliance with far-reaching consequences. The nickname 'Unraed' ('badly advised' rather than 'unready') was applied after his death and was a pun on his name Aethelred, which meant 'well advised'. His failures came largely from Scandinavian threats, including invasions by Ólaf Tryggvason, Thorkell the Tall and Sweyn Forkbeard. Ólaf won the Battle of Maldon in 991. Aethelred has been widely criticised for paying danegeld on five occasions, but these tributes bought time. He did combat the Scandinavians at sea. Internal opposition from Eadric Streona weakened England against outside attack. Aethelred was accused of attempting to kill all the Danes in England in the St Brice's Day Massacre of 1002, though his aims were probably more restricted. Nevertheless the act provoked Scandinavian retaliation. Sweyn Forkbeard invaded England in 1013 and forced Aethelred into exile in Normandy. He returned on Sweyn's death but soon died, leaving his son Edmund to dispute the kingdom with Cnut.

AETHELSTAN (ATHELSTAN) (894–939)

King of England from 924 (crowned 925), on the death of his father Edward the Elder. He continued to rule all the English. His father's base was Wessex but Aethelstan was brought up in Mercia. The kingdom of England was practically completed by his northern conquests. He ruled Northumbria, Wessex and Mercia and took over the Viking kingdom of York. In 934 he invaded Scotland. At Brunanburh in 937 he overcame his northern enemies – the Scots, Irish and men of Strathclyde. Under him the Wye became the Anglo-Welsh frontier. Aethelstan established power over British Cornwall. He had continental interests and his fleet intervened in Francia. He issued four law codes. He had neither wife nor children and died on 27 October.

AËTIUS (c.390–454)

A general during the collapse of the western Roman Empire, sometimes called 'the last of the Romans'. He was the main power in Gaul after his victory over his rival Boniface. He halted Visigothic expansion towards the Rhône in 436. He used barbarian troops in his armies, including the Huns, defeating the Burgundians who had established themselves on the Rhine. They moved instead to Burgundy, between Lyons and Geneva. In alliance with Burgundians, Visgoths and Franks, he defeated Attila the Hun in 451 at the Catalaunian Plains, keeping the Huns out of Gaul. In 454 he was assassinated through Valentinian III. His followers in turn killed the emperor in 455.

AFONSO ENRIQUES, KING OF PORTUGAL (1110–85)

Ruler of the county of Portugal and its first king – son and successor of Henry of Burgundy count of Portugal, who died in 1112. He overcame the hostile force of his mother Teresa. He won victories over the Muslims, notably at Ourique in 1139. In 1140 he declared himself King of Portugal, recognised by Castile in 1143. By 1147 he extended his authority south to the Tagus. He took Lisbon in 1147 with aid from the Second Crusade. He was captured by the Muslims at Badajoz 1169 but was later released. He captured Santarem in 1171. In 1184 Yūsuf invaded Portugal but his death in that year ended the attempt. Afonso died on 6 December and was succeeded by his son Sancho I.

AISTULF, KING OF THE LOMBARDS (d.756)

King from 749, he contributed to making the Lombard Laws, including that men should possess arms appropriate to their wealth. In 751 he seized the Exarchate of Ravenna from the Byzantines. Aistulf posed a threat to the papacy, invading the duchy of Rome in 752. He was forced to accept peace but broke the agreed terms. In 754 Pope Stephen II travelled to Francia seeking aid against him. Pepin the Short, by the Donation of Pepin, promised to restore what the Lombards had taken. In return the pope made Pepin and his sons patricians and recognised the dynastic change in Francia from Merovingians to Carolingians. Carloman, brother of Pepin the Short, represented the Lombards in negotiations but was imprisoned for his trouble. Aistulf

refused to yield to Pepin's demands and the latter invaded Lombardy to fulfil his promise to the pope. The Lombards were defeated in the Valley of Susa in 755 and the Franks besieged Pavia where Aistulf took refuge. He agreed terms while Pavia was still holding out but broke his promises within the year. Pepin with Tassilo of Bavaria invaded again in 756. Pavia was besieged and Aistulf surrendered, dying shortly afterwards when thrown from his horse against a tree while hunting. He left no heir. Pepin the Short initiated the process that would lead to Frankish rule of Lombardy.

ALARIC I, KING OF THE VISIGOTHS (c.370–410)

King from 395 who sacked Rome. He established authority over the Visigoths in the Balkans, acting as commander for the Eastern Emperor Theodosius I, fighting in the victory at Frigidius in 394. He defeated the usurper Eugenius but rebelled against Theodosius and moved west with his people, invading Italy in 401. He was defeated by the Roman commander Stilicho at Pollentia in 402, making peace in 407. Alaric was disappointed not to receive greater recognition within the Roman Empire. When Stilicho was executed by the Western Emperor Honorius in 408, Alaric rebelled again. His people caused devastation in Italy and attacked Rome, which he besieged three times, taking it in 410 – seen as a vital moment in the collapse of the Western Empire. It was the first time that outsiders had taken the city since the Gauls in 390 BC. Alaric planned to invade Sicily and Africa but storms destroyed his fleet. He died at Cosenza and was buried in the bed of the River Busentus.

AL-ASHRAF, SULTAN OF EGYPT (d.1293)

Al-Malik al-Ashraf Khalil was the son of Qalawun, whom he succeeded in 1290 as Mamluke Sultan. Qalawun on his deathbed made him promise to continue attacking the Christians. Al-Ashraf overcame a palace plot and led the final assault on the crusading state, besieging Acre in 1291. He brought a large army and a hundred siege engines, camping opposite the Tower of the Legate. Acre fell in less than a month and was razed to the ground. The few remaining Christian strongholds soon surrendered or were taken. Al-Ashraf made advances in Armenia in 1292. He was murdered on 13 December by his own emirs, fearing his ambitions. He was succeeded by his son al-Nasir who brought trophies from Acre to decorate his father's tomb in Cairo.

ALBERT (ALBRECHT) II, HOLY ROMAN EMPEROR (1397–1439)

King of the Romans from 1438, establishing Habsburg rule of the Holy Roman Empire until its collapse in 1806 (with a gap 1742–65). The last Luxembourg emperor died in 1438. Albert had shown himself an able military commander. He was made Margrave of Moravia by Emperor Sigismund, whose daughter he married. He shared rule of Austria with his brother Leopold. Leopold was killed at Sempach against the Swiss. Albert duke of Austria was elected emperor at Frankfurt. He succeeded Sigismund as king in Hungary and Bohemia. His reign was disturbed by the break-up of imperial power and the separate claims of Poland, Hungary and Bohemia. Albert died on 27 October having become ill campaigning against the Turks in Hungary. Albert's posthumous son, Ladislas, succeeded to Bohemia.

ALBOIN, KING OF THE LOMBARDS (d. c.572)

He led the Lombards from Pannonia (Hungary) to invade and settle Italy from 568. He besieged Pavia while other Lombards attacked the Franks. It was three years before Pavia surrendered. Alboin defeated the Ostrogoths and married Rosamond, daughter of the King of the Gepids. He established the kingdom of Lombardy in northern Italy, with his capital at Verona. His wife, previously made to drink from the skull of her murdered father, poisoned him in revenge and then married her fellow conspirator.

ALBRET, CHARLES D' (d.1415)

Leader of the French army at Agincourt, Constable of France. In 1368 his father, the Lord of Albret in Gascony, appealed against the authority of the Black Prince to the King of France. Charles' mother was Margaret of Bourbon, related to the Valois kings. He fought for Charles VI at Roosebeke in 1382 and in 1390 went on crusade to Tunis. He inherited the Albret lordship in 1401. He married Marie de Sully. Charles opposed the English in the south, extending French control to the Dordogne by 1405. He was appointed Constable in 1403. He advanced from Poitou and captured all the fortresses south of Saintonge. After 1407 he switched to the Orléanist party and lost his position as Master of Crossbowmen and Constable. He turned to Henry IV of England for aid. In 1412 he was besieged in Bourges. In 1413 he regained the Constableship and was made castellan of Melun. He was with the royal army that besieged Compiègne in 1414. When Henry V invaded Normandy Charles pursued Henry V. When the French attacked at Agincourt Charles commanded the French van with Marshal Boucicaut. He was killed in the battle and buried in the Friary Church at Hesdin. His son Charles succeeded to the lordship.

ALEXANDER II, KING OF SCOTS (1198–1249)

King from 1214 on the death of his father, William the Lion. Alexander invaded England against John in alliance with English rebels and Louis of France. Alexander won territory in the north but was beaten in 1216 near London. In 1222 he took Argyll from its Viking rulers. He made peace with England, marrying Henry III's sister Joan. In 1237, by the Treaty of York, he abandoned claims to Northumberland, Cumberland and Westmorland, defining the Anglo-Scottish frontier. He sought to win the Western Isles but died on the island of Kerrera in Oban Bay on 8 July and was succeeded by his son Alexander III.

ALEXANDER III, KING OF SCOTS (1241–86)

King from 1249 on the death of his father Alexander II though he only assumed power in 1260. His mother was Margaret de Coucy, Alexander II's second wife. There were divisions during the minority between the Comyns and the Durwards. Alexander continued efforts to win the Western Isles and the Isle of Man from Norway. He won the Battle of Largs in 1263 and Norway submitted in 1266 by the Treaty of Perth. Alexander married first Margaret daughter of Henry III and then Yolande de Dreux. The reign was later seen as a golden age. Three of his children died in the 1280s and Alexander died on 19 March when thrown from his horse, leaving no male successor.

ALEXIUS I COMNENUS, BYZANTINE EMPEROR (1048–1118)

Emperor from 1081, restoring much imperial territory. He was emperor during the First Crusade and the hero of his daughter Anna Comnena's *Alexiad*. His wife was Irene. He commanded armies before becoming emperor and was an able diplomat. He succeeded through a coup against Nikephorus III. He faced attacks on Byzantine territory by the Italian Normans under Robert Guiscard, including an attempt on Durazzo that was held off. He defeated the Pechengs at Levunium. He employed Turkish mercenaries and allied with Venice, to whom he granted privileges. Alexius recovered territory in Europe. He rebuilt the navy, regaining Crete and Cyprus. He manoeuvred the Franks on the First Crusade through his territory and into Asia Minor. As a result of the Crusade's success he recovered much of Anatolia from the Turks. He received some recognition from the new crusading states. His son John II succeeded.

ALEXIUS IV ANGELUS, BYZANTINE EMPEROR (d.1204)

Emperor during the Fourth Crusade. He sought aid from the west for his father, the deposed and blinded Isaac II. He attended a conference that led to the Fourth Crusade. When the crusaders attacked Constantinople in 1203, Alexius III fled. Isaac II was released from prison, and his son Alexius IV became co-emperor. He broke his promises to the crusaders and failed to destroy the Venetian fleet. Murzuphlus, son-in-law of Alexius III, led a rebellion in Constantinople. Alexius IV was garrotted and Murzuphlus became Alexius V. The crusaders captured Constantinople and set up the Latin Empire.

ALEXIUS V DUKAS (MURZUPHLUS/BLACK-BROWED), BYZANTINE EMPEROR (d.1205)

Took power during the attack on Constantinople in the Fourth Crusade. Alexius III fled from the attackers. The nickname Murzuphlus referred to his bushy black eyebrows. He rebelled against Alexius IV and Isaac II. Alexius IV was put to death. Murzuphlus took the throne as Alexius V in 1204. He led the defence against a renewed Frankish attack but, when the Franks broke in, he fled to Thrace. He married Eudocia, daughter of Alexius III. He quarrelled with his father-in-law who had him blinded. He was captured by the Franks, taken to Constantinople, and thrown to his death from the column of Theodosius.

ALFONSO I, EL BATTALADOR (THE BATTLER), KING OF ARAGÓN (1073–1134)

King of Aragón and Navarre from 1104, succeeding his brother Pedro I. He married Urraca of Castile in 1109 but the marriage failed. Alfonso may have been impotent. He defeated Urraca's troops at Sepúlveda in 1111. His efforts advanced the *Reconquista* and made Aragón a major Iberian power. He conquered the Ebro Valley and captured Zaragoza in 1118. From 1125 he raided south against Valencia, Granada and Málaga. He established Extremadura on the frontier, organised in new military zones. In 1133 he captured Mequinenza but was defeated by the Muslims at Fraga in 1134. He died on 7 September, when his lands were divided.

ALFONSO III, THE GREAT, KING OF ASTURIAS (d.910)

King from 866 of the small northern Iberian kingdom of Oviedo. He advanced the Christian frontier, defeating the Muslims of Toledo in 874. He took over Zamora and Toro on the Duero. His power extended westwards to Coimbra. His name is attached to a chronicle of early medieval Spain. He was succeeded in turn by his sons García and Ordoño II.

ALFONSO VI, KING OF CASTILE AND LEÓN (1030–1109)

King from 1065, initially in León, son and successor of Ferdinand I. He called himself King of León and later Emperor of all Spain. He defeated his brother Sancho II and took over Castile in 1070. Sancho died in 1072. Alfonso married first Agnes daughter of the Duke of Aquitaine, then Constance of Burgundy and four other wives. El Cid commanded his army with success before he quarrelled with the king and was exiled in 1081. Alfonso captured Toledo in 1085, a major step in the *Reconquista*, but was defeated by Yūsuf at Zalaka in 1086. In 1093 he took over Santarem, Lisbon and Cintra. He died on 30 June and was succeeded by his daughter Urraca.

ALFONSO VII, KING OF CASTILE AND LEÓN (1105–57)

King of Galicia from 1112, of Castile and León from 1126, son of Urraca. He married Berengaria daughter of the Count of Barcelona. He imposed his power on Aragón and Navarre. He recognised the independence of his cousin Afonso Enriques in Portugal in 1143. Alfonso invaded the southern Muslim territories, taking Zaragoza in 1134. He claimed to be Emperor of Spain in 1135. He took Córdoba in 1144 but lost it again. He was defeated and killed at Muradel on 21 August. His lands were divided between his sons, Sancho III in Castile and Ferdinand II in León.

ALFONSO VIII, KING OF CASTILE (1155–1214)

King from 1158, son of Sancho III. His minority was troubled by civil war until 1169. He married Eleanor daughter of Henry II of England. He was defeated at Alarcos by the Muslims in 1195. He also fought off invasions by León and Navarre. He conquered the Basque region. He formed an alliance of Christian powers, agreeing boundaries with Aragón in 1179. He captured Cuenca in 1177. He was a commander at Las Navas de Tolosa in 1212 and Fabraegen in 1213. He patronised the Order of Santiago. He was succeeded by his son Enrique I.

ALFONSO X, EL SABIO (THE WISE), KING OF CASTILE AND LEÓN (1221–84)

King from 1252, son and successor of Ferdinand III. His attempt to introduce succession by the eldest son and his descendants caused civil war with his younger son Sancho. His daughter Eleanor married Edward I of England. Alfonso was known as 'the Wise' from his intellectual interests; he was a great patron, a poet and a supporter of universities. He claimed the Holy Roman Empire through his mother Beatrice of Swabia and was elected in 1257, abandoning the claim in 1275. He captured Cádiz in 1262 and Cartagena in 1263. Following agreement with Jaime I of Aragón he invaded Granada in 1265. He conquered Murcia in 1266. Through his son Sancho he was declared deposed in 1282. Alfonso died on 4 April and, against his wishes, Sancho IV succeeded.

ALFONSO XI, KING OF CASTILE AND LEÓN (1310–49)

King from 1312, son and successor of Ferdinand IV. The minority was disturbed by civil war until 1325. Alfonso overcame this and advanced the *Reconquista*. In alliance with Portugal he defeated the Muslims at Salado in 1340. He won at the River Palmones in 1343. He captured Algeciras in 1344. He died of the Black Death on 26 March when attempting to recover Gibraltar, which the Muslims had recaptured earlier in his reign.

ALFRED THE GREAT, KING OF WESSEX (849–89)

King from 871, when the Vikings were threatening to take over all the English kingdoms. Only Wessex survived. The fifth son of King Aethelwulf, Alfred succeeded his brother Aethelred I (865–71). After defeat at Reading, Alfred won his first important victory at Ashdown in Berkshire. He led the army into action for his brother who was praying. In 878 Alfred was surprised by the Danes at Chippenham and retreated to Athelney in Somerset marshland. A later tale had him burning the cakes of a peasant woman. He eventually raised a force and advanced against the Danes. Alfred's most famous victory was at Edington in 878, where he besieged and defeated the enemy. England was then divided and Guthrum agreed to conversion, confirmed by the Peace of Wedmore. Alfred relieved Rochester in 885 and took London in 886. According to the *Anglo-Saxon Chronicle* he was accepted as king by all the English claiming independence from the Danes, a vital step towards a unified kingdom of England. Alfred reorganised the army on a rotation basis with forces on call throughout the year. He organised a fleet, seen as the beginning of an English navy. Alfred fortified strongholds or burhs throughout his lands as garrison centres; most became urban centres. Alfred was noted for cultural and literary interests. He died on 26 October and was buried at Winchester. His son Edward the Elder succeeded. Alfred's successors provided the first kings of England.

AL-KAMIL, AL-MALIK, SULTAN OF EGYPT (1178–1238)

Al-Malik al-Kamil was nephew of Saladin and son of al-Adil, succeeding as Ayyubid Sultan in 1218 when his brother al-Mu'azzam inherited Damascus. Al-Kamil led troops for his father. Al-Adil reunited the lands ruled by Saladin. Al-Kamil opposed the Fifth Crusade, recovering Damietta after its loss to the crusaders. In 1229 al-Kamil agreed a treaty with Frederick II (HRE), making concessions that were unpopular with his own people. He took over Baghdad, capturing Damascus in 1238. He died on 8 March at Damascus, leading to civil war between his sons.

AL-MANSŪR (ABŪ AMIR MUHAMMAD IBN ABĪ AMIR AL-MAAFIRI) (940–1002)

Regent of the Caliphate of Córdoba from 976 on the death of al-Hakim II when he became vizier for Hishām II. He was the son of a scholar, becoming tutor to Hishām and lover of the Queen Mother (the Basque Subh or Aurora). He ruled the caliphate, commanding the Umayyad forces against the Christians. He employed Berber mercenaries. In 981 he conquered León, winning at Simancas and capturing Zamora. He sacked Barcelona in 985 and Santiago de Compostella in 997. In North Africa he captured Fez in 998 and suppressed rebellion in Morocco. The name al-Mansūr means 'the victorious'. He died at Medinaceli after a victorious raid against Castile.

ALP ARSLAN, SELJUK SULTAN (d.1072)

Sultan of the Seljuk Turks from 1063, presenting a new threat to Byzantium. He was the son of Chagrai Beg, whom he succeeded as Governor of Khurasan in 1058. He succeeded his uncle Toghril Beg as Sultan. He defeated the Byzantines in the significant Battle of Manzikert 1071. His long moustaches had to be tied behind his back when he hunted. He invaded Armenia in 1064. He defeated the Byzantines at Media in 1069 but was beaten at Heraklea. He captured the border town of Manzikert but failed to take Edessa. At Manzikert in 1071 he decisively defeated Romanus IV, who was captured though later released on terms. Alp Arslan captured Nicaea and Antioch, winning most of Anatolia and Syria. He captured Jerusalem from the Fatimids in 1071, provoking the Christian crusading movement. Alp Arslan invaded Turkestan, defeating Yakub at Berzem 1072. Yakub was captured, but killed Alp Arslan when brought before him. Alp's son Malik Shah succeeded.

AMALASUNTHA, QUEEN OF THE OSTROGOTHS (d.535)

Ruler after the death of her father, Theoderic the Great, on behalf of her son Athalaric, until his death, 534. Her control included the conduct of military affairs. She continued to have power during the reign of her cousin, Theodehad, but was finally put to death on his orders, at the behest of nobles seeking revenge for deaths she had ordered when in power. She was imprisoned and strangled. Her death was the excuse used by Justinian for his invasion of Italy.

AMALRIC I, KING OF JERUSALEM (1136-74)

Son of Fulk king of Jerusalem and Melisende; brother and in 1162 successor to Baldwin III. He was Count of Jaffa and Ascalon. He married Agnes of Courtenay daughter of Joscelyn II of Edessa. He strengthened the crown's legal position by issuing the *Assise sur la ligece*, insisting on direct allegiance from lesser vassals. He invaded Fatimid Egypt three times. The Syrian Muslims under Nur ed-Din, Shirkuh and Saladin sought to block his efforts. The Egyptians, fearing domination, allied with Amalric to besiege the Syrian camp – though without success. The alliance was renewed in 1167, leading to the capture of Alexandria in 1167 and Bilbeis in 1168. When the Syrians won Egypt, Amalric was isolated. He allied with Byzantium and led an expedition against Egypt in 1169. He besieged Damietta but withdrew. On the death of Nur-ed-Din, Amalric arranged for an attack on Egypt by a Norman Sicilian fleet. The plans were dropped when Amalric caught dysentery and died on 11 July. After his death the power of the kingdom weakened. His son succeeded as Baldwin IV and his daughter Sibylla was mother to Baldwin V.

AMBROSIUS AURELIANUS

A leader of Romano-Britons and precursor of Arthur, who resisted the Anglo-Saxon advance in the 5th century. According to Gildas he was the victor of the Battle of Mount Badon. The name is Latin but otherwise little is known of him. According to Gildas he was 'perhaps last of the Romans . . . a gentleman . . . whose parents had worn the purple'. Possibly he had imperial ancestors. An Ambrosius had rivalled Vortigern in the 430s and may have been our Ambrosius' father. Gildas also says his descendants still ruled in his own day, the mid-6th century, which might suggest Ambrosius was a Romanised Briton. To confuse the picture further, an Irish version of *Nennius* makes Ambrosius a ruler in Brittany. It is not easy to reconcile these references. His fate is unknown.

ANDRONICUS I COMNENUS, BYZANTINE EMPEROR (1128-85)

Emperor from 1183, the last of the Comneni, nephew of John II. He was over six feet tall. He was renowned for his efforts in bed and battle. He once serenaded the beautiful Philippa of Antioch (28 years younger than him) beneath her window. He married Theodora, widow of the King of Jerusalem. He became Governor of Pontus. He led a rebellion in 1182, marching on Constantinople and becoming regent for and then co-emperor with the young Alexius II. He killed Alexius and married his widow Anna (he was 64, she 12). This caused a Norman invasion of Greece in which Thessalonika was captured, turning feeling against Andronicus. He attacked the

Latin residents in Constantinople – a popular policy – but later made terms with the Venetians. Andronicus attempted to reduce noble power and commenced a reign of terror. Eventually the mob turned on him. He was found hiding behind casks of wine and was paraded through the streets riding backwards on a camel. He was hacked to death, his remains thrown into the sea. He was replaced by Isaac II Angelus.

ANDRONICUS II PALAEOLOGUS, BYZANTINE EMPEROR (1257–1330)

Emperor 1282–1328, son of Michael VIII. He repudiated his father's acceptance of Roman Christianity but married the Frankish Princess Yolanda (renamed Irene). Under him Byzantine power and territory declined. He attempted economies by reducing army and navy numbers while employing mercenaries. The Ottoman Turks advanced in Anatolia. There were attacks by Charles of Anjou, the Serbs and Venice – the latter capturing Mediterranean islands. Andronicus made peace with the Serbs, marrying his daughter to King Milutin. He employed the Catalan Company against the Turks but it became discontented and turned against the Byzantines, seizing Athens. A crusade was prepared by Charles of Anjou but did not occur. Andronicus made peace and began a slow recovery, interrupted from 1321 by civil war against his grandson Andronicus III. Andronicus II was deposed in 1328. He remained in Constantinople until 1320, when he took the name Antonius and entered the monastery where he died.

ANDRONICUS III PALAEOLOGUS, BYZANTINE EMPEROR (1296–1341)

Emperor from 1328, co-emperor since 1325, grandson of Andronicus II. His second wife was Anne of Savoy. He held a western-style tournament to celebrate his son's birth. He planned to kill his mistress' lover but killed his own brother Manuel by mistake. Their father Michael IX died of grief. Andronicus'

grandfather rejected him as heir. Andronicus rebelled and seized the throne, causing civil war with his grandfather for seven years. Andronicus took Constantinople in 1328 and deposed his grandfather. His leading minister was the general John Cantacuzenus. Andronicus campaigned against the Ottomans under Orhan, attempting to recover territory, but was defeated at Pelekanos when wounded in the leg by an arrow. Nicaea and Nicomedia were lost. Andronicus made an agreement with the Bulgars, who were then beaten by the Serbs and posed less of a threat. Some territory was recovered in east and west, including Thessaly and Epirus. Andronicus died of fever in a monastery in Constantinople on 15 June. His son John V succeeded.

ARTHUR (d. c.537)

Arguments will always rage over the historicity of Arthur. There are sources that mention him but they are unreliable. The 12th-century tales of Arthur and later embroideries added a mass of fictional detail – Camelot, the round table, Guinevere, Galahad, Sir Lancelot, Merlin and so on. It is reasonable to assume there was an historical Arthur even if we know little about him. A British poem of c.600 (*Y Gododdin*) compared a later leader unfavourably with Arthur – the first time he was named. In *Nennius* 12 battles are listed that Arthur, a 'leader of battles' (*dux bellorum*), won. The sites are difficult to locate but suggest activity over a broad area. He probably flourished in the late 5th and early 6th centuries as military leader of the British resisting English invasion. In *Nennius* he fought at Mount Badon but it is not clear that he led the British. He probably played a part in halting the English advance in the 6th century. Division among the Britons led to the Battle of Camlann in c.537 where Arthur was killed. It was claimed that Arthur's remains were found at Glastonbury in 1190, but this is not trustworthy.

ATHAULF, KING OF THE VISIGOTHS (d.415)

Brother-in-law of Alaric the Visigoth, succeeding him as king in 410. In 412 he led the Visigoths from Italy to Gaul. He supported the usurper Jovinus in alliance with Alans and Burgundians, but transferred his allegiance to the Emperor Honorius and killed the usurper. While in Italy he married the emperor's captive sister, Galla Placidia. He is supposed to have claimed 'I once aspired to change the face of the universe, to obliterate the name of Rome', but came to prefer the survival of the Roman Empire. He took over Toulouse and Bordeaux, establishing a kingdom at Narbonne. In 415 he moved to Spain, but was assassinated by a follower in Barcelona.

ATTILA THE HUN (c.406–53)

Leader of the Huns, called 'the scourge of God'. From 434 Attila shared kingship with his brother Bleda, whom he killed in 445. From a base in Pannonia (Hungary), he won authority over other groups, including Slavs and Germans. The Huns attacked the Balkans in 441 and defeated the Eastern Emperor Theodosius II at Gallipoli in 447. Attila attacked Greece, and in 451 invaded Gaul. He besieged Orléans, but was defeated at the Catalaunian Plains in 451 by Aëtius. He invaded Italy in 452 and razed Aquileia. Pope Leo I paid tribute to Attila to save Rome. Attila died, covered in his own blood, from an apparently innocuous nosebleed. His empire disintegrated.

AUDLEY, JAMES TOUCHET, LORD (1398–1459)

A Lancastrian supporter with lands in the west midlands. Under Henry VI he was Justiciar and Chamberlain for South Wales. He led the 1431 expedition to France. For Henry he raised forces in Kent against Richard of York in 1452. In the Wars of the Roses he was active on the Welsh border. He was killed on 23 September at Blore Heath fighting for Queen Margaret. The fatal blow was delivered by Sir Roger Kynaston, who assumed the Audley arms –

though James' son John succeeded to the title. James was buried at Darley Abbey.

BALDWIN I, LATIN EMPEROR OF BYZANTIUM (BALDWIN IX, COUNT OF FLANDERS) (1171–1206)

First Latin Emperor of Byzantium from 1204. He became Count of Flanders in 1195. He was defeated by Philip Augustus and agreed the Treaty of Péronne. He joined the Fourth Crusade, participating in the attack on Zara. After the capture of Constantinople he was elected Latin Emperor. Baldwin besieged Adrianople in 1205 but was faced by a relief force under Kalojan the Bulgar. Baldwin was defeated, captured and killed – his arms and legs chopped off and thrown to vultures. His brother Henry succeeded.

BALDWIN I, KING OF JERUSALEM (1058–1118)

Baldwin of Boulogne was the brother and successor of Godfrey de Bouillon in 1100. It was Baldwin who established the extent of the kingdom of Jerusalem. He was intended for the Church but chose to crusade. He established the first crusader state at Edessa. Godfrey became the first ruler of Jerusalem but died a year later. As king Baldwin captured Arsuf and Caesarea. He defeated the Egyptians at Ramleh in 1101 but was beaten at the same site in 1102. He recovered with victories at Jaffa in 1102 and Ramleh again in 1105. He extended Christian control over the Syrian ports. On 2 April 1118 he died of dysentery when leading an expedition against Egypt.

BALDWIN II, LATIN EMPEROR OF BYZANTIUM (1217–73)

The last Latin Emperor to hold Constantinople, from 1228 to 1261, son of Peter of Courtenay who was elected Emperor in 1217 in his absence and never arrived in Constantinople. Peter was captured by Theodore of Epirus and died in captivity. Baldwin's mother, the Empress Yolanda, bore him in Constantinople. John de Brienne acted as regent and co-emperor until his own death in 1237, while Baldwin was in the west seeking aid. He returned for coronation in 1240. The army of the Greek claimant Michael VIII recovered the city in 1261, breaking in while Baldwin was asleep. Baldwin fled on a Venetian ship. He sought aid from the west, allying with Charles of Anjou in 1267. Baldwin died in 1273. His son Peter claimed the Empire – but unsuccessfully.

BALDWIN II, KING OF JERUSALEM (d.1131)

Baldwin of Le Bourg was cousin and successor of Baldwin I in 1118. He was so pious that he developed hard skin on his knees from praying. He succeeded his cousin as Count of Edessa. He married an Armenian princess, Morphia. At Harran in 1104 he was captured by the Turks and released in 1108. He contended with Tancred for Edessa. As king he won the Battle of Hab and was regent of Antioch to 1126. He tried to extend the kingdom's power but was captured by Balak (later Emir of Aleppo) in 1123, only ransomed after the latter's death in 1124. Tyre was taken from the Egyptians in 1124. In 1125 he defeated the Syrian Muslims at Azaz. Baldwin unsuccessfully attacked Aleppo in 1126 and Damascus in 1127. Under him the military orders had their origin. He died on 21 August and was succeeded by his son-in-law Fulk of Anjou.

BALDWIN III, KING OF JERUSALEM (1130–62)

King from 1143 on the death of his father, Fulk. His mother Melisende was regent until he came of age in 1145, when relations between them became strained. He joined the Second Crusade's disastrous attempt to take Damascus in 1148. His reign saw the rise of Nur ed-Din. Baldwin built his power around Tyre and Acre. He saved Antioch, where he acted as regent. He was temporarily regent of Tripoli. He defended the remnant of the county of Edessa against the Muslims, in 1150 selling to Byzantium lands long claimed there.

Baldwin married the Byzantine Princess Theodora, daughter of Emperor Manuel. In 1153 Baldwin gained Ascalon from the Egyptians. He allied with Damascus against Nur ed-Din and prevented the latter from taking it. Baldwin defeated Nur ed-Din at Banyas, and at al-Batihah in 1158. He died at Beirut on 10 February and was succeeded by his brother Amalric I.

BALDWIN IV, THE LEPER, KING OF JERUSALEM (1162–85)

Son and successor in 1174 of Amalric I while still a child, with Raymond of Tripoli as regent. Baldwin had ability but from childhood suffered from leprosy, which weakened his political position. The activities of Rainald of Châtillon deepened the crisis. Baldwin still resisted Saladin. In 1177 he defeated Saladin at Montgisard but was beaten by him at the Litani in 1179. They fought an indecisive battle at Belvoir in 1182. Baldwin was succeeded by his nephew Baldwin V.

BALIAN II, LORD OF IBELIN

Crusading lord at the time of Saladin. He married Queen Maria Comnena, widow of Amalric I, heiress of Nablus. Balian's squire was the chronicler Ernoul. Balian mediated between King Guy and Count Raymond of Tripoli. Balian fought at Hattin, commanding the rearguard. He escaped to Jerusalem where his wife had taken shelter. He knighted noble boys over 16 and burgesses in efforts to marshal a defence. Balian saved the lives of many in Jerusalem by agreeing surrender terms with a reluctant Saladin. Saladin later presented him with a fief at Caymon (Tel Kaimun). Balian supported Conrad of Montferrat as king, and later Henry of Champagne. His son, John of Ibelin, was named as successor to King Henry. Balian's family remained important in the kingdom of Jerusalem and in Cyprus.

BARDAS CAESAR (d.866)

Brother of the regent Theodora and uncle of her son, the drunkard Emperor Michael III the Sot. He was Michael's military commander and chief adviser and was appointed Caesar by him. Bardas virtually ruled the Empire for a decade. He pushed back the Bulgars and Slavs. He refounded the University of Constantinople. His success against the Saracens began a period of Byzantine recovery in Asia Minor. He rebuilt the Byzantine navy and prepared an expedition against Crete in 866. He came into conflict with Basil (I), ending with Bardas' assassination on 21 April when setting out for Crete.

BARDAS PHOKAS CAESAR (878–968)

Made Caesar in 963 by his son Nikephorus II. He was Governor of the Armeniakon Theme under Romanus I, defending it against the Rus in 941. Romanus rewarded him with command in the east against the Saracens in 945. He was wounded in the face in 953 by Sayf ad-Dawla near Germanicea, when his son took over command. Bardas died aged 90 during the reign of his son.

BARDAS PHOKAS, SON OF LEO PHOKAS, BYZANTINE EMPEROR (d.989)

A rebel against John I Tzimisces and Basil II; the nephew of Nikephorus II Phokas. Bardas' father, the general Leo Phokas, was exiled to Lesbos for opposition to John, while Bardas was sent to Pontus. Bardas escaped to Caesarea in Cappadocia, his family lands, and proclaimed himself Emperor in 971. His father and brother gave support but were arrested. When a force was sent against him, his men deserted and he fled to Tyropoion. It was besieged and he surrendered. He and his family were exiled to Chios. He was brought out of exile by Basil II to counter rebellion in 976. In 979 he defeated the rebel Bardas Sclerus in single combat. Phokas split his opponent's head with a sword. In 987 Bardas Phokas, believing himself overlooked, again rebelled, proclaimed himself Emperor and marched on Constantinople. In 989, with Bardas absent, Basil destroyed his army at Chrysopolis with aid from Vladimir of Kiev

– the origin of the Varangian Guard. With his surviving men Bardas tried to take Abydos, which Basil came to relieve. Bardas, after twice falling from his horse, rode forward and issued a challenge to single combat (which Basil was unlikely to accept). Bardas suffered a sudden dramatic stroke, falling dead from his horse. His body was cut in pieces and the head presented to Basil.

BARDAS SCLERUS, BYZANTINE EMPEROR (d. c.989)

A commander under the Byzantine Emperor John I, whose wife Maria was Bardas' sister. He won two victories against the Rus under Sviatoslav in 970 at Adrianople and Arcadiopolis. Bardas in the latter split a Russian horseman in two with his sword – the halves falling on opposite sides of the horse. He suppressed the rebellion of Bardas Phokas for John. In 976 he rebelled against Basil II, proclaiming himself Emperor. He won two battles against Basil in 978 at Pancalia and Basilica Therma. He captured Nicaea and besieged Constantinople. Bardas Phokas was brought out of exile to fight him. In 979 in single combat Phokas wounded Sclerus in the face. The rebellion was over but Sclerus survived to become a prisoner in Baghdad, until his captors released him. He proclaimed himself Emperor again in 987. Bardas Phokas treacherously invited Sclerus to negotiate and then arrested and imprisoned him for two years. On the death of Phokas, Sclerus, now almost blind, was released by Phokas' widow. He submitted to Basil and was allowed to retire. Brought before Basil he advised him not to allow too much power to governors and generals, dying soon afterwards.

BASIL I THE MACEDONIAN, BYZANTINE EMPEROR (812–86)

Emperor from 867, founder of the Macedonian dynasty though an Armenian peasant (from the Theme of Macedonia) by birth. He rose to high office under Michael III and killed his rival, Bardas

Caesar. Basil's wife Eudocia was Michael's mistress. Basil became co-emperor in 866 and killed Michael in 867 – taking power. He initiated a period of recovery and expansion. In 870 he was nearly killed at Tephrike, saved by the bravery of Theophylact the Unbearable. He defeated the Muslims at Samosata in 873. He overcame the Paulicians, a breakaway Christian group that had set up an independent state, capturing Tephrike in 872. He improved the Byzantine navy, winning control of much of the Mediterranean. He recovered territory in Italy, taking Bari and Taranto and expelling the Saracens from Calabria – though he failed to recover Sicily. Basil re-established control in the Balkans against Slavs, Bulgars and Serbs. The Bulgars and Serbs converted to Orthodox Christianity. Basil was killed on 29 August in suspicious circumstances when hunting. He was succeeded by his son (or possibly Michael III's son) Leo VI. The dynasty survived until 1055.

BASIL II THE BULGAR SLAYER, BYZANTINE EMPEROR (954–1025)

Emperor from 976, son of Romanus II, one of the greatest rulers of Byzantium. As a young man he was reputed to be a womaniser. Psellus said he was a villain in time of war but an Emperor in times of peace. Basil taxed the nobility to improve the army. He repressed the rebellions of Bardas Sclerus and Bardas Phokas. On the second occasion he used mercenaries from Kiev – the origin of the Varangian Guard. He fought to maintain power in the Balkans. He was defeated by the Bulgars at Trajan's Gate in 986 but recovered to conquer Greece, Albania and Bulgaria. He defeated the Bulgar Tsar Samuel in 1003 and again at Kleidion in 1014, where he blinded his captives except for one in every hundred left with one eye to lead the others home. Basil conquered Georgia. His empire stretched to the Adriatic and the Danube. He restored control in Syria and recovered Antioch and Aleppo. The Empire was larger than at any time since Justinian I. Basil died

in Constantinople on 15 December and was succeeded by his brother Constantine VIII.

BAYBARS (BAIBARS) I, AL-ZAHIR, RUKN AD-DIN, BUNDUKDARI, SULTAN OF EGYPT (d.1277)

Mamluke Sultan from 1261 though probably a Kipchak Turk. He took over Egypt and Syria and planned the downfall of the kingdom of Jerusalem, the Muslim Ayyubids and the Assassins – fundamentally altering the political situation in the Middle East. He repulsed the Mongols from the region. He built the first navy for the Sultanate. The nickname Bundukdari meant 'the arbalestier'. He served the Mongols early in his career. For the Egyptians he fought at Mansurah and Ayn Jalut. He came to power by assassinating Sultan Qtuz in 1260. He re-established puppet Abbasid caliphs in Cairo. He took over most of the surviving Christian territory in Palestine and Syria. He attacked Acre in 1263, captured Caesarea and Arsuf in 1265, Safed in 1266, Jaffa and Antioch in 1268 and Krak in 1271. He surrounded Safed with severed Christian heads. He frustrated the crusade of Jaime the Conqueror of Aragón in 1269 and opposed Edward I. In 1272 he made peace with the surviving kingdom. In 1277 he invaded Anatolia, defeating the Mongols at Elbistan, but withdrew. He died at Damascus on 1 July, possibly poisoned.

BAYEZIT (BAYEZID) I (YILDIRIM/THE THUNDERBOLT), OTTOMAN SULTAN (1347–1403)

Sultan 1389–1402, son of Murad I and a Greek mother. Bayezit was granted the title Sultan by the Egyptian Caliph in 1394. He commanded part of his father's army to victory over the crusaders at Kosovo in 1389. On the death of Murad, Bayezit's supporters murdered his older brother Yakub. Bayezit married a Serbian princess, Maria Despina. He developed the Janissary system begun by his father. Bayezit extended Turkish power in Europe, threatening Byzantium. He isolated

Constantinople and surrounded it with forts. Much of eastern Europe became Ottoman and remained Turkish for centuries. He became overlord of Bosnia and Wallachia in 1391. He conquered Macedonia and part of Albania. Serbia, Bulgaria and Byzantium recognised his suzerainty. He dominated previously Byzantine areas of Asia Minor and conquered most of Anatolia. The main threat to his position came from the Mongols under Tamberlane, whose interest however turned elsewhere. The West sought to aid Byzantium by a crusade. Bayezit defeated their army in 1396 at Nicopolis. In 1394 and then 1396 he besieged Constantinople but failed to take it. Bayezit campaigned successfully in Anatolia but Tamberlane returned in 1400. In 1402 Bayezit was defeated and captured near Ankara. He was carried around in an iron cage and used as a stool and mounting block by Tamberlane. Maria Despina had to serve Tamberlane at table naked. Bayezit suffered a stroke and died, possibly by his own hand, in captivity at Aksehir on 9 March. His son Mehmet I succeeded.

BEAUFORT, EDMUND, SELF-STYLED DUKE OF SOMERSET (d.1471)

Styled himself duke after the execution of his brother Duke Henry in 1464, but was never created duke. After Henry VI's defeat by the Yorkists, Edmund went into exile and fought for Charles the Bold of Burgundy. He joined Queen Margaret's invasion of England in 1471, raising troops in the west. He fought at Tewkesbury in 1471, making an unsupported advance that helped cause the Lancastrian defeat. He was captured and executed at Tewkesbury on 6 May, illustrated in the 15th-century *Historia of the Arrivall of Edward IV*.

BELISARIUS (505–65)

General of Justinian I, who reconquered much of the Western Roman Empire for Byzantium. Belisarius married Antonina, a charioteer's daughter. He rose to prominence by defeating the Persians at Dara in 529 though he was beaten at Kallinicum 531. He retrieved the situation at Sura and peace was made. He suppressed the Nika riots in Constantinople in 532. In the west Belisarius' first success was in North Africa, defeating the Vandals at Decimum and Tricamarum 533, capturing Gelimer, and ending Vandal power in Africa. Mediterranean islands were added – Sardinia, Corsica and the Balearics. Belisarius invaded Italy against the Ostrogoths. He took Palermo in Sicily in 535, Naples and Rome in 536, and captured Vitiges. Belisarius was recalled in 541 with only Verona and Pavia still independent. Justinian was jealous of Belisarius, suspecting treachery. In 542 Belisarius was sent east. He recovered Mesopotamia and invaded Persia, causing Chosroes to make peace. When the Ostrogoths recovered, Belisarius was sent west again. He regained Rome but was recalled in 549. Much of Spain was taken from the Visigoths. Belisarius was brought from retirement again and sent to Spain in 554. He was recalled to tackle a Bulgar threat in 559. He received little gratitude from his master and was unjustly imprisoned in 562, his property confiscated. He was released in 563 and died on 13 March in retirement in Constantinople.

BIGOD, HUGH, EARL OF NORFOLK (1094–1177)

Earl from 1140 or 1141, a difficult and troublesome baron who swore that Henry I in Normandy had declared for the succession of his nephew Stephen rather than his daughter Matilda. He took over Norwich Castle in 1136 but surrendered it to Stephen on demand. When Matilda invaded he joined her and was made earl. He later assisted Matilda's son, Henry Plantagenet. In the peace of 1153, Stephen's son William received Norwich Castle. Henry II confirmed Hugh as earl in 1155 but left Norwich under William, and Hugh discontented. Hugh joined the 1173 rebellion but submitted, escaping with a fine. The dispute over the succession to the earldom was settled by Richard I in favour of Hugh's son Roger.

BLANCHE OF CASTILE, QUEEN OF FRANCE (1188–1252)

Queen and regent, daughter of Alfonso VIII of Castile and Eleanor. She married Louis (VIII) in 1200. She acted as regent for her son Louis IX during his minority from 1226 to 1234, and continued to have influence afterwards. She did much to form St Louis' character. She dealt with rebellion by nobles including Peter Mauclerc count of Brittany, concluding with the Treaty of Vendôme 1227. She acted against the Cathar heretics and Raymond VII of Toulouse. At times she led the army. She opposed Henry III's ambitions in France. She was regent during St Louis' absence on crusade from 1248 to 1252. She had 12 children; her sons included Robert of Artois, Alphonse of Poitiers and Charles of Anjou – all significant figures. She died on 27 November at Melun and was buried at Maubuisson Abbey.

BOABDIL (ABŪ 'ABD ALLĀH MUHAMMAD/MUHAMMAD XI), KING OF GRANADA (1464–1536)

King from 1482, when he deposed his father Abū'l-Hasan. Civil war followed against his father and uncle. In 1483 Boabdil tried to take Lucena from the Christians but was captured. The concessions made to obtain release made him unpopular in Granada, and civil war ensued. He was captured at Loja in 1486 and again made concessions in return for freedom. Ferdinand and Isabella invaded Granada. Málaga was taken in 1487; Granada besieged and taken in 1492. Boabdil was granted a lordship in the Alpujarras but preferred exile in Morocco. He was killed fighting for the Caliph of Fez against the Berbers, his body placed in the river to flow out to sea.

BOHEMOND OF TARANTO, PRINCE OF ANTIOCH (1050–1111)

Prince from 1098 through the First Crusade, the son of Robert Guiscard and Alberada. Anna Comnena described the impact on the Byzantine court (and herself) of the tall, muscular, stooping, blond Norman. He fought for his father against the Byzantines in the unsuccessful attack on Albania in 1081. His younger brother Roger received the Apulian lands, and Bohemond inherited little. On the First Crusade, leading the Normans from Sicily, he fought at Dorylaeum and Antioch. The author of the *Gesta Francorum* was probably in his retinue. Bohemond founded the principality of Antioch despite Byzantine claims, but by the Treaty of Devol in 1108 recognised Byzantine overlordship. He was captured by the Turks near Aleppo in 1100 and imprisoned in Anatolia until ransomed in 1103. He was defeated by the Turks at Harran in 1104. He returned to the west in 1106, seeking reinforcements, and married Constance daughter of Philip I of France. With a new force Bohemond besieged Durazzo from 1107 but failed to take it. He returned to Italy and died in Apulia. His nephew Tancred and then his own son Bohemond II succeeded to Antioch.

BONIFACE II, MARQUIS OF MONTFERRAT (d.1207)

Boniface of Montferrat, called by Villehardouin 'one of the world's finest knights', led the Fourth Crusade. His brothers William and Conrad distinguished themselves in the Holy Land. Boniface was related to French and imperial royalty. He possessed family lands in Italy. When others died he became the leader of the Crusade. The Crusade captured Constantinople but Baldwin of Flanders, rather than Boniface, was elected Latin Emperor. In 1204 Boniface married Margaret daughter of Béla II of Hungary, widow of the Byzantine Emperor Isaac II. Boniface established the kingdom of Thessalonika in Thrace and Macedonia, previously held by his brother Rainier. Boniface's authority covered Thebes and Athens. He quarrelled with Emperor Baldwin. He was ambushed by the Bulgars in the Rhodope Mountains in 1207, caught without time to don his armour, and died from a wound in the arm.

BORGIA, CESARE, DUKE OF ROMAGNA (1475–1507)

Duke from 1501, the illegitimate son of the Borgia Pope Alexander VI. Cesare was intended for an ecclesiastical career but preferred politics. His ruthlessness became a by-word – accused of murders by poison, stiletto and garrotte. At Sinigaglia he ordered a massacre. Machiavelli served him for a time and wrote of his experiences. Cesare married the daughter of the King of Navarre. He tried to reconquer papal lands from local lords and establish his own state. He took Urbino treacherously and captured Forli in 1500 with cannons. His attempts to form a state failed after the death of his father in 1503. He was imprisoned by Julius II but escaped to Navarre and was killed fighting in Castile.

BOUCICAUT, JEAN LE MEINGRE, MARSHAL OF FRANCE (1364–1421)

Marshal from 1361, famed for knightly accomplishments, subject of the *Book of His Deeds*, and founder of the Order of the White Lady with the Green Shield. He himself wrote, contributing to *Les Cent Ballades*. He showed remarkable athleticism during the Hundred Years' War when he somersaulted in full armour, climbed a scaling ladder to the top by hand jerks only, and repeated the feat (without armour) using one hand. The English captured him again in 1352 in Gascony. He was imprisoned in England for three years before the ransom was paid. In 1356 he defended Romorantin to delay the English before Poitiers, but was again captured and ransomed. He was ambassador to England in 1362 over the release of John II. He participated in the Nicopolis Crusade of 1396, again captured and ransomed. He defended Constantinople against the Ottomans in 1398-9. He led the French van at Agincourt in 1415; he argued against fighting but was overruled. He was again captured, to die in prison.

BRUNHILD (567–613)

Daughter of Athanagild, King of the Visigoths in Spain. She married the Frankish King Sigebert of Austrasia. On Sigebert's murder she married Merovech, son of Childeric, who was killed in 577. She acted as regent for her son Childebert and for her grandsons, Theudebert II of Austrasia and Theuderic II of Burgundy. She played a part in setting them against each other, leading to Theudebert's death. Theuderic died and she supported his son, Sigebert II. She was the rival to Fredegund, regent for Neustria. In 598, on the death of Fredegund, Brunhild took over Neustria. She was accused of many political murders, including those of ten kings – probably an exaggeration by hostile sources. The Austrasian nobles rebelled and joined Fredegund's son, Chlothar. Brunhild and Sigebert II were captured and put to death. She was paraded on a camel's back and pulled apart by wild horses to which she was tied.

BUCKINGHAM, HENRY STAFFORD, DUKE OF (1455–83)

Rebel against Richard III. His father was killed at St Albans in 1455 supporting Henry VI. He turned Yorkist and married Edward IV's sister but became hostile to Edward IV after the latter married Elizabeth Woodville and promoted her relatives. He supported Richard for the throne in 1483 and was rewarded with lands and offices. The reasons for his subsequent opposition to Richard are unclear though he did move to support Henry Tudor. Presumably he had become disillusioned, perhaps believing Richard was doomed. He joined the rising now known as Buckingham's Rebellion, which was suppressed by Richard. Buckingham was betrayed by his own servant and beheaded at Salisbury on 2 November.

BYRHTNOTH, EALDORMAN OF ESSEX (d.991)

Ealdorman from 956, commander against the Danes at Maldon. There is a tradition that he won a battle against the Vikings on the River Blackwater in 988. According to the poem of Maldon, Byrhtnoth refused to pay tribute and assembled the fyrd of Essex. The Danes on the island of Northey were led by Ólaf Tryggvason. Three Englishmen barred the causeway to the mainland that appeared at low tide but Byrhtnoth allowed the Vikings to cross it and fight. He expected victory but was defeated and killed. The date of his birth is unknown but he was an old man by 991.

CADOC (LAMBERT OF)

Mercenary captain for Philip Augustus. Little is known of his background, birth or death. He supposedly received £1,000 a day – presumably as wages for his band (of several hundred men), but still an exaggeration. When Richard the Lionheart reconnoitred Gaillon, Cadoc (its castellan) shot the king in the knee with a crossbow bolt. He received the lordship of Gaillon as reward. Cadoc participated in the capture of Château-Gaillard, and afterwards held it for Philip. Following the conquest of Normandy he was granted the fiefs of Tosny and Pont-Audemer. His daughter married a Norman knight. He helped conquer Anjou from John. Cadoc became *bailli* of Pont-Audemer. In 1210 he campaigned against the Count of Auvergne for Philip, defending local churches against the Count. In the campaign before Bouvines, Cadoc was blamed for the loss of the French fleet at Damme in 1213, plundering the town while the fleet was attacked in harbour. He took no part at Bouvines. He was arrested in 1219 for profiteering as *bailli* and probably not released until 1227 though some believe he campaigned for Louis VIII in the south and at Avignon, which would mean an earlier release.

CANE, FACINO (1350–1412)

A *condottiere* with a ruthless reputation. His nickname, Cane, meant dog. He was born and began his career in Piedmont, moving to Savoy before taking employment for Genoa in 1394. From 1397 he served Milan under Gian Galeazzo Visconti. He proved his worth as a captain though captured by Hawkwood three times. After Gian Galeazzo's death in 1402 Facino played a major part for Milan under Giovanni Maria Visconti, threatening to seize power – prevented only by his death. Giovanni was assassinated but Facino became ill when besieging Brescia. On his deathbed in Pavia he urged his men to join Filippo Maria Visconti, who had married Facino's daughter Beatrice. Cane died on 16 May.

CANGRANDE DELLA SCALA (d.1329)

His family, the Scaligeri, ruled Verona from 1259, an early example of dynastic rule in the Italian city-republics; a patron of Dante. He was appointed imperial Vicar of Verona by Henry VII (HRE) in 1311. He made peace with Padua in 1318. Frederick of Austria besieged Padua in 1319 but failed to take it, and Verona made peace again in 1320. Under him Verona gained Padua and Vicenza. He died on 22 July, succeeded by his nephew Mastino. His equestrian statue stands in Verona.

CARLOMAN, BROTHER OF CHARLEMAGNE (751–71)

Son of Pepin the Short, four years younger than Charlemagne but, unlike his brother, legitimate. He was given imperial anointment by Pope Stephen II in 754 along with his father and brother. He assisted his father to govern. After Pepin's death in 768 Carloman shared rule for three years with Charlemagne. Carloman's portion included Burgundy, Provence, Septimania, Alsace and Alemannia. He was crowned at Soissons. He shared Aquitaine with Charles. In 769 they planned a joint expedition against the rebel Duke Hunoald II in Aquitaine. The brothers quarrelled at Moncontour and Carloman returned home. Charles sought allies against his brother. The latter died suddenly on 4 December at Samoussy and was buried in Reims. Carloman left a widow, Gerberga, and two sons. On his death Charlemagne became sole ruler.

CARLOMAN, UNCLE OF CHARLEMAGNE (d.754)

Son of Charles Martel, brother of Pepin the Short. On the death of Martel his sons shared power, Carloman becoming Mayor of the Palace for Austrasia. Pepin and Carloman imprisoned their half-brother Grifo and denied him any inheritance. They restored the Merovingian ruler Childeric III in 743. In alliance with his brother Pepin, Carloman attacked Aquitaine. They defeated the duke of the Alemans in 746 and imposed authority on Bavaria. Carloman may have been a more successful military leader than Pepin but lacked his political skills. In 747 Carloman retired to a monastic life in Monte Cassino, a move probably forced upon him. Carloman was also performing penance for the execution of thousands of defeated Alemans. He hoped his son Drogo would inherit, but after a short period Pepin the Short took control.

CARLOMAN/PEPIN, SON OF CHARLEMAGNE, KING OF ITALY (778–810)

King from 781 at the age of three. With the disgrace of Pepin the Hunchback, Carloman was renamed Pepin. He was made King of Italy. He died before his father. His son Bernard succeeded to Italy.

CEAWLIN, KING OF WESSEX (d.593)

He consolidated the founding of the kingdom of Wessex. He was a son of Cynric who had arrived with Cerdic to win Wessex. Bede named Ceawlin as second *Bretwalda*, the leading king of his age. He advanced the boundaries of Wessex following the lull after Badon. The traditional account of his career is that with Cynric he fought the Britons at Beranbyrg, becoming king in 560. In 568 he defeated a rival in Aethelbert of Kent at the Battle of Wibbandun. Ceawlin's greatest victory was alongside Cuthwine at the Battle of Deorham, 577, which was

followed by Wessex taking Bath, Gloucester and Cirencester. In 584 he fought at Fethanleag, where his ally Cutha was killed, and where the English were probably defeated. He died after a further defeat. There are problems over the dating of Ceawlin's reign, which may have only lasted seven years. He was probably expelled as king after defeat at Woden's Barrow in Wiltshire in 592, probably by Ceol who became King of Wessex.

CERDIC, KING OF WESSEX (d.534)

Founder of the kingdom of Wessex. The *Anglo-Saxon Chronicle* states that Cerdic landed in Wessex with his son Cynric and five ships in 495, probably near Southampton, fighting a battle on the same day. His name is British though there is no evidence to explain why. In 508 he defeated Natanleod at Netley. In 519 he won the Battle of Cerdic's Ford. A further battle is mentioned at Cerdicesleag in 527. He captured the Isle of Wight in 530. However Cerdic was elsewhere recorded as reigning until 516 or 530. There is a problem over records that mention a certain Creoda, who may have been the son of Cerdic and the father of Cynric, though Cynric is generally believed to have been Cerdic's son. As so often in this period we can appreciate the problems but not resolve them.

CHARLEMAGNE, HOLY ROMAN EMPEROR (747–814)

Emperor from 800, builder of the Carolingian Empire and crowned as Western Emperor. His father took the throne and initiated the Carolingian dynasty. Charlemagne was the greatest of the dynasty. He was born to Bertrada before she married Pepin. His given name was Charles. We know him as Charlemagne or Charles the Great (*Carolus magnus*). His first major campaign was fought on behalf of his father against the rebel Duke Hunald of Aquitaine. Charles' brother Carloman refused to take part, and credit for the success of the expedition went to Charles. Hunald fled to Gascony and then submitted. Pepin died in 768. Charles and Carloman shared rule of the Frankish lands until Carloman's death in 771 left Charles in sole command. He was crowned Western Emperor by Pope Leo III in Rome on Christmas Day 800.

Charlemagne's capitularies included rules for the formation and maintenance of armies, for the performance of military service and duties due according to land held, with fines for non-attendance in the army when due and regulations on the provision of weapons and supplies. There was a ban on exporting military gear.

Charles fought a series of wars, adding considerably to his territories. His most prolonged war, against the Saxons, was in essence a frontier struggle and a religious war against pagans – devil-worshippers according to Einhard. The war lasted over 30 years from 772, involving 18 expeditions. Charles won two pitched battles, both in 783, at Detmold and on the River Haase, after which the Saxons avoided battle. The Saxon war-leader was Widukind. Charlemagne destroyed the Saxon idol of the Irminsul. The Franks suffered setbacks, including the capture of the fort of Eresburg. In 782 a Frankish army under royal officials joined Charles' relative Count Theoderic. The officials, acting rashly without Theoderic, were beaten by the Saxons at the Süntel Mountain. Charles took revenge at Verden, executing 4,500 Saxons. Further rebellion in northern Saxony led to his deportation of the Saxon population from 804.

Charles fought an eight-year war against the Avars on his eastern frontier, blocking their advance. Two leaders fighting for Charles were killed in the war, Eric duke of Friuli and Gerold governor of Bavaria. Franks under Charles' son Carloman/Pepin defeated the Avars in 791. Charles advanced along the Danube without opposition. Expeditions in the 790s pushed into Avar territory, destroying the religious stronghold of the Ring. A campaign to Pannonia in 811 defeated the Avars who were forced to convert to Christianity.

Charles followed up his father's defeat of the Lombards. He invaded Lombardy in 773 after an appeal from Pope Hadrian I. He besieged Pavia 773–4 until King Desiderius surrendered. Desiderius' son Adalgis was exiled. Charles claimed the Iron Crown of Lombardy for himself. In 775 the Lombard duke of Friuli revolted but was killed in battle the following year. In 787, on papal urging, Charles attacked the Lombard duchy of Benevento, which submitted.

Charlemagne intervened in the duchy of Bavaria, insisting on lordship over his cousin Duke Tassilo III. Tassilo, after refusing to co-operate, was attacked and captured in 788. He was deposed in 794. Charles defended Bavaria against the Avars.

In 777 the Emir of Zaragoza sought Charles' aid against his rival in Córdoba. Charles took an army to Spain in 778 but failed to take Zaragoza. At the approach of an Ummayad army Charlemagne retreated. The returning Frankish army was ambushed by the Basques, the rearguard defeated and massacred at Roncesvalles. Charles' son returned south and in 801 Barcelona was captured. Louis took Tortosa in 811 and the Spanish March was established south of the Pyrenees.

Charles strengthened Frankish coastal defences against the Vikings after their raid on Aquitaine. He arranged the building of coastal forts and a defence fleet. He fought the Danes in 810 following provocation by King Godfred in Schleswig and Frisia. Godfrid was assassinated and his successor made peace.

Other campaigns took Charles to the Baltic, Dalmatia and Corsica. His son, Young Charles, fought against the Czechs and Slavs. Charlemagne conquered and subjugated a belt of territory to north, east and south, forming a buffer on the fringes of the original Frankish lands.

Charlemagne's wives were Himiltrude a Frankish noblewoman, the unnamed daughter of Desiderius of Lombardy, Hildegard who died in childbirth, Fastrada the daughter of a Frankish count, and Liutgard from Alemannia. He had various concubines including Maltegard, Gerswinda, Adalhaid and Regina. Our knowledge of his offspring is probably incomplete. He had numerous children, including Pepin the Hunchback by Himiltrude, five daughters and four sons by Hildegard, and several illegitimate children including the sons Drogo, Hugo and Theoderic. Charlemagne died at Aachen on 28 January and was buried there.

CHARLES (I) THE GOOD, COUNT OF FLANDERS (1080–1127)
The murder of Charles (I) the Good on 2 March 1127, during Lent when kneeling at prayer, created a crisis in northern Europe and made a martyr of the victim. Galbert of Bruges, a member of the comital household, wrote an account. Charles was the grandson of Robert the Frisian, count from 1119, succeeding his cousin Baldwin VII. He suppressed a revolt by the rival claimant William of Ypres. He extended the Peace of God to peasants and prohibited carrying arms in towns and market places. He was a noted participant in tournaments. The powerful Erembald family was behind his assassination in the Church of St Donatian in Bruges. The citizens besieged the Erembalds in the castle, which they stormed on 19 March. The Erembalds were either killed on the spot or hunted afterwards and executed. With no clear heir, Louis VI of France intervened for the succession of William Clito (son of Robert Curthose).

CHARLES IV, HOLY ROMAN EMPEROR (1316–78)
King of the Romans from 1346 and Holy Roman Emperor from 1355. He became Margrave of Moravia in 1334. Of the house of Luxembourg, he was raised in France. His father, Blind King John of Bohemia, was killed at Crécy, where Charles was wounded. He succeeded John as King of Bohemia and was elected King of the Romans with support from Pope Clement VI. Only the death of Lewis of Bavaria allowed Charles to take control. He

conciliated the Wittelsbachs and Habsburgs. Charles was crowned Emperor in Rome. He married first Blanche the sister of Philip VI of France, second Anne of the Rhine Palatinate, third Anna of Scweidenitz niece of the King of Hungary and finally Elisabeth daughter of the Duke of Pomerania. His marriages demonstrate an interest in eastward expansion. He favoured Prague and issued the Golden Bull of 1356, whereby the King of Bohemia became an Elector of the Empire. In 1365 he defended the Rhineland against threats from the Free Companies. Charles expanded the territory of Bohemia and his family. At his death on 29 November his son Wenceslas succeeded.

CHARLES VI, KING OF FRANCE (1368–1422)
King from 1380 as a minor, son and successor of Charles V. He married Isabella of Bavaria in 1385. It was rumoured she had an affair with Charles' brother Louis. Two of Charles' daughters married English kings. In 1396 he agreed the Peace of Paris with Richard II, who married Isabelle. In 1392 when on campaign in Brittany, possibly suffering from sunstroke, the sound of a lance on a helmet provoked a violent fit followed by bouts of mental instability. Sometimes he believed himself made of glass that would shatter. His brother and uncles vied for power in a civil war between Burgundians and Armagnacs. Henry V invaded France, and Charles' army under D'Albret and Boucicaut was defeated at Agincourt. By the Treaty of Troyes Charles agreed to his daughter Catherine marrying Henry V, with the succession going to their offspring. At Meaux, under siege by Henry V 1421–2, a defender pushed a donkey on to the wall and beat it until it brayed. The man declared this was their king (Charles). Charles died on 21 October, leaving a disputed succession between his son Charles and Henry VI of England. An effigy of Charles VI wearing his crown is at St-Denis.

CHARLES VII, KING OF FRANCE (1403–61)
Son of Charles VI, king by his own claim
from 1422 though not crowned until 1429.
He was Count of Ponthieu, Duke of
Touraine and in a divided France called the
Dauphin of Vienne or the King of Bourges.
Charles transformed France from its nadir
under English control to a new greatness.
During his father's madness and weakness,
France suffered civil war and defeat by
Henry V. Charles married Marie of Anjou.
His mistress was Agnes Sorel. In 1418 he
became regent for his unstable father. In
1419 John the Fearless of Burgundy was
murdered at a conference with Charles.
Charles VI agreed at Troyes in 1420 to
disinherit his son. Charles held on in the
south. Henry V's death in 1422 and French
success, inspired by Joan of Arc at Orléans
in 1429, heralded French recovery. Charles
was crowned at Reims in 1429. He
reconquered Normandy and Guyenne. In
1435 at Arras he made terms with
Burgundy, weakening England's position.
Charles entered Paris in 1436, the citizens
declaring 'Long live the king!' He entered
Rouen in 1449, when a mechanical stag
bowed before him. Charles reorganised the
army through ordinances, producing a
standing army, a more professional force,
and the free archers. In 1444 he sent troops
to defeat the Swiss at St Jakob leading to
peace. By 1453 France emerged victorious
from the Hundred Years' War. A French
force under Pierre de Brézé attacked the
English coast in 1457. French interest in
Italy developed and Genoa was taken in
1458. Charles died on 22 July, succeeded by
his son Louis XI. A portrait, painted by Jean
Fouquet in 1444, survives.

**CHARLES OF ANJOU, KING OF SICILY
(1220–85)**
Brother of St Louis. He conquered the
Norman kingdom of Sicily and ruled it as
Charles I from 1266. In 1246 he married
Beatrice heiress to Provence. The papacy
offered Sicily to Charles against the
descendants of Frederick II. He invaded and
was crowned in 1266. He defeated Manfred

at Benevento and Conradin at Tagliacozzo.
He suppressed revolts in Sicily. He
developed Mediterranean interests. He
took Corfu in 1267 but failed to recover the
Byzantine Empire for the Franks. He was
involved in St Louis' crusade to Tunis in
1270. He was crowned King of Jerusalem in
1278 and became Prince of Achaea. He
developed interests in northern Italy,
becoming Imperial Vicar in Tuscany and
Senator of Rome in 1268. He was defeated
by the Genoese in 1273, and in 1275 at
Roccavione. His greatest setback followed
the Sicilian Vespers in 1282 with the
French loss of Sicily. His fleet was defeated
off Naples by the Genoese in 1284. He died
on 7 January and was succeeded by his son
Charles II. His descendants ruled in Naples
and Hungary.

CHARLES MARTEL (688–741)
A founder of the Carolingian dynasty.
Martel was a 9th-century nickname,
meaning the hammer. He was an
illegitimate son of Pepin II of Heristal,
Mayor of the Palace of Austrasia. Charles
helped the Merovingian king to reunite
Austrasia and Neustria. He increased
Merovingian power over the Alemans, the
Saxons, the Aquitanians, the Bavarians, the
Burgundians and the Thuringians. His
greatest victory was against the Muslim
invaders of Gaul near Tours. He became
virtually King of Francia, though never
crowned, governing without a king from
737. He was buried at St-Denis. He was
father of Pepin the Short and grandfather of
Charlemagne.

**CHARLES THE BALD, CAROLINGIAN
KING OF WEST FRANCIA, HOLY ROMAN
EMPEROR (823–77)**
Youngest son of Louis the Pious by Judith,
king (Charles II) from 843 and Holy Roman
Emperor from 875. His baldness has been
questioned. In alliance with his half-
brother Louis, he fought against his half-
brother Lothar, defeating him at Fontenoy
in 841. Charles gained the West Frankish
kingdom by the Treaty of Verdun. He

subjected Aquitaine, becoming its king in 848. He took over Provence but failed to gain Brittany, where he was beaten by Nominoë at Ballon in 845. Charles fought off attempts on his kingdom from Louis the German. Charles had 11 children by Ermentrude, including Louis the Stammerer, and three by Richildis. In 871 he suppressed a revolt by his son Carloman, whom he blinded. Charles led an expedition to Italy resulting in coronation as emperor by Pope John VIII in 875. He became King of Italy the following year. He paid tributes to the Vikings but improved coastal defences against them with forts and fortified bridges on the Seine, Oise and Marne. He led campaigns against their raids. The establishment of a March for his son-in-law Baldwin was the origin of the county of Flanders. Charles' capitularies included military measures. The Edict of Pîtres in 866 required men of appropriate wealth to appear mounted in the host, increasing its cavalry element. In 876 Charles was defeated at Andernach by Louis of Saxony. Returning from Italy because of problems caused by his nephew Carloman, he was taken ill and died at Brides-les-bains. Because of the stench of the corpse he was buried quickly at Nantua, but later the bones were taken to his chosen resting-place of St-Denis in Paris.

CHARLES THE BOLD, DUKE OF BURGUNDY (1433–77)

The last Duke of Burgundy, from 1467, son of Philip the Good. He fought in the French civil war at Montlhéry in 1465. At Liège he was nearly captured while his men were dicing. In 1466 at Dinant aspersions were made on his birth, suggesting illegitimacy. In response he bombarded the centre of the town and hounded many to death by drowning in the Meuse. He won at Brustem in 1467. He hoped to revive Burgundy's greatness as an independent kingdom. He reorganised the Burgundian army, issuing Military Ordinances in 1471–3 for a well-balanced force in uniform, supported by powerful artillery. One problem was the

need to rely on mercenaries. He married the sister of Edward IV of England. He supported the League of the Public Weal against Louis XI of France. His ambitions threatened the Holy Roman Empire. He besieged imperial Neuss in 1474–5 but had to abandon it. He conquered Lorraine in 1475, dominated the Low Countries and invaded Switzerland. He was defeated by the Swiss at Grandson and Morat in 1476. He besieged Nancy and was killed in battle there on 5 January. His naked body was found two days later in the frozen mud, half eaten by wolves, the head split by a Swiss halberd. The collapse of Burgundy followed, its territory divided between France and the Empire.

CHILDERIC I, MEROVINGIAN KING OF FRANCIA (456–c.481)

He allied with the Romans as a federate and was appointed as a Roman official. He was chieftain of the Salian Franks based at Tournai (now Belgium). He fought for Aegidius against the Visigoths at Orléans in 463, and for Count Paul against the Saxons under Odoacer at Angers in 469. Later Childeric came to an agreement with Odoacer. Childeric was exiled for eight years in Thuringia, taking the king's wife into his own bed. Their offspring was Clovis I. Childeric's grave was discovered outside Roman Tournai in 1653, part of a Frankish cemetery that included horse burials. A ring was found with his name and the title 'rex' (*Childerici regis*), the clothes of a Roman official and Frankish weapons including axe and sword. Most of the grave goods were stolen in 1831, the gold objects melted down. The ring has been reconstructed from a plaster cast.

CHLOTHAR I, MEROVINGIAN KING OF FRANCIA (498–561)

Son of Clovis I who reunited Francia. On his father's death in 511 the kingdom was divided between Chlothar and his three brothers, leading to a prolonged civil war between the brothers, and then between Chlothar and his son Chramm. On the death of his last surviving brother, Childebert I, in 558, Chlothar reunited the kingdom. He died of fever at Compiègne, when Francia was divided in four between his sons.

CHLOTHAR II, MEROVINGIAN KING OF FRANCIA (584–629)

Arguably the most powerful Merovingian monarch, son of Chilperic I and Fredegund – though there were rumours of illegitimacy. He established his position in Neustria, capturing Paris in the 590s. In 613 he reunited the realm, defeating Brunhild, who was put to death. Under pressure from the magnates, he appointed his son Dagobert as sub-king for Austrasia – an important division for the future. In 626, during his war against the Saxons, early reference was made to a Frankish cavalry charge under Chlothar near the River Weser. Chlothar killed the opposing Saxon leader Bertwald in personal combat. He issued the first Alemannic law code. He was buried at St-Vincent in Paris.

CHOSROES I (KHUSRAU/KHUSRU) ANUSHIRVAN (IMMORTAL SOUL), GREAT KING OF PERSIA (d.579)

Ruler of the Sassanid Empire from 531, son of Kavadh. He sought to improve the army through better training with emphasis on payment and mercenaries. He made 'Eternal Peace' with Justinian I in 532, which lasted eight years. He sacked Antioch in 540 and attacked the Armenians. In 542 he was beaten by Belisarius. Chosroes was the greatest of the Sassanids. He overcame internal opposition. He allied with the Gök Turks against the Ephthalite Huns and defeated them. He defeated the Khazars. He conquered the Yemen. Justin I initiated war with Persia, which was eventually lost after Chosroes' death. Chosroes was succeeded by his son Hormisdus.

CHOSROES II PARVIZ, KING OF PERSIA (d.628)

King from 591, son of Hormisdus IV and grandson of Chosroes I. He suppressed revolt by Prince Bistram 591–6. Chosroes took over after the Byzantines under Maurice defeated Bahram. After Maurice's death in 602, Chosroes captured Dara, Edessa and Aleppo from Byzantium. He conquered Armenia and raided Anatolia. The Persians reached the Bosphorus against Phokas. Chosroes captured Damascus in 613, Jerusalem 614 and Chalcedon 616. He conquered Egypt. Late in his reign Heraclius invaded Persia and Chosroes fled when Ctesiphon was taken. In 628 his son Kavadh-Siroes rebelled. Chosroes was thrown into the Tower of Darkness, fed on bread and water, and killed by arrows.

CLOVIS I (CHLODOVECH), MEROVINGIAN KING OF FRANCIA (c.465–511)

Son of Childeric, creator of the kingdom of Francia, founder of the Merovingian dynasty. His portrayal by Gregory of Tours about a century later was idealised. He succeeded his father in 481, ruling a group of Salian Franks based at Tournai. There were competing lesser rulers in northern Gaul. Clovis' victory over Syagrius at Soissons 486 completed the defeat of Roman political units in Gaul. He subjected the Thuringians in 491. He married the Burgundian Princess Chlothilde in 493. In 496 he defeated the Alemans at Tolbiac (Zülpich) and gained control of the upper Rhine. The Franks captured Bordeaux in 498. Clovis' victory over the Visigoths under Alaric II in 507 at Voulon won southern Gaul to the Pyrenees. Clovis' advance was halted by Theoderic the Great and the Ostrogoths at Arles. He converted to Roman Catholicism in 496 though most barbarian leaders were Arian heretics. As a result he won the support of the Church for the dynasty that he established. He was reputed to be a severe disciplinarian. A soldier is said to have disputed Clovis' right to a valuable vase and broken it with his axe. Later at a military parade Clovis split the man's skull with an axe, shouting 'that's what you did to my vase'. He made Paris his base, helping the emergence of that city as capital, and died there when his lands were divided between four sons.

CNUT (CANUTE/KNÚT/KNUD) THE GREAT, KING OF ENGLAND, DENMARK AND NORWAY (995–1035)

Maker and founder of a great Scandinavian and western empire consisting at its peak of Denmark, Norway, parts of Sweden, the northern Scottish isles, Scotland and England. Cnut accompanied his father Sweyn Forkbeard on the invasion of England in 1013. Cnut became King of England in 1016 following the conquest by and death of his father. Cnut returned to Denmark before renewing his claim to England. Aethelred II resisted but died in 1016. Cnut agreed a division with Aethelred's successor Edmund Ironside after defeating him at Assandun. Following Edmund's death in the same year Cnut ruled England. In 1017 he married Emma of Normandy, widow of Aethelred II, though also taking an English 'wife' Aelfgifu. On the death of his older brother Harold, Cnut became King of Denmark in 1019. Cnut invaded Scotland in 1027 and forced Malcolm III to accept his overlordship. He conquered Norway in 1028, causing the flight of St Ólaf. Cnut ruled England firmly but was defeated by the Swedes in 1025. He lost Norway. In England he instituted earls (jarls) as his leading nobles. The story of Cnut using the tide to demonstrate his human weakness appeared in the 12th century and was later distorted to make Cnut appear arrogant. He died at Shaftesbury and was buried at Winchester. In England he was succeeded in turn by his sons Harold I Harefoot and Harthacnut.

COLLEONI, BARTOLOMEO (1400–75)

An Italian *condottiere*, born at Solza near Bergamo into a Guelf family of lesser nobility. Bartolomeo was orphaned early. He became a captain of mercenaries, serving Milan and Venice during their conflict against each other. He is chiefly remembered in Venice, which he served for 20 years from 1429, though defecting temporarily in 1443. He captured San Luca in 1431 and defeated Milan on Lake Garda in 1439. After his defection he quarrelled with the Milanese and spent a year in prison. He escaped to Venice and through a contract in 1457 became *generalissimo* for life. His last battle was against Federigo of Urbino in 1467. He is said to have invented a type of small cannon on a carriage. He spent his last years in comfortable retirement at his castle of Malpaga, where he died on 3 November. He was buried in Bergamo. His equestrian statue by Verrocchio stands in Venice, raised by his own family with permission of the Republic.

CONRAD II, HOLY ROMAN EMPEROR (990–1039)

King of the Romans from 1024 on the death of Henry II and Emperor from 1027. Conrad was Henry's nearest relative and founded the imperial Salian dynasty. He was the son of the Count of Speyer and became Duke of Franconia. His son Henry became Duke of Bavaria and Swabia. Conrad brought Poland and Bohemia under his authority. In 1032 he took over Burgundy and was crowned its king in 1033 (thereafter the kingdom of Arles). Conrad faced disturbances in Italy after 1036. In that year he defeated the Wends under Lyutitzi. His biographer Wipo called him the new Charlemagne. Conrad died on 4 June and was succeeded by his son Henry III. He was buried at Speyer.

CONRAD III, HOLY ROMAN EMPEROR (1093–1152)

Son of Frederick of Swabia, elected King of the Romans in 1138, founder of the Hohenstaufen dynasty. He made himself King of Italy. In Germany he faced a Welf rebellion under Henry the Proud duke of Saxony and Bavaria until the latter's death in 1139. Conrad defeated Henry's uncle, Welf VI, at Weinsberg in 1140. Conrad participated in the Second Crusade in 1147, when he became ill. The crusaders failed to take Damascus 1148. Conrad allied with the Byzantines against Roger of Sicily. He died on 15 February, when his nephew Frederick Barbarossa succeeded. Conrad was buried at Bamberg.

CONRAD IV, HOLY ROMAN EMPEROR (1228–54)

Son of Frederick II, King of the Romans from 1237 and of Jerusalem. His mother was Isabelle of Brienne, heiress to the kingdom of Jerusalem. He became Duke of Swabia 1235. Frederick II was still alive when Conrad was elected King of the Romans. There was intermittent opposition in Germany, from Henry Raspe and later William of Holland – both supported by the papacy. On Frederick's death in 1250 Conrad succeeded to Sicily and Jerusalem. He married the daughter of the Duke of Bavaria. In 1252 he claimed his rights in Sicily, though the papacy refused to recognise him. Conrad died of malaria in Apulia on 21 May, aged 26, when planning a return to Germany. He was buried at Messina. In Germany a 20-year interregnum followed his death.

CONRADIN, KING OF SICILY (1252–68)

Son of the Holy Roman Emperor Conrad IV who died in 1254 and descendant of Frederick II. He was named Duke of Swabia, King of the Romans, and King of Sicily from 1254 though his position was challenged by his uncle Manfred. He was named as King of Jerusalem but never ruled there. After the invasion of Sicily by Charles of Anjou, Conradin tried to recover his kingdom in 1268. He was defeated at Tagliacozzo, captured and executed on 29 October.

CONSTANTINE I, THE GREAT, ROMAN EMPEROR (c.280–337)

Founder of Constantinople and of the Byzantine Empire, born at Naissus (Nis) in Serbia, son of Constantius the Western Caesar and Helena. He served his father in Britain. When his father died at York in 306 Constantine was proclaimed co-emperor by the army. He defeated his rival and brother-in-law Maxentius in 312 at the Milvian Bridge. He proclaimed Christianity as the official Roman religion. He defeated Licinius the Eastern Emperor in a series of battles culminating at Chrysolopolis 324, when Licinius surrendered and was executed. Constantine was sole ruler of the Empire from 324. He defeated the Goths and allied with them against other barbarians. Having dreamed of an old woman becoming a beautiful girl, he rebuilt old Byzantium from 324, making it his capital as Constantinople by 330. He put to death his wife Fausta and his son Crispus – some said for an affair between them. He died on 22 May at Nicomedia when on campaign against the Persians and was brought to Constantinople for burial. He was succeeded by three sons – Constantius, Constantine and Constans – Constantius emerging as sole Emperor by 353. The speed with which Constantinople had been built showed in its rickety structures; the church where Constantine was buried cracked and the body had to be moved.

CONSTANTINE V, COPRONYMUS (NAMED AFTER DUNG), BYZANTINE EMPEROR (718–75)

Emperor from 741, son of Leo III. His nickname came from defecating during baptism. He became co-emperor in 720 when Byzantium was iconoclastic (destroying religious icons). He married three times and had seven children. His relative Artabasdus attacked and defeated him in 742, declaring himself Emperor, but was defeated by Constantine at Sardis in 743 and then blinded. He was said to indulge himself indiscriminately with boys and girls. Despite frequent illness he became a successful military commander. He recovered part of Syria and Armenia. He defeated the Arabs at sea, regaining Cyprus. The Umayyad dynasty at Damascus ended and Islam turned to the east. Constantine led nine campaigns against the Bulgars, winning a series of victories culminating at Anchialus in 763. During the 775 campaign his legs became swollen and he died while

being carried home on a litter on
14 September. His son succeeded as Leo IV.

CONSTANTINE VII, PORPHYROGENITUS, BYZANTINE EMPEROR (905–59)

Emperor from 913, son of Leo VI and Zoe
Carbonopsina – who married three days
after his birth, a fourth marriage frowned
on in Byzantium. The nickname meant
'born in the purple'. He was seven when his
father died and an alcoholic uncle became
Emperor Alexander. Constantine succeeded
when Alexander collapsed during a polo
match. Zoe was regent until 919.
Constantine's reign began in 944. He
married Helena, daughter of Romanus
Lecapenus. Despite being a fat historian
and intellectual, he proved popular. He was
fortunate in having the services of the
generals, John Tzimisces and Nikephorus
Phokas, who successfully fought the
Bulgars and Arabs. The Rus were beaten at
sea, as were the Saracens off Lemnos.
Constantine caught a fever travelling to see
the bishop of Cyzicus, returning to
Constantinople to die on 9 November. He
was succeeded by his son Romanus II
Lecapenus.

CONSTANTINE VIII, BYZANTINE EMPEROR (960–1028)

Emperor from 1025, son of Romanus II,
brother and successor to Basil II, an
excellent horseman and athlete but 65 at
his accession. He was co-emperor with
Basil from 976. He commanded a force
against the rebel Bardas Phokas in 989. He
made an agreement with the Egyptian
Caliph in 1027 allowing the Byzantines to
rebuild the Church of the Holy Sepulchre in
Jerusalem. The Pechenegs invaded over the
Danube but were defeated and driven back.
He died on 9 November and was succeeded
by his daughter Zoe who married
Romanus III.

CONSTANTINE IX, MONOMACHUS, BYZANTINE EMPEROR (d.1055)

Emperor from 1042 as third husband of Zoe
(though retaining his mistress Sclerina). He
sought to reduce noble power. He had to
make economies, reducing the army and
the defence of the Armenian Themes.
Despite increased Turkish attacks he
gained Ani in Armenia. The Normans made
advances in Sicily. Constantine used
mercenaries and barbarian troops. The
Pechenegs crossed the Danube in 1048 but
were given lands by Constantine and
formed a buffer state. The recall of George
Maniakes from Italy led to his rebellion,
but Maniakes was killed in 1043.
Constantine suppressed a rising in
Constantinople in 1044, coincident with a
siege of the city by Leo Tornices. An arrow
shot by a mounted archer from outside
missed the watching emperor by an inch.
Leo was captured and blinded. Constantine
repulsed Russian attacks on
Constantinople in 1043, defeating the
enemy at sea with Greek Fire. The final
split with the Roman Church occurred in
1054. The threat from the Seljuk Turks first
emerged. Zoe died in 1050. He died on
11 January from a chill after staying too
long in the bath. Zoe's sister Theodora
succeeded.

CONSTANTINE XI, PALAEOLOGUS DRAGASES, BYZANTINE EMPEROR (1404–53)

Emperor from 1448, son of Manuel II and
the Serbian Princess Helena. He was the
last Emperor of Byzantium, succeeding his
brother John VIII. He married first
Magdalena renamed Theodora, niece of the
Lord of Epirus, and second Catherine
daughter of the Prince of Lesbos. He was
Despot of the Morea and rebuilt the wall
protecting the isthmus (the Hexamilion).
Mehmet II succeeded as sultan in 1451 and
prepared to take Constantinople.
Constantine appealed to the west and
attempted union of the two churches. The
siege began on 7 April 1453. Constantine
conducted the defence. As the situation
worsened he made a speech, suggesting
causes worth dying for and reminding his
hearers of their descent from ancient Rome.
When the Turks broke in on 29 May

Constantine, rather than be taken alive, asked his companions to kill him. They refused, so he threw off his robes and joined the fight. No one can be certain of his fate, though it was claimed his body was recognised from his imperial boots and socks.

DAGOBERT I, MEROVINGIAN KING OF FRANCIA (605–39)

A late Merovingian king, son of Chlothar II. He became sub-king of Austrasia under his father in 623 and succeeded to Francia in 629. He restored authority to the crown, winning control over the Bavarians. A king of the Bretons recognised Dagobert's lordship but refused to dine with such an immoral person. Dagobert had at least five wives. The Austrasian nobles opposed centralisation, so Dagobert appointed his son Sigebert III as sub-king of Austrasia in 634. Dagobert sent expeditions against the Slavs and Wends. The Wendish leader Samo had 12 wives and 37 children but retained enough energy to defeat Dagobert. The latter was a patron of St-Denis in Paris, where he was buried.

DECIUS, ROMAN EMPEROR (d.251)

Victim of an early Roman disaster against barbarians. Gaius Messius Quintus Trajanus Decius was a rebel who became emperor in 249. He was defeated and killed by the Goths at Forum Terebronii in Maesia. His body was not found after the battle.

DESIDERIUS, KING OF THE LOMBARDS (d. c.780)

King 757–74. He was seen as a threat by the papacy. In a political move favoured by his mother, the young Charlemagne married a daughter of Desiderius. Charlemagne repudiated her in 772 and turned hostile to Lombardy. His enemies sought refuge there. Pope Hadrian I appealed for Frankish aid against the Lombards. Desiderius had destroyed the independence of the Lombard duchies of Spoleto and Benevento. Charles' negotiations with Desiderius failed and he invaded Italy in 773. Desiderius blocked Charles' route from the Mont Cenis Pass, but a second force under Charles' uncle, Bernard, entered Lombardy via the Great St Bernard Pass. Desiderius retreated to Pavia, which was besieged. After ten months Desiderius surrendered. He was sent to a series of monasteries, finishing at Corbie in Francia, and Charles seized the Lombard crown in 774. The date of Desiderius' death is unknown. His son Adalgis fled into exile and continued to trouble Charles. Desiderius' daughter Liutperga married an opponent of Charles in Tassilo III of Bavaria.

EDMUND II, IRONSIDE, KING OF ENGLAND (981–1016)

He succeeded his father Aethelred II as king while Sweyn Forkbeard and Cnut were challenging for the throne. Edmund rebelled against his father in 1015, opposing Eadric Streona. Edmund married the widow of a northern thegn killed by Eadric. Father and son were reconciled. Edmund resisted Cnut's invasion in 1015. Edmund succeeded on his father's death in 1016 but died that year. During that brief period he fought six battles against Cnut, including Penselwood and Sherston, neither being decisive. The Danes were beaten at Brentford, and at Otford in Kent. At Ashingdon Eadric deserted to Cnut. Edmund was defeated but escaped. The Peace of Alney followed, when England was divided. Edmund was probably wounded at Ashingdon. He died in London on 30 November and was buried at Glastonbury.

EDWARD THE ELDER, KING OF ENGLAND (c.870–924)

King of Wessex and the English from 899, crowned in 900, son and successor of Alfred the Great. He fought campaigns for his father. He continued the policy of fortified burhs. He extended English power into the Danelaw, winning Mercia and East Anglia. The most important victory of the reign occurred in his absence at Wednesfield near

Tettenhall, a key moment in the rise of Wessex at the expense of the Danes. Edward's authority was recognised by the Scots. He was in effect the first King of England, with power over all the land south of the Humber. His sister Aethelflaed assisted him until her death in 918. Edward married three times. He died on 17 July at Farndon on Dee and was buried at Winchester.

EDWARD I, KING OF ENGLAND (1239–1307)

King from 1272, son of Henry III and Eleanor of Provence, arguably the greatest medieval military King of England. He was over six feet tall, known as 'Longshanks'. He married Eleanor of Castile and secondly Margaret of France. He saved his father from the control of Simon de Montfort. After defeat at Lewes Edward won at Evesham in 1265, when de Montfort was killed. Edward went on one of the last crusades, during which his father died. In France he strengthened settlements as *bastides.* He invaded and conquered Wales from 1282, building a series of castles. He sought and won control over Scotland. At first he attempted to control the Scottish succession and the king but this failed. He conquered Scotland with victories at Dunbar 1296 and Falkirk 1298. The Scots resisted under William Wallace, who defeated the English under Warenne at Stirling in 1297. Robert the Bruce continued opposition into the next reign. Edward died on 7 July heading for Scotland to suppress rebellion. He was succeeded by his son Edward II.

EDWARD II, KING OF ENGLAND (1284–1327)

King from 1307, son of Edward I and Eleanor of Castile. In 1301 he became the first English Prince of Wales. He married Isabelle of France in 1308. He was probably homosexual and favoured friends, notably Piers Gaveston. The baronial opposition seized power and executed Gaveston in 1312. Edward was defeated in Scotland at Bannockburn in 1314. Power in England fluctuated between the opposition and the king supported by favoured ministers, the Despensers father and son. His leading opponent, Lancaster, was beaten at Boroughbridge in 1322 and later executed. Edward was defeated in Gascony in the War of St-Sardos, 1324–5. Queen Isabelle was hostile to the Despensers. She went to her native France for peace negotiations but deserted her husband for Roger Mortimer. They invaded England in 1326. The Despensers were executed and Edward forced to abdicate in favour of his son Edward III. He was imprisoned and killed in Berkeley Castle.

EDWARD III, KING OF ENGLAND (1312–77)

King from 1327, son of Edward II and Isabelle of France. He founded the Order of the Garter. He married Philippa of Hainault. Despite considerable success he faced troubles in his last years. Edward became king as a figurehead for his mother and Mortimer after the deposition of Edward II. He proved less amenable than expected and seized power. He renewed the war in Scotland, developing methods later employed in France. He won at Halidon Hill in 1333 but never completely suppressed the Scots. He had victories against the French in the early Hundred Years' War, winning at Crécy in 1346 and taking Calais in 1347. His son won at Poitiers in 1356. The first phase of the war concluded with the Treaty of Brétigny in 1360, largely favourable to England. Edward's achievements were diminished in his last decade, when health and ability declined. The economic consequences of the Black Death worsened the situation. His son the Black Prince died in 1376. Edward died on 21 June and was succeeded by his grandson Richard II.

EDWARD IV, KING OF ENGLAND (1442–83)

King from 1461, born at Rouen, son of Richard duke of York and Cecily Neville. He was Earl of March, succeeding his father as Duke of York in 1460. He fought against Henry VI at Northampton and assumed the crown that his father had sought but not gained. Edward confirmed the position with victories at Mortimer's Cross and Towton. He married Elizabeth Woodville in 1464, antagonising his brother the Duke of Clarence and the Earl of Warwick. He differed with Warwick over foreign affairs, favouring Burgundy rather than France. Warwick rejoined the Lancastrians and Edward fled the country in 1470. He returned in 1471 and won at Barnet and Tewkesbury, resuming the throne. In alliance with Burgundy he invaded France in 1475, making a favourable peace. He recovered Berwick from the Scots in 1482. In later life he conducted a scandalous affair with Jane Shore. He died on 9 April, possibly from a stroke. He was buried at Windsor, where he had built St George's Chapel. He was succeeded briefly by his son Edward V but his brother Richard III seized the crown.

EDWARD THE BLACK PRINCE, PRINCE OF WALES (1330–76)

Edward of Woodstock, Prince of Wales from 1343, son of Edward III and Philippa of Hainault. With his father he fought at Crécy in 1346, and commanded at Poitiers in 1356. He was Earl of Chester from 1333, Duke of Cornwall from 1337, and Prince of Aquitaine from 1362. In support of Pedro the Cruel he invaded Castile against Henry of Trastámara, winning at Nájera in 1367. Pedro's death in 1369 negated these efforts. After a *chevauchée* through France, he conducted the ruthless sack of Limoges in 1370, which has been condemned but followed normal practice in contemporary warfare. His death from dropsy on 8 June led to the succession of his son Richard II.

EDWARD BRUCE (d.1318)

Brother of Robert the Bruce. When Robert became King of Scots in 1306, Edward was his most trusted commander. Edward was Earl of Carrick from 1313 and a commander at Bannockburn in 1314. He invaded Ireland in 1315 with support from Ulster nobles. He claimed to be King of Ireland but never fulfilled the claim. He was defeated and killed on 14 October at Faughart near Dundalk.

EL CID, RODRIGO DÍAZ DE VIVAR, KING OF VALENCIA (1043–99)

Born near Burgos. He married Jimena Díaz daughter of the Count of Oviedo and niece of Alfonso VI. His fame chiefly comes from his portrayal in the *Poema del mío Cid*. The Muslims called him *El Cid* (the lord) or *El Cid Campeador* (the warrior lord). He served Alfonso VI of Castile but they quarrelled and he went into exile in 1081. After reconciliation he was exiled again in 1089. He became a captain of mercenaries (taking 60 knights with him), serving the Muslim King of Zaragoza. He won victories against the Count of Barcelona. His main achievement was the capture of Valencia in 1094, which he ruled until his death. He defeated the Almoravids at Cuarte in 1094 and Bairen in 1096. He captured Almenara in 1097. His widow Jimena returned Valencia to Muslim control in 1102. She removed Rodrigo's body to Burgos.

ENGUERRAND VII DE COUCY (1340–97)

Lord of Coucy to the north of Soissons. By the 1360 Treaty of Brétigny Enguerrand became a hostage in England, where he later chose to live. He married Isabella, daughter of Edward III, and became Earl of Bedford and Count of Soissons. He broke with England and ended his marriage. Isabella died and he married Isabelle, daughter of the Duke of Lorraine. He was a champion in tournaments. He was Captain General of Auvergne and Guienne for Charles VI. In 1390 he besieged Barbary in the Tunis Crusade. He besieged the pirate base at Mahdia, using a belfry. A Berber relief force was beaten but after ten weeks the siege was abandoned. In 1394 he occupied Savona for Louis II of Anjou. He went on the Crusade of Nicopolis and was captured in 1396. Arrangements for a ransom proceeded slowly and he became ill while a prisoner at Brusa, where he died on 18 February. Parts of him (how much is unknown) were returned in separate parcels to France for burial at Nogent and Sainte-Trinité Soissons (the heart).

ENRIQUE (HENRY) II DE TRASTÁMARA, KING OF CASTILE AND LEÓN (1333–79)

Illegitimate son of Alfonso XI who sought the throne in civil war against his half-brother Pedro the Cruel. Enrique declared himself king in 1366. He became involved in the Hundred Years' War, with support from France while England backed Pedro. He invaded Castile in 1366 but was defeated at Nájera in 1367. Enrique won at Montiel in 1369, stabbing Pedro to death in single combat, while Bertrand du Guesclin unchivalrously held Pedro by the leg. Enrique was thus confirmed King of Castile. He fought inconclusive wars against Portugal and Aragón. John of Gaunt married Pedro's daughter and claimed Castile, but could not substantiate the claim. Enrique besieged Lisbon, breaking the alliance between Portugal and John. In alliance with France, Enrique defeated the English fleet at La Rochelle in 1372. He raided the English coast in 1377. He died on 29 May and was succeeded by his son Juan I.

ERIK HAROLDSSON, BLOODAXE, KING OF NORWAY AND YORK (c.930–54)

King of Norway 942–47, the last Scandinavian King of York from 948. He succeeded to Norway on the abdication of his father, Harold Finehair. Erik married Gunnhild, sister of Harold Bluetooth of Denmark. Erik's brother Hákon the Good deposed him in 947, when he fled to England to become King of York. He was expelled in 949, returned by 952, and was expelled again in 954 through pressure from Eadred of Wessex on the Northumbrians. Erik was killed at Stainmore, a significant moment in the decline of Viking rule in England. Snorri's account of Erik is biased and hostile. The nickname Bloodaxe was applied after his death.

ERIK TORVALDSSON, THE RED (d.1002)

Leader of the first settlement in Greenland, giving the land its name. His nickname is said to derive from the colour of his hair. Born in Norway, he was a persistent troublemaker. Either Erik or his father was exiled for manslaughter in c.970, going to Iceland. Erik was forced to leave his home at Haukadalur for feuding, and then exiled for manslaughter. He attacked a neighbour in a private battle, leading to several deaths. Greenland had been sighted by Gunnbjörn earlier in the century. Erik sailed there in exile in about 982. He returned to Iceland and his successful colonisation occurred at the second attempt in 986 (though 11 of his 25 ships were lost). Erik built a farm at Brattahlid in the Eastern Settlement. He died from a disease brought by ship from Norway. He featured in two Icelandic sagas, *Greenlanders' Saga* and *Erik the Red's Saga*. His son Leif Eriksson was the first Viking to land in North America.

ESTE, NICCOLÒ III D', MARQUIS OF FERRARA (1383–1441)

Lord from 1393, a member of the Este dynasty that ruled Ferrara. He employed Muzio Sforza and educated his son Francesco Sforza. Niccolò was a noted patron. Lord of Ferrara from the age of ten, he fought to keep his position. He was renowned for numerous illegitimate offspring (at least 23) – 'On this side and that of the Po, all are the children of Niccolò'. Ferrara was often in the shadow of more powerful neighbours but emerged to greater prominence. Niccolò was ruthless and his armies successful. He brought decades of peace to Ferrara. Three sons succeeded him in turn – Leonello, Borso and Ercole.

EYSTEIN ÓLAFSSON, FART, KING OF VESTFOLD

Possibly an ancestor of Harold Finehair. The nickname refers to his wanderings rather than his indigestion. We know of him through Snorri Sturlusson using an ancient verse compilation. Eystein was knocked overboard by a passing ship's boom and drowned. He was said to be buried at Borre.

FAUCONBERG, THOMAS NEVILLE, THE BASTARD (d.1471)

Illegitimate son of William Neville Lord Fauconberg. Thomas was closely allied to his cousin Warwick the Kingmaker. He commanded a fleet in the 1470s, making piratical attacks on Spanish and Portuguese shipping. After Warwick's death he led a rising in Kent and unsuccessfully besieged London in 1471 for the Lancastrians. He surrendered to Edward IV, was pardoned, but then executed for breaking the agreement. His head was placed on London Bridge.

FAWKES DE BRÉAUTÉ (d.1226)

A mercenary captain for John and Henry III, probably the illegitimate son of a Norman knight. He was nicknamed after the *falx* (scythe) with which he killed a knight in Normandy. John granted him a position on the Welsh border and knighted him. In 1218 he was granted custody of the lands of the earldom of Devon. He fought at Lincoln for Henry III in 1217. Through the hostility of Hubert de Burgh he was deprived of his main lands and rebelled. Henry III besieged and took Bedford Castle in 1224, held by Fawkes' brother William, who was hanged with 80 of the garrison. Fawkes surrendered at Elstow, lost his lands, and was exiled to France. He sought restoration through appeal to the pope but died in Rome.

FERDINAND (FERNANDO) I, THE GREAT, KING OF CASTILE (d.1065)

King from 1035, son and successor of Sancho III. Sancho divided his territories between his sons. Fernando fought his brothers and reunited Castile with León and Navarre by victories at Tamarón in 1037 and Atapuerca in 1054. He advanced Castile eastwards to the Ebro. He captured Coimbra in 1064. He won control of the *taifas* of Zaragoza, Toledo, Seville and Badajoz. He attacked Valencia and won at

Paterna. He died on 27 December, dividing his territories between his sons. He was buried in the Cathedral of St Isidore in León.

FERDINAND (FERNANDO) II, KING OF ARAGÓN AND CASTILE (1479–1516)

King of Aragón from 1479, son and successor of Juan II. He married Isabella of Castile in 1469. He claimed Castile on the death of Enrique IV in 1474 but agreed to rule jointly with his wife, becoming Ferdinand V of Castile. The marriage led to the uniting of Spain under *Los Reyes Catolicos* (the Catholic monarchs). They conquered Granada, the last Muslim kingdom in Iberia, concluding the *Reconquista* with the capture of the city of Granada in 1492. After Isabella's death Ferdinand married Germaine, heiress to Navarre, in 1506. He ruled the kingdoms of Naples as Ferdinand III and Sicily as Ferdinand II. He patronised the voyages of Columbus.

FERDINAND (FERNANDO) III, KING OF LEÓN AND CASTILE (1200–52)

He fought a succession war 1214–17. He advanced the *Reconquista*, gaining Córdoba in 1236, Seville after a siege 1247–8 and Jaén. Only Granada survived as a Muslim state in Iberia. Ferdinand was canonised for piety, becoming *San Fernando Rey*. He died on 30 May and was succeeded by his son Alfonso X.

FERRAND OF PORTUGAL, COUNT OF FLANDERS (d.1233)

Son of Sancho I of Portugal. He married the heiress Joanna of Flanders in 1212 with the support of Philip II of France. Philip knighted Ferrand and received his homage. Ferrand's aunt, Matilda, widow of Philip count of Flanders, suggested the marriage. The French took Aire and Omer, antagonising Ferrand and making him unpopular in Flanders. Ferrand allied with John of England and Otto IV (HRE). Ferrand refused to join Philip's projected invasion of England in 1213. Philip made an abortive invasion of Flanders. The French fleet was destroyed at Damme. Ferrand fought against Philip at Bouvines in 1214, leading the allied left. He was unhorsed, wounded and captured. He was chained on a cart pulled by two *ferrands* (grey horses), the crowd jeering as he passed. On Philip's death, Ferrand was released by Louis VIII in 1227. He died, a broken man, from an illness contracted in prison.

FRANÇOIS DE SURIENNE (d.1462)

Born in Aragón, known as *L'Arragonais*, a mercenary captain, a specialist in fortification and artillery. He fought for the English in the Hundred Years' War, serving Henry VI from 1424. Henry made him Captain of Montargis and granted him a pension. He was encouraged to attack Fougères in Brittany in 1449, with the intention of releasing Gilles who had been imprisoned by his brother the Duke of Brittany. Surienne took and sacked Fougères, ruling it for seven months until it surrendered to France after a siege. His attack broke a truce between England and France. The English disclaimed him. He returned his Order of the Garter and went to Naples. He served Charles VII of France from 1450 as the French completed their triumph in the Hundred Years' War.

FREDEGUND, QUEEN OF NEUSTRIA (d.597)

Second wife of Chilperic I of Neustria, and mother of Chlothar II, the rival of Brunhild. Fredegund was set aside by Chilperic for Brunhild's sister Galswinth. Galswinth was murdered and Fredegund restored. She was accused by Gregory of Tours (whom she summoned to court for slander) of various tortures and murders but she was praised by Venantius Fortunatus as 'illustrious'. She ruled during the minority of Chlothar II, whose succession she ensured, taking military command. After her husband's murder she ordered the Saxons of Bayeux to cut their hair and dress as Bretons. They joined the Breton ranks and assisted their victory. She organised resistance to Wintrio duke of Champagne, advising a surprise attack with an advance camouflaged by men carrying branches that led to success. She died a natural death.

FREDERICK I, BARBAROSSA, HOLY ROMAN EMPEROR (1123–90)

King of the Romans from 1152 and Emperor from 1155. His nickname means redbeard. He was a Hohenstaufen, son of Frederick duke of Swabia and nephew of Conrad III. His mother was Judith daughter of the Duke of Bavaria. He thus united the rival interests of Guelf and Ghibelline. Frederick succeeded to Swabia in 1147. He developed the imperial demesne to include 400 castles. His major opponent in Germany was Henry the Lion of Saxony, whom Frederick failed to placate by recognising him as Duke of Bavaria. Henry did not attend Barbarossa's 1176 Italian expedition and was summoned to answer for it. Other nobles assisted the emperor in defeating Henry, who was exiled. Saxony was divided in two. Frederick married Beatrice heiress to Burgundy, which he took over. Family lands and marriage gave him interests in southern Germany and Italy. He sought to impose control over northern Italy, making four major expeditions. He undertook long sieges at Crema 1159–60 and Milan 1161–2. In 1167 Italian cities formed the Lombard League and defeated Frederick at Legnano 1176. He arranged the marriage of his son Henry to Constance heiress to Sicily, leading later to imperial rule. Barbarossa twice went on crusade, in 1146–8 and 1189–90, when he died *en route* on 10 June when crossing or swimming in the River Saleph (Göksu) in Cilicia (Turkey).

FREDERICK II, HOLY ROMAN EMPEROR (1194–1250)

Emperor from 1215 and King of Jerusalem from 1229, known as *stupor mundi* (wonder of the world), son of Henry VI (HRE) and Constance of Sicily. He was not elected in Germany on his father's death but succeeded in Sicily in 1198. Rebellion was suppressed and Frederick built castles in Sicily and Apulia. There was civil war in Germany between his uncle, Philip of Swabia, and Otto of Brunswick, the latter becoming Otto IV. Frederick received support in Sicily from the pope and maintained his position. Otto tried to seize Sicily but failed. Frederick claimed the Empire but only succeeded after Otto's defeat by Philip Augustus at Bouvines in 1214. Frederick's second wife was Isabelle of Brienne, heiress to the kingdom of Jerusalem. Though excommunicated by the pope, Frederick went on crusade and was crowned King of Jerusalem. His son Henry, elected King of the Romans, joined a rebellion in Germany. Frederick destroyed his opponents in 1234 and dethroned his son who was imprisoned in Sicily, where he died in 1242. Henry was replaced by his brother Conrad. In 1237 Frederick defeated the Lombard League at Cortenuova but the League took Parma in 1248. In 1249 Bolognese troops captured Frederick's illegitimate son Enzio. Frederick died of dysentery in Apulia on 12 December and was buried at Palermo. His wide-ranging interest in learning, including that of the Arabic world through Sicily, earned him his nickname.

FREDERICK III, HOLY ROMAN EMPEROR (1415–93)

King of the Germans from 1440, the last Holy Roman Emperor crowned in Rome, in 1452. His father was Ernst duke of Styria. In 1422 he inherited the Habsburg lands as Duke of Austria. Frederick failed to secure Hungary, while the Turks invaded in 1469 and 1475. He tried to suppress the Hussites in Bohemia. He married his son Maximilian I to Mary daughter of Charles the Bold of Burgundy, creating the base of later Habsburg power. He fought for and won the release of Maximilian after his capture at Bruges in 1488. Frederick's foot was amputated because of gangrene and he died on 19 August.

FULK III, NERRA, COUNT OF ANJOU (d.1040)

Count from 987, son of Geoffrey I Greygown, he was only eight at the time of his succession. The name 'Nerra' probably came from 'Niger' meaning the Black – though we have no explanation of its origin. He made Anjou a major political unit, an example of the growing power of the counts when the West Frankish monarchy was losing authority. Anjou began as a minor county but a series of great counts brought it to the forefront. Much of Fulk's career was spent fighting rival neighbours. In 992 Fulk defeated Conan I of Brittany at Conquereux, where Conan was killed. Fulk was thrown from his horse but recovered. Nantes, which had been besieged, surrendered. In alliance with Maine he defeated Odo II of Blois at Pontlevoy in 1016. Fulk imprisoned his former ally, Herbert Wakedog, Count of Maine, who was released on recognising Fulk's overlordship. Fulk was an important builder of early castles, including Langeais built in 994 and Montboyau. He captured the earliest-known European castle, Doué-la-Fontaine, from Blois in 1025. He twice made pilgrimages to Jerusalem. His first wife was burnt to death for adultery. His second wife was sent a cup with the message that it was from the man she loved best. Believing Fulk had found her out she leaped from a window. In fact Fulk had sent it from himself but luckily she fell into the moat and survived. Fulk died at Metz on return from Jerusalem. His body was embalmed and buried at Beaulieu Abbey. Fulk was succeeded by his son Geoffrey II Martel, who had previously rebelled against Fulk and been defeated. Fulk had kicked and beaten him before their reconciliation.

FULK IV LE RÉCHIN, COUNT OF ANJOU (1043–1109)

Count of Anjou from 1068, son of the Count of the Gâtinais and Ermengarde daughter of Fulk Nerra. Translation of his surname is uncertain, possibly meaning 'Quarreller', 'Rash', 'Exile' or 'Hissing' –

but probably 'Sour-Faced' (from a stroke that affected his appearance). He is said to have written an historical account known as the *Fragment*. He was knighted by his uncle, Geoffrey Martel, in 1060. He initiated a fashion in shoes with long pointed toes to hide his deformed feet. He was criticised for having too many wives (three to five by various reckonings – and not always consecutively). One wife, Bertrade de Montfort, ran off with King Philip I in 1107. Fulk's older brother became Count of Anjou as Geoffrey IV. They quarrelled, Fulk emerging victorious in 1068. Fulk released his brother, who rebelled again and was imprisoned for 28 years. Though criticised by historians, Fulk ruled firmly through a difficult period. He was responsible for wresting Maine from Normandy. He dealt firmly with internal risings, taking Amboise from its lord, Sulpice, after a siege in 1106. His son, Geoffrey Martel II, died before Fulk, who was succeeded by his younger son Fulk V, later King of Jerusalem.

FULK V, LE JEUNE, COUNT OF ANJOU, KING OF JERUSALEM (1092–1143)

Count from 1131, king from 1129, son of Fulk IV le Réchin. He defeated Henry I of England at Alençon in 1118. He was the first Count of Anjou to rule Maine directly. In 1120 he made a pilgrimage to the Holy Land. In 1128 he made peace with Henry I, and his son Geoffrey (V) married Henry's daughter the Empress Matilda – laying the foundation for the Angevin Empire. His first wife was Eremburg, heiress of Maine, his second Melisende daughter and heiress of Baldwin II King of Jerusalem. Anjou was left under his son Geoffrey V, and Fulk became King of Jerusalem in 1131 on the death of Baldwin II. Early in the reign he suppressed rebellions by Roman du Puy and Hugh du Puiset. He protected the kingdom by alliance with Damascus and Byzantium. In 1137 he surrendered Montferrand to Zangi after a siege, on condition of his release. He died on 10 November, falling from a horse when hunting hares. He was succeeded by his sons Baldwin III in Jerusalem and Geoffrey V, who was already Count of Anjou.

GAISERIC, KING OF THE VANDALS (c.390–477)

He established the Vandal realm in Africa. He was lamed in a fall from his horse. Noted for cruelty, he cut off the nose and ears of his daughter-in-law for conspiring against him. He became king in succession to his brother Gunderic in 429 and led the Vandals and Alans from Spain to Africa in 429. The division between Aëtius and Count Boniface in Africa provided an opportunity for invasion. Gaiseric captured Hippo in 431 and won Mauritania and Numidia. In 439 Carthage fell, becoming his capital. He established a realm that dominated the western Mediterranean, capturing Sardinia and Sicily. He beat off attacks by the eastern and western Romans on land and sea. He allied with Attila the Hun against the Romans. In 455 he led an attack on Rome, which was sacked. His son Huneric succeeded but Vandal power quickly declined.

GATTAMELATA (ERASMO DA NARNI) (1370–1443)

A *condottiere*, son of a baker from Umbria, generally known by his nickname, which means 'honeyed cat'. He served under Montone and Piccinino and alongside Colleoni. He was employed by Florence, the papacy and Venice. For Venice he opposed Milan under the Visconti. He became Captain General for Venice and was awarded lands and a castle for his services. His statue by Donatello stands in Padua. His son Gian Antonio served Venice as a *condottiere*.

GAUNT, JOHN OF, DUKE OF LANCASTER, DUKE OF AQUITAINE (1340–99)

Duke of Lancaster from 1362, of Aquitaine from 1390, son of Edward III, born at Ghent (hence Gaunt) in Flanders. He married Blanche daughter and heiress of Henry duke of Lancaster. He fought in France, leading a *chevauchée* to Bordeaux in 1373. His second wife was Constance of Castile, heiress to Castile and León, but his attempts to gain the kingdom failed. His daughter Katherine married Henry III of Castile. He married his mistress Katherine Swynford in order to legitimise their children, the Beauforts. He wielded considerable power in the last years of Edward III and in the reign of Richard II. Gaunt remained loyal to Richard but his death on 3 February led to invasion and the seizure of the throne by his son Henry Bolingbroke.

GEOFFREY I VILLEHARDOUIN, PRINCE OF ACHAEA (1209–29)

He did not participate in the Fourth Crusade, arriving in Greece after the fall of Constantinople. He was the nephew of the chronicler Geoffrey de Villehardouin. Geoffrey established a new Latin state in Greece, subject to the Latin Emperor. His territory was Achaea in the Peloponnese (the Morea) with its capital at Andravida in Elis. His main castle was Clermont (Khloumoutsi/Castel Tornese). He was succeeded by Geoffrey II. A number of historians confuse the three Geoffreys.

GEOFFREY III DE MANDEVILLE, EARL OF ESSEX (d.1144)

Rebel against King Stephen, who had restored Geoffrey's family possessions and appointed him sheriff of Essex, Hampshire, London and Middlesex, given him guardianship of the Tower of London, and made him earl in 1140. He was seen as the prime example of a self-seeking baron but his reputation has recovered a little. He probably did not change sides so readily and frequently as thought. He joined Matilda after Stephen's capture at Lincoln but returned to the royal allegiance. Stephen had Geoffrey arrested in 1143 possibly for an insult to Stephen's daughter-in-law Constance. Geoffrey may have been conspiring with Matilda. Geoffrey agreed to hand castles to the king but, on release, rebelled and took refuge in the Isle of Ely.

He seized Ramsey Abbey as a base, turning out the monks. Stephen came against him, building a castle at Burwell on the fringe of the fenlands. Geoffrey tried to prevent its completion and was wounded by a crossbowman. He was taken to Mildenhall and died a week later on 26 September.

GEOFFREY V, LE BEL, PLANTAGENET, COUNT OF ANJOU, DUKE OF NORMANDY (1113–51)

Count from 1129, duke from 1144, son of Fulk V King of Jerusalem. John of Marmoutier's *Historia Gaufredi Ducis* narrated his career. He was a noted participant in tournaments, a 'grant chevalier e fort e bel'. His father left to marry and to inherit Jerusalem in 1129, leaving Geoffrey to rule Anjou. Geoffrey's mother, Eremburg of Maine, strengthened his right to Maine. In 1128 he married the Empress Matilda, widow of Henry V (HRE) and daughter of Henry I of England. Geoffrey was knighted by Henry I. Geoffrey conquered Normandy from Stephen between 1135 and 1145 in a series of campaigns involving many sieges but no battles. The taking of Rouen in 1144 was the climax. Arques surrendered in 1145. He did not assist Matilda's attempt to win England from Stephen. He had to deal with rebellion by Gerard Berlai, besieging Montreuil-Bellay for three years. He used Greek Fire (for the first time in the west) and the castle surrendered in 1151. He was inspired to this by reading Vegetius' *De Re Militari*. Geoffrey died on 7 September and was succeeded by Henry. An image of Geoffrey appeared on an enamel for his tomb at Le Mans, showing as his arms those that became the arms of England (possibly derived from Henry I). His son and successor in Anjou became Henry II of England, founder of the Angevin Empire.

GODFRED, KING OF DENMARK (d.810)

The first main King of Denmark from c.800. His kingdom included southern Norway. After Charlemagne defeated the Saxons his power extended to Godfred's border. Godfred assembled an army at Hedeby in eastern Jutland, a town whose importance dates from the time, but failed to meet Charlemagne as agreed. In 808 Godfred attacked the Abodrites, Slav allies of Charlemagne, burning the settlement at Reric and capturing their chief Drasko, who was promised freedom but executed. Godfred's motive was apparently to destroy Hedeby's trade rival. Godfred strengthened the earthwork defence across the Jutland Peninsula against the Franks. Dendrochronology shows that the earthwork was begun earlier in c.737 – suggesting previous kings we know nothing of. In 810 Godfred attacked Frisia by sea and imposed tribute. There were fears that he intended attacking Aachen but he was killed by a retainer and the Danes made peace with Charlemagne.

GODFREY DE BOUILLON, DUKE OF LOWER LORRAINE (1061–1100)

Son of Eustace II of Boulogne, a leader of the First Crusade, elected Advocate of the Holy Sepulchre in 1099 – the first ruler of the kingdom of Jerusalem. He decided not to wear a crown in the Holy City. He fought for Henry IV (HRE), who made him a duke. Godfrey was at the sieges of Nicaea, Antioch and Jerusalem. He and Raymond of Toulouse led the decisive charge at Dorylaeum. He commanded at Ascalon in 1099. He established the kingdom and extended its territory. He died on 18 July and was buried in Jerusalem. He was succeeded by his brother Baldwin I.

GODWIN (GODWINE), EARL OF WESSEX (1018–53)

Earl of Wessex under Edward the Confessor, a powerful figure who threatened the king's position. Godwin's brood of offspring included Harold II Godwinson, King of England in 1066. Godwin's beginnings are unclear but his base was in Sussex under Cnut. His father was Wulfnoth, probably Wulfnoth Cild thegn of Sussex. Godwin seems English rather than Scandinavian but Cnut made

him Earl of Wessex and Godwin married into Cnut's family. Godwin had presumably helped Cnut gain the throne and was involved in the succession of Cnut's sons, Harold I Harefoot and Harthacnut. Under Harold Harefoot Godwin was involved in the arrest of Aethelred II's son Alfred, brother of Edward the Confessor, at Guildford in 1036. Alfred was blinded and died. When Edward became king there was a reconciliation. Edward married Godwin's daughter Edith in 1045. Antagonism continued and in 1051 Godwin refused to harry Dover, whose citizens had attacked Eustace of Boulogne. Edward exiled Godwin and his sons. Godwin went to Flanders, returning in 1052 to force a new reconciliation. Godwin's sons were earls of East Anglia and Northumbria, with new earldoms created in the southern midlands and in the south-east for Leofwin and Sweyn. At his death on 15 April Harold succeeded as Earl of Wessex. Godwin's son Tostig became involved in the events of 1066, allying with his brother's rival Harold Hardrada.

GORM THE OLD, KING OF DENMARK (d.958)

Probable founder of the kingdom. Sagas described him overcoming lesser kings and ending Swedish power over Jutland. Gorm made peace with Henry I (HRE) in 934 but resisted Christian efforts in Scandinavia. The memorial stone to his wife Thyri for the first time mentions 'Denmark'. Gorm was succeeded by his son Harold Bluetooth. Gorm's daughter Gunnhild married Erik Bloodaxe. A burial mound at Jelling, where royal power was based, is associated with Gorm. A stone set up to him by his son is dated c.985. A skeleton found in 1979 at Jelling is thought to be Gorm – if so he died in his forties.

GRANT (GRANDE/GRANDO), JOHN (JOHANNES)

Best known from his appearance in the fiction of Dorothy Dunnett, but an actual historical figure. Little is known of him. He may have been a Scot but one chronicler calls him 'the German'. He appears as Johannes Grant (Grande/Grando) in the sources. He arrived at Constantinople in 1453 in a Genoese relief force under Giovanni Giustiniani. He was an engineer, specialising in mining and counter-mining. He countered a Turkish mine on 16 May, digging into it and firing the props. The Turkish tunnel collapsed, killing many. On 23 May a Turkish officer was captured and, when tortured, revealed the mining plans. Within two days Grant had destroyed all the Turkish mines. As a result the Turks abandoned mining.

GREGORY I, SAINT, THE GREAT (540–604)

Pope from 590, during the time of the Lombard invasion of Italy. He defended Rome against the Lombard advance in 592–3. He intervened outside Rome, appointing a military governor in Nepi and instructing military commanders. He made peace with the Lombard Duke Ariulf in 592 and with King Agilulf in 593. The Byzantines undermined his efforts, opposing peace. He sent St Augustine to England.

GUESCLIN, BERTRAND DU, COMTE DE LONGUEVILLE AND DUKE OF MOLINA (1323–80)

A leading general for Charles V, Constable of France from 1370. His family was Breton. He became a captain of *routiers*, knighted for his efforts at Montmuran in 1354. He defended Rennes 1356–7. He was taken prisoner by the English but released. For Charles V he defeated Navarrese rebels at Cocherel 1364. He recovered the Cotentin. Under Charles of Blois he was defeated and captured by the English at Auray in 1364. He fought for France in the wars in Spain, supporting Enrique de Trastámara. He was defeated and captured by the Black Prince at Nájera in 1367. He tried to hamper John of Gaunt's *chévauchée*. He captured La Rochelle in 1372. He ended his days

fighting in Brittany where the French gained the upper hand. He died in July at the siege of Châteauneuf-de-Randon in the Auvergne. His reputation became legendary despite his defeats. He was a champion crossbowman, an able strategist, respected by his troops. His tried to avoid pitched battle against the English. His career matched the recovery of France in the Hundred Years' War. His image appeared on his tomb at St-Denis.

GUNDERIC, KING OF THE VANDALS (d.428)

He increased Vandal power in Spain, defeating the Suevi in Galicia in 420, though Roman forces imposed peace. In 422 he defeated the Romans and captured Cartagena in 424. He raided the Balearic Islands in 425 with a captured fleet, making possible the Vandal move to North Africa. By the time of his death he ruled most of Iberia.

GUNDOBAD, KING OF THE BURGUNDIANS (d.516)

Son of Gundioc, supporter of his uncle Ricimer, he became *magister militum* in Italy 472–3. The *Lex Gundobada* legal code was named after him. He supported Glycerius for emperor, but the latter preferred to be bishop of Salona. He gained power in Italy by murdering Emperor Anthemius, later killing his own brothers Chilperic II and Godgisel – though this scenario comes from Frankish propaganda. Another source has him weeping over his brothers' deaths. Godgisel had been in arms against him in alliance with Clovis I in 500. At Dijon Gundobad was defeated, but took refuge in Avignon, which Clovis besieged. Avignon held out and peace was agreed. On Clovis' death in 511, Gundobad held power in Gaul. Burgundy declined under the rule of his son, Sigismund.

GUNDOBAD, KING OF THE VANDALS

Led the Vandal invasion of Gaul in 406. He moved to Spain and fought the Suevi. He was succeeded by Gaiseric.

GUNTRAM BOSO (d.587)

Austrasian magnate and commander. The chroniclers refer to him as *dux*. His base was Tours, whose local levy he led. His followers were referred to as 'armed men' and 'friends'. The support of such troops was vital to the power of Merovingian princes. Boso fought for Sigebert I and Childebert II. On Sigebert's behalf he helped defeat and kill Theudebert in 575. He helped cause the death of Chilperic's son, Merovech, in 577. He was captured by King Guntram of Burgundy, accused of bringing Gundovald into Gaul. To retrieve his position he promised to capture the commander Mummolus in 582. Mummolus sabotaged the boats for Boso's crossing of the Rhône – many sinking in mid-stream. Boso proceeded to besiege Avignon, nearly drowning in a moat Mummolus had dug there. The siege ended with an agreed peace. Boso was an opponent of Queen Brunhild, and Childebert ordered him to be condemned to death at Trier. The house where he took shelter was put to the torch, and in trying to escape he was hit by a javelin and killed with spears, on which his body was propped upright.

GUTHRUM (GUTHORM), VIKING KING (d.890)

Leader of the Vikings against Alfred the Great. He led part of the Great Army that attacked England in 871, becoming king in East Anglia. He participated in the Viking conquest of Mercia, 873–4, the advance into Wessex in 876 and success at Chippenham in 878, which resulted in Alfred's retreat to Athelney. Guthrum was defeated at Edington in 878. The Danes retreated to Chippenham and agreed the Peace of Wedmore, by which England was divided. Guthrum and 30 followers agreed to be baptised, Guthrum taking the Christian name of Aethelstan. After the expulsion of the Vikings from London a new agreement was made in 886. Alfred was to have the south-west and Guthrum the north-east, with Watling Street as the dividing line. The Viking area became the Danelaw.

Guthrum made the agreements with Alfred but there is no evidence that he ruled all Viking lands in England. He ruled East Anglia and possibly Mercia but probably not Northumbria. Guthrum minted his own coins, a model for later Viking rulers in England.

GUY I DE LUSIGNAN, KING OF JERUSALEM (d.1194)

King of Jerusalem 1186–92, Lord of Cyprus 1192–4. His family had lands in southern France, vassals of Richard the Lionheart. A branch established itself in the kingdom of Jerusalem. In 1180 Guy married Sibylla, eldest daughter of Amalric I, sister of Baldwin IV and mother of Baldwin V, thus becoming king. When Saladin besieged Tiberias in 1183 Guy attempted a relief that resulted in his defeat and capture at Hattin. He was ransomed in 1188. He besieged Acre from 1189. His wife and two daughters died in the epidemic of 1190. Acre fell to the Third Crusade in 1191. There were political divisions within the kingdom, exacerbated by the westerners. In 1192 Guy was replaced by Conrad of Montferrat, and later by Henry of Champagne. Guy was offered Cyprus (conquered by Richard the Lionheart) in compensation – though he had to buy it. He established the Lusignan dynasty there. He held Cyprus from Richard but his successors became independent kings. Guy joined abortive plots to recover Jerusalem but died in Cyprus and was succeeded by his brother Amalric.

GUY, COUNT OF BRIONNE

Cousin and rival of William the Conqueror during his minority, son of Rainald count of Burgundy and Adeliza, Robert I's sister. William granted him Vernon and Brionne, both in Eure. Guy, 'puffed up in pride and arrogance', scorned William as a bastard unfit to rule. He allied with discontented nobles from Lower Normandy. Guy's hopes were ended with the Conqueror's victory at Val-ès-Dunes in 1047. He was wounded and retired to his castle at Brionne. It took the

Conqueror three years to eject him. Guy was exiled, probably to Burgundy.

HÁKON, EARL OF ORKNEY

According to a saga account he was the treacherous killer of St Magnús, then Earl Magnús, on the island of Egilsay in 1117.

HAROLD II GODWINSON, KING OF ENGLAND (c.1020–1066)

King from the death of Edward the Confessor on 5 January until his defeat and death at Hastings on 14 October, the son of Godwin earl of Wessex. He became Earl of East Anglia in 1045. On his father's death in 1053 he became Earl of Wessex. He shared his father's exile in 1051–2 but became a lieutenant to Edward the Confessor, his brother-in-law. Harold led campaigns against the Welsh with some success. Edward probably designated him as successor on his deathbed. Harold compromised his position by a trip to Normandy probably in 1064, possibly seeking to release relatives held hostage by William of Normandy. He went on William's Breton expedition, demonstrating valour and was probably knighted by William. He made an oath, possibly under duress, promising aid to William. The Normans claimed he broke the oath in taking the throne, for which Harold had English support – even the northern earls acquiescing. Harold was the Confessor's brother-in-law though without a claim by descent. His reign was short and eventful. He faced two major invasions. The first was by Harold Hardrada King of Norway, allied to Harold's resentful brother Tostig, former Earl of Northumbria. They defeated an English army under the northern earls at Gate Fulford on 20 September. Harold Godwinson marched north and on 25 September defeated the invaders at Stamford Bridge, where Hardrada and Tostig were killed. Harold had been expecting invasion from Normandy but was forced to disband the fleet. On news of William's arrival, he marched south. At Hastings Harold was hit in the head by an arrow and died. It was later claimed that the altar of Battle Abbey was built on the spot. The fate of Harold's body is uncertain. It was claimed that his mistress, Edith Swanneck, recognised him from certain private marks. There was a story of burial on the shore (the most likely version), and another of burial at Waltham Abbey, which Harold had founded. A more recent theory is that he was buried at Bosham. There were also tales of Harold's survival after the battle. He was almost certainly killed in the battle but the Normans wanted to keep quiet the place of burial. Harold's brothers Gyrth and Leofwin were killed in the battle.

HAROLD GORMSSON, BLÁTÖNN (BLUETOOTH), KING OF DENMARK (c.910–c.986)

King from c.958 on the death of his father Gorm the Old. The nickname 'Bluetooth' was given later. Dating this period in Scandinavian history is difficult. Harold married at least twice, once to the Wendish princess Tovi. He unified Denmark from a base in Jutland. He was converted to Christianity by Bishop Poppo in 965, marked by the Jelling Stone. He enforced the religion on Denmark. He erected a church and mounds to his mother and father at Jelling. Dendrochronology suggests he was responsible for the circular military fortifications at Trelleborg and elsewhere in 980–1, whose function was probably internal control. Other military and town defences are dated to the reign plus the building of roads and bridges. Harold resisted attacks from Norway and the Holy Roman Empire. He gained ground in Norway but submitted to Otto II (HRE) in 974. In Norway, in alliance with Earl Hákon of Lade, he defeated Harold Greycloak at Hals, when Greycloak was killed. Harold established Roskilde as his base. He was deposed by his son Sweyn Forkbeard in c.983, fleeing wounded to die in exile.

HAROLD HÁLFDANSSON, HÁRFAGRI (FINEHAIR/FAIRHAIR), KING OF NORWAY (c.865–c.933)

King c.870–930. The dating of events is difficult because of the sources and it is unwise to trust later saga information. Harold's power base was Vestfold. The *Heimskringla Saga* says he was ten when his father Hálfdan the Black died in c.870. He married Gyða. Harold established the kingdom of Norway, confirming control by the sea Battle of Hafrsfjord in c.890. Harold's ruthless rule forced many to migrate westwards. Iceland was probably first colonised in his reign. He claimed the Scottish islands though it is uncertain he visited them. He abdicated in favour of one of his 29 sons, Erik Bloodaxe. Later sagas suggest the nickname Finehair was descriptive.

HAROLD III SIGURÐSSON, HARDRADA/HARÐRÁÐI (HARD RULER), KING OF NORWAY (1015–66)

King from 1045, half-brother to St Ólaf, invading England in 1066. The nickname 'hard ruler' described the nature of his rule. He featured in sagas, including *Heimskringla* and *St Ólaf's Saga*. He fought alongside his brother at Stiklestad in 1030, in which Ólaf was killed and Harold wounded. Harold took refuge with Magnús the Good in Kiev. He went on to Constantinople and joined Michael IV's Varangian Guard, later becoming its commander. He fought for Michael in Greece, Sicily, Bulgaria and the Holy Land. In 1045 he returned to Norway to claim the throne, which his nephew Magnús the Good agreed to share. Harold became sole ruler in 1047. He fought against Sweyn II Estrithsson of Denmark, defeating him at Nissa in 1062. In 1066 Harold claimed the English throne, sailing with a large fleet and receiving support from Vikings of the Scottish islands. He defeated the northern earls at Gate Fulford in 1066 but was caught at Stamford Bridge by Harold Godwinson when he was defeated and killed. His body was returned to Norway for burial in St Mary's church near Nidaros. Harold married at least twice and was succeeded by his son Magnús II.

HAWKWOOD (ACUTO), JOHN (1320–94)

A *condottiere* in Italy (where he was known by various names including Acuto). He was a younger son from Essex in England who fought for the Black Prince, probably at both Crécy and Poitiers. After the 1360 peace he became a mercenary captain, travelling via Avignon to Italy in the White Company. He was employed by various cities, including Pisa, Milan and the papacy. For Pisa he raided Florence in 1364. In 1368, fighting for Milan, he was captured but released within the year. He served the papacy, on papal orders comitting atrocities in the sack of Cesena, after which he departed. His second marriage was to Donnina, illegitimate daughter of Bernabò Visconti. He was the victor for Milan against Florence at Cascina but, once attached to Florence, served that state for life. He became Florence's most trusted captain, winning a series of victories – often using English methods including longbowmen and dismounted knights. An outstanding victory was Castagnaro in 1387 for Padua (on loan from Florence) against Verona. His victories were often against other noted *condottieri*, including Dal Verme. He captured Facino Cane three times during a short space of time. He planned to retire to England but after a stroke died in Italy on 16 March. On request from Richard II the body was sent to England for burial at his birthplace, Sible Hedingham in Essex – though the tomb does not survive.

HENGEST (HENGIST) (d.488) AND HORSA (d.455)

Supposed initiators of the Anglo-Saxon invasion of England. Various dates are provided by sources, but concur for the mid-5th century. The battle dates here are from the *Anglo-Saxon Chronicle*. Hengest and Horsa are associated and best treated together. Some have doubted their existence, particularly of Horsa – names meaning 'stallion' and 'mare' being suspicious. However, the number of sources mentioning them suggests some truth in their existence. Bede named them sons of Wihtgils, descended from Woden. They were invited to England by Vortigern (now thought a title rather than a name). They arrived with three ships. They won successes against the Picts. The *Anglo-Saxon Chronicle* makes them joint kings of Kent, overthrowing its British king. They were not the first English to arrive but the first to seize independent power. Horsa was killed at Aegelesthrep (possibly Aylesford) in 455, which won Kent. Horsa was succeeded by Hengest's son, Aesc (Oisc). Bede claimed that in his day there was a monument to Horsa in Kent. Hengest and Aesc defeated the Britons at Crecganford in 456, consolidating their position. In 465 they won at Wippedsfleot, where 12 British chiefs were killed. According to *Nennius*, Hengest's son Octha succeeded him (possibly another name for Aesc though some consider Octha the son of Aesc). Aesc succeeded in 488, the presumed date of Hengest's death.

HENRY I, KING OF ENGLAND (1068–1135)
King from 1100, youngest son of William the Conqueror. His nickname 'beauclerk' depended on an ability to write his name. He succeeded on the killing of his brother William Rufus, of which Henry has been suspected but not convicted. He married Edith-Matilda, daughter of Malcolm III of Scots, descended from the old English royal family. Henry suppressed rebellion fostered by his elder brother Robert Curthose. Its leading figure was Robert of Bellême, whose castles at Shrewsbury and Bridgnorth were captured. Henry halted an invasion of England by Curthose and counter-attacked Curthose in Normandy, defeating and capturing him at Tinchebrai in 1106. Curthose was imprisoned and Henry became Duke of Normandy. He was defeated by Fulk V of Anjou at Alençon in 1118 but beat his enemies, including

Louis VI of France and Curthose's son William Clito, at Brémule in 1119. Waleran of Meulan's rebellion was defeated at Bourgthéroulde in 1124. Henry had over 20 children but the only legitimate son, William the Aetheling, was drowned in the *White Ship* disaster of 1120. Henry's daughter was the Empress Matilda. Henry made a second but childless marriage to Adela of Louvain. He died near Rouen from eating lampreys (eel-like fish), which always disagreed with him. He insisted on eating them, became ill, and died a week later. He was buried at Reading Abbey, his entrails removed for burial at Notre-Dame-du-Pré.

HENRY I, KING OF FRANCE (1008–60)
King from 1031, son of Robert II, crowned in his father's lifetime in 1027. He married Matilda, niece of Henry III (HRE), and in 1051 Anna of Kiev, daughter of Jaroslav grand duke of Kiev. Henry was 'vigorous in arms' but achieved little military success. He became Duke of Burgundy in 1015. He granted Burgundy to his brother Robert in 1032 but then clashed with him. In 1038 he avoided an attempted coup by his brother Odo, backed by Blois and Champagne. Henry sought refuge and help in Normandy and in return aided the young William the Conqueror, defeating Norman rebels at Val-ès-Dunes in 1047. Worried at William's growing power and ambitions, and his dealings with Henry's enemies, Henry supported William of Arques' abortive rebellion in 1053. Henry attempted to relieve Arques but was beaten at St-Aubin-sur-Scie. In 1054 and 1058 Henry and Geoffrey Martel of Anjou invaded Normandy but were defeated at Mortemer and Varaville. Henry died on 4 August and was succeeded by his son Philip I.

HENRY I THE FOWLER, KING OF THE ROMANS (876–936)
Elected king at Fritzlar in 919, when no representatives from Bavaria or Swabia were present, founder of the Ottonian Saxon dynasty. He became Duke of Saxony in 912. He established a state recognisable

geographically as Germany, bringing in the southern duchies and Lotharingia. He reorganised the army and built castles, especially on the eastern frontier. He attacked the pagans threatening his north and east frontier – Danes, Magyars and Slavs. Schleswig was taken from the Danes in 934. He defeated Wencelas of Bohemia. He overcame the Wends at Lenzen 929 and the Magyars at Riade 933. Otto had plans for coronation in Rome but died on 2 July before this was accomplished. His son Otto I succeeded.

HENRY II, KING OF ENGLAND (1133–89)

The first Plantagenet King of England from 1154, son of Geoffrey V count of Anjou and the Empress Matilda. His father conquered Normandy and passed it with his other lands to Henry on his death in 1151. Through marriage in 1152 to the heiress Eleanor he took over the duchy of Aquitaine. He invaded England and became king in 1154, establishing the Angevin Empire. He took Northumbria from Malcolm IV of Scotland. Henry invaded Ireland with papal approval in 1171. He invaded Toulouse but was forced to make terms with Louis VII. He had disputes with his own sons, the chief rebellion (which he suppressed) occurring in 1173–4. Henry was blamed for the killing of Thomas Becket, archbishop of Canterbury. Both rebels and foreign opponents used it to embarrass him. His reign was relatively peaceful, his greatest achievements legal and administrative rather than military. In 1189 he submitted to the allied opposition of his son Richard and Philip II King of France. He died soon after on 6 July. Young Henry had died in 1183 and the succession went to Richard I.

HENRY II, THE SAINT, HOLY ROMAN EMPEROR (973–1024)

King of the Romans from 1002, emperor from 1014, last of the Saxon dynasty, son of Henry the Wrangler duke of Bavaria. He married Cunegarde of Luxembourg, becoming involved in war against her brothers. His reputation for piety came from his wars against pagans. He was canonised in 1146. He suppressed an anti-German revolt when in Rome for the coronation. He defeated the Lombard Ardoin, replacing him as King of Italy in 1004. He defended the eastern frontier against Boleslaw of Poland with less success. He suppressed a revolt by Baldwin IV of Flanders, capturing Valenciennes in 1007 and Ghent in 1020. Henry suffered frequent illness, dying at Castle Grona on 13 July without an heir. He was buried at Bamberg.

HENRY II, THE WRANGLER/THE QUARRELSOME, DUKE OF BAVARIA (951–95)

Nephew of Otto I, rebel against Otto II from 973. He succeeded to Bavaria as a minor, with his mother Judith as regent. He conspired against Otto II, was captured and imprisoned. He was deprived of Bavaria in 976. He escaped and took refuge with Boleslav of Bohemia. He tried to regain power in Germany on the death of Otto II but failed to become regent for Otto III. He proclaimed himself King of the Romans in 984 but failed to establish his claim. He recovered a reduced Bavaria in 985, renouncing his claim to the crown. His son became Henry II (HRE) in 1002.

HENRY III, KING OF ENGLAND (1207–72)

King from 1216 on the death of his father, John. During his minority the efforts of William the Marshal and Hubert de Burgh retrieved the royal position after the Magna Carta crisis. Henry married Eleanor of Provence in 1236. He made two unsuccessful invasions of France, in 1230 and 1242. He was defeated at Taillebourg and Saintes in 1242 and agreed the Treaty of Paris in 1259, abandoning most of the Angevin Empire. He agreed to intervene in Sicily on behalf of his son Edmund, another failed venture. The English barons rebelled and Simon de Montfort defeated Henry at Lewes in 1264. Henry was released and restored through the victory of his son Edward at Evesham in 1265. His main achievement was perhaps the rebuilding of Westminster Abbey. He died on 16 November and his son Edward I, then on crusade, succeeded.

HENRY III, HOLY ROMAN EMPEROR (1017–56)

King of the Romans from 1039, crowned Emperor on Christmas Day 1046, perhaps the greatest of the Salians, son and successor of Conrad II. He used ministeriales as unfree administrators and for garrisons. His second marriage, to Agnes of Poitou daughter of William duke of Aquitaine, led to interest in Burgundy and Italy. Henry won control of Franconia, Bavaria, Swabia and Carinthia. He defeated Bratislav of Bohemia in 1041, becoming King of Bohemia and Moravia. He suppressed revolt by Baldwin V of Flanders and Godfrey of Lorraine in 1047. Henry attempted to conquer Hungary but was frustrated by Andrew I. He died on 5 October and was buried at Speyer. His son Henry IV succeeded.

HENRY IV (BOLINGBROKE), KING OF ENGLAND (1367–1413)

King from 1399, usurping the throne from Richard II to establish the Lancastrian dynasty. He was known as Henry of Bolingbroke from his birthplace in Lincolnshire. He became Earl of Derby and Duke of Hereford. He was the son of John of Gaunt, from whom he inherited the duchy of Lancaster. He married first Mary de Bohun, heiress to the earldom of Hereford, then Joan of Navarre. He joined the baronial opposition to Richard II and fought at Radcot Bridge in 1387. He participated in the Baltic crusade in 1390 and went on pilgrimage to Jerusalem in 1392. He was banished for ten years by Richard II in 1398 before an intended joust with the Duke of Norfolk. After Gaunt's death he returned to England in 1399, seeking his inheritance, and seized the throne. Richard was imprisoned, deposed and killed. Henry IV faced baronial revolt by the Percies, who allied with Owen Glendower. Henry

defeated the allies at Shrewsbury in 1403, where Henry Percy (Hotspur) was killed. The Percy rising of 1405 was suppressed. A royal army under Sir Thomas Rokeby defeated the surviving Percies at Bramham Moor in 1408. Henry died on 20 March. He was buried at Canterbury and succeeded by his son Henry V.

HENRY IV, HOLY ROMAN EMPEROR (1050–1106)

King of the Romans from 1056, emperor from 1084, son of Henry III and Agnes of Poitou. His minority ended in 1065. He married Bertha of Saxony. He clashed with Pope Gregory VII in the Investiture Controversy, damaging both Church and Empire. The clash was initiated by Henry's attempt to impose control on the archbishop of Milan. The pope had support from princes in Germany, who used this to gain demands from Henry. Henry submitted to the pope at Canossa in 1077, wearing a woollen shirt, barefoot in the snow. In 1077 the princes elected Rudolf of Swabia as king but Henry deposed him. Henry was defeated at Flarcheim and Hohen-Mölsen, but here Rudolf was fatally wounded. Henry marched on Rome, which he besieged in 1082 and 1083–4. Gregory VII was deposed and an anti-pope elected. The Normans from southern Italy rescued the pope and departed with him. Henry tried to keep control in northern Italy, taking Mantua in 1090–1 and defeating Matilda of Tuscany at Tricontai. Henry faced a second anti-king in Herman of Luxembourg. Saxony rebelled in 1073 and submitted in 1088. Henry faced rebellion by his sons Henry and Conrad. Henry IV was forced to abdicate but escaped to Liège, where he died on 7 August. The pope refused him Christian burial but he was buried at Speyer.

HENRY V, KING OF ENGLAND (1387–1422)

Son and successor of Henry IV in 1413, probably the best-known English military king thanks to Agincourt. He was born at Monmouth, becoming Prince of Wales in

1399. He fought for Henry IV against rebels at Shrewsbury in 1403, and against the Welsh. He suppressed the Oldcastle Rising in 1414. He renewed English ambitions in the Hundred Years' War. He captured Harfleur in 1415. At Agincourt he defeated the French, using archers and dismounted men-at-arms. He took Rouen 1418–19, completing the conquest of Normandy by 1420. By the Treaty of Troyes 1420 the succession to the French throne passed to him and his heirs. He married Katherine, Charles VI's daughter. He caught dysentery at the siege of Meaux in 1422. Meaux surrendered but Henry died on 31 August. He was succeeded by his son Henry VI.

HENRY V, HOLY ROMAN EMPEROR (1081–1125)

King of the Romans from 1105, emperor from 1111, last of the Salians. He rebelled against his father, Henry IV, in 1093, who was deposed in 1105. In 1114 he married Matilda, daughter of Henry I of England. He fought wars to the east, with success in Bohemia but not in Hungary or Poland. He was defeated by Boleslav III of Poland at Wroclaw in 1109. He led an Italian expedition in 1110 to receive the imperial crown. He suppressed revolts in Germany, though defeated several times. He sought to gain territory in the Netherlands and France but with little success. He was beaten by Louis VI 1124. Henry died of cancer on 23 May without offspring. He was buried at Speyer.

HENRY VI, KING OF ENGLAND (1421–71)

Son and successor of Henry V, king from 1422 when nine months old. With the death of Charles VI in 1422 he claimed to be King of France. He married Margaret of Anjou in 1445. His mental frailty and lack of military ability caused problems. Under him the French recovered all English-held land except Calais. In England Cade's Rebellion occurred and baronial opposition centred around Richard of York. In the first major battle of the Wars of the Roses, at St Albans, Henry was wounded by an arrow and captured. York ruled as Protector but Henry regained power. He tried to crush York in 1459 but failed. The Yorkists won at Blore Heath in 1459 and Northampton 1460. There was a brief Lancastrian recovery with York's defeat and death at Wakefield in 1460. The Lancastrians won the Second Battle of St Albans. York's son Edward retrieved their position, proclaiming himself Edward IV and winning at Mortimer's Cross and Towton. Henry was recaptured in 1465 when riding in Lancashire. In 1470 Henry's friends, reinforced by Warwick the Kingmaker, invaded England. Edward fled and Henry was released but his freedom was brief. Edward, allied with the Burgundians, invaded England in 1471, defeating the Lancastrians at Barnet and Tewkesbury. Warwick was killed at Barnet. Somerset was executed after Tewkesbury, where Henry's heir Prince Edward was killed. Queen Margaret was captured. Henry VI was probably put to death in the Tower on 21 April, the end of the Lancastrian dynasty.

HENRY VI, HOLY ROMAN EMPEROR (1165–97)

King of the Romans from 1190, emperor from 1191, King of Sicily from 1194. He was the son of Frederick Barbarossa, husband of Constance of Sicily and father of Frederick II. He imprisoned the returning crusader, Richard the Lionheart, and ransomed him. Henry the Lion of Saxony rebelled but made peace in 1194. Henry fought Tancred in Sicily, which Henry claimed through his marriage. He was crowned king at Palermo on Christmas Day 1194 – his son Frederick born next day. Here too there was revolt. While planning to crusade he died on 28 September at Messina, probably of malaria. He was buried at Palermo. Civil war followed in Germany though his son Frederick held Sicily.

HENRY VII, KING OF ENGLAND (1457–1509)

King from 1485, founder of the Tudor dynasty, posthumous son of Edmund Tudor

earl of Richmond by Margaret Beaufort. He
and his uncle, Jasper Tudor earl of
Pembroke, supported the Lancastrians.
Henry was captured at Pembroke in 1461 by
Edward IV and put under the guardianship
of the Yorkist Earl of Pembroke. After the
Yorkist triumph in 1471 Henry went to
Brittany. He became the focus of
Lancastrian opposition to Richard III. His
attempt at invasion in 1483 failed. He
returned in 1485, landing at Milford Haven
and winning at Bosworth where Richard
was killed. Henry took the throne. He faced
Yorkist rebellions, nominally under
Lambert Simnel and Perkin Warbeck, plus
risings in Yorkshire and Cornwall. He won
at Stoke in 1487 and suppressed all the
risings. In 1486 he married Edward IV's
daughter Elizabeth, uniting Lancaster and
York. He made peace with France in 1492
after a brief continental campaign. He
established his claim to Ireland by 1494. His
health deteriorated with poor eyesight and
declining mental capacity. He died on
21 April and was buried in Westminster
Abbey. His eldest son Arthur died before
him and his younger son succeeded as
Henry VIII. There is a bust of Henry by
Torrigiano, a portrait by Sittow, and a death
mask.

HENRY VII, HOLY ROMAN EMPEROR (1274–1313)

King of the Romans from 1308, emperor
from 1312. He was Count of Luxembourg,
French rather than German. He was elected
in opposition to the French Charles of
Valois. His son John married Elizabeth,
heiress to Bohemia. From 1310 he was in
Italy. His efforts were lauded by Dante but,
despite initial success, were largely
ineffectual. He took Brescia 1311 but failed
against Florence 1313 and was opposed by
Robert King of Naples. He died on
24 August near Siena, probably of malaria
when heading for Naples, though it was
claimed that a monk poisoned him with
sacramental wine. He was buried at Pisa.

HENRY THE LION, DUKE OF SAXONY (1129–95)

Duke of Saxony from 1142, of Bavaria from
1156, of Lüneberg from 1180, son of Henry
the Proud of Saxony who was dispossessed
for opposition to Conrad III. Henry's mother
Gertrude was daughter of Emperor Lothar II.
Frederick Barbarossa granted him Bavaria,
seeking his allegiance. He accompanied
Frederick to Italy and Poland. In 1160 Henry
defeated the Obodrites to the east. He
married Matilda, daughter of Henry II of
England, as his second wife in 1168. He
went to the Holy Land in 1172. In 1176
Henry refused to accompany Barbarossa to
Italy. The nobility supported the emperor
and Henry was condemned in 1180 and
deposed in 1181. Henry's son was elected
King of the Romans as Otto IV. Henry spent
part of his exile in England. He made his
peace with Henry VI (HRE) in 1194 and died
of dysentery the following year on 6 August.
He was buried at Brunswick. He built
Brunswick Castle, erecting the statue of a
lion as a family symbol.

HENRY RASPE, LANDGRAVE OF THURINGIA (1204–47)

Landgrave from 1231, granted by
Frederick II. He was elected 'King of the
Romans' (anti-king) in 1246. He was
excommunicated for supporting the
emperor and reneged to the pope in 1245.
With papal support he defeated Frederick's
son Conrad near Frankfurt in 1246. He died
on 17 February. William of Holland was
elected anti-king. Henry's death meant the
end of an independent Thuringia.

HERACLIUS, BYZANTINE EMPEROR (575–641)

Emperor from 610, victor over the Persians,
noted for a bushy beard and moustache. He
reorganised the army, cutting pay but
issuing arms and uniforms. He became
emperor when he and his father, Heraclius
Exarch of Africa, deposed and killed the
usurper Phokas the Tyrant. Heraclius
married first Fabia, renamed Eudocia, and
then controversially his niece Martina. The

Empire was in such a low state that
Heraclius considered removing his capital
to Carthage. From 622 he campaigned
against Persia, winning at Issus and Halus
in 623 and decisively at Nineveh 627. Much
territory was recovered and the True Cross
returned to Jerusalem. He had to defend
Constantinople against the Avars, aided by
the Persians, in 626. He improved the city's
defences. Ironically, having defeated Persia,
the strongest and most threatening rival in
Byzantium's history, the balance of power
in the Middle East changed with the
emergence of Islam. Heraclius' armies were
defeated by the Arabs at Yarmuk 636, losing
Syria, Egypt and most of the regained lands.
Heraclius died on 11 February of dropsy and
was buried in Constantinople. His dynasty
survived for 70 years.

HEREWARD THE WAKE

Rebel against William the Conqueror and
subject of literary romance. He may have
been a king's thegn from Lincolnshire, son
of Leofric of Bourne, descended through his
mother from an Earl of Northumbria.
Hereward was outlawed by Edward the
Confessor in 1062, going to Flanders where
he married. He rebelled on his return,
attacking Normans who took his family's
lands. He probably took part in the 1069
rebellion. In 1070 from the Isle of Ely he
attacked Peterborough Abbey, seizing its
wealth. Morcar earl of Northumbria sailed
to join him. Troops from Sweyn
Estrithsson, King of Denmark then in
England, came to Ely. The Conqueror
negotiated with Sweyn for the Danish fleet
to leave England. William attacked Ely in
1071. He brought a fleet while the army
approached via a causeway near Aldreth
made with trees and inflated sheepskins.
The rebels fled and Morcar submitted, to be
imprisoned for life (though released briefly
in 1087). Hereward escaped, fighting his
way out, and no more is known of him. Ely
Abbey was punished for its part in the
rebellion. The *Gesta Herewardi (Deeds of
Hereward)* is a 12th-century poem of which
he is the hero.

HERMAN OF LUXEMBOURG, COUNT OF SALM, COUNT OF LÜTZELBURG (d.1088)

Lotharingian rival to Henry IV (HRE). After
Henry defeated anti-king Rudolf of Swabia,
Herman was elected anti-king in 1081. He
was nicknamed 'King Garlic' (because of
his breath?) and said 'to bear the name of
king emptily'. He took refuge in Denmark
in 1085. He was killed on 28 September
when besieging a Lotharingian castle.

HOTSPUR, HENRY PERCY (1364–1403)

A leading opponent of Henry IV, son of the
Earl of Northumberland. His nickname
came from Scottish opponents. He was
appointed Warden of the East March on the
Scottish border in 1384. He commanded the
English at Otterburn in 1388 when defeated
and captured by the Scots. He was
ransomed and made Warden of the West
March. He supported Henry Bolingbroke in
1399. He commanded the victory over the
Scots at Homildon Hill in 1402, after which
Henry IV denied the Percies money from
the ransoms. Hotspur fought, as Justiciar of
North Wales, alongside Prince Hal against
Owen Glendower. Hotspur fought for the
rebels at Shrewsbury on 21 July 1403, when
he was defeated and killed.

HUGH CAPET, KING OF FRANCE (938–96)

King from 987, founder of the Capetian
dynasty, which endured until 1328. Three
of his Robertine ancestors ruled France,
including his grandfather Robert I, but from
987 Capetian rule was continuous. The
nickname of Capet possibly came from
wearing the cape of St Martin of Tours as a
lay abbot (or from a type of cap). On the
division of his father Hugh the Great's
lands in 960, Hugh received Neustria. He
succeeded as Duke of the Franks in 956. In
985 he suppressed rebellion against King
Lothar. He was elected king by an assembly
at Senlis on the death of the last
Carolingian, Louis V, and crowned at
Noyon. He defeated rebellion by Charles of
Lorraine in 991. Charles was captured and

imprisoned until his death in 993. Hugh died on 24 October and was succeeded by his son Robert II.

HUGH DU PUISET III (d.1132)
Lord of Le Puiset (south-east of Chartres) from 1109. His father Evrard went on the First Crusade. The lordship within the royal demesne was one that threatened Capetian power: Hugh was 'a snake among eels' according to Suger. In 1080 his grandfather Hugh I defeated Philip I in battle, pursuing the royalists to Orléans. Hugh fought the Count of Blois, attacking Chartres in 1111. Louis VI sought to impose authority over Hugh, demanding his castle. Hugh was captured and imprisoned at Château-Landon. Hugh supported Henry I of England against Louis VI and was defeated by Louis in 1112. Hugh remained a threat and Louis had to destroy his castle three times.

HUMPHREY IV OF TORON (TIBNINE) (1166–c.1205)
Stepson of Rainald of Châtillon, husband of Isabella daughter of Amalric I. He was Lord of Toron in the north of the kingdom of Jerusalem. He spoke Arabic. He married at Kerak when Saladin was attacking it. His mother sent Saladin food from the wedding feast and Saladin in turn ordered his artillery to avoid the honeymoon tower! Kerak was relieved. Some plotted for Humphrey's succession but Humphrey preferred to submit to Guy in 1186. He fought at Hattin and was captured, later ransomed. Humphrey joined Richard I during the Third Crusade and negotiated for him with Saladin. Through internal kingdom politics Isabella had to divorce Humphrey and marry Conrad of Montferrat in 1190 so the latter could succeed. Conrad was murdered in 1192 – some suspecting Humphrey. Isabella married the new candidate for the throne, Henry of Champagne. Both Henry and her fourth husband, Amalric II, predeceased her.

HUNALD II, DUKE OF AQUITAINE (d. c.775)
Rebel against Carolingian rule, probably the son of Duke Waiofar. Some believe Hunald II was simply Hunald I returned from the monastery on the Île-de-Rhé, but this is unlikely. Aquitaine rebelled on the death of Charles Martel, and the efforts of Pepin the Short had not brought submission, partly because of the alliance of Aquitaine and the Basques. On the death of Pepin, rule was shared by Charlemagne and his brother Carloman. In 769 they planned an expedition against the new rebel leader in Aquitaine, Hunald II. The brothers met at Moncontour de Poitou for the campaign, but quarrelled, and Carloman returned home, leaving Charles to continue alone. Charles took Angoulême and built a fortress at Fronsac. Hunald fled over the Garonne and sought refuge with the Basques. Lupus duke of Gascony handed over Hunald to the Franks and his fate is unknown – probably confinement in a Frankish monastery.

HUNYADI, JOHN (JÁNOS) (1387–1456)
Hungarian military commander, leader of anti-Turkish crusades, regent in Hungary 1445–52. He is famed for fighting the invading Ottoman Turks. In 1442 he expelled them from Transylvania. He won at Niš in 1443 and Mount Kunovica in 1444. He was defeated by Murad II at Varna in 1444, but escaped. He was defeated at Kosovo in 1448, leaving the Turks in control of the Balkans. He assisted King Ladislas after he assumed power in 1452. He defended Belgrade against Turkish invasion in 1456, thus also saving Hungary. He died on 10 September.

IDA, KING OF BERNICIA (d. c.560)
The first known King of Bernicia, from 547. His grandfather, Oesa, was said to be the first of the line in Britain. Bernicia was surrounded by Celtic British enemies – the kingdoms of Rheged, Manau Gododdin and Dalriada. Ida opposed the British king, Dutigern, who probably ruled in the

Strathclyde area. Ida built the fortress at Bamburgh, which is said to have provoked war with Dutigern. Ida had 12 sons, including Theoderic and Aethelfrith. Ida's son (or possibly grandson), Aethelric, was founder of Northumbria (combining Bernicia and Deira).

ISABELLA I, QUEEN OF CASTILE (1451–1504)

Queen from 1474, daughter of Juan II. She married Ferdinand of Aragón in 1469. Her half-brother Enrique IV died in 1474. Ferdinand sought Castile but agreed joint rule with his wife. The papacy named them *Los Reyes Catolicos*. The couple overthrew the last Muslim power in Iberia, Granada, and sponsored the voyages of Columbus. In the war against Granada Isabella accompanied her husband, riding a horse and wearing armour. At the siege of Málaga an unsuccessful attempt on her life was made by a Dervish prisoner. She died on 24 November and her husband ruled the two kingdoms.

IVAR YNGVARR (THE BONELESS)

Son of Ragnar Hairy-Breeches, brother of Hálfdan and Ubbi. Most of our information comes from sagas. He and his brothers were leaders of the Great Army, arriving in East Anglia in 865. He may be the Ímar of Irish history. It was said the brothers came to England to avenge the killing of their father Ragnar by Aelle of Northumbria, who threw him into a snakepit. They took York in 866, defeating Aelle and his allies in 867. Aelle was supposedly killed by the blood-eagle – ribs cut from spine, lungs pulled on to back like wings. Ivar and Ubbi defeated the East Angles, killing King (later St) Edmund in 869. Nothing is known of Ivar's subsequent career. Possibly he returned to Ireland. The later nickname may connect with the Viking who plundered a French monastery and was punished by his bones shrivelling.

JAIME (JAUME/JAMES) I, THE CONQUEROR, KING OF ARAGÓN (1208–76)

King from 1213, son and successor of Pedro II, born at Montpellier in southern France, belonging to Aragón through Pedro's marriage to Marie of Montpellier. The civil war of his minority ended in 1227. He played a part in the *Reconquista*, conquering the Balearic Islands from 1228 – Mallorca in 1229, Minorca 1232 and Ibiza 1235. He set up the kingdom of Mallorca for his son Jaime II. In alliance with Alfonso X of Castile he captured the *taifas* of Valencia and Murcia. He was wounded at Valencia by a crossbow bolt in the head. In 1258 he agreed the Treaty of Corbeil with St Louis, settling the frontier. He made two abortive crusades to the Holy Land. His *Libre dels feyts* (Book of Feats), in Catalan, is a unique work – a royal autobiography with political and military details. He died on 25 July, succeeded by his son Pedro III.

JOANNA (JOAN) II, QUEEN OF NAPLES (1371–1435)

Queen from 1414 in succession to her brother Ladislas, noted for her amorous affairs. She employed the *condottiere* Attendolo Sforza, said to be her lover. He expelled Braccio da Montone from Rome. She adopted Alfonso of Aragón as heir but became discontented with his actions and switched her favour to Louis III of Anjou. Her favourite (and lover) Giovanni Caraccioli was murdered in 1432. She died on 2 February, naming René of Anjou as heir, though Alfonso succeeded in taking control and uniting Naples and Sicily.

JOAN OF ARC (JEANNE D'ARC), ST, LA PUCELLE (MAID OF ORLÉANS) (1412–31)

Daughter of peasants from Champagne living at Domrémy in Lorraine. At 13 she heard the voices of saints and believed herself the saviour of France. She won support from Robert de Baudricourt. Wearing men's clothes she met Charles VII at Chinon in 1429, persuading him to make her *chef de guerre* (commanding a company). She accompanied the army to Orléans in 1429. The relief succeeded and she made a triumphal entry in white armour. In an attack on a fort at Orléans she was wounded. She suffered wounds, including a blow from a stone on the head at Jargeau (saved by her helmet) and a leg injury at Meung. The French won at Patay, though Joan was not present. She encouraged the coronation of Charles at Reims and had plans to take Paris (which according to some accounts she reached). She tried to relieve Compiègne in 1430 but was dragged from her horse, captured by the Burgundians and handed to the English. She was tried for heresy and sorcery, found guilty and burned at the stake in Rouen on 30 May. She inspired French recovery in the Hundred Years' War. In 1456 a French court reversed the court decision against Joan. In 1928 she was canonised.

JOHN, KING OF ENGLAND (1167–1216)

Son of Henry II, king from 1199 in succession to his brother Richard I, known as 'Softsword'. He was made Lord of Ireland by Henry II but his 1185 expedition failed. He was Count of Mortain. He joined rebellions by his brothers against their father. He rebelled against his brother Richard, who pardoned him. He married Isabella of Gloucester and then Isabella of Angoulême. He was accused of murdering his nephew Arthur of Brittany. He failed to defend the continental lands against Philip Augustus of France. Most of the Angevin Empire, including Normandy, was lost by 1206. John attempted recovery but was defeated by Philip's son Louis, his allies beaten at Bouvines in 1214. He faced baronial rebellion in England, leading to Magna Carta. The rebels allied with Prince Louis, who invaded England. John attempted recovery but died on 19 October at Newark after losing his baggage and treasure crossing the Wash. He was buried at Worcester and his son Henry III succeeded.

JOHN I TZIMISCES, BYZANTINE EMPEROR (925–76)

Emperor from 969, an Armenian noble who became Domestic of the Schools and had an affair with the Empress Theophano. He killed the Emperor Nikephorus II Phokas, his uncle, and replaced him. Religious leaders forced him to exile his mistress. He married Theodora sister of Romanus II in 971. He suppressed the rebellion of Bardas Phokas in 971. John resisted attacks on Bulgaria by the Russians under Sviatoslav, winning at Silistra in 971, when John led the decisive charge in golden armour. He recovered Damascus and much of the Holy Land from the Saracens, defeating the caliphs of Baghdad and Cairo. He became ill and returned to Constantinople, dying on 10 January of a mystery disease – some said of poison.

JOHN I DE BRIENNE, LATIN EMPEROR OF BYZANTIUM, KING OF JERUSALEM (1148–1237)

King from 1210, Emperor from 1228, leading figure in the Fifth Crusade. His daughter Isabella married Frederick II (HRE) in 1225. He was pressured to leave France after a scandalous affair with Blanche Countess of Champagne. He was involved in a scandal with his own niece. He married Maria, heiress to the kingdom of Jerusalem, and was crowned king. At Damietta he was outvoted over accepting a peace offer from al-Kamil. Damietta was taken in 1219 but the Christians were defeated and Damietta lost. John quarrelled with Frederick II, who claimed Jerusalem. John became co-emperor of Byzantium with Baldwin II in 1228. In 1229 he commanded papal troops in the invasion of Sicily, but was defeated by Frederick II. John did not arrive in Constantinople until 1231. The Greeks besieged the city against John in 1235 but had to abandon in 1236. John died on 23 March.

JOHN II COMNENUS, BYZANTINE EMPEROR (1087–1143)

Emperor from 1118, son of Alexius I. He was small and ugly, so dark-skinned he was nicknamed 'the Moor', deeply religious. He married the Hungarian Princess Piroska (renamed Irene). He revived Byzantium after defeat at Manzikert in 1071. He made agreements to preserve Byzantium and gained a little territory. He fought off the Danishmend Turks in 1119 and recovered much of Anatolia. He tried to restrict the growing power of Venice in Byzantium but had to give way. He defeated the Hungarians under Stephen II, who recognised his suzerainty. He received homage from Raymond Prince of Antioch. He fought the Pechenegs over Thrace and, though wounded in 1121, defeated them. John received a wound in the hand when hunting, from which he later died on 8 April. His body was returned to Constantinople for burial. He was succeeded by his son Manuel I.

JOHN II, THE GOOD (LE BON), KING OF FRANCE (1319–64)

King from 1350, succeeding his father Philip VI. He was Duke of Normandy. He was defeated and captured by the Black Prince at Poitiers in 1356, imprisoned in the Tower. France and England agreed the Treaty of Brétigny in 1360. A ransom was partly paid and John released in 1360. He took over Burgundy, which he granted to his son Philip. His son the Duke of Anjou, hostage for him, escaped – so John returned voluntarily to captivity in 1364. He died on 8 April and was succeeded by his son Charles V. Respected by his captors, his body was returned for burial at St-Denis.

JOHN III DUKAS VATATZES, BYZANTINE EMPEROR (d.1254)

Emperor based at Nicaea during the period of the Latin Empire, the last great Byzantine Emperor. He succeeded his father-in-law Theodore Lascaris as emperor in exile in 1222, with territory in western Anatolia. He doubled the size of his lands.

He defeated a rebellion supported by the Franks at Poimanenon in 1225, taking over the rival despotate of Epirus. He recovered Asia Minor, most of the Balkans and much of the Aegean. He married a second time to Constance (renamed Anna), illegitimate daughter of Frederick II (HRE), 40 years younger than him. He attacked Constantinople but failed to take it. He suffered from epilepsy and bad health. He died on 3 November and was succeeded by his son Theodore II. John's efforts made the Greek recovery of Constantinople almost inevitable. He was buried near Nymphaeum, his capital.

JOHN VI CANTACUZENUS, BYZANTINE EMPEROR (1295–1383)

Emperor from 1341 to 1354, the empire's guiding force for 35 years. He possessed ability but lacked a sound dynastic right. He was Grand Domestic, adviser and military commander to Andronicus III from 1320, practically ruling. He was proclaimed co-emperor with noble backing, leading to civil war with supporters of John V. John VI conquered Thrace in 1343, taking Constantinople in 1347. The Black Death hit Byzantium. John married his daughter Helena to John V. He rebuilt the Byzantine fleet but could not remove the Venetian and Genoese threat. He improved the defences of Constantinople, adding a moat. The Ottomans, his allies in the civil war, seized Gallipoli to become his main threat. John VI lost popularity and abdicated in 1354, leaving John V on the throne. John VI entered a monastery as Joasaph and wrote a history of his times. His wife Irene became a nun. Without him the Byzantines found difficulty in coping with the Ottomans. He died on 15 June at Mistra aged 88.

JOHN VII PALAEOLOGUS, BYZANTINE EMPEROR (d.1408)

Emperor in 1390, nephew of Manuel II and son of Andronicus IV, acting as co-emperor from 1377. He succeeded to his father's property in 1385. He took over Constantinople in 1390 but within months yielded to Manuel II. Relations between the two remained generally good. John and Manuel performed military service as vassals in the Turkish army 1390–2 and in return Sultan Bayezit gave John support within Byzantium. However, John defended Constantinople against the Ottomans and the disgruntled Bayezit from 1394 to 1402. John ruled Constantinople while his uncle sought aid from the west in 1399. The Byzantines were saved by Tamberlane's defeat of Bayezit in 1402 – but it was only a temporary respite. John supported Isa against his brother Mehmet I, but the latter proved victorious. John was banished to Lemnos by Manuel II in 1403 for reasons that are not clear (possibly his Turkish connections). He was allowed to move to Thessalonika and restored as co-emperor. He made terms with Sultan Suleiman. He became a monk and took the name Joasaph.

JOHN VIII PALAEOLOGUS, BYZANTINE EMPEROR (1390–1448)

The penultimate Byzantine Emperor from 1425. Son of Manuel II, he inherited little besides Constantinople. He resisted Murad II's siege in 1422 and a siege in 1442 by his brother Demetrios, supported by the Turks. The Ottomans overran Thessalonika. Seeking western aid, John tried to sell his claim to the throne to Charles VI of France, agreeing to union of the Orthodox and Catholic Churches. He travelled west for aid in 1437, trailing round Venice, Ferrara and Florence, not returning to Constantinople until 1440, when he repaired the land walls. The defeat of western crusaders at Varna and Kosovo negated all his efforts. He married three times but died childless on 31 October in Constantinople, where he was buried. He was succeeded by his brother Constantine XI.

JOHN OF LUXEMBOURG, KING OF BOHEMIA (BLIND KING JOHN) (1296–1346)

Son of Henry VII (HRE), he married the daughter and heiress of Wenceslas II of Bohemia, whose king he became in 1310. After early internal problems he expanded and strengthened Bohemia. With Lewis of Bavaria he defeated and captured Frederick of Austria at Mühldorf in 1322. He fought in Italy as Lord of Brescia from 1330, with little success. He fought for the Teutonic Knights on two crusades, during the second of which he became blind. He allied with Philip VI of France in the Hundred Years' War against the English. He was killed at Crécy on 26 August. His son was Charles IV (HRE).

JOHN THE FEARLESS (JEAN SANS PEUR), DUKE OF BURGUNDY (1371–1419)

Duke from 1404, succeeding his father Philip the Bold. As John of Nevers he joined the Nicopolis Crusade in 1396, where he earned his epithet. He fought bravely, was captured and ransomed, returning in 1398. His ducal territories included Flanders and Artois. He opposed his cousin Louis Duke of Orléans, brother of Charles VI. John gained control of Paris and the king in 1405. Louis' ambush and assassination in 1407, for which John was responsible, caused civil war between the parties. John suppressed rebellion against the bishop of Liège at Othée in 1408. At St-Cloud in 1411 he defeated an attempted coup by the Armagnacs (Orléanists). The Armagnacs recaptured Charles VI in 1414. John allied with Henry V at the time of Agincourt. In 1418 he regained Paris and purged the Armagnacs. At a meeting with the Dauphin Charles (VII) on the bridge at Montereau over the Yonne John was stabbed to death on 10 September. His skull was kept in the mausoleum at Dijon. Burgundy returned to its English alliance. John was succeeded by his son Philip the Good.

JUAN (JOHN/JOAN) I, KING OF ARAGÓN (1350–95)

King from 1387, son and successor of Pedro IV, born at Perpignan and appointed Duke of Girona. He had five children by his first wife Mata of Armagnac, four of whom died in infancy. Five of his six children by his second wife Yolande de Bar died young. Juan probably had epilepsy. He settled the boundary at the Pyrenees. He tried to protect the Jews in the kingdom against attack. He died on 19 May after falling from his horse when hunting. He was succeeded by his brother Martin I.

JUAN (JOHN) I, KING OF LEÓN AND CASTILE (1358–90)
King from 1379, son and successor of Enrique II. He married Beatriz of Portugal, which he claimed. He besieged Lisbon in 1382 but made terms. He tried again on the death of Ferdinand I of Portugal in 1383, and again failed, defeated at Aljubarrota in 1385. He ended Castile's involvement in the Hundred Years' War by truce in 1389. He died on 9 October and was succeeded by his son Enrique III.

JULIAN THE APOSTATE, FLAVIUS CLAUDIUS JULIANUS, ROMAN EMPEROR (332–63)
Emperor from 361, son of Julius Constantius and a Greek mother Basilina, grandson of Constantius Chlorus, the only pagan Byzantine Emperor. He was born in Constantinople and studied in Greece. As western Caesar he defended Gaul against barbarian attack from 356 and, although lacking military experience, proved successful. He defeated the Alemans at Argentorate in 357. He pushed the Franks back over the Rhine. Constantius gave him command in the east in 359. Julian succeeded Constantius. He revived paganism and reversed the policies of Constantine the Great. Julian invaded Persia. He beat Shapur II near Ctesiphon but failed to take the city. He retreated and on 26 June, fighting when not fully armed, was wounded by a spear near Samarra. He died in the night and was buried at Tarsus. The return to paganism proved temporary.

JUSTIN II, BYZANTINE EMPEROR (d.578)
Emperor from 565, nephew and successor of Justinian I. He stopped subsidies to the Avars, provoking attacks on the Balkans.

The Avars assisted the Lombard invasion of Italy. Justin was too preoccupied with other problems to resist – though he opposed their invasion of Dalmatia. He allied with the Turks against the Persians, ending tribute to the Persians. He fought Chosroes I in 572. The war went badly – Dara was lost and Justin made peace. In the late reign the general Maurice (later Emperor) recovered some lost ground. From 571 Justin suffered from some mental problem. He liked to sit in a cart, pulled around his palace while listening to music. He indulged in bouts of violence. The government was taken over by his wife Sophia. He died on 4 October.

JUSTINIAN I, FLAVIUS ANICIANUS JUSTINIANUS, BYZANTINE EMPEROR (482–565)
Emperor from 527, nephew of Justin I, he tried to recover the lost Western Empire. He is pictured on a mosaic in San Vitale Ravenna dated 546. He built the Haghia Sophia and revised imperial law. Justin had no sons and Justinian succeeded. It is difficult to know how far to trust the bitchy account in Procopius' *Secret History* – he said Justinian had 'no more sense than a donkey', was 'prone to evil-doing, easily led astray' and 'two-faced'. Justinian married Theodora, an actress and prostitute. Justinian was a great Emperor but with personality flaws. He was vain, indecisive and did not trust his lieutenants. Yet his vision of a reunited Empire had enormous impact. He was noted for hard work – 'the emperor who never sleeps'. He created a new army of Armenia. In the Persian War from 527 his general Belisarius won at Dara in 530, but was defeated and recalled. Justinian hesitated in face of the Nika Riots of 532, suppressed by Belisarius. Belisarius invaded Africa in 533 and conquered the province, defeating the Vandals at Decimum and Tricamarum. Gelimer was captured and taken to Constantinople. In 535 Belisarius invaded Italy, capturing Naples and Rome in 536, and Ravenna in 539, from Vitiges and the Ostrogoths.

Justinian's lack of trust led to the recall of Belisarius. New commanders, Germanus and Narses, completed the conquest, defeating Totila at Busta Gallorum in 552. Justinian ordered troops to Spain when Athanagild appealed for aid in 554. The Byzantine 'allies' stayed on as rulers in southern Spain. Justinian regained Dalmatia and Sicily, Sardinia and the Balearics. On the eastern frontier he made the 'Everlasting Peace' with Chosroes I in 532, though it only endured until 540. Justinian held the line, building 25 forts in every province, and strongholds along the Danube. He died on 14 November, probably from a heart attack, and was buried in Constantinople. His nephew Justin II succeeded.

JUSTINIAN II RHINOMETUS (SLIT-NOSED), BYZANTINE EMPEROR (d.711)

Emperor from 685, son of Constantine IV, last of the Heraclian dynasty. He resisted Arab attempts to regain Armenia but they defeated him at Sebastopolis, retaking Armenia. He campaigned against the Slavs, regaining part of Thessalonika. He employed Slavs in the army. His general Leontius deposed him in 695, slit his nose and tongue and exiled him to the Crimea – but was then overthrown by Tiberius III. The Arabs overran North Africa, taking Carthage. Justinian escaped to ally with the Khazars, marrying the khan's daughter, renamed Theodora. He allied with the Bulgars and in 705 recovered Constantinople. He was refused entry but entered via a conduit. He made a Bulgar Caesar and initiated a reign of terror, executing Leontius and Tiberius. Justinian wore a sinister false gold nose. He antagonised the Khazars, who allied with rebels. Justinian marched against the Arabs and was captured and executed. The rebel Philippicus became emperor and killed Justinian's son Tiberius.

KERBOGHA (KARBUQA/QAWAM AD-DAULA KERBUQA), ATABEG OF MOSUL (d.1102)

A Turk who rose through military ability, he fought the First Crusaders. He assembled an allied Muslim force to save Antioch in 1098. On the way he failed to recover Edessa. He arrived after the crusaders had taken Antioch, and besieged them within it. He was defeated outside the walls by a sortie under Bohemond. Kerbogha escaped.

KILIJ ARSLAN I, SULTAN OF RUM (d.1107)

The Seljuk Turkish Sultan from 1086, son and successor of Suleiman. Kilij married the daughter of Chaka of Smyrna. He killed his father-in-law at Nicaea and took over. He captured Nicaea and Smyrna in 1092. His successes provoked Byzantium to seek aid from the west, initiating the Crusades. Kilij annihilated the People's Crusade at Civetot in 1096. In 1097 the First Crusaders defeated him at Nicaea and Dorylaeum, capturing Iconium (Konya), which he later recovered for his capital. He was killed in battle by rival Turks near Mosul. He was succeeded by his brother Malik Shah.

KRUM, KHAGAN OF BULGARIA (d.814)

Khagan from 808, the first great ruler of Bulgaria, probably an Avar who united his people with the Bulgars. He united Pannonian and Balkan Bulgaria to threaten Byzantium. He sacked Serdica (Sofia) in 809. The Byzantines retaliated by invading Bulgaria. Krum was defeated and his capital Pliska captured, but he trapped the Byzantines in a mountain pass, where the Emperor Nikephorus I was killed in 811 – his skull later used as a drinking cup. The victory established Bulgaria. Krum invaded Thrace, taking Mesembria (Nesebur) in 812. He defeated an army sent by Michael I at Versinikia in 813. Krum approached Constantinople. The new emperor, Leo V, tried to kill him during negotiations. Krum had demanded a selection of the most beautiful maidens the Byzantines could provide. He raided Thrace, deporting the population of Adrianople. He planned an attack on Constantinople on 14 April but suffered a stroke and died. His son Ormortag succeeded.

LADISLAS, KING OF NAPLES AND HUNGARY (1376–1414)

King of Naples from 1386 in succession to his father Charles III of Durazzo. He resisted a claim by Louis II of Anjou, who was expelled in 1399. Ladislas intervened in the Papal States, taking over much of central Italy including Rome from 1408. His ambitions were halted when Florence joined his southern enemies. He claimed the throne of Hungary and was crowned in 1403 – though soon forced to leave. He died on 6 August and was succeeded by his sister Joanna II.

LANCASTER, THOMAS, EARL OF (1278–1322)

Son of Edmund Crouchback earl of Lancaster whom he succeeded in 1296, receiving the earldoms of Leicester and Ferrers. Under Edward I he fought in Scotland. He became Earl of Lincoln in 1311 through his marriage to the heiress Alice de Lacey. He was a cousin of Edward II and became the leading opponent of that king as a Lord Ordainer. He participated in the murder of Edward's favourite Piers Gaveston in 1312. He dominated England after Edward's defeat at Bannockburn in 1314. Edward recovered, relying on the Despensers. Thomas took to arms but was defeated at Boroughbridge in 1322. He was captured and executed for treason on 22 March at Pontefract. He was buried at Pontefract Priory, which became a cult centre. His brother Henry inherited the earldom.

LEO V, THE ARMENIAN, BYZANTINE EMPEROR (d.820)

Emperor from 813. He was Strategos of the Anatolic Theme, who seized power after Michael I's defeat by the Bulgars, when Leo deserted. Leo tried to kill Krum in negotiations outside Constantinople. Krum failed to take the city but devastated Byzantine territory in revenge. Leo strengthened the walls of Constantinople. After Krum's death Leo defeated his son Ormortag at Mesembria (Nesebur) in 817, after which a truce was agreed. He recovered Thrace. He reintroduced iconoclasm. He was assassinated on Christmas Day by supporters of Michael II, formerly one of his commanders. They struck off his head, exposing the body naked in the Hippodrome, before placing it on board ship to accompany his wife Theodosia into exile. Leo's sons were castrated.

LEO VI, THE WISE, BYZANTINE EMPEROR (866–912)

Emperor from 886, son of either Basil I or Michael III, by Eudocia – who was generous with her favours. This probably accounts for Basil's harshness to Leo. Friends of Leo may have killed Basil in a hunting 'accident'. Leo's marriage to Theophano was forced on him by Basil. On becoming emperor he married his mistress Zoe who lived only a year. He married a fourth time, against Byzantine custom, after his mistress Zoe Carbonopsina produced a son. He wrote a military handbook, the *Taktika*, but may never have commanded in person. He increased the proportion of cavalry in the forces. Leo allied with the Magyars against the Bulgars who invaded Byzantine territory and won at Bulgarophygon in 896. Leo agreed to pay tribute. He attacked Tarsus in 900 and advanced into Armenia. He resisted the Saracens in southern Italy and Sicily but lost Taormina in 902. Thessalonika was sacked in 904. Leo tried to recover Crete in 911 but his fleet was defeated by the Saracens. He died on 12 May and his brother Alexander succeeded.

LEOVIGILD, KING OF THE VISIGOTHS (d.586)

He restored Visigothic power in Iberia, ruling alone after the death of his brother, Liuva I, in 572. His main enemies were the Suevi to the north and Byzantines in the south. Toledo was his capital. His second wife was Goiswinth, widow of Athanagild and mother of Brunhild. His son Hermenengild rebelled in 580. Leovigild besieged Seville in 583, defeating his son who attempted to relieve it. Hermenengild was imprisoned in Tarragona and put to death in Seville. The Suevi were defeated in 585, their last king deposed. Leovigild made the Visigothic kingdom the major power in Iberia. He raided into Gaul. His son Reccared succeeded him.

LEWIS IV, WITTELSBACH, THE BAVARIAN, HOLY ROMAN EMPEROR (1283–1347)

King of the Romans from 1314, emperor from 1328, son of Lewis duke of Upper Bavaria. He faced civil war with Frederick of Habsburg duke of Austria, whom he defeated and captured at Mühldorf. Pope John XXII excommunicated Lewis in 1324. He was crowned in Rome in 1328, but not by the pope. In 1327 he invaded Italy and was crowned King of the Lombards in Milan. He attacked and took Rome, setting up the anti-pope Nicholas V. Civil war with Charles IV of Luxembourg marked the late reign, leading to Lewis' deposition. He died on 11 October when hunting and was buried in Munich.

LINCOLN, JOHN DE LA POLE, EARL OF (1462–87)

Earl from 1467, son of Elizabeth of York and the Duke of Suffolk, nephew of Edward IV and Richard III. Under Richard he led the Council of the North and was Viceroy in Ireland. Richard proclaimed him heir in 1484. John led Yorkist opposition to Henry VII. On Henry's accession he fled abroad, returning with an army including German mercenaries. He led the Lambert Simnel Rebellion and was defeated and killed at Stoke in 1487.

LLEWELYN AP GRUFFYDD, PRINCE OF WALES (1240–82)

Son of Gruffydd ap Llewelyn, successor to his uncle Dafydd in 1246, prince from 1258,

he sought to revive the position of his grandfather Llewelyn the Great as ruler of all Wales. He allied with Simon de Montfort against Henry III, then with Simon's sons and the Earl of Gloucester in 1267, invading Glamorgan in 1270. In 1278 he married Eleanor, daughter of Simon de Montfort. He refused homage to Edward I, who invaded Wales in 1277. They agreed the Treaty of Conway but war was soon renewed. Llewelyn used guerrilla tactics. He escaped a trap in South Wales but was killed attacking Builth on 11 December.

LLEWELYN AP IORWERTH, THE GREAT, PRINCE OF GWYNEDD (1173–1240)

Prince from 1201, having already taken Anglesey, son of Iorwerth Drwyndwn (Flatnose). In 1205 he married Joan, illegitimate daughter of King John. He conquered Powys and Ceredigion in 1208. John invaded Wales in 1211 but retired in 1212. During the conflict between John and the barons, Llewelyn took Swansea, assuming lordship of South Wales. Henry III made two expeditions against Llewelyn but both failed. Llewelyn was acknowledged as overlord of the Welsh princes, eventually recognised by Henry III. He died on 11 April, succeeded by his son Dafydd.

LOTHAR III (LOTHAR II BY SOME COUNTS), OF SUPPLINBURG, HOLY ROMAN EMPEROR (1075–1137)

King of the Romans from 1125, emperor from 1133, inheriting lands in Saxony. He rebelled against Henry IV (HRE), after whose death he became Duke of Saxony in 1106. His election was disputed by Frederick of Hohenstaufen duke of Swabia. Conrad of Hohenstaufen was elected anti-king in 1127. Civil war against the Hohenstaufen continued to 1135, when Lothar was successful. This initiated the Welf/Ghibelline conflict. Lothar invaded Bohemia in 1126 but was defeated at Kulm. He led an Italian expedition in 1133 and was crowned in Rome. He invaded southern Italy against Roger II and made

Rainulf Duke of Apulia. Roger recovered after Lothar's departure. Lothar became ill in Italy and died on 4 December in an Alpine peasant's hut during his return. He was buried at Königslutter near Brunswick.

LOUIS I, THE PIOUS, HOLY ROMAN EMPEROR (778–840)

Son of Charlemagne, emperor from 814 to 840. His name 'the Pious' comes from self-description in documents as 'piisimus' (most pious), emphasising the Christian nature of his empire. In France he is known as 'le Débonnaire'. He was King of Aquitaine from 781. He led campaigns into Spain for his father, and took Tortosa in 811. Charlemagne's plan was to divide the Carolingian Empire between his sons, but Louis was the sole survivor and inherited his father's position. Charles passed the imperial crown to Louis at Aachen in 813. After Charlemagne's death in 814, Pope Stephen IV re-crowned Louis in 816. Viking raids caused major concern. Louis' nephew Bernard of Italy rebelled, submitting in 817, and was blinded – he died soon afterwards. Louis did penance for it in 822. Louis tried to subdue the Bretons, with incomplete success though Nominoë did homage in 826. Louis was successful in clashes on the eastern frontier against the Slavs and Bulgars. His sons Pepin and Louis the German rebelled in 830, but made their peace, though rebelling again in 832. In 833 his rebel sons confronted Louis at the Field of Lies in Alsace. He was deposed and imprisoned but restored in 834 after quarrels between his sons. On return from another clash with his son Louis the German, Louis died at Ingelheim. Pepin predeceased him, but Lothar, Louis the German and Charles the Bald survived to divide the empire between them.

LOUIS VI, THE FAT (LE GROS), KING OF FRANCE (1077–1137)

King from 1108, son and successor of Philip I. He married Adelaide of Maurienne. He became so fat he could not mount a horse but was a noted warrior. His main struggles were against barons of the royal demesne, notably Hugh du Puiset. Louis encouraged William Clito, son of Curthose, to rebel against Henry I of England. Allied to Fulk of Anjou, Louis invaded Normandy but was defeated by Henry I at Brémule in 1119. Escaping, he became lost in a wood, but was led to safety at Les Andelys by a peasant. Louis' support gained the county of Flanders for Clito in 1127. In 1137 Louis arranged marriage between his son Louis and the heiress Eleanor of Aquitaine. He supported Stephen of Blois to become King of England. Louis died on 1 August and was succeeded by his son Louis VII.

LOUIS VII, THE YOUNG (LE JEUNE), KING OF FRANCE (1120–80)

Crowned in his father Louis VI's lifetime in 1131 (after his older brother Philip died), king from 1137. He married the heiress Eleanor of Aquitaine in 1137. In 1142 he invaded Champagne against Theobald of Blois, burning the church at Vitry (which he later repented) but gaining nothing. His marriage foundered during the Second Crusade and ended in 1152. Eleanor then married Henry of Anjou (soon to be King of England), who claimed Aquitaine. Louis married twice more, to Constance of Castile and Adela of Champagne (mother of Philip Augustus). The Second Crusade was a disaster, failing to take Damascus in 1148. Henry II invaded Toulouse but avoided confrontation when Louis came to defend it in 1159. Louis and Henry made peace in 1169. Louis established greater influence in the south. He sheltered two popes (Eugenius III and Alexander III), and Becket in exile. Louis encouraged the rebellion against Henry II by his sons in 1173–4, but made peace in 1174 at Montlouis. He insisted on homage from rulers of the great principalities. He died on 18 September after a stroke and was buried at his Cistercian foundation of Barbeau. His son Philip II succeeded.

LOUIS VIII, THE LION, KING OF FRANCE (1187–1226)

King from 1223 on the death of his father, Philip Augustus. He married Blanche of Castile. Louis participated in war against Otto IV (HRE) and John of England, defeating John at La Roche-au-Moine in 1214 while Philip won at Bouvines. Without his father's overt blessing Louis invaded England, in alliance with the Magna Carta barons, in 1216–17. His army was defeated at Lincoln in 1217 and his fleet at sea off Sandwich. Louis abandoned the invasion. As king he invaded the south of France, taking over from the Albigensian Crusade and declaring war on Henry III of England. Louis besieged and took Avignon. Amaury de Montfort surrendered the county of Toulouse to Louis who held most of southern France including Poitou. He became ill at Avignon. He was offered a wench in bed to warm him but primly refused. He never recovered, dying at Montpensier in the Auvergne on 8 November. His son Louis IX succeeded.

LOUIS IX, SAINT, KING OF FRANCE (1214–70)

King from 1226, son and successor of Louis VIII. His mother Blanche of Castile was regent in his minority. She suppressed baronial revolt and defeated an English invasion. He married Margaret of Provence. He gained more through diplomacy than war. He settled the frontiers with England and Aragón through treaties in 1258–9. His brother Alphonse became Count of Toulouse in 1249 through marriage to the heiress. His brother Charles of Anjou became ruler of the kingdom of Sicily. Louis saw off the invasions of Henry III, winning at Taillebourg and Saintes in 1242. His two crusades were unsuccessful. On the first in 1249 Damietta was taken, but lost after defeat at Mansurah in 1250 by Baybars, when Louis was captured. He was ransomed and released in 1250. He went to the Holy Land, whose defences he improved, returning to France in 1254. On his second crusade in 1270 the Emir of Tunis failed to surrender as expected. Louis became ill and died in North Africa. The boiled body was returned to Paris. The heart and entrails were buried at Monreale near Palermo by his brother Charles. Louis was succeeded by his son Philip III. He was canonised in 1297.

LOUIS XI, THE SPIDER KING, KING OF FRANCE (1423–83)

King from 1461, son and successor of Charles VII. He rebelled against his father several times and was exiled in 1456. He annexed the southern territories of Cerdagne and Roussillon in 1463 and suppressed a rebellion there. He faced internal revolt in 1465 in the War of the Common Weal, surviving the indecisive Battle of Montlhéry. He made an abortive attempt to take Brittany in 1468. His chief opponent was Charles the Bold of Burgundy. Louis invaded Picardy against Charles in 1471. Louis won and caused the collapse of Burgundy, which Louis seized on the death of Charles. Louis bought off an English invasion in 1475 through the Treaty of Picquigny. He failed to gain Burgundian lands in Flanders, where he fought the indecisive Battle of Guinegate against Maximilian (HRE) in 1479. He died on 30 August and was succeeded by his son Charles VIII. Louis was buried at his own wish in the church he had built at Cléry.

LUDOVICO IL MORO (THE MOOR), SFORZA, DUKE OF MILAN (1451–1508)

Son of Francesco Sforza, ruler of Milan as regent for his nephew from 1480. 'Il Moro' was probably a pun on his second name Mauro allied to his dark complexion. He kept his nephew Gian Galeazzo a virtual prisoner until his death in 1494. He fought to control Milan, which he lost for a time from 1476. He assumed the title 'Duke' in 1494. He allied with Charles VIII of France against Naples in 1494. This involvement of the French in Italy led to Ludovico's downfall and Milan's loss of independence. Ludovico was expelled by Louis XII in 1499, ending his life as a prisoner at Loches. He was a patron of Leonardo. Ludovico's son Massimiliano temporarily recovered Milan from Louis XII.

MAGNÚS I ÓLAFSSON, THE GOOD, KING OF NORWAY AND DENMARK (1024–47)

King of Norway 1035–47, Denmark 1042–7, the last Norwegian king to rule Denmark. He was an illegitimate son of St Ólaf, thought to be named Magnús after Charlemagne (*Carolus Magnus*). As a child he was exiled with his father through pressure from Cnut. Ólaf was killed at Stiklestad in 1030 and Magnús fled to Kiev. He returned to Norway in 1035 as king. From 1042 he ruled Denmark after the death of Harthacnut. In 1043 he defeated the Wends at Jumne (Wolin) and Lürschau Heath, where he fought in a red costume wielding his father's axe, *Hel*. In 1045 he shared Norway with his uncle, Harold Hardrada. Magnús died on campaign against Sweyn Estrithsson in Denmark.

MALATESTA, SIGISMONDO (1417–68)

Illegitimate son of Pandolfo of Fano. He succeeded his uncle, Carlo, as ruler of Rimini in 1432. He was a *condottiere* who served Francesco Sforza. He erected several military buildings, including the castle at Rimini (Castel Sigismondo). His reputation for disloyalty came from abandoning Alfonso of Naples in 1447. He lived down to the family name of 'evil head', accused of murder, incest, rape and sodomy among other sins. The pope excommunicated him for ignoring the peace of 1459, calling him the 'worst scoundrel' who had ever lived. He was a noted patron. He was defeated by an alliance of enemies at the River Cesano in 1462. In 1463 he lost all his possessions except Rimini. Late in life he served again as a mercenary, for Venice against the Turks in Greece. He died in Rimini on 9 October and was buried in the Tempio Malatestiano. He was succeeded by his son Roberto.

MALIK SHAH, SULTAN OF PERSIA (1055–92)

Seljuk Sultan from 1072, son of Alp Arslan. His successes against Byzantium provoked the First Crusade. He conquered the Middle East, invading Asia Minor from 1073. His brother Tutush took Damascus, Jerusalem, Acre and Aleppo from the Fatimids. Malik moved far to the east, winning Transoxiana and reaching China. He made Baghdad his capital in 1091. He was succeeded by his son Mahmud I, when civil war led to the break-up of the empire, leaving a patchwork of emirates.

MANFRED, KING OF SICILY (1232–66)

King from 1258, illegitimate son of Frederick II (HRE). His mother was Bianca Lancia from the comital family of Loreto. He held the Regno from 1250 on his father's death, nominally for his half-brother Conrad. In 1254 he took Lucera from the papacy and defeated a papal army at Foggia, winning Apulia. He intervened in Roman politics, supporting rebellion in 1257. He claimed Sicily in 1258 and was crowned. He found allies in northern Italy, including Siena. He defeated Florence at Montaperto in 1260 and took over Lucca in 1264. The papacy invited Charles of Anjou to attack Manfred in 1265. He was defeated and killed at Benevento on 26 February when, though beaten, he refused to leave the field. His daughter Constance married Pedro of Aragón.

MANIAKES, GEORGE (d.1043)

Byzantine general. He was very tall (reportedly ten feet!) – with a violent temper. As Strategos of the Theme of Teluch he tricked and killed attacking Saracens and was appointed Catapan of Lower Media. Romanus III was defeated at Aleppo but Maniakes recovered Aleppo and captured Edessa in 1032. Michael IV sent him to Sicily in 1038. Using Norman mercenaries Maniakes won victories at Rametta 1038 and Dragina 1040, taking Messina in 1038 and Syracuse in 1040 – only to be arrested for treason. Michael V released him and sent him to southern Italy in 1042. The situation deteriorated in his absence but he advanced again, ruthlessly destroying everything in his path. In his absence he heard that Romanus Sclerus had seduced his wife, which so enraged him that he stuffed the ears, nose and mouth of the messenger with dung and tortured him to death. When recalled by Constantine IX in 1043 he rebelled and was proclaimed Emperor by his troops. An imperial force blocked the way at Ostrovo in Bulgaria. Maniakes was winning when fatally wounded. His head was displayed in Constantinople.

MANUEL I COMNENUS, BYZANTINE EMPEROR (1118–80)

Emperor from 1143, youngest son of John II and a Hungarian mother Piroska (renamed Irene). He was a noted diplomat and womaniser. He married first the Bavarian Bertha, sister-in-law of Conrad III, and then the Frankish Maria of Antioch. He granted lands (pronoia) for military service, comparable to western feudalism. He faced a revival of Turkish power. He had to rely on Venetian naval aid, which later caused problems. Roger II of Sicily took Corfu in 1147 but was repulsed in 1149. Manuel invaded Italy in 1155, capturing Bari. He achieved little of permanence, making peace in 1158. William I of Sicily threatened Constantinople in 1156. The Turks took Edessa in 1144, provoking the Second Crusade. Manuel sought western aid against the Seljuks but the Crusade was a disappointment. Manuel allied with Amalric King of Jerusalem. He entered Antioch in 1159 but was defeated by Kilij Arslan at Myriocephalum in 1176. His general John Vatatzes recovered the situation in 1177. Manuel invaded Hungary ten times, and his overlordship was recognised from 1156. Success was completed by victory near Belgrade in 1167. He subdued Dalmatia in 1172. He became a monk before dying on 24 September. His son Alexius II succeeded.

MANUEL II PALAEOLOGUS, BYZANTINE EMPEROR (1348–1425)

Emperor from 1391, when he escaped from the Turks. He had to fight for the Turks as a vassal. His father John V made him Governor of Thessalonika. He married the Serbian princess Helena. From 1396 Constantinople was besieged by the Turks but saved by the appearance of Tamberlane. Hope of western aid faded with the failure of the Crusades of Nicopolis and Kosovo. In 1399 Manuel travelled west to seek aid against the Turks, visiting Venice, Paris and London. He returned in 1403. The Byzantines won at sea in 1413. Manuel rebuilt the Hexamilion wall across the Isthmus of Corinth. In 1423 he ceded Salonika to Venice. He faced an increasing Ottoman threat from Bayezit, Mehmet I and Murad II. By the time of his death he held little beyond Constantinople. Most of Byzantium was held by the Ottomans. Surviving fragments were held by his brothers and sons. He had a stroke in 1423 and, having become a monk, died two years later on 21 July. His son John VIII succeeded.

MARCEL, ÉTIENNE (d.1358)

Leader of popular opposition to the Dauphin Charles (VII). A wealthy cloth merchant, he became Provost of the Merchants in Paris, effectively Mayor. He made speeches critical of the crown at meetings of the Estates-General in the 1350s. In 1357 Charles agreed to a reforming ordinance. Charles declared himself regent. In February 1358 Marcel raised a mob of thousands, wearing red and blue hoods. He forced his way before Charles and ordered the execution of officials and courtiers. Charles had to confirm the ordinance, after which he fled. The Jacquerie, the French Peasants' Revolt, erupted in May. On 31 July Marcel, suspected of dealings with the peasants and planning to hand Paris to the Navarrese, was murdered on return from examining the city's defences.

MARGARET OF ANJOU, QUEEN OF ENGLAND (1429–82)

Wife of Henry VI, tougher and more effective than her husband, daughter of René duke of Anjou and King of Naples. She married Henry in 1445. She often replaced her husband as effective commander during his illness, incapacity and imprisonment. One chronicler thought she 'ruled the realm as she liked'. Her supporters were the dukes of Somerset and Suffolk. She removed York from the Protectorate and initiated the Wars of the Roses. She virtually commanded the victory at Ludford Bridge in 1459. When Henry was captured in 1460 she fled to Scotland. She brought an army south in 1461 to win the Second Battle of St Albans, rescuing Henry. She sought support from Scotland and France, never seeing Henry again. With the support of Warwick the Yorkists were defeated and Henry released but in 1471 Edward IV recovered power. Her son Edward was killed at Tewkesbury. Henry VI was put to death. Margaret was captured and taken to London in a cart. She remained a prisoner until 1476 when Louis XI ransomed her. She died in Anjou and was buried in Angers Cathedral.

MATILDA, THE EMPRESS (1102–67)

Daughter of Henry I and Edith-Matilda. She married Henry V (HRE) in 1114, becoming Empress. After his death she remarried Geoffrey Plantagenet, who became Count of Anjou. After the death of her brother, William the Aetheling, Henry I made Matilda his heir. There was opposition from nobles who preferred his nephew Stephen of Blois. Matilda and her husband disputed Stephen's succession. Geoffrey conquered Normandy from Stephen in a ten-year campaign. Matilda arrived at Arundel in 1139, initiating civil war. Her prime lieutenant was her half-brother, Robert of Gloucester. Stephen was captured at Lincoln in 1141 but Matilda was never crowned queen. She left London for her safety and retreated from Winchester, where Robert of Gloucester was captured covering her flight. She rode off astride a horse in male fashion. Stephen was released in exchange for Robert. Matilda was besieged in Oxford 1142, escaping in a white cloak through the snow. The war gradually petered out. Matilda left England. Geoffrey died in 1151. Her son, Henry Plantagenet, took up the cudgels and having become Duke of Normandy and Count of Anjou, won the throne as Henry II. Matilda continued to have influence with her son. She died on 10 September.

MAURICE (MAURICIUS), BYZANTINE EMPEROR (d.602)

Emperor from 582, an Anatolian who rose to prominence through war against Persia. Tiberius II married Maurice to his daughter Constantia and chose him as successor. Maurice is the supposed author of the military handbook, the *Strategikon*. He reformed the Byzantine army, reducing the *buccellarii* and incorporating Avar tactics. He fought against the Persians and strengthened the frontier, gaining Armenia. He faced attack from the Avars, whose advance under Baian he halted. In 592 he invaded Avar territory over the Danube, defeating Baian at Viminacium in 601. He improved the Byzantine fortifications of Ravenna and Carthage – each under a military exarch. The mob in Constantinople shouted rude verses at Maurice about his numerous illegitimate children. The cost of warfare caused rebellion under Phokas, who marched on Constantinople. Maurice agreed to abdicate but Phokas executed him and four of his sons, displaying the heads and throwing the bodies in the sea.

MAXIMILIAN I, HABSBURG, HOLY ROMAN EMPEROR (1459–1519)

Archduke of Austria, King of the Romans from 1486, emperor from 1493, son of Frederick III and Eleanor of Portugal. He sought to revive the glories of the imperial past. By the Perpetual Edict he tried to stop private war in Germany, with only partial success. He married Mary of Burgundy, daughter of Charles the Bold, in 1477, bringing considerable territory to the empire, including most of the Netherlands – a move with important consequences. Maximilian defeated the French at Guinegate in 1479, fighting on foot with his Flemish infantry. His second marriage, to Anne of Brittany in 1490, was annulled. He was in constant conflict with Charles VIII and Louis XII, coming into conflict with France over Italy. He recovered part of Austria from the Hungarians, mainly former Habsburg lands. Marriages arranged with Spanish royalty brought imperial expansion in the 16th century. He granted independence to the Swiss in 1499 after defeat at Dornach. He was buried at Innsbruck and his grandson Charles V succeeded.

MEDICI, COSIMO DE', *PATER PATRIAE* (1389–1464)

The first Medici ruler of Florence. From a wealthy Florentine family, he ruled Florence with popular support, disguising the disappearance of republican rule. He was exiled by the Albizzi in 1433 but returned in triumph the following year. He dealt with several attempted coups against him. He allied with Francesco Sforza of Milan, helping to make the Peace of Lodi in 1454. He died on 1 August, succeeded by his son Piero.

MEDICI, LORENZO DE', IL MAGNIFICO (THE MAGNIFICENT) (1449–92)

Joint ruler of Florence with his brother Giuliano from 1469, son of Piero. Giuliano was killed in the Pazzi Plot in 1478. Lorenzo made peace with Naples in 1480. Florence became arguably the greatest power in Italy under Lorenzo. One son became Pope Leo X. Lorenzo was a patron of Michelangelo. He is portrayed in a famous bust by Verrocchio.

MEHMET II, THE CONQUEROR, OTTOMAN SULTAN (1430–81)

Sultan from 1451, son of Murad II, who captured Constantinople in 1453 and destroyed the Byzantine Empire. He built the Rumeli Hisar fortress in 1452 on Byzantine territory, commanding the Bosphorus. In the siege of Constantinople he used enormous cannons and employed the western engineer Urban. He had ships dragged overland into the Golden Horn. The city fell on 29 May. Mehmet, before entering the Haghia Sophia, picked up a handful of earth to sprinkle over his head in humility. Entering the imperial palace he muttered lines of a poem – 'the spider weaves the curtains in the palace of the Caesars'. The city was pillaged for three days. He conquered Serbia by 1459 and the Balkans. He took the remaining Byzantine territories including Mistra and the Morea in 1460, and Trebizond in 1461. He faced resistance from Hunyadi and Vlad Tepes. In 1479 he invaded Italy. He also conquered the Crimea.

MELUS OF BARI (MELES/MELO) (d.1020)

A Lombard noble, among the first to employ Norman mercenaries for his rebellion against the Greeks in Apulia in 1017. Bari under Melus revolted against Byzantium in 1009. Melus took refuge in Salerno and then Capua. He met Norman pilgrims visiting the shrine of St Michael at Monte Gargano and sought their military aid. Another version has the Normans fleeing from their own duke. With their aid he won five battles against the Byzantines, demonstrating their value. Melus was defeated at Cannae in 1018. This led to the establishment of the first Norman lordship in the region by Rainulf. Melus fled to Germany where he died.

MERCADIER

Mercenary captain serving Richard the Lionheart from 1184, when he sacked Excideuil; he was a Provençal and leader of a band of Brabançons that caused problems in the Limousin. He fought in Richard's war against Philip Augustus in France, at Fréteval in 1194 and Vernon 1198. In 1195 he captured Issoudun. In 1197 he took Milly-sur-Thérain and captured the bishop of Beauvais. Richard granted him lands in Périgord, previously held by Adhémar de Beynac. When Richard was fatally wounded he pardoned the crossbowman responsible, but later Mercadier (who completed the taking of Châlus) had the man flayed alive. Mercadier claimed 'I fought for him [Richard] loyally and hard . . . and was placed in command of his army'.

MEROVECH, KING OF THE SALIANS (fl. c.450)

(Note: this Merovech is not to be confused with later members of the dynasty given the same name – one a son of Chilperic I, one a son of Theuderic II.)

The Merovingian dynasty that ruled Francia until 751 was named after him, though he was not the first king. He succeeded Chlodion as ruler of the Salian Franks. Their base was probably in Belgium (Toxandria, around Tournai), though some place it in Thuringia. Merovech belonged to the same family as Chlodion, though whether he was his son is uncertain – as is practically everything about his life. A legend had his mother raped by a sea monster, the Quinotaur, that fathered him – his name meant 'son of the sea'. He was probably the unnamed Salian who came to Rome seeking aid and was described as having long, fair hair over his shoulders. The Salians aided Aëtius against Attila the Hun, and fought in the victory at the Catalaunian Plains in 451. His son, Childeric I, succeeded.

MICHAEL I, RHANGABE, BYZANTINE EMPEROR (d.845)

Emperor 811–13 on the defeat and death of his father-in-law Nikephorus I (when Michael escaped) and the abdication of his brother-in-law Stauracius (paralysed in the battle). Michael's wife was Prokopia. He recognised Charlemagne as Western Emperor. On 21 June 813 the Bulgars defeated him at Versinikia. He escaped to Constantinople but was deposed by his general Leo V, who had deserted at Versinikia. Michael took the name

Athanasius to enter a monastery on the Princes' Isles, where he died on 11 January.

MICHAEL II, THE AMORIAN, THE STAMMERER, BYZANTINE EMPEROR (d.829)

Emperor from 820, from Amorium in Asia Minor. A critic considered 'he was an excellent judge of mules'. Accused of plotting against Leo V, he was arrested and sentenced to death. Michael's supporters assassinated Leo on Christmas Day and proclaimed Michael emperor, though still in manacles. He married twice, first Hekla and then Euprosyne, whom he took from a nunnery. He enlisted Bulgar aid to defeat the rebel Thomas the Slav, who besieged Constantinople in 821. Michael used Greek Fire against the enemy fleet, defeating their men on land at Keduktos in 823. At Arcadiolpolis Michael besieged Thomas, who was handed over and executed. The Saracens captured Crete and Sicily. Michael died on 2 October and his son Theophilus succeeded.

MICHAEL III, THE SOT, BYZANTINE EMPEROR (840–67)

Emperor from 842, last of the Amorians, son of Theophilus. The reason for his nickname is self-evident. Aged 15, advised by his uncle Caesar Bardas, he put his mother and regent, Theodora, in a convent and seized power. In 863 he defeated the Saracens at Poson, where Emir Omar was killed. An army for Michael defeated the Saracen Governor of Armenia. The Russians besieged Constantinople in 860. Michael invaded Bulgaria and forced Khazan Boris to make peace and accept Christianity in 864. On 24 September 867 his co-emperor, Basil I, killed Michael and took power.

MICHAEL IV, THE PAPHLAGONIAN, BYZANTINE EMPEROR (d.1041)

Emperor from 1034, son of a eunuch. He married his mistress Zoe, widow of Romanus III. He suffered from epilepsy and dropsy. George Maniakes was sent to Sicily in 1038, capturing Messina and Syracuse in

1040. He was recalled and the gains lost. Michael led a force against Bulgar rebels in 1040. He provoked them to sortie, then beat them, capturing Bojana and Peter Deljan – who was blinded and had his nose slit. Michael died on 10 December and was buried in Constantinople. His nephew Michael V succeeded.

MICHAEL VIII, PALAEOLOGUS, BYZANTINE EMPEROR (1234–82)

Emperor from 1258 at Nicaea and from 1261 in Constantinople, founder of the dynasty of the Palaeologi. He recovered Constantinople for the Greeks from the Latins. He rose through military command. In 1258 he deposed and blinded Theodore II, who ruled at Nicaea, and acted as regent for his son John IV. Michael defeated a coalition including Greeks from Epirus and Latins at Pelagonia in 1259, taking over Thessaly and Epirus. He tried to regain Constantinople in 1260 but failed. He allied with the Genoese against Venice in 1261 – though later he restored Venice's privileges. A Nicaean force entered Constantinople on 25 July 1261 and the Latin Emperor Baldwin II fled. Michael entered the city on 15 August to be crowned emperor. He blinded, deposed and imprisoned John IV. His fleet defeated the Latins at Demetrias in 1275. Michael sought reunion with the Roman Church but, for his troubles, was declared deposed – though it could not be enforced. He successfully resisted Charles of Anjou, King of Sicily, who tried to regain Constantinople for the Latins. Michael made peace with the Mongols. He allied with Aragón and encouraged the Sicilian Vespers in 1282, leading to the downfall of Charles in Sicily. Michael died of disease on 11 December while campaigning in Thrace. His son Andronicus II succeeded.

MILES OF GLOUCESTER, EARL OF HEREFORD (d.1143)

A leading baron for Matilda in the civil war against Stephen. He succeeded his father as sheriff of Gloucester, holding Gloucester Castle for Henry I. He welcomed Stephen as king but deserted to Matilda once she arrived. She spent much of her time at Gloucester, protected by Miles. He helped Robert of Gloucester to take Worcester in 1139. He captured Winchcomb, South Cerney and Hereford but failed to win Sudeley. He nullified Stephen's early success by swift action at Wallingford, which he relieved. Miles fought at Lincoln in 1141, commanding the left wing, when Stephen was defeated and captured. In 1141 Matilda made him Earl of Hereford. The bishop of Hereford excommunicated him for attacks on the Church. On Christmas Eve 1143 Miles went hunting and was killed by a stray arrow in the chest.

MONTAGU, JOHN NEVILLE, EARL OF NORTHUMBERLAND, LORD (1431–71)

Earl from 1464 to 1470, Lord Montagu from 1470, supporter of his brother Warwick the Kingmaker. Fighting for the Yorkists, he was captured at the Second Battle of St Albans and later released. He helped establish Yorkist power in the north, becoming Warden of the East March in 1463. In 1464 he defeated Lancastrian attackers at Hedgeley Moor. Then he won at Hexham and was rewarded with the earldom. He surrendered the title in 1470, when it was restored to Henry Percy. In compensation he was made Marquis of Montagu. Still resentful, in 1470 he deserted to the Lancastrians. After Edward's return Montagu was killed on 14 April at Barnet along with his brother.

MONTFORT, SIMON DE, THE ELDER (1160–1218)

Leader of the Albigensian Crusade against Cathar heretics. He claimed the earldom of Leicester through his mother. He played little part in England but his son was the Simon de Montfort of the Barons' Wars. Simon joined the Fourth Crusade but refused to attack Christian Zara in 1202, going on to the Holy Land. He commanded the Albigensian Crusade from 1209. He concluded a series of sieges against well-defended strongholds such as

Carcassonne, Minerve and Lavaur. His greatest victory was at Muret in 1213. He claimed the county of Toulouse from 1215 in place of Raymond VI, recognised by Philip II in 1216, though lacking local support. Simon became Duke of Narbonne and Viscount of Béziers and Carcassonne. He besieged Toulouse in 1218, and was killed on 25 June by a stone from a trebuchet operated by women. His son Amaury succeeded but was unable to sustain his position.

MONTFORT, SIMON DE, EARL OF LEICESTER AND CHESTER (1208–65)
Son of Simon de Montfort the Elder who came to England in 1230. He married Eleanor sister of Henry III in 1238 and was recognised as earl in 1239. He fought in Poitou in 1242 and as Henry's Governor in Gascony 1248–52, suppressing a rebellion in 1251. Complaints against him led to his recall. He became leader of the baronial opposition, defeating and capturing Henry III at Lewes in 1264. Simon virtually ruled England, assembling the Parliament of 1265. He became Earl of Chester. In 1265 he was defeated by Prince Edward (I) on 4 August at Evesham where he was killed. His body was dismembered and buried at Evesham Abbey, where a cult of pilgrimage developed.

MULEY HASAN (ABŪ'L-HASAN 'ALĪ), KING OF GRANADA
King from 1464. He had been at the court of Castile. He provoked the final stage of the *Reconquista* by attacking Zahara in 1481, which led to the Christian invasion of Granada. His son Boabdil rebelled in 1482. Muley recovered the throne after Boabdil's capture in 1483. Muley, ill and nearly blind, abdicated in favour of his brother Muhammad in 1485, who in gratitude gave Muley a pauper's burial!

MURAD (MURAT) II, OTTOMAN SULTAN (1402–51)
Sultan from 1421, son of Mehmet I. He increased Ottoman territory in the Balkans and Anatolia at the expense of Byzantium. By his death the fall of Constantinople looked inevitable – it survived so long because he let it. He developed the Janissaries and greater use of guns. His brother Mustafa rebelled with Byzantine aid but was defeated at Ulubat, captured and executed in 1423. Murad besieged Constantinople in 1421 but failed to take it. In 1423 he broke through the Hexamilion Wall across the Isthmus of Corinth. Serbia, Wallachia and Hungary accepted Ottoman suzerainty. One of his wives was the Serbian Maria. In 1430 he took Thessalonika, where 'chaste virgins fell into the embraces of profligates' and 7,000 inhabitants were enslaved. He took Salonika and conquered Albania in 1432, though it rebelled in 1443. In 1442 he aided the rebel Demetrios despot of Mesembria to besiege Constantinople, again failing. In 1444 and 1448 Murad defeated the Crusades of Varna and Kosovo – Byzantium's last hope of rescue. In 1444 he abdicated in favour of Mehmet, his son by a slave girl. He retired to Manisa, but took power again in 1446. The Byzantine Emperor was his vassal and fought for him. Murad died at Edirne (Adrianople) of a stroke on 3 February, succeeded by his son Mehmet II.

NEVSKY, ALEXANDER, OF SUZDAL (1220–63)
Prince of Novgorod from 1236, Prince of Kiev from 1247, Grand Duke of Vladimir from 1252, a successful military leader and victor over the Teutonic Knights, son and successor of Jaroslav II of Novgorod. He fought off Mongol attacks but was prepared to compromise. He defeated the Swedes at the Neva in 1240, earning the name Nevsky. The Knights tried to extend control eastwards against the Russians. Alexander recaptured Pskov and beat the Knights at Lake Peipus in 1242, leading to their decline. He defeated the Lithuanians in 1245. He suppressed a riot in Novgorod against a Mongol census in 1258 and kept Novgorod independent. He died at

Gorodets on 14 November. He was canonised by the Russian Orthodox Church in 1547.

NIKEPHORUS II, PHOKAS, BYZANTINE EMPEROR (d.969)

Co-emperor from 959, emperor from 963. He restored the Byzantine position in the Mediterranean and by victories against the Saracens, earning the nickname 'White Death of the Saracens'. He favoured archers, developed the wedge-shaped formation of heavy cavalry cataphracts and wrote a military handbook, the *Precepts*. His improved fleet recovered Crete in 960–1, clearing it of pirates. Candia (Heraklion) was besieged and taken in 961. He succeeded Romanus II in 963, marrying his widow Theophano. He took Cyprus in 965. He won back Anatolia and Syria, taking Aleppo in 962, Tarsus in 965 and Antioch in 969. He promised 'soon I shall conquer Egypt' but, though he forced the Fatimids to make peace, could not fulfil the promise. Later famine caused rioting in Constantinople. Nikephorus was deposed by his wife's lover, his nephew John I. On 10 December conspirators attacked Nikephorus, slashing his face with a sword, kicking him, pulling out his hair, punching him in the face and despatching him with a sword.

NOMINOË (d.851)

Ruler of the Bretons. Louis the Pious failed to subdue him, though Nominoë did homage in 826. Louis recognised him as *missus dominicus*. Charles the Bald was also foiled by Nominoë who defeated him at Ballon in 845. Charles recognised him as *dux* in Brittany by treaty. Nominoë's death encouraged further invasion by Charles the Bald, but the king was defeated by Nominoë's son, Erispoë.

NORTHUMBERLAND, HENRY PERCY I, EARL OF (1341–1408)

The first Percy earl from 1377. The family had long defended England against the Scots. He deserted Richard II to aid Henry IV and was appointed Constable of England and Warden of the West March. He opposed Henry cautiously. He was not at Shrewsbury in 1403, when his son Hotspur was killed, or in the Scrope Rebellion of 1405. He sought safety in Scotland, returning with an army to be defeated and killed on 19 February at Bramham Moor.

NORTHUMBERLAND, HENRY PERCY II, EARL OF (1393–1455)

Earl from 1416, grandson of Henry Percy I, a staunch Lancastrian loyal to Henry VI. He fought at St Albans in 1455. The Nevilles, rivals of the Percies, were among the Yorkist opponents. He was captured and put to death on 28 May.

NORTHUMBERLAND, HENRY PERCY III, EARL OF (1421–61)

Earl from 1455, in succession to his father Henry Percy II, Warden of the West March for Henry VI. He was killed fighting for Henry VI at Towton on 29 March, his slow advance contributing to the defeat.

NORTHUMBERLAND, HENRY PERCY IV, EARL OF (1449–89)

Restored to the earldom in 1470. His father, Henry Percy III, was killed at Towton when Edward IV passed the earldom to John Neville. Edward IV's brief downfall in 1470–1 led to the restoration. The Nevilles turned against Edward, so Henry became the first Yorkist Percy. His allegiance remained uncertain. He came to Bosworth at Richard III's summons but failed to aid the king. Henry Tudor showed no gratitude and had Percy imprisoned. He was killed at Topcliffe in Yorkshire by a mob opposing the war tax. Percy's son Henry succeeded to the earldom.

NUR ED-DIN, EMIR OF ALEPPO (1118–74)

The son of Zangi of Mosul, ruling Aleppo from 1146. He dominated Syria, taking Mosul in 1170. He married the daughter of the ruler of Damascus. He successfully resisted the Second Crusade. In 1147 he defeated the Count of Edessa and razed the city. He won at Inab in 1149, when Count Raymond was killed. He captured and blinded Joscelin of Edessa in 1150. He captured Damascus in 1154 but was beaten at Homs in 1163. He was the Lord of Shirkuh and of his nephew Saladin. Shirkuh conquered Egypt for him, taking Cairo in 1169. Nur ed-Din had differences with Saladin. He died in Damascus on 15 May and Saladin took over Egypt.

ODOACER, FLAVIUS, KING OF ITALY (433–93)

A Goth who commanded Roman troops, the first barbarian ruler of Italy. In 476 he defeated Orestes, deposing his son Romulus Augustulus, last Western Emperor. Odoacer became king in 476, with his capital at Ravenna. He annexed Dalmatia in 481 and Noricum in 488, attempting to bring the Eastern Empire under his authority too but antagonising the Eastern Emperor Zeno, who sent Theoderic against him, in 489. Odoacer beat Theoderic at Faenza and besieged him in Pavia. Diverted by other problems, Odoacer was defeated by the Ostrogoths in 490 at the Adda, taking refuge in Ravenna, which was besieged 490–3. Peace was agreed. At a subsequent banquet Theoderic had Odoacer murdered. Odoacer made Italy the only surviving section of the Western Roman Empire.

OFFA, KING OF MERCIA (d.796)

The greatest of the rulers of Mercia, king from 757, claiming descent from the continental Offa. Offa was an aetheling of the ruling family and emerged to power following a civil war in Mercia. He expanded his kingdom by conquering Lindsey, Essex, Surrey, Kent and Sussex. He may have been defeated at Otford in 776 but recovered to take over Kent. He defeated Wessex under Cynewulf at Bensington in 779, giving Mercia domination in the south and calling himself King of the English. He corresponded with Charlemagne, showing his stature in Europe. Offa defeated the Welsh, establishing the frontier known as Offa's Dyke. Under Offa the silver penny was established as the basic coinage in England, enduring until Tudor times. He died on 26 July.

ÓLAF I, TRYGGVASON, KING OF NORWAY (c.964–1000)

King from 995, probably brought up in Russia after the killing of his father. He took part in raids in the Baltic and on expeditions to England. He was probably the victor of Maldon in 991. He allied with Sweyn Forkbeard. Ólaf converted to Christianity in England, promising not to return. He overthrew Hákon to become King of Norway, encouraging the conversion of Norway and Iceland. He was killed at Svöld, fighting an alliance of Danes and Swedes. It was said that, recognising defeat, he leaped from his ship the *Long Serpent* (the largest ship recorded in the sagas) and drowned. *Ólaf Tryggvason's Saga* is part of the *Heimskringla*. There were tales that he survived.

ÓLAF II, HAROLDSSON, THE STOUT/ST ÓLAF, KING OF NORWAY (c.995–1030)

King from 1015, a descendant of Harold Finehair, son of Harold Grenske (a minor king in Norway), half-brother to Harold Hardrada. He was known as the Stout or the Fat, and after canonisation as St Ólaf. He participated in expeditions to England in 1009–11. He served Thorkell the Tall and Aethelred II of England. He was a leader of those who overran East Anglia, said to be responsible for destroying London Bridge. He turned Christian in Normandy in 1013. He won the throne of Norway by defeating Sweyn Hákonsson at Nesjar near Oslo in 1015. In c.1025 he made an agreement with the colonists in Iceland, ensuring Norwegian interest there. He forced conversion on Norway, arousing opposition. He married Astrid, illegitimate daughter of Olof Skötkonung of Sweden. He won at the Holy River against Cnut. Internal enemies allied with Cnut to oppose Ólaf who was exiled. He returned but was defeated at Stiklestad, where he was killed. He was buried secretly at

Trondheim, becoming the patron saint of Norway. His sword, *Hneitir*, was picked up by a Swede and placed over the altar of St Ólaf's Church in Constantinople.

ORDOÑO II, KING OF LEÓN (d.923)

King from 912, son of Alfonso III of Asturias, who divided his lands. Ordoño extended his territories and transferred the capital from Oviedo to León, giving the kingdom its name. In alliance with Navarre he was defeated by the Muslims at Val de Junqueras in 920 but successfully defended León against Muslim invasion. He advanced his control to Mérida, approaching Córdoba. His brother, Ramiro II, succeeded.

ORHAN, OTTOMAN SULTAN (1288–1362)

Sultan from 1324, succeeding his father Osman I. He established a new state in Anatolia and Thrace, posing a threat to Byzantium. In 1326 he captured Bursa, which became his capital. In 1328 he defeated Andronicus III at Pelekanos. He captured Nicaea in 1329 and Nicomedia in 1337, after a long siege. In 1344 he married Theodora, daughter of Emperor John Cantacuzenus, forming an alliance. When John fell from power in 1355 Orhan invaded Europe, establishing Turkish rule there. He captured Gallipoli in 1354 and Adrianople in 1362, settling Turks in Thrace and the Balkans. His son Murad I succeeded.

OTHMAN I (OSMAN), OTTOMAN SULTAN (1259–1324)

Sultan from 1280, founder of the Ottoman dynasty and Empire. His ancestors ruled a small territory in northern Iran, fleeing before the Mongol advance. Othman's father Ertugrul settled in Anatolia, serving as a mercenary captain for the Seljuks. The Ottomans were ghazi leaders, commanding troops of bandits and mercenaries, fighting the infidel. Othman's son, on his tomb, called his father 'ghazi son of ghazis'. He was born at Sogrut in Anatolia, developing his emirate at the expense of Byzantium. He occupied Dorylaeum in c.1300. Othman

captured Yenisehir, which became his capital. In 1301 he defeated the Byzantines at Baphaeum near Nicaea. In 1304 he captured Nicaea, in 1308 Ephesus, and then towns along the Black Sea coast. His final triumph was at Bursa, which he besieged from 1317. It was taken in 1326 by Othman's son Orhan and became his capital. Othman was brought there for burial. The Ottomans rose as the Seljuks declined – the Seljuk Sultanate ending in 1308. Othman died on 6 April and Orhan succeeded.

OTTO I, THE GREAT, HOLY ROMAN EMPEROR (912–73)

King of the Romans from 936, emperor from 962, son of Henry the Fowler. He ruled Saxony for his father. In 930 he married Edith, daughter of Edward the Elder of England. His second wife was St Adelaide, daughter of Lothar II King of Italy. He fought two wars to keep the crown, against his half-brother Thankmar, and then his brother Henry, the latter supported by Louis IV of France. Otto won victories at Xanten 940 and Andernach 941. He gained control over Lotharingia. He invaded West Francia in 942 when peace was agreed. Bavaria revolted and Otto was defeated by Duke Bertold at Wels. In 948 he intervened in West Francia to support Louis IV. In 950 Otto invaded Bohemia and Duke Boleslav submitted. Otto made three Italian expeditions, and was crowned King of the Lombards in 952. Otto revived the Holy Roman Empire of the Carolingians, initiating its history as a German empire. His reputation was enhanced by victory over the Magyars at the Lechfeld. He died on 7 May and his son Otto II succeeded. He was buried at Magdeburg.

OTTO II, HOLY ROMAN EMPEROR (955–83)

Crowned emperor during his father's lifetime in 967, succeeding Otto I in 973. He married Theophano a Byzantine princess. In the early reign he fought against Henry the Wrangler of Bavaria and

Boleslav of Bohemia. After victory Otto divided Bavaria. He disputed West Francia with the Capetians. The West Franks invaded, occupying Aachen, but were beaten off. Otto invaded West Francia and besieged Paris. Illness in the army forced him to retreat but he kept control over Lotharingia. In Italy he was defeated by allied Muslims and Byzantines at Crotona 982. He died of malaria in Italy on 7 December and was buried in Rome. His son Otto III succeeded.

OTTO III, HOLY ROMAN EMPEROR (980–1002)

King of the Romans from 983, emperor from 996, son of Otto II and the Byzantine princess Theophano. At his father's death he was three. His mother defeated rebellion by Henry the Wrangler. Otto took over in 994. He campaigned against the Slavs on the Elbe in 997. He made Italian expeditions in 996 and 998, in the second suppressing an anti-papal rebellion by John Crescentius. The latter and his followers were captured and hanged. Otto admired Charlemagne, whose tomb he re-opened, keeping one of his teeth. Otto died childless on 23 January, while trying to suppress rebellion in Rome. As he wished, he was buried beside Charlemagne at Aachen.

OTTO IV, HOLY ROMAN EMPEROR (1174–1218)

King of the Romans from 1198, emperor from 1209, son of Henry the Lion and Matilda daughter of Henry II of England. Following Henry's downfall, Otto was made Count of Poitou by Richard the Lionheart. On the death of Henry VI, Otto contested the throne with Philip of Swabia. Otto won and Philip was assassinated in 1208. Henry VI's son Frederick ruled Sicily. Otto invaded southern Italy in 1210 but failed. Frederick sought power in Germany and the issue was decided by Otto's defeat at Bouvines in 1214. Frederick was elected King of the Romans in 1215. Otto retired to family lands in Brunswick. He died on 19 May and was buried in Brunswick.

OTTOKAR I, KING OF BOHEMIA (d.1230)

King from 1198. Henry VI (HRE) made him Duke of Bohemia in 1192. Ottokar sought independence and won it from Philip of Swabia. He was crowned king at Mainz – confirmed by Otto IV in 1203 and by Frederick II in the Golden Bull. Ottokar's son Wenceslas succeeded.

OTTOKAR II, THE GREAT, KING OF BOHEMIA (d.1278)

King from 1253 in succession to his father, Wenceslas II. He allied with the Teutonic Knights against the Prussians in 1255. The Knights named their foundation at Königsberg in his honour. He won Styria from Béla IV of Hungary at Kressenbrun in 1260. During the interregnum in the empire he won Carinthia, Carniola and Istria. He fought against Rudolf of Habsburg, the successful rival for election as King of the Romans in 1273. Ottokar was defeated and abandoned some of his conquests. In 1276 Ottokar recognised Rudolf's overlordship but then rebelled to be defeated and killed at the Marchfeld on 26 August.

OWEN GLENDOWER (GLYNDŴR), PRINCE OF WALES (1354–1415)

Rebel against Henry IV, claiming to be prince from 1400, descended from the princes of Powys and Deheubarth, but beginning life modestly. He was educated in London and fought for the English in Ireland and Scotland. He married Margaret Hanmer the daughter of an Anglo-Welsh judge. He supported Richard II but rebelled against Henry IV. He quarrelled with Lord Grey of Ruthin and raided England to be beaten at Welshpool. His allies captured Conway Castle in 1401. In 1402 he defeated and captured Lord Grey and Edmund Mortimer at Pilleth. Mortimer married Owen's daughter. Owen captured Carmarthen Castle and Cardiff in 1403, Aberystwyth and Harlech in 1404. He allied with the French against Henry IV in 1404. He made terms with the Percies in 1405, giving him rule of a newly defined principality of Wales. Owen was defeated at Grosmont and Usk in 1405, and lost Carmarthen. Harlech Castle surrendered to the English. The Percies were defeated and Owen went into hiding. His life ended in obscurity on 20 September.

PEDRO I, THE CRUEL, KING OF LEÓN AND CASTILE (1336–69)

King from 1349 in succession to his father, Alfonso XI. He had his father's mistress Leonor murdered in 1351 and killed his own wife in order to enjoy his mistress without complaint. He intervened in Granada in 1362, supporting Muhammad V, whom he restored. He fought a succession war against his illegitimate half-brother Enrique de Trastámara. Castile entered the Hundred Years' War, with France supporting Enrique, and England supporting Pedro. The Black Prince invaded Castile in 1367 and won at Nájera but, after his departure, the war continued. John of Gaunt married Pedro's daughter. Enrique gained his revenge, defeating Pedro at Montiel in 1369 and stabbing him to death, while Du Guesclin hung on to Pedro's leg.

PEDRO III, THE GREAT, KING OF ARAGÓN (d.1285)

King from 1276, son and successor of Jaime I. He established a protectorate over Tunis in 1280. Pedro married Constance, daughter of Manfred of Sicily. He was offered the crown of Sicily in 1282 after the Sicilian Vespers. He was excommunicated but fought off a French invasion of Aragón in 1284. He died on 2 November when his son Alfonso III inherited Aragón, and his son Jaime Sicily.

PENDA, KING OF MERCIA (d.655)

The first important ruler of Mercia (the kingdom of the frontier), from 632. The dates are not certain. Penda remained pagan during the period of the conversion. He held his own against the great kingdoms. He expanded his territory. He fought against the West Saxons at Cirencester in 628, gaining lands from them before becoming king. He defeated the East Angles and installed his son Peada over them. He defeated the Hwicce and conquered their kingdom. His greatest conflict was with the English north of the Humber. The *Anglo-Saxon Chronicle* calls him 'the Southumbrian'. He defeated and killed Edwin and his son Osfrith at Hatfield Chase, 633, and beat and killed Oswald at Maserfeld (possibly Oswestry) in 641. Penda was defeated and decapitated by Oswy at Winwaed. His son Peada succeeded.

PEPIN (PIPPIN) I OF LANDEN, MAYOR OF THE PALACE OF AUSTRASIA (d. c.639)

(Note: this Pepin I is not to be confused with Pepin I King of Aquitaine; note also that Pepin III, the Short, is also Pepin I of Francia.)

Mayor of the Palace in Austrasia when mayors were challenging the dominance of the Merovingian dynasty. He came from a noble family with land in the Moselle valley. His daughter Gertrude married into the Arnulfing family, whose descendants were the Carolingian rulers of Francia. He was adviser to Dagobert I and Chlothar II, but became the enemy of Brunhild. It is believed that he lost influence during the later part of Dagobert's reign.

PEPIN II OF AQUITAINE (d.864)

Son of Pepin I, self-proclaimed King of Aquitaine, grandson of Louis the Pious. Pepin II succeeded his father in 838, retaining the backing of nobles who had supported his father. By the 839 Division at Worms, Charles the Bald received Aquitaine, but was opposed by Pepin II. Charles defeated Pepin in 840. The latter supported Lothar against his brothers, but was defeated with Lothar at Fontenoy in 841. An expedition against Pepin by Charles the Bald in 844 failed to take Toulouse and Charles was defeated near Angoulême. In 845 Charles and Pepin II reached agreement. Pepin recognised Charles and was in turn accepted by him, though part of Aquitaine was separated off under the Count of Poitou.

In 848 Pepin II's position collapsed through discontent with his defence against the Vikings. Charles in contrast made strenuous efforts against them. Charles took over Aquitaine and Pepin sought refuge with the Basques. He was handed over to Charles, deposed in 852 and sent to the monastery of St-Médard at Soissons. He escaped, seeking restoration, in 854. Pepin gained some support but not complete authority. In 855 Charles the Child, son of Charles the Bald, became King of Aquitaine. Pepin continued to struggle, allying with the Bretons in 859 and with the Vikings on the Loire from 857. A hostile source claimed he had abandoned Christianity but probably only because of this alliance. He joined the Vikings and, it was said, 'lived like one of them'. In 863, with the Vikings, he attacked Toulouse but failed to take it. In 864 he was captured by the Count of Poitou and handed to Charles. He was brought before an assembly at Pîtres and condemned to death as a traitor. He was imprisoned at Senlis where he probably died, but the nature of his death is unknown.

PEPIN II OF HERISTAL, MAYOR OF THE PALACE OF AUSTRASIA AND NEUSTRIA (d.714)

Son of Pepin I, and mayor in both Austrasia and Neustria, grandson of both Pepin I and Arnulf of Metz. He first became mayor in Austrasia. He was beaten by Ebroin in the Bois du Fays, but later defeated the Neustrians under Berchar and Theuderic III at Tertry in 687. Pepin's authority ran through most of the Frankish lands though later pro-Carolingian writers exaggerated his dominance. There was opposition from magnates, and the Merovingians were not entirely moribund. He led campaigns against the Frisians, the Bretons and the Alemans. His illegitimate son, Charles Martel, succeeded.

PEPIN III, THE SHORT, PEPIN I KING OF THE FRANKS (c.714–768)

The illegitimate son of Charles Martel, father of Charlemagne, first Carolingian

King of Francia. After Martel's death he was mayor in Austrasia. He and his brother, Carloman, dealt with rebellions and frontier troubles, restoring the authority formerly wielded by Martel. They fought against the Aquitanians, Bavarians, Alemans and Saxons. Carloman entered a monastery for life in 746. Childeric III's deposition in 751 brought Merovingian rule to an end. Childeric was probably set up by Carloman in the first place after an interregnum, but removed by Pepin. Childeric went into a monastery. Pepin was crowned at Soissons. In return for papal recognition, he fought the Lombards, leading an expedition to Italy in 754 when King Aistulf submitted. Pepin won control over Aquitaine and Septimania. He fought the Saxons in the north, the Goths and Saracens in the south. Throughout the 760s he fought the Aquitainians under Waiofar until they both died in 768 – Pepin in Paris.

PETER THE HERMIT (d.1115)

Leader of the People's Crusade, born near Amiens, nicknamed 'Little Peter' and probably small in stature, said to look like a donkey. He was known as 'the Hermit' from his spartan clothes, unwashed appearance and lifestyle. An itinerant preacher in France and Germany, he inspired many to join the crusading movement. He led the People's Crusade via Constantinople to Asia Minor. He was in Constantinople when the disaster at Civetot occurred. He went on to join the First Crusade. He fled from the siege of Antioch in 1098 but was captured and forced to return. He was chosen envoy for a failed negotiation with Kerbogha. He preached before the successful attack on Jerusalem was made. He returned to Europe in 1101 and died on 7 July.

PHILIP I, KING OF FRANCE (1052–1108)

King from 1060, son and successor of Henry I of France, crowned in his father's lifetime in 1059. His mother was Anna of Kiev, hence his Greek name. Like several early Capetians he grew corpulent, said to be too keen on eating and sleeping to fight. He succeeded as a minor with Baldwin V count of Flanders as guardian. Philip sought independence of Flanders but was defeated by Arnold III at Cassel in 1071 (though Arnold was killed). In 1076 Philip blocked William the Conqueror's invasion of Brittany. He encouraged Curthose's rebellion, leading to William's defeat at Gerberoi in 1079. Philip first married Bertha of Holland, stepdaughter of Robert the Frisian count of Flanders. In 1092 he seized Bertrade de Montfort, wife of Fulk IV of Anjou, for which he was excommunicated. He thwarted the ambitions of Rufus in Normandy in 1194. In his demesne Philip was defeated by Hugh du Puiset in 1080 but increased the royal demesne with part of the Gâtinais, Corbie and Bourges. He gained control of Montlhéry in 1104. He died at Melun on 29 July. His son Louis VI succeeded. Philip was buried, by his own wish, at the Abbey of Fleurie.

PHILIP II, AUGUSTUS, KING OF FRANCE (1165–1223)

King from 1180, son and successor of Louis VII, crowned during his father's lifetime in 1179. He married first Isabelle of Hainault, second Ingeborg of Denmark (whom he repudiated), and third Agnès de Méran his mistress. He destroyed the Angevin Empire. He went on the Third Crusade with Richard the Lionheart. They captured Acre but he returned home soon after. He eventually brought Henry II to his knees, by allying with his sons. Philip suffered minor defeats in the war with Richard the Lionheart at Fréteval and Vernon. Against John he triumphed, capturing Château-Gaillard, taking Rouen and regaining most of the Angevin lands in France. In his conflict with the Count of Flanders, the French fleet was destroyed at Damme in 1213. This ruined plans for an invasion of England. His greatest victory was at Bouvines in 1214 where Otto IV (HRE) and his Flemish and English allies were defeated. Meanwhile John was

defeated by Philip's son Louis in the south. Louis invaded England in alliance with the Magna Carta barons, though the invasion was abandoned. Philip encouraged the Fourth Crusade. He permitted the Albigensian Crusade, leading to increased royal power in the south. Philip improved the defences of Paris and built castles throughout France. He died in Mantes on 14 July. He was buried at St-Denis. St Louis later had the tomb covered in gold and silver. His son Louis VIII succeeded.

PHILIP IV, THE FAIR (LE BEL), KING OF FRANCE (1268–1314)

King from 1285, son and successor of Philip III. In 1284 he married the heiress Joan of Navarre, claiming Navarre. He fought Edward I over Gascony, which Philip seized in 1294 but later returned. When Flanders revolted, Philip was beaten at Courtrai in 1302, gaining revenge at Mons-en-Pévèle in 1304. He was blamed for a scandalous attack on Pope Boniface VIII. He attacked the Knights Templar from 1307 and the order was suppressed in 1313. He died on 30 November and was succeeded by three sons in turn – the last Capetian Kings.

PHILIP VI, KING OF FRANCE (1293–1350)

King from 1328, the first Valois King, son of Charles of Valois, nephew of Philip IV, cousin of Charles IV. He married Jeanne of Burgundy. He defeated the Flemings at Cassel in 1328. His right to the throne was challenged by Edward III of England in 1337, leading to the Hundred Years' War. Philip banished Robert of Artois in 1332, one cause of dispute since Robert was supported by Edward. As a counter Philip sheltered David II King of Scots in 1334. Philip declared the English possession of Gascony forfeit in 1337. Philip suffered the first major defeats of the war, including Crécy in 1346 and the loss of Calais 1347. Philip died on 22 August at the Abbey of Coulombs near Dreux and was buried at St-Denis. His son John II succeeded. The dynasty endured until 1498.

PHOKAS, BYZANTINE EMPEROR (d.610)
Proclaimed emperor by his army on the Danube in 602. The troops mutinied when ordered to winter north of the Danube, overthrew their commander Priscus, and followed the centurion Phokas. He had a scarred face but was 'not as pleasant as he looked'. He marched on Constantinople, deposing Maurice. Phokas was illiterate. He became a ruthless tyrant, torturing and mutilating his victims, marking the further decline of Byzantium after Justinian I's death. Maurice and his family fled, were captured and put to death. A reign of terror followed. The Persians under Chosroes II overran Armenia and Anatolia, capturing Dara, Edessa and Aleppo. The Avars advanced and were paid tribute. Narses rebelled but was defeated and burned alive. Phokas was overthrown by the rebellion of Heraclius, son of the Governor of Carthage. Phokas was killed by the mob and chopped into pieces 'until fit for the hounds'.

PROKOP (PROCOPIUS), ANDREW, THE SHAVEN (d.1433)
Hussite general, successor to Žiška despite his own blindness. He was a Hussite priest who opposed Emperor Sigismund, winning at Ústi 1425, Tachov 1431 and Domažlice 1431. He raided Saxony and Franconia. He used the tactic of defensive wagon circles and pikemen. He lost trust and, allied with the radical Taborites, was defeated and killed by Utraquists and Catholics at Lipany on 30 May 1433.

QALAWUN, SULTAN OF EGYPT (d.1290)
Mamluke Sultan from 1279 who brought the Crusader kingdom to its knees. He won at Homs in 1281, defeating the Mongols. He captured Margat in 1285 and Tripoli in 1289. He planned to attack Acre but died *en route* on 10 November. His son al-Kalil succeeded.

QTUZ, SAYF ED-DIN, SULTAN OF EGYPT (d.1260)
The first Mamluke Sultan from 1259, having been general for his predecessor. He took over through a coup. He assembled a force from Egypt and Syria to defeat the Mongols at Ayn Jalut. He captured Damascus in 1260, halting Mongol advance in the Middle East. Though the Christians did not obstruct him, they gave no aid and therefore received no benefit from his victory. Qtuz was assassinated by Baybars on 24 October.

RADBOD, KING OF THE FRISIANS (d.719)
He extended the kingdom, seeking to remain independent of the Merovingian Franks. Pepin II defeated him at Dorestad in 689. The conversion of Frisia to Christianity then gathered momentum. Radbod rebelled against the Franks but was defeated by Charles Martel in 718.

RAEDWALD, KING OF EAST ANGLIA (d. c.627)
Probably the king commemorated in the Sutton Hoo burial. Bede made him the fourth *Bretwalda* from 616, the major king of his day. He defeated and killed Aethelfrith of Bernicia on the River Idle in 616 but his own son was killed in the battle. Raedwald accepted Christian baptism but did not ban paganism, erecting Christian and pagan altars in the same building. No body was found at Sutton Hoo but Raedwald may have been buried there, though this is supposition.

RAGNAR LOÐBRÓK (HAIRY BREECHES) (864)
Possibly the attacker of Paris in 845. During this raid over a hundred Franks were hanged and Paris was sacked on Easter Sunday. The Frankish king Charles the Bald paid the first recorded tribute to Vikings to halt the attack. Ragnar Loðbrók features prominently in sagas. It is not certain that all the exploits attributed to him are those of one man. The historian Gwyn Jones calculated that if all the stories were accepted he would be 150 by his death. Ragnar was active in Ireland, Scotland, England and Francia. He was the father of Ivar, Hálfdan, Ubbi and Björn. It was

claimed that to win his wife, the Swedish princess Thora, he killed two serpents while wearing protective hairy trousers. In England Aelle King of Northumbria captured him and put him to death in a snakepit while he sang his own death lay! The dual tales of serpents and snakes arouse suspicion. His sons invaded in revenge in 865, killing Aelle in 867.

RAINALD OF CHÂTILLON, PRINCE OF ANTIOCH (d.1187)

Adventurer in the Holy Land, younger son of the Count of Gien, he joined Louis VII on the Second Crusade. He stayed to serve King Baldwin. Rainald married Constance Princess of Antioch. He allied with the Templars and proved his military ability by victory over the Armenians. He treated the Patriarch Aimery with cruelty. He invaded Cyprus in 1156 with military and financial success before withdrawing. He took Shaizar in 1157. Relations worsened with Baldwin, who allied with Byzantium against him. Rainald was captured by Nur ed-Din in a raid in 1160 and imprisoned at Aleppo until 1175. He married a second time to Stephanie of Oultrejourdain. Rainald became a lone bandit, mainly against Saladin. From 1181 Rainald attacked Muslim caravans, ignoring Christian criticism. He built a fleet to capture Aila on the Dead Sea. He attacked merchant shipping and caravans, sinking a Muslim pilgrim ship. His fleet was destroyed and Aila retaken. In 1183 he was besieged at Kerak but escaped when it fell. His activities provoked the campaign leading to Hattin, where he fought in Guy's army. Rainald was captured and decapitated by Saladin with a sword.

RAINULF (RANNULF) DRENGOT OF AVERSA (d.1045)

The first independent Norman lord in southern Italy, hired as a mercenary by Melus of Bari. Rainulf was 'a man adorned with all the virtues that become a knight'. He fought in the campaigns of Melus, including the disaster at Cannae. He was employed by Sergius IV of Naples, fighting to recover his territory. In 1030 Sergius rewarded Rainulf with the lordship of Aversa, where Rainulf built a castle. Rainulf married Sergius' sister, widow and heiress of the Duke of Gaeta. Rainulf encouraged new arrivals from Normandy. He changed his allegiance to the Prince of Capua, marrying his niece, and then to the Prince of Salerno. Conrad II (HRE) recognised Rainulf as Count of Aversa in 1038. His son Richard became Prince of Capua.

RALPH THE TIMID, OF MANTES, EARL OF HEREFORD (d.1057)

Son of Drogo count of the Vexin and Godgifu, sister of Edward the Confessor. Edward brought Ralph to England, making him Earl of Hereford in 1050. Ralph married Gytha and had a son Harold. He was a possible successor to the childless Edward. He co-commanded the fleet against the Godwins in 1052. His main claim to military significance came from fighting the Welsh under Gruffydd and Aelfgar on 24 October 1055 near Hereford. Ralph had trained his men to fight on horseback in the Norman and Frankish fashion, which was 'against their custom', and they were beaten. His flight earned the nickname 'the Timid'. He died on 21 December.

RAMIRO II, KING OF LEÓN (d.952)

King from 927 on the abdication of his brother Alfonso IV. He captured Madrid from the Muslims in 932. Zaragoza was lost in 937 to Abd-al-Rāhman. Ramiro gained revenge with victories at Simancas and Alhandega in 939, and Talavera in 951. His son Ordoño III succeeded after a civil war.

RAYMOND, COUNT OF POITIERS, PRINCE OF ANTIOCH (d.1149)

Raymond went to the Middle East in 1136, the year he inherited Poitiers. He married Constance heiress to Antioch and became its ruler. As uncle of Louis VII's wife, he was expected to assist the Second Crusade but argued with Louis over its objectives and was suspected of having an affair with Louis' wife, Eleanor of Aquitaine. Raymond left the Crusade to its own disasters. He defeated Nur ed-Din at Famiya in 1148 but was defeated and killed by Shirkuh the following year at Inab on 29 June, his head sent in a silver case to the Caliph of Baghdad.

RAYMOND OF ST GILLES, IV COUNT OF TOULOUSE, I COUNT OF TRIPOLI (d.1105)

Leader of the largest contingent on the First Crusade. He fought in Spain against Muslims. He was at the siege and capture of Antioch, quarrelling with Bohemond over its control. He became ill but was at the taking of Jerusalem. He was not elected as ruler of the new kingdom but became Count of Tripoli. In 1101 he captured Ankara but was defeated by the Turks at Mersivan in Anatolia. He was taken by Christian enemies and handed to Tancred who imprisoned him at Antioch, though soon released. He won outside Tripoli in 1102, establishing the new county. He took Tortosa but failed to take Tripoli itself – though he continued to attack it. A burning roof fell on his head in 1104. He never recovered, and died on 28 February, still hoping to take Tripoli.

RAYMOND VI, COUNT OF TOULOUSE (1156–1222)

Count from 1194, succeeding his father Raymond V. The papal legate Peter de Castelnau was killed in 1208 at St Gilles and Raymond was blamed as a sympathiser though not himself a Cathar. The pope called a Crusade. Raymond submitted and humiliated himself with a public flogging. The Crusade went ahead to invade southern France. Raymond joined the crusade for a time but then deserted. He and his Spanish allies were defeated by the crusaders at Muret in 1213. Raymond lost his county in 1215. He spent time in Spain. He failed to recover his county. He died in Toulouse in 1222, excommunicate, so his

body remained unburied in its coffin. By the 16th century rats had eaten the coffin and the bones had vanished.

RAYMOND VII, COUNT OF TOULOUSE (1197–1249)

Count from 1215 to 1249. His father was dispossessed in 1215 when Simon de Montfort the Elder, claimed the county. Simon was recognised by Philip II. Raymond retained a reduced territory. In 1217 he was welcomed when returning to Toulouse. Simon died in 1218 when besieging Toulouse. Raymond recovered much of his territory including Carcassonne and Béziers. He defeated Simon's son Amaury at Baziège in 1219. Prince Louis besieged Toulouse in 1219 but abandoned the attempt. Raymond was condemned by the papacy for supporting heretics. Louis VIII led a new Crusade south and conquered Toulouse. Louis IX granted Raymond the county for life in 1229. He rebelled in 1242 but his supporters were defeated. The succession was settled by the marriage of Raymond's daughter, Joan, to Alphonse of Poitiers, Louis' brother. Raymond died in Milau and was later buried at Fontevrault.

RECCARED I, KING OF THE VISIGOTHS (d.601)

Son of Leovigild, whom he succeeded in Spain in 586. This was arguably the high point of Visigothic power. Reccared converted from Arianism to Roman Catholicism in 587. He was instrumental in resisting Frankish invasion. Reccared in turn invaded Francia, plundering near Toulouse. He raided along the Rhône, capturing Cabaret and Beaucaire, and occupying Nîmes. He won victories over the Basques and the Byzantines.

RENAUD DE DAMMARTIN, COUNT OF BOULOGNE (1165–1227)

Renaud's family were castellans in the Île-de-France from the 11th century. His parents were Aubry and Mabille. He was brought up at the court of Louis VII, who knighted him. He repudiated his first wife, Marie de Châtillon the king's cousin, to marry the heiress Ida of Boulogne in 1190. Renaud was recognised as count by the king but was then involved in a quarrel at court. He allied with Richard the Lionheart and then paid homage to King John as a counter to Philip Augustus in 1199, making peace in 1201. Philip Hurepel, Philip Augustus' illegitimate son, was to marry Renaud's daughter Matilda (then aged one). Renaud returned to his French allegiance, receiving John's former county of Mortain. He became embroiled in war against Philip's cousin, the bishop of Beauvais. Renaud was accused of various crimes and sins, including attacks on the Church and parading his concubines in public. Philip demanded the return of Mortain, which Renaud refused. Philip seized Mortain and exiled Renaud, who did homage to John in 1212. He recruited allies against Philip, joining the attack on the French fleet at Damme. He opposed Philip at Bouvines in 1214, though he argued against fighting. He was among the commanders of the right. Renaud, on horseback bearing an ash lance, fought on to the end with his knights and mercenaries. He formed pikemen in a circle, two men deep. He and his knights issued from this circle to fight, withdrawing inside it for protection. Numbers told and Renaud was unhorsed and captured. Philip promised him his life but learned that Renaud was plotting against him. Renaud was imprisoned in a tower, chained to a log that had to be lifted for him to move to the toilet. Boulogne went to Philip Hurepel. After Philip Augustus' death, Renaud's hopes of release were dashed and he committed suicide on 21 April.

RICHARD I, COEUR DE LION (THE LIONHEART), KING OF ENGLAND (1157–99)

One of the greater military kings. King from 1189 on the death of his father Henry II. During Henry's reign he governed Aquitaine, his mother Eleanor's inheritance. He rebelled against his father in 1173–4, and in 1189 when allied to Philip II of France, bringing Henry to a humiliating submission. He and Philip led the Third Crusade in 1190. Richard travelled via Cyprus, which he conquered and later passed to Guy of Lusignan. In Cyprus he married Berengaria of Navarre. In the crusade Acre was taken and the Muslims defeated at Arsuf in 1191 and Jaffa in 1192. However, Richard turned back before reaching Jerusalem. He made an agreement with Saladin. During his return he was captured and imprisoned by Henry VI (HRE). He was ransomed and released in 1194. His brother John created problems in England but Richard resumed power and pardoned John. During his imprisonment Philip II had made gains in France. Richard fought to recover the losses. He built the castle of Château-Gaillard. He won minor engagements at Fréteval in 1194 and Gisors in 1198. The gains were negated by his sudden death when besieging Châlus-Chabrol. He received a fatal crossbow wound, dying in his mother's arms on 6 April. His body was buried at Fontevrault, his heart at Rouen. His brother John succeeded.

RICHARD I, DUKE OF NORMANDY (932–96)

Son of William Longsword, whom he succeeded in 942. As a boy he was sent to learn the Scandinavian tongue at Rouen. He married Gunnor, of Viking descent. His daughter Emma married Aethelred II of England in 1002, paving the way for the Norman Conquest. Richard was 'a tall man, handsome and strongly built, with a long beard and grey hair'. He faced a coalition of enemies from 954, including King Lothar and the Counts of Anjou and Flanders. He defeated them at Rouen and called in Viking aid. Vikings were still allowed to use Norman ports. Richard was a supporter of the Capetian family. A peasant revolt in Normandy in 996 was suppressed by the nobility.

RICHARD II, KING OF ENGLAND (1367–1400)

King 1377–99, called Richard of Bordeaux from his birthplace, son of the Black Prince who died in 1376, so that Richard succeeded his grandfather Edward III in 1377. His uncle, John of Gaunt duke of Lancaster, dominated the minority. The imposition of a Poll Tax led to the Peasants' Revolt in 1381, when Richard's courage defused the situation. He married Anne of Bohemia in 1382. He was opposed by the Appellants, who removed his Chancellor Michael de la Pole and defeated royalist forces at Radcot Bridge in 1387. He recovered power with the aid of John of Gaunt. Richard made an agreement with France in 1396. He was not a successful military commander, having gained nothing in France and led a failed expedition to Ireland. The banishment of Henry Bolingbroke led to the latter's return to seek his inheritance. Richard surrendered to Henry and was imprisoned. He abdicated and Bolingbroke became Henry IV. Richard was probably put to death in February at Pontefract Castle. He was buried in the Dominican Priory at King's Langley in Hertfordshire. Henry V later moved the body to Westminster Abbey.

RICHARD II, DUKE OF NORMANDY (996–1026)

Son of Richard I. His sister Emma married Aethelred II in 1002 and then Cnut in 1017. Aethelred's exiled sons by Emma, Edward (the Confessor) and Alfred, were brought up at the Norman court. The Normans assisted their attempts to recover the English throne, which Edward later succeeded in doing. Richard maintained links with the Vikings, still allowed to use Norman ports. They aided him against the Count of Blois-Chartres in 1013–14. In the 1020s Richard joined a coalition against that count. He supported the Capetian dynasty. He liked to work in the tower at Rouen and was 'in the habit of looking down over the city walls, the fields and the river'. He married the Breton, Judith, and then the Norman Papia. His sons by Judith, Richard and Robert, succeeded in turn.

RICHARD III, KING OF ENGLAND (1452–85)

King from 1483, son of Richard duke of York. He became Duke of Gloucester in 1461. On the death of his brother, Edward IV, Richard seized the throne rather than protecting the rights of his nephews, the Princes in the Tower. His supposed deformities, including a hunchback, probably came from Tudor propaganda rather than fact. In 1472 he married Anne Neville, daughter of Warwick the Kingmaker. The manner of his nephews' death is uncertain but Richard was probably responsible. He resented Edward's marriage to their mother, Elizabeth Woodville. Under Edward he had played a major part in the victories at Barnet and Tewkesbury. He accompanied Edward to France in 1475. He defended the Scottish border. As king he suppressed the 1483 rebellion and executed Buckingham. Richard's son Edward died in 1484. When Henry Tudor invaded in 1485 Richard was defeated and killed at Bosworth on 22 August, due largely to baronial treachery. His naked corpse was exposed to public view in Leicester for two days before burial. During the Dissolution of the Monasteries his remains were removed from their tomb and thrown in the River Soar.

RIDWAN, EMIR OF ALEPPO (d.1113)

Emir from 1095, son and successor of Tutush. He ruled this region of northern Syria at the time of the First Crusade. He and his brother Duqaq were bitter enemies. Ridwan suffered losses from the Crusade. He failed to relieve Antioch and was defeated there in 1098. He recovered part of the principality of Antioch. He won at Ma'arrat al-Numan and assisted in the victory at Mersivan in 1101. He increased his power by defeating and killing Kilij Arslan of Rum at the River Khabur in 1107.

He was prepared to compromise with either side and his death made Christian Edessa more vulnerable.

RIENZI (RIENZO), COLA DI (NICHOLAS) (1313–54)

A populist leader in Rome, claiming to be a bastard of Henry VII (HRE) but said to be the son of an innkeeper and a laundress. He opposed the papacy's move to Avignon from Rome but his chief enemy was the nobility. He roused support by public speeches, seeking self-rule for Rome, acting as a dictator with the title of Tribune. Rome briefly became a self-governing republic. He suppressed a rising by the Colonnas in 1347 but was forced to flee. He took refuge with Charles IV (HRE) who handed him to the pope. Rienzi was imprisoned at Avignon in 1352. Innocent VI restored him as Senator in Rome under Albornoz in 1353. A rising against the regime in 1354 led to Rienzi's death, torn to pieces, on 8 October. He became a hero of those seeking Italian unity, subject of a Wagner opera.

ROBERT I, THE BRUCE, KING OF SCOTS (1274–1329)

Earl of Carrick from 1292, king from 1306, son of Robert Bruce the Elder and Marjorie Countess of Carrick. He fought for Edward I against William Wallace. He sought the throne and killed his rival, Red John Comyn, in 1306. He was defeated by the English under Aymer de Valence at Methven in 1306. He took refuge in Ireland, returning in 1307. He defeated the Earl of Argyll at Loch Etive to control most of Scotland. He aimed against Stirling and brought Edward I north to die *en route*. In 1314 he defeated Edward II at Bannockburn, a major step to independence. His brother Edward invaded Ireland from 1315, where Robert joined him in 1317 – though the venture failed. Robert captured Berwick in 1318. He warded off an English invasion in 1322 by victory at Byland. He died on 7 June, possibly of leprosy. His son David II succeeded.

ROBERT I (THE MAGNIFICENT/THE DEVIL), DUKE OF NORMANDY (d.1035)

Father of William the Conqueror, son of Duke Richard II, the weakest link in a chain of great dukes. He was described as having a good physique with 'an honest face and handsome appearance'. He married Cnut's daughter, Estrith, but repudiated her. His mistress Herlève, reputedly a tanner's (or undertaker's) daughter from Falaise, bore his son William. There was a rumour that he poisoned his brother Richard III, who died a year after inheriting the duchy. Robert became duke in 1027. There was much disturbance in the duchy under him. A number of castles were built. In 1033 he organised a fleet at Fécamp for the sons of Aethelred II, Edward (the Confessor) and Alfred, against England. A storm ruined its chance. His support helped Edward to gain the throne later. Robert went on pilgrimage to the Holy Land but died at Nicaea when returning.

ROBERT II THE PIOUS, KING OF FRANCE (970–1031)

King from 996, crowned during his father Hugh Capet's reign in 987. His reign established the Capetian dynasty. His nickname came from an interest in Church affairs. The belief that French kings could heal by touch began with Robert. He married three times, to Suzanna of Italy (repudiated), Bertha of Burgundy (separated) and Constance of Arles (divorce attempted). Constance was the mother of his successor. Robert made an unsuccessful attack on Baldwin IV of Flanders in 1006 after the latter took Valenciennes. Robert turned royal interest on the south. He gained the duchy of Burgundy for his son Henry in 1015. He died on 20 July and his son Henry I succeeded.

ROBERT II, CURTHOSE, DUKE OF NORMANDY (1052–1134)

Son of William the Conqueror, duke from 1087. He helped complete the conquest of England, establishing the castle at Newcastle in 1080. He rebelled against his father in 1078, allying with the King of France. In 1079 Curthose defeated his father at Gerberoi, where Curthose had been besieged before making a sortie. Curthose unseated his father and wounded him. Later they were reconciled. On the Conqueror's death Robert succeeded to Normandy, but not England, which he sought unsuccessfully to take from Rufus. Curthose joined the First Crusade in 1096. He led an important charge at Ascalon in 1099, capturing the Egyptian banner. He returned without seeking territory in the Holy Land. He married Sybil of Conversano. He tried to recover England from his youngest brother, Henry I, who succeeded in his absence. Robert invaded England in 1102 but agreed terms. In 1106 he lost the battle and Normandy to Henry at Tinchebrai. Henry imprisoned him for life. Robert's son, William Clito, remained a threat to Henry I until his death in 1128. Robert was kept at Wareham, Devizes and finally Cardiff, where he died probably on 3 February. He was buried at Gloucester, where his effigy is in the cathedral.

ROBERT OF BELLÊME, EARL OF SHREWSBURY

A noted rebel against the sons of William the Conqueror, son of Roger of Montgomery and Mabel of Bellême, he inherited their lands in England and Normandy. He became Earl of Shrewsbury on the death of his brother Hugh in 1098. He brought warhorses from Spain to England and was a great castle builder, responsible for Bridgnorth, Shrewsbury, Arundel and Tickhill, noted for their broad moats. Orderic Vitalis says he was a 'resourceful engineer' who designed Gisors. At Bréval he employed an ingenious invention as a siege engine. He held 34 castles and was lord of thousands of men. He was noted for harshness – putting out eyes, hacking off hands and feet, and torturing. He opposed Henry I in support of Robert Curthose and lost his English lands as a result. He then rebelled in Normandy but made peace and fought for Curthose at

Tinchebrai in 1106, escaping from the defeat. He made terms with Henry but supported Curthose's son William Clito. Possibly acting for Louis VI of France he fell into Henry I's hands, was brought to trial and chained in a dungeon. He was imprisoned at Cherbourg and then Wareham. He was alive in 1131 but when he died is unknown. Robert's son William Talvas continued to oppose Henry.

ROBERT OF GLOUCESTER (OF CAEN, FITZROY), EARL OF GLOUCESTER (c.1090–1147)

Eldest illegitimate son of Henry I. His mother was probably Sibyl, daughter of Robert Corbet, a burgess of Caen. Robert was made Earl of Gloucester by his father in 1122, marrying the Gloucester heiress of Robert Fitz Hamon. Robert was slow to recognise Stephen as king but eventually came to his court. Robert's declaration for his half-sister Matilda in 1138 marked the start of civil war. Robert, 'the chief of the king's enemies', gave Matilda her best hope. He brought her to England, landing at Arundel, and remained a loyal supporter. He commanded for her in the war against Stephen from 1139 with notable successes, including Lincoln in 1141 when Stephen was defeated and captured. The Rout of Winchester was a victory for Stephen's supporters, when Robert was captured. Stephen and Robert were exchanged and released. Robert undertook a mission to bring Matilda's husband Geoffrey of Anjou into the war, but failed. Robert took Wareham and defeated Stephen at Wilton in 1143. Robert's death marked the end of Matilda's hopes of victory. She abandoned the country, leaving her claim to her son Henry. Robert died at Bristol on 31 October. His son William succeeded to the earldom.

ROBERT GUISCARD (THE WARY/WILY), DE HAUTEVILLE, DUKE OF APULIA (c.1025–1085)

Norman duke in Italy, of humble origin, the son of a lesser knight, Tancred de

Hauteville in Normandy, by his second wife Fredesendis. He was one of the many Hautevilles to go to southern Italy, arriving in 1047. He began in Calabria as a landless brigand leader. Anna Comnena described him as cunning and brave, tall, well built, with ruddy complexion and fair hair, his eyes sparkling. He gained lands to become the major Norman leader. He married Aubrée from a southern Norman family. He repudiated her for Sigelgaita, sister of the Lombard ruler of Salerno. Robert received the castle of Scribla but abandoned it for San Marco Argentano. He fought the papal army at Civitate in 1053, leading the left wing. He expanded Norman control in southern Italy, taking Calabria and Apulia. At Melfi in 1059 the pope recognised Robert as Duke of Apulia and Calabria and 'future Duke of Sicily'. He took Amalfi in 1073 and Salerno in 1076, the last major Lombard principalities. All Byzantine territories in the region fell to him. Bari was besieged and taken by 1071. He led the invasion of Sicily from 1060 and the capture of Palermo in 1072. Thereafter he concentrated on the mainland, delegating Sicily to his brother Roger. He expanded Norman power in the Mediterranean, mainly at the expense of Byzantium. He captured Dyrrachium (now in Albania) in 1082 and Corfu in 1084. In 1084 he rescued Gregory VII from Henry IV (HRE), sacking Rome and selling citizens into slavery. In Cephalonia he caught typhoid, from which many of his men died. He was taken to Cassiopi in Corfu and died on 17 July. His tomb was at Venosa, his favoured abbey. The tomb, now gone, carried an inscription to 'Guiscard, the terror of the world'.

ROBERT DE MOWBRAY (MONTBRAY), EARL OF NORTHUMBERLAND (d. c.1125)

Rebel against William Rufus in 1088 and 1095, son of Roger de Mowbray. William the Conqueror made him Earl of Northumberland in c.1085. He was 'a man of great bodily stature, strong, dark and shaggy, bold and crafty, with an austere and melancholy countenance' who hardly ever smiled when he spoke. His castles included Bamburgh. With his uncle, the bishop of Coutances, he seized Bristol Castle in 1088. From there he raided Gloucestershire, Somerset and Wiltshire and sacked Bath. The rebellion was suppressed and Mowbray was exiled to Normandy, allowed to return in 1093, when Malcolm Canmore King of Scots raided England. Robert ambushed him near the River Alne, where Malcolm was killed. In spring 1095 Robert again rebelled. He had seized four Norwegian ships, whose owners appealed to Rufus. Robert was summoned to court and his refusal to come initiated the rebellion. Rufus marched north. Mowbray seized Newcastle. Rufus besieged Tynemouth, which surrendered after two months (some historians believe it was Newcastle not Tynemouth). Rufus approached Mowbray in Bamburgh, leaving troops to continue the siege. Mowbray tried to escape but only to his own monastery at Tynemouth, where he held out six days before being wounded and captured. Robert was taken before the walls of his castle, where his wife Matilda still held out. They threatened to put out his eyes unless she surrendered, which she did. He was kept in Windsor Castle for the rest of his life, another 30 years.

RODRIGO I (RODERIC), KING OF THE VISIGOTHS (d.711)

King during the Arab invasion of Spain, previously *dux* of Baetica. He was at war with Agila, son of the king, when the Arab invasion began. Rodrigo won broader but not complete support. Possibly his political enemies invited in the Arabs. Rodrigo became king in 710 and immediately faced serious invasion from Africa, while rebel Visigoths and Basques threatened the north. The Arab invaders under Tāriq defeated and killed Rodrigo at the Transductine Promontories (or Guadalete). The Arabs took Toledo and the Visigothic kingdom collapsed, leaving most of Iberia in their hands within ten years.

ROGER I, DE HAUTEVILLE, THE GREAT, COUNT (c.1040–1101)

Leading figure in the Norman conquest of Sicily, youngest son of Tancred de Hauteville. He arrived in Italy in 1056. He was tall and well built with a cheerful, open manner. He married Judith daughter of the Count of Evreux, Eremberga daughter of the Count of Mortain, and Adelaide daughter of Manfred. Roger's older brother Robert Guiscard established him at Mileto. The invasion of Sicily with Guiscard began in 1060. Roger won at Cerami in 1063 and Miselmeri in 1068. Palermo was captured in 1072. Guiscard saw himself as the overall ruler, appointing his brother Count of Sicily while retaining suzerainty – but Guiscard did not return to Sicily. The completion of the conquest was Roger's work. He allied with Muslims, whom he used as mercenaries. Taormina was taken in 1079 and Syracuse in 1086. With the fall of Noto, Sicily was in Norman hands by 1091. In 1090–1 Roger invaded and conquered Malta and Gozo. After the death of Guiscard, Roger extended his power on the mainland, becoming the dominant Norman ruler in the south. His position was recognised by the papacy. He died on 22 June and was buried in Santa Trinita at Mileto. His son and successor was Roger II.

ROGER II, KING OF SICILY (1095–1154)

King from 1130, son of Roger the Great Count by his third wife Adelaide. He succeeded his older brother as Count of Sicily in 1105. Adelaide defended his position until he came of age. He became Duke of Apulia in 1127. Roger was recognised as king by Anacletus II and crowned on Christmas Day. Anacletus lost his struggle against a rival pope, but Roger retained the crown though having to suppress numerous revolts. He was opposed by Pope Innocent II and Lothar III (HRE), who made Rainulf of Alife Duke of Apulia. Roger was defeated at Nocera in 1132 and Rignano in 1137. In 1139 he gained revenge by winning the Rout of Galuccio. Innocent II was captured and, in return for release, recognised Roger. Sicily was a cosmopolitan state, with the right to worship for Greek Orthodox, Muslims and Christians. Sicily became a Mediterranean naval power. During the Second Crusade Roger attacked Byzantium, recovering Corfu and raiding Corinth and Athens. He conquered lands in North Africa. In 1146–7 he captured Tripoli, Tunis and Algeria, taking Bona in 1153. He died at Palermo on 26 February, probably of heart disease. The body was taken to Cefalu and then Palermo. His tomb survives. He married three times and his only surviving son, William I, succeeded.

ROGER DE FLOR (RUTGER VON DER BLUME) (d.1305)

Captain of the Catalan Company, a German by birth. His father was falconer to Frederick II. Roger joined the Knights Templar and was at the siege of Acre in 1291. He sold escape places on his ship, for which he was expelled from the Templars. He became a leader of pirates and then mercenaries. The Catalan Company (of mercenaries) was employed by Pedro of Aragón in 1281 in North Africa and Sicily, and by Byzantium in 1302 – when its leader, Roger, was made a *megas dux*. He married the emperor's niece Maria. Roger rose in the middle of his wedding night to stop a fight between his men and the Genoese. The Catalan Company inflicted defeats on the Turks. Failure of pay led to mutiny. Roger's fleet occupied Chios, Lemnos and Lesbos. His men killed the son of Byzantium's Alan mercenary commander, George Gircon. Michael IX negotiated but, when Roger came to Adrianople, Gircon murdered him on 6 April. The Catalan Company attacked Byzantine territory, taking the Latin duchy of Athens.

RÖGNVALD, EARL OF MØRE

Earl of Møre in Norway and founder of the earldom of Orkney. He passed Orkney to his brother Sigurd, the first earl. Rögnvald was killed in a dispute with Hálfdan son of

Harold Finehair. According to saga he cut Harold's hair (the origin of the nickname). Harold gave Orkney and Shetland to him. Rögnvald's illegitimate son, Torf-Einar, later succeeded to Orkney. A second son was possibly Rollo (Hrólfr), founder of Normandy.

ROLAND (HRUODLAND) (d.778)

Hero of Roncesvalles, better known in literature than history through the *Chanson de Roland*. He figures in Ariosto's *Orlando Furioso*. The fictional story is that Roland died bravely at Roncesvalles. The historical event was recorded in two contemporary sources. Charlemagne's army was returning from an expedition to Spain. In a pass through the Pyrenees the rearguard was attacked by Basques (not Muslims), who inflicted a damaging defeat. Roland was *Praefectus* or Count of the Breton March, responsible for the Breton border. He came from a noble Frankish family in which this position was hereditary.

ROLLO OF NORMANDY (ROLF THE GANGER/GÖNGU-HRÓLFR) (c.860–c.928)

The Viking leader who founded the duchy of Normandy though not himself called duke. His nickname (the ganger) was said to come from being too big to ride so that he always had to walk. He may have been the son of Rögnvald of Møre, exiled from Norway by Harold Finehair. Rollo probably joined raids on Scotland, Ireland and England. He led a war-band to attack the Frankish coast. His group settled on the Seine. In 911 the West Frankish King, Charles the Simple, agreed the Treaty of Saint-Clair-sur-Epte with Rollo, probably granting the area around Rouen in return for defending Francia against Viking attacks and converting to Christianity. Rollo was defeated at Chartres and could not bargain from strength, so Dudo's version of the event should not be accepted without question – where he seized the king's foot and pulled him over. The territory granted was probably Upper Normandy. Rollo was

baptised in 912. Normandy's capital, Rouen, is named after him. He and his descendants extended their territories and established the duchy of Normandy (the land of the Northmen). His son, William Longsword, succeeded. William the Conqueror was a direct descendant.

ROMANUS I, LECAPENUS, BYZANTINE EMPEROR (d.948)

Co-emperor from 920 to 944 with Constantine VII, admiral for Leo VI, co-emperor and effective ruler for Leo's son Constantine VII, who married Romanus' daughter. Romanus was the son of Theophylact the Unbearable – an Armenian peasant and soldier. In 921 Symeon the Bulgar was defeated. Symeon's son and successor, Peter, married Romanus' granddaughter and Serbia became subject to Byzantium. Byzantine power recovered in the east. The Saracens were pushed back, Melitene and Manzikert captured. Romanus' naval experience paid dividends. In 924 at Lemnos he defeated a Saracen fleet under Leo of Tripoli, and in 941 the Russians were beaten in the Bosphorus. In 944 Romanus was deposed and entered a monastery at Proti, having himself scourged for his sins before 300 monks. He tried to promote his numerous sons but without success. He died on 15 June and was buried beside his wife in the monastery in Constantinople that he had founded.

ROMANUS II, PORPHYROGENITUS, BYZANTINE EMPEROR (939–63)

Emperor from 959, son of Constantine VII. When his first wife died, Romanus married Theophano, an innkeeper's daughter. Nikephorus Phokas, his general, recovered Crete from the Saracens in 960–1. Another general, Nikephorus' brother Leo, defeated the Saracens under Sayf ad-Dawlah at Kulindros. Romanus' brief reign saw considerable success. He died on 15 March in a hunting accident. Theophano married Nikephorus Phokas. Both Romanus' sons survived to be emperors – Basil II the Bulgar Slayer and Constantine VIII.

ROMANUS III, ARGYRUS, BYZANTINE EMPEROR (d.1034)

Emperor from 1028. Constantine VIII wanted Romanus to succeed him and marry his daughter Zoe. On threat of blinding, Romanus put his wife of 40 years in a nunnery, and agreed. Constantine died three days after the marriage. Romanus came from a family of Anatolian landowners. He was a judge and administrator but was interested in the science of warfare (though completely ignorant of it). In 1030 he campaigned against the Emir of Aleppo but was defeated. In 1031 George Maniakes defeated the emir and recovered Edessa. Both husband and wife took lovers. Romanus drowned while swimming on 11 April, though murder was suspected. Zoe married her lover who succeeded as Michael IV.

ROMANUS IV, DIOGENES, BYZANTINE EMPEROR (d.1072)

Emperor from 1068 through marriage to Constantine X's widow Eudocia. His family had estates in Cappadocia. His father, accused of treachery, jumped to his death from a cliff. Romanus was a general and Governor of Sardica for Constantine X. He defeated the Pechenegs but Constantine accused him of conspiracy, recalled him and sentenced him to death – commuted to exile. Eudocia chose him to replace Constantine. Romanus made efforts to save Byzantium. He organised expeditions against the Seljuk Turks, winning at Sebastia and Heraclea. In 1071 he was defeated and captured by Alp Arslan at Manzikert, one of the greatest disasters in Byzantine history. The Seljuks took Armenia and most of Asia Minor. Romanus was released on agreeing to cede lands and pay tribute. In 1071 Bari, the last Byzantine territory in southern Italy, fell to the Normans. Before Romanus returned to Constantinople after Manzikert, Michael VII was proclaimed emperor. Romanus raised a force but was defeated, captured, blinded, and sent to the monastery at Proti, where he died on 24 October.

ROMULUS AUGUSTULUS, ROMAN EMPEROR (d. c.510)

The last Western Emperor, though the replaced Julius Nepos survived in Dalmatia until his murder in 480. His father, the commander Orestes, raised Romulus to the purple in 475. Odoacer defeated and killed Orestes. Romulus was deposed by Odoacer in 476 but allowed to retire to southern Italy.

RUDOLF I, HABSBURG, KING OF THE ROMANS (1218–91)

The first Habsburg ruler of Germany. His election in 1273 ended the interregnum in Germany. He sought but failed to achieve imperial coronation. He opposed Ottokar II of Bohemia. In 1276 he besieged Vienna, forcing Ottokar to do homage. The latter was defeated and killed at the Marchfeld in 1278. Vienna became the Habsburg capital of lands including Austria. In 1285 Rudolf suppressed the rising of Dietrich Holzschuh, who claimed to be Frederick II reincarnated. Rudolf died on 15 July and was buried at Speyer.

RURIK (RIURIK) (d. c.880)

The main Viking leader in Russia, probably from Sweden, possibly brother or nephew of Harold Klak – who was active in Frisia and Jutland in the 850s. The later *Russian Primary Chronicle* said the tribes of northern Russia asked for a Scandinavian leader from the Rus in c.860–2. Three brothers came, including Rurik who became ruler of Novgorod. By another version he came first to (Staraya) Ladoga and later founded Novgorod. His brothers died within two years. Rurik ruled the state based on Kiev that is seen as the beginning of the state of Russia. His relative Oleg and then his son Igor succeeded.

SALADIN, SALĀH AL-DĪN YŪSUF (1138–93)

Founder of the Ayyubid dynasty, reuniting Syria and Egypt, and winning Hattin. He reduced the size and strength of the kingdom of Jerusalem. He was a Kurd, son of Ayyub, serving Nur ed-Din under his uncle, Shirkuh. Saladin had a reputation for fairness and honourable conduct. He assisted the conquest of Egypt, in 1169 becoming vizier under the Fatimid ruler on behalf of Nur ed-Din. He brought the Fatimid dynasty to an end. After the death of Nur ed-Din, Saladin took over Syria. He won Damascus in 1174 and Aleppo in 1183. He suffered a surprise defeat by the Franks at Montgisard in 1177. His greatest victory was at Hattin in 1187 over King Guy, as a result of which the kingdom of Jerusalem came near to collapse – much of it (including Jerusalem) conquered by Saladin. This provoked the Third Crusade. The Christians recovered Acre and defeated Saladin at Arsuf. They concluded a truce whereby Saladin kept Jerusalem. He suffered from a long illness, dying on 1 March. He left 17 sons and one known daughter.

SALISBURY, RICHARD NEVILLE, EARL OF (1400–60)

Earl from 1429 through marriage to the heiress Alice Montacute, son of Ralph earl of Westmorland. He was appointed Warden of the West March. He fought in France in 1431–2 and 1436–7. He fought for Henry VI against the Yorkists, but he changed sides through hostility to the Percies. He fought a private battle with them at Stamford Bridge in Yorkshire in 1454. He was dismissed as Chancellor in 1455 and joined the Yorkists in their victory at the First Battle of St Albans. He commanded the Yorkist victory at Blore Heath in 1459. He escaped from the defeat at Ludlow to Calais and participated in the Yorkist invasion of 1460, taking London. He opposed York taking the crown but remained Yorkist. He fought in the Yorkist defeat at Wakefield in 1460 and was beheaded the following day, New Year's Eve. His son was Warwick the Kingmaker.

SANCHO III, EL MAYOR (THE GREAT), KING OF NAVARRE (d.1035)

King from 1000, son and successor of García II. He made Navarre the major Iberian Christian power. In alliance with León he defeated al-Mansur at Calatañazor in 1002. With the collapse of the Caliphate he demanded parias as tribute from the Muslim *taifa* states. In 1028 he conquered Castile and united most of Christian Spain, setting the political pattern for centuries by dividing his lands between his sons, Castile with part of León to Ferdinand I, Aragón to Ramiro I, and Navarre to García III.

SFORZA, FRANCESCO, DUKE OF MILAN (1401–66)

Duke from 1450, establishing the Sforza dynasty, son of the *condottiere* Attendolo – who gained the name Sforza (the force) through his exploits. Francesco fought as a *condottiere* for Milan and Venice, taking over his father's men. He served Filippo Maria Visconti, marrying his daughter Bianca in 1443. He commanded the victories over Venice at Soncino in 1431 and Caravaggio in 1448. On Filippo's death he served for Venice against Milan, which he then took over after a siege, becoming Duke. He agreed the Peace of Lodi with Venice and Florence in 1454. He won Genoa in 1463. He died on 8 March and his son Galeazzo Maria succeeded.

SHIRKUH, ASAD ED-DIN (d.1169)

Kurdish general serving Nur ed-Din, uncle of Saladin. He had damaged eyesight and was considered fat. He killed Raymond of Antioch in single combat in 1149 at Inab. Saladin served his military apprenticeship under Shirkuh, including the conquest of Egypt despite Christian opposition. Shirkuh beat a Frankish and Egyptian force at Hermoupolis in 1167, taking Cairo in 1169. He ruled Egypt as vizier in 1169, a promotion that caused a difference with Nur ed-Din. Shirkuh maintained a Fatimid figurehead in al-Adid. Shirkuh died on 23 March from over-eating and was succeeded in Egypt by Saladin.

SIGISMUND, HOLY ROMAN EMPEROR (1368–1437)

King of Hungary through marriage from 1387, King of Bohemia from 1419, King of the Romans from 1410, King of the Lombards from 1431, the last Luxembourg emperor from 1433. He was the son of Charles IV. Sigismund was defeated by the Hussites at Prague in 1419, Lutitz and Kuttenberg in 1421 and Nebovid and Nemecky Brod in 1422. Sigismund was responsible for executing Hus. He joined the Crusade of Nicopolis in 1396, retreating before the concluding battle. He recovered Bosnia, Herzegovina and Serbia from the Turks. He was one of the few emperors to visit England, coming in 1416 in the reign of Henry V. He died in Bohemia on 9 December and was buried at Nágy Varad in Transylvania.

SIGTRYGG ÓLAFSSON (SILK BEARD), KING OF DUBLIN (d.1042)

King from 989, son and successor of Ólaf Kvaran. In 997 Ireland was divided between native kings, Brian Boru and Maél Sechnaill. Sigtrygg ruled Dublin, issuing his own coinage (which oddly shows him beardless). He came under the power of Brian Boru. He allied with Leinster against Brian but was defeated in 999. He submitted and was recognised as subking, marrying Brian's daughter. Brian had married Sigtrygg's widowed mother. In 1012 Sigtrygg rebelled. Brian failed to take Dublin in a siege. Sigtrygg organised a coalition against Brian leading to the Battle of Clontarf in 1014, though Sigtrygg was not present. Brian was killed, despite being the victor, but Maél Sechnaill claimed overlordship of Dublin. In 1036 Sigtrygg abdicated in favour of his nephew. He was murdered during a second visit to Rome.

SIMNEL, LAMBERT (1475–1525)

Nominal leader of the 1487 rebellion against Henry VII. The Earl of Kildare protected him in Ireland, where he was presented as the Earl of Warwick in an effort to have the real earl released. Lambert was probably the son of an Oxford tradesman, trained by the priest Richard Simons to impersonate Warwick. Simnel was crowned in Dublin as 'Edward IV' and used as 'leader' of the 1487 rebellion. The invaders landed at Furness in Lancashire and were defeated at Stoke. Simnel was captured and employed in the royal kitchen, later being promoted.

SOMERSET, EDMUND BEAUFORT, SECOND DUKE OF (1406–55)

Minister of Henry VI, Earl and Marquis of Dorset, Earl of Somerset from 1444, Duke from 1448. He fought in the closing stages of the Hundred Years' War and was appointed Captain General and Governor of Anjou and Maine. He failed to hold Normandy and his surrender of Rouen was condemned. Henry VI made him Constable of England and Captain of Calais. When the Duke of York triumphed in 1454 he arrested Somerset. Henry VI's recovery brought Somerset's release. He commanded for Henry at St Albans in 1455 on 22 May. He took refuge in a house and was killed trying to escape.

STEPHEN, OF BLOIS, KING OF ENGLAND (c.1096–1154)

King from 1135, son of Stephen-Henry count of Blois and Adela, daughter of William the Conqueror. He came to England and was given lands by his uncle, Henry I. He married the heiress Matilda of Boulogne in 1125. On the death of Henry I, with the recognition of most of the nobility, he succeeded in England and Normandy. He faced baronial rebellions in England but they were suppressed. A Scottish invasion was defeated on Stephen's behalf at the Standard in 1138. Matilda (daughter of Henry I) claimed England. Her second husband, Geoffrey of Anjou, invaded Normandy and conquered it by 1145. Stephen resisted Geoffrey but gave priority to England. Matilda came to England in 1139, initiating civil war. In 1141 Stephen was captured at Lincoln and imprisoned. He was released in exchange for Robert of Gloucester, captured at Winchester. Stephen kept the upper hand. His fenland campaign against Geoffrey de Mandeville ended in success. After the death of Robert of Gloucester, Matilda left England. Her son, Henry, continued the war. By 1153 Stephen's wife and eldest son Eustace had died and he agreed at Winchester that Henry succeed. Stephen died in the Augustinian Priory at Dover of a 'flux of haemorrhoids' on 25 October and was buried alongside his wife at his foundation, Faversham Abbey. Stephen's younger son, William, kept the family lands and Henry II took England.

STEPHEN IV DUŠAN (UROS), KING AND EMPEROR OF SERBIA (1309–55)

King from 1336, emperor from 1346, Serbia's greatest medieval ruler. His father, Stephen III, conquered Macedonia after victory at Velbuzd in 1330. Stephen IV killed his father to seize power. He took advantage of civil war in Byzantium to conquer Epirus, Albania, Bulgaria, Thessaly and part of Bosnia. He called himself 'lord of almost the whole Roman Empire' – his territories greater than those of Byzantium. He aimed to become Byzantine emperor. He built a fleet against Byzantium. He took Adrianople and was threatening Constantinople at his death. He adapted Byzantine landholding methods to raise troops for Serbia. His son Stephen V succeeded but could not retain the whole empire.

STILICHO, FLAVIUS (365–408)

Vandal general for the emperor Honorius. His father fought for the Romans at Adrianople in 378. Stilicho was employed by Theodosius I and fought at Frigidus in 394. He was made *magister militum*, and guardian for the young Honorius in the west. His daughter married the emperor. The division between Eastern and Western Empires grew. Stilicho defeated Alaric's Visigothic confederacy, when it invaded Italy, at Pollentia in 402 and Verona in 403. Alaric survived and came to terms. A monument was raised in the Roman Forum to commemorate the victory at Pollentia, but later Stilicho's name was erased from it. He resisted the Germanic invasion by

Radagaisus. He failed to prevent the Vandals, Suevi, Burgundians and Alans from crossing the Rhine in 406–7. Stilicho's troops mutinied and he was accused of letting barbarians into the empire. Honorius ordered his execution at Ravenna. His bodyguard wished to save him but he stopped them, offering himself for decapitation.

STRONGBOW, RICHARD FITZGILBERT DE CLARE, EARL OF PEMBROKE, KING OF LEINSTER (d.1176)

Earl from 1148 in succession to his father; king from 1171. He lost the earldom on the accession of Henry II in 1154. Strongbow led a private invasion of Ireland, capturing Dublin and Leinster in 1170–1. He married Aoife, daughter of Dermot King of Leinster, and succeeded him in 1171. He defeated the Irish High King Rory O'Connor at Castleknock. Henry II went to Ireland in 1171–2, forcing Strongbow to submit but restoring his earldom.

SUFFOLK, WILLIAM DE LA POLE, DUKE OF (1396–1450)

Earl of Suffolk in succession to his father Michael; duke from 1448. He married Alice Chaucer. He fought in France for Henry V and John duke of Bedford. Under Henry VI he became Steward of the Royal Household. He received military command but failed to distinguish himself. He planned the attack on Fougères in 1449 and was largely responsible for the subsequent loss of Normandy. He was impeached in Parliament, though the accusations were exaggerated – including that he seduced a nun. Henry VI intervened to banish Suffolk. Privateers, who shared popular antagonism to him, caught him at Dover. On 2 May he was dragged into a boat and beheaded across the gunwale with a rusty sword. His son John regained the dukedom in 1463.

SULEIMAN AL-ARABI, GOVERNOR OF BARCELONA

The Muslim Abbasid governor who appealed to Pepin the Short for aid. He led an embassy to Paderborn to appeal to Charlemagne. Suleiman was threatened by the growing power of the Umayyads. He promised to allow Frankish entry to his cities. Charlemagne went to Spain in 778. Some places surrendered, but Zaragoza refused entry. Suleiman had taken over Zaragoza, but the citizens shut their gates. Charles abandoned his attempt to take the city. Roncesvalles occurred during the return to Francia.

SWEYN I HAROLDSSON (FORKBEARD), KING OF DENMARK (d.1014)

King from 987, son of Harold Bluetooth from whom he seized the Danish throne. He led raids against England in 991 and 994 with Ólaf Tryggvason. He opposed his former comrade in Norway. Sweyn's ally, Jarl Erik of Lade, defeated Ólaf at Svöld in 1000. As king Sweyn took over Hedeby and dominated the Wends. He led expeditions to England in 1003 and 1006. In 1013 he came to defeat Aethelred II, who fled. He controlled England but died in February 1014 at Gainsborough in Lincolnshire. In Denmark his son Harold succeeded but his most famous son was Cnut the Great.

SWEYN II (SVEIN/SVEN) ESTRITHSSON (ÚLFSSON), KING OF DENMARK (d.1074)

King from 1047, nephew of Cnut, son of Jarl Úlf. As a young man he was hostage for his father's loyalty in England. He served the King of Sweden. He claimed Denmark through his mother, Estrid, sister of Cnut and daughter of Sweyn Forkbeard. Sweyn was appointed to rule Denmark under Magnús the Good in 1042 but rebelled and was defeated. He allied with Harold Hardrada on his return to Scandinavia but Magnús won Harold over by offering half of Norway. When Magnús died, Sweyn gained control of Denmark. Harold fought against him, and Sweyn was defeated but not overthrown. Harold recognised Sweyn's rule. In 1069 Sweyn joined the English opponents of William the Conqueror. He raised an army, claiming England as successor to Cnut. He took York in 1070

but his invasion failed. He made peace with the Conqueror and returned to Denmark. Adam of Bremen was at Sweyn's court. He described Sweyn's intelligence and good memory and says Sweyn told him about Vinland. Five of his sons succeeded in turn, one of whom was St Cnut.

SYAGRIUS (d.486)

A Gallo-Roman magnate, 'King of the Romans' during the collapse of the Western Empire, son of Aegidius, a Roman general who established a 'kingdom' at Soissons. Count Paulus acted as regent before Syagrius took over. He ruled Frankish subjects. Syagrius inherited this kingdom in c.465. He was rather a soldier of fortune than a territorial king. He defeated a rival called Syrivald. The extent of his authority is unknown, but was probably not great. He fought against Childeric I, King of the Salian Franks, and was defeated by his son Clovis I in 486. He sought refuge in the Visigothic kingdom of Alaric II at Toulouse. Clovis demanded that Syagrius be handed over. He was delivered in chains, imprisoned, and killed secretly.

SYMEON, BULGAR KHAN (d.927)

Khan from 893 when Khan Boris abdicated for his son Vladimir, whom he then blinded and deposed in favour of the younger son Symeon. Symeon allied with the Pechenegs against the Magyars who were forced from Bulgaria. He took over Serbia. Symeon threatened Byzantium, demanding tribute after a series of victories culminating with Anchialus in 917. He conquered Macedonia, Thessaly and Albania. He was crowned Byzantine Emperor by the patriarch and married his daughter to Constantine VII. A coup placed Romanus I on the Byzantine throne in 919, ending the marriage and the tribute. Symeon attacked Constantinople until Constantine recognised him as Tsar of Bulgaria. His forces were beaten when invading Croatia. He died on 27 May. Symeon's son Peter succeeded and married the granddaughter of Romanus I.

TAILLEFER (INCISOR-FERRI)

Only known from (probably) later sources. The *Carmen de Hastingae Proelio (Song of the Battle of Hastings)* is probably the earliest source to mention him but probably does not date before 1100. He appeared in 12th-century sources including Wace's *Roman de Rou* and works by Gaimar, Benoit and Henry of Huntingdon. He is described in the *Carmen* as a minstrel who juggled with his sword before the assembled armies at Hastings. When an Englishman approached him, Taillefer pierced his shield with a lance and cut off his head with the sword, displaying the head to the Normans who 'all rejoiced' and were encouraged for the battle. Some historians accept this as fact; others see the man and the incident as fictional.

TAMBERLANE (TAMERLANE/ TAMBERLAINE/TIMUR LENG/TIMUR THE LAME), MONGOL KHAN (1335–1405)

Khan of Jaghatai (Turkestan/Uzbekistan) with its capital at Samarkand, from 1369, who won a vast Mongol-Turkish Empire. He was a Muslim who encouraged the spread of Islam. He was born at Kesh near Samarkand, of Mongol descent, but Turkish in speech and culture. He was noted for ruthlessness, often massacring the populations of captured cities. He conquered Transoxiana, Persia, Iraq, India, Syria, Armenia and Georgia. In 1395 he defeated the Mongol Golden Horde under Toktamish at Terek. In 1398 he sacked Delhi. In 1400 at Aleppo he won Syria from the Mamlukes. In 1401 he took Baghdad, defeating and capturing Bayezit I at Ankara in 1402 and winning Anatolia. Tamberlane died at Otrar on 19 February when returning to the east to invade China. His Empire fragmented but his descendants ruled India and Persia.

TANCRED, PRINCE OF GALILEE AND ANTIOCH (1077–1112)

A Norman from southern Italy, grandson of Robert Guiscard, nephew of Bohemond of Taranto, whom he accompanied on the First Crusade. Tancred found difficulty in reconciling a warrior's life with Christian beliefs. The Crusade was a welcome solution. He captured Tarsus and was at the taking of Antioch and Jerusalem, and the Battle of Ascalon in 1099. He gained Tiberias and Nazareth, which became part of the principality of Galilee. When Bohemond was captured Tancred ruled Antioch from 1101. He took Cilicia from Byzantium. In 1103 he besieged and captured Lattakieh – though the Byzantines regained much of their territory. From 1104 to 1109 Tancred was regent of Edessa. He remained regent of Antioch after Bohemond's release, when the latter returned west. After Bohemond's death in 1111 Tancred succeeded to Antioch. He probably died of typhoid. His nephew Roger succeeded.

TASSILO III, DUKE OF BAVARIA (742–c.794)

Cousin and opponent of Charlemagne, son of Odilo who died in 748. Bavaria was an independent duchy under the Agilolfings. Tassilo's mother, Hiltrud, was the sister of Charlemagne's father Pepin the Short. Tassilo, aged six, was overlooked for the succession. With Pepin the Short's support he later became duke and swore an oath of vassalage to Pepin at Compiègne. When Tassilo reached manhood he tried to restore Bavaria's independence, refusing to send troops for Pepin's campaign to Aquitaine. Tassilo married Liutperga, daughter of King Desiderius, and allied with Lombardy. To the east of Bavaria were pagan Avars and Slavs. Tassilo conquered the Slavs of Carinthia and assisted the spread of Christianity. Charlemagne sought to impose closer control. He used his influence with the papacy to demand allegiance from Tassilo. Tassilo had come to Worms when requested in 781, but when summoned in 787 he refused. Charlemagne then invaded Bavaria with a three-pronged attack, massing the army on the border. Tassilo was forced to surrender and swear vassalage. Charles returned Bavaria to him but Tassilo plotted against him. At an assembly in Ingelheim in 788, Charles arrested him, accused him of treason and sentenced him to death. Tassilo asked mercy. Charles forced him to renounce his rights to Bavaria and sent him into a monastery (probably Jumièges in Normandy). Charlemagne ruled Bavaria directly. A Council at Frankfurt in 794 confirmed Tassilo's deposition. Tassilo appeared at the assembly, admitted his faults and begged forgiveness before returning to his monastery. The date of his death is unknown.

TELL, WILLIAM
Legendary figure of the Swiss resistance to Austrian Habsburg control, supposed to have shot an apple from his son's head with a crossbow – a similar tale appears in Norse and English legends. He represents the Swiss infantrymen who won independence. In 1307 he is said to have killed Hermann Gessler, Austrian Governor of the Tyrol. There are comparisons with Robin Hood, and similar uncertainty over whether the hero lived. *The Ballad of William Tell* dates from 1465.

THEODORE ANGELUS DUKAS COMNENUS, DESPOT OF EPIRUS (d.1254)
Despot 1215–30, claiming to be Byzantine Emperor as great-grandson of Alexius I. The despotate was founded by Michael Comnenus Dukas when the Byzantine Empire fragmented after the Latin capture of Constantinople. Theodore was Michael's half-brother and succeeded. Michael won parts of Greece and Thessaly. Peter of Courtenay was elected as Latin Emperor. On his way to Constantinople Peter tried to take Durazzo from Theodore but was defeated and captured in 1217. Peter was imprisoned and never heard of again. Theodore took over most of Macedonia and captured Thessalonika in 1224, which became his capital. He claimed to be emperor but could not impose his authority beyond his own territories. In 1230 he invaded Bulgaria but was defeated and captured by John Asen at Klokotnitsa. Asen

married his daughter Irene, despite having blinded Theodore for plotting against him. Theodore was exiled to a country estate but continued to plot and was imprisoned to die in captivity. His son Demetrius took over Thessalonika but the despotate was broken up.

THEODERIC I, KING OF THE VISIGOTHS (418–51)
Beaten by the Romans at Toulouse in 439. He allied with Aëtius against Attila and was killed at the Catalaunian Plains.

THEODERIC, KING OF THE OSTROGOTHS, THE GREAT (455–526)
King from 471 after the collapse of Attila's empire when the Ostrogoths inhabited the Danube region. His position was strengthened by the death of one rival, Theodoric Strabo (the Squinter), and by the killing of another, Recitah. Theodoric spent years as a hostage in Constaninople and imbibed Roman ways. He was twice named as *magister militum*. The Byzantine emperor, Zeno, encouraged him to invade Italy, and made Theodoric *patricius*. Theodoric invaded in 489, defeating Odoacer at Sontius and Verona in 489, but beaten at Faenza in 490. He allied with the Visigoths and Burgundians, and finally beat Odoacer at Adda in 490. Odoacer continued to resist but made peace in 493. Theodoric invited him to dinner and killed him with his own sword. Theodoric acted as King of Italy and settled the Ostrogoths there. He undertook a programme of restoration, including in Rome. He established his capital at Ravenna. His authority extended to north of the Alps. He was an Arian Christian and put to death the philosopher Boethius. He thought he recognised a murder victim in the face of a cooked fish presented to him, took to bed with shock, and died.

THEODOSIUS I THE GREAT (FLAVIUS), EASTERN EMPEROR (346–95)
Emperor from 379, reviving the empire after Adrianople in 378. Son of a general

who suppressed revolt in Britain, he was a Spaniard who rose through military ability. Theodosius defended Moesia for Valentinian. He commanded for Gratian and became co-emperor in the east. Theodosius was a baptised Christian who opposed paganism and heresy. He rebuilt Constantinople including the Harbour of Theodosius. He massacred 7,000 citizens of Thessalonika after his captain had been killed. Theodosius defeated Maximus at Aquileia in 388. He reunited the Roman Empire, defeating Eugenius and Arbogast at the Frigidius (Vipacco) in 394. Theodosius was the last ruler of a united Roman Empire. He allowed the Visigoths to settle in Thrace in return for military service. He employed barbarian troops and, during the Hun threat to Persia, partitioned Armenia with Persia, stabilising the frontier. Theodosius died on 17 January in Milan and was taken to Constantinople for burial. The empire was divided between his sons Arcadius in the east and Honorius in the west.

THEODOSIUS II, BYZANTINE EMPEROR (401–50)

Emperor from 408, supposed son of Arcadius but possibly of a lover of his mother. He was seven at his father's death. Anthemius and Theodosius' older sister Pulcheria governed in the minority. Theodosius married Athenais, renamed Eudocia, a Greek philosopher's daughter. Under Anthemius the Theodosian Walls were built to defend Constantinople, enclosing seven rather than four hills. Theodosius sent an expedition to support Valentinian III as Western Emperor in 425. In 431 he sent Aspar to North Africa, where he was defeated by Gaiseric. The Byzantine navy had some success against the Vandals. Theodosius paid tribute to halt Attila the Hun in 441. Theodosius died on 28 July, falling from his horse when hunting.

THORKELL HAVI (THE TALL) (d. c.1023)

Leader of armies invading England. He may have led Baltic Jómsvikings but the evidence is unreliable. Thorkell's background remains shadowy. He was a mercenary serving various masters, probably a man of standing in Scandinavia. He and his brother Hemming arrived in England in 1009 with mainly Danish troops. He caused trouble in East Anglia, the midlands and the south-east. Ólaf Haroldsson served under him. In 1010 Thorkell defeated Ulfketel the ealdorman of East Anglia at Ringmere in Norfolk. He led the sack of Canterbury in 1111 when Archbishop Aelfheah was captured, though Thorkell distanced himself from the killing of Aelfheah. In 1212 Thorkell served Aethelred II. In England he made a fortune from pay and tribute. He helped to defend London against Sweyn Forkbeard in 1013. After the death of Aethelred, he joined Cnut and was rewarded in 1016 with the earldom of East Anglia. Thorkell rebelled and was outlawed. In 1023 they made peace and Thorkell became Cnut's regent in Denmark. He probably died soon after.

THÓRÓLF LOUSEBEARD

Too good a name to omit, foster father of Astrid, Ólaf Tryggvason's mother, and exiled with her. He was captured by pirates and killed because they thought him too old to work. Ólaf later killed Thórólf's murderer with a blow from a hand-axe to the head.

TOTILA (OR BADUILA), KING OF THE OSTROGOTHS (d.552)

King from 541, who recaptured Rome and defended Italy against Justinian. He only desisted from destroying Rome on Belisarius' plea. Totila survived but was defeated and killed at Busta Gallorum by the Byzantine general, Narses.

TUDOR, JASPER, EARL OF PEMBROKE AND DUKE OF BEDFORD (1430–95)

Uncle of Henry VII, a staunch Lancastrian, son of Owen Tudor and Katherine of France, born at Hatfield, the first Tudor Earl of Pembroke from 1452. He fought for Henry VI at St Albans in 1455. Through his

Lancastrian allegiance he twice lost the earldom and twice regained it. He fought against Edward IV at Mortimer's Cross and was exiled. He continued to support Henry VI and then his nephew Henry Tudor. He invaded with Henry Tudor, fighting at Bosworth. Henry made him Earl of Bedford in 1485. Jasper married Katherine Woodville, sister of Edward IV's Queen. He became Lieutenant in Ireland and helped govern Wales for Henry. He died in December.

VISCONTI, FILIPPO MARIA, DUKE OF MILAN (1392–1447)
Duke from 1412. He married Beatrice daughter of Facino Cane, the mercenary who controlled Milan under Giovanni Visconti. Cane and Giovanni died in 1412, when Filippo inherited Milan and Cane's mercenaries. Beatrice was put to death in 1418 for adultery, probably unjustly. The lost Lombard lands were regained. Filippo took over Genoa in 1421 and defeated the Swiss at Arbedo in 1422. He employed various *condottieri*, including Francesco Sforza, Carmagnola (Francesco Bussone) and Niccolò Piccinino. He fought against the other major northern Italian powers, Venice and Florence, from 1423. Some earlier gains, including Genoa, were lost. He won Bologna in 1438, holding it until 1443. His daughter married Francesco Sforza, the mercenary who succeeded him. Filippo died on 13 August.

VISCONTI, GIAN GALEAZZO, DUKE OF MILAN (1351–1402)
Perhaps the greatest of the Visconti, ruler of Milan jointly from 1378, alone from 1385, first Duke from 1395 – when he bought the title from Wenceslas King of the Romans. He ruled Milan with his uncle, Bernabò, from 1378 after the death of his father Galeazzo II. He married Isabelle de Valois, becoming Conte de Virtù, and then Caterina, his cousin. In 1385, through a coup, he imprisoned Bernabò for life. He employed various *condottieri*, including Jacopo dal Verme. In 1387 he took Verona

and Vicenza, and in 1388 Padua. Milan became dominant in northern Italy, taking over Lucca, Pisa, Siena and Bologna. He defeated Rupert of Bavaria's invasion at Brescia in 1401, and Florence at Casalecchio in 1402. He died of plague on 3 September, when his son Giovanni succeeded.

VORTIGERN
According to Bede, Vortigern was a Romano-British leader based in Kent who invited in the English to aid him against the Picts and Scots, the English then turning against him to begin the Anglo-Saxon conquest. Bede and the *Anglo-Saxon Chronicle* treat Vortigern as an individual but historians believe 'Vortigern' is a title meaning 'overlord' rather than a name. His descendants Vortimer and Guorthemer might also be vortigerns. It then becomes easier to reconcile accounts referring to a number of vortigerns. It is thought that our Vortigern equates with Gildas' 'proud tyrant'. Others though believe it could be a personal name, appearing in Celtic areas as Foirtchernn and Foirtgirn. In *Nennius*, Vortigern ruled from 425 and invited in the English in 428. Some believe the date is also wrong and should be decades later in 449. What we can conclude is that an individual British ruler whose title or name was Vortigern invited Saxons to help him militarily, and was later overthrown by them. Power in Vortigern's kingdom passed to Hengest and Horsa in the mid-5th century.

WAIOFAR, DUKE OF AQUITAINE (d.768)
Duke from 745, son of Hunald I. He allied with Pepin the Short's half-brother, Grifo, against Pepin. Grifo was killed in Aquitaine in 753. Waiofar was accused of taking church land in Aquitaine. Waiofar attacked territories outside his own lands, including Narbonne in 751. From 760 Pepin made seven destructive expeditions against Aquitaine. Pepin took control in the border regions of Berry, the Auvergne and the Touraine. He attacked the strongholds of

Escorailles, Chantelle, Turenne and Carlat. Waiofar dismantled some fortifications and retreated south. Waiofar's uncle, Remistian, joined Pepin but returned to Waiofar. Remistian was captured in 768 and hanged at Bourges. Waiofar had local support but was forced to seek refuge in the forest of Ver and killed in Périgueux by his own men – possibly with Pepin's connivance. Pepin became ill during the campaign and died on return to Paris. Aquitainian resistance continued under Waiofar's son Hunald II.

WALERAN, COUNT OF MEULAN, EARL OF WORCESTER (1104–66)

Waleran of Meulan led a rebellion in Normandy against Henry I. He was the son of Robert I de Beaumont, inheriting Meulan from him in 1118. He was the first-born of twins, his brother being Robert II de Beaumont earl of Leicester, who inherited the English lands. In the rebellion against Henry he attacked Vatteville but was defeated at Bourgthéroulde in 1124. He was captured and imprisoned though later released. With the succession of Stephen, Waleran was appointed Earl of Worcester in 1138. In the early years of Stephen's reign Waleran defended Normandy against Geoffrey V of Anjou. He joined Matilda in 1139 and was a rival in the west to Robert of Gloucester. Waleran fought for Stephen at Lincoln in 1141 but fled and escaped. He made his peace with Matilda in 1141. In Normandy he made terms with Geoffrey in 1141. Waleran went on the Second Crusade with Louis VII of France in 1147, escaping from a shipwreck. He shifted his allegiance to Louis, aiding him against Henry Plantagenet. Waleran lost influence in Normandy. In 1153 his nephew, Robert de Montfort, captured him. His earldom was confiscated. Henry II pardoned Waleran by 1162. Before his death he became a monk at Préaux.

WALLACE, WILLIAM (1272–1305)

His family were men of the Stewarts near Paisley. He rebelled against Edward I in 1297, defeating the English under Earl Warenne at Stirling. He was knighted in 1298. Edward I defeated him at Falkirk in 1298. He escaped and continued to resist, going to France for aid. He was defeated in a skirmish in 1303. He was betrayed and captured in 1305, executed on 23 August at Smithfield.

WALTER I DE BRIENNE, DUKE OF ATHENS AND THEBES (d.1311)

Duke from 1309 during Latin rule in Constantinople, succeeding his cousin Guy II. In 1310 he employed the Catalan Company to conquer Thessaly. In 1311 the Company rebelled when he failed to pay them. He offered land for military service, which was not acceptable. Walter was defeated and killed on 15 March at Kephissos in Boeotia. The Catalans ruled the duchy until 1388. Walter's son Walter II tried to recover the duchy but failed.

WALTER THE PENNILESS (SANSAVOIR) (d.1096)

A leader of the People's Crusade, from Poissy. 'Penniless' is a misnomer (or joke?), for he was a knight from the family of the Lords of Poissy whose cognomen was Sansavoir. He initiated the crusading trek to Hungary and Constantinople. He advised caution. When this was ignored he still fought at Civetot against the Turks on 26 October, and was killed.

WALTHEOF, EARL OF THE EAST MIDLANDS AND BAMBURGH (d.1076)

Son of Siward of Northumbria who died in 1055. Waltheof did not succeed to the earldom because he was young. He was created earl of a group of east midland shires in 1065. He did not oppose the Norman Conquest and kept his earldom. When William returned to Normandy in 1067, Waltheof went with him as a hostage. In 1069 he joined the northern rebellion. He made his peace with William, whose niece Judith he married in 1070. In 1072 he became Earl of Bamburgh. He was accused of involvement in the rebellion of 1075, though possibly innocent. The rebels were defeated and Waltheof imprisoned at Winchester. A year later, on 31 May, he was executed, permitted to say the Lord's Prayer but breaking down in tears before completing it. The executioner would not wait and cut off his head with a sword, when it was said the severed head completed the final words. The body was reburied at Crowland in 1092. Legends grew, miracles were reported, and the site became a cult centre.

WARBECK, PERKIN (1474–99)
Nominal leader of a rebellion against Henry VII in 1497, probably born in Flanders and taken up by exiled Yorkists. He claimed to be Edward earl of Warwick, Edward IV's nephew. Henry VII brought Warwick from the Tower and displayed him in public. A Breton merchant took Perkin to Ireland in 1491 where he impersonated Richard duke of York, the younger of the Princes in the Tower. Perkin was taken around Europe seeking aid against Henry. He married Katherine Gordon, a cousin of James IV of Scots. He received promises but little aid. Twice invasions were attempted but failed. On the third try in 1497 he landed in Cornwall but support evaporated. Perkin was captured when taking refuge in Beaulieu Abbey. At first he was treated leniently but then tried for treason and hanged at Tyburn on 29 November.

WARWICK, RICHARD NEVILLE, EARL OF (THE KINGMAKER) (1428–71)
Son of Richard Neville earl of Salisbury. The nickname 'Kingmaker' was given in the 16th century. He gained the earldom in 1449 through marriage to the heiress Anne Beauchamp. With his father he joined the Yorkists, opposing Henry VI and the Percies. He fought at the First Battle of St Albans in 1455, leading the attack that surprised the Lancastrian rear. He was appointed Captain of Calais and gained a naval reputation. He fled when York failed in 1459 but assisted Edward IV to become king, regaining his earldom. Warwick

captured Henry VI at Northampton in 1460. Warwick was wounded in the leg by an arrow at Ferrybridge but fought in the victory at Towton in 1461. His earldom was restored. He was defeated by Queen Margaret at the Second Battle of St Albans in 1461. With Edward's success Warwick became powerful in the north but felt inadequately rewarded. He opposed Edward's marriage to Elizabeth Woodville. He allied with Clarence who married his daughter. Warwick rebelled, joining the Lancastrians in exile. His daughter Anne married Henry VI's son. Warwick invaded with the Lancastrians in 1470 when Henry VI was restored. Edward returned the following year. Warwick was defeated and killed on 14 April at Barnet.

WENCESLAS II (WENZEL), KING OF BOHEMIA AND POLAND (1271–1305)
King of Bohemia from 1278, of Poland from 1300, son of Ottokar II. He established Bohemia as a major central European power. He took the crown of Hungary for his son 1301–4. His father was killed in battle and Wenceslas faced civil war in Bohemia. The three kingdoms separated again through the efforts of Albert of Austria. Wenceslas died on 21 June. His son Wenceslas III succeeded.

WENCESLAS IV (WENZEL), KING OF BOHEMIA AND OF THE ROMANS (1361–1419)
King of Bohemia from 1378, King of the Romans as Wenceslas I from 1376. He was of the House of Luxembourg, son of Charles IV who died in 1378. Wenceslas was reputed a drunkard. He was twice defeated by Bohemian coalitions, but each time recovered. He fought a civil war in Germany with Rupert of Wittelsbach and was deposed in Germany in 1400. He was rivalled by his brother Sigismund, elected King of the Romans 1410 and allowed to hold the position by Wenceslas from 1411. Wenceslas sold the duchy of Milan to Giangaleazzo Visconti for 100,000 florins. Radical Hussites were provoked into

attacking the Town Hall in Prague, throwing councillors out of the window. It was said Wenceslas died of shock on 16 August on hearing the news, suffering a stroke and roaring like a lion. He was buried in Prague.

WIDUKIND

Saxon military leader, Charlemagne's toughest opponent. His family was probably Westphalian nobility, possibly ducal. He allied with the Danes, related by marriage to the Danish royal family. From 777 he raided Frankish territory with attacks on monasteries and churches. In 778 he raided along the right bank of the Rhine from Deutz to Koblenz, attacking Charles' forces at Hesse. Widukind made attacks whenever Charlemagne was elsewhere. The frequency of Charles' expeditions against the Saxons is testimony to Widukind's threat. In 782 on the Weser he defeated a Frankish army led by three of Charles' officials. After Charlemagne's revenge in the massacre at Verden, Widukind escaped – it was said by reversing the shoes on his horse to mislead pursuers. He took refuge with the Danes. Charles won further victories but Widukind remained at large. He finally made an agreement with Charles in 785, agreeing to baptism at Attigny. He retained his lands but no more is heard of him, though he lived on in Saxon legend.

WILLIAM I, THE CONQUEROR, KING OF ENGLAND, WILLIAM II DUKE OF NORMANDY (c.1027–87)

Duke from 1035, King from 1066, known as the Bastard and the Conqueror, born in Falaise, the illegitimate son of Robert I duke of Normandy and Herlève – daughter of either a tanner or an undertaker. William succeeded as a minor and faced opposition. Some Norman nobles and the King of France protected his position. William's first major victory was against rebels at Val-ès-Dunes in 1047. In 1051–2 he captured Domfront and Alençon. The King of France became hostile but was defeated at St-Aubin-sur-Scie 1053. William captured Arques. Normandy was invaded in 1054 and 1057, but William won at Mortemer and Varaville. The deaths of Henry I of France and Geoffrey Martel of Anjou in 1060 left William freer. He took over Maine in 1063 and campaigned in Brittany in 1064. When Edward the Confessor died and Harold II took the throne, William accused him of treachery and invaded England, landing at Pevensey. Harold was defeated and killed at Hastings. By the end of 1066 he controlled the south-east of England, crowned in London on Christmas Day. Numerous castles were built in England, including stone ones at Colchester and London. He suppressed a series of rebellions, taking Exeter in 1068. Rebellion in 1069 led to the harrying of the North. Rebellion in East Anglia in 1071 was suppressed though Hereward escaped punishment. There was rebellion by the earls in 1075, leading to the execution of Waltheof. William defeated invasions from the sons of Harold Godwinson, and Scandinavia in 1069. William imprisoned his own half-brother, Odo of Bayeux, in 1083 for plotting against him. In 1072 William invaded Scotland, when Malcolm Canmore submitted. William married Matilda of Flanders, by whom he had nine children. He quarrelled with his oldest son Robert Curthose who rebelled. Robert defeated and unhorsed his father at Gerberoi 1079. The Conqueror injured himself on the pommel of his saddle when attacking Mantes. He was taken to Rouen where he died on 9 September. His body would not fit the stone sarcophagus and burst when forced in. He was buried at his foundation of St-Étienne, Caen. His sons Robert Curthose (Normandy) and William Rufus (England) succeeded.

WILLIAM I, THE LION, EARL OF NORTHUMBERLAND, KING OF SCOTS (1143–1214)

Son and successor of Henry earl of Northumberland from 1152, king from 1165 in succession to his brother

Malcolm IV. He invaded England in alliance with Henry II's sons in 1173. He experimented with military weapons, though with little success. When he threw fire from an engine at Wark in 1174, the wind blew the flames back in the Scots' faces. When he used an early trebuchet the stone tumbled from the sling and killed one of his men. He was captured at Alnwick. By the Treaty of Falaise in 1174 he recognised the overlordship of the King of England. He married Ermengarde de Beaumont in 1186. He repressed rebellions in Scotland, extending royal power north of the Moray Firth. He died on 4 December at Stirling and was buried in Arbroath Abbey. His son Alexander II succeeded.

WILLIAM I, LONGSWORD, DUKE OF NORMANDY (c.924–942)

Duke of Normandy from 927 (more properly Count of Rouen), son of Rollo the founder of Normandy and Poppa. He extended Normandy's boundary. By 933 he gained western Normandy to the Couesnon from the Bretons, adding the Cotentin and Avranchin – recognised by Ralph, King of the West Franks in 933. William claimed to be Duke of Brittany. In 933–4 the Scandinavian Rioul rebelled and was defeated. William married Liégarde, the Christian daughter of the Count of Vermandois. He was murdered on 17 December on the Somme island of Picquigny, through the treachery of the Count of Flanders. This led to a pagan revival. His illegitimate son Richard I succeeded.

WILLIAM II, RUFUS, KING OF ENGLAND (c.1058–1100)

Son and successor of William the Conqueror in 1087. His nickname means 'the Red' either from his complexion or his hair. He was also called Longsword. William fought for his father against Curthose at Gerberoi in 1079 and was wounded. On the Conqueror's death, Curthose became Duke of Normandy and felt England should be his. There were rebellions in England in 1088 and 1095, which were suppressed. Rufus sought to win Normandy in 1094 but failed. In 1096 Curthose raised money from Rufus to finance his participation in the First Crusade. Rufus was left in control of Normandy, recovering Maine in 1098. Rufus was killed on 2 August by an arrow when hunting in the New Forest. His brother Henry, who succeeded him, was suspected but without conclusive evidence. The body was taken to Winchester for burial. Rufus had not married and had no children to succeed him.

WILLIAM V, THE GREAT, DUKE OF AQUITAINE, COUNT OF POITOU (d.1029)

Son and successor of William IV, duke from 990, virtually an independent ruler from his capital at Poitiers, treating as equals kings of France, Holy Roman Emperors and rulers of Spain and Italy. His second marriage, to Prisca daughter of the Duke of Gascony, united Gascony with Aquitaine. His first wife was Adelmode of Périgueux, his third, Agnès of Burgundy. He accepted the crown of Italy for his son but gave it up. He imposed the Peace of God on lords engaging in private war. He sought to limit the power of his vassals by control of castles, leading to conflict with Boso II count of La Marche. William VI, and four sons in turn, succeeded.

WILLIAM IX, THE YOUNG, DUKE OF AQUITAINE AND GASCONY, COUNT OF POITOU (d.1126)

Duke of Aquitaine from 1086 as a minor, son of William VIII, a patron of troubadours and a poet. He married Philippa of Toulouse in 1094. He went on Crusade in 1101–2 when he was defeated at Heraclea in Asia Minor, though escaping to Jerusalem. Castellans of Poitou sought independence of Aquitaine, building castles. He fought his vassals the Lords of Parthenay and Lusignan, and his neighbour Fulk IV of Anjou. He became Lord of Toulouse through marriage, but only until 1119. In

1120 he was defeated in Gascony. He invaded Spain, reaching Granada in 1125. His son William X succeeded.

WILLIAM CLITO, COUNT OF FLANDERS (1102–28)

Son of Robert Curthose and Sybil of Conversano. Clito equates to 'Aetheling' or Prince. He was 'dogged by misfortune from his earliest years'. His mother was probably poisoned. He resented the conduct of his uncle, Henry I, who defeated and imprisoned his father and then seized Normandy – which Clito saw as his inheritance. He was protected in exile by the King of France and participated in rebellions and invasions of Normandy against Henry. He accompanied Louis VI on the 1118 campaign leading to Brémule when the French were defeated but Clito escaped. The 1124 Norman rebels supported Clito but were defeated at Bourgthéroulde. The marriage of Henry's daughter, Matilda, to Geoffrey of Anjou was intended to block an alliance between Clito and Anjou. Clito married the half-sister of Queen Adela of France in 1127. Louis VI gave him lands including the Vexin. After the murder of Charles the Good in 1127 Louis made William Count of Flanders, reclaiming the Vexin. Clito lived another 16 months. He hunted down the murderers of Charles but his hold on Flanders was uncertain. He alienated some by punishing the murder suspects, Bruges by the removal of privileges, other cities by ignoring their liberties. At the siege of Aalst in Flanders Clito, after fighting bravely, wounded himself grasping a lance. The arm turned black to the elbow (probably gangrene). Five days later on 27 July, after becoming a monk, he died. He was buried in the abbey of St-Bertin at St-Omer. His epitaph described him as 'an honoured knight'.

WILLIAM DE CHAMPLITTE, PRINCE OF ACHAEA (d.1209)

Ruler of the principality of Achaea or the Morea, established after the Latin capture of Constantinople. William was of French nobility. He and Geoffrey de Villehardouin captured the territory, consisting of most of the Peloponnese, in 1204–5. The capital was at Andravida, the principality divided in 12 baronies. Among its new castles was Mistra near Sparta. Women could inherit and rule, and Achaea had six female rulers. The principality passed to the Villehardouin family, surviving until 1341 when it surrendered to Byzantium. It passed to Thomas Palaeologus in 1432. The despotate of Morea fell to the Turks in 1460.

WILLIAM DE HAUTEVILLE, BRAS DE FER (IRONARM), COUNT OF APULIA (d.1045)

Eldest son of Tancred de Hauteville, the first to go to Italy in c.1035. He was employed by the Lombard Pandulf of Capua and then by the Byzantines. He unhorsed and killed the Muslim Emir of Syracuse in single combat at Troina, earning the nickname 'Ironarm'. On the mainland he assisted Lombard victories in 1041, commanding at Monte Maggiore on 4 May, despite a fever. At Melfi in 1042 he took the title Count of Apulia. He married Guida, daughter of the Lombard Duke of Sorrento. His brother Drogo succeeded.

WILLIAM FITZ OSBERN, EARL OF HEREFORD (d.1071)

Steward of Normandy, Viceregent in England for William the Conqueror, called 'the bravest of the Normans', related to the ducal family. His father Osbern was William's steward, murdered in his service. His territorial base was in central Normandy. He was a significant supporter of William before 1066, one of the few named in contemporary sources as fighting at Hastings. He received the Isle of Wight and the county of Hereford in 1067. After the northern rebellion Fitz Osbern was castellan at York. Philip I of France summoned him to represent the Conqueror against Flanders. He took only ten men and was killed on 20 (or 22) February at Cassel. His body was returned to Normandy for burial at Cormeilles.

WILLIAM OF HOLLAND, GERMAN ANTI-KING (1227–56)

Count of Holland, opponent of Frederick II in Germany, supported by Pope Innocent IV, the son of Count Florence IV. He married the daughter of the Duke of Brunswick. He was elected anti-king against Frederick to replace Henry Raspe in 1247 and re-elected in 1252. He fought a civil war against Frederick and his son Conrad IV until the latter's death in 1254. William died on 28 January, fighting the Frisians, when his horse sank into a frozen marsh.

WILLIAM OF YPRES (d.1162)

The military lieutenant of King Stephen. He was not created earl but held the position in Kent. The illegitimate son of Philip of Ypres, grandson of Robert the Frisian count of Flanders, he twice sought to become Count of Flanders but failed. He was captured and imprisoned, then exiled in 1133. He became a mercenary captain for Stephen count of Boulogne. His birth and military ability earned him a senior position. For Stephen as king William defended Normandy. In the civil war against Matilda he captured Devizes Castle in 1139. He led the left wing for Stephen at Lincoln and escaped. With Stephen captured William acted for him with Stephen's wife, Queen Matilda. They forced the Empress Matilda to flee from London and defeated her troops at Winchester, leading to Stephen's release. William became blind, playing no part in the war against Henry Plantagenet but was one of the few to suffer under Henry II. His lands in England were confiscated and he retired to his castle of Loo in Flanders to spend his last years.

WILLIAM THE MARSHAL, EARL OF PEMBROKE, REGENT OF ENGLAND (1147–1219)

Regent from 1217 to 1219 for Henry III, son of the royal Marshal, John fitz Gilbert, a famous knight and subject of the *Histoire de Guillaume le Maréchal*. He rose through success in tournaments, accumulating wealth (the medieval equivalent of a football star). He fought in the 1173–4 rebellion, first for Young Henry and then for the king. He unhorsed Richard the Lionheart in 1189 but Richard permitted his marriage to the heiress of Richard de Clare (Strongbow) that brought his earldom. He helped defeat Prince Louis' invasion, defeating the French at Lincoln in 1217. He died on 14 May possibly of cancer of the bowel. His English lands went to his son William. He was buried in the Temple in London, which retains his effigy.

YAGHI-SIYAN, EMIR OF ANTIOCH (d.1098)

Made Seljuk Emir of Antioch in 1087 by Sultan Malik Shah and thus emir at the time of the First Crusade. The Seljuks were conquerors in the region and not popular with a population of mainly Greek, Syrian and Armenian Christians. Yaghi-Siyan defended Antioch, when besieged by the crusaders, improving the fortifications. When the crusaders were treacherously let in on 3 June, Yaghi-Siyan escaped on horseback but fell fainting from his horse to be decapitated by an Armenian shepherd, who presented the head to the Franks.

YORK, RICHARD PLANTAGENET, DUKE OF (1411–60)

Son of Richard earl of Cambridge who opposed Henry VI to initiate the Wars of the Roses. He succeeded his uncle as duke in 1415. He married Cecily Neville, sister of Richard earl of Salisbury. He was knighted by Henry VI in 1426. York became Governor in France in 1436, and also in Normandy from 1440. He captured Pontoise in 1437. In 1447 he reluctantly became Lieutenant in Ireland. In 1450 he tried to control the royal Council but failed. In 1452 he took arms against the king but submitted without fighting. When Henry lost his mind in 1454 York became Captain of Calais and Protector of England. Henry's recovery ended the Protectorate. York took to arms in 1455, defeating the royalists at St Albans, where Henry was captured. The Protectorate was revived but Henry recovered and dismissed York. In 1459, lacking support, York fled to Ireland and was attainted as a traitor. After Warwick's success at Northampton, York prepared to assume the crown but was defeated and killed on 30 December at Wakefield. His sons became Edward IV and Richard III.

YŪSUF I, ABŪ YA'QŪB, ALMOHAD CALIPH (d.1184)

Caliph in Spain and North Africa from 1163, son and successor of 'Abd al-Mu'min. He recovered the Muslim position in Spain, taking Córdoba in 1164. In 1179 he attacked Lisbon but failed to take it. He attacked Portugal in 1184 but died from a wound. His son Abū-Yūsuf succeeded.

YŪSUF IBN-TĀSHFĪN, EMPEROR OF MOROCCO (1030–1106)

Emperor from 1061, founder of the Almoravid Empire. In 1068 he founded Marakesh as his capital. He invaded Spain in 1086 on appeal from the *taifa* ruler of Seville. He defeated Alfonso VI of Castile at Zalaka. In 1090 he took Granada and Málaga, in 1091 Córdoba and Seville, establishing a Spanish sector to his empire. Of the *taifas* only Zaragoza with aid from El Cid resisted successfully, while the Cid took Valencia which Yūsuf recovered after the Cid's death. Yūsuf died on 2 September and his son 'Alī succeeded.

ZANGI (ZENGI), IMAD AL-DIN, ATABEG OF MOSUL (1100–46)

Atabeg from 1127, under Alp Arslan, said to be the son of the captive Frankish Ida of Austria. His father was Aqsonqor emir of Aleppo. Zangi won control of much of northern Syria. In 1137 he besieged and took Montferrand from the Franks, in 1138 Homs. He failed to take Muslim Damascus in 1130, 1135 and 1139. He declared Holy War against the Franks, taking Edessa in 1144 and massacring the garrison – the kingdom of Jerusalem's first major loss.

The Caliph made Zangi King of Mosul in place of Alp Arslan. On campaign against Damascus he was murdered on 14 September by a Frankish eunuch he had rebuked for drinking wine. His son, Sayf ad-Din, succeeded in Mosul while another son, Nur ed-Din, held Aleppo. The dynasty survived until 1262.

ZENO THE ISAURIAN (TARASICODISSA), EASTERN EMPEROR (d.491)

Emperor from 474. He was employed by Leo I as a commander of Isaurian troops from Anatolia. He led the Excubitors, the imperial guard, the Army of Thrace, and later the Army of the east. He changed his name from Tarasicodissa Rousoumbladeotes to Zeno and married Leo's daughter Ariadne. Leo had no sons and, with Zeno, killed rivals for the throne, including Aspar. Zeno was co-emperor with his own son Leo II (grandson of Leo I) – aged seven and shortly to die. Zeno made peace with Gaiseric the Vandal. He fought off three coups. The Western Empire ended but Zeno maintained the Eastern Empire, persuading Theoderic and the Ostrogoths to move on and invade Italy. Zeno died in an epileptic fit on 9 April and was buried in Constantinople. A later tale had him buried alive, his calls from the tomb ignored.

ZOE CARBONOPSINA (BLACKEYES), BYZANTINE EMPRESS

Mistress of Leo VI, whom he married when she became pregnant. Her uncle was the Admiral Himerius. It was a fourth marriage for Leo, not normally allowed in Byzantium. Leo died in 912 and his brother Alexander banished Zoe. Alexander died in 913 and Zoe returned to replace Nicholas as regent for her son Constantine VII. She stopped the marriage between Constantine and the Bulgar Symeon's daughter, leading to an invasion of Byzantine territory. Zoe allied with the Pechenegs, encouraging them to attack the Bulgars but they were defeated at Anchialus in 917. The Byzantines defeated the invading Saracens near Tarsus and in Italy near Capua. In 920 Romanus Lecapenus put Zoe in a convent, where she was known as Sister Anna, and his daughter married Constantine.

ZOE PORPHYROGENITA, BYZANTINE EMPRESS (979–1050)

Empress from 1028, daughter of Constantine VIII. Constantine forced Romanus Argyrus to marry her before his death in 1028, when she was 50 and Romanus 61. She took Michael the Paphlagonian as a lover. Romanus III died in 1034, possibly killed by Zoe. Next day she married Michael, who became Michael IV but died in 1041. Zoe's adopted son became Michael V. In 1042 he forced her into a convent but popular protest led to the release of Zoe and her sister Theodora, enclosed in a convent for 15 years. They reigned together for three months. In 1042 Zoe married, her husband becoming Constantine IX. She was the more popular, and there was a revolt against him in 1044. Under Romanus III, George Maniakes emerged as a general, recovering the situation. Zoe takes some credit for his successes during the reigns of Romanus and the two Michaels that include defeating the Emir of Aleppo, capturing Edessa, taking towns in Sicily, and campaigning against the Bulgars.

PART II

Military events

Gallic warrior fleeing, temple frieze, terracotta,
2nd century BC Celtic, from Civitalba, Italy

1 | Romans and barbarians, 400–750

GENERALS AND LEADERS

See in Part I: Aegidius, Aëtius, Alaric, Alboin, Amalasuntha, Athaulf, Attila the Hun, Brunhild, Charles Martel, Childeric I, Chlothar I, Chlothar II, Clovis I, Dagobert I, Decius, Fredegund, Gaiseric, Gregory the Great, Gundobad, Guntram Boso, Leovigild, Merovech, Odoacer, Pepin I, Pepin II, Pepin III, Radbod, Reccared I, Rodrigo I, Romulus Augustulus, Stilicho, Syagrius, Theoderic I, Theoderic the Ostrogoth, Totila.

BATTLES AND SIEGES

Adda 490, Aquileia 452, Busta Gallorum 552, Cartagena 424, Carthage 695–8, Catalaunian Plains 451, Dorestad 695, Frigidius 394, Naissus 269, Orléans 451, 463, Pavia 476, 568–71, Pollentia 402, Ravenna 490–3, 537, 539–40, Rome 410, 455, 472, 537–8, 593, Soissons 486, 719, Tertry 687, Tolbiac 496, Tours (Poitiers) c.732, Transductine Promontories 711, Voulon 507.

OUTLINE OF EVENTS

There is debate over the nature, speed and effect of the collapse of the Western Roman Empire. The Eastern Empire continued, transforming itself into the Byzantine Empire. Before the losses of the west, the Eastern Empire had already become dominant with a new capital at Constantinople.

We are concerned with the course and impact of the barbarian invasions, and the degree of continuity of Roman military methods. The barbarians were large, tribal units, many nomadic – though now often seeking land to settle. We know little of their history from their own point of view as they were mostly non-literate. Information comes from their enemies.

Barbarian pressure was greatest on the river boundaries of the empire such as the Rhine and Danube, a pressure that was almost constant in the Middle Ages. In the early medieval period came the Huns, Franks and Visigoths; later the Mongols and Turks – among others.

Barbarian captives were employed within the empire, often militarily. By the 4th century many leading defenders were barbarians, such as the Vandal Stilicho. Many barbarians settled within the Roman world and became part of it.

The Romans had been threatened by barbarians from the 1st century AD, when they defeated the legions of Augustus. In the 3rd century the frontier began to collapse under Goth and German attack. The Goths killed the Emperor Decius in 251 but were beaten at Naissus in 269. A revived Empire delayed barbarian progress but in the 4th century a new advance began. The Visigoths defeated and killed the Emperor Valens at Adrianople, 378, and were given lands to settle.

The last Roman Emperor, Romulus Augustulus, was deposed in 476 by Roman forces under a barbarian commander, Odoacer, who went on to rule Italy. By then barbarians were well established in the west. The Roman Empire was divided into units under barbarian kings. Odoacer ruled Italy, the Visigoths southern Gaul and Spain, the Vandals Africa, the Anglo-Saxons Britain, and the Franks northern Gaul.

Gaul was invaded in 406, Spain in 411. The Goths separated into two groups: the Ostrogoths invaded Italy and established a kingdom under Theoderic at Ravenna by the 6th century; the Visigoths moved into Italy, sacking Rome in 410. They moved on west to Toulouse and then Spain. The Vandals came via Gaul to Spain, capturing Cartagena and an imperial fleet in 425. In 429 they crossed to North Africa. In 455 they sailed from Africa to the Tiber and sacked Rome.

In the 5th century the Huns under Attila attacked the empire. They were described as 'stunted, foul and puny . . . scarcely human', short and hairy with large noses and pinhole eyes. Attila employed Slavs and Germans. The Huns attacked the Balkans in 441, winning at Gallipoli in 447. Attila raided Greece, and then Gaul in 451. The Huns besieged Orléans but Attila was halted at the Catalaunian Plains in 451 by Aëtius. Attila withdrew to raid Italy, destroying Aquileia. On his death the Hun Empire disintegrated.

The Saxons, Alemans and Franks crossed the Rhine in the 3rd century. Many went on to the Low Countries and France. In the north other groups came from the Baltic. The Norse, Swedes and Danes moved into Scandinavia. The Angles, Saxons, Jutes and Frisians went on to Britain. A later arrival in the west were the Burgundians, tall and blond, greasing their hair with rancid butter. In general it was an enormous migration into western Europe.

The Franks, one of the major barbarian groups, moved to northern Gaul in two main groups – the Salians on the Yssel and the Ripuarians along the Rhine. Franks reached the lower Rhine by the 3rd century. The greatest early Frankish king was the Salian Clovis I, descended from Merovech, of whom we know little but who gave his name to the Merovingian dynasty. Merovech and his son, Childeric I, allied with the Romans and settled in Toxandria. Childeric fought under Aegidius against the Visigoths at Orléans in 463 and against the Saxons at Angers in 469. In 486 his son Clovis I took over the Seine valley, defeating the Romans under Syagrius at Soissons in 486. Clovis defeated the Ripuarians in 491 and by 511 was king of all the Franks with a capital at Soissons, later moved to Paris.

Clovis defeated the Alemans at Tolbiac (Zülpich) in 496, and the Thuringians, to take over the middle Rhine and the Main valley. He defeated Gundobad king of the Burgundians in 500, but failed to win control of their region. In 492 he married a Christian Burgundian princess, was baptised at Reims on Christmas Day 496 and became an orthodox Catholic Christian (as opposed to the Arian hereticism of most barbarians). In 507 he defeated the Visigoths at Voulon and won Aquitaine. He was then checked by the Ostrogoths under Theoderic. Clovis claimed authority over most of what would become the kingdom of France. The first great Church Council in Francia was held under him in 511.

Clovis died in 511 when the kingdom was divided between his four sons. Chlothar survived his brothers to reunite his father's kingdom. On Chlothar's death came another four-fold division. Under the later Merovingians followed a long civil war with succession disputes and political murders. Francia re-formed in two regions – Austrasia in the east and Neustria to the west. Below the king, mayors of the palace became powerful.

Some late Merovingian kings, notably Chlothar II and Dagobert I, were more significant than once thought. Charles Martel, one of the mayors, earned a great military reputation. During an interregnum he ruled virtually as king, crushing rebellion in Francia and defeating the Muslims near Tours. His son Pepin III deposed Childeric, the last Merovingian, in 751. He was crowned in 754. He aided the papacy against the Lombards in Italy.

The Huns were nomadic Turks from the Asian steppes. The Romans used them against Germanic tribes. The Huns defeated the Goths and established a kingdom in Hungary. In 441, after a dispute, the Huns defeated Roman forces sent against them. Then Attila led his people west until checked at Châlons by Aëtius. Attila then invaded Italy, destroying Aquileia. He died in 453.

A series of tribes attacked Italy, including the Vandals. In 476 the last Roman emperor was deposed and Odoacer the Rugian took the title King of Italy. Theoderic the Ostrogoth, with backing from the Byzantines, invaded Italy against Odoacer in 489. They came to an agreement in 493 but Theoderic had Odoacer killed. An Ostrogothic kingdom was set up around Ravenna. Theoderic temporarily established authority over the Visigoths in Spain. Under Justinian, the Byzantines sought to re-establish Roman control in Italy and the west. Italy was invaded in 535 and the Gothic Wars followed. The Ostrogoths besieged Belisarius in Rome in 537–8, but Totila was killed and by 553 the Byzantines had conquered Italy.

The Lombards came to Italy via Hungary and the Elbe. They allied with the Byzantines. Under Alboin they established the kingdom of Lombardy based on Pavia from 568. The Byzantines recognised Lombardy in 680 and it endured to 774. The Lombards also established semi-independent duchies at Spoleto and Benevento. The Lombards became Catholic in the 7th century under Aribert I. The Byzantines retained power at Ravenna and in parts of central and southern Italy. The kingdom of Lombardy was destroyed by the Franks.

The Vandals appeared in the Baltic in the 1st century and took over Pannonia in the

4th. They crossed the Rhine into Gaul. With the Alans and the Suevi, they reached Spain in the 5th century. They captured a Roman fleet and attacked the Balearic Islands. In southern Spain the Vandals gave their name to Andalusia. In 428 under Gaiseric they crossed to North Africa, captured Carthage in 439 and established a kingdom. From there Gaiseric raided Sicily, Sardinia and Corsica. He sacked Rome in 455, removing half the bronze roof of the temple of Capitoline Jove. The Vandals threatened Greece and the eastern Mediterranean but met problems from the Moors. The Byzantines reconquered North Africa in the 6th century.

The Visigoths were forced west by the Huns, entering Roman territories in the 4th century and defeating Valens at Adrianople. They invaded Italy under Alaric, attacking Rome in 410. After Alaric's death, his brother-in-law Athaulf led the Visigoths to Gaul and Spain. In Spain the Romans employed them against the Vandals and the Alans. They returned to Gaul to settle in Aquitaine from 418. The Visigoths were the first barbarians officially settled in Gaul. Under Theoderic II they invaded Spain in 456, taking most of the Iberian Peninsula by 480, though disputes and civil wars caused division. From 551 the Byzantines invaded. Leovigild reinforced control over northern Spain and won victories over the Byzantines.

The Visigoths founded kingdoms in Gaul and Iberia. They were at their most powerful in the 6th century. Leovigild established a kingdom centred on Toledo. His son Reccared became Catholic and the region followed. In the 8th century Visigothic rule crumbled before Muslim invasion from Africa. In 711 King Rodrigo was defeated and killed at the Transductine Promontories. The Arabs took over Toledo and the kingdom.

The emergence and expansion of Islam altered the political framework of the Middle East, North Africa and parts of western Europe. Roman Africa was conquered, Egypt fell, and Carthage was taken in 695. In 711 the Muslims invaded Spain, destroying the Visgothic kingdom by 720. They moved north into Gaul until the Franks checked their advance. Islam became a major Mediterranean naval power. In 750 the Umayyad dynasty was overthrown and replaced by the Abbasids. The Islamic Empire fragmented, the Umayyads surviving in Spain while North Africa fell to the Aghlabids.

BATTLES AND SIEGES

ADDA, BATTLE OF, 11 AUGUST 490
Fought by the river in northern Italy, establishing Ostrogothic power in Italy. After defeat at Faenza, Theoderic and the Ostrogoths retreated to Pavia, which Odoacer besieged. He had to send some troops to deal with invasion by Visigoths and Burgundians. Theoderic then sortied. Odoacer was beaten and retreated to Ravenna.

AQUILEIA, SIEGE OF, 452
Destroyed by Attila the Hun during the invasion of Italy. Aquileia, the largest and richest Roman city in the region, at the northern end of the Adriatic, resisted and was besieged. The Huns used a range of siege weapons. The siege lasted three months and absorbed Hun efforts in Italy. Attila saw a stork flying away and claimed that it was deserting the doomed city. The Huns broke in and sacked Aquileia, which did not recover for decades. Attila died within the year and the Hun threat to the west evaporated.

BUSTA GALLORUM (TAGINAE/TADINAE), BATTLE OF, 552
Byzantine victory over the Goths, giving control of Rome. The site is known also as

Taginae or Tadinae, a valley in the Apennines near Gubbio. The site is on a small plain. The Byzantines used archers, infantry and cavalry. The larger Byzantine army was commanded by Narses for Justinian I and included barbarian Huns and Lombards. Narses outmanoeuvred the Goths, defending the mountain pass by taking an alternative route. The Goths under Totila sought to occupy a hill on the enemy flank but were prevented by Byzantine infantry. Narses formed his army in a crescent, with archers and cavalry on the wings. Totila tried to break through the centre with a cavalry charge, but was foiled by archery. Several charges failed and Narses counter-attacked from the flank. The Goths were broken and Totila killed.

CARTAGENA, SIEGE OF, 424

Taken by the Vandals in Spain under Gunderic, signalling the establishment of their power. The Romans under Castinus tried to halt their advance but were defeated and fled to Tarragona, leaving Cartagena open. Gunderic captured a fleet in the harbour, making possible the invasion of the Balearics and the attack on North Africa.

CARTHAGE, SIEGE OF, 695–8

Taken by the Arabs during their invasion of North Africa. Carthage is in modern Tunisia, near Tunis, the ancient port of the Phoenicians and the Romans, according to Salvian the sink for vices from every country. It became the Vandal base from 438. Carthage was captured by Belisarius for the Byzantines in 534. The city had declined by the late 7th century, but resisted the Arabs for three years. It was destroyed and never recovered, later replaced by Tunis.

CATALAUNIAN PLAINS (CHÂLONS), BATTLE OF, 451

Checking Attila the Hun's advance into Gaul, probably near Châlons-sur-Marne in eastern France, often called the Battle of Châlons. The Romans were probably under Aëtius but included Burgundians, Franks and especially Visigoths. Previously Aëtius had allied with the Huns. Attila crossed the Rhine in 451, sacking Metz and advancing to Orléans. The Alans broke a promise to assist him and he retreated. Soothsayers forecast that Attila would win but would be killed. The battle was probably fought on a flat plain with large forces on both sides. There was a hill to the Roman right, which they held after a struggle. Theoderic I, King of the Visigoths, was killed by an Ostrogoth javelin. A charge from the hill decided the battle. Attila prepared for himself a funeral pyre of wooden saddles. It was growing dark and the Huns retreated without pursuit to move on to Italy.

DORESTAD, BATTLE OF, 695

Victory of Pepin II over the Frisians under Duke Radbod. Dorestad was on the old course of the Rhine, south of Utrecht, a major port in Frisia on the Frankish border. The victory increased Frankish control over Frisia and aided the spread of Christianity.

FRIGIDIUS, BATTLE OF THE RIVER, 5 SEPTEMBER 394

Victory for Emperor Theodosius I over Emperor Eugenius at an unidentified site, which reunited the Eastern and Western Roman Empires temporarily. Eugenius' force included the commanders Nicomachus Flavianus and the Frank Arbogast, while Theodosius' had the Vandal Stilicho and the Goth Alaric. Theodosius was encouraged by a vision of the mounted saints, John and Philip. Before the battle he prayed from a cliff top, making the sign of the cross. Arbogast tried to block the route from the Alps to Aquileia and the battle was fought north of the city. Theodosius, whose force consisted largely of Goths, attacked but received heavy casualties. Next day Theodosius renewed his attack. The battle was decided by the sudden gusting of the Bora, a wind that blew in the faces of Arbogast's men. Flavianus and Arbogast committed suicide. Eugenius was captured and beheaded. When Theodosius died the empire was divided again east and west between his sons Arcadius and Honorius.

NAISSUS, BATTLE OF, 269

Victory over the Goths by the Romans, a setback for barbarian advance into the empire, fought at modern Niš in Serbia. The Emperor Claudius II defeated Goths returning from sea raids around the Mediterranean. The battle was close, but a hidden reserve saved the day. Claudius was afterwards known as 'Gothicus'.

ORLÉANS, BATTLES OF, 451, 463

Attila the Hun besieged the recently re-fortified Orléans during his raid into Gaul in 451 but failed to take it despite using battering rams. Its bishop, Ananius, played a prominent role in the defence. It was here in 463 that Aegidius, recent victor over the Saxons at Angers, defeated the invading Visigoths under Theoderic II's brother Euric. Aegidius' army included Franks under Childeric the Merovingian. Aegidius was killed by poison the following year.

PAVIA, SIEGES OF, 476, 568–71

The key city during the Lombard invasion, an important stronghold. It was besieged and taken by Odoacer in 476, leading to the deposition of Romulus Augustulus. The Lombards besieged Pavia from 568 when led to Italy by Alboin. After three years the city fell and became the Lombard capital as they dominated northern Italy, with duchies at Friuli, Spoleto and Benevento.

POLLENTIA, BATTLE OF, 6 APRIL 402

Defeat on Easter Day of Alaric I, King of the Visigoths, by Stilicho. Alaric moved into Italy in 401, a migration rather than an invasion, accompanied by many non-combatants. Alaric camped near Pollentia (Piacenza), which the Romans attacked. Stilicho's Roman force included Alans and Vandals. Stilicho sent his Alans on a cavalry attack, which was held – the Alan leader being killed. The Romans did not break, and their infantry advance won the battle. The Visigoth camp was taken and

Alaric's wife was captured. Alaric escaped and Pollentia was not decisive. He was defeated at Verona and agreed to leave Italy, returning to make a peace with Stilicho that lasted until the latter's death.

RAVENNA, SIEGES OF, 490–3, 537, 539–40

Ravenna's significance as an early medieval stronghold in northern Italy is reflected in the frequency of the sieges. Classis, Ravenna's port, controlled a major harbour on the Adriatic. Ravenna was difficult to take, surrounded by water and marsh. In 490 Odoacer sought refuge here after Adda and was besieged by Theoderic the Great, King of the Ostrogoths. They agreed terms in 493. Theoderic was allowed into the city and murdered his rival. Ravenna became his capital. It was besieged in 537, when the Byzantines under Belisarius were shut in by Witiges. In 539 the position was reversed and Witiges was besieged. Witiges executed all the captive Roman senators because he distrusted them. He made terms and surrendered in 540. Magnificent buildings and works of art survive from the period of Byzantine control, when an independent exarchate was established. The Byzantines held on for many years against the Lombards.

ROME, SIEGES OF, 410, 455, 472, 537–8, 593

Rome was a city over which control was always sought. It was a target for the barbarians – sacked in 386 by the Gallic Senones, and by the Visigoths under Alaric in August 410 after a two-year blockade, during which many starved and a stench arose from unburied corpses. Alaric was provoked by broken promises. When taken, there were killings but the monuments were generally respected. The act was a vital point in the collapse of the Western Empire. The Vandals under Gaiseric captured Rome in 455. During a 14-day occupation the damage done was less than often presented, though the plunder was considerable. Gaiseric led his force from North Africa in response to an appeal from Eudoxia, widow of Valentinian III who had been forced into a marriage with her husband's killer, Petronius Maximus. Petronius was killed by a citizen heaving a brick at him. Ricimer besieged Rome in 472, during a civil war against the Emperor Anthemius. Ricimer broke in after three months. Anthemius was captured taking refuge in a church and beheaded. Rome was also a major prize in the fight between Ostrogoths and Byzantines in the 6th century. Belisarius took the city in 536 and was then besieged within it by Witiges in 537–8. There were skirmishes outside the walls, when wooden towers on wheels were used, but the Byzantines held out and the Goths departed. The Goths tried again in 545. Belisarius returned but failed to relieve his troops, who surrendered. The Byzantines recaptured Rome in 546, the Goths in 549, and the Byzantines in 553 through Narses. In 593 the Lombards under Agilulf besieged Rome but came to agreement with Pope Gregory the Great. Eventually the Carolingian Franks guaranteed Rome's independence of the Lombards.

SOISSONS, BATTLES OF, 486, 719
The key battle for Clovis I, King of the Salian Franks, in his rise to power. He attacked and defeated the Roman Syagrius. Syagrius and his predecessors ruled a Roman enclave, sometimes called a kingdom, based on Soissons in the region of Belgica Secunda. It was a major centre, producing coins and arms. Soissons became Clovis' early capital. His formal challenge to Syagrius was accepted. The victory gave Clovis control of the Seine valley. It was the end of independent Roman political units in Gaul. Syagrius escaped to Toulouse but was handed to Clovis who had him killed. Soissons was also the site of a victory for Charles Martel in 719, when he defeated the Neustrians and Aquitainians to reunite Francia.

TERTRY, BATTLE OF, 687
Victory by Pepin II of Heristal over the Neustrians under Berchar and Theuderic III King of Francia. Pepin was mayor of the palace of Austrasia, and Berchar of Neustria. Pepin had made demands which Berchar refused. Pepin invaded Neustria. At Tertry, near St-Quentin, the negotiations broke down. A year after the battle Berchar's mother-in-law had him murdered. Berchar's widow, Adaltrude, married Pepin's son, Drogo. Pepin appointed the mayor in Neustria and ruled both regions in the king's name. The two regions were united, paving the way for the rise of Pepin's descendants, the Carolingians.

TOLBIAC (ZÜLPICH), 496
Victory by Clovis I and the Franks against the Alemans to give control over the upper Rhine. Zülpich (the German form of the name) otherwise known as Tolbiac (the *civitas Tulbiacensis*) was a fortress in Austrasia south of Köln. Some historians have thought the correct date should be 506, when the Alemans moved on into Ostrogothic territory. Others have suggested that Clovis may not have fought at Tolbiac. The traditional version still seems the likeliest. Clovis spent ten years fighting the Alemans and this was the climax of his efforts. The battle went badly for Clovis until he called upon the God of his Roman Catholic wife from Burgundy, Clothilde, after which he went on to victory. Sigebert King of the Ripuarian Franks, who fought alongside Clovis, was wounded in the knee. The King of the Alemans was killed. On the following Christmas Day Clovis and 3,000 of his men were baptised at Reims.

TOURS (POITIERS), OCTOBER c.732
Victory by Charles Martel over the Islamic forces invading Francia. The battle was fought between Tours and Poitiers and is sometimes named after one, sometimes the other but most often Tours (though probably fought nearer to Poitiers). The traditional date is 732, but some historians believe 733 or 734 to be correct. The Muslims conquered Visigothic Spain and threatened Francia, capturing Nîmes and Septimania. Under Abd al-Rahman ibn

Gafiqi they defeated the Aquitainians near Bordeaux. Aquitaine under Duke Eudo allied with Martel to halt the advance. The Muslims retreated from Tours and were caught approaching Poitiers. The Franks stood like a wall, their infantry holding Muslim attacks. Abd al-Rahman was killed and his army broke and fled. The sources differ over whether or not there was a pursuit. The effect halted the Islamic threat to Francia and extended Martel's authority in the south. This battle was once seen as the critical moment for turning to the stirrup and cavalry, a view no longer held.

TRANSDUCTINE PROMONTORIES, BATTLE OF THE (GUADALETE), 19 JULY 711

King Rodrigo I was defeated and killed in this battle which brought the downfall of Visigothic Spain. Rodrigo had been king only a year and faced internal problems. Muslims from North Africa under Tariq ibn Ziyad invaded Spain in 711. Tariq had Berbers, Arab cavalry and aid from Byzantium and dissident Visigoths. It was probably fought on the River Guadalete near Medina Sidonia. During the battle, discontented Visigoths deserted Rodrigo whose fate is uncertain. He may have been killed during or after the battle or he may have survived. He played no further part in the history of Iberia. The Arabs took Toledo and the kingdom.

VOULON (CAMPUS VOGLADENSIS), BATTLE OF, 507

Victory by Clovis I and the Franks against Visigoths under Alaric II. Voulon, near Poitiers, is probably the correct site rather than Vouillé, which is usually named. Gregory of Tours says it was fought at the tenth milestone outside Poitiers. The Visigoths held Toulouse and land north to the Loire. The Burgundians allied with Clovis against them. Chloderic, son of Sigebert the Lame King of the Ripuarian Franks, was in Clovis' army. Clovis posed as the champion of Roman Catholicism against the Arian Alaric, ordering his troops not to damage Church lands and to take only water and grass for their horses. Clovis killed with his sword a man who ignored his order. Clovis had difficulty crossing the River Vienne, but caught the Visigoths near Poitiers. Javelins were used in the fighting, both sides closing. Alaric was killed, possibly by Clovis in person. Clovis had a close escape when attacked by spearmen but was saved by his leather armour and the speed of his horse. The victory gave Clovis control over Aquitaine and most of southern Gaul to the Pyrenees, a step in the formation of France. Theoderic the Ostrogoth kept Septimania (between the Rhône and the Pyrenees) and denied Clovis access to the Mediterranean.

Carolingian sieges

2 | Charlemagne and the Carolingians, 750–850

GENERALS AND LEADERS

See in Part I: Aistulf, Carloman uncle of Charlemagne, Carloman brother of Charlemagne, Carloman/Pepin son of Charlemagne, Charlemagne, Charles the Bald, Desiderius, Fulk Nerra, Hunald II, Louis the Pious, Nominoë, Pepin II of Aquitaine, Pepin the Short, Roland (Hruodland), Suleiman al-Arabi, Tassilo III, Waiofar, Widukind.

BATTLES AND SIEGES

Andernach 876, Angoulême 844, Ballon 845, Barcelona 800–1, Conquereuil 992, Fontenoy 841, Jengland 851, Pavia, 755, 756, 773–4, Pontlevoy 1016, Roncesvalles 778, Süntel Mountains 782, Valley of Susa 755, Tortosa 811, Verden 782, Zaragoza 778.

OUTLINE OF EVENTS

Merovingian rule in Francia was dogged by the tradition of dividing lands between sons, with resulting civil wars. After the death of Clovis I in 511 Francia was not reunited until 558, by which time his son Lothar was 70. The situation was repeated on the death of Lothar in 561, with wars between his sons. Eventually unity returned with Lothar II in 613.

Another factor for instability was the development of the semi-independent principalities of Neustria, Austrasia, Burgundy and Aquitaine. Neustria was in the north-west and included Paris; Austrasia was in the north-east. In the later Merovingian period mayors of the palace were appointed to govern the regions. Although the mayors were subject to Merovingian kings, they often rivalled them in power.

Late Merovingian rulers were called *rois fainéants* (idle kings), supposedly left to 'enjoy their mistresses, their meat and their wine' while others ruled. Historians believe this has been exaggerated and that some were able and important. Nevertheless the mayors became increasingly powerful. Their families established dynasties, one of which eventually took the throne – that of Pepin I of Landen. Pepin's rise began as mayor of Austrasia. Pepin II continued the rivalry with Neustria, triumphing at Tertry.

Pepin II's son, Charles Martel, defended Francia against the Muslims in the south, winning at Tours in 732. He also campaigned against the Alemans and the Frisians. In 738 he made the eastern frontier more secure by defeating the Saxons, from whom he demanded tribute. Missionary work was encouraged in this pagan region.

The Carolingians continued to divide the inheritance between sons, but there were fewer sons and shorter periods of conflict. Carloman and Pepin III the Short, the sons of Martel, shared rule for a time. Merovingian kingship was revived briefly. Carloman entered a monastery and Pepin III finally ended Merovingian rule by deposing Childeric III. Pepin took the crown and initiated the Carolingian dynasty, supported by the papacy. Pepin the Short was crowned as Pepin I King of the Franks by Bishop Boniface in 751 and by Pope Stephen III in 754. In return Pepin attacked the Lombards who threatened the papacy in Italy, twice defeating Aistulf.

Charlemagne (Charles the Great) was the son of Pepin the Short and Bertrada his concubine (whom he married later). Despite Christianity the Frankish rulers lived polygamously. Charlemagne's military education began early and he commanded for his father. He and his younger brother Carloman campaigned in Aquitaine, when Carloman turned back and Charles went on to defeat the rebels under Hunald. On the death of Pepin the Short in 768 his sons shared rule until Carloman entered a monastery to die in 771, leaving Charles as sole ruler.

The Vikings threatened Francia. Charlemagne developed defences against them, building ships for the 'rivers which flow out of Gaul and Germany into the North Sea' plus forts and coastguard stations 'at all the ports and at the mouths of all rivers considered large enough for the entry of ships'. He prepared coastal defences on the Mediterranean against the Saracens.

A threat to internal stability came from Charlemagne's sons. The eldest, Pepin the Hunchback, was the offspring of a concubine. His nickname suggests some physical deformity, which may explain why he was overlooked and sought revenge against his father. Fardulf, a Lombard poet at court, revealed the plot. Fardulf found the king with his women, who burst out laughing at the sight of him, stuffing their dresses in their mouths and hiding in the corners of the room. There was an odd similarity between reward and punishment. Pepin was sent into a monastery while Fardulf was made an abbot. Charlemagne's younger son Carloman was renamed Pepin to become the heir.

As arranged by his mother, Charles married the daughter of Desiderius King of the Lombards. The papacy looked to Francia for aid and feared an alliance between the two kingdoms. Charles had no enthusiasm for the marriage and little for the peace. The betrothal was broken off after a year. The papacy appealed for help against the Lombards when Charles was involved in Saxony. The Frankish assembly voted for an

Italian expedition and Charles went in 774. The Lombards were defeated and Charles entered Rome as King of the Franks and Lombards. In response to papal appeals he made further expeditions against the Lombards. In 780 he declared his son Carloman (now Pepin) King of the Lombards. When Pepin died, Pepin's son Bernard replaced him. Charlemagne was rewarded by the pope on Christmas Day 800 in Rome when declared 'Charles Augustus, crowned by God, the great and pacific Emperor of the Romans'. His territories had become the Holy Roman Empire.

Charlemagne's greatest problem outside Francia came from the Saxons, who threatened the north-eastern frontier. War against them lasted over 30 years, involving 18 expeditions. 'Never was there a war known to last so long, nor one that demanded such efforts on the part of the Franks.' A Saxon attack on a Christian mission was the excuse to open the war in 772, with support from the Frankish assembly. The Franks would fight the Saxons 'until they were conquered and converted or totally annihilated'. The Saxons were in three groups – Westphalians, Eastphalians and Angrians – with no overall king. They elected a war leader, Widukind. He allied with the Danes, to whom he was related by marriage. Charles destroyed the revered Saxon idol, the Irminsul, a carved column.

Charlemagne had setbacks. In 782 a Frankish army led by his officials was defeated. Charles took revenge at Verden, executing 4,500 Saxons. Widukind escaped by reversing the horseshoes of his mount to fool pursuers. The atrocity of Verden united the Saxons against Charlemagne but Widukind was persuaded to convert to Christianity. The Frankish laws of 785 provoked rebellion in Nordalbingia, and 'like a dog that returns to its vomit they returned to the paganism they had once thrown up'. Charles defeated them and deported every third Saxon from the north to Gaul and Germany. Charles also had success against the nomad Avars, some of whom were baptised – though Einhard commented: 'what use is baptism without faith?'

Charles sought control of Bavaria under his cousin Tassilo, from whom he demanded an oath of allegiance. Tassilo refused a summons from Charles, who invaded. Tassilo was defeated and surrendered Bavaria. Charles returned it to him as a subordinate. Relations remained difficult and Tassilo plotted against Charles. At the assembly in Ingelheim Tassilo was arrested and threw himself on Charles' mercy, renouncing his rights to Bavaria and entering a monastery.

Charlemagne's efforts in Iberia were less effective. The Muslims had broken from eastern Islam and were under the Umayyads, who had been overthrown elsewhere. There were divisions between the Muslims, and the Abbasid ruler Suleiman appealed for aid to Charlemagne's father Pepin. Charles undertook the expedition and temporarily gained Barcelona. His army was defeated during its return from Spain in 778, when the rearguard was ambushed at Roncesvalles in the Pyrenees by the Gascons. Hruodland (Roland), warden of the Breton Frontier, was killed. Charles established some control south of the Pyrenees over the Spanish March, vital in the later *Reconquista*.

Charlemagne's succession plans favoured his sons by Hildegard. Charlemagne had four wives and probably many mistresses. Einhard remarked on a daughter 'by a concubine whose name I cannot remember'. His many children included several illegitimate sons. Hildegard, 'a woman of most noble family from the Swabian race' (probably his third wife), married Charles when she was 13. She provided Charlemagne with four sons – including Carloman (renamed Pepin), Louis and Charles, his chief heirs. By the 806 Division of the Realm, Louis was to have the south (Aquitaine, the Spanish March and southern Burgundy), Pepin the east (Lombardy, Bavaria and eastern Germany), while the younger Charles would have the western territories including northern France. These plans were foiled through deaths, and by 813 only Louis the Pious survived to inherit the empire in 814.

Louis the Pious ruled from 814 to 840. His sons quarrelled during his lifetime. By a division of 840 Louis planned like his father to divide the empire between three sons. After his death a new division was agreed at Verdun, 843 – the west to Charles the Bald, the east to Louis the German, and the centre to Lothar. The eastern and western divisions, deriving from Austrasia and Neustria, were the origins of France and Germany.

BATTLES AND SIEGES

ANDERNACH, BATTLE OF, 8 OCTOBER 876
Defeat of Charles the Bald by his nephew, Louis the Younger, son of Louis the German. Louis the German, Charles' brother, died in August 876. Charles wanted to inherit but was opposed by Louis the Younger, who held Saxony and Franconia. At Deutz Charles threatened Louis across the Rhine so Louis crossed the river and camped on Andernach, a Rhine island between Koblenz and Köln. Charles attempted surprise but failed. Louis donned armour and ordered his men to wear white for recognition. They awaited Charles, whose cavalry was slowed by rain. The spurs of Charles' men 'scored and gashed the flanks of the horses' but failed to speed them through the mud. The East Franks on the wings of Louis' army performed well. Charles' standard-bearers were killed and his army broke and fled. Many were trapped, with the abandoned baggage train blocking their way. Louis captured four counts plus treasure and equipment. Local peasants seized spoils, including clothes. Charles escaped though 'almost naked'.

ANGOULÊME, BATTLE OF, 7 JUNE 844
Defeat for men of Charles the Bald. He undertook an expedition against Pepin II of Aquitaine in 844. He besieged Toulouse but failed to take it, though capturing and beheading Bernard of Septimania. Reinforcements for Charles were ambushed at Angoulême by William, son of Bernard of Septimania. The leaders were killed and the troops, who had begun to desert before the battle, were captured or allowed to go home. The historian Nithard, Charlemagne's illegitimate son Hugh and the standard-bearer Hrabanus were among the dead. Nithard's skull, found at St-Riquier in 1989, bears the sword mark that killed him. By agreement in 845 the Angoumois went to Pepin.

BALLON, BATTLE OF, 22 NOVEMBER 845
Defeat of Charles the Bald by the Bretons under Nominoë, Louis the Pious' *missus dominicus*. A Breton dispute led Charles to intervene with a small force. It was a 'rash attack'. Some of his men deserted. In marshy country at Ballon, north of Redon, Charles was beaten and retreated to Le Mans, barely escaping. Nominoë's victory ensured Brittany's independence of the Frankish king, later recognised by treaty. Charles was acknowledged as overlord and Nominoë as *dux* in Brittany.

BARCELONA, SIEGE OF, 800–1
Captured from the Muslims by Louis the Pious for his father Charlemagne. Louis besieged Barcelona, building earthworks to protect his troops. Barcelona was the main port on the northern Catalan coast. A Frankish archer shot a Moor who was insulting them from a tower. Louis hurled a javelin with such force that it stuck in the

city wall. Part of Louis' army stayed throughout the winter. The garrison ran short of provisions and surrendered on 4 April 801. Louis was not present but arrived for a triumphal entry. It was a satisfying revenge for Roncesvalles. Barcelona became the base of a Spanish March that lasted two centuries. Count Bera, a Goth, was placed in control.

CONQUEREUX, BATTLE OF, 27 JUNE 992
Fulk Nerra of Anjou defeated Conan I of Brittany. Fulk besieged Nantes, whose citizens resisted – throwing missiles. After three weeks the town surrendered but the castle held out. The Bretons dug trenches in front of their lines as a trap, into which the Angevins fell. They retreated. In the fighting Conan was killed and his army broke. Fulk, though thrown from his horse, recovered to rally his men like 'the force of a gale sweeping through corn'. The castle then surrendered.

FONTENOY, BATTLE OF, 25 JUNE 841
Defeat of Lothar and Pepin II of Aquitaine by Lothar's brothers Charles the Bald and Louis the German. Lothar succeeded Louis the Pious in 840. The brothers combined against Lothar, who sought 'supreme rule' by preventing their inheritance. Charles crossed the Seine while Louis defeated the Duke of Austria. They joined forces near Auxerre. The brothers claimed to be seeking the judgement of God by battle. They met at Fontenoy-en-Puisaye near Auxerre on a Saturday. The brothers advanced at dawn, occupying a hill over Lothar's camp. It was a large-scale battle in which many were killed. The poet Angilbert wished that 'neither dew nor rain nor shower should moisten that meadow where men most skilled in war did fall'. The fields were white with the linen of the dead. One annalist wrote 'no one can recall a greater loss among the Frankish people in the present age'. Lothar's men fled over a brook and Lothar escaped to Aachen. The brothers celebrated mass on the field. It was claimed they did not pursue from Christian

mercy. A three-day fast was imposed on all the participants. Fontenoy was not decisive and the struggle continued. Later, not entirely accurately, the battle was said to have established the division between France and Germany.

JENGLAND, BATTLE OF, 22 AUGUST 851
Defeat of Charles the Bald in Brittany. Nominoë, the Breton ruler, died in March 851 and Charles invaded Brittany. His force included Saxon infantry. He was met by Nominoë's son Erispoë by the River Vilaine near Redon. Charles was defeated. Among the dead were Hilmerad count of the palace and Count Vivian the chamberlain. Charles tried to retreat, in cowardly fashion according to the Bretons. Charles' rearguard was attacked. Afterwards he recognised Erispoë in Rennes and Nantes, in return for homage.

PAVIA, SIEGES OF, 755, 756, 773–4
After the Lombards were defeated at Susa in 755, the Franks besieged Pavia, the Lombard capital in which King Aistulf took refuge. He agreed terms while Pavia was holding out but broke his promises within the year. Pepin III, with Tassilo of Bavaria, returned in 756 and Aistulf surrendered, dying shortly afterwards in a hunting accident. King Desiderius took refuge there when Charlemagne invaded Lombardy in 773. Charles and his men (Charles went to Rome during the siege for a time) besieged Pavia in 773–4, building a temporary camp and a chapel. When Charlemagne arrived, the sun gleamed from his weapons. Charles' wife Hildegard joined him at Pavia, and their daughter Adalhaid was born there. The blockade, made more acute by plague, succeeded. Desiderius surrendered in June and Charlemagne became King of the Lombards.

PONTLEVOY, BATTLE OF, 6 JULY 1016
Victory of Fulk Nerra count of Anjou. In the summer Odo II count of Blois attacked Montrichard. Fulk allied with Herbert Wakedog count of Maine. They blocked

separate approaches, Fulk in the woods near Pontlevoy, Herbert at Bourré. Odo chose Fulk's approach and was getting the upper hand. Fulk was unhorsed and knocked unconscious. News reached Herbert who came to the rescue, charging Odo's left. Odo's army broke. The cavalry fled, leaving the infantry to be slaughtered. Odo's baggage was captured and the victors returned to Amboise. The victory secured Fulk's eastern border, giving him the advantage over Blois.

RONCESVALLES, BATTLE OF, 778
Subject of the *Song of Roland*, when Roland was killed. Charlemagne undertook a Spanish expedition in 778 but withdrew. During the return his rearguard was attacked at Roncesvalles in the Pyrenees by Basques or Gascons. The rearguard was wiped out and a number of court officials were killed, including seneschal Eggihard, Anselm count of the palace and Roland warden of the Breton March.

SÜNTEL MOUNTAINS (SÜNTELGEBIRGE), BATTLE OF, 782
Defeat of Charlemagne's army commanded by royal officials. In 782 the Franks entered Saxony under Adalgis the chamberlain, Worad count of the palace and Geilo the marshal. They aimed to attack Slavonic Sorbs in Thuringia but met with rebel Saxons. Men sent by Charlemagne under Count Theodoric reinforced the Franks near the River Weser, moving to the foot of the Süntel Mountains. The Saxons, probably under Widukind, took a defensive position on the slopes. The Franks ignorerd orders and attacked without waiting for Theodoric, to deny him a share in the glory. Adalgis and Geilo were killed, plus four counts and 20 nobles. Charlemagne took revenge at Verden.

VALLEY OF SUSA, BATTLE OF, 755
A step in the Frankish conquest of Lombardy. Pepin the Short, responding to papal request, invaded Lombardy against King Aistulf. Pepin's vanguard held the entrance to the Mont Cenis Pass through the Alps in the Susa valley. Aistulf confronted them and was defeated, escaping by sliding down a rocky slope. Pepin only arrived when the Lombards were already beaten. Aistulf took refuge in Pavia and agreed terms.

TORTOSA, SIEGE OF, 811
The key event in establishing the Carolingian Spanish March. After Roncesvalles the Franks tried to establish control south of the Pyrenees. Charlemagne's son Louis the Pious took Barcelona in 801. In 806 Pamplona and Navarre surrendered. Tortosa at the mouth of the Ebro was the main surviving stronghold, withstanding sieges in 809 and 810. In 811 Louis besieged Tortosa again, employing rams, balistas and mantlets. After 40 days Tortosa surrendered its keys, which Louis delivered to Charlemagne. The Spanish March was established, including Catalonia, with Barcelona as the capital.

VERDEN, MASSACRE OF, 782
Verden was neither a siege nor a battle, though some modern works of history treat it as a battle. It was Charlemagne's response to the massacre at the Süntel Mountains. Charlemagne summoned the Saxon nobles to Verden, at the confluence of the rivers Aller and Weser, demanding they hand over Widukind. They could not, but 4,500 Saxons, who had taken part in the recent battle, were handed over and beheaded in cold blood. Some historians, unwilling to accept Charlemagne's guilt for an atrocity, suggest the annalist meant 'deported' rather than 'decapitated', but we prefer the text as it stands. The Carolingian annalist saw the rebellion, rather than the executions ordered 'in vengeance', as the 'outrage'. Widukind escaped and the atrocity steeled him to fight on.

ZARAGOZA, SIEGE OF, 778
The failure to take Zaragoza in 778 preceded the return to Francia and Roncesvalles. In 777 the Governor of

Barcelona, Suleiman ibn al-Arabi, sought aid from Charlemagne against Córdoba. Suleiman became Emir of Zaragoza. Christians in Zaragoza welcomed the Frankish alliance. Charles intervened and the Franks later established the Spanish March south to the Ebro though this particular attempt failed. The Frankish armies joined forces at Zaragoza. Charles' allies were overthrown inside Zaragoza, which resisted – as did Barcelona. Charlemagne took Suleiman to Francia with him, possibly as a hostage. A Saxon rebellion required Charlemagne's presence in the north. The approach of a hostile Umayyad force led to Frankish retreat. Charlemagne razed Pamplona during the return, before the disaster at Roncesvalles.

The death of St Ólaf at the Battle of Stiklestad, Flateyjarbok

3 | The Vikings, Scandinavia and northern Europe, 850–1050

GENERALS AND LEADERS

See in Part I: Cnut the Great, Erik Haroldsson (Bloodaxe), Erik Torvaldsson (the Red), Eystein Ólafsson (Fart), Godfred of Denmark, Gorm the Old of Denmark, Guthrum, Hákon of Orkney, Harold Gormsson (Bluetooth), Harold Hálfdansson (Fairhair), Harold III Sigurdsson (Hardrada), Ivar Yngvarr (the Boneless), Magnús I Ólafsson (the Good), Ólaf I Tryggvason, Ólaf II Haroldsson (St Ólaf), Ragnar Hairy-Breeches, Rögnvald of Møre, Rollo of Normandy, Rurik, Sigtrygg Silk-Beard, Sweyn I Forkbeard, Sweyn II Estrithsson, Thorkell the Tall, Thórólf Lousebeard.

BATTLES AND SIEGES

Clontarf 1014, Constantinople 860, Dorestad 834, the Dyle 891, Gate Fulford 1066, Hafrsfjord c.890, Hals (Limfjord) c.974, Hjörungavágr c.980, Holy River c.1026, Jeufosse 852–3, Jómsborg and the Jómsvikings, London 842, 851, 886, 982, 994, 1010, 1013, 1016, Nantes 843, Nissa 1062, Oissel 858–61, Paris 885–6, Skyhill 1079, Stainmore 954, Stamford Bridge 1066, Stiklestad 1030, Tara 980, Trelleborg forts.

OUTLINE OF EVENTS

We take the Vikings to be the people from Scandinavia who expanded into western Europe and elsewhere from the late 8th century. The term 'Viking' is thought to come originally from the people of Viken in southern Norway. Its more common meaning was that applied to their activities, meaning something like 'sea raiders'.

The Vikings are less significant in land than sea warfare. Their pagan religion had an important military impact, with belief in the warrior heaven of Valhalla and aggressive gods such as Thor, generally portrayed with his war hammer. There were important conflicts in Scandinavia and with settled peoples in western Europe. The Scandinavian expansion to the Scottish islands, Russia and eastwards, Iceland, Greenland and America was mostly accomplished without the traditional means of invasion and conquest. The Vikings contributed to naval development and warfare, and to the production of arms and armour. Their earthwork camps probably contributed to the development of castles. Scandinavians caused havoc in western Europe, not only as pirates and brigands. Forces also appeared under nobles and kings, and were not all small in number.

The main Scandinavian nations – Denmark, Sweden and Norway – did not emerge until a relatively late date for European states. Their early medieval history is not well documented and we rely considerably on outside accounts and on archaeology for much of the Viking period.

The Viking Age is that when Scandinavians attacked, raided, settled and colonised beyond Scandinavia, from 800 to 1100. The first recorded raid was against Lindisfarne. The 9th century saw waves of Viking attacks. Sawyer and others suggest that Viking armies were much smaller than once claimed, but larger numbers have recently been accepted again – at least for the great armies that invaded and conquered in western Europe.

There has been debate over the motives of the Vikings and the nature of their impact, a tendency to play down rape and pillage in favour of trading and settlement. Archaeology in such towns as York and Dublin has shown the truth in this, but one cannot ignore contemporary chronicle accounts of violence. The fact that initial Viking clashes pitted pagans against Christians influenced hostile western accounts. Immediate gain such as the acquisition of monastic wealth was one motive, and profit from tributes was another.

To civilised regions the Vikings brought violence and war. They often settled but rarely for long. Their most enduring impact was on eastern England, Ireland and Normandy. Elsewhere the Vikings were usually ejected. In settled areas they tended to be integrated into the existing population. Conversion to Christianity hastened the process. They left an important heritage, not least in the development of towns and trade. Little or no warfare was required to establish themselves in sparsely populated or uninhabited parts, such as the Scottish islands, the Faroes, Greenland and Iceland – even (it now seems certain) in North America, though this episode was of short duration.

Francia, England, Scotland and Ireland were civilised regions that faced severe Viking attacks, especially in the 9th century. Stronger governments resisted. In England the kingdoms of Northumbria, East Anglia and Mercia fell but Wessex resisted under Alfred the Great. Alfred's descendants united England but Viking influence remained strong in the eastern Danelaw. The Scandinavian threat returned with large invasion forces. Aethelred the Unready was defeated and a Scandinavian, Cnut the Great, became King of England. His successors could not sustain the position, and the Anglo-Saxon dynasty returned. Even by 1066 a Viking threat loomed. A major invasion of England by Harold Hardrada was ended at Stamford Bridge. Viking threats appeared intermittently into the 12th century.

In Francia the Vikings advanced along the rivers, using coastal and riverine islands as bases. They attacked Frankish cities, taking plunder and tribute, initially concentrating on trading settlements such as Dorestad. From Charlemagne on, Frankish rulers improved defences with fortified bridges. Blockades of Viking Seine island bases at Jeufosse and Oissel failed to dislodge them. The Vikings besieged Paris in 885–6. They failed to take it but accepted tribute to move on. Seemingly, the payment of tribute was the only effective response.

Viking settlements were established along the coast but gradually the Franks had more success. In 891 Arnulf King of the East Franks defeated the Vikings at the Dyle. In time Viking settlements were overcome or absorbed. Only one more lasting Viking state emerged, in the duchy of Normandy, founded c.911. The Viking dynasty there survived and a direct descendant was William the Conqueror.

In Ireland the Vikings established themselves in new coastal ports, as in Dublin and Wexford. The Irish resisted and won two major battles, the second at Clontarf in 1014, when Brian Boru was the victor though he himself was killed.

The Vikings entered the Mediterranean and caused panic in Spain, North Africa, France and Italy, but made no long-term impact. There is debate over the degree of Viking influence in Russia. They sailed east down the rivers for trade and provided mercenaries for Byzantium. The Rus were probably Vikings, but Russian historians have stressed the Slav role in the origins of a Russian state, minimising the Viking contribution. The truth probably lies in between. The Vikings may not have founded the Russian state, or even cities such as Kiev and Novgorod, but they established trading settlements and helped develop cities. They provided rulers for a time though it is likely that Scandinavians were absorbed in Slav society, as they were in Normandy.

In England Danes provided the main Viking element. The emergence of the Viking threat paralleled that of Scandinavian nations. The origins of the Scandinavian states are unclear, in the absence of local contemporary accounts. In England and Francia writers mentioned Denmark as an entity from the late 9th century. The oldest Scandinavian reference is a 10th-century runestone at Jelling. In the early Middle Ages Denmark was the most advanced Scandinavian region, with kings from the 8th century, though the extent of their realm is unclear. By the 9th century there was probably a kingdom of Denmark though it did not include Bornholm, Skåne and Halland. It included part of what is now Norway. Denmark threatened Carolingian Francia, and Charlemagne sought to secure the frontier. The founder of Denmark was King Harold Bluetooth, seen now as building the Trelleborg forts and promoting Christianity. His son Sweyn Forkbeard invaded England where his son Cnut became king. After Cnut's death Denmark came briefly under Norway but independence was re-established by Sweyn Estrithsson. The elective nature of the monarchy caused civil wars. There was a tripartite division in 1156. Denmark emerged as the major Scandinavian state in the 13th century. Civil wars hindered development until Waldemar IV re-established monarchical power in the 14th century. The Union of Kalmar in 1397 united Scandinavia under Denmark until 1523. Denmark took over Greenland and the Faroe Islands in the 14th century. The Faroes became self-governing under Denmark in 1948, as did Greenland in 1979.

Norway means 'the North-way', the sea route to the north. It emerged as a kingdom at about the same time as Denmark. There were royal burials from the 8th century in Vestfold. The founder of the kingdom was Harold Finehair from Vestfold through his victory at Hafrsfjord. Chieftains in Norway resisted central power. After defeat by

Harold Bluetooth Norway came under Denmark until the rise of Ólaf I Tryggvason who supported the establishment of Christianity. Following defeat, Norway was divided but reunited by Ólaf II Haroldsson (St Ólaf). Cnut brought Norway under Denmark, and St Ólaf was killed at Stiklestad. His son, Magnús the Good, restored Norwegian independence. The northern expansion of the Vikings was exploited by Norway, which took over the Orkneys, the Faroes, Iceland and Greenland. Harold Hardrada invaded England but failed. Hákon IV improved the internal strength of Norway in the 13th century

Sweden was the last Scandinavian state to emerge, partly because of divisions between the Svear of Uppsala and the Götar in the south. The first ruler of both was Ólof Skötkonung from 995, but complete union was not achieved until 1172. Sweden was the last Scandinavian kingdom to become Christian, with paganism surviving into the 12th century.

BATTLES AND SIEGES

CLONTARF, BATTLE OF, GOOD FRIDAY 23 APRIL 1014

Once considered the battle that ended Viking power in Ireland. It was fought between Irish kings rather than against the Vikings, but it did signal the end of Viking power in Ireland. Brian Boru of Munster beat Maél Sechnaill of Leinster. The site was north of Dublin. Sigurd of Orkney and most Vikings allied with Maél, though some joined Brian. Sigurd carried a raven-shaped banner into battle. Sigtrygg Silkbeard organised the opposition to Brian but did not fight in the battle. Brian was ageing and his son commanded. Maél's Irish formed the centre of his force, with Vikings on the wings. The Irish centre advanced and was forced back, the decisive moment. Both Irish leaders were killed, as was Sigurd and virtually every leading figure, but Brian's side won. In the words of a saga: 'Brian fell but won at last'. He was killed with an axe by the Viking Bródir of Man, while praying for victory and refusing to fight on Good Friday. The Viking settlements had accepted Irish rule before the battle but Dublin continued under a Viking king.

CONSTANTINOPLE (MIKLAGARÐUR/THE GREAT CITY), SIEGE OF, 860

The Byzantine capital was a focus for attack over centuries but in this period was never taken. The eastward movement of the Vikings brought contact with Byzantium. Vikings served in the emperor's Varangian Guard and traded with Byzantium, making trading agreements. There were several Viking attacks on Constantinople, the first in c.860. On 18 June a Viking fleet, probably from Kiev, under Askold and Dir appeared off the city. 'This sudden hailstorm of barbarians' attacked monasteries, seeking removable wealth. There were further raids before 907 under Oleg, and in 941 under Igor, preceding trading agreements in 907 and 945. The latter attack was repulsed by Greek Fire.

DORESTAD, SIEGE OF, 834

A trading settlement in Frisia attacked by the Vikings. Dorestad became involved in internal Scandinavian politics. It stood at the junction of an arm of the Rhine and the Lek. It is now Wijk bij Duurstede near Nijmegen in the Netherlands. It emerged as a settlement in the 7th century. In 834 the Vikings 'destroyed everything'. It was under Carolingian protection but suffered when that protection was weak in 835, 836, 837 and 846. Danes occupied the town in 847. In 850 the Emperor Lothar granted Dorestad to the Viking Rurik, but Vikings attacked in 857 and 863, and Rurik was expelled in 867. A natural disaster, the alteration in the course of the Rhine, brought Dorestad's final decay.

DYLE, BATTLE OF THE, 1 SEPTEMBER 891

Danes were beaten in Flanders by the East Franks under Arnulf. It was in effect a siege ended by storming. The Danes raided down the Seine, killing the archbishop of Mainz. They made a fortified camp in marshy land on a loop of the River Dyle near Louvain, now in Belgium. The Franks arrived mounted, but fought on foot – an early example of the tactic, with little option since they had to climb over ramparts. The Franks made a surprise attack, breaking through. Many Vikings tried to escape but were drowned and 'their corpses blocked the river bed'. Their kings, Siegfried and Godfred, were killed. It was claimed only one Frank died. The survivors went via Boulogne to England in 892.

GATE FULFORD, BATTLE OF, WEDNESDAY 20 SEPTEMBER 1066

The first of three major battles in England in 1066, a victory for Harold Hardrada over the northern earls. Hardrada landed at Riccall with a force from Norway, his allies including Godwinson's brother Tostig and men from the Orkneys. He advanced on York. The northern earls, Edwin of Mercia and Morcar of Northumbria, came from York to bar the crossing of the Ouse. The site is just south of York in what are now suburbs. It lasted 'a long time'. The earls were defeated and many killed trying to escape, making 'a causeway of corpses' over the river.

HAFRSFJORD, NAVAL BATTLE OF, c.890

Victory for Harold Finehair, King of Vestfold, uniting Norway for the first time, though some claim he ruled only a part. The traditional date is 872 but 890–900 is now preferred. Harold was faced by a coalition of jarls and kings from Norway, one of whom was Kjotvi the Rich. They resented Harold's attempts to impose authority. The opposing fleet entered the fjord west of modern Stavanger when Harold attacked. His enemies included the berserker Thorir Hakland, whose death decided the result. Many losers went to settle Iceland. Timbers found under water are thought to be from ships in the battle.

HALS (LIMFJORD), NAVAL BATTLE OF, c.974

Fought off the narrow eastern entrance of the Limfjord in north-eastern Jutland, in which Harold Greycloak of Norway died. He was opposed by an alliance of Danes and Jarl Hákon with men from Trøndelag. Harold's death led to a division of Norway between Harold Bluetooth and Jarl Hákon.

HJÖRUNGAVÁGR, BATTLE OF, c.980

A defeat for Harold Bluetooth of Denmark by Jarl Hákon Sigurdsson of Lade, Norway. The dating is uncertain and some place it later. The event became part of the Jómsviking legend. They supposedly fought for Harold and were defeated, ending their heroic tale. Afterwards many were beheaded on a log – a famous tale frequently repeated. Wends allied with the Danes to oppose Harold, probably the origin of the Jómsviking connection. Thorkell the Tall may have fought for Harold. Bluetooth assembled a fleet in Limfjord and sailed north to Horundafjord seeking to control Norway. Hákon and his son Erik prepared a trap into which the Danes fell.

HOLY RIVER (HELGAÁ), NAVAL BATTLE OF THE, c.1026

The dating varies between 1025 and 1027. Ólaf Haroldsson (St Ólaf) of Norway and his ally Önund of Sweden, son of Olof Skötkonung, harried Denmark. Cnut the Great commanded an English fleet reinforced by Danes to Limfjord. His enemies retreated to the mouth of the Holy River on the Baltic coast of Skåne, now in Sweden. Both sides claimed victory but Cnut came out better despite heavy losses. Jarl Úlf, Cnut's regent in Denmark, was killed. Ólaf abandoned his fleet to return home overland. In 1028 Ólaf fled, leaving Cnut to take over his kingdom.

JEUFOSSE (FOSSA GIVALDI), SIEGE OF, 852–3

The Danes under Godfrid made a base on this peninsula in the Seine near Bougivae not far from Paris. Here they wintered in 853, building a fortification by 856. Charles the Bald attacked Jeufosse with 'very great slaughter' but the Vikings held on through the winter and the Franks gave up. The Vikings moved on to the Loire, returning to attack Paris in 856 and 857. By payment of tribute in 857 Charles persuaded them to move to Oissel, a Seine island further from Paris.

JÓMSBORG AND THE JÓMSVIKINGS

It is unclear whether Jómsborg, the home of the legendary Danish Jómsvikings, ever existed. Once this group, which appeared in sagas, was thought historical. They lived as a band with special rules in a sworn fellowship. Only men between 18 and 50 could belong. They acted as mercenaries, wintering at Jómsborg and campaigning in the summer. Booty was shared equally. No women were allowed to enter Jómsborg. In Danish tradition Harold Bluetooth founded Jómsborg on the Baltic coast. The Jómsvikings' downfall came with defeat at Hjörungavágr fighting for Harold Bluetooth. In the saga the Jómsvikings were seated on a log and beheaded in turn. One young man asked an enemy to hold his fine fair hair forward so as not to stain it with blood. He jerked backwards so that the man's hands were cut off rather than his own head. He and the remaining Jómsvikings were pardoned. If the Jómsvikings existed then Wolin, now in Poland, is a possible site for Jómsborg though it dates from before Bluetooth. Wolin at the mouth of the Oder was called Jumne, fortified in the 9th century. It was a Wendish Slav town though Viking remains have been found there. Palnatóki was the most famed Jómsviking leader. Thorkell the Tall was associated with them and fought in the Baltic region. Probably Scandinavian activity in the Baltic gave rise to later embroidery and legend.

LONDON, SIEGES OF, 842, 851, 886, 982, 994, 1010, 1013, 1016

London became a major city in the Viking Age, the target for control by Scandinavians and English and the subject of several sieges. It was attacked by Vikings in 842 and 851. They made it a winter base in 871. It was retaken by Alfred in 886. Vikings fired London in 982. When Ólaf Tryggvason and Sweyn Forkbeard invaded in 994 they besieged London but failed to take it, though a tribute was agreed. Ólaf Haroldsson (St Ólaf) failed to take London but is said to have pulled down London Bridge in 1010, the origin of *London Bridge is Falling Down*. London resisted attack by Sweyn Forkbeard and Cnut in 1013 when Thorkell the Tall fought for Aethelred. He went over to Cnut before the siege of 1016 against Aethelred II. The English king died in London but the citizens under his son Edmund Ironside continued to resist. Cnut brought up ships, dug ditches and built ramparts. The town surrendered but the 'citadel' held out. It was agreed that Cnut could use London as a base before Edmund Ironside died, after which Cnut became sole ruler of the kingdom.

NANTES, SACK OF, 24 JUNE 843

After the death of Louis the Pious the Vikings renewed attacks on Francia, now divided in three with Charles the Bald ruling West Francia. A Viking fleet appeared on the Loire in 842 under Oskar, allied with the rebel Count Lambert, son of the Count of Nantes exiled by Louis. Lambert's pilots led them along the river, past Noirmoutier to Nantes, which they attacked and took on St John the Baptist's Day. Many were killed, including the bishop. The Vikings took plunder and slaves, returning to Noirmoutier before raiding Aquitaine.

NISSA, NAVAL BATTLE OF, 1062

Defeat of Sweyn Estrithsson by Harold Hardrada, fought near the River Nissa in Halland, Sweden. Hardrada's ship had 70 oars and moved 'like an eagle with wings flapping'. He used a bow in the battle. The Danish fleet broke ranks and 'blood gushed into the ocean'. Sweyn survived and two years later Hardrada recognised him as King of Denmark.

OISSEL (OSCELLUS), SIEGES OF, 858–61
Oissel was a Viking Seine island base near Rouen. Sidroc and Berno wintered there in 856. Charles the Bald besieged it in July 858 but trouble from his brother Louis the German caused him to abandon the attempt after 12 weeks. In 860 the Somme Vikings under Weland were offered 3,000 pounds of silver (later increased to 5,000 pounds) to eject the Oissel band. The Oissel Vikings raided Paris and Melun. In 861 Weland besieged Oissel and agreed a ransom of 6,000 pounds. Weland joined his 'enemy' and together they probably raided in the Mediterranean. Charles constructed fortified bridges over the Seine against Viking raids, including one at Pont de l'Arche near Oissel.

PARIS, SIEGE OF, 885–6
Viking attacks on Paris included plundering by Ragnar in 845, a sacking in 857 and renewed attacks in 861 and 865. After the death of Louis III in 882 the Vikings advanced along the Seine, sacking Rouen and reaching Paris in 885. The city's rulers, Count Odo and Bishop Gozlin, led the defence. Siegfried arrived with 700 ships on 24 November. The bishop refused to let the Vikings through. Paris on its island had fortified bridges to both banks. The Vikings attacked the tower guarding the bridge on the right bank, begun in 870 but unfinished. They failed to take it and the defenders added a wooden upper storey overnight. The Vikings tried siege engines, fire and mining. A bolt from a Parisian balista transfixed seven Vikings like a kebab, which a humorous defender ordered to be taken to the kitchen. After three days the attack on the tower was abandoned and the Vikings built a new siege camp. They attacked from three directions while a ship approached the bridge. On land they used

belfries, two of which were captured. The Vikings could not blockade the city completely. Plague broke out and Bishop Gozlin died. A relief force arrived but one of its leaders, Duke Henry of Saxony, was killed. Charles the Fat claimed victory. Paris was saved but at the expense of a tribute and permission to raid into Burgundy. The fullest account of the siege appears in a poem by the monk Abbo, in Paris during the siege. In 889 Count Odo became King of the West Franks.

SKYHILL, BATTLE OF, 1079
Battle to decide the fate of the Isle of Man. Godred Crovan, an Icelander who had fought for Harold Hardrada at Stamford Bridge, went on to Man. 1079 was his third attempt to win Man and at Skyhill near Ramsey he emerged the victor. His dynasty ruled Man for two centuries.

STAINMORE, BATTLE OF, 954
In which Erik Bloodaxe and five other Viking kings were killed. Erik, King of York, was driven out in 948. He returned in 952 to face opposition from Osulf of Bamburgh, who supported the English King Eadred. Erik was ambushed and killed by a certain Marcus. The battle in Northumbria ended Viking rule of York, Northumbria becoming part of the English kingdom. Erik's widow Gunnhild took their sons to her brother Harold Bluetooth in Denmark.

STAMFORD BRIDGE, BATTLE OF, 25 SEPTEMBER 1066
In which Harold Hardrada was defeated and killed. He claimed the English throne, assembled a fleet at Bergen and sailed in September. He received help from the Orkneys including the sons of Thorfinn. He raided the east coast, joined by Harold Godwinson's dissident brother Tostig. Hardrada landed at Riccall in Yorkshire, advancing on York. The northern earls emerged to be beaten at Gate Fulford. Godwinson marched north and surprised the Vikings near Stamford Bridge on the

Derwent. He rested overnight at Tadcaster, ten miles from York. On 25 September he marched through York and approached the bridge, defended by a tall Norwegian who was killed by the spear of an Englishman passing under the bridge in a boat. Hardrada wore a blue tunic in the battle. His army held the slightly higher ground of Battle Flats. The English charged and broke through. The battle was prolonged by Eystein Orri taking up Hardrada's fallen banner, *Landwaster*. There was massive slaughter. Hardrada's marshal, Styrkar, escaped. The invaders had arrived in 300 ships; 24 sufficed for the survivors. England's fate now lay in the coming conflict between Harold Godwinson and William of Normandy.

STIKLESTAD, BATTLE OF, 29 JULY 1030
In which Ólaf Haroldsson (St Ólaf) was killed seeking to recover Norway. King Ólaf fled from Norway on the approach of Cnut the Great in 1028. In 1030 Cnut's regent in Norway, Jarl Hákon, drowned. Ólaf with Swedish allies and Norse supporters sought to regain Norway. The battle was fought in the Tröndelag, north-east of Trondheim in Norway. The traditional date is 29 July but some accounts report an eclipse of the sun, making it 31 August (the eclipse may have been introduced to enhance Ólaf's saintliness). Ólaf's men cried 'Press on, prince's warriors!' and decried the enemy as 'farmers' men'. They had a larger force. The battle began at half past one in the afternoon and was over by three. Ólaf was killed and his personal warriors fought to the death. His death was seen as martyrdom. Hardrada, Ólaf's brother, was wounded but escaped.

TARA, BATTLE OF, 980
Defeat of Ólaf Sigtryggson King of Dublin by Maél Sechnaill II King of Tara in north-east Ireland. The battle was fought on or near Tara Hill, an ancient hill fort (Teamhair na Ríogh/Tara of the Kings) in county Meath north of Dublin. The Viking force included men from the Hebrides. There was 'a red slaughter'. Ólaf left Ireland for Iona where he died. It was a key moment in the success of Irish kings over the Vikings. Dublin was besieged and made terms. It was retained by Ólaf's sons but paid tribute to the Irish kings.

TRELLEBORG FORTS, THE
The forts have been the subject of archaeological and historical debate over when and why they were built. There are five earthwork fortifications in Scandinavia of large scale and similar design. They are Trelleborg at Sjaelland in Denmark (the first to be found), Fyrkat and Aggersborg in Jutland, Nonnebakken in Odense on the island of Fyn and a second Trelleborg at Skåne in southern Sweden. The latter, the only non-Danish one, is of different design though it is circular. The name Trelleborg probably meant 'slave fort'. They are circular in shape, quartered by roads leading to gates. A ditch protected the exterior. Aggersborg is at least twice the size of the others. The quadrants of each fort contained boat-shaped timber buildings. The layout, size and design of the buildings varied. The scale suggests that they were royal. It was believed they were built by Sweyn Forkbeard as barracks for his invasion of England in 1013. Dendrochronology dates the timbers to c.980 and Harold Bluetooth. This suggests their function was to control his Scandinavian lands. Archaeology has provided evidence of stores and workshops. The buried skeletons of women and children suggest a residential or governmental purpose. They only survived for a generation. The inspiration for them remains a mystery as they have no clear precursors.

The English shield wall on the Bayeux Tapestry

4 | The Anglo-Saxon invasions and England, 450–1066

See in Part I: placeholder

GENERALS AND LEADERS

See in Part I: Aelle of Sussex, Aethelred II, Aethelstan, Alfred, Ambrosius Aurelianus, Arthur, Byrhtnoth, Ceawlin of Wessex, Cerdic of Wessex, Edmund Ironside, Edward the Elder, Godwin, Harold Godwinson, Hengest and Horsa, Ida of Northumbria, Offa of Mercia, Penda of Mercia, Raedwald of East Anglia, Vortigern.

BATTLES AND SIEGES

Aclea 851, Aegelesthrep 455, Ashdown 871, Bamburgh 651, Beorhford 752, Biedanheafde 675, Billington 798, Brunanburh 937, Camlann c.517, Catraeth 598, Chester c.604, Cirencester 628, Cleobury 1056, Crecganford 456, Degsastan c.603, Deorham 577, Edington 878, Eildon 761, Ellendun 825, Fethanleag 584, Galford 825, Hatfield Chase 633, Heavenfield 633, Idle 616, Llanfaes 817, Lumphanan 1057, Maldon 991, Maserfield 642, Mearcredesburna 485, Moira c.639, Mount Badon c.500, Nechtanesmere 685, Netley 508, Otford 776, 1016, Peonnan 658, Pevensey 491, Sandwich 851, Trent 679, Wednesfield 910, Winwaed 655, Wippedsfleot c.465.

OUTLINE OF EVENTS

Some historians now refer to the English rather than the Anglo-Saxons, partly because we see a complex mix of peoples coming to Britain as the Western Roman Empire fell apart. We retain the traditional label since it refers us to a period, from the end of Roman Britain to the Norman Conquest, taking us traditionally from 410 to 1066 – though the first date now seems flexible. The Anglo-Saxons first came to Britain before 410, probably well before, while the withdrawal of central Roman control did not mark the end of Roman Britain – which occurred through obscure events over some two centuries.

The Anglo-Saxons came to Britain during Roman rule, some as regular Roman forces, some as mercenaries. Archaeology has shown remains from Germanic peoples, especially in the east and south, during the Roman period – including evidence of settlement. The origins of the newcomers are hard to disentangle. Bede gave a precise description of the tribes in three main groups – Angles, Saxons and Jutes – the Angles settling in the north, the east and the midlands, the Saxons in the south and southern midlands, the Jutes in the Isle of Wight, the Hampshire coast and Kent. Archaeology has generally confirmed this picture though it seems likely other groups were involved – notably Frisians, Scandinavians and Franks. The Anglo-Saxon tribes had moved west over the continent before migrating to Britain. They had moved from such areas as the estuary of the Elbe, Schleswig, the Baltic and Jutland towards the North Sea coast, to Frisia and the Netherlands. During this movement tribes had mixed.

The early stages of the development from Roman Britain to Saxon England were less of a conquest than a takeover. Roman Britain now lacked centralised control. A British leader was defeated in 367 by an alliance of enemies including Anglo-Saxons, Picts and Scots, and the Count of the Saxon Shore was killed. There was rebellion against Roman control as well as British attempts to win power on the continent, as by Magnus Maximus in 383–8. In the 5th century there were British usurpers who seized independent power in Britain, notably Marcus and Constantine III. In 410 the Emperor Honorius declared that Britain must defend itself but contact did not end altogether. Links with the continental Christian Church continued through Bishop Germanus from 428–9, and as late as 445–6.

The Saxons came as soldiers and mercenaries in various Roman army units, including three Frisian *numeri*, and on the Saxon Shore coast – possibly named after settlers rather than invaders. They were employed by villa owners and were among the *laeti*, auxiliaries and federates. The Romans employed tribesmen against their own kind. As central authority crumbled, the newcomers attached themselves to British leaders and the British rulers called in Germans to their aid. The Anglo-Saxons settled in increasing numbers, as relatives from the continent moved in seeking land and homes.

Some writers believed the fatal moment was when British leaders called in Saxon support. Others blamed the rebellion of Saxons against British leaders. The story of Hengest and Horsa is such a tale. The names, meaning Horse and Mare, seem suspect yet accounts suggest they existed. Hengest was a relatively common name and the English Hengest may be known in his previous continental existence. Hengest and Horsa were called as federates to aid Vortigern in 449. Horsa was killed but Aesc succeeded his father Hengest in 488.

Late Roman Britain had its defenders though their history is shrouded in fragmentary accounts. Gildas wrote of a 'superb tyrant' who brought in Saxon mercenaries 'like wolves into the fold'. One probably aristocratic leader was Ambrosius Aurelianus. The British won at Mount Badon. Bede wrote of Vortigern, possibly a title rather than a personal name so that there may have been more than one 'vortigern'. Bede's Vortigern brought in mercenaries, including Hengest in the mid-5th century.

Vortigern married Hengest's daughter. New migrants came under Hengest's son Octha. Hengest and Horsa rebelled against their British masters and took over Kent. They advanced inland, met a setback, then advanced again. Horsa was killed at Aegelesthrep in 455 but Hengest won at Crecganford in 456 and Wippedsfleot in 465.

The arrival of groups in eastern England was less well recorded but they probably arrived first. Archaeological evidence shows Germanic settlement in the 5th century, with a second wave in the 6th. Saxons and others were involved though the Angles were the dominant group. Norfolk (north folk) and Suffolk (south folk) may have set up two separate kingdoms initially. The East Anglian royal family was the Wuffings after their founder Wuffa. Probably a member of this dynasty, possibly Raedwald a *Bretwalda*, was buried at Sutton Hoo, a site that suggests Swedish origins as well as British influence, with information on arms and armour.

Angles dominated Mercia (the middle kingdom/kingdom of the frontier) though Saxons also settled there. The ruling dynasty was the Islings, claiming descent from the continental Angle Offa. An early King of Mercia was Penda who won against the West Saxons at Cirencester in 628. Several separate groups settled the north. Frisians may have reached the Firth of Forth. Two major northern kingdoms emerged in Deira and Bernicia, later uniting as Northumbria.

Other Germanic groups arrived. There are doubts over the dating but we have kept to that from the *Anglo-Saxon Chronicle* for the most part. In 477 the South Saxons under Aelle and his three sons came to *Cymenes ora*, probably on Selsey Bill. They drove the Britons into the Weald and captured Pevensey in 491, killing all within. Aelle founded the kingdom of Sussex, the first invader recognised as *Bretwalda* (wide ruler), a title granted to individual rulers seen as overall leaders of their time. The title passed from one kingdom to another but otherwise there was no overall command and the kingdoms developed independently.

The founders of Wessex, Cerdic and Cynric, were reported as arriving in 495 at *Cerdices ora*. Interestingly Cerdic is a British name. The mixing of tribes and groups within the new Anglo-Saxon arrivals was widespread. The West Saxons killed a British commander, Natanleod, in 508. Arthur's defence set them back but Wessex developed into a major kingdom. In the late 6th century Ceawlin defeated the British at Fethanleag, when three of their kings were killed. He became the second *Bretwalda*.

The earliest English kingdoms were established around the east and south coasts. Most contained people of mixed origins but we tend to see some as mainly Angle, others as primarily Saxon. Thus East Anglia, Northumbria (from Deira and Bernicia) and Mercia are chiefly Angle. Lindsey should be included though it probably had British influence in its origins – including its name from Roman Lincoln. Essex, Sussex, Middlesex and Wessex were Saxon.

Some Britons lived within the new kingdoms while others remained independent and resisted further English expansion. Thus emerged the misty figure of Arthur. Some historians question if he existed. Most of the stories are later embroideries, and contemporary evidence is thin though probably sufficient to accept an historical figure who led Roman Britons against the English. *Nennius* provides a list of 12 battles, including Mount Badon, with the Britons under Arthur 'the commander [*dux*] of battles'. The identification of sites for these battles is difficult and historians come to differing conclusions, but they seem to cover a wide area, suggesting that Roman

Britons saw some unity among themselves. Arthur's downfall came through internal conflict that led to Camlann.

Roman Britain was threatened by Scots and Picts as well as Anglo-Saxons. Through the 5th and 6th centuries the invaders settled and new kingdoms emerged. The British survived independently in the west of England, in Wales, and in parts of the north.

The British victory at Mount Badon was probably followed by an agreement to divide control between the Britons and the English. After a lull in the English advance, they pushed forward again from the 6th century. Little is known in detail about the battles, even their locations are often unidentifiable, but they established the new kingdoms and their boundaries.

Three major English kingdoms emerged, Northumbria in the north, Mercia in the midlands and Wessex in the south – all at times extending their authority widely. Mercia emerged as a major kingdom with Penda's victory over the West Saxons at Cirencester in 628. He played a part in defeating the Northumbrians near Oswestry. He was finally defeated at the battle of Winwaed in 655. Aethelbald consolidated the strength of Mercia but its period of dominance came under Offa who claimed descent from the continental Angles. His standing was such that he could correspond with Charlemagne on something like equal terms.

Northumbria was formed by the union of two earlier kingdoms, Deira and Bernicia. Deira covered the plain of York to the south, while Bernicia lay north of the Tees. In the north there were threats from surviving Britons, Picts and Scots. King Ida won an important victory over the British at Bamburgh. His son Theoderic defeated Urien of Rheged, a surviving British kingdom. The Northumbrians won a further victory at Catraeth in c.600. By this period most of the north was under Northumbrian control.

The Viking invasion nearly wiped out Anglo-Saxon control. Northumbria and Mercia collapsed while Wessex narrowly escaped. After being forced back to Athelney Alfred advanced to win at Edington. He made peace with Guthrum, dividing England. He established a naval force, thus nullifying one Viking advantage. Alfred's successors consolidated and extended the boundaries of Wessex to establish a new kingdom of the English. Edward the Elder ruled all the English south of the Humber. Aethelstan took over Northumbria, Viking York and Cornwall and established frontiers with the Scots and the Welsh.

Unity was threatened by rebellion, division and Scandinavian invasion, but survived. For a period England came under Scandinavian control through Sweyn Forkbeard and his son Cnut. Two of Cnut's sons succeeded him but the Scandinavian dynasty ended with the return of Edward the Confessor. Edward had some political success despite disturbance within his realm, largely through the power of the Godwin family. Harold Godwinson, on Edward's behalf, extended English control into Wales. 1066 was the critical year. Edward died. Harold succeeded. Invasion threatened from Scandinavia under Harold Hardrada and from Normandy under William the Conqueror.

BATTLES AND SIEGES

ACLEA, BATTLE OF, 851

The Vikings attacked Canterbury and entered the Thames. An attempt to relieve London by a force under Berhtwulf of Mercia was defeated. The Vikings moved into Surrey and were then met by Aethelwulf of Wessex and his son Aethelbald at Aclea. The location is probably in Surrey but has not been identified and is probably not Ockley. The victory established Aethelwulf's pre-eminence among the English rulers. The *Anglo-Saxon Chronicle* called it 'the greatest slaughter [of a heathen army] that we ever heard of until this present day'.

AEGELESTHREP, BATTLE OF, 455

Victory for Hengest and Horsa over Vortigern, turning rebellion into conquest. Horsa was killed but Hengest and his son Aesc succeeded to the kingdom of Kent. The meaning of 'threp' is not known. Aylesford in Kent has been accepted by some as the location but without clear evidence. *Nennius'* Set Thirgasbail is probably the same but does not solve the location.

ASHDOWN, BATTLE OF, 8 JANUARY 871

A victory against the Vikings by King Aethelred I of Wessex, when his younger brother Alfred took active command. It was fought on Ashdown ridge in Berkshire near a thorn tree that Asser said he had seen. This was probably in the *Domesday* hundred of Nachededorn (naked thorn) where one finds Louse and Lowbury Hills. The battle occurred four days after a clash at Reading, where the Vikings kept the field – a sign of victory. At Ashdown the Vikings were in two groups, one under Halfdan and Bagsecg, the other under jarls. They held the ridge. In one account Aethelred was praying while Alfred fought, though it was intended that he should lead half the force. Events dictated that Alfred had to begin the fight. However, in the *Anglo-Saxon Chronicle*, Aethelred participated in the fighting. In Asser the English formed a shield wall, charging uphill with Alfred like a 'wild boar'. Bagsecg and five jarls were killed. The pursuit continued to nightfall. The Vikings retreated to Reading. Although not decisive, the battle brought Alfred to the fore and gave hope for the future. Alfred soon succeeded to the throne of Wessex.

BAMBURGH, SIEGE OF, 651

A stronghold in the Cheviots that resisted a siege by Penda of Mercia. The *Anglo-Saxon Chronicle* says it was built by Ida, King of Bernicia and was later called Bebba's Fort after Aethelfrith's queen. Irish sources called it Dinguoaroy. It had probably been a Celtic promontory fort. The chronicler added that it was surrounded first by a fence and later by a wall. It was taken over by the English. Paulinus used Bamburgh as a base for preaching Christianity. Penda of Mercia besieged Bamburgh in 651 when campaigning in Northumbria. He had no time for a long siege and failed to break in. He tried to fire Bamburgh with planks, beams, wattle and thatch, building a pyre that was fired when the wind was in the right direction. Bishop Aidan on the nearby island of Farne saw smoke and prayed for Bamburgh. The wind changed direction and the fire blew on the besiegers. The attack was abandoned. Bede says the site had been abandoned before his own day. It revived, became a burh, and was attacked by Vikings in 993.

BEORHFORD, BATTLE OF, 752

Victory by Cuthred King of Wessex over Aethelbald King of Mercia. Cuthred rebelled against Aethelbald after assisting him in war against the Britons. The Mercians were put to flight. The location is no longer thought to be Burford in Oxfordshire. Beorhford marked the rise of Wessex, previously subordinate to Mercia. Cuthred maintained independence until his death in 756.

BIEDANHEAFDE, BATTLE OF, 675

Between Wulfhere King of Mercia, son of Penda, and Aescwine of Wessex, who was seeking to halt Mercian domination. Wulfhere advanced Mercian power to the Isle of Wight. The location is unknown and the result is not recorded. Wulfhere died in the same year. Aescwine seems to have achieved some success in protecting Wessex.

BILLINGTON, BATTLE OF, 2 APRIL 798

The conspirators under Ealdorman Walda who opposed Aethelred King of Northumbria, and had him murdered, re-formed in the hope of making Osbald king rather than Eardwulf. They fought Eardwulf on Billington Moor near Whalley in Lancashire. Eardwulf won and established himself as king while Osbald entered a monastery and died in 799.

BRUNANBURH, BATTLE OF, 937

Victory for King Aethelstan against the Scots. The location is unknown but was in the north, possibly in Yorkshire or Scotland. To the Vikings the site was Vinheiðr, to the English Wendun. A saga described it as heathland with a stream to the west and woodland to the east. The English sheltered in a burh or fortress. The Scots threatened Aethelstan's position in Northumbria. In 937 the Scots under King Constantine allied with Welsh, Vikings from Dublin and Northumbria (including Ólaf of York) and men from Strathclyde to invade Northumbria. They defeated a local English force but were halted by Aethelstan with his brother Edmund the Atheling. Aethelstan held the narrowest point between the stream and the woods. The English held firm against attack and countered. The *Anglo-Saxon Chronicle* says the field was darkened by blood and 'there lay many a man destroyed by the spears'. In the pursuit on horseback five kings were killed. Brunanburh allowed Aethelstan to claim the kingdom of England.

CAMLANN, BATTLE OF, c.517

In which King Arthur was killed. The information is from the *Annales Cambriae* in the *Nennius* collection. The entry reads 'the Battle of Camlann, where Arthur and Medraut fell'. It is not even clear if they fought on the same side or which side was victorious. It is suggested that the battle was between Britons, rather than against the English, and that Medraut (a British name) was Arthur's opponent. The name for the battle means crooked glen (or valley). The same name was used for a site in Merioneth and for the fort of Birdoswald on Hadrian's Wall. The site has not been identified. The date is uncertain, placed between 515 and 537. It marked the close of the main British resistance to English conquest.

CATRAETH, BATTLE OF, 598

An account of this battle appears in the poem *Y Gododdin* by the poet Aneirin who it was said alone survived the battle. The Angles from Deira and Bernicia fought against the British under the Votadini from Edinburgh. The British warriors were the Gododdin, attacking Angle territory. Catraeth (possibly Catterick) was an Angle victory. The British 'were killed; they did not grow old'.

CHESTER, BATTLE OF, c.604

A victory by Aethelfrith of Bernicia over the men of Powys. Aethelfrith united Bernicia and Deira, playing an important part in the expansion of Angle power in the north. Aethelfrith advanced against Powys and defeated its army under King Selyf ap Cynan. The *Anglo-Saxon Chronicle* recorded that 'a countless number of Britons was killed'. The victory was said to fulfil St Augustine's prophecy that if the Britons did not make peace with the Saxons they would perish. The British kings Cetula and Selyf were killed. Monks from Bangor, who came to pray for British victory, were put to death – though their leader Brocmail and 50 others escaped. The victory brought the English to the Irish Sea, separating the

Britons of Wales from those of the north. The date is uncertain, possibly a decade later.

CIRENCESTER, BATTLE OF, 628

The *Anglo-Saxon Chronicle* recorded that 'Cynegils and Cwichelm fought against Penda at Cirencester and afterwards came to terms'. Cynegils and Cwichelm were kings of the Gewisse (the West Saxons). Their relationship is uncertain, possibly father and son. Penda became King of Mercia in 632. Penda won and his authority over Cirencester and region was recognised by the West Saxons. The battle demonstrated the expanding power of Penda and Mercia. The dating has been questioned and may have been a few years later.

CLEOBURY, BATTLE OF, 17 JUNE 1056

A victory for Gruffydd of Wales over the English under Leofgar, bishop of Hereford. Leofgar was killed. Harold Godwinson led a force to avenge this battle. Gruffydd was then beaten and recognised the overlordship of Edward the Confessor.

CRECGANFORD, BATTLE OF, 456

Fought during the English advance in the south-east towards London. The British were defeated. The *Anglo-Saxon Chronicle* recorded, 'Hengest and his son Aesc fought against the Britons in the place that is called Crecganford and killed 4,000 men; and the Britons then deserted Kent and fled with great fear to London'. The identification of the site as Crayford in Kent is no longer generally accepted.

DEGSASTAN (DEGSASTONE), BATTLE OF, c.603

A victory for Aethelfrith of Bernicia over the Scots of Dalriada (in Argyll, western Scotland). These Scots had arrived from Ireland and sought to expand south. Under King Aedan they tried to block the contemporaneous English advance north by Aethelfrith. The sources say Hering of Bernicia led the army, though it is generally

assumed that Aethelfrith was present. Aethelfrith took over Deira to form Northumbria. The location (called Degsastone by Bede) is uncertain, possibly Dawston in Liddesdale. The Scottish army was larger. Aethelfrith's brother, Theodbald, was killed but the Scots were beaten, halting their advance into Northumbria. 603 is given by Bede and the *Anglo-Saxon Chronicle*, but 604 is also possible.

DEORHAM (DYRHAM), BATTLE OF, 577

Victory by Ceawlin and Cuthwine (possibly Ceawlin's son) of the West Saxons over the Britons. The lower Severn region fell under English control through the battle. The *Anglo-Saxon Chronicle* gives Deorham, probably Dyrham north of Bath. Three British kings – Coinmail, Condidan and Farinmail – were killed. They may each have ruled one of the cities named – Gloucester, Cirencester and Bath – which fell to the English. The Britons north and south of the Bristol Channel were separated.

EDINGTON (ETHANDUN), BATTLE OF, MAY 878

Victory over the Danes, Alfred's comeback battle after the Danish advance into Wessex and his retreat to Athelney in Somerset. Reinforced by men from Somerset, Wiltshire and Hampshire he marched east. The armies met at Edington in Wiltshire, south of the Viking base at Chippenham. The English formed a shield wall. Many Vikings were killed. Alfred pursued the Danes to Chippenham, which he besieged for a fortnight until Guthrum agreed to give hostages and accept baptism. He withdrew to East Anglia. Wessex was saved and the future of England lay with the Wessex dynasty.

EILDON, BATTLE OF, 6–9 AUGUST 761

Fought in the reign of Aethelwald Moll king of Northumbria, lasting three days, which makes one wonder if it was a siege. It was caused by Oswine's rebellion against

Aethelwald. Oswine was killed on the third day.

ELLENDUN (WROUGHTON), BATTLE OF, 19 AUGUST 825

Victory for Egbert of Wessex over Beornwulf of Mercia. Beornwulf had taken the offensive, and met Egbert at Wroughton in Wiltshire to the south of Swindon, the place confirmed from charter place-name evidence. Many were killed, including Aethelweard Hun, Ealdorman of Somerset, who was buried at Winchester. Egbert then subdued Kent, Surrey, Sussex and Essex, establishing the authority of Wessex. Stenton called it 'one of the most decisive battles of Anglo-Saxon history' because it ended the dominance of Mercia.

FETHANLEAG, BATTLE OF, 584

The West Saxons under Cutha and Ceawlin against the Britons. Ceawlin was attempting to expand north. Cutha was killed but Ceawlin went on to capture many towns. According to the *Anglo-Saxon Chronicle* Ceawlin returned in anger, which suggests that Fethanleag was an English defeat. The name may mean 'warriors' wood'. It was fought near Stoke Lyne in Oxfordshire, where a 12th-century document mentions a wood called Fethelée.

GALFORD, BATTLE OF, 825

Between the British of Devon and Cornwall, weakening the west against the advance of Egbert of Wessex.

HATFIELD CHASE, BATTLE OF, 14 OCTOBER 633

Fought on the same day as Hastings (Bede has 12 October), in which Edwin king of Northumbria was killed. The allied victors were Cadwallon ap Cadfan, King of Gwynedd in North Wales, and Penda then aetheling of Mercia. Penda was a pagan and Cadwallon a barbarian. Cadwallon responded to Edwin's invasion by a counter against Northumbria. Edwin's son Osfrith was killed. The victors laid waste Northumbria. Paulinus took the dead king's widow, Aethelburh, to Kent where he became bishop of Rochester. Ryknield Street passed through Hatfield Chase and was on the route from Northumbria to the south. The site of the battle was close to Edwinstowe in Northumberland. The battle marked the downfall of a great northern king and the rise of Penda, soon to be King of Mercia. Edwin's head was taken to York, to the Church of St Peter.

HEAVENFIELD, BATTLE OF THE, 633

Victory for Oswald over the British under Cadwallon of Gwynedd. Cadwallon advanced north. The battle was fought near Hexham at Denis' burn (from Bede). Cadwallon had the larger force. Oswald held a cross while it was erected, and then prayed for victory. He claimed to have seen a vision of St Columba. Cadwallon was killed. The name was given after the victory. Oswald won fame for his piety and was recognised as King of Northumbria.

IDLE, BATTLE OF THE RIVER, 616

In which Aethelfrith of Northumbria was killed by Raedwald of East Anglia, fought on the east bank of the river, the climax of a struggle between the leading kings of the northern English. Aethelfrith of Bernicia took over the lands of Deira. Raedwald's authority extended over the Middle Angles. Aethelfrith's rival, Edwin, fled for protection to Raedwald's court. Aethelfrith offered money to Raedwald to kill Edwin, but it was refused. In the summer of 616 Raedwald advanced north with the larger army and surprised Aethelfrith before he could assemble all his troops. The battle was fought near to the crossing point of the Roman road from Doncaster to Lincoln. Aethelfrith was defeated and he and his son Regnhere were killed. Edwin became King of Deira and then Northumbria while Raedwald became *Bretwalda*.

LLAN-FAES, BATTLE OF, 817

During the Mercian invasion of Anglesey, one of a series of battles named in Welsh sources but not described. The scenario is invading English gaining the upper hand over British resistance.

LUMPHANAN, BATTLE OF, 15 AUGUST 1057

In which Macbeth king of Scots was defeated and killed. He had killed Duncan I in 1040. In 1054 Siward of Northumbria invaded, defeating Macbeth to install Duncan's son, Malcolm III Canmore. Macbeth was brought to bay by Macduff and Malcolm Canmore, who gained revenge for his father's death. The site is in Mar.

MALDON, BATTLE OF, 11 AUGUST 991

Recounted in a celebrated poem, a disastrous defeat for the English by the Vikings under Ólaf Tryggvason. Although in verse, this is the most detailed account of an Anglo-Saxon battle before Hastings. The fyrd of Essex under Ealdorman Byrhtnoth, aged over 60, blocked the way inland of invading Vikings. The Vikings established themselves on Northey Island, with the Blackwater to the north and Southey Creek to the south, and a causeway uncovered at low tide the only way to the mainland. They demanded tribute but Byrhtnoth refused. Three English warriors blocked the causeway. Byrhtnoth unwisely agreed to let the Vikings cross and fight a battle, no doubt recalling his victory at the same spot in 988. The battle was fought on the bank of the river. In the poem Byrhtnoth sent away the horses and the English fought on foot. He ordered the formation of a shield wall. Soon 'bows were busy' though the poet does not say on which side, possibly both. The English fought with spears though Byrhtnoth drew his 'bright-edged' sword with its golden hilt. Byrhtnoth was wounded and killed. The shield wall was broken and the English vanquished, though some fought on to the death. In 1769 a six feet nine inch skeleton, found in Ely Cathedral, was claimed to be Byrhtnoth.

MASERFELD (MASERFELTH/MAES COGWY), BATTLE OF, 5 AUGUST 642

Probably the same as Maes Cogwy in *Nennius*. The dating is uncertain. Bede gave 642 for the 'great battle' but the *Welsh Annals* had 644. Penda of Mercia, called by the *Anglo-Saxon Chronicle* 'the Southumbrian', fought against Oswald King of the Northumbrians. Cynddylan a Prince of Powys allied to Penda. Oswald of Northumbria prayed for victory as the enemy closed but was killed in the battle and his body dismembered. His brother Eowa was killed. Because (at least some of) his enemies were pagan, Oswald was treated as a martyr. Bede said many collected dust from where Oswald had fallen to mix with water, which 'did much good to their friends who were sick'. The grass was greener than elsewhere. The victor was Penda of Mercia. The site may be Oswestry in Shropshire. Oswald was buried at Bardney. Oswald's brother Oswiu succeeded him. Penda was thereafter the most powerful ruler in Britain, taking sole power over the Mercians.

MEARCREDESBURNA, BATTLE OF, 485

The entry in the *Anglo-Saxon Chronicle* is brief. 'In this year Aelle fought against the Britons near the bank of Mearcredesburna'. The site has not been identified, the result not given. The battle follows the landing of the South Saxons in 477 and precedes the taking of Pevensey in 491. This would suggest progress from west to east. Aelle was recognised as the first *Bretwalda*, implying a career of successful conquest. One is inclined to see this as a Saxon victory though the *Chronicle*'s failure to record a result allows the possibility of defeat. *Burn* means a waterway, and the Arun, Ouse and Cuckmere have been suggested as possible sites.

MOIRA, BATTLE OF, c.639

Marked the failure of the Scots of Dalriada to recover power in their homeland in Antrim, Ireland. Domnall Brecc of Scottish Dalriada was defeated by the O'Neill,

Domnall King of Tara. The weakened Scots of Dalriada kept on good terms with Oswy of Northumbria.

MOUNT BADON (MONS BADONICUS), SIEGE AND BATTLE OF, c.500

The most famous battle of early English history. Gildas said it was fought in the year of his birth, a victory for Ambrosius Aurelianus over the Saxons. He said it arose from a siege, presumably of a British stronghold. *Nennius* lists Badon as one of Arthur's victories where 'he carried the cross of Our Lord Jesus Christ on his shoulders for three days and three nights'. Some think 'shoulders' should read 'shield'. It is suggested the English came from Kent, Sussex and Wessex – but there is no specific evidence of the composition of the force. It has been thought possible the English leader was Aelle of Sussex. The battle halted the English advance for a generation. Gildas wrote 'our people regained their strength'. The dating is between c.490 and 516. The site is unknown but a fortification must mark the place and Badbury Rings in Dorset or Solsbury Hill at Bath have been suggested.

NECHTANESMERE (DUIN NECHTAIN/ DUNNICHEN/THE LAKE OF HERON), BATTLE OF, 20 MAY 685

In which Ecgfrith of Northumbria was defeated and killed in Pictish country near Forfar in the kingdom of Circinn. Ecgfrith led a raid – 'rashly against the advice of his friends'. The Irish name was Duin Nechtain now Dunnichen; it was also known as the Lake of Heron. Ecgfrith advanced through Strathmore. The Picts gave ground and drew the English into a trap in mountainous country. The victor was the Pictish King Bruide. Many English were killed, others enslaved. The battle halted the English advance north, a setback to the Northumbrians who never regained all the lost ground. The Picts recovered land and the Scots regained their independence.

NETLEY (NATANLEAG), BATTLE OF, 508

In the *Anglo-Saxon Chronicle* 'Cerdic and Cynric killed a British king, whose name was Natanleod, and 5,000 men with him; and the land right up to Cerdicesford was called Natanleag after him'. Cerdicesford has been identified as Charford on Avon, and Natanleag as Netley, both in Hampshire. Cerdic and his son (or grandson) Cynric arrived in England in 495 and founded the kingdom of Wessex.

OTFORD, BATTLES OF, 776, 1016

The first is the only battle of Offa of Mercia that the *Anglo-Saxon Chronicle* records in the south. It does not record the outcome. Offa had come to dominate Kent. Stenton thought it a Mercian victory but more recently a setback for Offa has been favoured. The Mercians fought against the men of Kent. Probably Kent and Sussex regained their independence temporarily. Later Offa directed affairs in Kent. A second battle occurred at the same place in 1016 when Edmund Ironside defeated a Danish force.

PEONNAN (PEONNUM), BATTLE OF, 658

Cenwealh of Wessex fought the Britons when he returned from three years' exile in East Anglia, driven out by Penda of Mercia. The Britons were beaten and fled to the River Parrett. The site has been suggested as Pen Pits in Wiltshire, or (with less credibility) Pinn Beacon or Pinhoe in Devon. Penselwood on the boundary of Somerset, Dorset and Wiltshire is the most likely site and, if correct, was at a traditional assembly point. The date may be a little later. The battle marked the progress of English power.

PEVENSEY (ANDREDESCEASTER/ ANDERIDA), SIEGE OF, 491

Climax of the conquest of Sussex by the South Saxons. The *Anglo-Saxon Chronicle* recorded that 'Aelle and Cissa besieged Andredesceaster, and killed all who were inside, and there was not even a single Briton left alive'. Aelle and his son Cissa were the leaders of the invasion of Sussex. Anderida was the Roman fort at Pevensey, a Saxon Shore Fort guarding south-east Britain. It became a Saxon burh and later a Norman castle. The Roman walls of the fort still stand and the report of the siege, though brief, is important. It shows that the Saxons were capable of storming and capturing walled fortifications. Aelle was named as the first *Bretwalda*, showing that the English viewed his role as significant. The *Chronicle* date has been questioned.

SANDWICH, NAVAL BATTLE OF, 851

The *Anglo-Saxon Chronicle* reported this victory by Aethelstan the sub-king of Kent and Ealdorman Ealhhere over the Vikings. 'They fought in ships and slew a great army at Sandwich in Kent, and captured nine ships and put the others to flight.' Asser called the enemy 'a great Viking army'. Stenton called this 'the first naval battle in recorded English history'.

TRENT, BATTLE OF THE RIVER, 679

A defeat for Ecgfrith of Northumbria by Aethelred of Mercia. The 'great battle', in Bede, halted the expansion of Northumbria to the south. Lindsey returned to Mercian control. Ecgfrith's 18-year old brother Aelfwine was killed. Bishop Theodore worked to reconcile the rival kings afterwards. A payment was agreed to atone for the death of Aelfwine. One of Ecgfrith's men, Imma, was left for dead on the field but recovered. He was captured and pretended to be a rustic, 'afraid of admitting himself a soldier'. Every time they tried to bind him the bonds miraculously loosed. They sold him as a slave but he was allowed to ransom himself.

WEDNESFIELD (TETTENHALL), BATTLE OF, 5 AUGUST 910

A victory by Edward the Elder over the Vikings. Northumbrian nobles allied with Wessex and Mercia. The *Anglo-Saxon Chronicle* claimed that the Vikings broke the peace to ravage Mercia. Edward

transported his men from Kent by sea, intercepting the Vikings on their return after crossing a bridge over the Severn. The Vikings fled and, according to the *Chronicle*, thousands were killed. Three Viking kings died – Halfdan, Eywysl and Ivar. The site was near Tettenhall, after which the battle is sometimes named. Wednesfield is in Staffordshire and means 'Woden's plain'. The battle marked the rise to dominance of Wessex in England.

WINWAED (WINWAEDFELD), BATTLE OF THE, 15 NOVEMBER 655

In which the Northumbrians defeated Penda of Mercia. Penda's aim was to destroy Oswy (Oswiu) with a coalition including Welsh from Gwynedd and Northumbrian dissidents. Oswy, originally King of Bernicia, led the Northumbrians. He sought to buy peace but Penda refused. The result was a decisive victory for the Northumbrians. Penda was killed and decapitated. Thirty princes died, including Anna of East Anglia's brother, Aethelhere, his body lost in the river. Cadfael of Gwynedd escaped. The Northumbrians were recent converts to Christianity and Winwaed was claimed as a triumph over pagans (Aethelhere was a lapsed Christian). Oswy (as he had vowed) gave the Church 12 estates free from military service, his daughter Aelfleda becoming a nun. The River Winwaed (possibly the Went, a tributary of the Don) was in the district of Loidis. According to Bede, at the time of the battle the river overflowed its banks from rain.

WIPPEDSFLEOT, BATTLE OF, c.465

Versions of the *Anglo-Saxon Chronicle* give different dates. The battle established independent English in Britain. Hengest and his son Aesc fought against the Britons. Twelve British chiefs were killed. The English thegn, Wipped, was killed but gave his name to the site. *Fleot* was Old English for an estuary, stream or creek. It may have been near the Wantsum Channel in Kent.

Coronation of King Roger II, Palermo,
Church of the Martorana

5 | The Norman Conquests in Britain and Europe, 911–1154

GENERALS AND LEADERS

See in Part I: Geoffrey de Mandeville, Guy de Brionne, Henry I, Hereward, Matilda, Melus of Bari, Miles of Gloucester, Rainulf Drengot, Ralph of Hereford, Richard I of Normandy, Richard II of Normandy, Robert I of Normandy, Robert II Curthose, Robert of Bellême, Robert of Gloucester, Robert Guiscard, Robert de Mowbray, Roger I of Sicily, Roger II of Sicily, Rollo, Stephen, Taillefer, Waleran of Meulan, Waltheof, William I the Conqueror, William II Rufus, William Clito, William I Longsword of Normandy, William Bras de Fer, William fitz Osbern, William of Ypres.

BATTLES AND SIEGES

Alençon 1118, Arques-la-Bataille 1052–3, Bamburgh 1095, Bari 1068–71, Bourgthéroulde 1124, Brémule 1119, Brionne 1047–50, 1124, Burwell 1144, Cannae 1018, Cerami 1063, Civitate 1053, Dinan 1064, Dol 1064, Domfront 1051–2, Dyrrachium 1081–2, Ely 1071, Exeter 1068, Faringdon 1145, Hastings 1066, Lincoln 1141, Mayenne 1063, Messina 1061, Monte Maggiore 1041, Mortemer 1054, Oxford 1142, Reggio 1060, St-Aubin-sur-Scie 1053, Standard 1138, Strymon 1185, Tinchebrai 1106, Val-ès-Dunes 1047, Varaville 1057, Venosa 1041, Wallingford 1139, 1152–3, Wilton 1142, Winchester 1141, York 1069.

OUTLINE OF EVENTS

Normandy was founded in c.911 when Charles the Simple, the West Frankish king, granted lands to the Viking leader Rollo. Viking raiders threatened western Francia, and Charles needed Rollo to form a buffer, repelling further Viking incursions. The grant at

St-Clair-sur-Epte may have been exaggerated in its extent – probably only Rouen and a region around it was granted. The early rulers were styled 'counts' rather than 'dukes' – but for convenience we shall refer to all Norman rulers as dukes, as they became.

Rollo and his successors established a powerful entity, which we shall call the duchy of Normandy. Rollo extended his power west to the Vire, taking in central Normandy with the Bessin. His son William Longsword took Breton lands, expanding Normandy west to the Couesnon, including the Cotentin and Avranchin. Ducal power remained weak in the west until William the Conqueror.

The Vikings were pagan invaders but the dukes converted, making Normandy an important component of the Christian west. In 996, when Richard II succeeded, there was a peasants' revolt, suppressed by the nobility. Peasant representatives who brought their complaints to the Count of Ivry had their hands and feet cut off. Some Scandinavian influence continued but Normandy reverted to Frankish language and culture. The Frankish nobility revived in a new form. In the 11th century the dukes and nobles built castles as residences and strongholds.

Richard III died in 1027, possibly poisoned. Under Robert I, Normandy suffered disturbances with invasions by the French king and internal rebellion. Robert left his troubled duchy for a pilgrimage to the Holy Land, but died during the return.

His illegitimate son, William the Conqueror, succeeded at the age of about nine. Instability continued. William's first battle, at Val-ès-Dunes in 1047, was a victory over rebels under Guy de Brionne. In 1053 the Conqueror's uncle, William of Arques, led another rebellion. Henry I King of France came to aid the rebels but was defeated at St-Aubin-sur-Scie. Arques surrendered and the Conqueror's uncle was exiled. A new invasion was halted by the victory of William's magnates against a secondary force at Mortemer in 1054. The invasion by Henry I in 1057 was beaten at Varaville.

The death of his leading enemies left William freer to pursue expansion. He established a stronger grip on western Normandy and attacked neighbouring areas. In 1063 Maine fell under Norman power. In 1064 William invaded Brittany, accompanied by Harold Godwinson. He took Dol, Rennes and Dinan and won control over eastern Brittany.

During this campaign William probably knighted Harold. Harold then, possibly under duress, swore an oath promising support. The English king, Edward the Confessor, had a Norman mother and had spent years as an exile in Normandy before becoming king. He gave Norman and French supporters positions in Church and government. He had no children and the Normans claimed, probably truthfully, that he promised the throne to William.

On Edward's death early in 1066 Harold Godwinson took the throne, though he had no claim by blood, apart from the fact that his sister had married Edward. The Normans protested that Harold was an oath-breaker and William claimed the throne. A Scandinavian attempt to take the kingdom by Harold Hardrada was beaten off at Stamford Bridge. William planned an invasion, collecting and building a fleet. He sailed while Harold was engaged against the Scandinavians.

Landing at Pevensey William established himself on the south coast. Harold marched south to be defeated near Hastings. The conquest of England followed. William's campaign after Hastings brought in much of the south. The climax was the submission of London and his coronation there on Christmas Day.

It took several years to complete the conquest. Castles were built as the Normans moved north. The northern earls, Edwin and Morcar, made peace. There were further rebellions and invasion attempts. Eustace of Boulogne broke with William and attacked Dover, only to be beaten off. The rebellions were serious but not united – in the north, East Anglia, Exeter, Hereford and Kent. William captured York. The 1069 rebellion by Earls Waltheof and Gospatric, Edgar the Aetheling, Scots and Danes was a major threat. They took York, which William recovered, laying waste to England north of the Humber. In 1072 he entered Scotland and Malcolm Canmore submitted. The surviving sons of Harold Godwinson rose in the west but failed. Probably the most famous rebellion was by Hereward the Wake in Ely in 1071, supported by Earl Morcar. William marched to the spot. Morcar submitted and Hereward escaped from history into legend. In 1075 some of William's earls rebelled – Roger of Hereford and Ralph the Breton of Norwich. They were defeated. Roger was captured and imprisoned for life. Waltheof, who had survived an earlier rebellion, was accused (perhaps wrongly) of conspiracy and was executed in 1076. Thereafter William's position was secure.

The other great Norman Conquest occurred in southern Italy, led by lesser nobles seeking their own advantage in a divided land. They included the Hautevilles from near Coutances, whose origins are obscure. A foretaste of Italian events occurred in Spain, where the Normans Roger de Tosny and Robert Crispin joined the Christian *Reconquista* of Iberia from the Muslims. The earliest Normans in Italy were passing through on pilgrimage to the Holy Land. They became embroiled as mercenaries in local struggles. Others came seeking gain, some exiled from Normandy. The region was fought over by Lombards, Byzantines and Muslims. The Normans proved useful mercenaries. Those employed by the Lombard, Melus of Bari, won five successive battles before defeat at Cannae in 1018.

The Normans established independent lords. The first was Rainulf Drengot who survived Cannae to become Lord of Aversa. He married the widow of the Lombard Duke of Gaeta, becoming Count of Aversa and Duke of Gaeta. His successor Richard I became Prince of Capua. In 1038 the Byzantines under George Maniakes attacked the Muslims in southern Italy. A number of Normans, including the Hauteville brothers, distinguished themselves. Normans also aided the Lombard Arduin against the Byzantines in 1041, winning at Venosa, Monte Maggiore and Monte Siricolo.

In 1042 the Norman leaders held a conference at Melfi and agreed to recognise three regional authorities – Rainulf Drengot as Duke of Apulia over Aversa, Gaeta and now Capua, Salerno and Monte Gargano; William Ironarm de Hauteville over Troia and Melfi (later overall leader as Count of Apulia); his brother Drogo de Hauteville over Venosa. The Normans took over Apulia and Calabria. The papacy awoke to the Norman threat and allied with the Byzantines. The papal army was beaten at Civitate in 1053 and peace was made, while the Byzantines withdrew from Italy. In the Norman army were late Hauteville arrivals, Richard of Aversa (nephew of Rainulf Drengot) and Robert Guiscard (half-brother to the early Hautevilles). Richard ended Lombard power in Capua, becoming Prince of Capua. Robert Guiscard became Duke of Apulia and Calabria.

Sicily was invaded in 1061 and conquered by 1091, ruled by Guiscard's brother Roger I as count. Roger II was recognised as King of Sicily, Apulia and Calabria by the anti-pope Anacletus II in 1130, crowned in Palermo on Christmas Day. The kingdom survived until the 19th century. Roger II extended his power through the Mediterranean and coastal North Africa. In 1194 Frederick (II) (HRE), son of the Norman Queen Constance, took over. The southern Normans played a major part in the Crusades, founding the principality of Antioch.

William the Conqueror and his successors made the link between England and Normandy a significant part of medieval history. The Norman kingdom may be taken as continuing until 1154 and the death of the Conqueror's grandson Stephen. Normandy remained an independent duchy until 1204, when Philip II of France took it from John.

The impact of the Conquest was considerable. The Normans introduced aspects of their social organisation to England, thought of as feudalism. They brought their own form of fortification, castles, especially motte and baileys. They altered the system of raising armies and their tactical use. Cavalry from the socially superior became a major part of armed forces.

The Conqueror's son, William Rufus, succeeded on his father's death but the older son, Robert Curthose, became Duke of Normandy, the kingdom and the duchy thus being divided. In 1088 there was rebellion against Rufus but it was suppressed. In 1096 Curthose joined the First Crusade, leaving his duchy in Rufus' care. The arrangements for its return were never put into effect. A further rising occurred in 1099 under Robert de Mowbray earl of Northumberland. It was put down with the capture of Bamburgh Castle. Rufus was killed in the New Forest, possibly by assassination involving his brother Henry.

Henry I succeeded in 1100 in England. His older brother Robert Curthose again opposed but was forced into an agreement after a failed invasion. Henry I dealt with Curthose's supporter Robert of Bellême and then attacked Normandy. At Tinchebrai in 1106 Curthose was beaten, captured and imprisoned for life, dying in 1134. England and Normandy were united under Henry I until his death in 1135. Henry was opposed in Normandy by Curthose's son, William Clito, who gained support from Louis VI of France and Fulk of Anjou. In 1118 Fulk besieged Alençon and defeated Henry when he attempted relief. Henry gained revenge at Brémule in 1119. A rebellion by Waleran of Meulan was beaten at Bourgthéroulde in 1124.

On the death of Henry I the throne went to his nephew Stephen, despite attempts to pass it to his daughter Matilda. She married Henry V (HRE), becoming empress, and then Geoffrey of Anjou. Stephen put down early rebellions and his men defeated the Scots at the Standard 1138. Matilda invaded England, leading to civil war in which neither side gained ultimate control though Stephen largely kept the upper hand. In 1141 Stephen was defeated and captured at Lincoln. He was imprisoned for a year. Matilda's lieutenant, her half-brother Robert of Gloucester, was captured at Winchester. Robert and Stephen were exchanged. Matilda's son, Henry Plantagenet, attempted invasions but Stephen survived until his death in 1154. By then he had agreed that Henry should inherit rather than his own son. During Stephen's reign Henry's father, Geoffrey of Anjou, conquered Normandy in a ten-year campaign.

BATTLES AND SIEGES

ALENÇON, SIEGE AND BATTLE OF, 1118

In which Anglo-Norman knights dismounted to fight on foot. The only detailed account is in an Angevin chronicle. Anglo-Norman chroniclers ignored it, except for a brief reference by Orderic Vitalis, probably because Henry I was defeated. Fulk V of Anjou besieged Alençon, held for Henry by his nephew, the future King Stephen. Henry came to its relief. Fulk camped within a defensible enclosure called the Park. He sent out his men group by group, including archers and knights, in three sorties. They made no serious impact until reinforcements arrived under Lisiard of Sablé. This force dismounted in a wood and attacked Henry from the flank. Henry's ally Theobald of Blois was wounded by an arrow in the forehead. Fulk sallied from the Park in a mounted charge. Under the dual attack Henry's force broke and fled. Alençon surrendered but Henry soon recovered.

ARQUES-LA-BATAILLE, SIEGE OF, 1052–3

The castle of Arques, near Dieppe, was besieged by William the Conqueror against his uncle, William count of Arques who built it c.1038 and rebelled in 1052. He deserted the ducal army before Domfront and shut himself in Arques. The Conqueror set up a blockade and built a belfry. He left Walter Giffard to conduct the blockade. The ducal victory at St-Aubin-sur-Scie removed hope of relief. Arques surrendered on terms late in 1053, the garrison promised their lives. They emerged with heads bowed, carrying their saddles. Count William was exiled to Boulogne. Arques was the last castle in Normandy to surrender to Geoffrey V in 1145 and resisted Philip Augustus in 1204.

BAMBURGH, SIEGE OF, 1095

Bamburgh and its castle are on the coast north of Alnwick, Northumberland. On a rock, surrounded by sea, marsh and pools, it was considered 'impregnable'. William Rufus besieged the castle when Robert de Mowbray took refuge there after his rebellion. Rufus blockaded, buiding a counter castle named *Malveisin* or *Yfel Nehbur* (Bad Neighbour). Robert shouted from the walls to shame those who had promised him allegiance. Rufus went to Wales, leaving the siege to continue. One night Robert and 30 knights escaped to Newcastle but he was refused entry, captured and taken to Bamburgh. Rufus threatened to put out his eyes unless the castle surrendered. Countess Matilda and Robert's steward, Morael, yielded. Robert spent the rest of his life in prison.

BARI, SIEGE OF, 1068–71

Bari was the final Byzantine obstacle to Norman control of Apulia and southern Italy, capital of the Byzantine catapan. It stands on a promontory with a harbour on the Adriatic. Robert Guiscard besieged it from 5 August 1068. Engines were brought against the walls. The defenders used precious metal plate to reflect the sun into Norman eyes. They made a successful sortie, firing the engines. A hired assassin attacked Guiscard with a poisoned javelin but his throw missed when Guiscard bent under a table to spit. The blockade became fully effective in 1071 when Guiscard's brother Roger count of Sicily brought a fleet. The Byzantines attempted relief by sea but failed. Bari surrendered on 16 April 1071 and Guiscard entered. His peace terms were generous. It ended five centuries of Byzantine rule.

BOURGTHÉROULDE, BATTLE OF, 1124

The climax of Waleran de Meulan's revolt against Henry I in Normandy. Waleran relieved his castle at Vatteville in the north and returned towards Beaumont. Henry's household troops collected a force from neighbouring garrisons to block Waleran near Bourgthéroulde. The royalists were under Odo Borleng (captain of household troops), William of Tancarville (Henry's chaplain) and Ralph of Bayeux (castellan of Évreux). The young Waleran ignored advice to retreat. Odo Borleng set an example by dismounting to fight on foot though others remained on horseback. He ordered archers to the van against the enemy attack. The charge was halted and Waleran unhorsed and captured. The rebellion was over.

BRÉMULE, BATTLE OF, 1119

Victory for Henry I of England in Normandy against an invasion force under Louis VI of France, allied with Fulk of Anjou. They intended to make William Clito, Curthose's son, duke. The battle was fought on a plain near the hill of Verclives, where Henry posted scouts. They informed him when the French emerged from the woods. He ordered some knights to dismount and fight on foot, placing himself with them. The French made an undisciplined charge that was held by the dismounted knights. Eighty French knights were killed. A second charge was also halted. Henry I was wounded in the head but saved from a worse fate by his mail hood. The French broke and Louis fled to Andely. He became lost in the woods but a peasant led him to safety. Henry was welcomed in Rouen with hymn singing and bells ringing. Normandy was safe.

BRIONNE, SIEGES OF, 1047–50, APRIL 1124

Brionne stood on the Risle in central Normandy. Guy of Burgundy count of Brionne, the Conqueror's cousin, shut himself behind barred gates in Brionne Castle in 1047 after a rebellion against the Conqueror was ended by William's victory at Val-ès-Dunes. Brionne had a stone walled enclosure. The Conqueror's siege lasted three years according to Orderic Vitalis. Some historians have queried the duration but there is no alternative evidence. William built counter castles on either side of the river. There were daily sorties but the blockade began to work. Guy surrendered on terms and returned to Burgundy. The castle was razed though later rebuilt. Henry I of England besieged Brionne in 1124 following the rebellion by Waleran of Meulan. The town was damaged by fire. Henry built two counter castles and Brionne surrendered. Henry ordered the castle to be razed.

BURWELL, SIEGE OF, SEPTEMBER 1144

Burwell Castle in Cambridgeshire was built by Stephen against Geoffrey de Mandeville in 1143. Geoffrey rebelled with the Isle of Ely as his base. Burwell was built to garrison royal troops and protect Cambridge. It had an unusual rectangular plan, with stone walls and gate and a wide ditch to be filled from a nearby stream. It was never finished. In 1144 Geoffrey attacked, making reconnaissance bareheaded because of the heat. He was hit in the head by a crossbow bolt shot by a low-born archer. He was taken to Mildenhall and died a week later. The rebellion was over and the castle left unfinished.

CANNAE, BATTLE OF, 1018

Defeat in southern Italy for the Lombard, Melus of Bari, with his Norman mercenaries. He won five battles with their aid but was beaten by the Byzantines at Cannae, on the right bank of the Ofanto, four miles from the coast. It was the site of Hannibal's victory over the Romans. The Greeks, including the Varangian Guard, were under the catapan Boiannes. Amatus described the Greeks swarming over the battlefield like bees from an over-full hive. Cannae ended the independence of Lombard Apulia. The Normans showed their military worth and some transferred to Byzantine service. One Norman who survived the battle was Rainulf Drengot.

CERAMI, BATTLE OF, 1063

Norman victory in Sicily, after which the papacy granted the Normans a papal banner. Cerami was a small settlement on the River Cerami, west of Troina near Nicosia. It was a victory for Roger I the Great Count with only 130 knights against a larger Muslim army. The enemy included troops from Sicily and Africa. They had advanced from Palermo against Roger's stronghold at Troina. Roger, his nephew Serlo and his lieutenant Arisgot of Pozzuoli covered themselves with glory. The small Norman force withstood a charge. The battle lasted through the day but in the evening the Muslims broke and fled. It was an important step in the Norman conquest of Sicily. They were now established on the island.

CIVITATE, BATTLE OF, 17 JUNE 1053

Victory for the Normans in Italy against a papal army. The Normans were under Robert Guiscard and his brother Humphrey. Pope Leo IX sought to diminish Norman power, advancing south from Monte Cassino. His mainly Lombard army included Byzantines and Swabian infantry with two-handed swords. The Germans jeered at the shorter Normans. Negotiations failed and the Normans attacked. They fought in three divisions: Guiscard on the left and in reserve, Humphrey in the centre and Richard of Aversa on the right. The Normans had success on the flanks but the Germans held the centre. Norman cavalry on the right outflanked the enemy centre. Guiscard was unhorsed three times but fought on with lance and sword. Leo was captured afterwards. The site is near San Severo, on a plain by the River Fortore. The papacy recognised Norman possessions in Italy. Leo was released but died the following year.

DINAN, SIEGE OF, 1064

Besieged by William the Conqueror during his expedition to Brittany, when it resisted. The *Bayeux Tapestry* shows a wooden keep on a motte while the Normans fire it with torches. The Bretons handed over the keys as a symbol of surrender.

DOL, SIEGE OF, 1064

Besieged by William the Conqueror during his expedition to Brittany, his first objective. Riwallon of Dol rebelled against

Conan II count of Brittany and appealed to William for aid. The *Bayeux Tapestry* depicts the castle as a wooden keep on a motte. Conan besieged Riwallon in Dol and the Conqueror came to its relief. The *Tapestry* shows Conan escaping by rope. Chronicles however make it clear that the count left before William arrived. The castle was saved. Conan recovered and exiled Riwallon.

DOMFRONT, SIEGE OF, 1051–2

Domfront Castle, built by William of Bellême, stands on a rock over the Varenne near Avranches, on the border with Maine. A large ditch cut off the only approach. William the Conqueror besieged Domfront, held for Geoffrey Martel of Anjou, in the late summer of 1051 and through the winter. While it continued he attacked Alençon, which he took, ordering the citizens who had reminded him of his bastardy to have their hands and feet chopped off. At Domfront William built four counter castles. During the siege William found time to go hawking. Martel attempted relief but had to retreat. The blockade worked and Domfront surrendered on terms. Later Henry I of England built a new keep, now in ruins.

DYRRHACHIUM (DURAZZO/ EPIDAMNOS), SIEGE AND BATTLE OF, 1081–2

Dyrrhachium (Durazzo to Italians, Epidamnos to Greeks) was the capital of Illyria, and is modern Durrês in Albania. Robert Guiscard and his son Bohemond besieged it in 1081 in the Norman attempt at Mediterranean expansion against Byzantium. Guiscard left Otranto with a fleet and army in May 1081. A Venetian fleet allied to the Byzantines to defeat the Normans in June, after the Normans suffered damage in a storm. Guiscard could not blockade from the sea as intended. The siege was an attempt by the Normans to gain safety within. The defence was led by George Palaeologus. The Normans built a belfry, countered by a wooden tower and later destroyed by fire. The defenders used catapults, pitch and Greek Fire. The Normans suffered illness and starvation. Alexius I Comnenus came to the relief. The battle was fought on 18 October. Against the odds the Normans won through using archers and cavalry against the Varangian Guard (including Anglo-Saxon exiles). Guiscard's wife Sigelgaita participated in the ensuing battle, brandishing a spear and helping to rally the troops. Alexius was wounded in the forehead but escaped to Ochrid. The Byzantines retreated and Dyrrhachium surrendered on 21 February 1082. Guiscard returned to Italy. Bohemond continued to Larissa where he was defeated by the Byzantines.

ELY, SIEGE OF, 1071
William the Conqueror besieged the rebel Hereward the Wake. Ely was a fen island, difficult to approach. The Danes allied with Hereward, who took over Peterborough Abbey and Ely in 1070. William negotiated with the Danes, who agreed to leave. He blockaded Ely with ships on the Ouse and built a causeway via Aldreth with logs and stones. The rebels were joined by Morcar earl of Northumbria but fled. Morcar submitted and was imprisoned for life. Hereward escaped.

EXETER, SIEGE OF, 1068
Besieged by William the Conqueror. Harold Godwinson's mother, Gytha, took refuge there after Hastings. The citizens refused to swear fealty to William or pay tax, shutting the gates against him. The Conqueror brought an army, including English troops, to besiege Exeter for 18 days. Negotiations failed. One defender on the wall bared his posterior and farted at the attackers. William blinded a hostage in the view of the defenders. He lost a considerable number of men. The walls were mined. Exeter surrendered on terms. The king forbade looting. He built Rougemont Castle inside Exeter for a garrison under Baldwin de Meules. Gytha escaped before the surrender to Flatholme. In 1069 there was a

local rising for an invasion by the sons of Harold Godwinson but Exeter remained loyal to William.

FARINGDON, SIEGE OF, 1145
Captured by Stephen in the civil war with Matilda. Faringdon Castle was built by Matilda's supporter Robert of Gloucester for his son Philip. It controlled Malmesbury and threatened Oxford, demonstrating the Angevin intention of advancing east. Stephen assembled a force at Oxford, including London militia. He besieged Faringdon, building a counter castle. Stone-throwing engines were set up and attacks made daily. Archers ringed the walls to shoot in arrows. Robert was not inside and made no attempt at relief. The royalists tried scaling but failed. The defenders were persuaded to surrender on terms. Matilda's hopes for triumph were crushed though her son Henry continued the fight. Possibly because his father failed to save Faringdon, Philip of Gloucester went over to Stephen.

HASTINGS, BATTLE OF, 14 OCTOBER 1066
Victory for William the Conqueror over Harold Godwinson, the major battle in the conquest of Anglo-Saxon England by the Normans. William invaded in the autumn, landing at Pevensey. Harold defeated a northern invasion by Harold Hardrada at Stamford Bridge. On news of Norman arrival he marched south, hoping to surprise William, but the latter was prepared. Harold fought without troops who could have taken part had he waited longer. The traditional site is the hill of Battle town, because the *Battle Abbey Chronicle* says Harold was killed where the altar of the abbey was built. The earliest sources are less clear, making Caldbec Hill the possible site. The English formed ranks on foot. The Normans had cavalry and infantry, including well-armed men and archers. William opened with the archers, who failed to break the English line. Cavalry charges were difficult because of the ground and failed to break through. A rumour William had been killed led him to

remove his helmet and prove he was alive. The Normans made feigned retreats, drawing troops after them and turning on them, thus depleting the English ranks. William made a last push and the English broke. Harold was killed by an arrow in the eye. Two of his brothers were killed. The English retreated but some made a stand, an event that is difficult to unravel from the sources – the Malfosse incident. A stand was made near a deep slope or ditch and some Norman cavalry came to grief, but it did not alter the outcome of the battle. The English never recovered from Hastings. William secured his position in the south east and was crowned in London by the end of the year.

LINCOLN, BATTLE OF, 2 FEBRUARY 1141
In which King Stephen was defeated and captured, giving the Empress Matilda her best opportunity to rule England. The royal castle of Lincoln was seized by the half-brothers Ranulf earl of Chester and William de Roumare by a ruse in 1140. The citizens of Lincoln appealed against the rule of the half-brothers. At Christmas Stephen besieged Lincoln. The citizens let him in but the rebels held the castle. Stephen used throwing engines against them. Robert earl of Gloucester, for Matilda, attempted relief, including Welsh allies. The battle was fought on a Sunday. Stephen was advised to retreat before a larger army but chose to fight. Robert crossed the Witham and Stephen emerged to fight to the west of the city. Baldwin fitz Gilbert made a pre-battle speech for Stephen. Stephen and some of his knights dismounted to fight on foot, with cavalry on each wing. Some Angevins dismounted and fought on foot. The royal cavalry saw off the Welsh infantry on the flanks but was routed by enemy cavalry. Stephen's lieutenants on the wings, including six earls and William of Ypres, escaped. Stephen fought on with a sword until it broke, and then an axe handed him by a citizen, which also broke. Stephen was felled by a rock on the head. The victors killed many citizens. Stephen was

imprisoned, later in irons, until exchange brought his release.

MAYENNE, SIEGE OF, 1063
Geoffrey de Mayenne's castle, on a rock over the Mayenne, was besieged by William the Conqueror to complete his conquest of Maine. William intervened in the succession dispute over Maine on behalf of his son. Geoffrey favoured a rival. The castle was south of Domfront near the border. William brought up cavalry and infantry. He used fire, shot into the castle to panic the garrison. Two boys also entered the castle to start a fire. The garrison surrendered next day. Geoffrey kept his lands and castle though the Conqueror placed a garrison there.

MESSINA, SIEGE OF, 1061
A major step in the early stage of the Norman conquest of Sicily. Muslim Messina stood on the east coast, an obvious target for invaders from the mainland. Count Roger made two unsuccessful attempts against the city in autumn 1060 and early 1061. In 1061 the Norman fleet was defeated and the army forced from retreat to flight. In May 1061 Roger returned, expecting aid from Robert Guiscard. Roger crossed with an advance force at night to find the walls deserted. A supply train for Messina was intercepted. Roger attacked without waiting for aid and took the city. Many Muslims departed. The Normans strengthened the fortifications and put in a garrison.

MONTE MAGGIORE, BATTLE OF, 4 MAY 1041
One of three battles in 1041 won for the Lombards against the Byzantines in southern Italy by Normans. The site was that of Cannae but the mountain name is generally used in this case. The Normans emerged victorious under William de Hauteville (Ironarm), who was suffering from fever and watched from a hill. Excitement overcame him and he charged into the fray. The victory was due to the

impact of Norman cavalry. The Normans took much loot.

MORTEMER, BATTLE OF, FEBRUARY 1054

A victory for William the Conqueror against an invasion of Normandy by Henry I of France and Geoffrey Martel of Anjou. William blocked the route of the main force. A second army reached Mortemer on the border, led by Henry I's brother Odo. Magnates from Upper Normandy, on William's behalf, faced this force, under William de Warenne and Walter Giffard. The invaders lacked discipline, being allowed to loot and rape. The Normans attacked by surprise and routed them. Guy of Ponthieu was captured and submitted. William ordered a herald, Rodulf de Tosny, to shout the result from a treetop at night. He began, 'I bring you dreadful news . . .' The king and count retreated. William's success was a blow for his enemies in Normandy.

OXFORD, SIEGE OF, SEPTEMBER TO DECEMBER 1142

The Empress Matilda was besieged by Stephen in the civil war. Oxford was a westerly outpost for Matilda. Her presence posed a threat. Stephen countered by besieging Oxford from 29 September. The castle possessed a high tower. Matilda's garrison shot arrows over the river. Stephen crossed by a ford, leading the way by swimming. He charged and burst into the town, which was fired. The blockade of the castle continued for three months. Siege engines battered the defenders. Robert of Gloucester planned a relief but Matilda escaped before Christmas. In one version she escaped by a rope, but probably she slipped through a postern gate with four knights. She crossed the frozen Thames in a white cloak, tramping through the snow to Abingdon. She rode to Wallingford and safety. The Oxford garrison surrendered. It was an exciting escape but a blow to Matilda's cause.

REGGIO, SIEGE OF, 1060

The Byzantine capital was the last Byzantine stronghold taken by the Normans in Calabria, captured by the Hauteville brothers, Robert Guiscard and Count Roger. Roger built siege engines the previous winter. The garrison surrendered on terms and went to Scilla where they resisted the Normans before going on to Constantinople. The conquest of Calabria paved the way for the invasion of Sicily.

ST-AUBIN-SUR-SCIE, BATTLE OF, 25 OCTOBER 1053

Victory for William the Conqueror's men over Henry I of France. Henry invaded Normandy to support rebellion by William of Arques. The Conqueror besieged Arques and Henry I attempted relief. Henry camped at St-Aubin. In the battle the Norman cavalry made a feigned flight to draw the enemy on before turning upon them. The Normans 'who seemed to be fleeing, turned round and began violently to cut down the French'. The Conqueror used the tactic at Hastings. Enguerrand II count of Ponthieu, brother-in-law of the Count of Arques, was killed fighting for Henry. Henry retreated from Normandy. Arques surrendered and the count was exiled.

STANDARD, BATTLE OF THE, 22 AUGUST 1138

The English for King Stephen against Scottish invaders. David I king of Scots was Empress Matilda's uncle. Dissident English barons took refuge at his court. This was the third Scottish invasion of England in 1138. Stephen was occupied in the south and a northern army countered the threat, summoned by Thurstan, archbishop of York, and led by magnates Walter Espec and William of Aumale. A force of royal household knights under Bernard of Balliol and reinforcements from the midlands joined the northern army. The English used a *carroccio*, a cart with a pole carrying northern church banners. At its top was a silver pyx containing the host. This was the Standard. The site was a plain north of

Northallerton, Yorkshire. David made the error of allowing the Galwegian claim to take the van. The English chose a defensive position on a hill, probably Standard Hill but possibly Red Hill. Some English knights dismounted to fight on foot, interspersed with archers – a similar formation to that used in the Hundred Years' War. The Galwegian infantry charged and was 'destroyed by arrows', looking like 'hedgehogs with spines'. Prince Henry of Scots led a cavalry charge from the flank but it was held. The Scots broke and the English pursued. The battle lasted two hours. A modern track, Scotpits Lane, reflects the tradition of bodies buried after the battle. The victory eased Stephen's worries about his northern frontier.

STRYMON (STRUMA), BATTLE OF THE, 7 NOVEMBER 1185
Marking the end of William II of Sicily's ambitions regarding the Byzantine Empire. He was encouraged by dissension within the empire when Isaac Angelus succeeded. A fleet and an army under the Sicilian Baldwin approached Constantinople. The Greek commander, Alexius Branas, made a surprise attack, routing the Norman advance force at Mosynopolis. Negotiations followed but the Greeks attacked the main army at the Strymon (which runs through Greece and Bulgaria) and routed it. Many drowned in the river. The Norman generals, Baldwin and Richard of Acerra, were captured. The Norman fleet was attacked by Thessalonians and much damaged.

TINCHEBRAI, BATTLE OF, 1106
The first Anglo-Norman battle when trained cavalry dismounted to fight on foot, a victory for Henry I over his brother Robert Curthose. Curthose invaded England, seeking the throne, and failed. Henry replied by invading Normandy in 1105. He besieged Tinchebrai Castle, held by William count of Mortain for Curthose. William appealed to Curthose who attempted relief. Henry constructed a counter castle. The battle was fought on

level ground. Henry formed two lines of infantry with dismounted men, himself in the second. He placed cavalry on the wings, with relief cavalry under Helias of Maine out of sight. Curthose dismounted some men but led a cavalry charge, which was held. The relief force attacked on the flank and broke the enemy. Curthose was captured and never released. Henry became Duke of Normandy.

VAL-ÈS-DUNES, BATTLE OF, JANUARY 1047
Victory for William the Conqueror and Henry I of France, who aided the young William against Norman rebels under Guy of Burgundy, William's cousin. Guy claimed the duchy, supported by Norman magnates. The rebels assembled in western Normandy and crossed the Orne to fight on flat ground near Caen. There were cavalry clashes. Ralph Taisson deserted the rebels to join the king. Henry I was unhorsed but survived. The young William fought well. The rebels fled, many drowning in the river. Loose horses galloped over the field. Guy of Burgundy escaped to Brionne Castle, which later surrendered. The battle saved the duchy for William.

VARAVILLE, BATTLE OF, AUGUST 1057
Defeat by William the Conqueror of Henry I of France and Geoffrey Martel of Anjou. They invaded Normandy, destroying and pillaging. They were crossing a ford of the Dives when the Conqueror attacked. Henry succeeded in crossing but tidal water prevented half the army from following. William assembled an army at Falaise. He attacked the stranded force with archers and knights, decimating it. The invaders retreated, not to return. The victory aided William's rise to dominance in western France, making possible his invasion of England.

VENOSA, BATTLE OF, 17 MARCH 1041
In 1041 the Lombard, Arduin, established Norman knights at Melfi in southern Italy. Within days they captured Venosa. That

year three battles were fought and won against the Byzantines, the first near Venosa at the confluence of the Olivento and Ofanto. The Byzantines, under Catapan Doceanus, challenged the Normans to fight or leave. When the messenger had finished, the Norman Hugh Tuboeuf punched his unfortunate horse between the eyes, felling it. The rider fainted and was sent back on a new horse with the reply. The battle was fought next day. Many Greeks and Varangian Guards were killed, some drowning in the river. The Byzantines withdrew.

WALLINGFORD, SIEGES OF, 1139, 1152–3
A stronghold on the Thames, built inside a Saxon burh, vital in the civil war between Stephen and Matilda, held by Brian fitz Count, a supporter of Matilda. Stephen besieged it in 1139. The king built two counter castles, leaving a garrison while he moved west. Miles of Gloucester, for Matilda, attacked the besiegers and defeated them. Wallingford remained an easterly salient for Matilda. She rode to Wallingford after escaping from Oxford in 1142. When Henry took over from his mother, Stephen besieged Wallingford in 1152, building two counter castles. In 1153 the Londoners gave Stephen aid. Brian fitz Count sallied but failed to break out. Stephen moved on, leaving Roger of Hereford to continue the siege but Roger deserted to the enemy. Henry Plantagenet now besieged the besiegers in their counter castle at Crowmarsh, guarding a bridge over the Thames, the last major clash of the war. Henry captured a wooden tower and beheaded 60 archers, but without gaining a decisive victory. Stephen approached and faced Henry over the river. A truce was agreed; the war was virtually over.

WILTON, BATTLE OF, 1142
A defeat for Stephen in the civil war with Matilda. The king built a castle here against Robert of Gloucester, a salient into Matilda's territory. Robert of Gloucester, for Matilda, besieged Wilton. The king led a sortie that became a battle. The site is now in the grounds of Wilton House. Stephen placed cavalry on each wing. Robert's force was in three divisions. The Angevin cavalry charged, forcing back the royalists. Stephen fled. His steward, William Martel, delayed the enemy while Stephen escaped, but was himself captured. Stephen surrendered Sherborne Castle in return for William's release. Wilton was ravaged by the victors.

WINCHESTER, THE ROUT OF, 14 SEPTEMBER 1141
A victory for Stephen in the civil war against Matilda, while Stephen was a captive. His brother Henry of Blois, bishop of Winchester, was besieged in his castle at Wolvesey in Winchester from 31 July by Empress Matilda. Henry escaped to join Stephen's queen, the other Matilda, who brought a relief force under William of Ypres, including London militia. There was a double siege – Angevins besieging Wolvesey while themselves surrounded by royalists. On 2 August royalists fired the city. On the first Sunday in September an intended Angevin retreat turned into flight. Robert of Gloucester fought a rearguard action. He saved Matilda but was captured. The Londoners sacked Winchester. Miles of Gloucester escaped by abandoning his armour to avoid identification. Empress Matilda escaped, riding astride to Ludgershall and then by litter to Devizes. Her cause had suffered a major blow. Robert of Gloucester was exchanged for Stephen.

YORK, SIEGE OF, 1069
York held a significant strategic position. It became a capital for Viking kings. Aethelstan captured it as a step towards becoming King of England. York recovered independence until the fall of Erik Bloodaxe in 954. Harold Hardrada's invasion against Harold Godwinson in 1066 aimed at York. Control of York remained vital and the Conqueror, after capturing it in 1068, built the castle known as Clifford's Tower. York was a base for rebellion and Danish

invasion in 1069. The castellan of Clifford's Tower, Robert fitz Richard, made a rash sortie and his force was wiped out. William Malet remained in the castle and sent to William for aid. William returned from Normandy and recovered York. He 'spared no man' and built a second castle, the Old Baile. The rebels attacked York again but were held off. William's response was the harrying of the north until 'there was no village inhabited between York and Durham'. This episode is a vital part of the imposition of royal control over northern England.

The Battle of Morat, 1476, from Diebold Schilling's *Chronicle*

6 | The Holy Roman Empire and central Europe, 850–1500

GENERALS AND LEADERS

See in Part I: Albert II, Charles IV, Charles the Bold of Burgundy, Conrad II, Conrad III, Conrad IV, Frederick Barbarossa, Frederick II, Frederick III, Henry I the Fowler (HRE), Henry II (HRE), Henry II the Wrangler of Bavaria, Henry III (HRE), Henry IV (HRE), Henry V (HRE), Henry VI (HRE), Henry VII (HRE), Henry the Lion, Henry Raspe of Thuringia, Herman of Luxembourg, John of Luxembourg, Lewis IV, Lothar III, Maximilian I, Otto I the Great, Otto II, Otto III, Otto IV, Ottokar I, Ottokar II, Prokop, Rienzi, Rudolf I, Sigismund, Wenceslas II, Wenceslas IV, William of Holland, William Tell.

BATTLES AND SIEGES

Alessandria 1174–5, Aussitz 1426, Benevento 1266 (p. 232), Brescia 1238, Cortenuova 1237, Deutschbrod 1422, Dornach 1499, Durben 1260, Flarcheim 1080, Grandson 1476, Hohenburg 1075, Hohen-Mölsen 1080, Lake Peipus 1242, Lechfeld 955, Legnano 1176, Lenzen 929, Liegnitz 1241, Marchfeld 1278, Merseburg 933, Milan 1158–62, Morat 1476, Morgarten 1315, Mühldorf 1322, Nancy 1477, Parma 1247–8, Saaz 1421, St Jakob 1444, Sempach 1386, Tannenberg 1410, Vysehrad 1420, Weinsberg 1140.

OUTLINE OF EVENTS

The Holy Roman Empire dated from the papal coronation of Charlemagne in Rome in 800. It claimed to be the descendant of the Roman Empire, controlling most of western Europe. This situation only endured with the Carolingians. The fall of the

Carolingians saw the division of their empire and the formation of new units. Three or four such units appeared, altered, merged and eventually became East and West Francia, the nuclei of Germany and France. At first neither of the new monarchies was very strong. East Francia established itself as the inheritor of Charlemagne's empire, becoming the Holy Roman Empire.

Lewis the Child was the last Carolingian ruler of the East Franks. He died in 911, when an assembly of East Franks at Fircheim elected Conrad duke of Franconia as Conrad I king of the East Franks. East Francia consisted of four main principalities, the stem duchies – Saxony, Bavaria, Swabia and Franconia. To the west was Lotharingia (Lorraine), initially separate but claimed by both East and West Francia. Conrad I favoured his own duchy against the others. He tried to win Lotharingia but failed. He tried to limit ducal power but with little success. He faced revolts in Saxony and Bavaria, which remained virtually independent.

While the West Franks established hereditary monarchy, East Francia remained elective, its ruler chosen from one duchy and family then another. This restricted the growth of power of the kings. On Conrad's death Henry the Fowler of Saxony was elected at Fritzlar, with the support of only two duchies. He fought to win wider recognition. Bavaria accepted his rule when he defeated Duke Arnulf in 921. Henry married the Duke of Lotharingia's daughter. His greatest achievement was against his pagan neighbours – Magyars, Slavs and Danes – including victory at Unstrut.

Henry the Fowler seemed to have established a Saxon dynasty. His son was elected as Otto I (the Great). In 962 Otto was crowned Holy Roman Emperor by Pope John XII, establishing East Francia as the heir to Charlemagne's empire. The ruler elected by the German duchies was called King of the Romans. Only if crowned by the pope could he properly be called emperor. In common parlance, however, the rulers of Germany are often referred to as emperors, and we shall follow this practice.

Otto I forced the papacy to give him imperial coronation but the need to have papal blessing caused problems for his successors. Otto faced internal revolt and external threats. Eberhard rebelled but was killed in battle and his duchy, Franconia, was added to the royal demesne. Otto extended his family power by establishing his brother in Bavaria, his son in Swabia and his brother-in-law in Lotharingia. From Lotharingia he developed German interest in Italy, which would dog imperial history through the Middle Ages. Otto had notable success over the Magyars at Lechfeld.

The son and grandson of Otto I continued family expansion. Otto II gained imperial prestige through marriage to a Byzantine princess. Otto III faced opposition from Henry the Wrangler of Bavaria. He made regular Italian expeditions, three in six years. He died without heir. The clash with the papacy reached crisis point under Henry IV who was elected as a minor, not reaching his majority until 1065. His clash with Gregory VII came over the archbishopric of Milan. Henry threatened to bring down the pope, calling him a false monk and demanding 'let another mount the throne of St Peter'. In turn Henry IV was excommunicated and deposition threatened. Henry submitted to the pope at Canossa in 1077. The death of his rival Rudolf of Swabia, killed at Hohen-Mölsen, was a turning point in his control of the German princes. In 1084 Henry attacked Rome and deposed Gregory, who was rescued by the Normans of southern Italy. Henry V (HRE) reached an agreement with the papacy to resolve the Investiture Controversy by the Concordat of Worms.

The Holy Roman Emperors found it difficult to maintain power in Germany. Constant changes of dynasty made it hard to establish a demesne. Frederick Barbarossa, arguably the greatest emperor, attempted to regain dominance in Germany and the west. He was elected after a period of frequently changing ruling familes – from Saxony, Bavaria and his own Swabia. His family was the Hohenstaufen. He was Conrad III's nephew, preferred to Conrad's young son. The Hohenstaufen lands were on the fringes of Germany. Frederick's second marriage, to Beatrice of Burgundy, directed his interest south. He built up the royal demesne and imperial administration through officials called ministeriales. A major threat came from the duchy of Saxony under Henry the Lion. Their early good relationship deteriorated. Frederick used other magnates to bring down Henry, who was exiled, while Saxony was split in two. Frederick was crowned emperor in Rome in 1155 but the Lombard League of Italian towns formed against him and rebelled. On his final expedition Frederick failed to take Alessandria and was defeated at Legnano. He recognised Lombard freedom. Frederick married his son Henry to the heiress Constance of Sicily, leading to imperial rule of the Norman kingdom.

Henry VI died in 1197. His young son Frederick was not elected. Frederick though, as the son of Constance of Sicily, inherited that kingdom, which became his base. In Germany power went to Otto IV of Saxony, though opposed by Frederick's uncle, Philip of Swabia, in a civil war that lasted until Philip died. Otto's fate was sealed when he joined an alliance against Philip Augustus of France and was defeated at Bouvines. The young Frederick was crowned at Aachen.

Frederick II had to compromise with the German princes to keep his throne while facing a rival in Henry Raspe. Frederick was excommunicated by the pope for failing to go on crusade, though he eventually went and was crowned King of Jerusalem. He defeated the Lombard League at Cortenuova in 1237. He suppressed a rebellion by his son Enzio and his chief minister Piero della Vigna.

After Frederick II the empire declined as a western power, becoming increasingly divided. The inherent weaknesses of its monarchical system became more apparent. The nobles and the towns of Germany and Lombardy became independent of imperial control. Frederick's descendants fought to keep Sicily but Anjou and Aragón ousted them. Imperial territory in Italy declined into a patchwork of lesser states – the kingdom of Sicily/Naples, the Papal States and the city states of Milan, Venice and Florence. Germany was weakened by internal division. The death of Conrad IV was followed by a 20-year interregnum, no ruler winning universal acceptance. Rudolf of Habsburg was elected in 1273 but his son was not. The Habsburgs remained powerful but were opposed by the Wittelsbachs.

Central Europe was an ever-changing patchwork of states through the Middle Ages, not unlike the Balkan region. Poland, Lithuania, Hungary and Bohemia were the major units (with the Empire) – power moving from one to the other. Magyars and Slavs formed a large part of the population. Christian wars against pagans marked the early Middle Ages. Later the Teutonic Knights and the Mongols (Tatars) joined the fray.

A political unit existed in Poland from the early Middle Ages. Mieszko I converted to Christianity in 966. His son Boleslaw I was the first crowned king though coronation remained difficult and intermittent. Feudal ties developed but power was often in the hands of dukes rejoicing in such names as Henry the Bearded, Boleslaw the Bashful, Henry the Honourable and Wladislaw Spindleshanks. Przemysł II duke of Kraków brought more unity, ruling Gdańsk (Danzig) and eastern Pomerania. He arranged for his own coronation only to be murdered before it could happen, in 1296. Wenceslas II of Bohemia was crowned king in 1300, uniting the crowns. A separate Polish monarchy returned in 1320 with the coronation of Wladyslaw the Short-Elbowed, who lost some territory but strengthened internal rule. Poland proper emerged with Casimir III the Great who increased royal power, fortified towns, built castles and regained Mazovia. After a succession crisis the throne went jointly in 1386 to Jadwiga daughter of Louis of Hungary and her husband Jagiełło, Grand Duke of Lithuania and previously pagan. The dynasty ruled Poland until 1572. The power of the Knights declined after their defeat at Tannenberg in 1410. The dynasty came to control Hungary and Bohemia as well as Lithuania and Poland.

In northern Europe a crusading movement led to the conversion of the pagan Baltic (north Germany, Poland, Lithuania, Livonia, Estonia). Christians from Scandinavia and the west with the Military Orders participated. The Sword Brothers were important early, later absorbed into the Teutonic Knights. They focused on the Baltic region. The Knights conquered Prussia. They were defeated by Alexander Nevsky at Lake Peipus. In 1410 they were beaten by the (now Christian) Lithuanians at Tannenberg. Western crusaders still came to Marienburg, where their shields were displayed on the walls, among them Henry Grosmont of Lancaster and Henry Bolingbroke. Ordinary people, especially from Germany, came for land. Crusading transformed into wars between Christians for territory. The Teutonic Order declined from 700 members in 1410 to 300 by 1453 but survived the Middle Ages.

Hungary was another major state in central Europe, formed from Magyar settlement. It had constant contact with the Holy Roman Empire to its west and Balkan countries to its east. The Mongols had overrun Hungary in the mid-13th century when the larger of the two-pronged Mongol invasion had defeated Béla IV at the River Sajó in 1241. In the same year, however, the Great Khān Ögedei died and the Mongols withdrew. There was still Mongol activity in Hungary in the later 13th century but the main threat had passed. A stronger western influence was felt with the succession of Charles Robert (Carobert) in 1310 as Charles I, the grandson of the Angevin Charles II of Naples. He restored Hungarian unity, defeating his internal opponents at Rozgony in 1319. He married Elizabeth, sister of Casimir the Great of Poland, and their son Louis ruled both kingdoms. In a 40-year reign Louis the Great recovered the Dalmatian coast from Venice, Wallachia, Moldavia, Bosnia and part of Serbia and Bulgaria. Hungary suffered under Sigismund, largely because of his wide interests elsewhere and his costly wars. After his death for a time the union with Poland was restored. Hungary was saved by the efforts of its general, John Hunyadi, despite the disaster at Varna in 1444 due to the king breaking the truce. Hunyadi saved Belgrade just before his death in 1456. Hunyadi's son, Matthias I Corvinus, was elected king despite having no claim by inheritance. He reformed the army, demanding service from a proportion of the serfs, and won back ground from the Turks. He crusaded against the Hussites. He recovered Moravia, Silesia and Lusatia. From Austria he won Salzburg and Styria, in 1485 besieging and taking Vienna, where he died in 1490.

The imperial concept crumbled in central and eastern Europe, where German claims of lordship were overthrown and smaller states established themselves, including Bohemia. Charles of Moravia succeeded his father John as king. He was elected as Emperor Charles IV in 1346. He is accused of favouring Bohemia at the expense of the empire, granting privileges to Prague. By the Golden Bull he recognised limitations on emperors, which were already apparent, defining the system for election. Seven electors were named, one being the King of Bohemia. The Czechs sought independence and revolted against Sigismund in the Hussite wars. Sigismund invaded Bohemia but was defeated at Vyšehrad by Žiška. Prokop took over as Bohemian commander. Sigismund finally captured Prague but recognised self-rule.

Switzerland also escaped from imperial grasp. The region was dominated by the Habsburgs from the 13th century. Three mountain cantons agreed to exclude Habsburg control. Their confederation grew. Their attempt at independence led to wars. They defeated the Austrians at Morgarten. Swiss military methods became a model for others and the papacy employed Swiss Guards. The cantons called their confederacy Schwyz and resisted the Habsburgs. The story of William Tell symbolises the fight but may be fictional. Sigismund recognised their independence in 1415. They still had to resist attempts at control by Burgundy. Charles the Bold of Burgundy was beaten at Grandson. Swiss independence was recognised by Burgundy in the Peace of Zurich.

BATTLES AND SIEGES

ALESSANDRIA (ALEXANDRIA), SIEGE OF, 1174–5

Frederick Barbarossa besieged Alessandria from 29 October on his fifth Italian expedition. Alessandria was founded on the Po by the Lombard League against Frederick and named after Pope Alexander III who was hostile to Frederick. On Good Friday Frederick broke the Truce of God to mine the wall. His men entered but were defeated. Frederick abandoned the siege on 13 April, Easter Sunday, burning his camp and siege equipment. Three days later he made terms with the Lombard League. There was a battle at Alessandria in 1391, when Milan defeated Florence.

AUSSITZ (AUSSIG/ÚSTI), SIEGE AND BATTLE OF, 1426

The Hussites besieged Aussitz on the Elbe in Bohemia. Frederick the elector of Saxony led the third anti-Hussite 'Crusade' and on 16 June sought to relieve Aussitz, which he had been granted by Sigismund. The Hussites under Prokop drew up wagons defensively on a hill. The Hussites held off Frederick with artillery fire. They then used cavalry to break and pursue the enemy.

BRESCIA, SIEGE OF, 1238

Besieged by Frederick II from 3 August to 9 October. Brescia is to the east of Milan, a stronghold that Frederick needed to control if he were to win Milan. Frederick brought siege engines and mining gear. An engineer, the Spaniard Calamandrino, was captured and was offered gifts (a house and a woman) to change sides. He showed the Brescians how to make catapults against Frederick's belfries. The besiegers tied captives to the front of their engines to discourage attack. The Brescians lowered captives on ropes before the walls at which Frederick's rams were aimed. A nocturnal sortie surprised Frederick. With winter Frederick retreated to Cremona.

CORTENUOVA, BATTLE OF, 27 NOVEMBER 1237

Victory for Frederick II against the Lombard League. He moved from Cremona to catch the enemy near the crossing of the Oglio at Cortenuova. Frederick's van was initially successful but the Milanese around their *carroccio* held on. With darkness the Lombards abandoned the field in heavy rain, leaving the *carroccio* stuck in the mud. Frederick made a triumphal entry into Cremona, pulling the *carroccio* by elephant. The success did not endure. Frederick failed to take Brescia the following year.

DEUTSCHBROD (NĚMECKÝ BROD), SIEGE OF, 10 JANUARY 1422
Victory for the Hussites under Žiška, leading to the expulsion of imperial forces from Bohemia. The Hussites had beaten Sigismund at Kuttenberg on 6 January but many escaped. A large number of these took shelter in Deutschbrod. It was stormed and those within massacred.

DORNACH, BATTLE OF, 22 JULY 1499
Defeat of Emperor Maximilian by the Swiss, the decisive battle in the Swiss struggle for independence which led to the Treaty of Basle, recognising that independence.

DURBEN (DURBE), BATTLE OF, JULY 1260
Defeat of the Teutonic Knights by the Lithuanians, leading to a revival of paganism in the eastern Baltic after the second Prussian revolt. The Knights tried to relieve besieged Christian garrisons. Their master, Von Hornhausen, was ambushed and killed in the battle. Kurland revolted and Livonia was lost. There followed a series of crusades and the revolt was not suppressed until 1283.

FLARCHEIM, BATTLE OF, 27 JANUARY 1080
An indecisive battle but Henry IV (HRE) withdrew from the field, leaving Rudolf of Rheinfelden duke of Swabia to claim victory. The pope declared Henry deposed but Rudolf was killed later in the year. Henry recovered power in Germany.

GRANDSON, 2 MARCH 1476
Swiss defeat of Charles the Bold duke of Burgundy. Charles captured Grandson and hanged its garrison. He advanced towards Neuchâtel when the Swiss van met him at the foot of Mont Aubert near Lake Geneva.

The Swiss formed a defensive square and made infantry charges with pikes. Charles tried to break them with artillery and cavalry but failed. The appearance of Swiss reinforcements on the flank decided the issue. The Burgundians fled, losing 400 pieces of artillery. The Swiss recovered Grandson.

HOHENBURG (HOMBURG-ON-UNSTRUT), BATTLE OF, 9 JUNE 1075
Defeat of the Saxons by Henry IV (HRE) during Henry's first war with the Saxons after Saxony and Thuringia rebelled. Henry raised support, especially from southern Germany. Rudolf of Swabia made a charge on Henry's behalf but had to be rescued by the Bavarians.

HOHEN-MÖLSEN, BATTLE OF, 15 OCTOBER 1080
Indecisive battle but Henry IV (HRE)'s rival Rudolf of Swabia was fatally wounded. A replacement anti-king was elected in Hermann of Salm but the battle established Henry's position in Germany.

LAKE PEIPUS, BATTLE OF, 5 APRIL 1242
Victory of Alexander Nevsky over the Teutonic Knights, fought over the ice at the crossing between Lakes Peipus and Pskov. The Knights had Danish, Livonian and Estonian allies. The Russians made the best of the conditions. Their horse archers forced back the enemy left. The Knights were surrounded and slaughtered. Their position in the Baltic declined sharply after the defeat.

LECHFELD, BATTLE OF, 10 AUGUST 955
Victory for Otto I against the Magyars, who had been raiding west into Europe under Karchas Bulcsu. It was fought by the Lech near Augsburg in Bavaria, which the Magyars had been besieging. Initially the Magyars were successful, surprising Otto with a sudden attack on his camp by a second force from the flank. Otto took up shield and lance to lead the charge that settled the battle. Conrad the Red of

Lorraine, fighting for Otto, was killed. Afterwards the Magyars settled in Hungary. Otto was now called 'the Great'.

LEGNANO, BATTLE OF, 29 MAY 1176

Defeat of Frederick Barbarossa by the Lombard League, the climax of Frederick's fifth Italian expedition. Frederick assembled at Como against Milan. Legnano is 15 miles north-west of Milan. Henry the Lion did not answer Frederick's summons. Some of Frederick's troops were employed elsewhere in Italy. Frederick had a small cavalry force and rashly accepted battle against a larger, better-balanced Lombard army. His charge was repulsed by pikemen and dismounted knights, holding steady round the *carroccio*. It was an early example of success for good infantry against heavy cavalry. New Lombard troops arrived on the flank. Frederick was unhorsed and for a time believed dead, but escaped to Pavia leaving behind shield, lance and treasure. He made peace with the papacy and recognised the liberties of the Italian communes. Afterwards Frederick took revenge on Henry the Lion.

LENZEN, BATTLE OF, 4 SEPTEMBER 929

A force for Henry I (HRE) defeated the Slavic Redarii who had revolted near the Elbe. Saxon success depended on their possession of a small cavalry force, which the Slavs lacked. Afterwards the Redarii paid tribute and converted to Christianity.

LIEGNITZ (WAHLSTATT), BATTLE OF, 9 APRIL 1241

Defeat for the Teutonic Knights by Mongols under Batu. The smaller of two Mongol armies raided through Poland and sacked Kraców. The Knights fought in alliance with Poles and Silesians. Duke Henry II the Pious of Silesia commanded the Christians, his infantry in four battles. The Mongols used horse archers in a feigned flight, drawing the Christians into a trap. Mongol cavalry then attacked. Duke Henry was killed. The Mongols invaded Silesia but were blocked by the Bohemians

and retreated to Hungary where Batu defeated Béla IV of Hungary at Mohi on the Sajó. A crusade was preached against the Mongols. Liegnitz ended the furthest advances of both the Mongols and the Teutonic Knights.

MARCHFELD, THE (DÜRNKRUT/STILLFRIED), BATTLE OF, 28 AUGUST 1278

Defeat of Ottokar II of Bohemia by Rudolf I Habsburg and Ladislas IV of Hungary. The Marchfeld is near Stillfried and Dürnkrut, by the Danube. Ottokar invaded Austria and camped near Stillfried, allied with Poles and German mercenaries. Rudolf was with his reserve. The conflict opened with Hungarian horse archers, for Rudolf, attacking the enemy flank. Infantry is not mentioned in the accounts. Ottokar was killed in flight. The Marchfeld ended the expansion of Bohemia and helped establish the Habsburgs.

MERSEBURG (RIADE/ALLSTEDT), BATTLE OF, 15 MARCH 933

Defeat of the Magyars by Henry I (HRE) at an unidentified site near Merseburg in northern Thuringia. The Magyars threatened western Europe. Henry refused to pay tribute, returning a dog without ears and tail. He blocked the invaders' route, placing light horse to the fore to mask the heavy cavalry, which made a successful charge.

MILAN, SIEGE OF 1158–62

During Frederick Barbarossa's second Italian expedition. Frederick could not surround the city but used three lines of men to shoot in missiles, starving Milan into submission. All those between 14 and 70 had to take an oath of loyalty to him. Milan was the leader of the Lombard League, opposing imperial authority. It revolted again in 1159. Frederick was occupied at the siege of Crema, which Milan tried to aid. He returned to Milan in September 1161 with reinforcements. He laid waste the surrounding area to disrupt food supplies. Five Milanese captives were blinded. A sixth lost his nose but kept his eyes to lead the others home. The city surrendered on 1 March 1162. Frederick promised mercy but destroyed much of the city.

MORAT (MÜRTEN), BATTLE OF, 22 JUNE 1476

Defeat of Charles the Bold of Burgundy by the Swiss. Charles advanced towards Berne, making a diversion to besiege Morat on its lake, a town recently taken by the Swiss, who now attempted relief. Their force consisted mainly of halberdiers and pikemen but also cavalry from Lorraine and Germany. Charles had a barricaded position with a camp outside. The Swiss made a surprise attack through a wood. They were hit by artillery, and some Swiss cavalrymen were cut in half by the shot, their lower halves remaining on horseback. The Burgundians broke and thousands were slaughtered, only the left wing escaping.

MORGARTEN (MORTGARTEN), 15 NOVEMBER 1315

Defeat of Duke Leopold of Austria by the Swiss near Lake Egeri. The Swiss supported Lewis of Bavaria against Frederick of Habsburg to rule Germany. The latter's brother, Leopold, sought revenge. He advanced towards Schwyz by a narrow path between the mountain and the lake at Morgarten to find his way blocked by a stone barrier. The Swiss hurled down boulders on the trapped enemy. Hidden Swiss closed off the rear. Swiss halberdiers demolished the Austrians. One source called it 'a butchery'. The only escape was into the lake, where many drowned. Leopold was one of the few to escape. This was the first major victory by Swiss infantry over German knights. Lewis recognised the Swiss confederation.

MÜHLDORF, BATTLE OF, 28 SEPTEMBER 1322

Defeat of Frederick of Habsburg duke of Austria by Lewis IV (HRE) after a divided election for King of the Romans between them in 1314. Frederick tried a pincer movement against Bavaria, the second force under his brother Leopold. King John of Bohemia fought for Lewis. Frederick crossed the Inn when Lewis attacked. The battle was fought mainly by cavalry, including Hungarian mounted archers for Frederick. A flank attack by the burgrave of Nuremberg decided the issue. Frederick was captured and became reconciled with Lewis. It was claimed Lewis ignored the laws of war by not remaining on the site for three days. The victory established Lewis' success, recognised at Nuremberg in 1323.

NANCY, BATTLE OF, 5 JANUARY 1477

Final Swiss defeat of Charles the Bold of Burgundy. René II of Anjou, having recovered his territories from Burgundy, was besieged by Charles at Nancy. The Swiss advanced to aid René. Count Campobasso, leading Charles' mercenaries, had once fought for Anjou and now deserted. The Burgundians were outnumbered three to one. The Burgundian position was between woods and the River Meurthe on the left. The battle was fought amid snow and ice – conditions that suited the Swiss. René's standard carried an image of the Virgin. Charles' artillery failed to stop a Swiss infantry advance. A flank attack through the woods against Charles' right decided the issue. The Swiss discharged culverins in the attack. The Burgundians tried to retreat. Austrian cavalry pursued, joined by Campobasso. Charles was killed trying to cover the retreat. A Swiss halberd cut through his helmet and skull. The body was found two days later in the frozen mud, partly eaten by wolves. The main beneficiary was Louis XI of France.

PARMA, SIEGE OF, 1247–8

Conducted by Frederick II from 16 June. He was heading for Lyons when Parma declared for the papacy and the Lombard League. He returned to besiege it, setting up camp on the left bank of the Po and optimistically calling his settlement Vittoria (Victory). He laid waste around but the blockade was only partial. Mantua sent a fleet to assist Parma. Frederick failed to break in. The new leaders of Parma spread false reports that relief was coming, to keep up spirits. Frederick's force was depleted by other demands. On 18 February 1248 he was defeated by a Parmesan sortie that broke into Vittoria, seizing the imperial treasure and crown. Frederick was nearly captured. His minister Taddeo da Suessa was taken, his hands cut off and he was left to die in prison. The siege was abandoned.

SAAZ (SAAS/ŽATEC), SIEGE AND BATTLE OF, 2 NOVEMBER 1421

Victory for the Hussites under Žiška, settling the second anti-Hussite crusade. Two forces invaded Bohemia from east and west. The German princes coming from the west besieged Saaz. Žiška brought a relief force. He had sight in only one eye and now became entirely blind.

ST JAKOB, BATTLE OF, 26 AUGUST 1444

Defeat for the Swiss by Armagnac écorcheurs for Charles VII of France, assisting Frederick of Habsburg. The French were under Charles' son, the Dauphin Louis (XI). A lull in the Hundred Years' War made troops available. The French invaded Switzerland. The battle was fought by the River Birs near Basle. A small Swiss infantry army crossed the river and attacked. They pushed back the French van but were surrounded by the larger army, which then made cavalry charges. The Swiss retreated to the ruined leper hospital of St Jakob. They held off cavalry but the French attacked with archers and artillery from a distance. The Swiss killed over twice their number of French but were wiped out by the bombardment. The French however retreated, not wishing to face further Swiss troops. One reported he had 'never seen or met men who resisted so strongly or were so willing to sacrifice their lives'.

SEMPACH, BATTLE OF, 9 JULY 1386

Duke Leopold III of Habsburg, ruler of Swabia, was defeated by the Swiss. The Swiss supported the Swabian League against Leopold. He invaded Swiss territory and was met in Luzern. The Swiss stood on a slope near Hildisrieden by Lake Sempach, later commemorated by a chapel. The Austrian van dismounted and fought on foot, seeking a solution to Swiss infantry tactics. The Austrians had initial success but their heavy armour made advance difficult. More Swiss arrived to attack from the flank. The Austrians broke and fled. Leopold rode forward in order to save the day but was killed. It was an important step towards Swiss independence. The legendary Arnold Winkelried is supposed to have played an heroic part in the battle.

TANNENBERG (GRUNWALD), BATTLE OF, 15 JULY 1410

Defeat of the Teutonic Knights by allied Slav forces under Jagiełło king of Poland and Vitold grand duke of Lithuania, joined by Tatars and Bohemians under Žiška. The Knights were led by Grand Master Ulrich von Jungingen. Tannenberg (now Grunwald) is in northern Poland. The Knights crossed the River Drewenz and initiated battle despite having the smaller force. The Knights stood with Tannenberg to their left and forest on their right. They had cannons in the van but a thunderstorm wet the powder. In the centre and on the right the Poles prevailed. The Knights had a wagon fort to the rear with cannons. The Poles overran it. Von Jungingen was killed. The Knights lost Old Prussia. They agreed the Treaty of Thorn in 1411, recognising Poland's independence but keeping their own lands. The defeat was a serious blow to the prestige of the Knights whose decline followed.

VYŠEHRAD (WYSCHEBRAD), BATTLE OF, 1 NOVEMBER 1420

Defeat for Emperor Sigismund by Hussites under Žiška. The Heights of Vyšehrad are near Prague. Sigismund besieged the garrison. The Hussites came from Prague against him. It was the first major Hussite victory, causing the failure of the first anti-Hussite crusade.

WEINSBERG, BATTLE OF, DECEMBER 1140
Defeat of Welf VI by Conrad III. Conrad deprived Henry the Proud of Bavaria and Saxony. Henry died in 1139. Welf was the uncle of Henry the Proud and opposed the grant of Bavaria to Leopold of Austria, Conrad's half-brother. The labels Guelf and Ghibelline are said to originate from this conflict, from Welf and Weibling. Saxony supported the Guelfs and Conrad invaded Saxony in 1140. In 1141 Conrad returned to besiege Weinbsberg, which surrendered. He agreed to let the women go with whatever they could carry. They took their husbands. In 1141 Leopold died and Conrad made an agreement with the Saxons. The divisions within Germany persisted.

Gentile Bellini, *Sultan Mehmet II*, 1480

7 | The Byzantine Empire and eastern Europe, 400–1453

GENERALS AND LEADERS

See in Part I: Alexius I Comnenus, Alexius IV Angelus, Alexius V Dukas (Murzuphlus), Alp Arslan, Andronicus I Comnenus, Andronicus II Palaeologus, Andronicus III Palaeologus, Baldwin I, Baldwin II, Bardas Caesar, Bardas Phokas Caesar, Bardas Phokas son of Leo, Bardas Sclerus, Basil I, Basil II the Bulgar Slayer, Bayezit, Belisarius, Chosroes I, Chosroes II, Constantine I, Constantine V Copronymus, Constantine VII Porphyrogenitus, Constantine VIII, Constantine IX Monomachus, Constantine XI Palaeologus, Grant (John), Heraclius, John I Tzimisces, John I de Brienne, John II Comnenus, John III Dukas Vatatzes, John VI Cantacuzenus, John VII Palaeologus, John VIII Palaeologus, Julian the Apostate, Justin II, Justinian I, Justinian II, Krum, Leo V, Leo VI the Wise, Maniakes (George), Manuel I Comnenus, Manuel II Palaeologus, Maurice, Mehmet II, Michael I Rhangabe, Michael II, Michael III, Michael IV, Michael VIII Palaeologus, Murad II, Nikephorus II Phokas, Orhan, Othman, Phokas, Roger de Flor, Romanus I Lecapenus, Romanus II Porphyogenitus, Romanus III Argyrus, Romanus IV Diogenes, Stephen Dušan of Serbia, Symeon, Tamberlane, Theodore Angelus Dukas Comnenus, Theodosius I the Great, Theodosius II, Walter de Brienne, William de Champlitte, Zeno, Zoe Carbonopsina, Zoe Porphyrogenita.

BATTLES AND SIEGES

Abydos 989, Adrianople 378, Arcadiopolis 823, 970, Chernomen 1371, Constantinople 1203–4, 1397–1402, 1422, 1453, Demetrias 1275, Kalamata 1415, Klokotnitsa 1230, Kosedag 1243, Kosovo 1389, 1448, Kulikovo 1380, Kustendil 1330, Larissa 1083, Levunium 1091, Manzikert 1071, Myriocephalum 1176, Nika Revolt 532, Pelagonia 1259, Pelekanos 1329, Phoenicus 655, Poimanenon 1204, 1224, Rovine 1395, Samosata 873, Spetsai 1263, Stilo 982, Struma (Kleidion) 1014, Thessalonika 1185, 1224, 1430, Trajan's Gate 986, Tricamarum 533, Versinicia 813, Yarmuk 636.

OUTLINE OF EVENTS

The Byzantine Empire was the surviving eastern part of the ancient Roman Empire. The history of the Eastern Empire began with the transfer of the capital from Rome to the renamed Constantinople by Constantine the Great. His chosen site was that magnificent setting between Europe and Asia protected by the Golden Horn to the north, the Bosphorus to the east, the Hellespont to the west and the Sea of Marmara to the south. The settlement was said to have been founded in c.600 BC by Greek colonists under Byzas but it had remained insignificant until Constantine. The Romans took it over in 73 AD.

The Roman Empire was divided for convenience in ruling. By the 4th century the east was more prosperous but endangered by Persia to the east. Constantinople rather than Rome became the emperor's base. Constantine recognised the value of the site for a city that expanded to become a major – sometimes *the* major – city in the known world. Constantine rebuilt Byzantium from c.324, settled there in 328 and inaugurated it as Constantinople in 330. He increased it fivefold with two and a half miles of defensive walls. His religious policy meant that 'new Rome' was Christian from its beginning.

Emperor Julian the Apostate declared himself a pagan and tried to revive the ancient religion. His failure was the last serious attempt of this kind. Julian tried to combat the Persians and won at Ctesiphon but the campaign petered out. The barbarian threat from Goths, Huns and others, which felled the Western Empire, was faced in the east too, which also encountered Bulgars, Slavs, Avars and others. The division of the empire became more pronounced as the barbarian threat increased. After the defeat of Valens by the Goths in 378 there was a clear division between the west under Gratian and the east under Theodosius. Again in 395 the empire was divided between east (Arcadius) and west (Honorius).

When the Western Empire collapsed into separate barbarian states in the 5th century, the Eastern Empire continued as *the* Roman Empire. Constantinople became *the* capital as Rome succumbed to barbarian control by Huns, Goths, Vandals, Lombards, Franks and so on. Constantinople became stronger, its walls improved by successive emperors such as Theodosius II. There were barbarian attacks on Constantinople, as in 447, but they failed. From 476 the Western Empire had collapsed into a patchwork of barbarian states and Odoacer took power in Italy while Zeno in the east was the surviving emperor.

The Eastern Empire developed its own characteristics. Its language and outlook became increasingly Greek. Outsiders referred to its people as Greeks – though ideas of a united empire had not vanished. In the 6th century, Justinian I's success against the Persians allowed him to indulge visions of a reunited empire. He set about reconquering the west under generals Belisarius and Narses. Africa, Italy and Spain were recovered, and Byzantine involvement in the west continued for centuries.

Justinian's successors found it hard to retain his hold in the west. The Lombards overran most of Italy while Avars and Slavs invaded the Balkans. Nor could Byzantium ignore the Persian threat. Emperors such as Maurice and Heraclius distinguished themselves in this struggle, holding off the attackers. Heraclius reorganised the government under military themes, defeating the Persian Chosroes in a series of battles.

New threats appeared from all directions, including new barbarian arrivals in Magyars, Bulgars and the Rus, the appearance of a new Western Empire under Charlemagne, and the rise of Islam. The latter's rapid expansion out of Arabia in the 7th century destroyed the Persian Empire and damaged Byzantium. The Slavs overran the Balkans while Islam took the Middle East. Byzantine territory was lost in Asia Minor, North Africa and Spain. Several times Constantinople was attacked but survived. At sea Greek Fire played a significant part in Byzantium's defence.

In the 8th century Byzantium recovered. Greece was regained from the Slavs. Some Slav groups and the Bulgars were converted to Christianity. In the Mediterranean Crete and Cyprus were retaken. There was recovery in Syria and Palestine, while Armenia and Bulgaria were conquered.

Byzantine expansion was halted by the disaster at Manzikert in 1071 against the newly arrived Seljuk Turks. Byzantine strength was diminished by religious disputes. The iconoclast feud divided Byzantium internally while there was also a separation from Rome. Imperial succession also caused trouble, with coups, court intrigues, civil wars, murders and mutilation of enemies (notably blinding). Few dynasties could endure for long.

The period of the Comneni emperors after Manzikert was a difficult one. Asia Minor was mostly lost. The Normans took southern Italy and Sicily while Byzantium had to cope with the Crusades. Byzantines might have hoped that western Christians after the Holy Land would bring relief. There was success with the First Crusade but crusading also brought new anxieties and threats for Byzantium.

The Fourth Crusade was one of the greatest disasters in Byzantine history. What began as a Christian attack on Islam was diverted against Constantinople, which the crusaders captured, installing a Latin Emperor. For a generation the descendants of former emperors were in exile from their own capital. Byzantium fragmented into Nicaea, Trebizond and Epirus, under Greeks, while the capital and other territory was under Franks. The Latin Empire was soon in trouble, with its first emperor, Baldwin, defeated by the Bulgars.

Byzantium recovered under the Palaeologi, beginning with Michael VIII. In 1261 the Greeks regained Constantinople. The Empire, however, was a reduced and weaker version of itself. A new western threat came from Charles of Anjou who took Sicily. In 1282 that was defused by the rising against Charles in the Sicilian Vespers and the fall of Sicily to Pedro of Aragón. Problems arose from employing the western Catalan Company of mercenaries which, having failed to obtain its anticipated rewards, turned on Byzantium. Also in the 14th century came the Ottoman Turks, the eventual destroyers of Byzantium. Nor did internal division help, with civil war between Andronicus II and his grandson Andronicus III.

The development of Russia began in the 6th century. The area was settled by Slavs who formed tribes in the 7th century. Scythians, Sarmatians, Alans, Huns and Avars all crossed the region and left a mark. In the 9th century came the Vikings or Varangians. Although the Scandinavian settlers became absorbed in the population, they provided leaders who formed states, in particular those around Novgorod and Kiev under the Rurik family. In c.900 Prince Oleg united Kiev and Novgorod. Expansion came under his grandson Sviatoslav, who defeated the Khazars in 965 though he was killed during the Pecheneg invasion. His son Vladimir the Saint, so called because he converted Russia to Greek Orthodox Christianity, formed the first recognisable state at Kiev as Grand Duke Vladimir I, 980–1015. Contacts were made with Constantinople though there was also conflict. Waves of nomadic invasion from the east continued with the Khazars and the Pechenegs. Kiev's dominance ended with its destruction in 1169 by Andrew Bogoliubski prince of Suzdal. Russian colonisation to the north-east had begun and continued until c.1300. The Battle of Kalka in 1223 led to Mongol (Tatar) domination until the late Middle Ages. Alexander Nevsky of Novgorod (a Mongol vassal) defeated the Swedes on the Neva in 1240 and the Teutonic Knights at Lake Peipus in 1242. Under the Mongols Russia fragmented under branches of the Rurik family into principalities – one of which was Moscow. The state of Muscovy was established under Ivan I Kalita (Moneybags) (1328–40). The Mongols were defeated by Dmitri Donskoi of Moscow at Kulikovo in 1380. Tamberlane invaded Russia from 1390 and defeated the Mongols before withdrawing. His actions damaged the Golden Horde. The grand dukes of Moscow, Basil I and II, began to escape Mongol lordship. Basil II defeated Novgorod in 1456. Ivan III (1462–1505) took the title Ruler of all Russia and took over Novgorod, becoming in effect the first tsar. He married Zoe daughter of Constantine XI, the last Byzantine emperor. In 1480 he refused tribute to the Mongols. He also invaded Finland from 1495.

The lesser states of eastern Europe fell under the sway of one or other of the greater powers or the invading hordes. The Slavs settled eastern Europe but were not united. Most lost their independence, though some smaller states emerged – sometimes becoming powerful though rarely for long. Constant new invasion from the east was a significant factor. Some areas, including Croatia, fell to Charlemagne in the 8th century. Croatia emerged independent under Tomislave in 925 but was usually subordinate to stronger powers. Lithuania suffered from attack from both directions. It was for a time a considerable power in both central and eastern Europe and much involved with Poland, with which for a time it united.

Bulgaria formed from the Slav settlements in the early Middle Ages, emerging as a state by the 9th century. It was a powerful unit for two centuries, under such rulers as Krum, though having to fight off Magyars and Pechenegs. Under Boris I it became Christian in 866. Symeon took over Macedonia and Albania. Bulgaria fell under Russian and Byzantine power and then revived under Samuel from 976 only to fall under Byzantium again by 1014. Bulgaria defeated the Byzantine Latin Empire and captured Baldwin I. The Mongols conquered Bulgaria after 1241 and it would fall under Byzantium, Serbia and finally the Ottomans from 1370. Ottoman victory at Kosovo in 1389 led to control of Bulgaria, Albania and Serbia. The Ottomans also invaded Greece from 1397. Albania regained independence from 1443 to 1468 under George Castricato (Skanderbeg), previously a Janissary for the Turks, but was taken over again on his death.

Serbia emerged in the 8th century and then fell to the Bulgars under Symeon. From 931 Serbia was independent under Chaslav only to fall to Samuel and remain under Bulgaria until the 11th century. From Milvutin who succeeded in 1281 Serbia rose again notably under Stephen Dečanski who beat the Byzantines at Kustendil in 1330, and Stephen Dušan who in the late 14th century took over Macedonia, Albania, Thessaly, Epirus, Bulgaria and part of Bosnia. He defeated the Hungarians. After Kosovo in 1389 Serbia fell under the Ottomans. It regained independence briefly in the

15th century under George Brankovic, Despot of Serbia 1427–56, but was swallowed again from 1459.

The Ottomans advanced relentlessly through the 14th and 15th centuries. They captured Gallipoli, took Thessalonica, defeated the Serbs at Kosovo and brought down the Bulgarian Empire. Constantinople was surrounded by Turkish territory though still able to survive attacks in 1397–1402 and 1422. Though Byzantium sought aid from the west, little came – the Italian cities still sought the best deals they could get.

The final, cataclysmic fall of Constantinople came in 1453 through Mehmet II. Eventually the city was taken and the last emperor killed. The Ottoman advance looked unstoppable, progressing across the Mediterranean and overland to central Europe but was eventually halted at Malta and Vienna.

BATTLES AND SIEGES

ABYDOS (ABYDUS), SIEGE AND BATTLE OF, 13 APRIL 989
Victory for Basil II over Bardas Phokas. Bardas Phokas, a pretender to the throne, was near Abydos in Anatolia, where he assembled support. He besieged Abydos and Basil came to its relief. The two armies met on a plain east of the city. Basil charged and scattered the enemy. Bardas rode by the emperor, intending to challenge him to personal combat, but fell from his horse apparently from a sudden stroke. His army fled and was cut to pieces.

ADRIANOPLE, BATTLE OF, 9 AUGUST 378
Victory for the Visigoths over the Romans. In 376 Goths, driven on by the Huns, crossed the Danube. Some were permitted into the empire in return for military service, but were treated badly, charged highly for supplies, some murdered at Marcianople and taking to arms. They failed to take Adrianople (Edirne in European Turkey). At The Willows (Ad Silices), they were attacked by Romans with no clear result. The survivors were joined by Alans and Huns crossing the Danube. The main force under Fritigern built a camp near Adrianople, in Thrace, west of Constantinople. The eastern emperor Valens, underestimating the size of the enemy, attacked their camp. Goth and Alan foragers, riding back to camp, made a surprise flank attack – 'like a

thunderbolt'. The Romans were massacred. Valens was wounded by an arrow and died when the building where he was taken was fired. The barbarians besieged Adrianople. The defenders replied with stones from a throwing engine and the attackers withdrew. Nevertheless, the battle created a shock through the empire and barbarians dominated the Balkans.

ARCADIOPOLIS (LÜLEBURGAZ), SIEGE OF, 823, BATTLE OF, 970
Capital of the Theme of Thrace, near Adrianople, its position made it a focus for conflict. In 823 the rebel Thomas the Slav took it and was besieged by the Byzantine emperor Michael II. Thomas expelled non-combatants and survived the summer. By October the garrison was eating dead horses; some climbed the wall to surrender. Thomas' men yielded and handed him over. Michael ordered Thomas to have his hands and feet cut off and be impaled on a stake. In the 970 battle Sviatoslav and the Russians invaded Thrace against the Byzantines and were defeated by Bardas Sclerus. The Byzantines pursued under John Tzimisces and won a second victory at Dorostalon in 971.

CHERNOMEN (MARITZA), BATTLE OF, 26 SEPTEMBER 1371
Victory for Murad I in the first pitched battle for the Turks in Europe. He defeated the Serbians under King Vukashin by the

Maritza west of Adrianople. The Serbs had Bulgar allies. The Byzantine emperor John V was in the west seeking aid. The Turkish force was smaller but surprised the Serbs, who broke and fled, the end of a powerful medieval Serbia and of the independent Serbian principality of Serres. Macedonia fell to the Turks while Byzantium and Bulgaria became Murad's clients. Constantinople was surrounded by Turkish territory.

CONSTANTINOPLE, SIEGES OF, 1203–4, 1397–1402, 1422, 1453

The capital of the Byzantine Empire saw numerous sieges throughout the medieval period, reflecting its political, economic and geographical importance. Books have been written on 1453 alone. One could easily double the number of sieges covered here, including earlier attempts by Persians and Avars 626, Saracens 674, 717–18, Scandinavian-Russians 860, 907, 941 – and many others. The sieges listed here mark the decline and fall of Byzantium. 1203–4 was the Latin siege in the Fourth Crusade, the first time Constantinople fell to an outside force. The crusaders arrived in June 1203. The ancient and blind Venetian Doge Enrico Dandolo was with them. On 17 July, following a vigorous assault on the walls, Alexius III fled and Isaac II was restored, with Alexius IV as co-emperor. In January 1204 the citizens proclaimed Nicholas Canabus, and Isaac II was killed. In February Alexius IV was killed and Nicholas imprisoned. Murzurphlus was proclaimed as Alexius V. On 12 April the crusaders stormed the city. Alexius fled and was later caught and killed. The Latins sacked the city. On 16 May they proclaimed Baldwin of Flanders as Baldwin I, the beginning of the Latin Empire that lasted until 1261. From 1397 the Ottoman Sultan Bayezit I made several abortive attempts to besiege Constantinople, being diverted by other problems. He built the fort of Anadolu Hisar on the opposite side of the Bosphorus. In 1399 Manuel II went west

seeking aid. Byzantium was aided by outside pressure on the Turks through Tamberlane. In spring 1402 Bayezit abandoned the siege and went east to be defeated, captured and later killed by Tamberlane. In 1422 Sultan Murad II besieged an isolated Constantinople from 8 June. He sent siege engines against the land walls. His attempt to storm the city failed and he abandoned the siege in August to deal with rebellion by his brother Mustafa. The 1453 siege was a significant event in world history though its outcome was easy to forecast. Sultan Mehmet II began the siege on 7 April, aided by the renegade Hungarian Urban who produced large cannons for him. A small Venetian fleet broke through to offer temporary relief. Mehmet entered the Golden Horn by taking ships overland on rollers. On 29 May the Ottomans broke in, some over the wall, others through a postern gate. Constantine XI was killed. The Turks sacked the city, which became their capital. It was the end of the long history of the Byzantine Empire, itself a continuation of the ancient Roman Empire, and marked the rise of Islam and decline of Christianity in eastern Europe. It has been seen as marking the end of the medieval world.

DEMETRIAS, NAVAL BATTLE OF, 1275

Generally seen as a sea battle though one source says it was fought on land. The Latins in Greece who were allied to John the Bastard of Thessaly fought against a Byzantine fleet in the Gulf of Volos. The Latin assault was successful until Greek reinforcements under Despot John the brother of Michael VIII arrived. The Latins were beaten – perhaps on land as well as at sea.

GALLIPOLI, BATTLE OF, 447

Hun victory over the eastern Romans. Attila had recently become khan. His victories over the Eastern Empire culminated in Gallipoli. He then raided into the Balkans. It was a prelude to invasion of the west, which came as a relief to the Byzantines, probably encouraged by them.

KALAMATA, BATTLE OF, JULY 1415

Byzantine emperor Manuel II planned to rebuild the wall of the Hexamilion across the Isthmus of Corinth as a defence against the Ottomans. The tax for it provoked rebellion but at Kalamata he defeated the rebels.

KLOKOTNITSA, BATTLE OF, APRIL 1230

Victory of John Asen II of Bulgaria over Theodore Dukas despot of Epirus on the Maritza in Thrace, near Adrianople. Theodore built up Thessalonika and aimed at recovering Constantinople from the Latins. He wished to wipe out Bulgar power and invaded John Asen's lands. He was captured and his empire broke up. Asen besieged Constantinople but failed to take it. Theodore was released when Asen married his daughter. In his lifetime Asen dominated the Balkans, claiming all the land between Adrianople and Durazzo – 'Greek, Albanian and Serbian'. The major effect of the battle was to eliminate Epirus as a contender for rule in Byzantium, leaving Nicaea as the chief challenger.

KOSEDAG, BATTLE OF, 26 JUNE 1243

Mongol victory over the Seljuk Turks of Rum under Kaikosru II, marking the decline of the Seljuk threat to Byzantium though Byzantines and Frankish mercenaries fought alongside the Seljuks. The Mongols took over Anatolia. The Sultan of Rum and the Emperor of Trebizond agreed to pay tribute to the Mongols. Mongol interest moved elsewhere but the Seljuks remained in subjection.

KOSOVO, BATTLES OF, 15 JUNE 1389, 17–18 OCTOBER 1448

In 1389 Sultan Murad I defeated an alliance of Serbs, Bulgars, Bosnians, Wallachians and Albanians under Tsar Lazar of Serbia. The site is in southern Serbia at 'the Field of the Blackbirds'. The Slav army was larger. Serbia became subject to the Ottomans. The Slavs began well but Vuk Brankovic deserted. Murad was killed by a captured Serb. His son Bayezit, who was there, succeeded. Lazar was captured and executed in the tent where Murad had been stabbed. The battle became a subject for heroic literature including the Serbian *Kossovo Cycle*. It broke major opposition to the Turks in the Balkans. In 1448 Murad II defeated the crusade under John Hunyadi in a two-day battle (some accounts make it three or four days). Hunyadi's force included western crusaders and eastern Christian allies. Hunyadi did not wait for the Albanians to arrive. Dan of Wallachia and George Brankovic of Serbia deserted Hunyadi. German and Bohemian handgunners fought for Hunyadi. The Turkish Janissaries relied chiefly on bows but afterwards took more to handguns. Both sides used palisades of stakes to protect their infantry. Half the Hungarian army was killed. Hunyadi escaped to take revenge on George by invading Serbia in 1449. Constantinople was isolated and vulnerable.

KULIKOVO, BATTLE OF, 8 SEPTEMBER 1380

Victory by Dmitri Donskoi grand duke of Moscow over Mamai the Mongol and the Golden Horde with Lithuanian allies. The site was on the upper Don. Mamai sought to recover losses to Russian rebels. The Lithuanians arrived late and the Russians then retreated. It nevertheless confirmed the strength of Moscow.

KUSTENDIL (VELBUŽD), BATTLE OF, 28 JULY 1330

Victory of Stephen Dečanski of Serbia over the Bulgars. The Bulgars expected aid from their Byzantine allies that did not materialise. The Serbs attacked while some Bulgars were foraging. Cavalry won the battle. Serbia then controlled the Varda valley and Stephen's position was confirmed.

LARISSA, SIEGE AND BATTLE OF, 1083
Byzantine victory over the Normans of
Sicily under Bohemond son of Robert
Guiscard. Guiscard returned to Italy,
leaving Bohemond in command. Bohemond
won two victories and besieged Larissa. The
Byzantine emperor Alexius I came to its
relief. He ordered a feigned flight by some
troops while he attacked the Norman
camp. Bohemond abandoned the siege
and retired to Kastoria before returning to
Italy.

**MOUNT LEVUNIUM (LEVUNION),
BATTLE OF, 29 APRIL 1091**
Byzantine victory for Alexius I with Kuman
allies against the Pechenegs. The site was
the foot of a hill near the mouth of the
Maritza. Anna Comnena described her
father's battle. The evening before, soldiers
lit torches and fixed them to their spears. A
massacre followed, when many Pecheneg
camp followers were killed or enslaved.
The Pecheneg threat to Byzantium was
erased.

**MANZIKERT (MALAZGIRT), SIEGE AND
BATTLE OF, 19 AUGUST 1071**
Decisive victory of the Seljuk Turks under
Alp Arslan over the Byzantine emperor
Romanus IV. The date is disputed but
19 August generally accepted. The site was
north of Lake Van in Armenia, now Turkey.
Romanus divided his forces, sending some
to forage while he besieged Manzikert. Alp
Arslan came to its relief. He offered peace
terms but Romanus refused. Romanus led
the first line and his nephew Andronicus
Dukas the second. The Turks retreated. At
night Romanus retreated but this caused
confusion. The Turks attacked and
Andronicus, with the second line,
abandoned the field and fled. The first line
was killed or captured. Romanus was
captured but freed on agreeing ransom and
tribute. The Seljuks conquered Armenia
and most of Asia Minor, overrunning Syria.
Later that year Romanus was deposed.
Byzantium never entirely recovered from
the disaster.

**MYRIOCEPHALUM (MYRIOKEPHALON),
BATTLE OF, 17 SEPTEMBER 1176**
Defeat of Byzantine emperor Manuel I by
the Seljuks under Kilij Arslan II. The site
was near the ruined fort of Myriocephalum
(modern Denizli in Turkey) in highlands
near the Tzibritze pass. Manuel invaded,
intending to gain lands and attack the
Sultan's capital of Iconium (Konya). He was
ambushed during a sandstorm when
approaching the pass, which he had failed
to scout properly. The Byzantines were too
dispersed and were surrounded. With
Manuel were Hungarian allies and his
brother-in-law Baldwin of Antioch.
Baldwin charged but was killed. The
Byzantines suffered heavy losses. Kilij
Arslan offered terms and the Byzantines
were allowed to withdraw. Manuel
recovered to some extent through the
efforts of his general John Vatatzes.

NIKA REVOLT, 532
Rising against the Byzantine emperor
Justinian in Constantinople, caused by
discontent at taxation. Justinian dealt
harshly with disorder by the Blue and
Green circus factions, supporters of the
chariot races. A riot began in the
Hippodrome on 10 January. On 13 January
large-scale fighting followed. The Blues
and Greens burst from the Hippodrome
against the imperial palace, shouting 'Nika'
(victory) – the cry used at the races.
Hypatius, nephew of the former emperor
Anastasius, was proclaimed emperor on
18 January. Justinian wanted to flee but his
wife Theodora persuaded him to stay. The
general Belisarius, recalled after defeat by
the Persians, used trained troops against
the rioters. Thousands were killed.
Hypatius was captured and executed. The
riots left the Haghia Sophia in ruins.

**PELAGONIA (BITOLJ/MONASTIR),
BATTLE OF, OCTOBER 1259**
Between the fragmented Byzantine states
during the period of Latin control in
Constantinople. The Greeks of Nicaea
under John Palaeologus, brother of

Michael VIII, defeated those of Epirus under Michael II Dukas. Michael of Epirus allied with Manfred of Sicily and William II Villehardouin prince of Achaia. John advanced from the south. Michael deserted his allies and fled to Cephalonia. The remaining troops were decimated by John's Cuman archers and many knights surrendered. The allies who continued to resist were cut down. William was captured. John sent a force against Epirus and took Arta. It helped the recovery of Constantinople by Michael VIII.

PELEKANOS (PELEKANON/MALTEPE/ MANYAS), BATTLE OF, 10–11 JUNE 1329

Defeat of Byzantine emperor Andronicus III by Sultan Orhan during the Ottoman advance. The Turks aimed at Nicaea and Andronicus intervened. He approached the Turkish camp but failed to break in. Next day Andronicus' retreat turned into a rout and his army was destroyed. He was wounded but escaped to Constantinople. Two years later Nicaea was taken and the Turks approached Constantinople.

PHOENICUS (FINIKE), NAVAL BATTLE OF, 655

Victory of Muawiyah over the Byzantines under Constans. Constans took a fleet to block the Turks off the Lycian coast. The Byzantine fleet was scattered. Constans escaped by changing clothes with one of his men, who was later killed.

POIMANENON, BATTLES OF, 6 DECEMBER 1204, 1224

1204 was a victory for the Latin Constantinople under Baldwin I over Theodore I Laskaris of Nicaea, son-in-law of Alexius III. After the Latin conquest of Constantinople, Theodore established himself in Asia Minor, in a state claiming to be the real Byzantine Empire. In attempting to recover the city he fought this battle 40 miles south of the Marmara. A group of western knights, for Baldwin, garrisoned Panormos, attempting to take

the surrounding land. Theodore came to prevent them. The Latin force numbered only 140 knights plus some mounted sergeants. The outcome damped the hopes of Theodore. In the 1224 battle the Nicaean emperor John Vatatzes defeated the Latins and took most Byzantine territory in Asia Minor.

ROVINE, BATTLE OF, 17 MAY 1395

Victory by the Hungarians and Wallachians over the Ottomans under Sultan Bayezit. The Christian army was led by Sigismund of Hungary and Mircea of Wallachia. It drew Bayezit away from Constantinople. Some Serbian princes and Greeks fought as Turkish vassals. The victory was not decisive and Mircea still recognised Turkish overlordship.

SAMOSATA (SAMSAT), BATTLE OF, 873

Victory for the Byzantine emperor Basil I against the Saracens in his advance through Asia Minor. Samosata was in the Euphrates valley. Basil extended Byzantine power to the Euphrates, capturing Samosata.

SPETSAI (SETTEPOZZI), NAVAL BATTLE OF, 1263

The Venetians defeated a Genoese and Byzantine fleet. Michael VIII allied with Genoa to reduce Venetian power in Constantinople. The Genoese sailed south towards Monemvasia. Off the island of Spetsai they met a smaller Venetian fleet. The allies refused battle but were attacked and broken up, losing a thousand men and their admiral.

STILO, NAVAL BATTLE OF, 982

Holy Roman Emperor Otto II's Italian expedition was halted by an alliance of Byzantines and Saracens. Otto failed to take Crotona and was defeated at Basientello in Apulia while his fleet was beaten at Stilo. Otto escaped by concealing his identity. He swam to a passing ship and then to shore. Otto died the following year in Rome.

STRUMA (KLEIDION/CIMBALONGUS), BATTLE OF, 29 JULY 1014

Victory by Basil II over the Bulgars under Tsar Samuel at the pass of Kleidion, leading from Serres to the Struma valley. Basil's entry was blocked by palisades. A force under Nikephorus Xiphias crossed the hills to attack the Bulgars from the rear while Basil stormed the palisades. The Bulgars were routed and Basil completed his conquest of Bulgaria. Samuel escaped, a broken man, dying soon after. Basil ordered the captives blinded – one in a hundred left with one eye to lead the others home.

THESSALONIKA (SALONIKA), SIEGES OF, 1185, 1224, 1430

Byzantine Thessalonika, a major Aegean port, was sacked by William II of Sicily in 1185. The Norman fleet was under Tancred of Lecce, and the army under his cousin Richard of Acerra. They sailed from Messina in June. Durazzo surrendered. In August the Normans arrived at Thessalonika to besiege the city. The garrison ran short of weapons and water. German mercenaries within were bribed to admit the attackers on 24 August. The Normans massacred the inhabitants and devastated the city. In 1224, during Latin rule in Constantinople, Thessalonika was taken from its Latin ruler, William de Montferrat, by Theodore Dukas, Greek Despot of Epirus. Theodore proclaimed himself Byzantine emperor. In 1246 the rival ruler of Nicaea, John Vatatzes, claimed Thessalonika. 1224 was the end of the Latin principality and significant in the decline of Latin rule. In 1430 Thessalonika fell to the Turks, having changed hands several times before being sold by Manuel II to Venice in 1423. Seven years later it was taken by Sultan Murad II, whose arrival on 26 March was met by a hail of arrows. On 29 March the Ottomans stormed the city. The citizens were slaughtered or enslaved, a major step in the fall of Byzantium.

TRAJAN'S GATE (SUCCI PASS), BATTLE OF, 17 AUGUST 986

Defeat of Basil II by the Bulgars. Basil's expedition sought revenge for the Bulgar massacre at Larissa. He followed the Maritza and headed for the pass at Trajan's Gate. He tried to take Serdica but gave up. On his return he was ambushed at the pass. Many were killed though Basil escaped. The defeat spurred Basil to vengeance. He defeated the Bulgars, gaining the name of Bulgar-Slayer.

TRICAMARUM, BATTLE OF, 15 DECEMBER 533

Final victory for the Byzantines under Belisarius against the Vandals under Gelimer in North Africa. The site was 20 miles west of Carthage. Belisarius undertook the reconquest of Roman Africa for Justinian I. The Vandals could not be provoked into attacking over a stream. In a largely cavalry conflict, the Byzantines made three charges. The Byzantine centre crossed first and when the Vandals engaged the wings, they crossed to attack from either flank. The Vandals broke. Gelimer's brother Gzazo was killed and Gelimer fled. Hippo was taken and Vandal Africa collapsed. Gelimer surrendered in 534 and was taken to Constantinople for Belisarius' triumph.

VERSINICIA (VERSINIKIS), BATTLE OF, 22 JUNE 813

Victory by the Bulgars under Tsar Krum against Michael I, 20 miles north of Adrianople. The Byzantine left attacked with initial success. The Anatolians on the Byzantine right, under Leo the Armenian, deserted. The Bulgars surrounded the remaining troops to win a resounding victory. Krum captured Adrianople. Leo took the throne as Leo V.

YARMUK, BATTLE OF, AUGUST 636

Victory for Islam under Khalid ibn al-Walid against Theodore, brother of the emperor, Heraclius. The Arab advance was halted by the arrival of a Byzantine army in 636.

Khalid retreated to the Yarmuk. He beat off an attack by Theodore's Persian allies. Theodore's army mutinied and Khalid attacked. Fighting continued over several days. The Byzantine cavalry was isolated and fled. The Byzantines ran out of arrows and were beaten. Many were driven to death over the cliffs rising from the river. Khalid took Syria and Damascus.

toute le feu dont dieu
le gart a peut pont.
Et disons dont q
ctaunt graee nous
fist dieu le tout puissa
quant il nous teffen
Ci deuise comment da
miete fu prinse.

di te mort et de peril a la
nuer la ou nous arriua
mes a pie et couurimes
sus a nos ennemis q
qui estoient a cheual.

Grant graee
nous fist
nostre seig
neur de da

miete que il nous te
liura. La quele nous
ne teuilions pas auoir
pule sanz affamer. Et

St Louis at Damietta

8 | The Crusades, 1095–1500

GENERALS AND LEADERS

See in Part I: Adhémar of Le Puy, al-Ashraf, al-Kamil, Amalric I, Baldwin I, Baldwin II, Baldwin III, Baldwin IV, Balian II of Ibelin, Baybars, Bohemond of Taranto, Boniface of Montferrat, Edward I, Geoffrey I Villehardouin, Godfrey de Bouillon, Guy of Lusignan, Humphrey of Toron, Kerbogha, Kilij Arslan, Louis VII, Malik Shah, de Montfort (Simon the Elder), Nevsky (Alexander), Nur ed-Din, Peter the Hermit, Philip Augustus, Qalawun, Qtuz, Rainald of Châtillon, Raymond of Poitiers Prince of Antioch, Raymond of St Gilles IV Count of Toulouse and I of Tripoli, Raymond VI Count of Toulouse, Raymond VII Count of Toulouse, Richard I, Ridwan, Saladin, Shirkuh, Tancred, Walter the Penniless, Yaghi-Siyan, Zangi.

BATTLES AND SIEGES

Acre 1189–91, 1291, Antioch 1097–8, 1268, Arsuf 1191, Ascalon 1099, Ayn Jalut 1260, Civetot 1096, Damascus 1148, Damietta 1218–19, 1249–50, Dorylaeum 1097, 1147 Edessa 1098, 1144, Field of Blood 1119, Harbiya 1244, Hattin 1187, Homs 1281, 1299, Jerusalem 1099, 1187, 1244, Krak des Chevaliers 1271, Ma'arrat al-Numan 1098, Mansurah 1250, Montgisard 1177, Montségur 1243–4, Nicaea 1097, Nicopolis 1396, Ramleh 1101, 1102, 1105, Tiberias 1187, Toulouse 1211, 1217–18, Tunis 1270, Tyre 1111–12, 1124, Varna 1444.

OUTLINE OF EVENTS

Crusading history has expanded in time and space. Once it included only certain numbered expeditions to the Holy Land, ending with the fall of Acre in 1291. Now it involves the study of various additional expeditions to the Middle East, crusades within Europe for example against pagans in the north or heretics in France, and is carried on into the early modern world and later, for example to the fall of Malta. Details of military events appear in the relevant geographical region, thus the northern crusades appear in Section 6, the *Reconquista* in Section 11 and so on. Here the main emphasis is on crusades to the Holy Land.

The main drive of the crusading movement was towards the Middle East, against Islamic control of Christian Holy Places, in particular of Jerusalem. It is generally agreed that the Crusades began with Pope Urban II's appeal at Clermont-Ferrand in 1095, followed by expeditions to the Middle East from 1096. Urban's interest was inspired by Byzantine appeals for aid against the Turks. Before this the pilgrimage movement from the west to the Holy Places had been growing. It is arguable that the war against Islam in Spain was an early example of crusading.

Urban's appeal led to the first military effort in the Middle East, the so-called 'People's Crusade'. It involved several groups making their own way to the Holy Land under Peter the Hermit, Walter the Penniless (a knight), Gottschalk, Folkmar and Count Emich of Leiningen. Massacred Jews in Europe were the first victims of the crusaders under Count Emich. A thousand Jews were killed in Mainz, 800 in Worms. The People's Crusade was inspired by Peter the Hermit. It attracted many non-knightly individuals, mostly lacking military training. These poorly organised treks ended in disaster at points along the way. Hungary proved difficult to pass through. The Byzantine emperor, Alexius I, moved crusaders on as quickly as possible. Those who got to the Middle East were wiped out at Xerigordon and Civetot. Older historians preferred to ignore this effort and called the subsequent knightly expedition the First Crusade.

The First Crusade was led by nobles rather than kings. The main crusade assembled at Le Puy in the Auvergne. Five main groups set out, the first under Godfrey de Bouillon and his brother Baldwin. A French group went under Hugh count of Vermandois, son of Henry I of France. The Counts of Blois and Flanders and Robert Curthose duke of Normandy marched to Italy, sailing from there. A fourth group was of southern Normans from Italy under Bohemond and his nephew Tancred. Finally the oldest leader, Raymond count of Toulouse accompanied the appointed church leader, Adhémar bishop of Le Puy. Various routes across Europe were taken, heading for Constantinople – the crossing point to Asia Minor. The First Crusaders faced fewer problems than the People's Crusade since they possessed greater military strength. Alexius took oaths of allegiance from the leaders and helped them on their way, breathing a sigh of relief as they went.

They passed Civetot, site of the disaster for the People's Crusade. Groups chose their own route. They took Nicaea and won at Dorylaeum in 1097. Baldwin went to Edessa, which he took over from its Armenian Christian ruler Thoros. The other crusaders besieged and captured Antioch in 1098, only to be besieged within it by Kerbogha of Mosul. The latter withdrew and the crusaders proceeded to take Acre, reaching Jerusalem in 1099, recently taken from the Seljuks by the Egyptians. Jerusalem fell to the crusaders and a massacre followed.

A new Christian state was established, the kingdom of Jerusalem. Godfrey de Bouillon was called advocate of the Holy Sepulchre, in effect the first King of Jerusalem. Linked principalities were established under Baldwin count of Edessa, Bohemond prince of Antioch, and Raymond count of Tripoli. Other baronies developed under the counts of Jaffa and Ascalon, the Prince of Galilee and the lords of Sidon, Caesarea,

Beisan and Kerak. Castles were built for defence, including Beaufort, Safed, Toron, Montréal, Ibelin and Krak. New immigrants came but the population remained mixed – Greek, Armenian, Saracen and Syrian. The courts used ten languages.

The success of the First Crusade depended on the weakness of Islamic states of the region – soon to change with the rise of Zangi emir of Mosul. In 1144 the Muslims took Edessa, provoking the Second Crusade, preached by St Bernard. This time kings responded – Louis VII of France, Conrad III (HRE), and Roger II of Sicily. The crusade was a disaster. Roger went his own way, attacking Corfu and the Greek mainland. Louis faced marital problems with Eleanor of Aquitaine. Conrad went ahead and was defeated at Dorylaeum in 1147. Together they attacked Damascus, under a friendly Islamic ruler, and failed to take it. The crusade broke up. At most it had temporarily distracted Islamic attention from the crusading states.

The Muslims made further inroads against the crusader states under Nur ed-Din, son of Zangi, who united Syria. For Nur ed-Din the general Shirkuh, with his nephew Saladin, pushed into Christian territory. On the death of Nur ed-Din, Saladin ruled Syria. He defeated the Christians under King Guy at Hattin in 1187. The kingdom of Jerusalem never entirely recovered. Jerusalem fell to Saladin and soon only Tyre remained of the great cities. This situation inspired the Third Crusade, under Richard the Lionheart, Philip Augustus and Frederick Barbarossa. It had more success than the Second Crusade. Barbarossa died before reaching the Holy Land. Richard stopped on his way to capture Cyprus, a major gain. The crusaders took Acre. Philip returned to the west. Richard won at Arsuf in 1191 but did not reach Jerusalem, concluding a treaty with Saladin in 1192. Richard was captured by the emperor while returning and ransomed. The kingdom of Jerusalem survived but in truncated form.

Saladin died in 1193, offering possibilities for a new crusade. Crusaders assembling in Italy found themselves so in debt to Venice for transport that they were persuaded to pursue the interests of the Republic. Instead of going to the Holy Land the Fourth Crusade attacked Christian Zara on the Adriatic and then Constantinople, which they took in 1204 installing the Latin emperor, Baldwin. The Latin Empire survived until 1261 when the Greeks recovered Constantinople. The episode provided little aid for the struggling remnant of the kingdom of Jerusalem.

One un-numbered episode was the Children's Crusade of 1212, which demonstrated surviving enthusiasm among ordinary folk. Thousands were led to Marseilles and were shipped to North Africa. Most were sold as slaves to Muslims! Others found their way to Italy. Some were lucky enough to return home.

The Fifth Crusade, concluded by Frederick II (HRE), was extraordinary. The crusade started without the emperor against Egypt. Damietta was taken but then lost. Frederick had long promised to crusade but was excommunicated by the pope for delays. He finally went while excommunicated! His Crusade was more a diplomatic mission than a campaign. With his knowledge of Muslims from Sicily, he negotiated with al-Kamil and in 1229 agreed a treaty. Both sides made concessions. The Christians received possession of the Holy Places with agreed Muslim access. Frederick was crowned in Jerusalem. His intervention helped create a civil war in Outremer and the treaty concessions were unpopular.

By the mid-13th century the kingdom had disintegrated. The monarchy's authority declined. It became the kingdom of Acre, power chiefly with lords and Italian merchants. After the Fourth Crusade the numbering system, always rather shaky, has less significance. The next crusades are better known as those of St Louis. Western aims became less clear. The Fourth Crusade ended at Constantinople. The Sixth Crusade was aimed at splitting the Muslims of Syria from those of Egypt. It was argued that control of the Holy Land depended on defeating the main Muslim power in the region. Louis sailed in 1248 to besiege Damietta, which was captured. Supplies ran short and disease attacked in the heat. In 1250 Louis was defeated and captured at Mansurah, though later ransomed. He may have been a great king but he was not a greatly successful crusader. He tried again, believing that the Emir of Tunis would become Christian. Louis was already ill and was carried on board by litter. Tunis resisted and Louis died before its walls in 1270.

The Mamlukes of Egypt halted the expansion of the Mongols in the Middle East. Qtuz won at Ayn Jalut to become Sultan, reuniting Syria and Egypt. He was assassinated and succeeded by the Turkish Mamluke, Baybars. The surviving crusader strongholds fell – Caesarea, Athlit, Arsuf, Safed, Jaffa and Beaufort. Edward I of England made a late expedition in 1271, when an assassin made an attempt on his life. Edward made a two-year truce to gain a little time. Western enthusiasm for crusading declined. Qalawun took over from Baybars. He defeated the Mongols at Homs and concentrated on the Latins. He captured Tripoli in 1289. His son al-Ashraf delivered the final blow, taking Acre in 1291. The surviving pockets were mopped up and the kingdom ended. Within a decade Acre was deserted, its ruins picked over by a few peasants.

Crusading history is now viewed more broadly. There were other areas of operation against Muslims and pagans – in Iberia, northern and eastern Europe – and continuing opposition to Muslims in Africa, the Middle East and the Mediterranean. The *Reconquista* proceeded throughout the Middle Ages. Crusading continued in the later Middle Ages. There were attempts to retake the Holy Land through Recovery Crusades. There were Crusades against enemies of the papacy – religious, political, heretical and schismatic. In southern France and northern Italy the heretical Cathars were attacked by the Albigensian Crusade. In eastern Europe the followers of John Hus, the Hussites, were declared heretical and crusades sent against them. Crusades were declared against the political enemies of the papacy, for example the descendants of Frederick II (HRE) attempting to retain Sicily. Crusading indulgences were offered to those opposing the rebels in the Sicilian Vespers, themselves supporters of Aragón. Crusades were declared against the Colonna family in Italy, Venice in 1309, Ferrara in 1321, Landau's mercenary company in 1357, Naples in 1382 and Castile in 1371. In Castile two rival popes declared crusades against each other. This distorting of the crusading ideal helped tarnish the image of the concept. The Recovery Crusades in eastern Europe came closest to retaining the concept of the movement in the later Middle Ages. The extension of Muslim power into Europe by the Ottomans can be linked to this, with crusades declared against them. One idea was to organise small expeditions with particular objectives.

The Baltic crusades were partly the work of the military orders, especially of the Sword Brothers and the Teutonic Knights. This is examined in Section 6. It led to the conversion of much of the surviving pagan areas of Europe.

After the fall of Acre and the kingdom a Christian state survived in Cilician Armenia, enduring to 1375. The Cilicians supported the Mongols in Syria and suffered with their defeat. A new threat emerged with Tamberlane, who captured Baghdad in 1392 and attacked Syria. He defeated the Mamlukes near Ankara in 1402, capturing Bayezit. Then the Ottomans overran Byzantine territory in Asia Minor and Europe. The Smyrna Crusade went against them in 1356. The Christians won a naval victory and captured Smyrna, which they retained until 1402. The Nicopolis Crusade went to northern Bulgaria in 1396, when Sigismund of Hungary was defeated by Bayezit. In 1444 Hunyadi besieged Varna. A Turkish relief force defeated this last major crusade from west to east.

BATTLES AND SIEGES

ACRE, SIEGES OF, 1189–91, 1291

Acre was the major port of the kingdom of Jerusalem, jutting into the sea, with walls to protect the land side. Its harbour was protected by a mole, on which stood the Tower of Flies. After the Battle of Hattin, King Guy was released. Acre was taken by the Turks after Hattin. Guy sought to restore his reputation by recovering Acre. He began the siege with 400 knights and 7,000 infantry on 28 August 1189. Saladin brought a relief force but could not get through. The crusaders, according to the enemy, were solaced by a shipload of beauties with fleshy thighs. Guy was reinforced by the arrival of the Third Crusade, first Philip Augustus and then Richard the Lionheart. Both kings fell ill during the siege. They broke in on 12 July 1191. Richard threw down the standard of Leopold of Austria from the wall. Philip returned to France. Saladin was slow to pay the ransom and Richard ordered the killing of 2,700 prisoners. The fall of Acre in 1291 was the deathblow to the crusader kingdom, sometimes called the kingdom of Acre. It was a base for the military orders and Italian merchants. The attack was planned by Qalawun and undertaken, after his death, by his son al-Ashraf from 6 April with 220,000 men. His engines included *Victorious* and *Furious*. Acre was taken on 18 May and razed to the ground.

ANTIOCH (ANTAKYA), BATTLE AND SIEGES OF, 1097–8, 1268

Antioch (now Antakya in Turkey) on the Orontes, 12 miles from the sea, was a major target for the First Crusade. It was a Byzantine city taken by the Turks in 1085. The garrison in 1097 was under Emir Yaghi-Siyan. The crusaders arrived on 21 October 1097. They beat off two relieving forces at Homs in 1097 and by Lake Antioch in 1098. To discourage the garrison, 200 Turkish heads were shot over the walls. The crusaders took Antioch on 3 June 1098, when a traitor opened the gate to the Tower of the Two Sisters, though the citadel on Mount Silpius resisted. The Christians were then besieged within the city by a newly arrived force under Kerbogha of Mosul. Some Christians escaped to return west, including Stephen-Henry count of Blois. In the battle on 28 June 1098 the crusaders made a sortie to attack the Muslim camp. Antioch became the centre of a new crusader principality. On 18 May 1268 Antioch was recovered by the Turks under Baybars after a brief siege. The garrison was under the constable, Simon Mansel. Simon led a sortie and was captured. The Muslims proclaimed 'the God who gave you Antioch has taken it away again'. Crosses were smashed, women sold four for a dinar, pages of holy books were scattered, tombs overturned and monks had their throats slit.

ARSUF, BATTLE OF, 7 SEPTEMBER 1191

Victory of Richard the Lionheart against Saladin during the Third Crusade, to the north of Arsuf. Arsuf was captured by the Franks in 1101. The crusaders were attacked when marching south from Acre to Jaffa along the coast. During the march Richard was wounded in the side by a spear. To the east of Arsuf was forest. The army was supplied from ships. Richard kept infantry on the left of the march to protect the cavalry from flank attack, especially by mounted archers. Saladin provoked the Hospitallers at the rear to turn and charge. This could have led to the break-up of the crusader formation but Richard followed up with a series of charges. The Muslim army broke but there was no pursuit, Richard continuing his march. Saladin avoided further pitched battle and Richard had the edge in negotiations over the future of the kingdom.

ASCALON, BATTLE OF, 12 AUGUST 1099

After Jerusalem was captured in the First Crusade, Egyptian Muslims under al-Afdal attempted its recovery. The Egyptians had the larger army. The hastily assembled Christian army captured the enemy supply train and next day attacked their camp near Ascalon at dawn. Godfrey de Bouillon blocked a flank attack. Robert Curthose and Tancred led the centre charge to win the battle. The Christians captured much wealth, including gold and precious stones. Ascalon settled the establishment of the kingdom of Jerusalem.

AYN JALUT (AIN JALUD/THE POOLS OF GOLIATH), BATTLE OF, 3 SEPTEMBER 1260

Vital in determining the future of the Middle East. Ayn Jalut was in Palestine (modern Israel) near Lake Galilee. The Mamluke Sultan Qtuz defeated the Mongols under Kitbuqa (a Christian) representing Hulagu. The Egyptians were allowed to march through Christian territory but given no aid. The Egyptians took position in a valley. Qtuz's general Baybars led a feigned flight, drawing the Mongols into a trap. Qtuz led the decisive charge. Mongol expansion was halted. The surviving crusader state was vulnerable to the Muslims. Qtuz was killed on the way home in a coup by Baybars.

CIVETOT (CIBOTUS), BATTLE OF, 21 OCTOBER 1096

The first major battle of the crusades that destroyed the People's Crusade. The crusaders took Xerigordon, which the Muslims under Kilij Arslan recovered. The Turks approached the remaining crusaders at Civetot, a disused Byzantine fort in Asia Minor on the Sea of Marmora. Peter the Hermit had gone to Constantinople and the leaders at Civetot included Walter the Penniless. Walter advised staying put but majority opinion favoured marching out to face the Turks. The Christians were ambushed near Dracon by archers. They broke and the Turks attacked the camp. Many were killed, including Walter; others were enslaved.

DAMASCUS, SIEGE OF, 1148

The Second Crusade besieged Damascus from 24 to 28 July. Conrad III (HRE) and Louis VII of France decided, unwisely, to aim for Damascus. Baldwin III of Jerusalem joined them. Their reason was probably to save it from Nur ed-Din. In one incident Conrad killed an opponent with a blow of his sword, removing head, shoulder and one arm. At first they attacked from the west. Muslim reinforcements arrived and entered Damascus. The kings moved to the east of the city. Orchards had made approach from the west difficult and they thought the east less well defended. They were now without shelter, food or water. The garrison made a sortie. Frankish corpses smelled strongly enough 'to make the birds fall out of the sky'. Fears of a relief army led to the abandonment of the siege and the collapse of the Second Crusade.

DAMIETTA, SIEGES OF, 1218–19, 1249–50

From 29 May 1218 the Fifth Crusade besieged Damietta in Egypt at the mouth of the Nile with its three enclosing walls. The leaders included John de Brienne and Leopold of Austria. The Egyptians blocked progress on the Nile at Damietta with a chain and a bridge of boats. The attackers tried to break through with a siege tower lashed on two ships to attack the defences from above. The besiegers suffered from a disease that turned their skin black and killed many. Al-Kamil attacked their camp but achieved little. A Muslim relief attempt failed. St Francis of Assisi acted as a Christian envoy – the Muslims thought the grubby saint a figure of scorn. On 5 November the crusaders broke in. Their attack on Cairo failed. The crusaders were isolated and surrendered Damietta in 1221. On 4 June 1249 St Louis' crusade arrived there. Louis leaped into the water up to his armpits rushing ashore. He used engines while the enemy hurled Greek Fire and fire-bolts like 'stars falling out of heaven'. On 6 June the crusaders entered the city but found it abandoned. After the crusaders were defeated at Mansurah, Damietta surrendered on 6 May 1250.

DORYLAEUM (ESKISHEHIR), BATTLES OF, 1 JULY 1097, 25 OCTOBER 1147

The first battle was the major victory of the First Crusade over the Seljuks. The crusaders took Nicaea and advanced south in two groups. They had not advanced far when the van, under Bohemond with the counts of Normandy, Flanders and Blois, was attacked by Kilij Arslan at a mountain pass near Dorylaeum (now in Turkey). The Turkish mounted archers were effective. Bohemond used infantry to protect the mounted warriors and allow them to charge. The second force, under Godfrey de Bouillon and Raymond de St Gilles, arrived to attack from the rear, winning the battle. The crusaders found much wealth in the Muslim camp. A second battle occurred near Dorylaeum in 1147 during the Second Crusade. A German force under Conrad III (HRE) was defeated by the Turks. The crusaders' retreat turned into a rout, greatly weakening the crusade.

EDESSA (URFA), SIEGES OF, 1098, 1144

Baldwin le Bourg (later Baldwin I of Jerusalem) reached Edessa in Mesopotamia on 6 February 1098. He struck east over the Euphrates, leaving the main army. Edessa was under the Armenian Thoros, who made Baldwin an ally and adopted him as his son. In the ceremony a large shirt was placed over them both while they rubbed breasts! Thoros was murdered by his citizens on 9 March. Baldwin declared himself Count of Edessa, the first principality in the kingdom of Jerusalem. The Muslims under Kerbogha tried to recover Edessa in May 1098 but Baldwin resisted successfully and delayed the Muslim army heading for Antioch. On Christmas Day 1144 Zangi recovered Edessa from Count Joscelin II (who was elsewhere), the first major loss for the crusader kingdom that provoked the Second Crusade. Zangi's bombardment was so intense that 'even the birds dared not fly near'. The walls were mined and the city stormed. The county of Edessa was not revived.

FIELD OF BLOOD (AGER SANGUINIS), BATTLE OF THE, 28 JUNE 1119

Ilghazi of Aleppo defeated Roger prince of Antioch. Roger tried to extend his power around Aleppo, advancing without waiting for reinforcements, against the advice of King Baldwin. Faced by Ilghazi, Roger took a defensive position in the hilly country west of Aleppo, in a valley with wooded slopes on each side. Ilghazi surrounded him. The battle opened with archers shooting from either side. The wind blew dust in the Christian faces. The Christians were routed and Roger was killed, only a few escaping. Most prisoners were tortured and killed. It demonstrated Muslim recovery since the First Crusade.

HARBIYA (LA FORBIE), BATTLE OF, 17 OCTOBER 1244

Victory for the Egyptians and Khorezmians under Emir Baybars over a combined army of Christians and Muslims from Damascus. The site was a sandy plain north-east of Gaza, now in Israel. Members of the Leper Hospital of St Lazarus took part. Walter of Jaffa favoured attack, believing his forces superior, but the charge failed. Under attack the Damascenes broke and fled. The defeat struck a serious blow to the crusader kingdom. Over a thousand knights were killed, including the grand master of the Templars. Eight hundred prisoners were taken. It inspired St Louis' crusade though his efforts were not very effective.

HATTIN, BATTLE OF, 4 JULY 1187

Defeat for Guy king of Jerusalem by Saladin. Saladin besieged Tiberias on Lake Galilee and Guy brought a relief army. The town was taken but the garrison, including Raymond of Tripoli's wife Eschiva, held out. Guy marched over difficult country, without water. Saladin harassed the march. Guy halted on the slopes of the twin-peaked Horns of Hattin, though others advised continuing to the lake. Saladin fired the scrub. In the morning the Muslims attacked, their archers bringing down many horses. Count Raymond, leading the van, broke out and escaped. Guy was captured and later released. Rainald of Châtillon was captured and executed. The defeat caused the near collapse of the kingdom, with Saladin taking Jerusalem and other territory. Tiberias surrendered on 5 July.

HOMS, BATTLES OF, 30 OCTOBER 1281, 23 DECEMBER 1299

Qalawun of Egypt defeated the Mongols under Mangu Timur in 1281. Homs was on the border of Tripoli and a target in the Christian–Muslim conflicts. The Mongols invaded Syria, joined by some Armenian and crusader Christians. The victory ended Christian hopes of escaping Egyptian domination after the Mongols withdrew. A battle occurred nearby at Salamia in 1299 when the Mongols again invaded and were faced by Egyptians. The Mongols under Ghazzan won but their domination was short-lived. In any case it was too late to save the crusader kingdom.

JERUSALEM, SIEGES OF, 1099, 1187, 1244

Jerusalem was besieged during the First Crusade from 7 June. The city had recently fallen to the Egyptian Fatimids. Its governor was Iftiqah ad-Dawla. The crusaders were under Godfrey de Bouillon, Raymond de St Gilles, Robert Curthose, Robert of Flanders and Tancred. The Muslims removed all animals from outside the city and poisoned the wells. The crusaders attacked from the north-west. Ships' timbers from the fleet at Jaffa were made into siege engines and towers because of the lack of trees. Jerusalem fell on 15 July and the crusaders carried out a sack and massacre, wading up to their ankles in blood. There were too many corpses to clear and a great stench arose. Iftiqah and a few others were allowed to leave, after surrendering to Raymond de St Gilles. Jerusalem became the capital of the new crusading kingdom of Jerusalem. In 1187 Saladin took Jerusalem from the Christians after Hattin. The defence was under the recently arrived Balian of Ibelin, who knighted young nobles and other residents to boost morale. The siege began on 20 September. Balian negotiated the surrender on 2 October. Many were ransomed. In 1244 Jerusalem was taken by the Khorezsmian Turks. The city fell but the garrison held out until 23 August when it surrendered. This ended the compromise that allowed Christians a place in the city.

KRAK (CRAC) DES CHEVALIERS (HUSN EL AKRAD), SIEGE OF, 1271

The great crusader castle, near Tripoli in Syria, was taken by Baybars. Built in 1115, it was held by the Knights Hospitaller from 1144. It resisted several sieges. That by Baybars, whose allies included the Assassins, began on 3 March. Rain prevented the siege engines working for a while but they broke the outer wall on 15 March. At the end of March the Muslims entered the inner bailey. On 8 April those in the only tower still resisting surrendered and were granted a safe-conduct to Tripoli. Baybars made repairs and garrisoned the castle.

MA'ARRAT AL-NUMAN, SIEGE OF, 1098

Besieged during the First Crusade before the attack on Jerusalem. Raymond de

St Gilles and Baldwin of Flanders arrived on 27 November. They attempted storm on 28 November but failed. Bohemond arrived that day but a second attack also failed. A belfry was built for an attack on 11 December. The crusaders broke in late in the day. Next day they carried out a massacre, torturing and killing prisoners, even eating their buttocks. Raymond and Bohemond quarrelled over who should have the town, which was finally left under the bishop of Albara.

MANSURAH (AL-MANSURA), BATTLE OF, 8 FEBRUARY 1250

Between Baybars (for Turan Shah) with an Egyptian army and St Louis on his first crusade. In 1249 Louis advanced from Damietta towards Cairo, reaching Mansurah in the Nile Delta in December. The Egyptians faced him over a tributary of the Nile. In February the Christians tried to cross. The Egyptians hurled barrels of Greek Fire. A traitor showed the crusaders a ford, which some crossed. Louis' brother, Robert of Artois, charged rashly into Mansurah and was killed, as was the Earl of Salisbury. The main army fought a difficult battle to hold their ground. Louis could claim a victory, albeit Pyrrhic. In March the crusaders retreated, suffering heavily on the way, especially the Templars who gave cover. Louis was captured and the crusade ended in disaster. Baybars seized power in Egypt.

MONTGISARD, BATTLE OF, 25 NOVEMBER 1177

Victory by Baldwin IV of Jerusalem over Saladin. Saladin, ruler of Egypt, invaded the kingdom of Jerusalem. He attacked Ascalon and aimed for Jerusalem. Baldwin summoned the Templars from Gaza. The brothers Baldwin and Balian of Ibelin were among the Christian leaders. King Baldwin caught the Muslims by surprise crossing a ravine near the castle of Montgisard, near Ramleh. The Muslims were scattered, some foraging. It was claimed that St George appeared to aid the crusaders.

Many Muslims were killed and Saladin retreated, the worst defeat of his career though the setback was only temporary.

MONTSÉGUR, SIEGE OF, 1243–4

Conclusion of the Albigensian Crusade. Montségur was a Pyrenean stronghold, 12 miles east of Foix, the last refuge of the Cathar heretics. Raymond VII of Toulouse besieged it in 1241 but abandoned the attempt. Its garrison of 20 knights and 100 sergeants was not Cathar but attacked inquisitors operating in the neighbourhood at Avignonet in 1242. A new siege was undertaken in May 1243 by Hugh des Arcis, seneschal of Carcassonne, for St Louis. The citizens defended the place vigorously, women operating throwing engines. For the besiegers the bishop of Albi operated a trebuchet. A traitor let in the crusaders, and a group of Basques scaled the difficult approach to knife the guards on duty. They took a tower but the garrison held on for several weeks before surrendering on 2 March. The heretics were given the option of recanting or being burned. On 16 March, 200 were executed on a huge pyre at the foot of the castle.

NICAEA (IZNIK), SIEGE OF, 1097

The Christians on the First Crusade besieged Nicaea (now in Turkey) from 6 May, as their first major target. It had been taken from Byzantium by the Turks after Manzikert. Kilij Arslan sultan of Rum held Nicaea but was absent when the crusaders arrived. He returned with a Seljuk relief force but was defeated on 21 May and withdrew. Heads of captive Turks were shot over the walls to demoralise the defence. The crusaders built siege engines and dug mines. A belfry was destroyed by rocks thrown from the walls. A Byzantine fleet aided the crusaders, attacking from the lake. On 19 June the garrison surrendered to the Byzantines in preference to the crusaders. Kilij Arslan's wife was captured trying to escape and sent to Constantinople.

NICOPOLIS (NIKOPOL/NIGBOLU), SIEGE AND BATTLE OF, 12 SEPTEMBER 1396

Victory by sultan Bayezit I over the crusade of Nicopolis. With Constantinople under threat from the Turks a mixed army of western Christians advanced to Nicopolis (now in Bulgaria) on the Danube, which they besieged. The allies included French, Burgundians, Wallachians, Poles, Germans and Hungarians. The leaders included John the Fearless of Burgundy and the French Marshal Boucicaut. Bayezit came to the relief. Sigismund of Hungary withdrew rather than fight the large Turkish army. The remaining crusaders charged into a disguised trap of stakes and horse archers and were defeated. Nicopolis diverted Ottoman attention from Constantinople for a while.

RAMLEH, BATTLES OF, 4 SEPTEMBER 1101, 17 MAY 1102, 27 AUGUST 1105

Ramleh, west of Jerusalem, was taken from the Muslims on the First Crusade in 1099. In 1101 Baldwin I of Jerusalem defeated the Fatimid Egyptians under Saad al-Dawlah. The Egyptians headed for Jerusalem but were caught by surprise at dawn. The Christians were in six divisions. Mounted charges won the battle, notably that of the reserve under Baldwin on his horse Gazelle. In 1102 Baldwin was defeated by the Egyptians under Sharaf al-Ma'ali. The Egyptians approached from Ascalon. Baldwin entered Ramleh for refuge and escaped at night. The Muslims attacked in the morning and took Ramleh, slaughtering those within, including Stephen-Henry count of Blois. He had escaped from Antioch during the First Crusade and returned west. Now he came back to the Holy Land and met his death. Ironically he is usually seen as a coward. In 1105 Baldwin gained his revenge at Ramleh on a Sunday against invading Egyptians under Sena al-Mulk with allies from Damascus. The Patriarch of Jerusalem was with Baldwin, bearing the True Cross, and blessed the Christians before battle. A charge by Baldwin decided the day. Sena al-Mulk escaped. The battle ended the Fatimid attempt to conquer Palestine.

TIBERIAS, SIEGE OF, 1187

The siege of Tiberias by Saladin led to Hattin. A force besieged Tiberias for Saladin from 2 July. The Lord of Tiberias was Count Raymond of Tripoli whose wife Eschiva was within the walls. The town was stormed but the citadel held out. King Guy with Raymond advanced to the relief but were defeated at Hattin. The garrison surrendered on 5 July. Eschiva was permitted to go to Tripoli.

TOULOUSE, SIEGES OF, 1211, 1217–18

Toulouse was the chief town in the region noted for Cathar heresy, a target for the Albigensian Crusade. It was Count Raymond VI's capital. Simon de Montfort the Elder besieged Toulouse from 16 June 1211 though he could not blockade the whole circumference. A storm attempt failed and the siege was abandoned on 29 June. In 1217 Simon made a second attempt after Raymond took refuge in Toulouse in September. The defenders made sorties. In May 1218 flooding proved more uncomfortable for the attackers than the defenders. Simon's attack from the River Garonne failed. On 25 June a stone from a defending trebuchet shot by women hit Simon on the head and killed him. The Capetian monarchy took over the attack on the heretics and benefited most in the long run.

TUNIS, SIEGE OF, 1270

St Louis' second crusade aimed against Tunis where Emir Mustansir was expected to convert to Christianity. The Christians camped at Carthage near Tunis on 18 July. They found that the emir had no intention of converting or surrendering. Joinville wrote 'I was not there, thank God'. Louis, along with many of his men, became ill probably with typhus, dying on 25 August. His brother Charles made terms with the emir on 1 November.

TYRE, SIEGES OF, 1111–12, 1124

The first major siege of Tyre by the Christians of the kingdom of Jerusalem failed. Tyre was almost an island, with three encircling walls and a narrow approach from land. Rocks protected the sea approach. It was held by the Fatimid Egyptians. Baldwin undertook the siege from November 1111. He lacked aid from sea and the Byzantine fleet gave little aid. A relief attempt under Toghtekin of Damascus succeeded. The siege was abandoned in April 1112. The second siege was undertaken by Baldwin II from 15 February 1124. The Turks from Damascus disputed control of Tyre from 1112 and came to take over the defence under Toghtekin in 1124. A Venetian fleet arrived to blockade from the sea. Relief attempts from Egypt and Damascus failed. The Christians operated throwing engines from belfries, one with five platforms. An Armenian Christian expert was paid to aim the engines. The Muslims used a device with hooks to catch the end of rams and turn them over. They shot Greek Fire at the Christians. Tyre surrendered on 7 July, when each side was allowed to view the other's fortifications. The Christians now held all the main ports on the Syrian coast. Tyre resisted an attempt against it by Saladin and was one of the last Christian strongholds to surrender, on 29 May 1291.

VARNA, SIEGE AND BATTLE OF, 1444

From November 1444 a crusade under Ladislas III of Hungary and Poland with the general John Hunyadi of Transylvania besieged the Black Sea port of Varna (in Bulgaria) during the Varna Crusade aimed at Constantinople. A Venetian fleet was supposed to take the crusaders on from Varna but failed to arrive. Varna was held by the Ottomans. Sultan Murad II came to relieve it. On 10 November the smaller crusading army was defeated. Ladislas was killed and Hunyadi escaped. It was not decisive but the siege and the crusade were abandoned. It was one of the last hopes of saving Constantinople from the Turks.

Joan of Arc directing operations

9 | The Capetians and the Valois, France 987–1500

GENERALS AND LEADERS

See in Part I: d'Albret (Charles), Blanche of Castile, Boucicaut, Cadoc, Charles the Good, Charles VI, Charles VII, Enguerrand de Coucy, Ferrand of Flanders, François de Surienne, Fulk le Réchin, Fulk V of Anjou, Geoffrey V of Anjou, Guesclin (Bertrand du), Henry I of France, Hugh Capet, Hugh du Puiset, Joan of Arc, John II, John the Fearless, Louis VI, Louis VII, Louis VIII, Louis IX, Louis XI, Marcel (Étienne), Mercadier, Philip I, Philip II, Philip IV, Philip VI, Renaud de Dammartin, Robert II the Pious, William V the Great of Aquitaine, William IX of Aquitaine.

BATTLES AND SIEGES

Agincourt 1415, Baugé 1421, Beauvais 1430, 1472, Bouvines 1214, Brémule 1119, Breteuil 1356, Caen 1346, 1417, 1450, Calais 1346–7, Candé 1106, Cassel 1071, 1328, Castillon 1453, Château-Gaillard 1203–4, Conquereux 992, Courtrai 1302, Cravant 1423, Crécy 1346, Falaise 1418–19, Formigny 1450, Fréteval 1194, Gisors 1198, Harfleur 1415, Herrings (Rouvray) 1429, Jacquerie 1358, Laon 986–7, La Rochelle 1372, Liège 1468, Mauron 1352, Meaux 1421–2, Mons-en-Pévèle 1304, Montboyau 1026, Montlhéry 1465, Montreuil-Bellay 1149–51, Morlaix 1342, Muret 1213, Neuss 1474–5, Orléans 1428–9, Patay 1429, Poitiers 1356, Rennes 1356–7, Roche-Derrien 1347, Roosebeke 1382, Rouen 1418–19, 1449, Saintes 1242, St-Pol de Léon 1346, Sluys 1340, Thurie c.1370, Valmont 1416, Verneuil 1424.

OUTLINE OF EVENTS

In 987 Carolingian rule ended after years of uncertainty. Hugh Capet duke of the Franks took the crown. His family, descended from Robert the Strong, had dominated the kingdom of the West Franks for some time. Hugh founded a dynasty that lasted until 1328, the Capetians. The early Capetians were relatively weak with little authority over the great principalities – Normandy, Flanders, Anjou, Brittany, Burgundy, Blois and Aquitaine. The monarchs endured through effort and luck. Among the factors helping them was the lack of external interests, a good relationship with the Church, and a series of long-lived kings with male heirs. Between 996 and 1180 there were only five kings, with a shortest reign of 29 years. This stability meant a permanent and increasing territorial family base for the monarchy.

Three Robertines (Odo, Robert and Raoul) were crowned kings before Hugh Capet. As Duke of the Franks Hugh possessed a base in the Île-de-France which, though restricted in extent, was larger than the demesne of the late Carolingian kings. The early Capetians resisted domination by the great princes – the dukes and counts. Odo count of Blois claimed he had no wish to be king, 'just always the king's master'. The principalities threatened to develop beyond the monarchy's control. The Duke of Normandy conquered England and became a king. Other principalities, especially Flanders and Burgundy, had important connections outside West Francia – in their cases with the Holy Roman Empire, which meant divided loyalties. Capetian independence was often threatened but the threats were shrugged off in the long run.

Control of lords within the royal demesne was a constant problem for the early Capetians (Hugh, Robert the Pious, Henry I and Philip I). Henry I of France quarrelled with his brother, but internal family differences were rare. The growing power of the monarchy encouraged Henry to invade Normandy but his limitations were exposed by defeat at the hands of William the Conqueror. The weakness of the early Capetians can be exaggerated and a policy of co-operation with the principalities was generally successful.

From the 12th century the monarchy emerged from relative humility. Philip I defended the Vexin against the Normans and by 1108 was recovering from his defeat by Hugh du Puiset. Louis VI gained revenge over Hugh. Louis developed a strong central administration with reasonable control over the barons of the demesne. By countering the local lords Louis forged closer links with the growing towns that wanted independence of the same lords. Communes and the monarchy gave each other mutual support, and both benefited. The value of the demesne became clear, not least the hold on Paris. Louis was now more on a par with the greater princes of Europe, and benefited from ecclesiastical support. Nevertheless a royal invasion of Normandy was defeated, this time at Brémule.

Louis VII married Eleanor of Aquitaine but failed to keep her or her inheritance of the duchy of Aquitaine. Yet monarchical power continued to increase and relations with the Church were cemented by the protection given to Pope Alexander III. Louis could not stop the growth of the Angevin Empire but he undermined Henry II through supporting Becket and encouraging Henry's rebellious sons. Louis went on the Second Crusade, a failure but a sign of his good relationship with the Church.

Medieval France became more significant under the great Capetians, the first of whom was Philip II. From a lengthy struggle with his rivals in Flanders, the Empire and England, he emerged victorious – conquering Normandy and winning at Bouvines. Philip's son continued and completed his father's work by bringing southern France more fully under Capetian rule.

Many see Louis IX as the greatest ruler of medieval France though he was not its most successful military leader. His two crusades were disasters. He is better known for his peace treaties, which settled the basic frontiers of France, than for his wars. He was fond of quoting 'Blessed are the peacemakers', and agreed that wars should be just. His mother, Blanche of Castile, was regent in the early reign, when Henry III of England unsuccessfully invaded France in 1230. She fended off opposition from the princes, including those of Boulogne, Brittany, Toulouse, La Marche and Champagne. Under Louis, the Cathar heretics were crushed with the taking of Montségur. The power of the counts of Toulouse was destroyed, the county going to Louis' brother Alphonse.

No prince in France could now match monarchical power. A second invasion by Henry III of England in 1241 ended in victory for Louis at Saintes. In 1258 Louis' treaty with Henry recognised the English loss of most of the Angevin Empire – including Normandy, Anjou, Maine, Touraine and Poitou. Henry III did homage for the lands he retained in France. Louis made a similar agreement with Aragón at Corbeil in 1258 with Jaime the Conqueror, agreeing the Pyrenees as the border. Jaime also performed homage. Louis' brother, Charles of Anjou, invaded Sicily in 1266 and became King of Sicily. The French ruled Sicily until the Sicilian Vespers of 1284.

St Louis' grandson Philip IV has a mixed reputation, known as Philip the Fair but noted for some dastardly acts – the bishop of Pamiers called him 'not a man but a beast'. He was nevertheless the last great Capetian. Flanders submitted to the monarchy. After defeat at Courtrai in 1302 Philip gained revenge at Mons-en-Pévèle in 1304. Lille, Douai and Béthune were ceded to the monarchy. Philip clashed with Edward I of England in southern France. Philip took Guyenne but thereafter Edward held his own and peace was agreed with the marriage of Edward's son to Philip's daughter Isabelle.

Philip's bad reputation comes largely from clashes with the Church. Most French bishops supported Philip against the papacy. Philip's agent Philip de Nogaret was responsible for an attack on Boniface VIII's palace, soon followed by the pope's death. However, Philip was then able to dominate and pressurise later popes, notably Clement V. French influence assisted the papacy's move to Avignon. Philip's most famous act was his attack on the Templars in 1307, leading to their suppression in 1311. His motives have never been satisfactorily explained – though criticism of their activities, accusations of heresy (unlikely to be true), and profit from their wealth were part of it. Scandals late in the reign, over the conduct of his daughters-in-law, did not improve the monarchy's reputation. Philip's three sons inherited the throne in turn and died quickly without leaving male heirs.

In 1328 Philip VI became the first Valois King of France. Under him the Hundred Years' War began. Philip partly provoked the war by continuing to seek expansion and allying with the Scots. Philip's victory in Flanders at Cassel in 1328 increased French domination and damaged English interests there. The two monarchs were involved in a succession dispute over Brittany. Edward III renounced homage to Philip for his French lands in 1336 and declared war in 1337. France was under attack. Edward won at sea off Sluys in 1340 and on land at Crécy in 1346 and Poitiers in 1356. At Poitiers King John II of France was defeated and captured – imprisoned in the Tower. France was harmed by the Black Death and the social upheaval of the Jacquerie. The 1360 Treaty of Brétigny recognised English holdings in Poitou, Gascony, Aquitaine and Calais.

France was ravaged by unemployed mercenaries. An even greater threat came from the growth of an independent duchy of Burgundy. The murder of Louis of Orléans in 1407 led to civil war between Burgundians and Armagnacs. Burgundy allied with England and encouraged Henry V's invasion France. He besieged Harfleur and won at Agincourt in 1415. By 1419 England had reconquered Normandy. By the 1420 Treaty of Troyes, Henry V married the French Princess Catherine.

The turning point in the war came in the 1420s. Henry V died suddenly and was succeeded by the minor Henry VI, who was no warrior. The English still won at Cravant and Verneuil, but the tide turned. Joan of Arc appeared and helped save Orléans. She was associated with a revived monarchy under Charles VII. The French, assisted by good generals and cannons developed by the Bureau brothers, began to win battles and recover territory. They defeated the English at Patay and Formigny. Burgundy made peace with France, deserting England. The French victory at Castillon in 1453 marked the end of the war. Of the territory once held by English kings in France, only Calais remained.

The duchy of Burgundy was a rival as well as an enemy of France. Its rulers retained high ambitions – perhaps too high. Charles the Bold led the duchy into a series of military disasters. Burgundy had hopes from renewed alliance with England but Edward IV's invasion of France, though it brought financial compensation to Edward, was concluded with a peace that excluded Burgundy. Charles the Bold failed to take Neuss in 1474 and was defeated by the Swiss at Grandson and Morat in 1476. At Nancy in 1477 he was defeated and killed. Louis XI could not suppress his pleasure at the news.

Louis XI was the last great medieval king of France. He dealt with the War of the Public Weal, a league formed against him that threatened Paris. He was defeated at Montlhéry in 1465 but escaped and recovered all lost ground. The fall of Charles the Bold led to an increase in royal authority and demesne but Charles' daughter, Mary, avoided a French marriage for one with Maximilian (HRE). The French were defeated at Guinegate in 1479. Louis gained Roussillon and Cerdagne in the south from Aragón to settle the Pyrenean frontier. Louis' son Charles VIII married the heiress Anne of Brittany in 1491 and the extent of modern France was established. French invasions of Italy take us into a new era.

BATTLES AND SIEGES

AGINCOURT, 25 OCTOBER 1415
Victory of Henry V over the French under Constable d'Albret, Marshal Boucicaut and the dukes of Orléans and Bourbon. Henry invaded France in 1415. After the siege of Harfleur he headed for Calais. He crossed the main rivers, shadowed by a larger French force. He crossed the Somme but was caught near Azincourt (Agincourt), 30 miles south of Calais. Henry took a defensive position but advanced to provoke enemy action. He was protected on either flank by woods. The French dismounted knights in the centre, with cavalry on each wing. English longbowmen, on the wings of the English army protected by stakes, halted French charges. The French centre advanced through muddy ground and was held. Henry countered. He saved one fallen brother, Humphrey, but another, the Duke of York, was killed. Eighteen French knights swore to kill Henry or die; they failed apart from denting his helmet (now in Westminster Abbey). Fearing for his

small force during an attack on the baggage train, Henry ordered the execution of French prisoners. Agincourt was a major victory, followed by the conquest of Normandy and the successful claim to the French throne. Henry and his troops received a triumph in London.

BAUGÉ, BATTLE OF, 22 MARCH 1421

Defeat on Easter Saturday of the English under Thomas duke of Clarence (Henry V's brother) in the Hundred Years' War while Henry was in England. Clarence had news of an Armagnac force in the vicinity. He rashly crossed the bridge over the Couesnon at Baugé in Anjou to attack. The English cavalry was separated from the infantry and met by the enemy, including Scots under Buchan. The English entered the town and rallied on the slope by the river. Buchan appeared with his larger force. Clarence charged forward and was killed, as was Lord de Roos. The earls of Somerset and Huntingdon were captured. The Earl of Salisbury with a force of archers recovered Clarence's body from the cart on which it had been thrown. The battle was a sign of changing fortunes for the French even before the emergence of Joan of Arc.

BEAUVAIS, BATTLE OF, 1430, SIEGE OF, 1472

What is known as the Battle of Beauvais was fought 20 miles west at Savignies. The French were defeated and pursued to Beauvais. The victory was won by English archers. The war was swinging in favour of France, but the traditional English formation still won some victories. Nevertheless the area was soon overrun by the French. Ironically it was in 1430 that Joan of Arc was brought before the bishop of Beauvais as judge (ejected from his see by Charles VII). In 1472 Beauvais was successfully defended by the French. Women, including Jeanne Laisné (model for the legendary Jeanne Hachette), helped the defence. It was besieged from 27 June by Charles the Bold of Burgundy against Louis XI. The besiegers' ladders were too

short and Charles lacked sufficient ammunition for his cannons. The siege was abandoned on 22 July. Louis XI rewarded Beauvais (and its women) with civic privileges – the women were allowed to wear what they chose and to precede the men in town processions.

BOUVINES, BATTLE OF, 27 JULY 1214

Victory of Philip Augustus king of France over allies under Otto IV (HRE). Otto allied with Flanders, England and dissident French lords and threatened to overwhelm Philip. Philip wanted to avoid battle but was caught at a river crossing near Bouvines, between Douai, Tournai and Valenciennes, a marshy area – and the weather had been wet. Philip was crossing the Marcq but recalled those who had crossed to face the enemy. The French right charged under Guérin de Glapion. The Flemish knights despised this attack by men of low rank, and Eustace de Mechelen challenged the French knights to fight him – he was then surrounded and killed. The head of a man who fell from his horse was buried to the neck in mud. The counts of St Pol and Melun charged and broke through. They turned to attack from the rear. On the French left Ferrand of Flanders (for the allies) was unhorsed and captured. Otto advanced in the centre and the battle was in the balance. Philip was unhorsed and fell with a lance sticking in his mail. He was not badly injured, and remounted. The allied right made an angled advance towards Philip but was held by the bishop of Beauvais, who clubbed down and captured the Earl of Salisbury (fighting for the allies). Otto IV was unhorsed but remounted and fled. Renaud de Dammartin (for the allies) fought a last ditch resistance, issuing repeatedly from a circle of pikemen – but numbers told. Most of Renaud's men were killed and he was captured. The battle lasted three hours. Otto's eagle standard was damaged and captured. Most major prisoners were ransomed. The defeat of Otto led to his replacement by Frederick II in 1215. Otto retired to Brunswick and died in 1218. Ferrand's defeat led to the division of Flanders between France and the Empire. Ferrand was not released until 1227, dying a broken man. Renaud, as a traitor, was imprisoned and when it became clear he would never be released he committed suicide. For King John, although not present, the defeat was a disaster, soon followed by Magna Carta. Philip proceeded to a triumph in Paris. The victory sealed his conquest of the Angevin Empire and removed the imperial threat for the rest of the reign.

BRÉMULE, BATTLE OF, 20 AUGUST 1119

Victory for Henry I of England over Louis VI of France. Louis and Fulk V of Anjou invaded Normandy in support of William Clito's claim to the duchy. Louis headed for Noyon but was seen by Henry's scouts on the hill at Verclives. They saw the French emerging from the woods and warned Henry, who moved to block them. The site was on a plain near the River Andelle. Henry I dismounted some knights to strengthen the infantry. He led the rear division. The French attacked, losing 80 knights in the first disorderly charge. The second charge broke through the front line but was halted by the dismounted men. Henry advanced into the fray. He was wounded by a blow on the helmet but survived. An attack by a reserve force (probably cavalry) under Henry's sons decided the battle. The French broke and fled. Louis got lost in a wood but was led to safety at Les Andelys by a peasant. One chronicler said that French knights were captured, rather than killed, on Christian principles. Louis' standard was captured. Henry went on to a triumph in Rouen. His control of Normandy was secured.

BRETEUIL, SIEGE OF, 1356

Besieged by King John II of France from 26 July after he had taken Evreux. He used engines and a three-storey belfry with 200 men on each level and loopholes for archers. Peasants collected wood to fill the moat, covering it with earth and straw so

the belfry could cross. The Navarrese garrison, allied to the English, halted the belfry with cannons and Greek Fire. It caught fire and was abandoned. Breteuil surrendered on 20 August, the garrison paid off and allowed to go.

CAEN, SIEGES OF, 1346, 1417, 1450

City and castle in western Normandy at the junction of the Orne and the Odon, vital in the Hundred Years' War. Edward III besieged it in 1346 on his Crécy campaign, approaching by land and water. The garrison included Genoese crossbowmen. The town was stormed on 26 July and many inhabitants killed. The castle surrendered on terms. Henry V besieged Caen in 1417 during his conquest of Normandy. He camped in monastic buildings. He used a collapsible bridge to cross the river. Defenders placed bowls of water on the walls to detect mining attempts. English scaling ladders proved too short. Caen was stormed on 4 September. Two hundred French were killed in the market place. The castle surrendered on terms on 20 September. Henry went on to conquer Normandy. In 1450 the French besieged Caen from June and recovered it from the English in the reconquest of Normandy. Somerset retreated to Caen from Rouen. The French bombarded with cannons for three weeks. One cannonball entered the chamber where Somerset's wife and children were staying. They survived but Somerset surrendered. By the end of the year Normandy was lost.

CALAIS, SIEGE OF, 1346–7

Besieged by Edward III from 4 September 1346 after Crécy. Calais belonged to the county of Boulogne. The English fleet arrived to blockade but was defeated by a Genoese fleet for France. Calais' defence was commanded by the Burgundian Jean de Vienne; 1,700 poor were expelled and allowed to pass through, provided with food. Cannons were brought from London and siege engines built. A 'new town' was constructed for the besiegers. Philip VI's attempts at relief in October 1346, May and July 1347 all failed. Calais surrendered on 4 August 1347. Edward demanded six leading citizens to execute. Six burghers with ropes round their necks approached Edward's Queen, Philippa of Hainault, and gained from her an appeal for mercy – probably staged to enhance Edward's reputation. The ordinary citizens were expelled and replaced by an English garrison. Calais remained English longer than any continental possession, until 1558 under Mary I.

CANDÉ, SIEGE OF, 1106

Marked by the death of Geoffrey Martel II, son and heir of Fulk IV count of Anjou. Candé lies on the Loire and the Angevins sought to control it. Geoffrey besieged Candé against Norman of Montevrault. He stormed and took the castle. During peace negotiations Geoffrey was treacherously shot in the arm by a crossbow bolt and died the next day. His brother Fulk V succeeded to Anjou in 1109.

CASSEL, BATTLES OF, 22 FEBRUARY 1071, 23 AUGUST 1328

In 1071 Flemings under Arnulf III count of Flanders, allied with Philip I of France, defeated Robert the Frisian, Arnulf's rival. Cassel, then in Flanders, is now in northern France. Arnulf had become count in the previous year. He was killed at Cassel. Philip recognised Robert the Frisian as count. In 1328 Philip VI defeated Flemings rebelling against French rule. The Flemings stood on a hill but chose to attack. The French took their revenge for Courtrai and thousands were killed. Louis of Nevers was restored as Count of Flanders. To commemorate the victory Philip had a statue of himself erected at Notre-Dame in Paris.

CASTILLON, BATTLE OF, 17 JULY 1453

Battle that ended the Hundred Years' War. The English commander was John Talbot earl of Shrewsbury. The French were under Jean de Bueil. Castillon is on the Dordogne. Talbot sought to recover Bordeaux. The French built a camp outside Castillon, which they were besieging. The camp, between the Dordogne and the Lidoire, was designed by Jean Bureau, protected by 300 cannons. The French had 700 handgunners. Talbot unwisely attempted to storm the camp and his force was decimated by the guns. Talbot was an obvious target with his white hair, purple hat and scarlet gown. He lacked armour, having sworn on release from captivity not to appear against the French in arms. A Breton force came to aid the French and the battle was soon concluded. Talbot's horse was hit and fell, trapping him underneath. He was despatched with a battleaxe. The corpse was returned to Shropshire. In 1860 the tomb was opened and the skull was found to have been split by a blow. Castillon surrendered and then Bordeaux. There was no treaty but the war was over.

CHÂTEAU-GAILLARD, SIEGE OF, 1203–4

Besieged and taken by Philip Augustus during his conquest of Normandy. The castle was built in 1196–8 by Richard the Lionheart on a cliff over the Seine by the Norman border at Les Andelys. Philip arrived in August 1203. The castle was held for King John by Roger de Lacy. John attempted relief with a land and river attack that failed. He returned to England. The outer bailey was mined in February 1204. The middle bailey was entered through a garderobe chute. The inner bailey was mined, the besiegers sheltering behind the rock bridge leading to it. The defenders surrendered on 8 March 1204. Within a year Philip held Normandy, and most of the Angevin Empire followed suit.

CONQUEREUX (CONQUEREUIL), BATTLE OF, 27 JUNE 992

Fought near Nantes between the Bretons under Conan I and the Angevins under Fulk Nerra. Some Bretons dismounted to fight on foot, an early example of the tactic. Fulk, seeking to expand Angevin power, intervened in Brittany to support the nephew of Guerech count of Nantes (killed in 988). The Breton tactic failed. Conquereux was the first in a series of victories by Fulk, aiding the growth of Anjou.

COURTRAI (THE GOLDEN SPURS), BATTLE OF, 11 JULY 1302

Defeat by the Flemish of the French under Robert of Artois for Philip IV. It followed the revolt of the Matins of Bruges. The Flemings besieged Courtrai whose castle was held by the French. The French attempted relief. A Flemish force, called 'weavers, fullers and the common folk', assembled under Guy of Namur, William of Jülich and Jean de Renesse. The Flemish army consisted mainly of citizen militias, infantry armed with crossbows and goedendags. The Flemings protected their position with ditches. The French charged but, faced by ditches and pikes, failed to break through. The garrison sortied against the Flemish rear but was beaten back. Robert led the rearguard into the fray. His horse was hit and he was dragged off and killed. Courtrai demonstrated the value of infantry against cavalry. The battle was known as that of the Golden Spurs, because 700 pairs were taken from French corpses as trophies. The defeat shocked France, but Philip IV gained his revenge at Mons-en-Pévèle.

CRAVANT, BATTLE OF, 31 JULY 1423

An English victory in the Hundred Years' War. The English were commanded by the Earl of Salisbury and fought in alliance with Burgundy. Charles VII invaded Burgundy with Scottish allies, besieging Cravant on the frontier by the Yonne. Salisbury came to its relief. The French held the high ground but came down to the river. Covered by shots from his archers, Salisbury crossed the Yonne to attack. The English garrison made a sortie. The Count of Ventadour and the Scot Sir John Stewart, who lost an eye, were captured.

CRÉCY, BATTLE OF, 26 AUGUST 1346

Victory of Edward III over Philip VI in the Hundred Years' War, the first major victory of the war. Edward took Caen and marched north to escape pursuit by a larger army. He crossed the Somme ford at Blanchetaque but was caught at Crécy by the River Maie. The English took a defensive position. The French used Genoese crossbowmen but rain lessened the effectiveness of their bows. The French charged through their failed archers to be halted by longbows and the ditches Edward had dug. Horses piled up 'like a litter of piglets'. Fifteen charges were made and all failed. The English used a few cannons but with little effect. The Black Prince was knocked down but saved by his standard-bearer. Philip VI was wounded in the neck by an arrow but escaped. The French losses were high, the English slight. Blind King John of Bohemia and Louis de Nevers count of Flanders were killed fighting for the French. Edward continued his march to Calais.

FALAISE, SIEGE OF, 1418–19

The castle near Caen, where William the Conqueror was conceived and born, was besieged in December 1418 during Henry V's conquest of Normandy. It was defended by Olivier de Maunay, Charles VII's standard-bearer. The English built huts against the icy weather. Henry's guns brought down the clock tower and breached the wall. The town surrendered on 2 January but the castle resisted. Blockade eventually succeeded and the garrison surrendered on 16 February. A captured Welsh captain, Edward ap Gruffydd, was hanged, drawn and quartered as a traitor. Falaise was recovered by the French in 1450 after a siege.

FORMIGNY, BATTLE OF, 15 APRIL 1450

Defeat for the English in the final stages of the Hundred Years' War near Bayeux, for which the English were heading. The French were under Clermont, the English under Thomas Kyriell. The English took a defensive position and held early French attacks. The main conflict was over the English attempt to capture French cannons. A second French force arrived under

Constable Richemont. It attacked from the flank and won the battle. Kyriell was captured, Normandy lost.

FRÉTEVAL, BATTLE OF, 3 JULY 1194

Defeat for Philip Augustus by Richard the Lionheart. Richard sought to recover ground lost in France during his captivity after the Third Crusade. Philip tried to avoid battle but Richard caught him near Vendôme. Richard attacked the French rearguard and captured the baggage train, including the royal archives, the royal seal, and letters revealing treachery by Angevin nobles. Fréteval was a skirmish rather than a battle and Philip, who was not involved in the fighting, escaped. Philip entered a church to pray while Richard chased elsewhere on false information. Fréteval assisted Richard's recovery of territory.

GISORS, BATTLE OF, 28 SEPTEMBER 1198

Victory of Richard the Lionheart over Philip Augustus. Gisors was a major castle on the Norman frontier. Richard de Vaux started to build a castle at Vaux for Philip in 1186, to threaten Gisors. Henry de Vere, castellan of Gisors, declared he would destroy it. The French came out to protect the building work and a skirmish followed in which Richard de Vaux' son Ralph was killed. Henry fled to Richard the Lionheart for protection. In 1193 Philip invaded Normandy and captured Gisors, which surrendered. In 1198 Richard invaded the Vexin and a skirmish occurred involving Philip Augustus. Philip was attempting to reach Gisors with a small force of 200 knights when Richard caught him. It was a minor victory for Richard since Philip escaped to Gisors. The incident is remembered because, as the surviving French knights crossed the bridge over the Epte into Gisors, it broke. Philip was among those who fell into the water. Eighteen were drowned. Philip was dragged to safety and soon moved on. Angevin chroniclers ridiculed Philip but it was an embarrassment rather than a serious defeat. Philip still held Gisors.

HARFLEUR, SIEGE OF, 1415

Besieged by Henry V from 13 August at the start of his invasion of Normandy. Harfleur is now part of Le Havre. Henry was well provided with arms and siege equipment. His fleet prevented approach from the sea. Harfleur had two and a half miles of walls. The French dammed the River Lézarde, creating marshy ground for the attackers. A relief force of 300 broke through to aid the defence. Henry bombarded with guns, including *London* and *Messenger*. The weather worsened and many besiegers sickened and died. The French agreed to surrender in three days if no help came. Harfleur fell on 22 September, providing a base for the conquest of Normandy.

HERRINGS, BATTLE OF THE (ROUVRAY), 12 FEBRUARY 1429

Defeat of the French by English heading for Orléans. An English supply train (with wagons full of herrings) under Sir John Fastolf was attacked by French under Clermont, with allied Scots under Sir John Stuart, between Rouvray and Janville. Fastolf made a barricade with wagons, protected by archers and stakes. The French attacked with guns while the Scots charged on foot. They were held and Stuart was killed. Fastolf's charge decided the battle. The English continued their march to Orléans with the supplies. The victory gave false hope since Joan of Arc was about to emerge from obscurity.

JACQUERIE, THE, 1358

Political and economic reasons provoked this French Peasants' Revolt, following French defeats in the Hundred Years' War, the capture of the French king, the Black Death, and pillaging and disorder caused by mercenary companies. The name comes from calling a typical peasant 'Jacques Bonhomme'. The peasants assembled on 28 May at St-Leu in the Beauvaisis. They marched on the local lord's residence, killing him and his family. A protest movement turned into violence throughout northern France. A leader emerged in

Guillaume Cale from Picardy. Attacks were made on castles and noble residences with looting, killing and rape. Compiègne was besieged but held out. In June the revolt was crushed by the nobles under Charles of Navarre. Cale was treacherously captured at a 'parley'. He was crowned with a ring of red-hot iron and beheaded. Peasants were massacred at Meaux and Clermont-en-Beauvaisis. There were troubles in Paris where Étienne Marcel was killed in riots in July.

LAON, SIEGE OF, 986–7
Besieged by Hugh Capet against the Carolingian Charles duke of Lower Lorraine. Charles entered the city and imprisoned its bishop. Hugh came to recover it in the autumn but decided it was too late in the year for a siege. He returned next spring. The bishop escaped from the tower by sliding down a rope and joined Hugh. When Hugh returned he used an engineer to build a belfry but the slope to the walls was too steep. One night Hugh's troops drank too much wine. The garrison took advantage to sortie, firing the besiegers' camp. Hugh abandoned the siege though he eventually triumphed over Charles to found the Capetian dynasty.

LA ROCHELLE, SIEGE AND NAVAL BATTLE OF, 1372
La Rochelle was besieged by the French under Du Guesclin. Enrique II of Castile, allied to France, defeated the English relief fleet under the Earl of Pembroke. Pembroke was captured and taken to Spain. The mayor of La Rochelle, Jean Caudourier, tricked the illiterate English commander Philip Mansel, inviting him to dinner to show him a letter supposedly from Edward III. Mansel could not read and believed what the mayor said – that the king ordered him to parade outside the castle. The English paraded in the town square and were set upon. They surrendered and the mayor handed town and castle to Du Guesclin, contributing to French recovery of morale and territory.

LIÈGE, SIEGE OF, 1468
Besieged by Charles the Bold duke of Burgundy from 1467, in alliance with a reluctant Louis XI. Liège rebelled against Burgundy in 1467, repeating the offence in 1468. The Burgundians made four expeditions against Liège in four years, culminating in 1468. It was winter and there was deep mud around the gates. On the night of 29 October Charles and Louis were nearly captured by a sortie made while courtiers were playing dice. Men were losing fingers from frostbite. The besiegers made a surprise attack on Sunday 30 October, taking the city. They found tables laid for Sunday dinner. Charles killed one of his own men for plundering a church on the Sabbath. The city was fired and buildings fell. The attackers found the wine frozen and carried it off in chunks. Louis XI, forced to accompany Charles, now returned to Paris. Relations with Charles worsened rather than improved.

MAURON, BATTLE OF, 14 AUGUST 1352
Victory for the party favoured by England in Brittany early in the Hundred Years' War. The site was on the Breton border by the River Ivel. The English were under Sir Walter Bentley, the French under Guy de Nesle. De Nesle raided Brittany and was halted near Rennes. Both sides dismounted some cavalry to fight on foot. The English took a defensive position. French cavalry on their right forced the opposing archers to flee. The English centre advanced to decide the battle. Eighty-nine members of the French Order of the Star, forbidden by its rules to retreat, were killed. Guy de Nesle was killed. Bentley was wounded. Thirty English archers who had fled were arrested by their own side and beheaded next day. The French withdrew from Brittany.

MEAUX, SIEGE OF, 1421–2
Besieged by Henry V from 6 October 1421. Meaux stands on either side of the Marne. It was the last major stronghold resisting Henry in northern France. Juvenal, on

Henry's firing of the neighbourhood, wrote 'war without fire is like sausages without mustard'. The garrison under the Bastard de Vaurus acted ruthlessly, hanging captives from an elm. Eighty bodies hung there when Henry arrived. Henry resided in the abbey of St Faro and built huts for his men. He made a bridge of boats for communication over the river. Sir John Cornwall's son was decapitated by a cannonball and Cornwall swore never again to fight Christians. Henry became ill. The defenders put a donkey on the wall and made it bray, saying this was their king, Charles VI. The trumpeter Orace blew raspberries at Henry through his instrument. Guy de Nesle attempting relief fell from a ladder into the moat and was captured. The English took the town. The French retreated to the Market, a fortified island, but surrendered on 10 May 1422. The Bastard was beheaded, his body hanged on the elm. The trumpeter Orace was taken to Paris and executed. The main significance of Meaux was that Henry never recovered from his illness and died in August, a blow to English progress in the war.

MONS-EN-PÉVÈLE, BATTLE OF, 18 AUGUST 1304

Victory of Philip IV of France over the Flemish under William of Jülich, Philip's revenge for Courtrai in 1302. The battle site is between Douai and Lille. Philip advanced to Flanders. The Flemish infantry took a defensive position. Philip was reluctant to attack and the Flemish advanced to provoke battle. It was so hot that men on both sides died of sunstroke. The French used cavalry in flank attacks. The Flemish broke into the French baggage train and Philip was unhorsed and had to defend himself with an axe passed to him. A knight who gave his horse to the king was decapitated. Philip's horse bolted but he was safe. The French charged. William of Jülich was killed. The Flemings withdrew from the field but both sides suffered heavy losses.

MONTBOYAU (LA MOTTE-MONTBOYAU), SIEGE OF, 1026

The castle with a motte (now St-Cyr-sur-Loire) was built near Tours by Fulk Nerra in 1017, to threaten Blesevin Tours. Odo II of Blois besieged Montboyau (possibly for a second time). He built a belfry but it collapsed, killing the men inside, and was fired by the defenders. Fulk diverted Odo's attention by attacking Saumur. In the peace settlement Fulk agreed to dismantle Montboyau but kept Saumur. An early example of a battle with a feigned flight occurred during fighting over Montboyau. Odo II of Blois later captured Montboyau and built a new wooden tower.

MONTLHÉRY, BATTLE OF, 16 JULY 1465

An indecisive battle in the War of the Public Weal, a rebellion against Louis XI of France. The site is south of Paris. The rebels allied with Charles the Bold. Louis hoped to avoid battle. Both sides used archers, the Burgundians copying English methods with dismounted men-at-arms. Charles was hit in the stomach by a pike, leaving a bruise that was evident in the evening – the pikeman was cut down. Charles was also cut on the throat by a sword, leaving a scar for life. The battle was technically a victory for the rebels who held the field when Louis returned to Paris.

MONTREUIL-BELLAY, SIEGE OF, 1149–51

Besieged by Geoffrey V of Anjou for nearly three years. Its lord Gerard Berlai rebelled. Montreuil-Bellay had double walls and a keep 'rising to the stars', isolated from approach by a chasm. Geoffrey ordered men from the fair at Saumur to bring stones and rubbish to drop in the chasm for a bridge. He breached the wall but it was patched overnight. Reading Vegetius, Geoffrey had the idea of using Greek Fire, which he hurled in pots from throwing engines. Geoffrey broke in and captured the castle – the first time Greek Fire was used in the west, knowledge of it probably coming from the Holy Land (Geoffrey's father was Fulk king of Jerusalem).

MORLAIX, BATTLE OF, 30 SEPTEMBER 1342

First main land battle in the Hundred Years' War, a partial victory for the English. The English and French supported opposing rivals for control of Brittany. Morlaix was a fortified port on the Breton coast, north of Brest. The English expeditionary force under the Earl of Northampton besieged the French garrison from 3 September. Charles of Blois, the French candidate for the duchy, came from Guingamp to relieve Morlaix. The English used archers with dismounted men-at-arms, a tactic that would become familiar. They took a defensive position near woods with ditches and a stream protecting their front. The French attacked in waves. Some were dismounted to fight on foot but their cavalry was halted by hidden trenches. English longbows proved more effective than Genoese crossbowmen for the French. The English ran out of arrows and retreated into the woods but Charles had withdrawn. Morlaix was neither relieved by Charles nor taken by Northampton.

MURET, BATTLE OF, 12 SEPTEMBER 1213

During the Albigensian Crusade, part of a frontier conflict between France and Aragón. Muret was a fortified town at the junction of the Louge and Garonne, south of Toulouse. Simon de Montfort the Elder commanded the crusaders. His opponents included southern French under Raymond VI count of Toulouse and Pedro II king of Aragón. Simon's garrison held Muret. The allied force came to recover Toulouse. Simon arrived to relieve his men and entered Muret, only to find himself shut in. Simon sortied at dawn. He enticed the enemy to attack a gate that was deliberately opened. Simon meanwhile appeared behind his opponents, who were routed. Pedro was slain by a group of knights who had sworn to kill him. Civil war followed in Aragón where Pedro's son Jaime I emerged successful. Muret aided the Capetian domination of southern France.

NEUSS, SIEGE OF, 1474–5

Besieged by Charles the Bold duke of Burgundy from 20 July 1474. Neuss is near Düsseldorf. The defenders used a three-stage rota system of duty. In May 1475 Frederick III (HRE) attempted relief but failed. Charles built a *grue* (a type of crane) to lower a ladder on the wall. The *grue* stuck in the mud and caused hilarity among the defenders. Neuss held out. On 13 June 1475 Charles abandoned the siege after a wasted year. The failure presaged his fate at the hands of the Swiss.

ORLÉANS, SIEGE OF, 1428–9

The turning point in the Hundred Years' War with the emergence of Joan of Arc. Orléans on the Loire marked the frontier between the English-held north and the lands controlled by Charles VII. The siege began on 7 October 1428. On 3 November the English commander, the Earl of Salisbury, was hit by debris from a cannon-ball shot and died eight days later. Talbot took over. The English constructed forts around the city. An English supply train broke through after winning the Herrings in 1429. Joan of Arc appeared, having persuaded Charles VII to appoint her to a military position. She entered the city on a white horse. The French took the fort at St Loup on 4 May. The English in the fort of Les Tourelles, by the bridge, surrendered on 7 May. Next day the siege was abandoned. Joan of Arc was wounded at Orléans but the victory boosted French morale.

PATAY, BATTLE OF, 18 JUNE 1429

A French victory confirming the change of fortunes marked by the English failure to take Orléans. Patay is north of Orléans. The French under the Duke of Alençon pursued the retreating English under Lord Talbot. Joan of Arc fought here, having encouraged the French to attack. The English archers were surrounded and Talbot was captured. Sir John Fastolf escaped only to have his Order of the Garter taken away, though later restored. Charles VII went to Reims for his coronation.

POITIERS, BATTLE OF, 19 SEPTEMBER 1356

Victory of the Black Prince over the French in the Hundred Years' War. The Black Prince led a *chevauchée* from Gascony. At Maupertuis (possibly La Cardinerie) near Poitiers he was faced by the French under King John II. Edward tried to avoid battle but the French attacked during his march. He formed a defensive position with archers on the wings, using a hedge as protection. The French could not break through. The English became short of arrows and archers ran forward to retrieve some. Edward's ally, the captal de Buch, led a reserve force behind a hill to attack the French by surprise from the rear. At the same time the Black Prince advanced. The French broke and fled into Poitiers. John and his son Philip were captured. John was imprisoned in the Tower. The first phase of the war was soon brought to an end.

RENNES, SIEGE OF, 1356–7

Besieged by Henry duke of Lancaster in the Hundred Years' War. Rennes was the chief target from 3 October. Storm, mining and bombardment by throwing engines all failed. The winter was harsh. Lancaster raided around. The young Du Guesclin harried the English from outside their lines. The English John Bolton went hawking and caught six partridges. He approached the walls and offered to sell them so ladies of the town could be fed. Olivier de Mauny offered to fight a duel for them and swam over the moat. Olivier was wounded but won and returned with the birds. Later Olivier became ill and Bolton persuaded Lancaster to let him through the lines for medical attention. Lancaster was ordered to abandon the siege by Edward III but refused. On 5 July 1357, with a relief force under Charles of Blois approaching, the siege was abandoned. Lancaster arranged a face-saving ceremony in which he received the city keys and returned them. Du Guesclin offered him a drink that was accepted and the English departed. The city voted Du Guesclin 200 livres per annum.

ROCHE-DERRIEN, LA, SIEGE AND BATTLE OF, 1347

Conflict in the early Hundred Years' War in Brittany. Charles of Blois, nephew of Philip VI, besieged La Roche-Derrien near Bégard by the River Jaudi. He used nine large engines and hit the governor Richard Totsham's house with a 300-pound stone. The English attempted relief under Sir Thomas Dagworth. He attacked from an unexpected direction on 20 June. The initial impact wore off. Dagworth was wounded and captured but soon rescued. The English garrison sortied and captured Charles of Blois. The siege was abandoned. Later the French took La Roche-Derrien and massacred its garrison.

ROOSEBEKE (WESTROZEBEKE), BATTLE OF, 27 NOVEMBER 1382

Victory by the French under Charles VI over rebel Flemings under Philip van Artevelde, 'regent' of Flanders – known by his enemies as 'Filthy Phil'. The Flemings besieged Oudenaarde in Flanders, held by a French garrison. Philip the Bold duke of Burgundy appealed to the French, who came to its relief. They met the Flemish army, mainly militia from Ghent, on the plain of Roosebeke. The French dismounted men in the centre, with cavalry on the wings. The Flemish drove into the French centre but did not break through. They became vulnerable to attack from the flank. Some, including Van Artevelde, were crushed to death. His unwounded body was brought before Charles VI, who kicked it and hanged it from a tree. Ghent continued to resist with aid from England. The war concluded in the duke's favour in 1385.

ROUEN, SIEGES OF, 1418–19, 1449

Besieged by Henry V from 29 July 1418 during his invasion of Normandy. He crossed the Seine, isolating the city, and began a blockade. A chain was placed to stop the French coming down the Seine from Paris. A contemporary verse described the state of the defenders: 'They ate up dogs, they ate up cats, / They ate up mice, horses and rats'. Girls sold their bodies for a crust of bread. The poor were sent out. Henry would not let them through though he provided food at Christmas. A Burgundian relief force abandoned its attempt. Rouen surrendered on 19 January 1419. Henry entered wearing black and gold, on a black horse. He soon completed his conquest of Normandy. Charles VII recovered Rouen in 1449. The Duke of Somerset took refuge there. The French battered with cannons while the citizens attacked the English garrison. Rouen surrendered on 29 October. Somerset was allowed to leave. The citizens made a mechanical stag that bowed its knees when Charles VII entered. Normandy had been recovered by the French.

SAINTES, BATTLE OF, 22 JULY 1242
Defeat of Henry III by Louis IX. Henry in alliance with French rebels, including the counts of La Marche and Toulouse, sought to regain lost territory. Taillebourg surrendered to Louis. On 21 July the two forces skirmished outside Taillebourg and the English retreated to Saintes. The armies were on opposite sides of the Charente, which Louis crossed by two bridges, one at Taillebourg, the other that he constructed. The English retreated to Blaye. Saintes surrendered to Louis and the rebels submitted. Henry's invasion had failed.

ST-POL DE LÉON, BATTLE OF, 9 JUNE 1346
Victory for the English in Brittany under Sir Thomas Dagworth against Charles of Blois in the Hundred Years' War. One of several battles early in the war when the French dismounted cavalry to fight on foot – a tactic formerly ascribed to the English in the period. Charles of Blois blocked Dagworth's march. The English were outnumbered and took a defensive position on a hill. A series of attacks until late in the day were held off. The French withdrew.

SLUYS (SLUIS), NAVAL BATTLE OF, 24 JUNE 1340
English victory at the start of the Hundred Years' War. Edward III's invasion force met a combined French and Genoese fleet off the port of Sluys (now in the Netherlands, then a harbour for Bruges) on the coast of Flanders. Neither of the French admirals, Quiéret and Béhuchet, were seamen. It was fought like a land battle, the French anchored in position by chained lines. English longbows made their first vital impact on the war. The archers were placed as on land, on the wings, with men-at-arms in a central squadron. After the archers' barrage, the French were boarded; 190 French and Genoese ships were captured. Both French admirals were captured and executed. So many French were pushed in the sea, it was said if fish could speak they could have learned French. Control of the sea aided England's subsequent successes.

THURIE (TERRY), SIEGE OF, c.1370
A castle near Albi captured by the bascot (bastard) de Mauléon, a Gascon mercenary. Among his employers were the captal de Buch and the Black Prince. The bascot disguised himself and six others as women with handkerchiefs over their faces, taking pitchers from the well and using falsetto voices so they would be let in. They then blew a horn, summoning their friends from outside. The bascot profited from the venture and told the tale to Jean Froissart at an inn with the sign of the Moon at Orthez in 1388, when Froissart says the bascot was about 50. Froissart did not date the event.

VALMONT, BATTLE OF, 11 MARCH 1416
The Earl of Dorset raided through Normandy after Agincourt. Near Valmont his march was blocked by French under Constable Bernard count of Armagnac. Dorset took a defensive position with dismounted men-at-arms and archers, planting stakes before his front. Dorset was badly wounded. After resisting charges, he formed his small force to face outwards (comparable to Scottish schiltrom and Flemish pike formations). Darkness fell and Dorset withdrew. Two days later near the Seine the English were caught by the

French, who charged expecting easy victory but were defeated. When Armagnac arrived with more troops, the English charged and routed them. The English, battered but victorious, reached Rouen.

VERNEUIL, BATTLE OF, 17 AUGUST 1424
Victory of John duke of Bedford (regent for Henry VI) over the French under the Count of Aumâle. The French marched from Tours, with allied Scottish archers under Alexander earl of Douglas and Lombard cavalry. They were let into Verneuil on the Avre in south-east Normandy. The armies met north of Verneuil as the English emerged from the forest of Piseux. Bedford assumed a formation of dismounted men-at-arms and archers, with stakes as protection. Bedford dismounted. The English did not attack until four in the afternoon. The Lombard cavalry broke the English archers on the left and attacked the baggage camp, but the main army held firm to win the subsequent conflict. Aumâle and Douglas were killed. Captain Young fled the field to announce premature news of defeat. He was hanged, drawn and quartered. It was an English triumph but was soon reversed. Charles VII lost his main army but Joan of Arc was about to appear.

A soldier's skull from the Battle of Towton, 1461

10 | The Angevins to the Tudors, Britain 1154–1485

GENERALS AND LEADERS

See in Part I: Alexander II, Alexander III, Audley (Lord), Bigod (Hugh), Buckingham (Duke of), Edward I, Edward II, Edward III, Edward IV, Edward the Black Prince, Edward Bruce, Fauconberg (the Bastard), Fawkes de Bréauté, Gaunt (John of), Henry II, Henry III, Henry IV, Henry V, Henry VI, Henry VII, Hotspur (Henry), John, Lancaster (Thomas, Earl of), Lincoln (Earl of), Llewelyn ap Gruffydd, Llewelyn ap Iorwerth, Margaret of Anjou, Montagu (Lord); Montfort (Simon de), Northumberland (I Earl of), Northumberland (II Earl of), Northumberland (III Earl of), Northumberland (IV Earl of), Owen Glendower, Richard I, Richard II, Richard III, Robert the Bruce, Salisbury (Earl of), Simnel (Lambert), Somerset (Duke of), Strongbow, Suffolk (Duke of), Tudor (Jasper), Wallace (William), Warbeck (Perkin), Warwick (Earl of), William the Lion, William the Marshal, York (Duke of).

BATTLES AND SIEGES

Bannockburn 1314, Barnet 1471, Bedford 1224, Blore Heath 1459, Boroughbridge 1322, Bosworth 1485, Bramham Moor 1408, Cade's Rebellion 1450, Dunbar 1296, Dupplin Moor 1332, Edgecote Moor 1469, Evesham 1265, Falkirk 1298, Faughart 1318, Fornham 1173, Halidon Hill 1333, Hedgeley Moor 1464, Hexham 1464, Homildon Hill 1402, Largs 1263, Lewes 1264, Lincoln 1217, London 1471, Loudoun Hill 1307, Methven 1306, Mortimer's Cross 1461, Myton 1319, Neville's Cross 1346, Northampton 1460, Otterburn 1388, Peasants' Revolt 1381, Pilleth 1402, Radcot Bridge 1387, Rebellion of 1173–4, Rochester 1215, St Albans 1455, 1461, Sandwich 1217, Shrewsbury 1403, Stirling 1297, Stoke 1487, Tewkesbury 1471, Towton 1461, Wakefield 1460.

OUTLINE OF EVENTS

Compared to other areas of Europe, Britain, and especially England, was relatively peaceful. Its political establishment was secure, its monarchs well established. There were three major kinds of warfare. The first came from claims to land on the continent, mainly looked at under France with the Hundred Years' War. Invasions of England from the continent were now rare, almost non-existent. The second main cause of war was English ambition to rule the British Isles. Wales was conquered by Edward I though some troubles followed. The conquests attempted in Ireland and Scotland were less successful but border conflicts more frequent. The third cause of war was internal risings and rebellions. Risings by lesser folk included the Peasants' Revolt and Cade's Rebellion. Weaker monarchs in particular faced several serious conflicts with rebel barons, including the conflicts that removed Edward II and Richard II from the throne. The most serious internal troubles came with the Wars of the Roses though even this warfare was intermittent and less damaging than once thought.

In this section we shall deal with the last two of these three sources of war, firstly regarding England's efforts at expansion. Norman barons established themselves throughout Britain, spearheading royal intervention. Henry II obtained papal permission to invade Ireland. Among the barons already there was Richard de Clare known as Strongbow. Henry was able to make his son John Lord of Ireland but the conquest was never as complete as the claims. The King of Connaught retained independence. English lords won lands in Ireland and caused antagonism between Irish and Anglo-Irish – later reinforced by religious differences. Parts of Ireland remained independent and several English kings met severe problems there, including John and Richard II.

Attempts to rule Scotland had initial success that proved illusory. Edward I won victories but his efforts were resisted. Scotland was politically more united than Wales or Ireland. By his death Edward's domination was still incomplete. His son Edward II was defeated at Bannockburn. There were further serious attempts to win Scotland, notably by Edward III, but the Scots kept their independence. In the later Middle Ages the Scots often allied with France against England, causing acute difficulties for the old enemy.

Even the strongest kings were likely to face baronial opposition, given the nature of political power in a feudal society. Henry II faced rebellion by his sons, notably during 1173–4, though he overcame it. An invading baronial army was beaten at Fornham. At his death Henry's son Richard was opposing him in alliance with France.

One of the most famous examples of opposition to a king was that leading to Magna Carta, linked to a French invasion by the rebel's ally Prince Louis. After John's death loyal barons saw off the invasion with victories at Sandwich and Lincoln. Henry III faced internal war against barons under Simon de Montfort. Simon was initially successful through victory at Lewes but his regime only survived a year until his defeat and death at Evesham. Henry III's son Edward I helped deal with De Montfort and became one of the most powerful of England's medieval kings. He faced some internal problems but concentrated on military efforts outside England, notably in France, Wales and Scotland. There was reaction after his death, and Edward II's defeat at Bannockburn had repercussions in England. The barons under Lancaster forced Ordinances upon the king but Lancaster was defeated at Boroughbridge in 1322. Edward II's queen, Isabelle of France, joined forces with the dissident baron, Mortimer. They invaded England, removed Edward's ministers, imprisoning and killing the king.

Edward III succeeded to the throne and in 1330 had Mortimer executed. Edward III was another great king. He made efforts in France and Scotland with some success. His powers declined in his later years when England suffered economic disaster with the Black Death.

The death of the Black Prince left a minor, his son Richard II, as king. An enigmatic character, Richard fought a long struggle with the barons, concluding in 1399 with his arrest and death. His main opponent, Henry Bolingbroke, took the crown as Henry IV, the first Lancastrian king. Henry IV's usurpation began a drawn out struggle for the throne. Usurpation invited further attempts to alter the succession. Henry's reign was marked by rebellions. There was a major rising in Wales under Owen Glendower, who allied with English rebels. Henry's leading opponent was the Percy family, powerful in the north. The Percies defeated the Scots at Homildon Hill in 1402. They were beaten by royalists at Shrewsbury in 1403. Then the Percy Earl of Northumberland was beaten and killed at Bramham Moor in 1408.

Henry V's success in France helped to overcome enemies in England but his death left the vulnerable Henry VI on the throne. The English position in France collapsed. His leading opponent was Richard duke of York who initiated the conflict between the houses of Lancaster and York that we know as the Wars of the Roses. After his victory at St Albans, York was beaten and killed at Wakefield. York's son claimed the throne as Edward IV in 1461. To his opponents he was a usurper. Edward survived until 1470, when he was taken by surprise and forced to flee the country. In 1471, with Burgundian aid, he returned to win at Barnet and Tewkesbury, recovering the throne. The leading baronial figure, Warwick the Kingmaker, was killed at Barnet. Henry VI either died, or was put to death, while a prisoner.

On Edward IV's death in 1483 his brother, instead of supporting Edward's sons, took the throne as Richard III. His former friend the Duke of Buckingham rebelled but failed and was executed. The invasion of Henry Tudor caused Richard's downfall in 1485, when he was beaten and killed at Bosworth. His opponent took the crown as Henry VII. There were half-hearted Yorkist rebellions. The main rebels were beaten at Stoke in 1487 and the Wars of the Roses came to their conclusion. The history of the Tudors belongs to early modern history.

BATTLES AND SIEGES

BANNOCKBURN, BATTLE OF, 23–4 JUNE 1314
During the Scottish War of Independence, defeat of Edward II by Robert the Bruce. Edward tried to relieve Stirling from a Scottish siege. Bruce took a defensive position behind the Bannock burn (stream) and dug pits against cavalry. Edward's attack on 23 June was held. He tried to catch Bruce from the flank by a night march but his troops became trapped in boggy ground. Edward's archers were to the rear rather than on the flanks. The English attacks on 24 June were held by the Scottish schiltroms (squares of pikemen). Scottish charges broke the English who fled. Edward escaped but English power in Scotland was broken.

BARNET, BATTLE OF, 14 APRIL 1471
Victory of Edward IV over the Lancastrians under Warwick. After a decade as king,

Edward fled England in 1470. He returned with mercenaries to reclaim the kingdom in 1471, landing in the north to march on London. Warwick raised an army and came south. Edward marched to Barnet just north of London. They met at four in the morning on a foggy day. Warwick overestimated the distance and his artillery overshot the Yorkist position. In the fog the armies overlapped, each right wing turning in on the enemy flank. Warwick's archers mistook the Earl of Oxford's rising sun badge for Edward's and shot at their own side, causing fears of treachery. Edward led the decisive charge. Warwick was killed, knifed in the eye trying to escape. His brother Lord Montagu was also killed. John Paston, a Lancastrian, was wounded by an arrow in the arm and paid a costly doctor's bill; he was later pardoned. Barnet and Tewkesbury resulted in Edward resuming power.

BEDFORD, SIEGE OF, 1224
Besieged by Henry III against Fawkes de Bréauté's garrison. Fawkes captured the castle for John and became its castellan. After John's death, Fawkes was accused of raiding from Bedford. The judge appointed to hear the charges was taken and imprisoned in Bedford. Fawkes refused to release him, and Henry began collecting siege materials. Fawkes was not in Bedford when the royal army arrived on 22 June; the garrison was under his brother William. The barbican was taken, then the outer and inner baileys. The garrison held the keep but surrendered when Henry mined it. William de Bréauté and 80 men were hanged. Fawkes was exiled. Bedford Castle was slighted.

BLORE HEATH, BATTLE OF, 23 SEPTEMBER 1459
Yorkist victory early in the Wars of the Roses. Lord Audley with Queen Margaret for the Lancastrians intercepted Yorkists under Salisbury marching to join the Duke of York. They met east of Market Drayton. The Yorkists had Wemberton Brook on the left and protected their right with wagons. Audley, with the larger force, attacked. Three charges, two cavalry and one infantry, were halted by Yorkist archers protected by stakes. Lord Audley was killed, Audley Cross marking the spot. Some Lancastrians deserted but others fought on under Lord Dudley. An anvil at Mucklestone is said to be where Queen Margaret reversed the shoes of her horse to fool pursuers.

BOROUGHBRIDGE, BATTLE OF, 16 MARCH 1322
Victory in Yorkshire for Sir Andrew Harclay sheriff of Cumberland against the rebel Thomas of Lancaster. Lancaster with the Earl of Hereford marched for Scotland. Harclay for Edward II stopped them at the bridge over the Ure, from which the battle is named. Both sides dismounted cavalry to fight on foot. Harclay's force included Cumbrian pikemen, who formed a square (a schiltrom on the Scottish pattern). Hereford was killed. Lancaster and over 20 rebels were executed on Edward II's orders, against custom. Harclay was made Earl of Carlisle.

BOSWORTH, BATTLE OF, 22 AUGUST 1485
Victory for Henry Tudor over Richard III, ending Plantagenet rule. Henry sailed from Harfleur to land at Milford Haven in Pembrokeshire. Richard took position on Ambion Hill near Market Bosworth in Leicestershire. The Duke of Norfolk, commanding the royal van, failed to prevent Henry deploying. The Stanley brothers, summoned by Richard, took position north and south of the royal army but finally joined Henry not Richard. Henry's right under the Earl of Oxford attacked the royal flank. Richard saw Henry moving across the field and charged at him, only to be killed. Lord Thomas Stanley found Richard's crown and presented it to Henry. Richard's body was stripped and displayed in public. He was buried in the Franciscan priory at Leicester. Henry took the crown as Henry VII.

BRAMHAM MOOR, BATTLE OF, 19 FEBRUARY 1408

The concluding battle of the Percy rebellion against Henry IV. After defeats for the Percies, Northumberland fled to Scotland and raised an army to invade England. A royal force under Sir Thomas Rokeby faced him near Tadcaster in Yorkshire. Northumberland was killed, then beheaded, and his body quartered.

CADE'S REBELLION, 1450

A rising against Henry VI, provoked by tax and failure in France. The Duke of Suffolk was killed in Kent, and Henry threatened the county with reprisals. *The Complaint of the Commons of Kent* was drawn up and sent to Parliament. The protesters assembled on Blackheath, joined by men from Essex and the south-east. A royal army came against them and was beaten. In July the rebels took London but antagonised the citizens. They executed the treasurer, Lord Saye. Cade was promised a pardon but it was ignored once the rebels disbanded. Cade was wounded and captured at Heathfield in Sussex and died on 12 July. His body was quartered, the head placed over London Bridge.

DUNBAR, BATTLE OF, 27 APRIL 1296

Defeat for the Scots under John Balliol against English under the Earl of Surrey. Edward I supported Balliol for the Scottish throne but Balliol rebelled. The English besieged and took Berwick. Balliol came to attempt its recovery but was blocked by Earl Warenne. English cavalry decided the battle. Balliol escaped but abdicated. Edward now sought to control Scotland directly.

DUPPLIN MOOR, BATTLE OF, 12 AUGUST 1332

Victory for Edward Balliol and 'disinherited' landowners against Scots under Donald earl of Mar, regent for David II. The site is by the River Earn south of Perth. Edward III supported Balliol, who took a defensive position with dismounted men-at-arms and archers probably on the flanks – what would become the typical English formation. Scottish pikemen halted an English attack. The Scots countered but suffered heavy losses against the archers. Mar was killed. Edward Balliol took the Scottish throne.

EDGECOTE MOOR, BATTLE OF, 26 JULY 1469

Defeat of a Yorkist army by Warwick the Kingmaker. Warwick allied with Edward IV's brother, the Duke of Clarence, who was married to Warwick's daughter. They invaded England to coincide with a rebellion in the north that Edward went to deal with. Warwick entered London and headed north to join the rebels under Robin of Redesdale. The Lancastrians camped at Edgecote Moor near Banbury in Oxfordshire. The armies met at a crossing of the Cherwell. A quarrel divided the royalists, leaving them in two groups with Humphrey Stafford earl of Devon absent from the battle. The group under William Herbert earl of Pembroke was beaten by Warwick. Pembroke was captured and executed. Edward IV was virtually a prisoner for a time.

EVESHAM, BATTLE OF, 4 AUGUST 1265

Defeat of Simon de Montfort by Prince Edward in the Barons' War. Edward escaped while his father Henry III was a prisoner. Simon planned to join forces with his son, taking Henry with him, but Edward trapped him in a loop of the Avon in Worcestershire. The royalists controlled the bridge, preventing escape. A thunderstorm preceded the battle. Edward's larger army outflanked and encircled the enemy. Simon was unhorsed and killed. His son Henry was killed. Simon's head and limbs were cut off, his remains buried in Evesham Abbey. Henry III was released.

FALKIRK, BATTLE OF, 22 JULY 1298

Victory of Edward I over the Scots under William Wallace. Edward found an answer to the Scottish schiltroms that had brought victory at Stirling. Wallace took a defensive position by the River Carron with pikemen in four schiltroms and archers on the flanks. He used stakes with ropes tied between them against the cavalry. Edward used his archers, longbowmen and crossbowmen, to break up the schiltroms from a distance and then attacked with cavalry. Wallace remained at liberty until 1305.

FAUGHART, BATTLE OF, 14 OCTOBER 1318

Defeat of Edward Bruce, brother of Robert the Bruce, by an English force under the lord lieutenant of Ireland, Richard Clare. Edward Bruce tried to conquer Ireland, taking the title of king. It was fought near Dundalk on the east coast of Ireland. Bruce intended to capture Dundalk. His force was in three divisions, widely separated from each other. He refused to retreat but disguised himself as an ordinary soldier. He was killed. Another corpse was mistaken for his and quartered.

FORNHAM, BATTLE OF, 17 OCTOBER 1173

Defeat of rebels against Henry II during the 1173–4 rebellion by his sons. With Henry II in Normandy, Robert Blanchemains earl of Leicester invaded England, landing at Walton in Suffolk. His force included Flemish mercenaries, marching to the song 'Hop, hop Willekin, England is mine and thine' – not endearing them to the locals. It was fought near Bury St Edmunds. The royal army was under Richard de Lucy and Humphrey de Bohun. The invaders were routed by cavalry. Local peasants attacked the Flemings with scythes and pitchforks. Leicester was captured and imprisoned at Falaise.

HALIDON HILL, BATTLE OF, 19 JULY 1333

Victory of Edward III over the Scots under Archibald Douglas. The battle was fought near Berwick, which Edward was besieging and Douglas sought to relieve. Edward formed groups of dismounted men-at-arms with archers on the flanks – what became the typical English formation later. Edward took a defensive position on Halidon Hill, dismounting with his knights. The Scots attacked over marshy ground and were destroyed by archers. Douglas and five earls were killed. Edward Balliol was made King of Scots. Berwick surrendered and remained English thereafter.

HEDGELEY MOOR, 25 APRIL 1464

A Yorkist victory in the Wars of the Roses. Henry duke of Somerset and Sir Ralph Percy deserted Edward IV. Their army, including Scots, was met by Lord Montagu for Edward. It was fought on moorland near Alnwick in Northumberland. Both sides began with archery. The Yorkists advanced and the enemy left broke. Somerset escaped but Percy was killed in a charge, when his horse made an amazing 12-yard jump over what was afterwards called Percy's Leap.

HEXHAM, BATTLE OF, 10 MAY 1464

A Yorkist victory in the Wars of the Roses for Lord Montagu against Henry VI and the Duke of Somerset. After Hedgeley Moor the Lancastrians regrouped at Alnwick to march south. They camped in a meadow called the Linnels, near the Devil's Water stream south of Hexham. Montagu marched from Newcastle and took them by surprise, occupying the high ground and charging downhill. The Lancastrians, with water behind, could not retreat. Somerset was captured, humiliated by a cook who struck off his spurs with a knife, and then executed. Henry VI escaped, leaving his helmet and crown. Edward IV rewarded Montagu with the earldom of Northumberland. The Lancastrian position in the north collapsed.

HOMILDON HILL, BATTLE OF, 14 SEPTEMBER 1402

Victory of the Percies over invading Scots under Archibald earl of Douglas. Douglas was stopped in Northumbria by Northumberland and his son Henry Hotspur. Douglas took a defensive position on Homildon Hill. English archers shot from a neighbouring hill. The Scots attempted a cavalry charge but it was halted by archery. Douglas was unhorsed and captured, hit six times and wounded in the eye. Henry IV refused to let the Percies benefit from ransoms, provoking them to rebel.

LARGS, BATTLE OF, 3 OCTOBER 1263

Between Alexander III king of Scots and Haakon IV of Norway. Haakon took Iceland and sought to conquer the Hebrides. He brought ships to Scotland but a storm forced some to land at Largs. The battle was fought on the beach by the Firth of Clyde, with no clear result. Haakon retired to Kirkwall in Orkney and died. Norse expansion halted and the Hebrides remained Scottish.

LEWES, BATTLE OF, 14 MAY 1264

Victory of rebels under Simon de Montfort against Henry III. The royalists camped at Lewes in Sussex. De Montfort attacked early in the morning. Prince Edward made a successful charge on the right against the Londoners – but returned four hours later to find the royalists beaten. Henry III, his brother Richard of Cornwall (having taken refuge in a windmill) and Edward were captured. For a year England was governed by the barons, who implemented the Provisions of Oxford.

LINCOLN, SIEGE AND BATTLE OF, 1217

Victory of William the Marshal for Henry III against Prince Louis of France and rebel barons. Prince Louis invaded England. He occupied Lincoln in 1216 but the castle resisted and was besieged. William came to its relief with Fawkes de Bréauté and Peter des Roches. William unblocked the unused west gate and entered the castle. On 20 May he made a surprise sortie against the French in the town. The French commander, the Count of Perche, was killed. The event was called the Fair of Lincoln, suggesting an easy victory. It led to the abandonment of Louis' invasion.

LONDON, SIEGE OF, 1471

Besieged during the Wars of the Roses by the Bastard Fauconberg. His cousin Warwick was killed at Barnet. Fauconberg led a rising in Kent and approached London seeking to rescue Henry VI. The rebels were faced by guns along the river and at the gates. Fauconberg tried to storm the city over London Bridge but was repulsed. He fired taverns near the Tower but had to move off. He marched to Kingston but abandoned a new attempt to cross the Thames when a relief force under Edward IV approached. On 14 May Fauconberg attacked London from the south. There was an artillery exchange and the rebels were repulsed. Fauconberg received reinforcements from Essex and tried a new attack in three places at once – London Bridge, Bishopsgate and Aldgate. Sixty houses on London Bridge were fired but again the attack was beaten off, retreat turning into rout. London had survived.

LOUDOUN HILL, BATTLE OF, 10 MAY 1307

Victory of Robert the Bruce over the English under Aymer de Valence earl of Pembroke for Edward I. The site is near Kilmarnock. Pembroke advanced from Ayr hoping to catch Bruce at Galston. Bruce took a defensive position on Loudoun Hill with boggy ground on either side and ditches dug in front. The English charge was halted by pikes and the ditches. A pike advance decided the issue. Pembroke escaped to Bothwell. Three days later Bruce defeated the Earl of Gloucester. Edward I died marching north against the Scots. Loudoun Hill marked a change of fortunes for Bruce after his defeat at Methven in 1306.

METHVEN, BATTLE OF, 26 JUNE 1306

Victory of Aymer de Valence earl of Pembroke for Edward I over Robert the Bruce. Bruce killed his rival Red John Comyn to become King of Scots. He camped at Methven in Perthshire. Pembroke made a sudden, treacherous attack. Bruce was captured but escaped and fled to Ireland, returning to triumph a year later.

MORTIMER'S CROSS, BATTLE OF, 2 FEBRUARY 1461

Victory for Edward duke of York over the Lancastrians under the Earl of Wiltshire and Jasper Tudor earl of Pembroke. Edward blocked the Lancastrian march at Mortimer's Cross in Herefordshire. Edward took a position on the River Lugg, with archers guarding the crossings. Edward's men claimed to see a parhelion in the sky – three suns that they took to represent York's badge of the sun in splendour, an omen of success. Pembroke on the Lancastrian right tried a flanking movement that failed. The Lancastrian left had initial success but could not halt Edward's drive through the centre. The Lancastrians were routed. Pembroke and Wiltshire escaped in disguise. Owen Tudor was captured and executed in Hereford, claiming 'that head shall lie on the stock that was wont to lie on Queen Katherine's lap'. The head was placed on the market cross where a woman combed its hair and washed off the blood. A month later Edward assumed the crown.

MYTON, BATTLE OF, 20 SEPTEMBER 1319

Victory at Swaledale in Yorkshire of invading Scots under Sir James Douglas for Robert the Bruce against an English force raised by the archbishop of York. The English attacked but were blocked crossing a bridge over the Swale. The Scots formed a schiltrom of pikes and advanced. The English broke, many drowning in the river. Because the English force included clergymen the battle was named the Chapter of Myton. The Scots burned and pillaged 84 villages before departing. Edward II abandoned his siege of Berwick.

NEVILLE'S CROSS, BATTLE OF, 17 OCTOBER 1346

Victory for the English under Ralph Lord Neville against Scots under David II.

Edward III was in France on the Crécy campaign. The Scots allied with France and invaded. The archbishop of York summoned an army that met the Scots west of Durham near an ancient cross. The English made a defensive formation of dismounted men-at-arms and archers. The Scots formed schiltroms and advanced with initial success but were held by archers then broken by cavalry. David II was wounded, captured and not released until 1357.

NORTHAMPTON, BATTLE OF, 10 JULY 1460

Victory for Edward, son of the Duke of York, and Warwick the Kingmaker against Henry VI and Buckingham. Warwick sailed from Calais and marched north. The battle was fought in a meadow south of Northampton near Delapré Abbey. The Lancastrians built an artillery camp by the Nene with trenches before it. Rain damaged the Lancastrian gunpowder. Warwick made a dawn charge and the Lancastrian guns failed. The Lancastrian Lord Grey of Ruthin was accused of treachery. The Lancastrians fled, many drowning in the river. Buckingham was killed defending the king and Henry VI was captured by an archer. Richard of York claimed the throne.

OTTERBURN (CHEVY CHASE), BATTLE OF, 5 AUGUST 1388

Victory for the Scots under James earl Douglas against the Percies, though Douglas was killed in the battle. The Scots raided south to avenge a raid into Scotland by Richard II. The Scots were stopped in Redesdale, Northumberland. The battle was fought late in the day, ending by moonlight. The English commander Henry Percy (Hotspur) was captured. The ballad *Chevy Chase* is supposedly about the battle but is inaccurate. The date may have been 15 or 19 August.

PEASANTS' REVOLT, 1381

Peasant rising in southern England. The discontent was roused by Poll Taxes imposed in Richard II's minority. The focus of rebellion was Kent and Essex with outbreaks in East Anglia and St Albans. The main leaders were Wat Tyler and John Ball. The rebels assembled, many armed with bows. They marched into London and created havoc. They fired John of Gaunt's Savoy Palace and released prisoners from Newgate and the Fleet. Archbishop Sudbury of Canterbury and Treasurer Robert Hales were executed. The rebels demanded the abolition of serfdom. The young Richard II courageously asked the rebels to disperse on 15 June. Wat Tyler was killed in a scuffle. The rebels dispersed but promises to them were broken. Many were executed, including John Ball. The government was persuaded that Poll Taxes were unwise.

PILLETH, BATTLE OF, 22 JUNE 1402
Victory of Owen Glendower over Edmund Mortimer. Mortimer was trapped in a pass through the mountains. He was taken prisoner, as was Lord Grey.

RADCOT BRIDGE, BATTLE OF, 20 DECEMBER 1387
Victory of Henry Bolingbroke earl of Derby and the Lords Appellant over Robert de Vere earl of Oxford for Richard II. Oxford brought an army from Cheshire and was met by Henry at the crossing of the Thames in Oxfordshire. Oxford's rear was blocked by the Earl of Gloucester. The royalists broke. Oxford escaped abroad. For the time being Richard was under the control of the Appellants.

REBELLION OF 1173–4
Rebellion by the sons of Henry II against their father. The sons were supported by their mother Eleanor of Aquitaine. In March 1173 Young Henry, the eldest son, left his father's court to join Louis VII in France. Henry II faced problems at home, abroad and with the papacy, since the killing of Becket in 1170. The sons disliked Henry's plans for the division of the Angevin Empire. Young Henry was joined

by his younger brothers Geoffrey and Richard. In October 1173 the Earl of Leicester invaded England with Flemish mercenaries but was defeated at Fornham. William the Lion king of Scots invaded England in 1174 but was captured in Northumberland. Henry agreed terms with Louis VII and made peace with his sons in September. Trouble arose again between father and sons, with rebellions before and after the death of Young Henry in 1183.

ROCHESTER, SIEGE OF, 1215
The Magna Carta barons took control of Rochester Castle. King John assembled siege equipment and marched along the Medway. Provisions in the castle were short. Robert fitz Walter sought to relieve Rochester but failed to break through and returned to London. William of Albini refused permission for a crossbowman in the castle to shoot at the king. The outer walls were mined and then the keep, whose south-east corner collapsed. An internal dividing wall allowed the defenders to continue resisting but they finally surrendered. John set up a gallows to execute the whole garrison but was persuaded against it, contenting himself with hanging some crossbowmen.

ST ALBANS, BATTLES OF, 1455, 1461
The First Battle of St Albans occurred on 22 May 1455, a victory for Richard duke of York against Henry VI, the opening battle of the Wars of the Roses. The Yorkists marched south towards London. Henry VI occupied St Albans. Negotiations failed and the Yorkists under Richard and Warwick the Kingmaker attacked. St Albans lacked walls but the royalists erected barriers. The abbey bells rang as the battle began. The Yorkists failed to break through the barricades. Robert Ogle for Warwick advanced through gardens to attack the Lancastrians on the flank. The Lancastrian duke of Somerset was killed. Henry VI was wounded by an arrow in the neck and captured. Richard of York claimed the throne but died without attaining it. The

Second Battle of St Albans was on
17 February 1461, a Lancastrian victory.
After the death of Richard of York, royalists
under Queen Margaret and Andrew
Trollope advanced south on London.
Warwick the Kingmaker, for York's son
Edward, advanced north from London to
St Albans. The Lancastrians attacked the
town at dawn in snow. They avoided
Warwick's traps but Yorkist archers halted
them. Warwick's left was defeated and his
right fled. Warwick was not engaged in the
fighting and escaped to join Edward. They
occupied London before the Lancastrians,
who failed to take advantage of their
victory.

SANDWICH, NAVAL BATTLE OF, 23 AUGUST 1217

Victory of an English fleet over the French.
Prince Louis invaded England in alliance
with the Magna Carta barons. After John's
death Louis was opposed by barons loyal to
Henry III. In May Louis was defeated at
Lincoln. The French fleet under Eustace the
Monk was carrying reinforcements for
Louis. Henry III and William the Marshal
watched from the clifftop. The English
under Hubert de Burgh and Richard of
Chilham gained the windward and threw
powdered lime into the wind, blinding the
enemy. The French were boarded. Eustace
was captured and executed on board with a
sword, his head placed on a pike and
paraded through Canterbury. Louis
abandoned the siege of Dover and his
invasion.

SHREWSBURY, BATTLE OF, 21 JULY 1403

Victory for Henry IV over baronial rebels
under the Percies, fought by a crossing of
the Severn north of Shrewsbury. Battlefield
Church was built to mark the spot. Both
sides used longbows. Henry commanded
the right, with his son Prince Hal
commanding the left. An attempt to split
the royalists was foiled by Henry IV. He
caught Hotspur separated from his allies.
Prince Hal was wounded in the face by an
arrow. Hotspur was killed and his men fled.

The earls of Douglas and Worcester were
captured. Hotspur's head was displayed in
York. Worcester was beheaded and Douglas
ransomed.

STIRLING, BATTLE OF, 11 SEPTEMBER 1297

William Wallace's defeat of the English
under Earl Warenne and Hugh de
Cressingham for Edward I. Wallace rebelled
against Edward I's conquest of Scotland.
The battle occurred at the bridge over the
Forth and is often called the Battle of
Stirling Bridge. The Scots deployed on the
slope of Abbey Craig behind a causeway
leading to the bridge. The English failed to
use a nearby ford, preferring the narrow
bridge. When half the English had crossed,
the Scots attacked in schiltroms (pike
squares). Cressingham was killed. His skin
was stripped off to make a sword belt for
Wallace. Warenne, fortunately for himself,
escaped. In 1298 Edward I won at Falkirk,
but Stirling remained an encouragement for
Scottish independence.

STOKE, BATTLE OF, 16 JUNE 1487

Postscript to the Wars of the Roses, a
victory for Henry VII over Lancastrian
rebels at East Stoke near Newark in
Nottinghamshire. The Simnel rebels, under
John earl of Lincoln, reinforced by German
and Swiss mercenaries, took position on a
hill. Henry's van under the Earl of Oxford
headed for Newark to meet the rebels.
Oxford's attack was held. A rebel advance
was halted by royalist archers. Royal
reinforcements arrived and the rebels
broke, many dying in the ravine known as
the Red Gutter. Lincoln was killed. Simnel
was captured and put to work in the royal
kitchen. It was the last major battle
between Lancastrians and Yorkists.

TEWKESBURY, BATTLE OF, 4 MAY 1471

Victory for Edward IV, confirming his
success at Barnet and completing the
Lancastrian collapse. After Barnet the chief
Lancastrian threat came from Queen
Margaret, whose force landed at

Weymouth. Edward moved west and met the queen's army in Gloucestershire near Tewkesbury Abbey. The Lancastrians took a defensive position on a slope. Edward provoked the enemy with archery. Somerset led a Lancastrian charge on the right, attempting surprise by coming from behind a hill. It had initial impact but was halted by Edward's brother Richard of Gloucester. Edward brought up men from Tewkesbury Park. Somerset's force was annihilated in what came to be called Bloody Meadow. Queen Margaret's son Prince Edward was killed in the pursuit. Somerset was captured and beheaded in Tewkesbury market place. The Queen was captured next day and sent to the Tower. Edward's recovery of the throne was secure.

TOWTON, BATTLE OF, 29 MARCH 1461
Yorkist victory reviving Edward IV's claim to be king after Warwick's defeat in the Second Battle of St Albans. It is claimed that more men fought here than in any other battle in Britain. Edward, after victory at Mortimer's Cross, marched from Wales. He and Warwick entered London where Edward was proclaimed king. The Lancastrian victors of St Albans marched back north and Edward pursued them. Approaching Towton the Yorkist Lord Fauconberg crossed the Aire to make a surprise attack at Dintingdale, where Lord Clifford was killed. The Yorkists spent the night at Saxton and advanced on Sunday morning through the snow. Henry VI and Queen Margaret were in York, so their army was under Somerset. The armies met south of Towton. The wind changed direction to favour the Yorkist archers, who provoked a Lancastrian charge. Lancastrian reinforcements arrived from Castle Wood and nearly turned the battle. The Yorkists held and were reinforced by the Duke of Norfolk. The Lancastrians broke and were massacred. Among those killed were Buckingham, Northumberland, Lord Dacre (when removing his hat to take a drink) and Sir Andrew Trollope. Somerset, Henry VI and Queen Margaret fled to Scotland. Edward entered York as king.

WAKEFIELD, BATTLE OF, 30 DECEMBER 1460
Defeat and death of Richard duke of York after claiming the throne. He left London for Sandal Castle, south of Wakefield. His way was blocked by Lancastrians under Somerset. Part of the Lancastrian army was hidden from view and York miscalculated its size and made a charge. He was surrounded and defeated. York was killed, his head placed on Micklegate Bar in York. His son Edmund was killed. The Earl of Salisbury was captured and beheaded in Pontefract. The Yorkist claim to the throne seemed to be destroyed but Warwick and Edward of York proved otherwise.

11th-century ivory carving from Cuenca (Spain) of a mounted
warrior and an archer with a shortbow

11 | Iberia and the *Reconquista*, 850–1492

GENERALS AND LEADERS

See in Part I: Abd-al-Rāhman III, Abū Yūsuf Ya'qūb, Afonso Enriques of Portugal, Alfonso the Battler of Aragón, Alfonso III of Asturias, Alfonso VI of León and Castile, Alfonso VII of Castile and León, Alfonso VIII of Castile, Alfonso X of Castile and León, Alfonso XI of Castile and León, Al-Mansūr, Boabdil, El Cid, Enrique de Trastámara, Ferdinand I of Castile, Ferdinand II of Aragón, Ferdinand III of Castile and León, Isabella of Castile, Jaime I of Aragón, Juan I of Aragón, Juan I of Castile and León, Muley Hasan, Ordoño II of León, Pedro I the Cruel of Castile and León, Pedro III of Aragón, Ramiro II of León, Sancho III of Navarre, Yūsuf I, Yūsuf ibn-Tāshfīn.

BATTLES AND SIEGES

Alarcos 1195, Algeciras 1342–4, Aljubarrota 1385, Cuarte 1094, Eppila 1348, Granada 1491–2, Huesca 1094, 1096, Las Navas de Tolosa 1212, Lisbon 1147, Loja 1482, Montiel 1369, Muradel 1157, Nájera 1367, Ourique 1139, Rio Salado 1340, Sepúlveda 1111, Simancas 939, Toledo 1084–5, Toro 1476, Zalaka 1086, Zaragoza 1118.

OUTLINE OF EVENTS

The most important military event in medieval Iberia is the *Reconquista* by the Christian states from the Muslims. There were also wars between Christian states and between Muslim states. Thirdly there were conflicts between inter-religious alliances, for example of individual Christian kingdoms allied to individual *taifa* states against their enemies – when priority was given to the welfare of the state rather than to religion. It must be pointed out that the populations of the kingdoms were generally very mixed. Muslims in Christian states were generally known as Mudéjares, and

Christians in Muslim states as Mozarabs. There were also strong Jewish communities in Iberia. Finally, in the military conflicts, there was intervention by outside Christian and Muslim powers, notably Moorish armies from North Africa and crusaders from western Europe, mainly France.

The *Reconquista* or Reconquest of Iberia by the Christian states occurred mainly between the 11th and 15th centuries. Muslims invaded Iberia from 711, at one extreme of Islamic expansion. Muslims swept through Iberia and into Gaul but were halted by Charles Martel at Tours in 732. The Christians gradually recovered, regaining southern France and part of northern Iberia. The Carolingians established a Spanish March, later the county of Barcelona. The kingdom of Asturias took over Galicia. The major Iberian power was the Umayyad caliphate of Córdoba under such as Abd-al-Rahman II and III. An early Christian advance was made by the kingdom of León under Ordoño II and Ramiro II. Abd-al-Rahman was defeated at Simancas in 934 and Zamora in 939. The caliphate recovered under al-Mansur, who sacked León in 988.

After the death of al-Mansur the caliphate declined, collapsing in 1031. It fragmented into smaller states known as *taifas*. At first there were seven – Seville, Granada, Murcia, Toledo, Badajoz, Zaragoza and Valencia. They lacked unity and found it difficult to resist the stronger Christian states. Often a *taifa* state recognised the overlordship of a Christian state, paying a paria tax or annual tribute. Often various religious communities were permitted their own system of law, the *fueros*. Only the intervention of stronger Muslim powers from North Africa gave renewed strength to Muslim Iberia.

The main thrust of the *Reconquista* went with the strengthening of Christian states, coalescing into more powerful units. Navarre came to dominance when Sancho the Great took over Castile, León and Barcelona. Two main powers emerged in Aragón and Castile (incorporating León). Aragón developed under Ramiro I and by the time of Alfonso VI was the chief Christian power. This was the age of El Cid, who served Christian and Muslim rulers in his career. The capture of Huesca by Pedro I of Aragón was a major advance for the Christians, as was the capture of Toledo by Alfonso VI in 1085. After being exiled from Aragón, El Cid besieged and took Valencia, ruling it in his own right.

The flow was not in one direction. The Christians captured two *taifas*, Toledo and Valencia, but the survivors invited in the Almoravids from Morocco. Yūsuf defeated Alfonso VI at Zalaka and recovered Valencia. Under Alfonso the Battler, Aragón expanded south, taking Zaragoza in 1118. Portugal emerged through the marriage of the French Count of Lorraine. What had been a county subject to Castile became an independent kingdom under Afonso Enriques, acknowledged by Castile in 1143.

A new wave of Muslim success followed the emergence in North Africa of the Almohads after a religious revolution, though North African problems allowed Christian recovery and a return to independence by the *taifas*. By the middle of the 12th century the Almohads emerged victorious in North Africa and turned their attention to Iberia, gaining the submission of the *taifas* and recovering the Balearics.

A major Christian revival and advance occurred in the 13th century. Possibly the greatest victory of the *Reconquista* was at Las Navas de Tolosa in 1212. Ferdinand III of Castile and León took over north and west Andalusia, capturing Córdoba in 1236, Jaén in 1246, and Seville in 1248. Jaime the Conqueror of Aragón recovered the

Balearics – Mallorca in 1229, Minorca in 1233 and Ibiza in 1235. He besieged and took Valencia. By the time the advance slowed, the only surviving *taifa* was Granada. Jaime I settled the frontier of Aragón with France by the Treaty of Corbeil with Louis IX in 1258 – each giving up territories on the other side of the Pyrenees.

The *Reconquista* seemed almost complete in the 13th century but it slowed to a halt. Muslim Granada survived, though as a vassal state to Christian Castile. A series of Muslim rebellions threatened the *status quo*, including those in Andalusia in 1264 and Valencia in 1274. A new wave of invasion came from North Africa with the emergence of the Marīnids under Yūsuf. The Marīnids declined after Yūsuf's defeat by Alfonso XI and assassination in 1354. Only Castile's internal problems allowed Granada to survive so long. Iberia became involved in the Hundred Years' War. In 1461 Castile finally took Gibraltar. In 1469 Ferdinand of Aragón married Isabella of Castile. Under their rule the two kingdoms were united and the *Reconquista* completed. Granada was besieged in 1491 and taken in 1492. The Christians ruled all Iberia though its population and customs remained mixed.

BATTLES AND SIEGES

ALARCOS, BATTLE OF, 17 JULY 1195

Victory by the Moroccan Almohad caliph Abū Yūsuf over Alfonso VIII of Castile. The caliph sought to recover Muslim territory. After success against Portugal he targeted Castile. It was fought near Ciudad Real. Alfonso began a fortress at Alarcos on the southern frontier of Castile, which the caliph came to destroy. Without waiting for reinforcements from León, Alfonso charged with some effect but the Muslim reserve attacked from the left to decide the issue. Alfonso escaped to Toledo. The fortress was abandoned and the caliph took the name al-Mansūr (the Victorious).

ALGECIRAS, SIEGE OF, 1342–4

Alfonso XI of Castile besieged Algeciras after his victory at Rio Salado in 1340. Algeciras controlled the northern shore of the Strait of Gibraltar. A Catalan fleet blockaded from the sea. Muslim defenders used cannons (the first recorded in Iberia), described as 'thunder engines', firing balls the size of apples. A Christian crusade resulted with aid from England, France and elsewhere. In *The Canterbury Tales* Chaucer's knight was at the siege. Algeciras surrendered on 26 March 1344. Alfonso attacked Gibraltar but his demise in the Black Death led to abandonment.

ALJUBARROTA, BATTLE OF, 14 AUGUST 1385

Victory for João of Avis king of Portugal and English allies against Juan I of Castile. Juan I invaded Portugal with French allies. He besieged Lisbon but his army was hit by plague. The Portuguese took a defensive position with English longbowmen on the flank, pits dug before them. Juan's charge failed. In 1386 England and Portugal made an alliance that was to endure.

CUARTE, BATTLE OF, OCTOBER 1094

Victory of El Cid over the Almoravids near Valencia. The Cid took Valencia, and Yūsuf ibn Tāshfīn's nephew Muhammad came to recover it. The Cid attacked at night and the defeated Muslims retreated to Jativa. Cuarte and the Cid's victory at Bairen in 1097 confirmed Christian control of Valencia, albeit only until 1102.

EPPILA, BATTLE OF, 1348

Victory by Pedro IV of Aragón over the Union of Valencian nobles. Pedro faced prolonged rebellion. After defeat he was trapped in Valencia. The Black Death caused his opponents to disband. Pedro gained revenge at Eppila with aid from Alfonso XI of Castile. Many rebels were killed, their banners displayed in Eppila.

The Union of nobles broke up while Pedro sought reconciliation.

GRANADA, SIEGE OF, 1491–2
The climactic event of the *Reconquista* when the last Muslim stronghold in Iberia fell to the Christians. In 1491 the Muslim ruler of Granada refused to pay the tribute. Ferdinand and Isabella attacked the kingdom of Granada, besieging the city in April 1491. It surrendered on 2 January 1492. Muslims were permitted their own worship. Boabdil received a small kingdom but left for North Africa. The Alhambra became a Christian palace.

HUESCA, SIEGES OF, 1094, 1096
In 1094 Sancho Ramírez I of Aragón was killed by an arrow when trying to take Huesca on his southern frontier. His successor Pedro I returned in 1096. Muslims under al-Mutamin attempted relief. Pedro defeated them and Huesca surrendered, becoming his chief city.

LAS NAVAS DE TOLOSA, BATTLE OF, 16 JULY 1212
Victory for the Christian kingdoms over the Almohads under al-Nāsir. The Christians were defeated at Alarcos in 1195. They formed a new alliance under Alfonso VIII of Castile, Sancho VII of Navarre and Pedro II of Aragón. French allies joined them in a crusade. Al-Nāsir believed he was safe behind the mountains of the Sierra Morena but the enemy approached through the pass of Despeñaperros to attack by surprise. The Christians made a cavalry charge against the mainly infantry enemy. The Muslims held but attack by the Christian reserve settled the issue. The Muslims broke and fled. Al-Nāsir escaped to North Africa. Central Iberia was now in Christian hands.

LISBON, SIEGE OF, 1147
Part of the *Reconquista* and the Second Crusade. Iberian Christians under Afonso I of Portugal besieged Muslim Lisbon from 28 June. They were joined by northern crusaders, including English, headed for the Holy Land. On arrival the crusaders built a 95 feet high belfry and siege engines. The Christians mined but the Muslims counter-mined. The Christians made a device like a large mousetrap with food inside to trap hungry Muslims. After 17 weeks the attackers entered on 24 October using a belfry to cross the wall. Lisbon surrendered to become the capital of Christian Portugal.

LOJA, BATTLE OF, 1 JULY 1482
Defeat of Ferdinand II of Aragón. The Christians besieged Loja in the final stages of the *Reconquista*. Muslims under the Granadan captain 'Ali al 'Attār, Boabdil's father-in-law, ambushed the besiegers under Ferdinand and drove them off. It was a late setback for the Christians but was soon reversed.

MONTIEL (MOUTIEL), BATTLE OF, 14 MARCH 1369
Defeat of Pedro the Cruel of Castile by his illegitimate half-brother Enrique de Trastámara, the climax of the succession war that had drawn Spain into the Hundred Years' War, with England supporting Pedro and France aiding Enrique. The site is near Ciudad Real. Enrique fought a personal combat against Pedro and, with Bertrand du Guesclin hanging on to Pedro's leg, stabbed his rival to death. Pedro had generally held the upper hand but now Enrique ruled.

MURADEL, BATTLE OF, 21 AUGUST 1157
Defeat of Alfonso VII of Castile by the Almohads. He invaded Muslim Iberia but in the retreat was defeated and killed at Muradel.

NÁJERA (NAVARRETTE), BATTLE OF, 3 APRIL 1367
Victory for Pedro the Cruel of Castile and the Black Prince over Enrique de Trastámara, Pedro's rival for the crown. The Black Prince, whose force included John of Gaunt and Sir John Chandos, avoided an attempt to block his route and crossed the Ebro. The armies met south of

the river and Enrique attacked. His cavalry was halted and routed by English archers. The French finally surrendered, their commander Bertrand du Guesclin being captured. Pedro was restored to his throne. The result was reversed by the Black Prince's illness and withdrawal from Spain.

OURIQUE, BATTLE OF, 25 JULY 1139

Victory by Afonso Enriques of Portugal over invading Murābit Muslims. It led to independence for the kingdom of Portugal. The location is uncertain and may not have been modern Ourique.

RIO SALADO, BATTLE OF, 30 OCTOBER 1340

Victory of Alfonso XI of Castile and his Christian allies, including his father-in-law Afonso IV of Portugal, against the Marīnid Sultan Abū'l-Hasan and the ruler of Granada, Yūsuf I. The Marīnids from Morocco retook Gibraltar and threatened Castile. Iberian and North African Muslims besieged Tarifa on the south coast of Spain. The Christians, seeking to relieve it, met the Muslims near the River Salado. The Christians made a cavalry charge with some impact but the Muslim line held until the Christian garrison from Tarifa sortied against the Muslim rear to turn the battle. The sultan returned to Morocco, while Yūsuf shut himself in Granada. North African intervention was never again a major threat to the *Reconquista*.

SEPÚLVEDA, BATTLE OF, 26 OCTOBER 1111

Victory of Alfonso the Battler of Aragón against the supporters of his wife Urraca, whom he had repudiated. She was the heiress to Castile but Alfonso seized power for himself. Urraca backed her son, another Alfonso. They failed in the battle but her son later became Alfonso VII of Castile and León.

SIMANCAS, BATTLE OF, 22 JULY 939

Victory by Ramiro II of León against Muslim invaders. The Caliph of Córdoba, Abd al-Rāhman, won a series of victories. He assembled troops in Iberia to invade León. Simancas was besieged and Ramiro came to its relief, the first of several victories.

TOLEDO, SIEGE OF, 1084–5

Captured by Alfonso VI of Castile. Toledo was the capital of a *taifa* state on the Tagus. It was allied with Castile but Alfonso wanted direct control. He assembled troops from Aragón, France, Italy and Germany. He deposed his former ally al-Qādir, after two rebellions against him in Toledo. The Christians appeared before the city in 1084 though Alfonso did not arrive until March 1085. Toledo offered little resistance and surrendered on 25 May. The Muslims were allowed their own worship. Al-Qādir went to Valencia with Alfonso's support. Alfonso's kingdom became the largest in Iberia. His success provoked the Muslims into seeking aid from the Almoravids of Morocco.

TORO, BATTLE OF, 1476

Fought for the succession to Castile on the death of Enrique IV between Ferdinand II of Aragón and Afonso V of Portugal. Ferdinand married Isabella, Enrique's sister, and Afonso married Juana, Enrique's daughter. It was fought near the Duero. Ferdinand's victory was a step towards the unity of Aragón and Castile.

ZALAKA (ZALLĀQA/AZAGAL/SAGRAJAS), BATTLE OF, 23 OCTOBER 1086

Victory near Badajoz of Yūsuf ibn-Tāshfīn over Alfonso VI of Castile. Alfonso VI advanced the *Reconquista*, capturing Toledo in 1085. The Muslims called for aid from the Almoravids of Morocco. Yūsuf brought an army in 1086 and the Iberian Muslims joined him. Alfonso abandoned the siege of Zaragoza. He ordered a charge but it was held. The Christians were routed but Yūsuf did not press his advantage. Alfonso retreated to Toledo. The battle marked a halt in the Christian advance. Some authorities date it to 1088.

ZARAGOZA (SARAGOSSA), SIEGE OF, 1118

Captured by Alfonso the Battler of Aragón. It was held by the Murābit Muslims as the capital of a *taifa* state. Alfonso led a crusade with Norman and French support. Gaston de Béarn had been on the First Crusade and built belfries and siege engines. The Muslims tried to relieve Zaragoza but were repulsed. It was starved into surrender on 19 December, leaving the *taifa* in Christian hands.

Statue of Bartolomeo Colleoni, Venice, by Verrocchio

12 | Renaissance Italy, 1250–1525

GENERALS AND LEADERS

See in Part I: Borgia (Cesare), Cane (Facino), Cangrande della Scala, Charles of Anjou, Colleoni (Bartolomeo), Conradin, Este (Niccolò d'), Gattamelata (Erasmo da Narni), Hawkwood (John), Joanna II of Naples, Ladislas of Naples, Ludovico il Moro, Malatesta (Sigismondo), Manfred, Medici (Cosimo de'), Medici (Lorenzo de'), Sforza (Francesco), Visconti (Filippo Maria), Visconti (Gian Galeazzo).

BATTLES AND SIEGES

Alessandria 1174–5, Alexandretta 1294, Anghiari 1440, Arbedo 1422, Atella 1496, Benevento 1266, Brescia 1238, Caravaggio 1448, Carthage 1280, Cascina 1364, Castagnaro 1387, Cerignola 1503, Chioggia 1378–81, Cortenuova 1237, Curzola 1298, Eight Saints 1375–8, Ferrara 1482–4, Fornovo 1495, Garigliano 1503, Legnano 1176, Marignano 1515, Messina 1283, Milan 1158–62, Naples 1284, Novara 1513, Pavia 1525, Pola 1379, Sapienza 1354, Seminara 1495, Sicilian Vespers 1282, Tagliacozzo 1268, Trapani 1264.

OUTLINE OF EVENTS

1250 was a dividing line in the history of Italy, the year Frederick II (HRE) died. He had united the German lands, the parts of northern Italy that came under imperial control, and the kingdom of Sicily. After his death this unity, never strong, could not be maintained. The southern kingdom was fought over by his descendants with each other and with interested outside powers. In the north his death gave new opportunities to imperial enemies. There were still struggles between supporters of the empire and the papacy (Guelf/Ghibelline). However, these were now more parties in local politics than groups dominated by outside powers. There were interventions by the emperors but these were less significant in Italy than previously.

Later medieval Italy is seen as the birthplace of the Renaissance – though there were previous developments in France. We note in passing that the political pattern of Italy played a large part in its cultural development. There was no state of medieval Italy, which was rather a geographical expression. Italy was a patchwork of small states, more of them than we can examine. We only note the foremost. Greater powers were always on the scene, either internally or on the fringes. At the beginning of our period the empire and the papacy were the greatest political powers concerned, though both declined so far as Italy was concerned. The power of emperors declined, even in Germany. The papacy was based outside Italy at Avignon for most of the 14th century though it returned and regained influence by the 15th century. The Papal States remained a political unit in Italy. In the north three greater states emerged from many lesser ones, always at odds with each other, their power and boundaries ebbing and flowing. In each of them there was conflict between existence as a republic or under dynastic tyrants. Such states as Padua, Verona, Bologna and Genoa were important at times but fell under the sway of one of the big three – Venice, Milan and Florence. Milan and Florence came under dynasties: the Visconti and the Sforza in Milan, the Medici in Florence. Venice retained its republican status. These northern states were almost constantly at war with lesser neighbours and each other, and at times with external powers. The three major powers were wealthy, and paid troops to defend their interests. In Italy emerged armed bands under captains, the *condottieri* – who made a *condotto* or contract to supply troops to the state concerned. It was the unique political pattern of Italy that brought about the unusual military system.

There was one further major power in Italy, in the south, the kingdom of Naples, the successor state to the Norman kingdom of Sicily. It became the target of external interests, falling in turn under the empire and princes from France (Anjou) and Aragón. Through much of the later Middle Ages the area was separated in two, the mainland as the kingdom of Naples, and the island of Sicily, sometimes called the kingdom of Trinacria.

Because of its political pattern the chief military events of Italy are best examined through the separate states – Venice, Milan, Florence, the Papal States and the kingdom of Naples. By the mid-15th century and the Peace of Lodi the boundaries of these states had more or less stabilised, only altered by intervention from European powers, in particular the invasion of Charles VIII of France – which takes us into the early modern period.

Venice was the only surviving republic among the greater states, a land and sea power with interests around the Mediterranean and in the Middle East. Venice played a part in the fall of Constantinople to the Fourth Crusade and depended on trade to the east, retaining links with Byzantium. Venice was wealthy and, it was said, housed 14,000 harlots. It swallowed up neighbouring smaller states including Padua, Vicenza and Verona. It had a complex constitution producing a great council and a doge (or duke), elected for life.

Milan became the dominant power in Lombardy, a leading industrial region in the medieval world. It suffered more than the rest of Italy from imperial interventions and benefited as these declined. It led the Lombard League against the emperors. From the

13th century Milan was dominated by dynasties – the Torre, the Visconti and the Sforza. The greatest of the Visconti, Gian Galeazzo, was named Duke of Milan by Wenceslas king of the Romans, and the title was retained. Gian Galeazzo took over Pisa, Siena, Perugia and Bologna. Milan's expansion provoked reaction from Venice and Florence. The greatest of the Sforza was Francesco, who married Filippo Maria Visconti's only daughter, the illegitimate Bianca Maria. Milan's independence was lost after the period of invasions, first to France and then to Spain.

Florence is renowned as the prime base of the Renaissance. It had strong republican traditions but fell under the partly disguised power of dynasties. On the death of Frederick II, Florence accepted popular government under *priori* (ruling magistrates). It could not sustain its position without surrendering to first the Albizzi and then the Medici, who replaced the Albizzi with popular support. They played down their real power – not unlike the way the earliest ancient Roman emperors had to pretend to be first among equals. Cosimo established the new regime and repulsed the threat from Milan. His grandson Lorenzo the Magnificent fended off an assassination attempt, the Pazzi Conspiracy. His success depended more on diplomacy than on war. In the 16th century Florence lost its independence, but a brief return to republicanism was ended with the appointment of Alessandro (son of the Duke of Urbino) as Duke of Florence in 1531.

The Papal States had little unity, despite their prestige in Christendom. The Avignon residence in the 14th century weakened papal power in Italy. Towns within the States were subject to attempts at control from other Italian powers. They also sought independence of the papacy, which itself fell into the hands of the Italian families, whose members were elected popes – including the Borgias and the Medici. Alum from Tolfa helped finance defence of the States.

The kingdom of Sicily or Naples was the only Italian monarchy, the largest of the states of Italy, but the most backward economically by the late Middle Ages. It suffered on the death of Frederick II with succession wars, involving his legitimate and illegitimate descendants based in the south and in Germany, and claimants to the kingdom from England, France and Aragón. His Staufen descendants lost the struggle. Charles of Anjou, brother of St Louis, conquered the kingdom. In 1282 the rebellion of the Sicilian Vespers led to loss of the island of Sicily to Aragón. The kingdom remained divided until the mid-15th century. Naples fell victim to foreign invasion – conquered by Charles VIII of France, reverting to Aragón in 1496, to Louis XII of France in 1500 and finally to Spain in the 16th century.

BATTLES AND SIEGES

ALESSANDRIA (ALEXANDRIA), SIEGE OF, 1174–5

Frederick Barbarossa besieged Alessandria from 29 October during his fifth Italian expedition. It was founded on the Po by the Lombard League against Frederick, and named after Pope Alexander III who was hostile to Frederick. The town resisted. On Good Friday, Frederick broke the Truce of God by mining the wall. His men entered but were defeated inside. He abandoned the siege on 13 April, Easter Sunday, burning his camp and siege equipment. Three days later he made terms with the Lombard League. There was a Battle of Alessandria in 1391, when Milan defeated Florence.

ALEXANDRETTA, NAVAL BATTLE OF, 1294

Victory off the coast of Cilicia near Alexandretta (held by Venice) for Genoa against Venice in the war between them. Venice soon recovered.

ANGHIARI, BATTLE OF, 29 JUNE 1440

Victory of an alliance between the papacy and Florence against Milan at the ancient walled town of Anghiari near Arezzo, a largely cavalry engagement. The Milanese army was led by the *condottiere* Piccinino, the allies by Francesco Sforza. According to Machiavelli it was an example of the kind of battle fought between mercenaries who would not kill each other – 'one man was killed and he fell off a horse'; in fact probably about 300 died. Over half the Milanese force was captured as well as all the baggage. The Medici position in Florence was strengthened. Leonardo painted a fresco of it in the Palazzo Vecchio Florence (now only known from a copy by Rubens). There is also a painting from the school of Uccello.

ARBEDO, BATTLE OF, 30 JUNE 1422

Milanese victory over Swiss invaders near Bellinzona, now in Switzerland. The Milanese were led by the *condottiere* Count Carmagnola for Filippo Maria Visconti. The Swiss came through the St Bernard Pass to besiege Bellinzona, held by Milan. They abandoned the siege to face the Milanese relieving army. After an abortive mounted charge, Carmagnola dismounted his cavalry and attacked on foot. Milan now held the Val d'Ossola. Until Arbedo the Swiss posed a threat to Milan and Venice. The Swiss used halberds and their defeat encouraged the future use of pikes.

ATELLA, BATTLE OF, 1496

Success of the Spanish in Italy under Hernández Gonzalo de Córdoba against the French under Gilbert duc de Montpensier. Charles VIII of France invaded Italy from 1494. A Spanish force came to aid the King of Naples. The Spanish gained revenge for Seminara. They besieged the French in Atella, outside which the battle was fought. Montpensier was captured.

BENEVENTO, BATTLE OF, 26 FEBRUARY 1266

Victory for Charles of Anjou in the kingdom of Naples near the road for Apulia. Charles invaded Italy and was crowned King of Sicily in Rome. He was opposed by Manfred, illegitimate son of Frederick II. Manfred claimed to be king but had been excommunicated by the pope. Charles took a defensive position on the bank of the River Calor, over which Manfred attacked. Charles' cavalry broke the enemy archers and surrounded their German cavalry. Manfred renewed his attack but was killed. It was the end of Norman and imperial rule in southern Italy.

BRESCIA, SIEGE OF, 1238

Besieged by Frederick II from 3 August to 9 October. He wanted to take Brescia, east of Milan, before attacking Milan itself. He brought siege engines and the Spanish mining expert Calamandrino, who was captured and offered gifts (a house and a woman) to change sides. He then showed the Brescians how to make catapults against Frederick's belfries. The besiegers tied captives to the front of their engines to discourage attack. The Brescians lowered their captives on ropes before the walls where Frederick's rams were aimed. A nocturnal sortie took Frederick by surprise. With winter Frederick retreated to Cremona.

CARAVAGGIO, BATTLE OF, 15 SEPTEMBER, 1448

Victory of Francesco Sforza for Milan over Venice. Sforza was attacked by surprise at dawn on the road from Brescia to Milan. Sforza held the attack and sent men through the woods to attack from the rear. This surprise was effective and the Venetians were beaten. Sforza made terms to gain Venetian support in his bid for power in Milan.

CARTHAGE, BATTLE OF, 1280
Victory of Charles of Anjou king of Sicily over the Moors in Tunisia. He made a feigned flight and turned on the pursuing enemy.

CASCINA, BATTLE OF, 28 JULY 1364
Victory of Florence over Pisa. The Pisans were not expecting attack and some were bathing in the Arno. Michelangelo painted an unfinished fresco of Cascina in the Palazzo Vecchio in Florence, of which a copy survives. Hawkwood won a victory here in 1369 for Milan against Florence, using a feigned flight.

CASTAGNARO, BATTLE OF, 11 MARCH 1387
Victory of Padua against Verona with Venetian support. Hawkwood commanded the Paduans for Francesco Carrara, Ordelaffi the Veronese with Cane among his captains. The Paduans were besieging Verona but abandoned the siege and retreated via the Adige. At Castagnaro the Veronese caught up. They had ribauds in their artillery – small cannons bound together to fire in concert. Ordelaffi hesitated before opening hostilities late in the day. Hawkwood's front was protected by a stream. He used archers to repel Veronese charges. He kept a cavalry reserve and, when it attacked from the flank, the Veronese broke. Their carroccio (symbolic chariot) was captured, as were Ordelaffi and Cane. The victory enhanced Hawkwood's reputation. Both opposing towns soon fell under Milanese control.

CERIGNOLA, BATTLE OF, 28 APRIL 1503
Victory of Aragonese over French for control of the kingdom of Naples, fought near Foggia in Apulia. The French, with Swiss mercenaries, were commanded by the duc de Nemours, the Spanish by Gonzalo de Córdoba. The Spanish marched from Barletta to take a defensive position on a hillside, defended by ditches and palisades. Their gunpowder blew up and they could not make full use of their cannons. Their arquebusiers still repelled the French charges. A Spanish counter with pikes and cavalry won the day. Nemours was killed.

CHIOGGIA, WAR OF, 1378–81
The fourth and last attempt by Genoa to challenge the domination of Venice. They were the main trading powers of Italy. They fought intermittent wars against each other from the mid-13th century. In October 1378 Venice captured Tenedos from Genoa. On 16 August 1379 Genoa, with aid from Padua, captured Chioggia on the Gulf of Venice. It was recovered by Venice on 22 June 1380. Venice's rivals by land (Hungary, Austria, Milan and Padua) encouraged making the Peace of Turin on 8 August 1381. Venice remained a great power for some time but Genoa's peak had passed.

CORTENUOVA, BATTLE OF, 27 NOVEMBER 1237
Victory for Frederick II over the Lombard League. He moved from Cremona and caught the enemy by the crossing of the Oglio at Cortenuova. Frederick's van had initial success but the Milanese around their carroccio held on. After dark the Lombards abandoned the field in heavy rain, leaving the carroccio stuck in the mud. Frederick made a triumphal entry into Cremona, pulling the carroccio by elephant. The success was neutralised in the following year when Frederick failed to take Brescia.

CURZOLA, NAVAL BATTLE OF, 8 SEPTEMBER 1298
Victory of Genoa over Venice in the Adriatic off the Dalmatian island of Curzola, during the wars between the cities. The Genoese fleet was under Lamba Doria. Peace was made in 1299, leaving Genoa to dominate the Black Sea. Venice decided to reorganise its government, making tighter rules for membership of the great council.

EIGHT SAINTS, WAR OF THE, 1375–8
Florence organised a league in the Papal States, causing rebellion against the papacy in 1375. The war is apparently named in error, confusing the eight who led Florence to war with the eight ('saints') who levied tax from the clergy. In 1376 Gregory XI declared the whole city excommunicated. In 1377 the papal legate, Robert of Geneva, captured Cesena and ordered his mercenaries to massacre the citizens. In 1378 a rising in Florence by the Ciompi under Michele di Lando took over the city. The new regime made the Treaty of Tivoli with the papacy, paying an indemnity. A rebellion against the new regime was suppressed.

FERRARA, WAR OF, 1482–4
The war resulted in invitations to foreign powers to intervene in Italy. Pope Sixtus IV invited Venice to give naval aid against Naples in return for territory belonging to Ferrara. Venice declared war on Ferrara, then under Ercole d'Este, occupying Rovigo and the Polesine. Florence and Milan declared for Ferrara and allied with Naples under its Aragonese ruler. The papacy ended its alliance with Venice, which sought French aid and revived Angevin claims to Naples. The war was ended by the Peace of Bagnolo in 1484.

FORNOVO, BATTLE OF, 6 JULY 1495
Venetian victory with Milanese allies over the invading Charles VIII of France, fought by the River Taro near Parma. Charles retreated and Gonzaga blocked his route through the Pontremoli Pass. The Venetians were under Francesco Gonzaga. The French had Swiss mercenaries. Venice won but not conclusively. The French escaped and Charles VIII departed from Italy. Gonzaga was fatally wounded.

GARIGLIANO, BATTLE OF, 29 DECEMBER 1503
Victory of the Aragonese under Gonzalo de Córdoba over the French with Italian allies to control the kingdom of Naples. Córdoba attacked in bad weather. His engineers constructed a bridge over the River Garigliano for a surprise attack. The French fled to Gaeta. Piero de' Medici, son of Lorenzo and on the French side, drowned in the river.

LEGNANO, BATTLE OF, 29 MAY 1176
Defeat of Frederick Barbarossa by the Lombard League, the climax of his fifth Italian expedition. He assembled at Como preparing to attack Milan. Legnano is 15 miles north-west of Milan. Henry the Lion failed to answer Frederick's summons to the expedition. Some of Frederick's troops were elsewhere in Italy. Frederick had few cavalry and rashly accepted battle against a larger and better-balanced Lombard force. His charge was repulsed by pikes and dismounted knights, the infantry holding steady round the *carroccio*, an early example of good infantry beating heavy cavalry. Lombard reinforcements arrived to attack the flank. Frederick was unhorsed and believed dead, but escaped to Pavia. His shield, lance and treasure were captured. He made peace with the papacy and recognised the liberties of the Italian communes. Later he took revenge on Henry the Lion.

MARIGNANO (MELEGNANO), BATTLE OF, 13–14 SEPTEMBER 1515
Victory for the French under Francis I in Italy against Milan and the papacy. The French were entrenched ten miles from Milan, their main target. The Swiss infantry, allied with the Italians, attacked, taking the French by surprise before they could make full use of their artillery. The Swiss were halted. The French victory came from their power in cannons, which proved more than a match for the Swiss pikes. It lasted two days because the Swiss, despite heavy losses, refused to break. Venetian reinforcements under Bartolomeo de Alviano for the French turned the battle. The French took control of Milan.

MESSINA, NAVAL BATTLE OF, 11 OCTOBER 1283

Victory for the Aragonese with a Catalan fleet under Roger de Loria, an exile from Calabria, against the Angevins. It followed the Sicilian Vespers rising against Charles of Anjou in Sicily. Pedro of Aragón entered Messina. Charles besieged Messina but his fleet was defeated and he retreated to the mainland. The Spanish won again at Naples the following year. The Spanish took over Sicily from the Angevins.

MILAN, SIEGE OF, 1158–62

During Frederick Barbarossa's second Italian expedition in 1158 he besieged Milan. His force included Italian allies. Frederick could not surround the city but used three lines of men to shoot in missiles and starved Milan into submission. All aged between 14 and 70 had to take an oath of loyalty. Milan was leader of the Lombard League, opposing imperial authority. It revolted again in 1159. Frederick was occupied at Crema, which Milan tried to aid. Frederick returned to Milan in September 1161 with reinforcements from Germany. He laid waste the area, disrupting food supplies. Five Milanese captives were blinded while a sixth lost his nose but kept his eyes to lead the others home. The city surrendered on 1 March 1162. Frederick promised mercy but destroyed much of the city.

NAPLES, NAVAL BATTLE OF, 5 JUNE 1284

Victory of Roger Loria for the Aragonese over Charles of Anjou in the Bay of Naples. The Angevins emerged but Roger captured 48 of their galleys. Charles the Lame, son of Charles of Anjou, was captured and later ransomed. The defeats for Charles at Messina and Naples confirmed his loss of Sicily with the Sicilian Vespers.

NOVARA, BATTLE OF, 6 JUNE 1513

Swiss victory over the French under La Trémoille in Italy, west of Milan. The French invaded Italy, seeking to evict Massimiliano Sforza from Milan. He sent against them Swiss mercenaries who linked up with the Milanese garrison at Novara to make a surprise dawn attack. The French infantry was destroyed though the cavalry escaped to France.

PAVIA, SIEGE AND BATTLE OF, 1525

Francis I invaded Italy in 1524, besieging Pavia on his way to attack Milan. An army for Charles V (HRE) came to the relief. The battle was fought on 24 February. The French charged with initial success but were held and defeated. Le Trémoille was killed. Francis was unhorsed, wounded and captured. Some French escaped under Charles duc d'Alençon. In 1526 Francis was released after agreeing the Treaty of Madrid, abandoning his claims in Italy.

POLA, NAVAL BATTLE OF, 1379

Victory off Pola for Genoa over Venice in the War of Chioggia. The Genoese were aided by Padua and commanded by Luciano Doria. The Venetians were under Vittorio Pisani. Doria was the victor but was killed. His brother Pietro went on to take Chioggia at the entrance to the Venetian lagoon. The Genoese success did not last.

SAPIENZA, NAVAL BATTLE OF, 4 NOVEMBER 1354

Victory of the Genoese fleet over Venice at Porto Longo off Sapienza, the largest island off Modon in the south-west Peloponnese. Sapienza was a noted pirate haunt. The battle was an early clash in a war between the cities that spanned the 14th century, concluding with the War of Chioggia. The Venetian fleet was virtually destroyed.

SEMINARA, BATTLE OF, 28 JUNE 1495

Defeat for the Aragonese under Gonzalo de Córdoba by the French. Swiss mercenaries for the French played a large part. Córdoba thereafter employed Swiss infantry and went on to a series of successes.

SICILIAN VESPERS, THE, 1282

On Easter Monday 30 March the local people attacked the unpopular Angevin garrison in Palermo. The revolt began as bells rang for evening worship, Vespers. A French sergeant insulted a local woman. Her husband knifed him and riot followed. The rebellion spread. Messina was taken. The French shut themselves in Mategriffon Castle. Charles of Anjou king of Naples and Sicily was expelled. He besieged Messina in 1293 but failed to take it. The crown was offered to Pedro III of Aragón, married to Constance daughter of Manfred of Hohenstaufen. Pedro relieved Messina. There was war between the two outside forces for 20 years, the Aragonese finally succeeding.

TAGLIACOZZO, BATTLE OF, 23 AUGUST 1268

Defeat for Conradin, son of Conrad IV (HRE), the last Hohenstaufen in Sicily. He invaded the kingdom of Sicily with German and Spanish allies in 1267, seeking to make good his claim against Charles of Anjou. Supporters revolted against Charles in Sicily. The battle was fought in central Italy as Conradin advanced south. Charles took position behind the River Salto. Conradin's men failed to take the bridge but others crossed further up and attacked the Angevins on the flank. Then the bridge was crossed. Charles recovered by leading a charge with a hidden reserve when many of the enemy, thinking victory theirs, pursued Angevins off the field. He then defeated the returning enemy. It was largely a cavalry battle, a costly victory: 'never was victory so bloody, for nearly his whole army had fallen'. Conradin fled but was captured and executed in Naples in October. It ended German Hohenstaufen rule in Sicily, leaving the Angevins in control.

TRAPANI (TREPANI/DREPANA), NAVAL BATTLE OF, 1264

Victory for Venice over Genoa in the first war between them. Trapani was a harbour in western Sicily. Venice increased its hold on trade to the east and improved its position in Constantinople.

PART III

Military topics

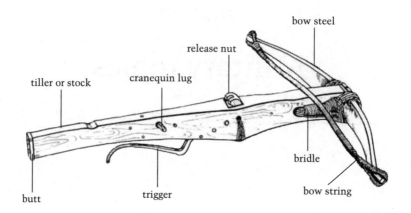

bow steel

release nut

tiller or stock

cranequin lug

bridle

butt

trigger

bow string

A crossbow with a steel bow

13 | Arms of the warrior

OUTLINE HISTORY

We are here concerned with the personal arms of individual warriors. The five main ways to know about medieval arms are from archaeological finds, surviving examples, manuscript illustrations, sculptures, and accounts in documents and chronicles. The evidence is scantiest early on and increases gradually through time.

Both Romans and barbarians contributed to early medieval arms development. Too many historians have stressed the contribution of one to the detriment of the other. Romans and barbarians also borrowed from each other and there is no clear distinction between the arms of one and the other. Both owed a debt to Bronze and Iron Age predecessors.

The medieval weapon *par excellence* is the sword. Other significant weapons were spears and axes. Some weapons declined in importance afterwards. The small throwing axe of the Franks is an example, probably because it proved less effective when used in larger infantry formations. Most weapons had their particular advantage – the bow was more effective at a distance than the spear, the sword less cumbersome in close combat than the axe.

With the increased significance of mounted knights more emphasis was placed on cavalry arms. The lance developed into a specifically designed weapon, longer and with a special grip. Swords needed to be adaptable, light enough to wield from horseback, and useful for the knight on foot. Smaller personal weapons such as knives and daggers were handy in emergencies.

There were changes in infantry tactics. It was necessary to find a way to counter the strength of mounted charges. Cavalry proved ineffective for this and various infantry tactics were developed, as with bows, spears and other weapons. Crossbows returned to favour and larger trained forces of archers were employed. Spears were retained for thrusting rather than throwing and became longer, the beginning of pike tactics. There were further changes in the later Middle Ages. Crossbows were improved. The ordinary bow, or longbow, came to its peak period, a riposte to mounted charges. Pikes had the same function, especially with large numbers of trained men forming a wall or square.

All these weapons had a long ancestry but lost some significance with the development of firearms. Gunpowder had been known of for a long time but was now used with effective weapons, both handguns and artillery. Artillery weapons for best effect in battle needed to be portable. The development of portable artillery and handguns proceeded in parallel.

A–Z OF TERMS

ANGON
A barbed javelin, only mentioned in connection with the Franks, described as not very long and used for throwing or stabbing. The angon was similar to the Roman *pilum* and may have derived from it. The head was iron and long in relation to the shaft. The point was small with two barbs. A head found in Germany was a metre long. The head was barbed and difficult to extricate from a wound or shield. If the angon struck a shield, the Frank could wrench away the shield using the angon as a handle.

ARQUEBUS (HARQUEBUS)
An early portable gun, first used as artillery but later a personal weapon. Its name comes from Middle Low German *hakebusse* (hook-gun), because a hook attached the gun to its carriage. The name was later commonly used for various portable guns and handguns. The arquebus was often placed on a carriage, trestle or rest. The main part was a metal tube. With an added wooden stock it became a hand weapon, fired from the shoulder via a touch-hole using a match. It was used from the mid-15th century. The Hussite hand culverin was probably the model for the arquebus. Charles the Bold of Burgundy employed arquebusiers in the 1470s. At the same time Matthias of Hungary claimed that a fifth of his infantry were arquebusiers. The arquebus became a favourite Spanish weapon. At first, loading was slow. In the late Middle Ages a mechanism was developed to carry a slow match to the powder, its lever shaped like a letter S or serpent, a name then used for the weapon.

AXE
The Franks possessed a small throwing axe, the franciska, about two feet long. They were used as missiles and thrown in unison. The Vikings used hand axes, as demonstrated on a gravestone from Lindisfarne. The larger battle-axe had a shaft of some five feet with an iron head fixed by socket. It was wielded with both hands. The battle-axe was popular with the Vikings and often called a Norse or Danish axe. Vikings sometimes named their axes, such as 'Witch' or 'Fiend', suggesting their personal nature. The Vikings used bearded axes named from the shape of the drooping lower edge, and broad axes. The latter

emerged in c.1000, sometimes with a steel edge welded to the blade. The blade was narrowest at the socket, broadening to a curved edge about a foot long. The bipennis was a double-headed blade. Axes were favoured by the English at Hastings and employed by English and Scandinavians in the Byzantine Varangian Guard. Byzantines and Muslims used axes, especially hand-axes such as the saddle-axe. The axe continued in use in the later Middle Ages but with decreasing importance. King Stephen at Lincoln in 1141 was handed an axe by a citizen, suggesting it was still a weapon for ordinary folk. Irish and Scottish troops used axes in the later period though the English by then saw it as primitive. An axe was employed by a Scot at Otterburn in 1388 – albeit a priest defending the Earl of Douglas. From the 13th century one finds smaller and lighter axe-heads. Axes did not disappear in the later Middle Ages, when they were still used in Scandinavia and eastern Europe. They were probably the predecessors of staff weapons. The later medieval type with a lighter head and a hammer at the rear of the blade suggests such a development. Mongols used small axes. A hand-axe known as the horseman's axe regained popularity in the late Middle Ages as a reserve weapon for cavalry.

BILL (BILLHOOK)
Formerly the name for a type of sword but more commonly meaning a staff weapon with a concave or curved blade, having a rear spike and a spear-like top. The name was applied to a variety of staff weapons. Initially it was like a scythe. Its distinctive feature remained the curved, crescent-shaped blade. The bill was replaced in popularity by the pike in the later Middle Ages.

BOLT (QUARREL)
Missile shot by a crossbow, shorter and heavier than an arrow, about a foot in length. It appears as Latin *bolta* or *quarellus* (*quadrellus*) – hence quarrel. The butt end was tapered and flattened. The

head or pile was usually of iron and pyramid-shaped. Bolts were described as 'four-sided'. Early shafts were often of ash or yew with feathered flights. Sometimes wood was used for the flight. The bolt was placed in the groove of the crossbow and over the nut. The string was pulled over the nut to lay against the butt end of the bolt. A vireton was a bolt with a spiral flight so that it rotated in flight, making it more accurate. Bolts had to be the correct size for the particular crossbow. An English inventory of 1298 lists three different sizes. The *Milemete Manuscript* illustration shows a type of bolt as an early missile for a gun. Incendiary bolts were known in the 15th century, constructed with a bomb-like shaft. They could be shot on to roofs to cause fire. The term bolt is used for the missile of a balista.

BOW (SEE ALSO CROSSBOW, LONGBOW, SHORTBOW, SPRING-BOW)
A weapon to shoot missiles – arrows, bolts, quarrels. The essential idea of all bows is to tense a string, which when released will propel a missile. The string is tensed against a solid but flexible stave. Longbows and ordinary wooden bows had a wooden stave, generally yew, while crossbows had wooden, and later steel, staves. The shortbow had a composite stave. The efficacy of the weapons at different points of time led to one kind of bow replacing another in popularity. In the early period the three main types of bow were all known. The longbow was not a later medieval invention as often suggested. The crossbow tended to be slower in operation, and early on was made of wood. The later use of a metal bow saw an increase in its velocity and impact. The shortbow gained its efficacy from bending a composite stave against its own spring. The shortness made it useful for horsemen. It was used by nomads from the east. The spring-bow was not really a weapon of the usual kind. It was a bow set as a trap ready to spring automatically when released by the victim accidentally.

COUSTEL

A dagger, descended from the seax, the derivation for the name of a warrior using a dagger or knife (a *coustiller* or *coutilier*). A coustiller was an armed personal servant of a higher class warrior. Coustillers fought at Bouvines and were common in France in the later Middle Ages. The name coustillers was also applied to brigands.

CROSSBOW (ARBALEST)

A bow with a mechanism to draw the string. The bow was small and bound to a wooden stock, which the archer held. The end of the stock is the tiller. The string was released by trigger. The string was drawn back over a nut on the stock. The trigger retracted the nut. The crossbow was known in the ancient world, used by the Chinese and the Romans. The T'ang dynasty had a Crossbow Office. Early crossbows were drawn by hand and foot, with the foot on the bow and the hands pulling the string. Various improvements were made to this process, such as a stirrup at the end of the stock for the foot to grip, or a claw on the belt to attach to the string so that the weight of the body could be used to draw. Mechanical devices were invented to draw the bow – a pulley, a goat's foot lever (with a cloven end fitting over pins fixed in the stock), a windlass (a winding device) and a cranequin (with a metal ratchet bar and cogs). The bow of early weapons was of wood. By the 13th century composite bows of wood, horn and sinew were used. From the 15th century steel bows were produced. The crossbow shot a bolt or quarrel, fitting into a groove on the stock. The nut was commonly of horn, shaped like a thick coin with a groove in the centre of the edge. It fitted into a socket in the box of the stock. The Latin for crossbow was *balista* (the same word as for a throwing engine that was in effect a large crossbow, causing confusion in translation). The Normans probably used crossbows at Hastings. Two English kings were killed by crossbow bolts: William Rufus in the New Forest and Richard the Lionheart in France. The papacy banned crossbow use (1096 and 1139) against Christians though this was often ignored. Later its use was permitted against heretics or in a just war – most rulers claimed their wars were just. The crossbow was widely used by the 13th century, often by mercenaries. The French used Genoese crossbowmen at Sluys and Crécy. It is said the crossbow was not commonly used in England but this is incorrect. With a steel bow the impact was considerable and the range from 400 to 500 yards.

CROSSGUARD

The transverse piece of metal that forms the first part of a sword hilt, separating it from the blade, protecting the swordsman's hand. It was commonly made from one piece of metal with a slot in the centre fitting over the tang of the blade. It varied in shape and style, for example straight, curved, or in shapes resembling bow ties. Oakeshott has produced a list of types of crossguard, an aid to dating swords.

DAGGER

Small knife for stabbing, usually a reserve weapon, often carried in a belt. It normally had two sharp edges and a sharp point, but single-edged weapons were known. It became more popular in the later Middle Ages. It descended from the earlier seax. Daggers were used by the Visigoths, Franks, Vikings and Anglo-Saxons. The Byzantines saw it as the assassin's weapon. Charlemagne's capitularies demanded that mounted warriors carry daggers. A Latin term for dagger was *cultellus* e.g. '*cultellum qui dicitur dagger*' (a knife that was called a dagger). Early daggers were longer than was later common, such as the 'long knives' used at Bouvines, 1214. The mercenaries known as *cottereaux* were probably so called because they carried daggers or knives (*couteaux*). Daggers were useful for piercing gaps in armour. *Misericorde* was a term for a dagger, probably from using it on anyone begging for mercy. From the 14th century one finds the kidney dagger or more properly (improperly?) the ballock dagger – from the shape of the hilt with two globular decorations. The *basilard* was a type of dagger with a blade broad at the hilt, popular in Italy. A dagger with an even broader blade at the hilt was the ox-tongue or *cinquedea* – five fingers in width. A common 15th-century dagger was the *rondel*, with discs at either end of the hilt, a slim, needle-like weapon. In the Renaissance period it was common to fight with sword in one hand, dagger in the other.

FALCHION
Sword with a curved, sharp outer edge broadening towards the point and then tapering so that it looked boat-shaped. The blunt edge was straight. The name was from Latin *falx* (scythe) from its shape. It descended from the Norse seax. Its period of prominence was the 13th and 14th centuries. The *faussar* of 12th-century Iberia might be an early example. The falchion was used by lower ranking infantry, men-at-arms and archers. One was found at the Châtelet in Paris with the Grand Châtelet arms on the pommel. The Conyers Falchion, at Durham, was used in tenure ceremonies.

FIREARMS
The medieval period saw the introduction to Europe of gunpowder and firearms. Experiments with gunpowder occurred in the 13th century. Initially used for portable artillery weapons, these inspired the invention of handguns. A culverin could be mounted on a tripod or used by hand, like the culverins *ad manum* mentioned in 1435. Early firearms were inefficient but by the late Middle Ages their value was clear. The Anatolian Turks had handguns in the mid-14th century, but guns developed faster in the west. By the 16th century the Turks regained the initiative. In 1364 Italians produced small handguns in Perugia and Modena. There is a record in England from c.1375 for the fitting of eight guns with handles like pikes. The term

handgun first appeared in 1386. Handguns were more common by the 15th century, in the Hundred Years' War and the Hussite Wars. At Caravaggio, Italy, in 1448 the smoke from Milanese handguns obscured the view. In that year Hungarian handgunners defeated the Ottomans under Murad II. Flemings and Germans were noted for supplying handgunners. Musketeers became significant in the early modern period.

FRANCISKA (FRANCISCA)
Small throwing axe associated with the Franks, named after them or they after it. The word is the Latin term found in chronicles. It was also called a *frakki*. It was used from the 5th to the 7th century, but then lost popularity. Examples have been found in graves. It was single bladed with a heavy metal head, commonly slim becoming wider at the blade. The Franks hurled their axes together at a signal. The Goths also used this weapon, borrowed from the Franks.

GLAIVE
A weapon with a blade or a head. It meant, at different times, a sword, spear, lance or bladed weapon on a handle. Glaive later meant a lance that was the winning mark in a race, the winner taking it as his prize. Glaive comes from Old French for lance or sword, probably from Latin *gladius* (sword). The term is commonly used now for the later medieval staff weapon with a long, curved single-edged blade attached to a long wooden staff. Its blade was broader than that of a bill, with the edge on the inner curve. The blade sometimes had additional hooks and projections.

GOEDENDAG (GODENDAC)
One of the names for a later medieval staff weapon; others include bill, halberd, pole-axe, gaesa, croc, faus, fauchard, faussal, pikte, guisarme and vouge. Some of the names may be variants for the same thing. Goedendag means 'good-day' or 'good morning' – the poet of the Battle of Courtrai

says it meant 'bon jour'. It was the main weapon of the Flemish at Courtrai in their victory over the French in 1302 when it was used two-handed. Because of the illustrations on the Courtrai Chest it is probably correctly believed that the weapon was a club or mace with an attached metal spike. It may be significant that the similarly named morning star was a type of mace. One chronicle says it could be used for cutting, so some historians believe it is a type of halberd. Luckily my friends do not greet me with it each day.

GUISARME (GISARME)

Staff weapon with a long blade, sharpened on both sides and ending in a long point, up to eight feet in length. It derived from the scythe and the prong. There is a Catalan reference to it in 977 and it may have originated in Andalusia. The name guisarme is Old French. The length of the blade allowed the addition of hooks and projections. With these additions it became a *fauchard* – probably its most common medieval form. It could be used for cutting or thrusting. It was similar to the glaive, but with a shorter blade. It was popular in Scotland. Sometimes bells were attached to frighten approaching horses.

HALBERD

A long-handled staff weapon with a blade that was both pointed as for a pike and edged as an axe, probably the most common staff weapon. Often a curved spike projected at the rear of the axe head. The name first appeared in a Swiss poem of the 14th century. The halberd was probably first used by the Swiss, as at Morgarten in 1315. At Sempach the halberd crushed the knights of Duke Leopold, and at Nancy a halberd slashed Charles of Burgundy across the face, causing him to be unhorsed and killed. It was replaced in popularity by the longer pike, more effective against cavalry. The Swiss are said to have lost faith in the halberd after their failure at Bellinzona in 1422.

HAMMER

Often referred to as the war-hammer. Like the axe it could be a tool or a weapon. It had a metal head with a flattened surface for striking. It reappeared in the 13th century and was much used during the Hundred Years' War. A hammer is represented on a 13th-century tomb effigy in Malvern Abbey Church, Worcestershire. This has a short handle and a spike at the back of the head. Several are depicted in later Spanish paintings, some with long handles. A 15th-century hammer head with a spike at the rear is in the Wallace Collection.

HILT

The handle or grip of a sword or dagger. Petersen detected no less than 26 types of hilt for swords of the Viking period. The hilt was formed over a tang from the blade, slotting over the guard, covering the grip, with a pommel to stop the end. The hilt was often decorated in patterns, for example with inlaid copper and brass. Thin sheets of tin, brass, gold, silver or copper might be used. Some were marked with a maker's or firm's name. On one lower guard is lettering '*Leofric me fec[it]*' (Leofric made me), possibly meaning the hilt rather than the whole sword. The transverse piece of metal forming part of a sword hilt is the crossguard, separating it from the blade.

LANCE

A cavalry weapon with a long wooden shaft and metal head. The name is from Old French via Latin (*lancea*), but possibly of Celtic origin. Initially it was a spear. By the end of the 11th century lances were used couched (i.e. held underarm) for concerted cavalry charges. This type of attack was known in the Middle East as the Syrian attack, though a Mamluke cavalry tactic was known as 'playing the Frank'. On the *Bayeux Tapestry* some lances are couched but others are used overarm, perhaps because the lance was not especially useful against infantry. In the later Middle Ages the lance became more specialised, thicker and heavier than a spear and with a shaped grip, balanced for holding at the centre. The forward part thickened before the grip, thus providing protection for the hand. A wing attachment to the head prevented the lance burying itself too deeply in its target. A lance rest was sometimes fixed to a knight's breastplate, to make carrying easier. The rest could be attached to a spring so that it clipped shut when not in use. It became common practice to place the lance across the horse with the lance head on the left of the horse. The 1277 brass of Sir John d'Abernoun shows a lance with a straight shaft, a spear-like head and an attached pennon. Lighter lances were still used in the later Middle Ages, for example by the fast moving *stradiots* of Byzantium. Plate armour lessened the killing power of the lance. Tournament lances were normally blunted, commonly with a head called a coronal, or replaced by relatively harmless substitutes such as canes. The lance was the chief weapon in jousting.

LONGBOW

The longbow is associated with English archers in the Hundred Years' War. Longbows were not then a new invention. Bows with long wooden staves, often of yew, had been produced for centuries and have been found, for example, in excavations in Scandinavia and Ireland from the Roman and the Viking periods. The Vikings were great exponents of the bow. Norman bows on the *Bayeux Tapestry* should probably be described as longbows though perhaps not as long as was later common. The crossbow became the most popular bow in the 12th and 13th centuries but the longbow reached its golden age during the Hundred Years' War. The Welsh used longbows but it is unlikely that the English learned of it from them. The longbow had a wooden stave and a string. The stave was commonly of yew, rounded with a D-shaped central section. The sapwood of the stave was on the outside, the heartwood towards the archer – giving the stave a natural spring. Longbow length needed to be in proportion to the archer's

height. Its typical length was about six feet. There was a thickened grip in the centre of the stave for the left hand, allowing the arrow to rest on the top of the grip. The right hand drew the string, normally of gut, sometimes hemp. The string was looped over each end of the stave. The centre of the string was usually strengthened at the nocking point. Pieces of horn or nocks were added at the ends of the stave to help hold the string in place. The best draw was to the chest and required considerable strength. A good longbowman needed strength and the knack of drawing and releasing at the correct moment. Woodland and forest areas produced the most experienced longbowmen. Whether or not Robin Hood actually lived, the tales link a forest area with the weapon. What made the longbow so effective was its tactical use by large groups of trained archers in selected forward positions, shooting in unison. The English used longbows both in sea warfare, as at Sluys, and on land as at Crécy, Poitiers and Agincourt. Longbowmen were used as mercenaries; Scots for example were hired by the French. The English were reluctant to abandon their famous weapon and continued its use into the Tudor period. Longbows were discovered aboard the *Mary Rose*. Elizabethan writers romantically sought to encourage its continued use, but in the real world gunpowder had taken over.

MACE

A heavy club with an added head, probably initially an infantry weapon, its prime use in the Middle Ages was by cavalry. It needed to be light and was often of bronze. The head sometimes had an added spike or projection. The mace was known in 10th-century Moorish Andalusia. It appears on the *Bayeux Tapestry*, as a clubbing weapon. Later the heads looked like dart flights, with wings projecting from a central spoke. One such is in the Museum of London. Often the head had a projecting spike like a spear. Maces are depicted on the *Maciejowski Bible* and on 13th-century sculptures at Lincoln and Constance. It was often used in ceremonies, for example by lawyers, clerics and royalty, and was a common weapon in tournaments. The later medieval Gothic Mace was metal, its shaft thickened at the grip, sometimes with a guard and pommel like a sword hilt. Animal-headed maces were used by steppe nomads and the Turks. Maces could be of bronze, iron or steel and for ceremonial use of silver or gold. The morning star was a type of mace.

MISERICORDE (MISERICORD)
A small dagger, a knight's reserve weapon, said to be named from its use for the death stroke, when the victim could ask for mercy or be killed. Alternatively it is suggested the name meant that the dagger was 'merciful', putting the injured victim out of his misery. The term appeared first in the Treaty of Arras of 1221, named alongside the knife. The misericorde often had a straight blade of triangular section with a sharp point. It is sometimes shown carried on the right side, fixed by chain to the belt.

MORNING STAR
A later medieval staff weapon, generally combining a mace with a spear point, named from the German *morgenstern* (possibly ironic – from seeing stars after being struck), but probably from its appearance, the head looking like a spiky pineapple, or with imagination a star. Hewitt suggests the morning star was a type of flail attached to the staff by a chain, the head being globular and spiked and looking like a star, but this is not generally accepted.

PIKE
A long wooden staff with a spear-like head, up to 18 feet long with a ten-inch steel head. Pike is the common English term for such weapons though variations include the goedendag and partisan. It was seen as the weapon of inferior ranks. Wace wrote of 'villeins with pikes'. It was originally an infantry weapon for defensive use. It was held with the butt on the ground, steadied by the foot, with the head towards the enemy. It proved useful against cavalry. Unlike archers, whose weapons were only useful when the cavalry was at a distance, pikemen could hold a charge. Special formations were developed, such as the hollow square or circle with men facing outwards all round. The pike was a standard defensive weapon in the 14th century. Its effectiveness was demonstrated by the Flemings at Courtrai in 1302. The Scots used pikes at Stirling in 1297 and Bannockburn in 1314, forming schiltroms, outward-facing groups. The English used this formation under Harclay at Boroughbridge in 1322. The Swiss won victories with pikes and became the favoured late medieval mercenaries. They developed offensive tactics of advancing phalanges. Charles the Bold of Burgundy's ordinance of 1473 detailed infantry tactics with pikemen kneeling while archers shot over their heads.

POLE-AXE
The pole-axe began life as an axe on a long pole, an infantry weapon. In its more familiar form it was a late medieval staff weapon, similar to a bill, *guisarme* or halberd. Its head was an axe blade with a spear point and hammer at the rear. The hammer distinguished it from similar weapons and it was used to stun or to poleaxe. It was also used by knights when fighting on foot.

POMMEL
The pommel was the extreme end of the sword hilt or dagger. Swords were constructed so that the blade had a projecting tang over which the parts of the hilt were threaded. The pommel completed the hilt and held it in place, the tang being hammered over the end of the pommel. The term came from Latin for a little fruit, in French a little apple. Pommel shapes help to distinguish types of sword – Oakeshott has identified 35. Modern attempts to

describe these shapes include cocked hat, tea cosy, scent-stopper and brazil nut. Pommels were often decorative; one from Sutton Hoo was decorated with gold and red garnets. A dagger from Paris was marked with arms on the pommel. The most common Viking pommel had three lobes. A disc-shaped pommel was popular in the later Middle Ages. After the medieval period old detached pommels proved useful for shopkeepers' weights. (Note: the word pommel was also used for the upward projecting front of a saddle.)

QUARREL (SEE BOLT)

SCABBARD
Container for a sword or dagger. The term is from Old French, the English equivalent being sheath. It protected the blade when not in use. Wood and leather were common materials, as in the Sutton Hoo example. The inside was sometimes lined with wool so that lanolin would prevent rust. The scabbard could have a locket at the top to grip the blade just below the hilt. The scabbard could be made of *cuir bouilli* (leather soaked and dried). The scabbard might be attached to a baldric, worn over the shoulder, or on a belt. Several scabbards survive. A 13th-century one from Toledo is made of two thin pieces of wood covered with pinkish leather. It ends in a chape of silver, a projecting piece of metal. Oakeshott believes the chape was meant to catch behind the left leg for ease in drawing the sword. It also protected the vulnerable end of the scabbard.

SEAX (SAX)
A short sword or knife with a heavy, single-edged blade wielded one-handed, associated with the Franks and Alemans. It was used by the Anglo-Saxons and Vikings. *Seax* was its Old English name, possibly from the Saxon folk as the *franciska* from the Franks though it may derive from the Latin *sica*, a Thracian weapon. Blade types included the angle-backed shape from the 7th century. The seax varied in length from 6 to 18

inches, with 12 inches the most common. The blade usually had a tang with a hilt, like a sword. The shorter seax is sometimes called a scramasax.

SHORTBOW
The composite bow favoured by mounted steppe nomads. The stave was of three pieces – a centre and two wings. The shape was formed over pieces of wood. Horn was glued to the inside of the wood, sinew to the outside, giving flexibility and power. The stave was bent backwards and secured with the string. Its smallness and power made it ideal for horsemen. The Saracens and Turks used shortbows. Shooting backwards over the shoulder was a skilled but common practice.

SLING
Used by David against Goliath and by medieval armies, made from a strap fixed to two strings, or to a staff. Whirling it built up speed before one end of the sling was released, projecting the stone. The sling of a trebuchet worked on the same principle. In ancient warfare slingers opposed cavalry. The sling appears in several manuscripts e.g. the *Psalter of Boulogne*, the 13th-century *Harleian MS 4751* and the *Bayeux Tapestry* (for hunting). It was used through the early and central Middle Ages. Geoffrey of Anjou used slings at Le Sap in Normandy, when 'many slingers directed showers of stones against the garrison'. Imperial forces used slings against Tortona in 1155 and Crema in 1159, when slingers operated from a belfry platform. Jaime I of Aragón used slingers like this in Mallorca. A cause of confusion is that a 'slinger' in Latin (*fundator, fundibalarius, fundbalista*) could be using a hand sling or a throwing engine. The 'Balearic slingers' probably worked engines. Richard the Lionheart was said to move on the march more swiftly than a Balearic sling. Slingers of uncertain type were used by Fulk le Réchin of Anjou at Le Mans. A 14th-century sling with a leather cup for the stone was found at Winchester.

SPEAR

A stave with a pointed end for thrusting or throwing. An ancient wooden weapon that could have just a sharpened and hardened end. Stone and bronze were used in prehistoric times for the head. By the Middle Ages the head was normally iron, with a sharp pointed blade, a tubular shank and a socket riveting it to the stave. Ash was a favoured wood, anything from 6 to 12 feet long. It was a common Germanic weapon. The word spear is Old English, though there were other OE words for it. It was the quintessential infantry weapon. It could be held and used in defence, for example against cavalry, or for thrusting, the basis for the pike. It could be hurled as a missile like a javelin. The missile spear would normally be lighter. It could be used from horseback and was the origin of the lance. Spearheads of varied shape, size and design have been found, including leaf-shaped, angular, triangular, lozenge-shaped, corrugated or barbed. Spearheads for thrusting often had wings to prevent the spear penetrating too far, so that it could be retrieved. Medieval armies frequently used spearmen, particularly in the earlier centuries. Spears figured prominently in warrior burials. The right to carry a spear was the mark of a free man. Throwing a spear against the enemy was a way of declaring hostilities.

SPRING-BOW

The exact nature of this device is unknown but it was probably a kind of crossbow triggered by the unsuspecting victim. It was a trap rather than a weapon. It was called *li ars qui ne fault* (the bow that does not fail). The first mention is by Gaimar in *L'Estoire des Engleis*, where the traitor Eadric devised one to kill Edmund Ironside. The king was shown into a privy where there was 'a drawn bow with the string attached to the seat, so that when the king sat on it the arrow was released and entered his fundament'. He died. The device became a figure of speech for any trap that could not fail.

SWORD

The medieval weapon *par excellence*. Iron made a significant difference, producing a thinner and more flexible weapon. The Roman sword was short and stout, primarily for thrusting. Its development probably came via the Greeks and Etruscans. Iron swords were found at La Tène on Lake Neuchatel. Styria was an important centre of manufacture. Early users were the Celts who developed the pattern-welded blade with strips of iron twisted together cold and then forged; twisted again and re-forged to the edges. The blade was then filed and burnished, leaving a pattern from the now smooth surface of twisted metal. Unlike bronze, iron was worked by forging rather than casting. Iron made possible a different structure for the sword, with a tang from the blade over which the handle could be slotted. Iron had advantages but a longer iron sword would bend and buckle if used for thrusting. Early European swords were long with cutting edges. When used by charioteers they needed length, best used with a cutting action. Much the same is true of cavalry swords. Swords from the first four centuries BC came from bog deposits in Scandinavia. Those at Nydam had pattern welded blades, about 30 inches long and mostly sharpened on both edges. A sword at Janusowice from the time of the Battle of Adrianople had a long blade and evidence of a leather scabbard. It had a large bronze, mushroom-shaped pommel. The sword at Sutton Hoo, old when buried, had a pommel decorated with gold and red garnets. It had rusted inside its scabbard, but X-rays showed it was pattern welded. The scabbard was of wood and leather.

Viking swords were outstanding in design and efficiency. What we call 'Viking' swords are common to those used over a wider area including Francia. They were of varied styles of blade and hilt. Petersen detected no less than 26 types of hilt. The hilt was formed over a tang from the blade, slotting over the guard, covering the grip, the end stopped with a pommel. The most common

Viking pommel had three lobes but there were many variations. Most Viking swords were plain but well designed. Some were decorated with patterns of inlaid copper and brass on the hilt. Thin sheets of tin, brass, gold, silver and copper might be used. Some had a maker's name or a firm's name. On one lower guard is lettering *Leofric me fec[it]* (Leofric made me). Other names are Hartolfr, Ulfbehrt, Heltipreht, Hilter and Banto. Ulfbehrt is found quite often, for example on a sword from the Thames. The name seems a Scandinavian–Frankish hybrid. Ulfbehrt swords date from the 9th to the 11th centuries. One should probably think of most as made by 'firms', no doubt family concerns, rather than by individuals. This manufacture probably originated in the Rhineland. Another name to appear in the 10th century, though less frequently, is Ingelrii – about 20 have been identified. A sword from Sweden reads *Ingelrii me fecit*. One finds other inscriptions and symbols, often enigmatic, including crosses, lines, Roman numerals and runes. Some names were of owners rather than makers, for example, 'Thormund possesses me'. Swords were sometimes named by their owners for example as millstone-biter, leg-biter. Viking swords became heavier from the 8th century, and in the 10th century there were design improvements. Later swords were not usually pattern welded and some were of steel, harder and more flexible. They were lighter and tougher with a more tapered blade, bringing the balance nearer to the wrist, and could be used for thrusting or cutting.

The sword became the weapon *par excellence* of the later medieval knight. The significance given to swords in literature, to Arthur's *Excalibur* or Roland's *Durendal* reflects this regard. It had symbolic value, in oath-making, dubbing, being blessed by the Church or promised to churches after the knight's death.

Late medieval swords were shorter and less flexible. Some survive – from burials, riverbeds and in churches, including 'Charlemagne's sword' which is probably 12th-century, the sword of Sancho IV of Castile late 13th-century, of Emperor Albert I c.1308 from his tomb, and of Cesare Borgia dated 1493.

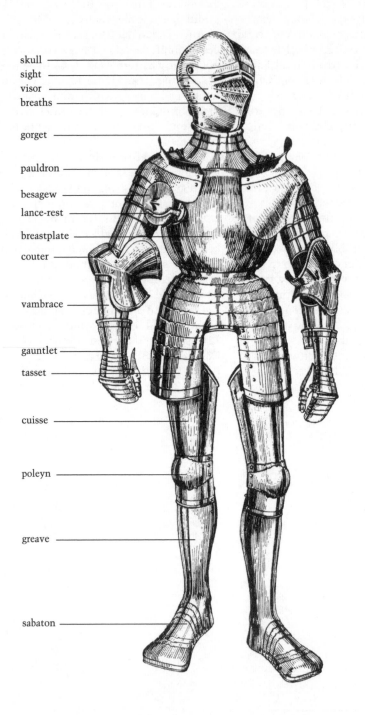

skull
sight
visor
breaths

gorget

pauldron

besagew
lance-rest

breastplate

couter

vambrace

gauntlet
tasset

cuisse

poleyn

greave

sabaton

A complete suit of late medieval plate armour

14 | Medieval armour

A–Z OF TERMS

Ailettes, aketon, armet, aventail, backplate, bard, bascinet, besagew, bevor, breastplate, brigandine, burgonet, byrnie, chausses, coif, cuirass, *cuir bouilli*, cuisses, espaliers, gambeson, gauntlets, gorget, greaves, haubergeon, hauberk, helmet, jack, kettle hat, lance-rest, mail, pauldron, plate, poitrine, poleyns, pourpoint, sabatons, sallet, shield, spangenhelm, spurs, surcoat, tabard, tassets, vambrace, visor.

OUTLINE HISTORY

There are close links between the development of medieval armour and medieval arms (see section 13). Again the influence of Roman and barbarian armour is obvious. The evidence comes from the same kind of sources: survivals, burials, manuscript illustrations and written accounts. It is equally true that the basic items of armour are of ancient origin – helmet, body tunic and shield. The Romans had separate items for limb protection, including greaves. Leather continued in use for certain items; shields were still commonly of wood and leather. In truth, early medieval armour saw little original development. Mail was not new and a mail tunic remained the main part of armour.

The major change in medieval armour came with social development, the rise of the aristocratic mounted knight. The knight used the best armour of his day, which came gradually to be a complete suit of armour. This occurred in parallel with improvement in metallurgy and manufacture, with the production of lighter and more flexible steel. Plate armour began with the introduction of single plates, probably first breastplates. The helmet came to cover the whole head and neck, with a movable visor for air and vision. Metal plates were produced for breast, back and limbs. Pieces were introduced to cover the gaps and protect the more mobile body parts – shoulders, elbows and knees. Laminated armour allowed flexibility to protect vulnerable parts. It consisted of separate strips or lames of metal, riveted together and overlapping, moving like a lobster shell. There was also constant change in style and fashion.

A–Z OF TERMS

AILETTES
Protection for the shoulders or neck, like epaulettes. The word is a diminutive from Latin *ala* via French *aile* for wing, describing their appearance. They were usually made of buckram or leather and sometimes carried metal plates. Ailettes became popular from the 13th century. They are generally depicted standing upright on the shoulder, so their purpose may have been to protect the neck rather than the shoulder itself. The German equivalents were *Tartschen*, meaning shields – suggestive of their purpose. They were generally rectangular but some were in lozenge form and others circular. Oakeshott believes they offered no protection and were for decoration. More commonly they have been considered to offer defence against a cut from a sword or axe, or a blow glancing off the helmet. Ailettes were sometimes decorated with arms and could have been for identification. In 1313 Piers Gaveston possessed ailettes decorated with pearls.

AKETON (HAQUETON/ACTON)
A stuffed jacket worn under mail, usually quilted or pourpointed, sometimes with sleeves, sometimes not. The name is from Arabic for cotton. The jacket was made of fabric, such as linen, and stuffed with tow or cotton. Saladin presented an aketon to Richard the Lionheart. It could be worn without armour as a protection in its own right for lesser infantry. The name was retained for a leather jacket with metal plate attached. The jupon was similar, sometimes worn over armour, and so was a gambeson – possibly just another name for aketon.

ARMET
A late medieval style of helmet with a visor, which replaced the bascinet in the 15th century. It had a skull-shaped cap made from a single piece of metal. The armet was worn with the brim resting on the ears, as with many modern helmets, but cheek pieces were riveted on and the rear covered the nape of the neck – all closing together to make a covering for the lower face. It had a visor with a forward point that could be raised and lowered, producing a rounded helmet with a beak-like projection. It probably originated in Italy.

AVENTAIL
Mail fixed to a helmet to protect the head or face, from French, meaning to let out air. The name was applied to mail covering the mouth or face in certain types of helmet. Mail aventails could be fixed inside late medieval bascinets with rivets, hung from rings or from a leather band that fitted over vervelles. This latter type of aventail had the advantage of being removable. The name was also applied to mail covering the head as in a type of coif or tippet.

BACKPLATE
Metal plate to protect the back in the later Middle Ages. There could be more than one backplate, as an upper and lower, or sometimes a three-piece arrangement. At first the backplate was joined to the breastplate by straps, hinges and buckles. Early and late a single plate was common.

BARD
A term for plate armour but generally used for the armour on a horse, commonly covering its breast and flanks. The Romans used mail for horse armour. One-piece coverings for the horse are called trappers. In the early Middle Ages the bard was shaped leather or a quilted cloth. In the 12th century Wace wrote of a horse

'covered in iron'. In the 13th century *cuir bouilli* was used and then separate plates of metal, but overmuch weight had to be avoided. The peytral was the plate for the chest, the crupper for the rear, and flanchards suspended from the saddle covered the flanks. Additional horse armour was a chanfron or *testière* for the head. The plates were generally attached by a mail crinet. A cloth with arms on was often put over the bard. A 14th-century chanfron is kept at Warwick Castle. A 15th-century Burgundian record mentions *une barde d'acier* (a bard of steel).

BASCINET (BACINET/BASINET)

A simple helmet to fit the skull, the most common helmet of the later Middle Ages. There were variations in shape. It could be pointed with ear pieces, have an added visor – either in a snout shape (pig-faced), or conical extending to the shoulders at back and sides. In later versions with visors, sometimes called great bascinets, the pointed top was at the rear not the centre. In the 15th century the rounded shape returned. Mail, including an aventail, was often attached to a bascinet for added facial or head protection. Early references are found in a statute of c.1295 (in French) as *bacynet*, and in 1298 (in Latin) in the will of Odo de Rossilion as *meum bassignetum*. Surviving examples are displayed in the Tower of London and the Wallace Collection. Bascinets were often worn by lower ranking soldiers, including archers. There are many medieval illustrations and brasses, including the miniature of Sir Geoffrey Luttrell from c.1340.

BESAGEW

Disc-shaped plates attached to a vambrace as part of plate armour. Besagews often had points at the centre like shield bosses. They protected weak points in plate armour but were also decorative. They were fastened by laces to the front of the shoulder and to the elbow. A late example is found on the Hastings brass at Elsing, Norfolk, of 1347. A later type was fan-shaped.

BEVOR

Plate protection for chin and neck, also known as a gorget, introduced in the 13th century. Its simplest form was a metal collar over the lower part of the head. The most common form had a forward point. Later examples were padded to protect the skin. In the 15th century the bevor could be a plate from visor to chest, usually with laminated plates at the bottom edge, strapped around the head and called a wrapper.

BREASTPLATE

Plate armour for the chest, probably the first plate armour and seen as the most vital. Ancient breastplates were of leather and bronze. Twelfth-century illustrations show warriors in mail but with plate chest protection, the *plastron de fer* or *poitrine*, generally fixed to the mail. At the same time we find plate armour for the chest worn under mail. From the 13th century came coats of plate, usually fitted to leather. In the 14th century occurred the move towards the suit of armour. The chest protection could be a single piece, often of pronounced rounded shape; sometimes more than one plate, the lower part called the plackart. Breastplates continued for less fully armoured troops. Swiss infantry, for example, often had only a helmet and breastplate. Two late medieval breastplates survive in the collection of the Tyrolean Trapp family. The first has plates fixed to a leather lining and was strapped to the body; the second is made of a single globular shaped piece of steel strapped directly to the body. Later breastplates often had lance rests attached.

BRIGANDINE

Body armour of metal rings or plates fixed to a garment of material such as leather, canvas or linen and also covered by material on the outside. It was similar to the coat of plates. The brigandine could be made from small overlapping lames and was flexible. It was the main body armour of infantry such as archers. Nobles also wore brigandines and the Earl of Shrewsbury was killed at Castillon in 1453 wearing only a brigandine for armour – not a great advert for replacing normal noble armour. The origin of the word is Italian, *brigantina*. It appeared in the 14th century in Italian records. Nicolle suggests that an early form was found in Russia in the 13th century. The first mention in England is of pairs of *briganters* in 1397. It was a common form of armour in the 15th century. Two late medieval brigandines survive in the Tower of London, both of plates placed between canvas on each side.

BURGONET

Both a steel cap worn mainly by pikemen and, more commonly, a type of helmet with a visor. The visor when raised resembled the peak of a cap and was riveted to the side of the skull piece. The word derives from French for Burgundian and it was also called a sallet of Burgundy. Its most common form was a close fitting helmet to cover the sides of the face but open at the front. It resembled certain kinds of classical helmet and was light in weight. It remained a popular form of helmet in the early modern period.

BYRNIE

A mail tunic. The word is from Old Norse, used for the Anglo-Saxon garment – the 'battle shirt' of *Beowulf* – the same in practice as the Norman hauberk. The byrnie could be made of leather, metal scales, rings sewn to leather, or mail. The term is used of Carolingian mail, its export forbidden in capitularies (Latin *brunia*). In 805 each man from 12 mansi called to the host must possess a byrnie. In the *Anglo-Saxon Chronicle* every eight hides must provide a helmet and a byrnie, seen as the vital armour. A mail byrnie was found at Sutton Hoo. The Viking in Harald Hardrada's army who defended the bridge at Stamford Bridge in 1066 wore a byrnie (OE *brunie*).

CHAUSSES

Leg armour, appearing when armour developed for the whole body. Leg mail is shown on some warriors on the *Bayeux Tapestry* and was common by the 12th century, when Wace wrote of 'chausses of iron' (*chauces de fer*). In Spain both Christians and Muslims wore chausses. Sometimes they covered the shins and were laced behind. Others were like stockings. The brass of Sir John d'Abernoun at Guildford shows mail chausses covering the feet. Fabric stockings were worn under them. Mail chausses continued in use after the introduction of plate armour but in the later Middle Ages were replaced by plate.

COIF

Armour for the head, from Late Latin *coifa/coifia* for helmet, usually of mail, shaped like a balaclava helmet and open at the front. It was a general word for any close fitting cap. The protective coif was often part of the body mail, made to lace or buckle at the side of the head. A woodcut from Willemin shows a mail coif over a cap of material. From at least the 13th century, it was a separate item. From the end of that century it covered more of the shoulders. The coif could be the only head protection but sometimes a steel cap was worn under the mail, and often a separate helmet was worn over the coif. In the late Middle Ages mail was attached to the helmet as a tippet.

CUIRASS (CUIRIE)

Armour to cover the upper part of the body, combining breastplate and backplate. Armour for this purpose was the main armour of ancient times. The term comes from Latin *corium* (leather), from which the cuirass was originally made, the term as armour first appearing in the 12th century. The fact that it consisted of breast and back armour is emphasised by references to pairs of cuirasses. Hardened *cuir bouilli* pieces were also used. It was worn over the hauberk and under the surcoat. With the development of plate armour, the piece that covered this part of the body continued to be called a cuirass, the plates commonly fastened at the side with laces or buckles.

CUIR BOUILLI

From the French, meaning boiled leather though it was in fact not boiled but treated with cold water, moulded into shape, and allowed to dry hard. It was used for armour, especially for difficult shapes, for saddles, sheaths, helmets, cuirasses, leg armour, armour plates and shields. Its use continued throughout the Middle Ages. Boiling was not the normal process since leather boiled in water is ruined and leather boiled in oil becomes permanently soft. Probably it was not boiled with wax either, though this is commonly said. A medieval document speaks of bottles made with leather *boulues de cire*, but the meaning of 'boulues' here is uncertain and it may not mean boiled. The actual process was to soak the leather in cold water for up to 12 hours. It was then kept damp until ready for moulding. It was dried at a low heat and given a wax finish. The reason for the term is a mystery but may come from a misunderstanding of the drying process. The resulting material was tough and light. The technique was ancient but armour made by the process was most common in the central Middle Ages.

CUISSES

Armour to protect the upper leg. Cuisses could be made of material, leather, plates or overlapping scales. Gamboised cuisses were of quilted fabric and worn either under or over chausses. They are illustrated in the *Maciejowski Bible* c.1250. They were tied, strapped or buckled round the leg. In the 14th century cuisses of plate metal were common. In the 15th century one finds more elaborate cuisses of scales or overlapping lames for greater flexibility. In London the makers of cuisses were known as kissers.

ESPALIERS (EPAULIERES)

Protection for the shoulders, consisting of a single plate or of overlapping plates.

Initially it may have been a term for shoulder padding underneath armour, possibly originating in the Middle East or Islamic world. Whalebone was sometimes used for espaliers in tournaments. They were common in the 13th and 14th centuries. An English form of the word was spaudler.

GAMBESON

Quilted jacket or tunic, normally worn under armour, probably the same as an aketon. The word may derive from Old Frankish *wamba* meaning belly. It could also be worn without metal armour, or over the top of armour. It emerged in the 12th century, mentioned by Wace and William the Breton. Gambesons were sometimes of silk, presumably for luxurious comfort, or for show. The Assize of Arms of 1181 (Henry II) expected gambesons for burgesses in contrast to mail coats for knights. A 1284 French document shows gambesons worn by the middling wealthy, as against hauberks for the wealthier. Initially the gambeson was worn in place of other armour. Later it was worn either under or over armour. The early 14th-century monument of Sir Robert Shurland shows an outer quilted gambeson as a short-sleeved tunic decorated with his lord's arms. One source described the *wambasia* as a thick tunic made from linen and tow or old cloths.

GAUNTLETS

Armoured glove from the French *gant* (glove). They could be of leather, comonly buff, but were usually leather or fabric with metal plates fixed over. A 1296 French record mentioned *gantelès* with plates fixed to fabric. Sometimes the part extending over the wrist and lower arm was of overlapping lames, resembling wicket-keeping gloves. A common form consisted of a larger plate over the back of the hand and smaller separate plates for the parts of fingers and thumbs, sometimes with spikes or gadlings over the joints. The surviving gauntlets of the Black Prince were of chamoised deerskin with gilt latten riveted on.

GORGET

Plate armour for the throat, from French *gorge* for throat or neck, the same thing as a bevor, protecting the gap between helmet and breastplate. It appeared in the 13th century, replacing the camail. A 1296 French document listed *gorgières* of plate, and one of 1302 referred to *gorgerets*. It was often in two pieces that fitted round the neck and joined together. The helmet rested upon the gorget, transferring pressure from the head to the shoulders. In later armour gorgets were of laminated pieces rather than single plates. Charles the Bold of Burgundy was killed at Montlhéry in 1453 when his gorget fell off and he was wounded in the throat.

GREAVES (JAMBS)

Armour for the lower leg, from Old French *greve* for the calf. Greaves like shin guards, strapped to the leg, are called demi-greaves. An English term was *schynbald*. Charlemagne wore iron leg armour at Pavia in 773. Greaves as plate armour appeared in the 13th century though the term is not known until the 14th century. Close greaves were of two hinged plates covering the lower leg, tied or buckled. Greaves were often shaped to fit over ankles and instep. Some were made of *cuir bouilli* and patterned.

HAUBERGEON (HABERGEON)

A small hauberk, an alternative word for hauberk, originally meaning a shorter mail tunic. Wace in the *Roman de Rou* has the Conqueror at Hastings wearing a hauberk, and his half-brother Odo a haubergeon. Some authorities suggest the haubergeon was a quilted garment worn underneath mail. A 15th-century riddle contradicts this suggestion – 'Question: what is heavier the more holes it has? Answer: a haubergeon' (suggesting that it was heavier when the mail rings were smaller and therefore more numerous). A 14th-century source described *hauberjons à mailles* (haubergeons of mail) – though this does not preclude haubergeons of other material.

HAUBERK

The quintessential armour for the earlier Middle Ages, a mail tunic, originally meaning only neck defence (Frankish *halsberg*, from *hals* for neck) but soon applied to the whole tunic. Hauberks often had attached coifs. An 837 southern French will mentioned a helmet with a hauberk (*halsberga*), which may have been simply a helmet with mail neck protection. Hauberks varied in shape and length, with short or long sleeves or no sleeves at all, and in construction. The skirt was usually split, sometimes only at front or rear, sometimes both, sometimes at the sides. Hauberks might be of banded mail (attached to leather or material) or riveted, of single, double or triple mail – referring to the way in which the links were joined. The mail tunic without material backing appeared from the 11th century. Illustrations of hauberks are common and appear, for example, on the *Bayeux Tapestry*. Some seem to have a rectangular neck opening with laces. Wace says that the Conqueror wore a hauberk (*haubert*) in the battle. Examples survive from the Battle of Lena in 1208, and one from Prague said to have been St Wenceslas' (d.935) – though it may be later. It is of riveted iron rings with the skirt split at the rear and a laced neck opening. Hauberks were found at Wisby from 1361. The edge of surviving mail often tapers into smaller links, causing the garment to cling to the body. Although we consider the hauberk to be mail armour, medieval writers used the term also for garments with scales or plates. Chaucer described a hauberk 'strong in every plate'.

HELMET

Armour for the head, an essential part of equipment. The Germanic and Old English word *helm* meant hidden, from covering the head. Early medieval helmets were often of leather with metal additions, sometimes of *cuir bouilli*. More exotic materials were not unknown, even crocodile skin. Later helmets were usually metal, though Waterer believes that leather, particularly *cuir bouilli*, continued in regular use, often covered by mail. Such helmets were lighter and useful in tournaments. Through the early Middle Ages a conical helmet was popular, as used by Vikings and Normans. Conical helmets commonly had a nasal projecting over the nose to guard the face. These helmets often had a metal frame and a strip round the bottom edge, like a birdcage without a bottom. This type is known as a *spangenhelm*. Such helmets sometimes had hinged cheek and neck pieces, like the Sutton Hoo helmet – which also had a face covering. The Coppergate helmet from York had mail attached for the neck. Some helmets were made from a single piece of metal. One such at Prague, supposedly St Wenceslas', has the nasal riveted on, while one in Vienna has helmet and nasal of one piece. With the development of plate armour the style of the helmet changed. From the 12th century a cylindrical flat-topped helm became common, covering more of the head. Late medieval helmets often had visors, riveted to the helmet and lowered when in action, protecting the face. Various styles of helmet appeared through the period, including bascinets (skull caps) and kettle hats. Kettle hats had broad brims and were common in the later Middle Ages. The late medieval knight normally wore a great helm, enclosing the head and protecting the neck. These were commonly made of separate plates riveted together, including a visor with a slit for the eyes and holes for breathing. In this later period the fashion of wearing crests on helmets returned, often in association with heraldic arms. The great helm of the Black Prince is preserved in Canterbury Cathedral. Helmets were often donned only at the last minute, as at the Marchfeld in 1278, when the order was given: 'Helms on'. At Tagliacozzo in 1268 Charles of Anjou's knights removed their helmets during a break in the fighting.

JACK (JAKKE)
A jacket or coat, similar to an aketon or brigandine, generally of fabric and quilted, commonly worn by late medieval infantry. Sometimes jacks had added metal plates. Although usually associated with common soldiers they were at times worn by others. In 1381 John of Gaunt's jack was set on a post in the Strand and used by archers for target practice.

KETTLE HAT
A type of helmet popular in the later Middle Ages, especially with common infantry, a metal hat with a broad brim, resembling a sun hat. The French called it a *chapel de fer* and the English a *shapewe* from the French *chapeau* or *chapel*. It appeared in the 12th century and became common in the 13th. The sloping brim offered defence from downward blows. It could be worn over a mail coif. Joinville loaned his kettle hat to Louis IX to replace an enclosing helmet so the king could get more air. Examples are illustrated in the *Maciejowski Bible*, where the brim is riveted to a skull cap and laced under the chin. In 14th-century examples the cap is domed like a fireman's helmet.

LANCE-REST
An addition to the late medieval breastplate to support the weight of a couched lance, which by this time had become heavier. The rest was generally a hinged bracket riveted to the right side of the breastplate though sometimes attached to staples. It resembled a projecting clothes hook. The earliest known example is on an effigy from c.1386, but lance-rests only became common in the 15th century. A fewter, or felt butt on the saddle bow, served the same purpose.

MAIL
Mail provided body defence throughout the Middle Ages, as in a hauberk or byrnie. The

word comes from the Latin *macula* (net) via the French *mailles*. It is 'the net of armour' in *Beowulf*. In the early Middle Ages mail was widely used for body armour, as in Scandinavia, Byzantium and the Islamic world. Mail was used to defend the head, as a hood attached to the hauberk or a separate coif. Pieces of mail were used to defend parts of the body, with gauntlets, chausses or pieces attached to the helmet to protect the neck. Mail could also protect the limbs. Charlemagne wore mail arm and thigh protection. It was also used for horse armour. Mail could be attached to material forming the garment or it could be unsupported. Mail usually consisted of metal rings joined together. The rings could be made complete and joined by riveted links, but more commonly the ring was placed around another ring and butted together or riveted to complete the circle. The typical construction was each ring joining four other rings. Mail was sometimes made stronger by joining more rings together and producing double or triple mail. It could be tailored to fit the body by reducing the size of rings at the edges. Some mail found at Vimose had rings one-eighth of an inch in diameter, others a quarter of an inch. Mail continued in use through the period of plate armour.

PAULDRON (POULDRON, SPAUDLER)
Armour for the shoulder, from Old French *espauleron* for shoulder, modern French *épaule*. This plate defence appeared as a separate item from the late 14th century and was common in the 15th century. The pauldron for the left shoulder was commonly larger than that for the right, because the knight rode left shoulder forwards and it allowed more freedom for the right arm. This is the case in Giovanni Cose's armour in the Louvre. The pauldron was often made from overlapping lames for flexibility.

PLATE
Plate armour was the main body defence in the later Middle Ages. Plate was a literal term for the thin sheets of metal from which the armour was made (Medieval Latin *plata*). The initial use of plate armour was for a breastplate. Additional pieces were made to protect other body parts. William the Breton in the early 13th century wrote of protection from 'worked iron plates'. Early on plates could be sewn to material to make a garment. From the 13th century the metal protection was sometimes constructed apart from material. By the 14th century the body could be completely protected by a suit of armour. This remained the main protection for knights even after the Middle Ages. Certain regions were noted for the manufacture of plate armour, including the Low Countries and Lombardy. Certain regional styles developed such as German and Italian. There were improvements in the production of metal so that late medieval armour was of good quality steel, the shine causing it to be known as white armour.

POITRINE
French term for breastplate.

POLEYNS (GENOUILLIERES)
Plate armour for the knees. Poleyns appear in 13th-century illustrations, such as the Trinity College *Apocalypse* from c.1230, but the term appeared first in the inventory of Hugh de Clermont in 1331. Possibly early poleyns were of leather or *cuir bouilli*, but iron plate may have been used from the beginning. Early examples show poleyns attached to chausses or cuisses. The plates became larger in the later 13th century, enclosing the whole knee. In the 14th century a smaller poleyn again became popular. Late medieval poleyns often had side wings and lames between them and the other leg armour.

POURPOINT
Quilting for padded armour, normally referring to the jacket worn underneath armour or as armour in its own right for poorer troops, the aketon or gambeson. The

jacket could itself be called a pourpoint, as in a record from Henry III dated 1252 (*unum purpunctum*).

SABATONS
Metal protection for the feet in the later Middle Ages, appearing first in the 14th century. A 1314 effigy has pointed shoes of metal plates joined by rivets. Plates for a sabaton were found at Wisby from 1361. More commonly sabatons were made of overlapping lames covering the top of the foot, as on the brass of Sir William Fitzralph of Essex, c.1330, the lames riveted together. The sabaton was laced to the foot. Fifteenth-century German examples had sharply pointed toes. Some had squarer or rounder toes such as the 'bear's-paw' type, and some take this to be the true sabaton, referring to earlier foot armour as sollerets. A sabaton was also a late medieval Flemish shoe with a broad toe.

SALLET
A late medieval semi-globular, skull-fitting helmet, especially in the 15th century, from Italian *celata*, also called a *salade* (salad) but the derivation is obscure. It was popular in Italy and Germany. The sallet was probably a development of the kettle hat. It normally had a shelving piece to protect the back of the neck and often a visor. It resembled the old coalman's hat. The German version has been compared to a sou'wester and was common in western Europe. The tail part over the neck was often made by adding lames. The sallet could be combined with a bevor to protect chin and throat. Surviving sallets are to be found at St Mary's Hall in Coventry, in the Wallace Collection, in Vienna and at the Tower of London. They also appear in many manuscript illustrations.

SHIELD
A vital part of protection though not truly armour. The shield was used for heraldic decoration. It was an ever-present part of the knight's gear through the central and later Middle Ages. The early medieval

shield derived from Roman and barbarian examples, including small bucklers or long curved semi-tubes. It could be made from wood and leather, *cuir bouilli*, or metal. The frame was generally wooden, and the covering leather sometimes horn. Metal was also used for frames and for the central boss and, when used for the shield itself, generally in the form of plates. Straps (*enarmes* and *guiges*) for holding and carrying were usually of leather but some shields had wooden or metal grips at the centre fixed to the boss so that the hand could fit in the hollow of the boss. The Sutton Hoo shield had a wooden frame covered with hide and decorated with bronze fittings. It was 92 cm in diameter. Lime, the linden wood, was popular for Anglo-Saxon shields. By the 11th century the common shield was kite-shaped as on the *Bayeux Tapestry*. From the 12th century the top became flatter and the shape triangular. With the growing prominence of cavalry, smaller shields became more popular. The late 12th-century shield of Arnold von Brienz survives in the Landesmuseum Zurich. It is made of lime, with leather covering and straps. A heraldic silver lion, moulded in *gesso duro*, stands on a blue background. In the later Middle Ages the shape that we recognise as shield-shaped was most common, and connected with heraldic decoration. Viking shields were frequently red and the *Bayeux Tapestry* shields have a variety of geometric and figurative designs. True heraldic shields appear in the 12th century, as on the enamel of Geoffrey V of Anjou. Many late medieval shields had a *bouche*, a notch in the right-hand corner to support the lance. In this period the shield was used in tournaments but often ignored in battle. The shield was the mark of a warrior and was commonly buried with its owner. It might be used to carry the warrior from the field. In eastern Europe the shield was a symbol of peace, perhaps deriving from its protective rather than offensive function.

SPANGENHELM

A type of helmet made from strips of metal (the *spangen*) forming a frame with a band of metal for the rim. The frame formed a conical shape. A nasal could be added by projecting the front piece of the frame downwards. The surface was covered with metal plates or sometimes horn. It was common in the central Middle Ages. The *Bayeux Tapestry* illustrates this type. The term is a modern German one.

SPURS

An attachment to the heels of a cavalryman for urging on the horse, usually of metal, commonly with a spike or wheel. The single spike or prick spur was most common through the central Middle Ages. The metal arms altered to a curved shape either side of the prick in the 12th century. The rowel spur appeared in the 13th century, as on a seal of Henry III, becoming popular in the 14th. It was argued that the appearance of the spur coincided with that of the knight, since the cavalry charge would be impossible without it. It now seems clear that spurs developed well before the social significance of the knight became marked in the 10th or 11th century. Spurs were in any case never exclusively for military use.

SURCOAT

Long coat of material with a loose split skirt worn over armour, then called coat armour (*cote à armer*). Some surcoats had sleeves, some not. It displayed the wearer's coat of arms or his lord's. It gave some protection from rain or sun. It appeared in the 12th century with heraldry, becoming common in the 13th. It may have been borrowed from the Saracens. An early example appears on the seal of Waleran of Meulan. Sometimes the surcoat was made into armour by adding metal plates. The surcoat could resemble a uniform, for example as worn by the Hospitallers.

TABARD

A garment worn over armour, shorter than the surcoat and open at the sides with short sleeves or no sleeves. It might be worn with a belt. It could be decorated with the wearer's arms. It was also worn by ordinary soldiers and could be non-military. Its was common in the 15th century. The tabard was also the coat worn by a herald or pursuivant.

TASSETS (OR TACES)

The skirt of plate armour, becoming longer in the 15th century. Tassets were usually made of riveted lames, and the description of one type as a lobster tail gives a good impression of the appearance.

VAMBRACE

Plate armour for the forearm, from the French *avant bras*. An early term for the whole arm protection was bracer, meaning arm defence, also an archer's wrist protector. Armour for the upper arm was the rerebrace (from *arrière bras*). After the Middle Ages the vambrace was applied to armour for the whole arm, the parts being upper and lower cannons. The vambrace appeared in the 14th century, though similar defences appeared in illustrations of Muslim warriors from the 9th century. Early western examples were gutter-shaped to cover the outer arm, as on the Fitzralph brass in Pebmarsh Church, Essex, c.1320. The German vambrace was more flamboyant, with flutes. The plates were usually strapped in position. Vambraces enclosing the lower arm were hinged so the plates closed over the arm, and were strapped together.

VISOR

The front part of the helmet over the face with an opening for vision and breathing, from *vis*, Old French face. It is normally taken to be the part of the helmet fixed at each side for lowering and raising. Some 14th-century examples were hinged to the helmet at the top of the visor (German *Klappvisier*). The visor would normally be lowered when the wearer was in action. A popular late medieval form (on the pig-faced bascinet) was shaped like a snout.

Early face protection was usually a fixed part as on the Sutton Hoo helmet. The Byzantine Emperor Manuel wore a visor in 1150. The will of Odo de Roussillon of 1298 mentions a *heaume a vissere*. Visors on helmets were common in the 14th century.

Jean Courtois, Sicily Herald for the King of Aragón, c.1420

15 | Heraldry

OUTLINE HISTORY

A complete history of heraldry would continue up to the present time showing its continued influence. Heraldry was a medieval invention and the Middle Ages its great time, when it was functional as well as decorative. It was essentially a military development, although it soon had other applications.

The origins of heraldry are obscure and there are virtually no records on how and when it began. Its probable line of development was from a fashion in decorating shields as one felt inclined, to the identification of individuals who always used a specific shield decoration, to the claim of such a design as exclusively the property of that individual and his family.

The first source for heraldry is literary, where coats of arms are described in words. Since the art of blazon was not developed these do not provide accurate information. The second, and perhaps most important, source is the armorial on a personal seal. This is usually an accurate source though for administrative not military purposes, and the use of seals may post-date that of coats of arms. Seals are also monochrome, lacking information on tinctures. The third source is manuscript illustrations, some in colour, but with relevant material even later than from seals. Many illustrations also related to fictional or pre-heraldic figures whose arms were invented.

A study of sources suggests some facts that can be accepted, but first we must

distinguish between true heraldic arms and pre-heraldic. There are, for example, decorated shields on the *Bayeux Tapestry* but they are not heraldic. Heraldic arms follow
certain rules of composition. To be heraldic there must be a hereditary element.

It is said that heraldic arms appear in the middle of the 12th century but we would
propose a slightly earlier date. The earliest known arms show similarities between
lateral members of families (such as brothers). This could be due to lateral borrowing
but it seems more likely that the similar arms of brothers or cousins derived from a
common ancestor. So if in the second quarter of the 12th century we find lateral arms
it seems probable that the origin is a generation back, that is at the start of the 12th
century. The shields depicted in the *Stephen Harding Bible* of c.1109 would support
this proposition. They are not truly heraldic, portraying biblical and not contemporary figures, but they seem to follow heraldic rules of composition. Recognisances
were mentioned in a chronicle source at Tinchebrai in 1106. John of Marmoutier
recorded that Henry I gave arms to his son-in-law Geoffrey of Anjou in 1128. This is
often discredited as written later but may be confirmed by the enamel of Geoffrey at
Le Mans, showing armorials with lioncels. That the arms borne by Geoffrey were
lioncels suggests possible evidence for the early use of what became the English royal
arms.

We should investigate the origin of heralds, later the arbiters of heraldic disputes
over the right to bear particular arms and the rules of heraldic design. The term herald
(Old French *herault/hiraut*; Old German *heriwald/hariwalt*; Latin *praeco*) was applied
to men who announced tournaments, made announcements for rulers or carried messages for commanders. Orderic Vitalis referred to a herald (*praeco*) at Jerusalem in the
First Crusade in 1098, who made a proclamation through the Christian camp. He was
called *Mala Corona*, which has the ring of a herald's title.

It is probable that armorials became important for identification though there is
little evidence to prove it. Armour became more enclosing and its wearer less visible
in the 12th century. Armorials on a shield, helmet or coat could distinguish the individual. This had not happened by 1066 when William the Conqueror removed his
helmet at Hastings to show his face in order to prove he was alive. Through the Middle
Ages armour progressively covered more of the body. Armorials became fashionable
with the growing popularity of tournaments, where heralds took charge.

The linking of relatives through their arms in heraldry developed at the same time
as the emphasis on hereditary right. By the end of the 12th century the passing of
armorials to sons was well established, along with differences to distinguish one
member of the family from another. It is the family possession of armorials that marks
heraldry – the idea that a particular design belonged to a family. There were later legal
cases when two or more claimed the same arms – showing that the concept of exclusivity had developed. In the 13th century the use of armorials became virtually
universal among the aristocracy. By the end of the Middle Ages lesser men could also
bear arms. In England there was more social exclusivity than in most regions, where
tradesmen and peasants might be allowed arms.

The collection and illustration of coats of arms was undertaken (often by heralds)
and provides evidence of individual arms and the extent to which the rules had
become established by the central Middle Ages. Armorial Rolls, showing coats of arms
belonging to individuals, were kept from the 13th century. Heralds became recognised

experts and arbiters, with their own uniform of tabards by the 14th century. In Europe by the late Middle Ages some million individuals had armorials.

The earliest known treatise on heraldry, by Bartolo de Sassoferrato, dates from c.1356. Edward III created Windsor Herald, Lancaster Herald and probably some pursuivants (the lesser heralds) – including Blue Mantle. Henry V created Rouge Dragon. The English College of Arms was founded in 1484 under Richard III.

A–Z OF TERMS

ACHIEVEMENT
The display of armorials in full, including crest and supporters.

BLAZON
The description of armorials in words. Emblazon is the painting of armorials – though the word blazon originally covered this sense too. Blazon means accurate heraldic language, describing the arms in full so that they might be emblazoned. The development of blazon came with the development of rules for heraldry. In England the language of blazon is largely Anglo-Norman. The blazon follows clear rules that must be obeyed with regard to layout and tinctures. The term comes from Old German *blasen* (to blow a horn), from the function of a herald. Initially it was more common to speak of blazing arms than of blazon.

CADENCY (SEE ALSO DIFFERENCE)
Marks of cadency distinguish or difference similar armorials within a family. The marks may be in the upper part of the shield, the crest or the supporters. Strict rules came to apply. For example the mark for the eldest son became the label, for the second son the crescent and so on. The label first appeared in the 13th century. Cadency is from Latin *cadere* (to fall), and means descending in order through the family cadets.

CANTING ARMS
Armorials where the choice of motif has a pun or play on words on the bearer's name. Examples are sheaves of cumin for Comyn, lucies (or pikes) for Lucy, a castle for Oldcastle, the fleur-de-lis (lily) for the city of Lille. A common reason was that the bearer had an easily portrayed name such as of an animal or bird, say Fox or Swan. The Italian Prince Orsini had a bear device because in Italian *orso* meant bear. The arms that Shakespeare had approved for his father bore a spear. The term is from Latin *cantare* (to sing), meaning repetition.

CHARGE
Whatever was placed on the field of a shield other than ordinaries and lines of partition. A shield could be charged with a chevron or other similar mark. A charge could be virtually anything. Common charges were animals such as a lion, plant or star. A charge could be placed on a crest or upon another charge.

COLOURS
Colours in heraldry are specific colours opposed to the metals. The permitted colours are gules (red), sable (black), azure (blue), vert (green) and purpure (purple). Certain colours were more favoured in certain countries, for example azure in France and sable in Germany. Gules was the most used colour and azure next.

CREST
An addition to the armorials on the shield, in origin the crest placed upon a helmet. Arms might be painted upon the helmet itself. A crest appears on the 1197 seal of Baldwin of Flanders, Latin emperor. Though not precisely a crest, the charge of lioncels on the arms of Geoffrey V of Anjou is depicted upon his hat in the enamel at Le Mans. In rolls from the 14th century the

crest was depicted above the shield in a complete achievement. Crests were popular additions to armorials for tournaments, when many weird and wonderful examples were produced, including models of beasts, winged birds, trees and horns – not unlike fashion hats at Royal Ascot. The crest was attached to the helmet by mantling, sometimes seen as part of the crest, or sometimes as a separate entity, but in any case part of the full achievement.

DIFFERENCE

Distinguishing similar coats of arms within a family. The differencing might be in tincture of either shield or charge, or in additional charges. The major example is cadency, distinguishing the sons from the father. Other means of differencing were to move the charge on the shield or add a border. Medieval differencing was freer. More restrictive rules of cadency were enforced in the 16th century.

FIELD

Surface of the shield, or any other object, on which all other parts of arms were placed. Shields were never blank, having at least a surface tincture. In general the field was the background to the arms. It could be divided but is the whole shield surface. The field of royal prerogative was entirely gules, as in some royal arms.

FURS

Tinctures deriving originally from furs used for armorials in the field. The two furs are ermine and vair. Ermine is the fur of the arctic stoat as it turns in winter, white with a black tip to the tail, an expensive fur. Ermine is shown as argent with sable spots or other shapes, placed in rows. Vair was shown as alternating blue and white bell shapes in rows, alternating as upright and upside down. Vair was a term for various furs for lining garments, particularly Siberian squirrel with its blue-grey and white.

HERALD

Initially the speaker for an important person such as a king (Old French *heraut*; Old German *heriwald*), meaning messenger or crier. He made announcements and delivered messages. Heralds were often involved in military affairs, where announcements and exchanges with the enemy could be vital, giving them a diplomatic function. They took on an important role in tournaments, making announcements, dealing with entries, and enforcing regulations. Heralds had to describe arms and regulate them. They became the experts on arms and the arbiters. Heralds made records of armorials for rolls of arms. They later conducted visitations on correct usage. They gave their name to the practice of heraldry. They have remained historians of heraldry, from William Dugdale and Elias Ashmore to Sir Anthony Wagner. From the 14th century heralds had their own 'uniform' in the tabard – a tunic bearing the arms of their lord. The College of Arms was set up in 1484. In England the College of Arms has three kings of arms (Clarenceux, Garter and Norroy), six heralds (Chester, Lancaster, Richmond, Somerset, Windsor and York) and four pursuivants (Blue Mantle, Rouge Croix, Rouge Dragon and Portcullis). These offices were established by medieval and Tudor kings, notably Edward III, Henry V and Henry VIII.

METALS

There are two metals in heraldry, or and argent (gold and silver), which may in practice be represented by yellow and white. They are tinctures and treated as separate from colours and furs. A basic rule is that a metal must not be placed upon a metal or a colour upon a colour. Thus if the field is argent the charge upon it, say a lion, must not be in or. This rule may have originated for visibility, so that the charge would stand out.

MOTTO
Words on an armorial, probably originating
from personal war cries. The cry of the
individual was transferred to his coat of
arms. Later, phrases were invented to apply
to a bearer, perhaps with a pun on his name.
In depicted armorials the motto is
sometimes placed above the arms, but more
usually in England in a scroll under the
arms. The exclusive rules of the shield do
not apply to mottoes, which may be altered
at will. Famous mottoes included those of
the English kings, *Dieu et mon droit* (God
and my right) and the Prussian kings *Gott
mit uns* (God with us).

ORDINARIES
Charges on the shield made from
geometric shapes by horizontal, vertical or
diagonal lines. Ordinaries are distinct from
lines of partition, which are simply a
division of the field. A charge could be
placed upon the ordinary. There is some
debate over the number of ordinaries but it
is generally thought there were nine
honourable ordinaries. The principal
ordinary is the chief, taking up the upper
third of the field. The pale is a band, taking
up one-third at the centre of the shield
from top to bottom. The bend is a band
taking up one-third of the shield from the
dexter chief – right top – to the sinister
base – left bottom (left and right on the
shield are always seen from the bearer's
point of view). The bend sinister (not an
honourable ordinary) is reversed, beginning
top left. The fess is a horizontal band
taking up a third of the shield at its centre.
The chevron is a band at the centre of the
shield shaped like an upside-down letter V.
The cross is in effect a pale plus a fess, as
the saltire is a bend plus a bend sinister.
The escutcheon is a shield within the
shield, one-fifth of the width of the main
shield. When this is in the exact centre it is
called the inescutcheon. The bar is the
same as the fess, but smaller, taking up a
fifth of the shield. There were variations on
all these major or honourable ordinaries.
There are some dozen sub-ordinaries or

general ordinaries, sometimes combining
two honourable ordinaries – thus the gyron
is a combination, quartered and divided per
cross and per saltire, the result being an
eight-fold division of the shield from a
central point. The pile is a wedge, with
point usually downwards – like an upside-
down pyramid, but the position can vary.
The quarter takes up a fourth of the shield
in the upper dexter of the shield. Other
general ordinaries are orle, canton and
flaunch.

PURSUIVANTS
Initially apprentices who attended the
heralds, from the French for candidates for
office or followers. In practice, pursuivants
were lesser heralds. The English
pursuivants are Blue Mantle, Rouge Croix,
Rouge Dragon and Portcullis. Edward III
probably created Blue Mantle and Henry V
Rouge Croix. The other two were
established by Henry VIII.

QUARTERING
The division of the shield to represent the
armorials for a different branch of the
family. The proportion of the shield for this
purpose may in practice be less than an
actual quarter. The son of a father and
mother both of whose families have arms
may quarter his shield, with the mother's
family arms in the second and third
quarters. Edward III claiming to be King of
France as well as England quartered the
royal arms of England with those of France.
This process continued after the 15th
century and could lead to multiple
quarterings – Queen Victoria had arms with
256 quarterings.

REBUS
Pictorial pun on the bearer's name,
sometimes with an object to portray each
syllable. Abbot Islip's arms had a man
falling from a tree calling 'I slip'. It was
usually a simple device; the more subtle
efforts being known as canting arms.

ROLLS OF ARMS

Collections of arms, usually with illustration, the best evidence for medieval armorials. A roll was a convenient reference for the identification of arms, and rolls became important evidence in family claims to hold certain arms. One reason for the early making of rolls was to identify combatants in a tournament. Another purpose was to list those appearing in a royal army. In England such rolls exist from the 13th century. There are about 30 medieval rolls for England, though most survive in later copies. Glover's Roll dates from c.1245. The Falkirk Roll lists those serving Edward I against the Scots in 1298. The Roll of Caerlaverock is unusual in its context, the poem *The Siege of Caerlaverock* (1300). It describes over a hundred coats of arms. A French royal herald, Gilles le Bouvier, made one compilation in the 15th century, recording arms for France and other western nations including England and Scotland. His method was by visitation of the bearers in their homes, which became practice in England for visits by heralds to check and correct claims to arms.

SHIELD AND ITS DIVISIONS, THE

The shield was probably the first area to be covered in heraldic arms, and the normal means of displaying them. To distinguish individual arms, one could add charges or make partitions of the shield in geometrical lines. Some of these divisions were known as ordinaries and sub-ordinaries, which were themselves charges. Others were simply partitions of the shield. The divisions were made apparent by the use of different tinctures. The upper third of the shield was chief, the central third fess, the lower third base. The right-hand third of the shield (to the bearer) was dexter, the left hand sinister, the central section pale. Such divisions could make patterns. A multiplication of horizontal bars made the shield barry. The use of horizontal and vertical lines produced the chessboard pattern known as checky. A multiplication of diagonal bends made a shield bendy; of the horizontal pale made paly; and of chevrons chevronny. A band around the edge of the shield is the bordure. A shield covered with regular diamond-shaped lozenges is lozengy. Quartering the shield was the means of adding family arms in separate partitions. These are only a few of the more common methods of dividing a shield.

SUPPORTERS

The figures or designs added on either side of the shield. They appear to be holding up the shield, so the term is literal. They appeared in the 14th century on seals, probably as an artistic fancy to fill out the space. Another, less likely, theory is that they came from human supporters dressed in fanciful costumes, carrying the shield at tournaments. Supporters are usually seen as an extra ornament and not a fundamental part of the coat of arms – but the right to use supporters is considered more exclusive than the right to coats of arms. In France supporters are divided into *tenants* (human), *supports* (animals) and *soutiens* (objects and plants). Lions are particularly popular. Supporters are associated with the arms of peers and certain knightly orders.

TINCTURES

Overall term for all the colours, metals and furs that may be used on a shield.

VISITATIONS

A largely post-medieval development in England, whereby heralds made tours to record, check and correct the use of arms, beginning in the 15th century as part of an attempt at central, royal control of the use of arms. From the 14th century kings of arms made surveys of arms borne. William Ballard, March King of Arms, made a limited visitation in 1480. Such local visitations began in the 15th century but became more official and thorough from 1530 under royal commissions. The last visitation occurred in 1686.

14th-century Flemish infantry on the Courtrai Chest

16 | Medieval armies

A–Z OF TERMS

Antrustiones, *arrière-ban*, bannerets, battle, *buccellarii*, *caballeros*, *carroccio*, cavalry, *comitatenses*, *comitatus*, *condottieri*, *conroi*, *écorcheurs*, federates, feudal service, *fief-rente*, *franc-archers*, free companies, *fyrd*, hobelars, household troops, *huscarls*, indenture, infantry, lance, medical provision, mercenaries, militia, *ministeriales*, scutage, *servitium debitum*, standards, stipendiaries, strategy, supply, tactics, uniforms, *vavassors*, war cries.

OUTLINE HISTORY

Medieval armies varied considerably in size and composition. One of the major problems is to find trustworthy sources. Chroniclers were notoriously unreliable on numbers – for a single battle one can have very different estimates. Even administrative sources are not necessarily accurate, usually incomplete and often pose problems of interpretation.

One needs to combat modern misconceptions about medieval armies, in particular to address the idea of what was a 'feudal' army, and the proportion and significance of heavy cavalry. In brief most armies of any importance contained both cavalry and infantry. There were obligations in most nations for men to provide military service, often a duty to serve in a national crisis. We need not broach arguments over the nature of feudalism but it was common in the central Middle Ages for rulers and princes to give land in return for obligations of military service. Commonly this was tied to the provision of a knight, a well-armed and trained cavalryman. There are similar arrangements in Byzantium and the Middle Eastern states and even further afield.

It is clear that armies were rarely composed only of feudal forces. Practically all armies contained an infantry element. In the later Middle Ages infantry, sometimes supplied by urban militias, became increasingly important. In English armies the ratio of archers to men-at-arms increased to about three to one. It was rare for a large medieval army to be without mercenaries or stipendiaries. Paid soldiers were employed in princely and noble military households. 'Allies' might also be paid, as were the hired troops in late medieval companies. By then whole armies often consisted of paid men.

Military households descended from the war-bands of barbarian kings or chieftains. Members owed allegiance to their lord, often reinforced by oaths. In return the lord gave shelter and sustenance. Practically all medieval rulers had military households, often expanded in war. Most household men needed the lord's wealth to support their living. One example is the *huscarl* of Scandinavian and late Anglo-Saxon kings. Perhaps their greatest significance is their permanence; trained soldiers, they were the precursors of professional troops and standing armies.

Mercenaries were also significant. An individual could easily exchange one status for the other. Basically a mercenary required pay in return for his fighting presence. Mercenaries might be employed short- or long-term. The increased financial resources of medieval rulers made possible the employment of more mercenaries more often. They replaced traditional forces raised through national duty or feudal obligation. Mercenaries could be employed throughout the year for long campaigns. National and feudal troops were not normally poorly trained and we should remember that medieval man was accustomed to a state of almost permanent war, so that most men were prepared and experienced in action. Nevertheless mercenaries came closest to being professional warriors. In the later Middle Ages they appeared in cohesive bands under captains, employed *en bloc* by a ruler. They were often engaged as specialists – heavy cavalry, light cavalry, archers, spearmen, pikemen and so on.

It has been argued that medieval armies were smaller than once assumed. Exact figures are rarely if ever available but reasonable estimates support this thesis in general. Medieval armies seldom consisted of more than a few thousand men and sometimes of only a few hundred. We must however be cautious, since large numbers were often available and we can rarely be certain how many were used.

It is important to analyse the composition of medieval armies. They were normally well organised in units, small and large. The major divisions were often called 'battles' – three, four, or more, to an army. Men often fought in regional groups – Bretons on the left, Normans on the right. There were smaller units, such as *conrois*, consisting of 10 or 20 men.

If armies were less feudal than has been thought, in their command they were mostly royal and aristocratic – social position taking precedence over military ability. No one could command an emperor or a king. Overall command of allied forces was a tricky affair and allied armies often, as a result, did not combine well. Kings were usually expected to lead their armies and it was rare for lesser men to receive the same respect. A sensible king could recognise military capacity in subordinates, and trusted lieutenants could improve their master's command ability or compensate for lack of it; one thinks of Mercadier serving Richard the Lionheart or Cadoc for Philip Augustus. The army was subdivided and commanders were required for the battles and divisions. These would commonly be nobles, who usually brought, under their personal command, a proportion of the whole army.

Armies needed organisation. There were numerous necessary tasks such as assembly, grouping, feeding, supply, weapons and clothing, accommodation, pack animals, arrangements for river crossing or transport overseas. The royal or noble household was often vital, with officials responsible for particular tasks. When one considers the problems of travel and transport one realises that organisation in some ways posed greater difficulties than in modern times.

A–Z OF TERMS

ANTRUSTIONES
Close followers of Frankish rulers in the Merovingian period, part of the ruler's *trustis*. The term derives from Salian *trust* meaning helper but the English idea of a trustee, someone who can be relied upon, is not far from explaining their status. They are much the same as early war-bands of chieftains, forming the nucleus of an army, ready for immediate employment. An *antrustio* had to appear at court in arms and make an oath of fidelity, taking the prince's hand – an obvious link with the oath of homage.

ARRIÈRE-BAN (RETROBANNUS/ ARIBANNUM)
A general call to attend the host – for example in national emergency, the military obligation on all free men to serve in the host – found chiefly in the 12th and 13th centuries. The *heriban*, a related term, was a Frankish tax on those who failed to perform their service. It sometimes had a more restricted significance, applying only to those holding certain lands. It made possible the raising of a large force by the ruler for a declared purpose.

BANNERETS
Knights with their own following, of perhaps 20 knights, who had the right to a banner, or square flag, carried before their group. It was thus a higher rank of knighthood, often granted by the king for deeds performed in battle. Bannerets formed the core of the royal military household. Edward II had 32 bannerets in his household plus 89 ordinary knights.

BATTLE
In addition to the usual meaning of an armed conflict, a battle was a division of a medieval army. Three to five battles made up a typical army. One battle could be the vanguard and one the rearguard. Each was normally under a leading noble, in England commonly an earl, under the overall command of the king.

BUCCELLARII
Household warriors, literally 'biscuit-eaters' – referring to the fact that the lord supplied their food. The term is found during the barbarian invasions and in Byzantium. The *buccellarii* belonged to lordly households and war-bands. They received arms from their lord, which had to be returned if they changed masters. In Byzantium in the 7th century *buccellarii* were incorporated into the imperial army.

CABALLEROS
Two types are found in Castile and León from the 11th century: the *caballero hidalgo* was of higher social rank, normally a fief-holder owing military service, though sometimes a mercenary; the *caballero villano* was a peasant knight used in light cavalry. *Caballeros* were used by Christian rulers against the Muslims, especially in border fighting.

CARROCCIO
A special kind of standard used by cities in Italy. It was normally a wagon or cart with banners on it, commonly of the local patron saints. It marked the central command and rallying point for an army. The *carroccio* of Milan was mentioned in

1039, coloured red and white, with the banner of St George, guarded by several hundred men, and drawn by white oxen. Florence's *carroccio* in 1260 was an ox cart bearing relics and banners that had been blessed, guarded by a gonfalonier and 50 knights. When Frederick II captured the *carroccio* of Milan in 1237 he had it dragged through Cremona in triumph. A *carroccio* made an appearance in England with the English army fighting for King Stephen at Northallerton in 1138 (the Battle of the Standard). The cart contained a ship's mast to which the banners of the local royalist bishops were fixed. At the top was a silver pyx containing the host. A *carroccio* with a dragon banner was used by the Latins on the Third Crusade at Arsuf in 1191.

CAVALRY
The mounted part of an army. Roman armies had been dominated by infantry, their cavalry seen as auxiliary and provided by barbarian troops. The barbarian states normally possessed cavalry. Heavy cavalry developed to become the élite in the army. The wealth to arm such troops brought a change in society. The socially privileged could afford to equip themselves well and provide the horses. Thus the landed wealthy became the military cavalry. This kind of force was often provided through feudal means, by the granting of land in return for military service. It saw the rise of the knight. Heavy cavalry, cataphracts, also developed in Byzantium and there too a kind of feudal tie emerged. The usefulness of cavalry was increased by training. Tournaments allowed practice at concerted charges, flank attacks or feigned flights. The breeding of war-horses was essential to the improvement of cavalry. The need for more permanent forces and larger numbers of cavalry led to the employment of lesser men as mounted sergeants – sometimes as light cavalry. Late medieval mercenary companies contained heavy cavalry, especially in Italy.

COMITATENSES
Originally those in the field army of a Roman emperor, later all Roman imperial troops based in provinces, as opposed to frontier troops. The term is also used for members of a barbarian *comitatus*.

COMITATUS
The war-band of a chieftain or king, from the 11th century a fief whose vassalage involved the right of ban. Such fiefs were granted, for example in France and Flanders, to great lords who were expected to attend the royal court.

CONDOTTIERI
Italian mercenary troops, derived from the *condotta* or contract of employment of these troops. Originally the *condottiere* was the captain of the force but *condottieri* became the general term for all the troops employed. They were first used by Italian city states, usually on short-term contracts. Later long-term contracts became more common. *Condottieri* were common in the last two medieval centuries, often in companies gathered from many nations. They consisted largely of cavalry. The *condottiere* Braccio developed a tactic of using his squadrons in rotation so that there were always fresh troops to throw into the fray. Famous captains included Michelotto, Sir John Hawkwood, Niccolò Orsini, Francesco Gonzaga and Roger de Flor.

CONROI
A small unit of the army, usually 10 to 20 knights, though sometimes larger. The term is from French, literally 'with the king'. A *conroi* could be a family group or the following of a lord. *Conrois* allowed tactical use of small groups, suggesting greater sophistication in medieval armies than once supposed.

ÉCORCHEURS
From medieval French, meaning 'flayers' or 'skinners', used of mercenary companies. They caused devastation in France in the

later Hundred Years' War, especially when not employed and supporting themselves by living off the land. They were renowned for ruthlessness and atrocities. Charles VII of France replaced the wide use of mercenaries by raising a larger standing army through ordinances.

FEDERATES (*FOEDERATI*)

Troops employed by the Romans in addition to regular forces, similar to later mercenaries or allies. They were mainly barbarians fighting for pay under their own chiefs. They were common in late Roman armies, especially against barbarian invaders. Some thought that Rome's reliance on them was too great for its own good. Federates were often the cavalry in a largely infantry army. Early Byzantium also relied heavily on federates.

FEUDAL SERVICE

Feudalism is a modern historical concept, deriving from the term for the land given as a *feodum* or fee. Attempts to define medieval society too closely are usually doomed to failure – there are always exceptions and modifications. 'Feudal' cannot describe all society or all the armed forces available. In military terms there were arrangements whereby land was given by a king or lord in return for military service from an individual. What began in a modest and haphazard manner spread to become common though not universal. Princes were able to raise large forces of well-armed men, the land supporting the cost. Feudal service is seen as the promise to give knight service as heavy cavalry for the parcel of land known as a knight's fee. It carried an obligation to serve for certain periods, sometimes 40 days a year. Such arrangements were never uniform and not a 'system'. Feudal service was one of several options open to a medieval prince in raising an army. Modern extensions of the term to mean something like 'medieval' or 'old-fashioned' have deprived it of almost any value.

FIEF-RENTE (MONEY FIEF/*FIEF DE CHAMBRE*/PURSE FIEF)

Term for a money payment as the equivalent or substitute for land, in return for military service, seen as a semi-feudal arrangement, illustrating the difficulty of defining medieval practice. Those who served in this way were virtually mercenaries. The money was usually paid on a regular, annual basis. For example Henry I of England promised £500 per annum to the Count of Flanders in 1101 for the service of a thousand knights.

FRANC-ARCHERS (FREE ARCHERS)

A system of militia created by Charles VII of France in 1448 to provide his army with trained archers. Localities contributing to the scheme were given tax privileges. The number of soldiers was linked to the number of hearths in each locality, for example one archer from every 80 hearths. It made about 8,000 men available. They had to train regularly and were organised under captains. The local community provided the equipment. The system included other infantry, pikemen, handgunners, longbowmen and crossbowmen. Louis XI extended it to new regions. The success of Swiss infantry, whom he now employed, led him to abandon the system after 1479.

FREE COMPANIES

Companies of mercenaries that acted independently, offering their services to any prince they chose. They appeared from the 12th century. They normally had a captain, a noble and/or leading military figure, who made an agreement or contract with the employing prince. They included *écorcheurs*, *condottieri* and the great companies such as the Catalan Company, the German Great Company, and the White Company in Italy. Over a hundred companies were formed. When unemployed they often created a nuisance, not least in France. Powerful governments suppressed them in their own states.

FYRD (FIERD)

The Anglo-Saxon army, though 'force' is a better translation, since the naval equivalent was the ship-*fyrd*. The term carried a sense of national military service. The free adult male population was available for service in the *fyrd*. Some have suggested there was a smaller force derived from this, a 'select' fyrd of the best-armed and -trained men. The whole force available was not generally called upon but there is no clear evidence that reduction was achieved by a distinction over the quality of the troops. Armies were normally assembled on a regional basis, and not all regions were called on at a given time. There developed some similarity to feudal arrangements, with military service tied to land – a man serving for every five hides. Norman kings continued to use the *fyrd* obligation for some time.

HOBELARS

Light mounted troops in Britain, either light cavalry or mounted infantry. In the latter case they were usually archers or spearmen who rode when the army was on the march. They were socially inferior to knights and not heavily armoured. They probably originated in Ireland – Irish troops, with horses known as *hobinos*, were employed by the English. Hobelars first appear for Edward I against the Scots. They were recognised as a specific group; a 1372 record refers to 'men at arms, hobelars, archers and others'.

HOUSEHOLD TROOPS (FAMILIA/MESNIE)

With the end of Roman domination the military household became the nucleus of most armies. Barbarian kings and chieftains led war-bands, and the military household (Latin *familia*; French *mesnie*) was a direct descendant. A king needed a household for administration, including for war. He maintained men to raise, organise and supply his armies. Members of the household, normally aristocratic, were commanders under the king. There were household men whose purpose was to fight, including bodyguards. The household lived and ate with the king and was supported by him. In return, members swore loyalty and gave service. In war the household became the nucleus of the army. There are many examples of loyal household troops fighting for their king to the bitter end, even after his death. Although paid and supported they were the most loyal troops that could be obtained.

HUSCARLS (HOUSECARLS)

Employed in the households of Scandinavian rulers, mainly as bodyguards. They were trained soldiers, provided with arms and armour. They were paid for their services and in this sense were mercenaries, the nearest thing to professional soldiers. The institution was brought to England by Danish conquerors of the 11th century and retained. The *heregeld* was a tax to raise money to pay *huscarls*. Many received land, tied to their military service – a similar development to feudalism, though *huscarls* fought as infantry. *Huscarls* fought for Harold at Hastings. They fulfilled a similar function to later household troops.

INDENTURE

A type of contract by which an individual or group was paid an agreed sum by an employer (king or lord) in return for a specified period of military service. Early indentures, in the 14th century, were for short periods but in the 15th they were more extended. Surviving indentures are useful historical military records.

INFANTRY

Often underestimated in medieval warfare, probably because it consisted of lower social ranks and was not given much attention in chronicles. Infantry was the mainstay of Roman armies, in which cavalry was treated as auxiliary. Through the early medieval period most armies depended chiefly on infantry, as in Viking and English armies. Even when knightly cavalry became significant, infantry remained important. It was the main counter to concerted cavalry charges. Sometimes the best-armed and -trained troops were dismounted to strengthen infantry against cavalry, as in Anglo-Norman warfare. Another major solution to heavy cavalry was more use of missile troops, especially archers, to strike the cavalry from a distance before it could make impact. The best medieval armies were balanced with good infantry as well as cavalry. In the later Middle Ages infantry became increasingly significant, from their use in greater numbers and from their specialist significance. Among the most respected were English longbowmen, Italian crossbowmen, and Flemish and Swiss pikemen. With the advent of guns, artillerymen and handgunners joined the list. One should note that sieges were more common than battles in medieval warfare, when the role of infantry was bound to be dominant.

LANCE

A kind of spear for cavalry and also a unit of fighting men. In the mid-14th century, for example, a lance could consist of one heavy armoured knight plus several mounted archers. In 15th-century Burgundy a lance could be a knight with his page, an armed sergeant, three mounted archers, a crossbowman, a handgunner and a pikeman. The lance was a group of men under a knight. Later medieval mercenary companies often consisted of lances; Michelotto's company contained 600 lances (*lanze*). Each company set up by Charles VII of France's ordinance in 1445 included 100 lances, each with a man-at-arms, a *coutillier* (with knife and sword), a page, two archers and a valet – all mounted.

MEDICAL PROVISION

Provision was often inadequate but some effort was made. Noble and royal households often included a doctor. The Church sometimes provided men to assist the wounded and dying. Medical knowledge, though limited and crude by

our standards, increased through the Middle Ages, not least with the spread of Islamic culture to the west and the growth of universities (notably Salerno and Montpellier). Hospitals also were funded. Warfare offered a practical field for medical research. In the 7th century a Byzantine manual covered the removal of arrowheads and how to deal with broken bones. Byzantine armies included surgeons in the 6th century. Richard the Lionheart, when wounded at Châlus by a crossbow bolt, was attended by a surgeon – albeit unsuccessfully. The monk Guyot de Provins expressed a common view of medieval medics – 'Woe is him who falls into their power'.

MERCENARIES

Soldiers who fought for pay. The problem in the Middle Ages is to define the rewards received. Feudal troops could receive pay for support and additional service. Allies and household men were often paid. We understand mercenary to mean one who would fight for any cause and see medieval mercenaries as fighting for another country or prince – a situation that made them as unpopular then as now. More populous areas, such as Flanders and Italy, often supplied mercenaries. Men from certain regions – such as Flanders, Gascony or Switzerland – were respected and in demand. A captain usually received pay from the prince for his company. Contracts were made to employ troops, including *condotta* and indentures. Companies appeared in the 12th century and were important in the later Middle Ages. From the 14th century paid troops were the core of most armies, though some were nationals rather than foreign.

MILITIA

Troops raised in towns or regions, not generally seen as professional troops. In the later Middle Ages many urban militias were well trained and effective. Some served as an obligation to their community and were supported financially by the community. By the 14th century uniforms were often provided; men of Tournai wore red tunics with a silver castle. Initially militias were to protect their town but they were also used in more broadly based armies, especially when trained and armed. Wealthy areas with growing cities, such as Flanders and Italy, produced excellent militias. Militias from the Lombard cities resisted German imperial armies. Militias of the Flemish communes defeated France at Courtrai in 1302. Swiss militias won victories against Burgundy, German and Austrian armies. Some militias were composed of a balance of troops; others were specialists, such as pikemen or archers. They still retained an amateur appearance. A captain of militia at St Albans in 1461 was a butcher (who hanged himself when his side was defeated).

MINISTERIALES (DIENSTLEUTE)

Knight-serfs, unfree soldiers (or servants) in Germany. *Ministeriales* is Latin for Dienstleute (servants), appearing under Conrad II (HRE) in the 11th century. They gave military service to their lords. Some held land to which the service was tied. They had to defend their lord's land, but were compensated for additional service.

SCUTAGE (SCUTAGIUM)

Tax paid instead of performing personal feudal military service, meaning shield money (Latin *scutagium*). The first English reference was in 1100 under Henry I for St Pancras Priory at Lewes in Sussex. By 1200 scutage had become a regular tax.

SERVITIUM DEBITUM

(Military) service owed in a feudal arrangement, literally the singular 'service owed', the plural being *servitia debita*. The term is associated with England after the Conquest, but existed elsewhere. The king agreed or imposed a quota of knights owed by a lord for his land. Taxes such as scutage, paid instead of service, were calculated according to the *servitium*. William the Conqueror, after the distribution of English lands, was owed *servitia* of about 6,000 knights, mostly for two months' service in war and 40 days in peace per annum. The service owed could include riding service, or watch service, as well as service in the army. Later the services were often reduced or commuted for money payments.

STANDARDS

Flags carried in battle. The 1138 clash at Northallerton is known as the Battle of the Standard because standards in a cart were used like an Italian *carroccio*. A standard was an ancient way of marking the leadership of a group. Each standard bore distinguishing marks – images, designs and sometimes text. Standards were used by the Romans and throughout the Middle Ages. A standard provided a signal flag for group manoeuvres and a rallying point. Standards could represent individual nobles or princes. In Italian urban militias each specialist group of soldiers (such as pikemen) had a standard. The loss of a standard meant disgrace while captured standards were valued trophies.

STIPENDIARIES

Soldiers, generally knights, serving for a stipend – a money payment or wage paid regularly. Some historians distinguish stipendiaries from mercenaries but this seems pedantic.

STRATEGY

The overall planning of warfare, particularly of campaigns, from Greek, the plan of the *strategos* or general. As with tactics so with strategy, older historians sneered at medieval methods, denying that strategy existed. More recent studies (for example Smail, Contamine, Gillingham) show this is untrue. It could normally only be a concept of princes and kings. Thus strategy might be determined by a ruler's decision to invade and conquer, as Edward I did in Scotland or Henry V in Normandy. Most princes followed a cautious strategy, avoiding pitched battle and favouring control through sieges and garrisons. Sometimes strategy was limited to creating damage and panic, as with the *chevauchées* of the Black Prince. Popular medieval military handbooks, such as those by Vegetius, Pierre Dubois and Christine de Pisan, contained views on strategy.

SUPPLY

The provision of what an army requires – food, drink, clothing, transport, camp gear, arms, armour, fodder and so on. Food and drink were the main necessity, with the need for fresh supplies. Well-organised supply was always a major factor in war. Supply for distant campaigns could be particularly difficult, requiring careful planning. When supply is insufficient, problems follow – desertion, atrocities, damage from foraging to compensate for failed supply, even death. Good supply is often the province of government and requires good communication with the army, with information on its changing needs. Medieval armies realised the need for good supply. Carolingian capitularies reserved two-thirds of grazing in some regions for the army and arranged for carts to transport supplies. Improvement came with the streamlining of taxation and bureaucracy. Ability in this area explains the military success of some rulers who may not have been great generals – Philip Augustus springs to mind. It was important to disrupt the enemy's supply, hence the emphasis on crop destruction, pollution of water sources, attacks on supply trains, and breaking lines of communication – destroying bridges, blocking roads and ports or barring river traffic. In England from about 1300 the development of prise (the compulsory purchase of food for armies, later called purveyance) was a move towards larger-scale organisation. Protection and storage mattered. On crusade in Cyprus, St Louis collected heaps of wheat and barley as large as hills. The corn on top sprouted after rain and was wasted but that underneath remained useable.

TACTICS

It was formerly believed that medieval armies had little planning or organisation. It is now acknowledged that strategy and tactics were a constant part of medieval warfare. There are so many factors involved in tactical decisions that one cannot give comprehensive cover in a brief note but there are countless examples of the use of tactical positioning – for example on a hill, or with flanking cover, as from marsh or river. The benefit of surprise was recognised, of using hidden forces and reserves. The past was studied for information. Geoffrey V of Anjou, while at a siege, studied the *De Re Militari* of Vegetius – a frequently copied work. The bishop of Auxerre expatiated on Vegetius before a crowd of knights in c.1200. The nature of weapons and troops available influenced tactics such as concerted knightly charges, dismounting men-at-arms, use of missile forces like archers, or defensive pike formations. The importance of training was understood, as shown in tournaments, or by practice manoeuvres of militias. Armies were formed from tactical units – major divisions such as battles and lesser groups such as *conrois* or lances, making possible battlefield moves including steady advance, angled advance, advance in echelon, flanking attack and organised retreat. Mistakes were made and some commanders lacked tactical ability but medieval warfare usually involved tactical thinking. The survival of a document on how Agincourt might have been fought (in the way it never was) shows that tactics were considered before battle as well as during it. There is evidence for the use of scouts to give advance warning of enemy movements (as at Brémule), and of messengers to keep the command informed during battle. Major considerations were how to use available forces, such as mounted knights or gunpowder weapons, to their best advantage, how best to counter enemy strengths, for example by taking good positions or presenting obstacles such as stakes, trenches or missile troops, and how best to attack the particular opposition.

UNIFORMS

It is not easy to know when uniform was worn in medieval times though the need to distinguish two sides was a constant. Ways of doing this, apart from wearing identifiable clothing, included following a standard, wearing a badge or plume, or using a war cry. Heraldic arms developed partly to identify an individual or a group during battle. This partly explains the use of similar arms for a family and its branches – usually fighting on the same side. The development of groups paid by a single source increased the likelihood of uniforms, as with mercenary companies. Urban militias were often provided with uniforms. The men of Tournai in 1340 wore blue jackets and white hats. The crusader cross was an identifying mark. In the 14th century forces from Wales and Cheshire wore green and white uniforms. Most medieval uniform was not reserved for military use but had social significance too. The use of uniforms increased in the final two medieval centuries. There were some national elements in symbols, like the cross of St George for English troops, but universal national uniform in the modern sense did not exist.

VAVASSORS (VAVASSORES)

Lesser vassals, similar in meaning to vassals but generally understood as 'vassals of vassals', called rear-vassals or under-vassals. In the *Bayeux Inquest* of 1133 a *vavassor* was a free tenant with military obligations who performed military service with arms, armour and a horse. *Vavassors* could hold land, sometimes a fraction of a knight's fee. They were found in England, France and Italy. They demonstrate the complexity of feudal arrangements.

WAR CRIES

Usually originating as a family or national signal in war, an appeal for support in action. With the development of heraldry the war cry was often incorporated as a text in family arms. Examples include the '*Hui hui*' of the Magyars. War cries were often to saints – the English 'St George', the French 'St Denis'.

Krak des Chevaliers seen from the north-west of the castle

17 | Castles and siege warfare

A–Z OF MAJOR CASTLES

Abinger, Aigle, Alhambra, Amboise, Arques, Arundel, Beaufort, Beaumaris, Bled, Bodiam, Bodrum, Bonaguil, Bouillon, Burghausen, Burwell, Caernarvon, Carisbrooke, Castel del Monte, Castello Sforzesco, Castel Sant'Angelo, Châteaudun, Château-Gaillard, Chepstow, Chillon, Chinon, Cochem, Colchester, Conway, Corfe, Domfront, Doué-la-Fontaine, Dover, Drachenfels, Falaise, Gisors, Grandson, Habsburg, Hälsingborg, Harlech, Hastings, Haut Koenigsbourg, Herstmonceux, Hochosterwitz, Hüsterknupp, Karlštejn, Kerak, Kirby Muxloe, Krak des Chevaliers, Langeais, Lewes, Linz, Loches, London, Louvre, Málaga, Mantua, Margat, Marienburg, Montréal, Montreuil-Bellay, Montségur, Muiderslot, Niort, Nuremburg, Nyborg, Orford, Plessis-Bourré, Plessis-Grimoult, Rhodes, Rhuddlan, Riga, Roche-Guyon, Rochester, Salzburg, San Gimignano, Saumur, Segovia, Silifke, Sirmione, Stirling, Stokesay, Tarascon, Thun, Trifels, Trim, Valladolid, Vincennes, Visborg, Wartburg, Werlar, Windsor, York.

A–Z OF TERMS

Adulterine castles, *archères*, artillery, ashlar, bailey, balearic sling, balista, barbican, *bastide*, bastion, belfry, *bergfried*, berm, bore, brattice, brigola, cannon, castellan, castle-guard, cat, catapult, combustibles, concentric castles, counter castles, crakkis, crenellation, curtain, donjon, drawbridge, *en bec*, fonevol, forebuilding, *funda*, Greek Fire, hoarding, keep, machicolation, mangonel, mantlet, merlon, *meutrières*, mining, moat, motte, parapet, paterell, pavise, pele, petrary, portcullis, postern, ram, rampart, ravelin, rendability, ribaudequin, scaling, scorpion, sow, spur, talus, testudo, trebuchet, ward.

OUTLINE HISTORY

Castle warfare is a phase in the history of siege warfare. Fortification existed from early times, as evidence of earthwork sites proves. Settlements have often been defended, by earth ramparts or timber stockades, by wet and dry moats, or by walls. European medieval siege warfare descended from Roman methods. Fortified towns and camps existed in the earliest medieval period. Equally ancient were methods of attacking and taking fortified places – by agreement, trick, blockade, storm and various methods of breaking in. Many siege weapons came from the Romans, including rams, bores and throwing engines.

A major medieval development was the emergence of the castle, a residence as much as a fortification, representing an exclusive element in society. Castles were built for kings and lords and were relatively small. They appeared from about the 10th century, probably modelled on town citadels. The first known European castles were noble residences turned into fortifications in the Loire valley at Doué-la-Fontaine and Langeais. Fulk Nerra of Anjou was an early castle builder. Over the next century such stone fortifications became more common as residences and strongholds of kings and nobles.

A more basic type of castle emerged, of earthwork and timber – the motte and bailey. It appeared first during the wars between the Carolingian Franks and the Vikings. Such castles could be built relatively quickly and cheaply and during a campaign, as in the Norman Conquest of England, or the English Conquest of Ireland.

By the 12th century the typical castle was a fortification with stone walls and a stone keep. Earlier earthwork castles were often transformed into stone. The Crusades influenced western castle architecture, from familiarity with Byzantine fortifications. Great stone castles were built in the Holy Land. Castle defence brought changes in methods of attack with powerful throwing engines and methods of breaking walls, including boring, ramming, mining, belfries and Greek Fire.

The history of castle warfare is a tit-for-tat affair: improve the defences; improve the weapons of attack. A major change in the 13th century was the introduction of round towers along with improvements to gatehouses and moats. The result was the concentric castle, with more than one surrounding wall. Edward I's castles in North Wales are excellent examples of concentric castles.

Then came an improvement in weapons of attack. Most throwing engines of the period – catapults, mangonels, balistas and so on – were adapted from ancient weapons. An original medieval machine was the trebuchet, using counterweights rather than torsion or tension. Trebuchets could hurl enormous stones and demolish walls. An even more powerful late medieval weapon was the cannon. Some cannons used in sieges were very large. Defenders improved walls and widened moats against cannons, while making platforms and loopholes to use cannons for defence.

Social change in Europe made the castle less desirable. Houses that were warmer, brighter and drier became preferred residences for the great and powerful. In England the castle is medieval, the country house later. In France the term château, which had meant castle, came to mean country house.

A–Z OF MAJOR CASTLES

ABINGER, SURREY, ENGLAND

A Norman motte and bailey castle, excavated in 1949. On the flat top of the motte was found a rectangle of postholes, remains of a timber keep. The castle dated from c.1100 though the keep was rebuilt in the 12th century. Other postholes showed that a timber palisade surrounded the edge of the motte platform. The keep was on four main corner posts like stilts, as at Dinan on the *Bayeux Tapestry*. A horizontal wooden bridge connected the bailey to the motte.

AIGLE, SWITZERLAND

Fairytale castle with conical roofed towers set against the snow-capped Alps south-east of Lausanne. The castle dates from the 11th century and was extended in the 13th century. It was captured by Berne in 1475 and rebuilt in its present form. The curtain wall is massive with round corner towers, one of which is the keep. There is a large rectangular building in the courtyard. There is brattice-work above the entrance.

ALHAMBRA (THE RED FORT), GRANADA, SPAIN

A Moorish fort, part of the Alcazaba citadel of Granada. The citadel dates from the 9th century, the Alhambra from the 13th. It is seen as a gem of European architecture. The Justice Gate was built in 1348 with a vaulted passage. The Alhambra, held by the Nasrid Sultan Boabdil (Muhammed XII), surrendered to the Christians in 1492, the climax of the *Reconquista*. The Alhambra became a palace for Ferdinand and Isabella.

AMBOISE, FRANCE

Near the Loire, between Tours and Blois. A Frankish fortress stood here. Fulk Nerra captured it from Blois in the late 10th century. He passed it to his treasurer Sulpice who built a new tower. Charles VIII of France was born here and rebuilt the castle in its present form in the 15th century. It is more a Renaissance château than a medieval castle. It became a prison and then the residence of the comte de Paris.

ARQUES-LA-BATAILLE, FRANCE

On a rocky coastal headland in northern Normandy, south of Dieppe, built by William count of Arques from 1038. He rebelled against William the Conqueror, who besieged Arques in 1052–3, accepting its surrender and suppressing the rebellion. From 1123 it was rebuilt in its present form by Henry I, who added a rectangular keep with flat buttresses. It was the last castle to resist Geoffrey V of Anjou's conquest of Normandy, 1135–45, falling in 1145. Philip Augustus captured Arques in 1204 during his conquest of Normandy after two sieges. It was taken by Henry V in 1419 and recovered by the French in 1449. The north-west barbican was added in the 16th century. The castle was damaged in the Second World War.

ARUNDEL, WEST SUSSEX, ENGLAND

By the River Arun, built by Roger of Montgomery earl of Shrewsbury soon after Hastings, the stronghold for a Sussex Rape. He built a motte and bailey castle, with a bailey on either side of the motte. It passed to the crown in 1101 after a siege by Henry I. The motte was crowned by a 12th-century shell keep. It was the first base for the Empress Matilda on her arrival in England. It was held by the Aubigny earls of Sussex, the Fitz Alan earls of Arundel, and the Howard dukes of Norfolk. It underwent frequent additions and alterations. The 19th-century work has left little of the original.

BEAUFORT, LEBANON

Crusader castle at Qalaat es-Shaqif south of Kefer Tibnit. The fortified site was captured by King Fulk in 1139. He passed it to the Lord of Sidon who built a castle on the precipice over the River Litani. The approach was protected by a ditch cut through the rock. The keep is rectangular, incorporated in the western section of the curtain wall. Saladin besieged it from 1189, starving it into submission by 1190. The Christians recovered Beaufort in 1240 and it was sold to the Knights Templar in 1260. It surrendered to the Muslims in 1268.

BEAUMARIS, ANGLESEY, WALES
The last castle Edward I built during his conquest of Wales. It stands on the island of Anglesey. Beaumaris was designed by Master James of St George and built from 1295 after Madoc's rising in 1294. There is a rectangular inner bailey. The outer bailey was added later. The inner bailey wall has massive mural drum towers and two double-towered gatehouses. The outer bailey has an enclosing wall with towers, making Beaumaris a concentric castle – though it was never completed. Beaumaris was never attacked though royalists held it during the English Civil War, surrendering in 1646.

BLED, SLOVENIA
North of Ljubljana, on a cliff over Lake Bled. A fortification existed here from the 11th century. Henry II (HRE) gave the castle to the bishop of Blixen. It remained an episcopal castle until the 19th century. It has an upper and lower bailey and a curtain wall.

BODIAM, EAST SUSSEX, ENGLAND
A late medieval castle. Richard II granted a licence of crenellation to Sir Edward Dalyngrigge in 1385 'for resistance against our enemies'. The coast was under threat from French invasion – Bodiam is 15 miles inland but by the River Rother. It stands on a rectangular platform surrounded by a wide moat. There are drum towers at each corner of the ashlar curtain wall. Three sides have a central rectangular tower. On the fourth side the central gatehouse has two rectangular towers, initially fronted by a barbican. The gatehouse is machicolated with gunports in the walls. A 14th-century wrought iron cannon was found in the moat and taken to Woolwich.

BODRUM, TURKEY
Sited on the Turkish coast opposite Kos. The site was given to the Templars in 1415 in return for Smyrna. On the peninsula by Bodrum Bay they built two rectangular towers (of France and Italy) and a high curtain wall. Heraldic Templar shields were carved on the walls. A bastion for guns was added in the 16th century. The Templars abandoned Bodrum for Malta in 1523.

BONAGUIL, FRANCE
In southern France west of Cahors, built in the 13th century with a thick wall and rounded corner towers. The pentagonal keep makes a spur to the north. In the 15th century was added machicolation, a buttressed artillery terrace, and towers with low-level loopholes.

BOUILLON, BELGIUM
South of Dinant on the River Semois. The 11th-century castle was held by Godfrey I of Bouillon before he went on the First Crusade. The entrance was protected by a ditch. Two 13th-century halls survive. The present building is largely late medieval with 17th-century modifications.

BURGHAUSEN, GERMANY
In Bavaria north of Salzburg, consisting of six ditched enclosures. The early 12th-century castle belonged to the counts of Burghausen and passed to the dukes of Bavaria. Some interior buildings are 13th-century. The surviving exterior dates largely from the late Middle Ages, when the region was threatened by the Turks.

BURWELL, CAMBRIDGESHIRE, ENGLAND
Built to a rectangular plan by King Stephen in 1143 as a base against Geoffrey de Mandeville. Excavation revealed a curtain wall and square tower gatehouse of stone. A 30-foot-wide moat surrounded the castle but was never filled. There were foundations for a keep in the courtyard. In 1144 Geoffrey attacked Burwell. He was hit by a crossbow bolt and later died. The king abandoned the unfinished castle.

CAERNARVON, CAERNARVONSHIRE, WALES

One of Edward I's Welsh castles, built as his major base by James of St George from 1283 on a peninsula between the River Seiont and the Menai Strait. It replaced Hugh of Chester's 11th-century motte and bailey castle. A moat separated the castle from the town. The castle formed a rough figure of eight. Building continued for 40 years and was not completed. Facing the town, the main entrance is the King's Gate. A second entrance, the Queen's Gate, faces east. Caernarvon reflected the imperial magnificence of Constantinople, with a banded stone wall and polygonal towers. In Madoc's 1294 rising Caernarvon was taken and damaged though soon retaken. Edward's son Edward II was born there and known as Edward of Caernarvon and Prince of Wales. Owen Glendower besieged Caernarvon 1401–3 but failed to take it.

CARISBROOKE, ISLE OF WIGHT, ENGLAND

On a Roman site, the 11th-century motte and bailey castle was built by William fitz Osbern. The crown took it over in 1077. In 1082 Odo of Bayeux was arrested here. It has two baileys. It was strengthened in stone in the 12th century, the motte topped by a shell keep. Baldwin de Redvers took refuge here against Stephen in 1136 but submitted when the water supply ran dry. (The deep well using donkeys to draw the water is of later date.) The French tried to take Carisbrooke in 1377 but failed. Charles I was imprisoned here.

CASTEL DEL MONTE, ITALY

On a hill south of Bari (Andria) in Apulia, built by Frederick II (HRE) to an unusual octagonal plan with octagonal corner towers. The residential rooms are highly decorated with coloured stone and marble. It reflected Frederick's artistic and architectural interests. It was called 'the crown of Apulia'. A later lord was Charles of Anjou king of Sicily.

CASTELLO SFORZESCO, MILAN, ITALY

A castle around three courtyards built by Galeazzo II Visconti from 1368, known as Castello di Porta Gloria. The revolutionary *Repubblica Ambrogiana* attacked and destroyed the castle. It was rebuilt by Francesco Sforza from 1450 and work continued after his death in 1466. Leonardo and Bramante were among the artists to decorate this Renaissance castle, and works by them survive. It has square towers to the north and round towers facing south into the city, with an impressive brick gate tower designed by Filarete and rebuilt in the 19th century.

CASTEL SANT'ANGELO, ITALY

Papal castle on the right bank of the Tiber in Rome, an urban citadel. It guards a bridge to the left bank. At its heart is the massive Mausoleum of Hadrian, a round tower on square foundations. Fortifications were added by the 6th century. In the loggia is a statue of the angel that appeared to Pope Gregory I (the Great) in 590, to give the castle its name. Pope Leo IV used it as a fortress in the 9th century. Italian families held it through much of the Middle Ages. Cencius Stephani built a new tower in the 11th century. Pope Gregory VII took refuge there from Henry IV (HRE) in 1084. It returned to papal control in the 14th century. Nicholas V in the mid-15th century added round towers to the corners of the tomb. Alexander VI added polygonal towers at the end of the Middle Ages. Further building in the 16th century turned it into an early modern fortress with angled bastions.

CHÂTEAUDUN, FRANCE

The site is north-west of Orléans on a plateau over the River Loire. Theobald le Tricheur count of Blois is said to have built it in the late 10th century. The surviving 12th-century castle, with its round keep, was built by Philip Augustus. It was from Châteaudun in 1194 that Philip marched against John at Le Vaudreuil. In the 15th century the Bastard of Orléans made it more comfortable for residence, adding the Sainte-Chapelle. The state took it over in 1939 and carried out restoration.

CHÂTEAU-GAILLARD, FRANCE
At Les Andelys in Normandy, south-east of Rouen, by the Seine. It stands on a cliff over the river. Richard the Lionheart built the castle on the frontier against Philip Augustus. Its name, 'cheeky castle', reflects its object of provoking France. It was also called Richard's 'beautiful daughter'. He poured in massive resources to complete the castle in two years, 1196–8. Ditches were dug to defend the only approach. It was an impressive and innovative structure, triangular in shape to fit the plateau. The inner defences command the outer by height, as concentric castles would later do. Philip Augustus besieged it against John's garrison from 1203, taking it in 1204, after which Normandy fell to him. It has a magnificent *en bec* round keep. The inner bailey is defended by large semicircular bastions, almost touching each other. The outer bailey forms a separate triangular enclosure, the point towards the direction of approach, cut off from the rest of the castle by a gully. Because approach was from one direction the outer bailey, middle bailey and inner bailey form consecutive obstacles to be breached in turn. A bridge of natural rock led to the inner bailey. Henry IV of France ordered it dismantled in 1603 but the ruins remain imposing.

CHEPSTOW (CASGWENT/STRIGUIL), MONMOUTHSHIRE, WALES
Beside the Wye, with a deep ravine (the Dingle) protecting the other side. A motte and bailey castle was built by William fitz Osbern (Earl of Hereford) from 1067, known as Casgwent or Striguil (from the Welsh for narrow vale), in the Norman invasion of Wales. A rectangular stone keep was built soon afterwards. From 1120 the defences were rebuilt in stone. Its famous lords included Richard de Clare (Strongbow) in the 12th century. In the 13th century, under

William the Marshal and Hugh Bigod, the barbican, middle bailey, lower bailey and Marten's Tower were added, and the keep enlarged. Some damage occurred in the 17th century, when demolition was ordered though not fully enforced. The Department of the Environment took it over in 1953.

CHILLON, SWITZERLAND
The most famous Swiss castle, on a small island in Lake Geneva (Leman) south of Montreux. The fortification is probably 10th-century in origin. The earliest remaining part is the Alinge Tower. The Duke's Tower was added in the 11th century. The surviving castle was built by Pierre Mainier for Peter II of Savoy. It has some magnificent wall paintings commencing from this period. The outer walls and towers have machicolation. Byron's poem 'The Prisoner of Chillon' concerns François Bonnivard, imprisoned here in the 16th century.

CHINON, FRANCE
Extended fortifications over a Roman site on a ridge over the River Vienne, consisting west to east of the Château du Coudray, the Château du Milieu and Fort St-Georges. The three enclosures are separated by moats. Coudray was built by the Count of Blois in the 10th century. Geoffrey Martel of Anjou took it in 1044. His descendant Henry II of England added Fort St-Georges and died there in 1189. Philip Augustus took Chinon in 1205 after a siege, adding a new keep in Coudray. The Valois kings added the Tour de l'Horloge. Here Joan of Arc met Charles VII in 1429.

COCHEM, GERMANY
On a rise beside the Moselle, south-west of Koblenz, controlling the passage of the river, begun in c.1020 with further work in the 12th century. The bishop of Trier enlarged it in the 14th century. It possesses a cluster of conical-topped towers. The castle was razed by the French in 1689.

COLCHESTER, ESSEX, ENGLAND

One of the only two stone castles begun by William the Conqueror in England. Colchester was built over a Roman temple. It is similar in plan to the Tower of London, with apsidal-ended chapels inside a rectangular keep. Some Caen stone was used. Under Henry II a bailey was added. Demolition in the 17th century reduced the height of the towers. It was held for Prince Louis of France during the Magna Carta rebellion and recovered by John in 1216.

CONWAY (CONWY), CAERNARVONSHIRE, WALES

The most expensive of Edward I's Welsh castles, built by Master James of St George, 1283–7, beside the Menai Strait on the foremost point between the rivers Conway and Gyffin. It was incorporated into the walls of the town built at the same time, separated from it by a moat, making the castle virtually an island. It has two major wards divided by a thick wall, with barbican extensions to east and west. The curtain wall incorporates eight drum towers. Conway was besieged by the Welsh under Madoc in 1294 but resisted successfully. Restoration was carried out in 1346. Richard II met Henry Percy here on his return from Ireland in 1399, when betrayed and captured. The castle was taken briefly for Owen Glendower in 1401. It decayed, passing into state hands in 1953, since when restoration work has been accomplished.

CORFE, DORSET, ENGLAND

A magnificent site on a hill. Here Edward the Martyr was murdered in 978. The castle was begun by William the Conqueror. Parts of the original curtain wall and hall survive. The rectangular keep was built by Henry I. Baldwin de Redvers, who came to England for Matilda against Stephen in 1139, shut himself in Corfe. Stephen besieged it but abandoned the attempt because of other problems. Further works costing £1,400 were added by King John, including La

Gloriette. The outer bailey with an outer gate was built in the 13th century. It was slighted by parliamentarians after the Civil War.

DOMFRONT, FRANCE

In southern Normandy, east of Avranches, over the River Varenne, begun by William de Bellême in 1011. A ditch protected the only approach. William the Conqueror besieged and captured it from the Count of Anjou. Henry I of England turned Domfront into a major border castle. The surviving ruins date chiefly from this period, including the rectangular keep. Geoffrey V of Anjou was handed the castle by its lord and it became a base for his conquest of Normandy. Henry II of England met the papal nuncio here to settle the Becket dispute.

DOUÉ-LA-FONTAINE, FRANCE

The site, La Motte, is south-east of Angers in the Loire valley. Excavation in 1967–70 revealed the earliest known stone castle, a keep, fortified by Theobald count of Blois in c.950. A residential stone hall was erected in c.900. It caught fire and was altered, the ground floor entrance sealed. An upper storey and forebuilding were added, protecting first floor entry. A motte was built around the foot of the tower. It was captured by Fulk Nerra of Anjou in 1025.

DOVER, KENT, ENGLAND

The coastal site was an Iron Age fort, a Roman lighthouse and an Anglo-Saxon burh, protecting an area vulnerable to continental attack. Harold Godwinson promised William the Conqueror to build a defence here but what he contributed is unknown. William built the castle after Hastings. Henry II's mason, Maurice the Engineer, added an inner curtain wall, the beginnings of the outer curtain, and the rectangular keep. King John continued the outer curtain. Hubert de Burgh successfully defended the castle against Prince Louis of France in 1216 during his invasion. Under Henry III the outer curtain was completed, the walls strengthened and the Constable's Gate (gatehouse) built.

DRACHENFELS, GERMANY
On a rocky crag over the Rhine, south of Bonn. Drachenfels means 'dragon's rock' and features in the legend of the Nibelungs, when Siegfried slays a dragon there. A fortification existed there in 1117 when it opposed Henry V (HRE). A tower was built by Arnold bishop of Köln in c.1147 and was passed to the monastery of Boon, then to the Count of Drachenfels, who rebuilt the castle. It was enlarged with a new curtain wall and round towers in the 15th century but abandoned after the Thirty Years' War and robbed in the 19th century. The ruins remain impressive.

FALAISE, FRANCE
In Normandy, south of Caen, over the Ante valley. The beginnings of the castle are obscure but it existed under Duke Robert I and was the birthplace of his son William the Conqueror in 1028. Henry I of England built the rectangular keep. Philip Augustus after the conquest of Normandy added the circular keep known later as the Talbot Tower, after the English commander who repaired it in the Hundred Years' War. Restoration was carried out in the 19th century though the castle suffered damage in the Second World War.

GISORS, FRANCE
In the Norman Vexin, south-west of Beauvais, built on the frontier against the Capetians in the 11th century. Robert of Bellême for William II of England built the motte in 1096. An octagonal shell keep and stone walls were added by Henry I of England. Philip Augustus captured Gisors in 1193, when it surrendered without a fight. He strengthened the defences, adding the circular keep known as the Prisoners' Tower.

GRANDSON, SWITZERLAND
On Lake Neuchâtel, built by the Lord of Grandson in the 11th century. The surviving castle dates chiefly from the 13th century. It passed to the Châlon-Orange family who rebuilt it in the later Middle Ages. The curtain wall is very high with five circular or semicircular corner and mural towers having conical caps. Outside Grandson Charles the Bold was defeated by the Swiss in 1476. The castle passed to Berne and Fribourg.

HABSBURG, SWITZERLAND
Built on the height of the Wülpelsberg, north-west of Zurich. The castle with its rectangular Bergfried (watchtower) probably dates from the 11th century though first recorded in 1108. In the 12th and 13th centuries a palace and outer wall were added. It was the original seat of the Habsburgs, who ceased to reside there from the 13th century. The castle passed to Berne in 1529 and later to the canton of Aargau. Alterations in the 16th century left a building that emphasised residence rather than defence.

HÄLSINGBORG, SWEDEN
On the south-west coast over the Ore Sund, controlling Baltic traffic. The fortifications at Hälsingborg and at Helsingør (Elsinore) on the opposite shore were built by the Danes in the 12th century. The Kärnan (keep) survives. Waldmar IV rebuilt the tower in brick in c.1370 to a height of 113 feet.

HARLECH, MERIONETH, WALES
On the estuary of the River Dwyryd, on the site of a former Welsh fort, built by Master James of St George for Edward I, 1283–90, costing £9,500. The sea was closer then to the castle. It had a concentric plan with a wide moat on two sides. A massive twin-towered gatehouse faces east. The inner curtain has round corner towers. The curtain to the narrow outer bailey is low, dominated by the inner bailey. Master James became constable of Harlech 1290–3. It was besieged by Welsh rebels in 1294 but relieved. Repairs were made in the 14th century. Harlech was besieged and taken in

1404 by Owen Glendower with French allies, to become his base, and recovered by Lord Talbot in 1408. In the Wars of the Roses Harlech was taken over in 1468 by Dafydd ap Ieuan, whose men were the original 'Men of Harlech'. The castle was besieged and taken by Yorkists under the Earl of Pembroke. It was held for the royalists in the English Civil War.

HASTINGS, SUSSEX, ENGLAND

Partly lost through demolition and erosion of the cliff on which the castle stands. The cliff stands above the modern town. It was an Iron Age fort. William the Conqueror built a motte and bailey castle after his landing and before Hastings. The building of the motte with a wooden keep is shown on the *Bayeux Tapestry*. There is dispute over whether this is the correct site, but Norman pottery has been found, and we accept it. It was held by Robert count of Eu from 1069 to 1088 as the centre of a Sussex Rape. Additions were made in the 12th century, including a stone keep. John ordered the slighting of the castle in 1216. Repairs were made by Henry III. There was an inner bailey and two outer baileys. The gatehouse had two semicircular towers. Damage from erosion occurred in the 14th century. In 1951 it was bought by Hastings Corporation.

HAUT KOENIGSBOURG (HOHKÖNIGSBURG), FRANCE

South of Strasbourg in Alsace, built by the Hohenstaufen emperors in the 12th century. Haut Koenigsbourg was burnt down in the Thirty Years' War and rebuilt for Kaiser Wilhelm II in the 20th century.

HERSTMONCEUX, SUSSEX, ENGLAND

Late medieval castle on a rectangular plan with octagonal towers at each corner and flanking the gatehouse, which is machicolated. Semi-octagonal towers stand at regular intervals on each wall. The whole is surrounded by a wide moat. Sir Roger Fiennes received a licence to crenellate in 1441. The name comes from earlier De

Monceux holders of the estate. The castle is designed more for comfort than was normal earlier, with more windows and brick rather than stone walls. It remained a residence until the 18th century. Herstmonceux was restored in the 20th century. It was for some years the home of the Royal Observatory.

HOCHOSTERWITZ, AUSTRIA

A hilltop castle in Carinthia, replacing a 10th-century fortification. The main castle is rectangular. In order to enter, one has to pass through 14 towers and cross three ditches. It was held in turn by the bishops of Salzburg and the lords of Osterwitz. Most of the surviving structure is 16th-century.

HÜSTERKNUPP, GERMANY

Near Frimmersdorf, a motte and bailey castle that developed from a 10th-century farmhouse. Excavation showed a farmhouse fortified in an enclosure. A mound was added at its heart and it became a motte and bailey, with a keep on the mound.

KARLŠTEJN, CZECH REPUBLIC

On a rocky hilltop by the River Morina, south-west of Prague, built 1348–57 by Charles IV (HRE) for his treasure and holy relics. The keep is large, with a chapel above containing medieval wall paintings including portraits of Charles and his wife. It had wooden hoarding, restored with the castle as a whole in the 19th century. Emperor Sigismund resisted sieges there in the Hussite Wars.

KERAK-IN-MOAB (EL KERAK), JORDAN

On a rocky spur south of Amman, built of volcanic stone on the far side of the Jordan by Pagan the Butler from 1142. It defended the approach to crusader lands from the plain of Moab. There were inner and outer baileys and rectangular towers. It was used by Rainald de Châtillon as a base to attack Muslim caravans. He was besieged there by Saladin in 1183 and 1184. It was finally taken by the Muslims in 1188 after Rainald's death following Hattin. There were later additions and repairs.

KIRBY MUXLOE, LEICESTERSHIRE, ENGLAND

A late medieval castle, begun in 1480 by William Lord Hastings, a Yorkist. When Hastings was executed by Richard III for treachery in 1483, work on the castle stopped. The west corner tower and the gatehouse were finished. It was planned as a rectangular platform in a moat fed from the nearby stream. During building there were worries about flooding. Kirby Muxloe has gunports for defence but stresses residential comfort, with brick rather than stone walls. It had a rectangular enclosure with square corner towers and a gatehouse surrounded by four octagonal towers to the north-west. The Hastings family held the castle until the 17th century. It came under state control in the 20th century and was repaired.

KRAK (KERAK/CRAC) DES CHEVALIERS, SYRIA

Crusader castle built on the mountain spur of Gebel Alawi, where an Arab fortress guarded a mountain pass. The Hospitallers received the castle from the Count of Tripoli in 1142. It had a rectangular plan with square towers. It was damaged by intermittent earthquakes and needed repairs. It was developed as a concentric castle with rectangular and round towers in the outer curtain, which has machicolation. It was besieged several times but resisted until 1271, when captured by Baybars.

LANGEAIS, FRANCE

Once thought the oldest castle in western Europe, and now the second oldest known. It is in Touraine in the Loire valley, on a spur between the Loire and the Roumer. It was built by Fulk Nerra of Anjou before 995, when Odo I of Blois besieged it. It has a rectangular tower keep on a mound, now in ruins. Work by Pierre de Brosse in the 13th

century has now gone. The English captured Langeais in 1427 and returned it on condition that only the ancient tower was left standing. From 1465 a Renaissance château was built on adjacent land by Jean Bourré for Louis XI, only two wings being completed. Here Charles VIII of France married Anne of Brittany in 1491. Rabelais lived nearby.

LEWES, SUSSEX, ENGLAND

Castle with two mottes, built by William de Warenne earl of Surrey soon after the Norman Conquest as the castle for a Sussex Rape. It appears in *Domesday Book*. It stands above the Ouse. The mounds were increased in size with chalk blocks. The smaller eastern motte, Brack's Mount, is oldest. A stone shell keep was added in the 12th century. In the 14th century a barbican and gatehouse with round towers and machicolation were built. In 1347 it passed to the Fitz Alans. In the 17th century the ruins provided material for local buildings. It was taken over by the Sussex Archaeological Society in 1850.

LINZ, AUSTRIA

On the south bank of the Danube, fortified by 799 and throughout the Middle Ages. In the 15th century Frederick III (HRE) built a new Renaissance castle. There were subsequent additions.

LOCHES, FRANCE

On a rocky plateau by the Loire near Tours. Gregory of Tours mentioned an early fortress here. Fulk Nerra built the first castle, including the rectangular keep. It was rebuilt by the 12th century. Philip Augustus took Loches in 1194 but Richard I recovered it. After Philip captured Loches from John in 1204, he added towers *en bec*. In the 15th century the round tower in the *Martelet* was built. The castle contains the white marble tomb of Agnès Sorel, mistress of Charles VII of France (d.1450). Ludovico Sforza was a prisoner here in the 16th century, when he painted geometrically patterned frescoes.

LONDON, THE TOWER, ENGLAND

There was a fortification in London called an *arx* in 899 – but its site is unknown. When Cnut besieged London in 1016 a garrison held out in the citadel. The castle was begun by William the Conqueror after London's surrender in 1066, built by the Thames in the south-east corner of the city walls as a keep and bailey castle. The rectangular keep is the White Tower. Like Colchester it has an extension for the apsidal end of a chapel. A new curtain wall was built in 1097. Bishop Ranulf Flambard was imprisoned in the White Tower under Henry I. He escaped on a rope that was too short and fell on his fat bottom, hands burned by the rope, groaning with pain. The fortification was extended west by Richard I and Henry III. Under Edward I it became a concentric castle with a new outer ward, outer curtain wall, moat (filled from the Thames but now dry) and water-gate. A royal menagerie was kept here. War engines were constructed here by Master Bertram in 1276. The Tower was an arms store, as under Edward III (when 100 cannons were kept) and Henry V. The princes in the Tower died here under Richard III, in the Bloody Tower. In Tudor times it was used as a prison for major figures, including Princess Elizabeth and Walter Ralegh. Several executions occurred either in the castle on Tower Green (including Anne Boleyn, Lady Jane Grey and Essex) or outside on Tower Hill. Rudolf Hess was imprisoned here in the Second World War. It now houses the crown jewels and a collection of arms and armour.

LOUVRE, PARIS, FRANCE

Built 1190–1202 by Philip Augustus with a round tower keep, the Tour Neuve. The castle was incorporated into the new defensive wall of Paris built by Philip. The round tower was surrounded by a quadrangular wall with round corner towers. Leading prisoners from Bouvines in 1214 were imprisoned here. Charles V turned it into a palace in the 14th century. Today it houses a great art collection.

MÁLAGA, THE ALCAZABA AND GIBRALFARO, SPAIN

On a rise at the foot of mountains over the harbour are two linked fortifications. The Alcazaba was a Moorish fortress built between the 8th and 11th centuries with a rectangular enclosure and citadel. The Gibralfaro (on the site of an ancient Phoenician lighthouse) has two further enclosures surrounded by a wall and towers. A double wall surrounds the whole. The fortifications surrendered to Ferdinand and Isabella in 1487, at the conclusion of the *Reconquista*.

MANTUA, CASTELLO DI SAN GIORGIO, ITALY

South of Lake Garda, a rectangular castle with square corner towers built from 1395 by Bartolino da Novara for Francesco Gonzaga. It has a moat and a drawbridge. It was turned into a Renaissance palace by Ludovico II. It contains frescoes by Mantegna.

MARGAT (MARQAB), SYRIA

On a hill at Qalaat Marqab near Baniyas on the coast. An 11th-century Muslim fortress was captured by the crusaders in 1118. It became a castle for the principality of Antioch, built by the Mazoir family in a triangular enclosure. Little of the original work survives. In 1186 it was bought by the Hospitallers who built new fortifications, a hall, a chapel and a massive two-storey round keep. The entrance tower is machicolated. Margat was besieged in 1204–5 by men of the Sultan of Aleppo but successfully resisted. A traveller in 1212 thought it 'the strongest [castle] in the whole of this country'. Qalawun besieged Margat in 1285 – the last major castle siege in the crusader kingdom. When Qalawun brought down the Tower of the Spur by mining, the castle surrendered on terms, the garrison allowed to go to Tripoli or Tortosa.

MARIENBURG (MALBORK), POLAND

At Malbork, south-east of Gdansk, by the River Nogat, begun by the Teutonic

Knights in 1280, becoming their base in 1309. The moat was filled from Lake Dabrowka. It is a brick-built rectangular castle with three main sections, the Hochschloss, the Mittelschloss, and the later Unterschloss. The inner gate has a magnificent portcullis. Marienburg was besieged in 1410 and taken after two months when the Knights were defeated at Tannenberg. In 1457 it was taken over by the Poles. It was used as Stalag XXB by the Germans in the Second World War, suffering damage in 1945. It has since been restored.

MONTRÉAL, JORDAN

On a hill over a valley at Shaubak, south of Amman and east of the Dead Sea. It was built by Baldwin I king of Jerusalem in 1115 as an outpost. It dominated the area, protecting the trade route between Syria and Egypt. Part of the curtain wall and two chapels survive. Water was supplied through a tunnel cut in the rock to cisterns fed by springs. After Hattin, Montréal was besieged by the Mamlukes and starved into surrender when the garrison went blind through lack of salt. The main fortification as it stands was added later.

MONTREUIL-BELLAY, FRANCE

By the River Thouet south of Saumur, built by Fulk Nerra of Anjou in the 10th century on a rocky rise protected by a natural chasm, the Valley of the Jews. It was handed to the Berlai family. It had double walls and a keep 'rising to the stars'. After rebellion by Gerard Berlai, Geoffrey V of Anjou besieged Montreuil-Bellay for three years from 1148. He brought people from the fair at Saumur to drop rocks and rubbish in the ditch so he could cross. Reading Vegetius, the Roman writer on warfare, Geoffrey had a new idea. He made the first known use of Greek Fire in the west, hurling it in pots from a throwing engine. The ploy worked and the castle was taken and demolished. The surviving white stone building is late medieval with rounded turrets and an interesting kitchen building.

MONTSÉGUR, FRANCE

On a Pyrenean peak east of Foix, the last stronghold of the Albigensian heretics. It was built in 1204 to a pentagonal plan with a square keep and a massive curtain wall. Unusual features were two unfortified gates and windows rather than loops. In 1241 it was besieged by Count Raymond VII of Toulouse, but he abandoned the attempt. It was besieged with more energy by the Albigensian crusaders in 1243–4. The bishop of Albi commanded the attackers' trebuchets. Women operated engines from the castle walls. The garrison (not heretics) was betrayed. Some Basques climbed inside and knifed the guards. The garrison surrendered and was allowed to depart. In 1244 over 200 heretics, who refused to recant, were burned alive at the foot of the mountain. The castle was demolished and left in ruins.

MUIDERSLOT (MUIDER), NETHERLANDS

At Muiden, east of Amsterdam, on an island in the River Vecht. The site was fortified in c.1000. A castle was erected from c.1280 by Count Floris IV, who was assassinated here in 1296, after which the castle was demolished. It was rebuilt from 1370 by Albert of Bavaria count of Holland, constructed in brick to a square plan with a moat. The round corner towers have conical caps. There is machicolation on the sunken entrance and a covered wall-walk on the curtain. It was captured by the Duke of Gelderland in 1508, and the Earl of Leicester in 1586.

NIORT, FRANCE

In Poitou on the bank of the Sèvre Niortaise near Poitiers, built by Henry II of England from c.1160 to an unusual plan with twin square keeps having rounded corner turrets. The later curtain had 16 round towers. The twin keeps, separated by a courtyard, were linked by a building in the 15th century. The southern keep has early machicolation. The French captured Niort in 1436. It was damaged in the 16th-century religious wars. The northern keep was rebuilt in the 18th century.

NUREMBURG, THE KAISERBURG, GERMANY

In Bavaria on a hill in the north-east corner of the city wall, with two main enclosures. The Kaiserburg is the imperial castle of Nuremburg. It was begun by Henry III (HRE) in c.1040 and controlled the trade route to the River Main. Additions were made by Conrad III and Frederick Barbarossa, including a round tower and a two-storey chapel. The palace building and the Kaiserstallung date from the 15th century under the Hohenzollern. It has been restored since the Second World War.

NYBORG, DENMARK

On the Baltic island of Fyn, south-east of Odense, believed to be the oldest royal castle in Scandinavia though little of the early building survives. It was the assembly-point for parliaments, the base of government in Denmark until 1416 and afterwards a royal residence. It was damaged in the 17th century but has since been restored.

ORFORD, SUFFOLK, ENGLAND

East of Ipswich, built by Henry II between 1165 and 1173 to protect the port that then existed. It countered baronial castles at Framlingham and Walton. Orford was built on a rectangular plan with a ditch, and a curtain wall with rectangular towers. The surviving keep is polygonal, with a circular interior. It had three rectangular buttress towers, with a forebuilding at the entrance containing a chapel. Orford was a base for Henry II during his suppression of Hugh Bigod's rebellion. In 1217 it was captured by the invading Prince Louis of France but returned to royal control when the invasion failed. Edward III passed it to the Earl of Suffolk in 1336. It came under state control in 1962.

PLESSIS-BOURRÉ, LE, FRANCE

At Écuillé north of Angers, built in the late 14th century. It was acquired in 1462 by Louis XI's minister, Jean Bourré, who rebuilt it. It was adapted for artillery warfare, with a wide moat, thick walls and gun platforms inside the moat. The castle is virtually a rectangular island. There are interesting interior decorations from the 16th century in what had become a Renaissance château.

PLESSIS-GRIMOULT, LE, FRANCE

An early earthwork castle in Normandy, examined by excavation. A circular rampart was built by the early 11th century. It was improved with stone walls, a stone gatehouse and at least one mural tower. The gatehouse was a rectangular tower with an entrance passage. It was held by the Du Plessis family until 1047 when its lord, Grimoult, rebelled against William the Conqueror. The castle was then abandoned.

RHODES, GREECE

On its island, Rhodes Town is a fortification with an internal stronghold known as the Grand Master's Palace. It was a crusader castle, constructed by the Hospitallers after the loss of the Holy Land and their move to Rhodes in 1309. It protected the best harbour on the island. Forward towers were built on projecting moles at Fort St Nicholas, the Tower of Naillac and the Tower of St Angelo. It was built to accommodate artillery. Egyptian attempts against Rhodes in 1440 and 1444 failed. After an earthquake in 1481 it was rebuilt with thick walls and towers. Rhodes resisted a siege by the Turks in 1480–1 but surrendered to an attack by Suleiman the Magnificent in 1522. It has been restored in modern times.

RHUDDLAN, FLINTSHIRE, WALES

South of Rhyl, possibly fortified from the 8th century. A Welsh stronghold here was taken by Harold Godwinson in 1063. By 1073 Robert of Rhuddlan built a motte

(Twthill) and bailey castle. Master James of St George rebuilt it from 1277 as a concentric castle for Edward I. The inner bailey is square with double towers to east and west, and single towers north and south. There is a lower outer bailey, protected by a surrounding rampart and a moat fed by the River Clwyd. It was attacked by Welsh rebels in 1282 but resisted successfully. It was besieged in the English Civil War and taken by Parliament under Mytton in 1646, after which it was dismantled. It was taken over by the state in 1944 and restored.

RIGA, LATVIA
Built from 1330 by the Teutonic Knights in the Baltic crusades. It was built on a rectangular plan with corner towers. The Pulvera or Gunpowder Tower, part of the first castle, was rebuilt in the 17th century. It was taken over by the Knights of the Sword. Riga was damaged in the Second World War and has since been restored.

ROCHE-GUYON, LA, FRANCE
Built from c.1190 north-west of Mantes on a cliff over the Seine near its confluence with the Epte. Roche-Guyon stands on an isthmus, the neck cut by a ditch. The keep is *en bec*.

ROCHESTER, KENT, ENGLAND
By the Medway, controlling a crossing point, probably the site of an early Norman motte and bailey castle. Odo of Bayeux was besieged here by William Rufus in 1088. The garrison surrendered and Odo was exiled. The first stone castle was built from c.1088 by Bishop Gundulf within the Roman walls. In c.1126, when held by the archbishop of Canterbury, a massive rectangular keep was erected with a forebuilding. In 1141 Robert earl of Gloucester was imprisoned here. In 1215 in a third siege by King John against rebel barons the south-eastern corner of the keep was brought down by mining. The keep had an internal dividing wall and resistance continued for a time but

eventually the garrison surrendered. This corner tower was rebuilt with a round tower, whereas the other corner towers are rectangular. At the same time a circular mural tower was added. Prince Louis of France held Rochester during his invasion from 1216. It survived a siege in 1264 by rebels in the Barons' Wars. Further towers and a bastion were added by Edward III and Richard II. It was taken briefly by rebels in the Peasants' Revolt. The castle remains an impressive ruin, the keep without ceilings and floors.

SALZBURG, FESTUNG HOHENSALZBURG, AUSTRIA
Above Salzburg on the Mönschsberg Ridge, fortified by archbishop Gerhard from 1077 when the central Altes Schloss was built. The castle was enlarged and strengthened in the 15th century. Round towers were added in the outer curtain wall. The Golden Room was decorated from 1501. Further work was done in the early modern period.

SAN GIMIGNANO, ITALY
In Tuscany, 14 high rectangular towers, mostly 13th-century. It is an extreme example of a group of between 50 and 80 competing towers. The town walls were built from 1251.

SAUMUR, FRANCE
Perhaps the best-known pictorial example of a fairytale castle with conically capped towers, as depicted to represent September in the illuminated manuscript the *Très Riches Heures*. It was fortified by Fulk Nerra of Anjou in the 10th century. The surviving castle was rebuilt by the duc de Berry in the 14th century, lavishly decorated with Gothic tracery, flying turrets and golden weathercocks – though the gilding has weathered. The castle was abandoned in the 17th century when the west wing collapsed. It became a prison and a barracks and has been restored in modern times.

SEGOVIA, ALCÁZAR, SPAIN
The citadel of Segovia, built on a height between rivers, fortified by the Moors in the early Middle Ages. The castle was built in the 11th century by Alfonso VI of León. It became part of the 15th-century royal palace, when the Torre del Homenaje was added by Juan II. It retains a Moorish appearance with conically capped towers, probably influenced by the Alhambra. It is a Gran Buque (Great Ship) castle, the whole shaped in outline like a ship with a pointed prow. Fire damage occurred in 1862, since restored.

SILIFKE (CAMARDESIUM), TURKEY
On the south coast by the River Saleph. The Byzantines built a fortification in 1111 though little remains. Frederick Barbarossa (HRE) died in the river in 1190 *en route* to the Third Crusade. In 1210 Byzantine emperor Leo II gave it to the Hospitallers, who constructed a castle modelled on Krak des Chevaliers. Silifke had an oval enclosure with a curtain, a keep, spaced horseshoe-shaped towers, all protected by a ditch. Cisterns were dug for water supply. The entrance up a ramp is protected by an outwork with a round tower. The wall-walk could only be reached through a tower. The Armenians took it in 1225 and Hethum I added to the defences.

SIRMIONE, ITALY
On a peninsula south of Lake Garda. A moat, fed by the lake, separates the castle from the mainland. The castle was built in brick by the Scaligeri in c.1300. It has a harbour protected by the outer walls and is best approached by boat. It has rectangular corner towers and two gatehouses. The keep is similar to family towers in Italian cities. The square tower overlooking the harbour has machicolation. The castle controlled traffic on the lake.

STIRLING, STIRLINGSHIRE, SCOTLAND
North-west of Glasgow on a rock above the town, controlling a ford over the Forth. The castle was built in c.1100. In 1304 it fell to Edward I. After Bannockburn the Scots dismantled it. Stirling was rebuilt in the 15th century with a gatehouse having flanking towers. The surviving Prince's Tower may be a reconstruction of the early Norman castle. It became a barracks in the 18th century and has been restored in modern times.

STOKESAY, SHROPSHIRE, ENGLAND
Built south of Shrewsbury by the De Say family, dating from c.1200, including the stone North Tower. Further buildings were added in c.1240. The surviving fortified manor house was built from c.1285 by the wool merchant Lawrence of Ludlow (d.1296), who bought the site. It has a deep ditch and a crenellated though weak curtain wall. It marks a move to more residential comfort. The interior buildings include a great hall and chambers with a tower at either end. The southern tower is larger, representing a keep. A timber gatehouse was added in the 17th century. In 1645 the parliamentarians captured Stokesay and slighted its defences.

TARASCON, FRANCE
On a rocky site by the Rhône south of Avignon. Louis II king of Naples rebuilt the castle from c.1400. After it passed to the French crown King René made additions from 1481. The curtain wall was raised to the level of the towers, allowing a continuous wall-walk, the type of the bastille, influenced by the Bastille in Paris. Machicolation was added and a postern gave access to the river. It was later used as a prison. Modern restoration work has been executed.

THUN, SWITZERLAND
South-east of Berne. The keep was built by the Duke of Zahringen in the late 12th century. It passed to the counts of Kyburg. It has a rectangular plan with corner towers. The large hall is now a museum.

TRIFELS, GERMANY
On a height near Annweiler, controlling the route between Speyer and the River Saar, linking the Rhineland to France. It was built on a roughly triangular plan. It is unusual for the region, with a western-style keep. It was taken over by Frederick Barbarossa who enlarged it from 1153. Richard the Lionheart was moved here from Dürnstein as a prisoner by Henry VI (HRE) in 1193 after his capture returning from the Third Crusade. He was released in 1194.

TRIM, MEATH, IRELAND
On the River Boyne north-west of Dublin, the largest castle in Ireland, built by Hugh de Lacy in 1173. In his absence the keep was burned down in 1174. It was rebuilt in stone as a triangular walled enclosure with towers and an interior square keep (the Great Tower), which was later increased in height. The north wall has rectangular mural towers, the south wall semicircular ones. A gatehouse was built to the east with a round tower. Here Henry IV stayed before his accession in 1399. It was heavily involved in Anglo-Irish wars.

VALLADOLID, LA MOTA, SPAIN
At Medina del Campo to the east of Valladolid, previously a Moorish fortification. It was rebuilt in the 12th century and again in the 15th. Only lower parts of the walls remain from the 12th century. The surviving castle is largely of brick in a roughly rectangular walled enclosure with corner towers. It became in effect a concentric castle. The later additions, the work of Fernando Carreño and then Alonso Nieto, included the Torre del Homenaje (the keep) in a corner of the inner bailey. The curtain wall has a vaulted *chemin de ronde* with stairs inside round towers. The castle was a model for others. In 1475 it passed to the Christian kings. Cesare Borgia was imprisoned here. It was restored in the 20th century.

VINCENNES, FRANCE
In the Île-de-France, east of Paris, originally a royal hunting lodge for the forest outside Paris. Louis IX added a keep but the surviving keep dates from the 14th century, with six storeys and circular corner turrets. The rectangular enclosing wall incorporates the keep and nine other towers. There are ditches protecting the keep and the curtain. It became a royal palace. Louis X, Charles IV and Charles IX died here, as did Henry V of England. Henry VI used it as a residence. The French recovered Vincennes in 1432. It became a prison, its residents including Diderot, Bonnie Prince Charlie and Mirabeau. In 1944 the Germans shot 30 men here.

VISBORG, SWEDEN
At Visby on the island of Gotland, in the south-west corner of the town wall. It was built in the 15th century, planned by the Teutonic Knights and built under King Erik from 1411. Erik sheltered here for ten years. The castle was demolished in 1679 but the town wall survives. (Note: not to be confused with Viborg at Jutland in Denmark, or Vyborg in Finland.)

WARTBURG, GERMANY
On a height at Eisenach, built by Ludwig von der Schauenburg in the 11th century – unusual as a baronial rather than an imperial castle in this region. It had two wooden towers. It was rebuilt by the Landgrave of Thuringia in the 12th century. It became a noted centre of patronage for the arts and has been restored in modern times.

WERLAR, GERMANY
Near Goslar in Saxony, built by Henry the Fowler in c.950. It had two long parallel outer enclosures and two nearly circular adjoining inner enclosures. All the enclosures were surrounded by stone walls, while stone towers defended the gateways.

WINDSOR, BERKSHIRE, ENGLAND
By the Thames near London, a royal castle begun by William the Conqueror. An

Anglo-Saxon royal residence stood nearby. William constructed a motte and bailey castle but with two baileys. It was strengthened with stone walls and a shell keep by Henry II. Prince Louis besieged Windsor in 1216 but failed to take it. The three drum towers were built by Henry III. The buildings in the upper bailey and the Round Tower were added by Edward III, who was born here. Windsor became a fortified palace. St George's Chapel dates from the 15th century. Henry VIII rebuilt the gatehouse in the Lower Ward. There has been much restoration work as under George IV and since the 1992 fire.

YORK, YORKSHIRE, ENGLAND

William the Conqueror built two motte and bailey castles in York in 1068–9 for his conquest of the north. There were originally timber towers on both mottes.

The two castles were built either side of the River Ouse – the Old Baile to the south, and the surviving York Castle with Clifford's Tower as its keep to the north. The Old Baile was probably built in 1068 and York Castle in 1069. They were both attacked and destroyed in the 1069 rebellion. After William's harrying of the north, York's castles were rebuilt. The Old Baile was still in use under Edward III, when repairs were carried out, but was later abandoned. York Castle, the surviving Clifford's Tower, was rebuilt in stone by Henry III in the 13th century with four circular turrets in close proximity. The curtain wall had five towers, a main gatehouse to the south and a lesser one in the north to the town. Damage was done during the Civil War by attacking parliamentarians. Clifford's Tower was damaged by fire in 1684.

A–Z OF TERMS

ADULTERINE CASTLES

Built without official permission when kings and princes sought to control castle building. They claimed rendability – that castles in their area must be handed over if demanded. Many baronial castles were built in the civil war under Stephen without permission and are called adulterine. Henry II claimed the right to destroy them. Later licences were issued for crenellation or fortifying buildings.

ARCHÈRES

Arrow loops, slits in fortified buildings for archers to shoot through, often made by leaving a narrow space between adjacent stones. They allowed the defending archer a good range and protected him. The shapes varied to accommodate various weapons, including crossbows. Usually they were narrow on the outside, sloping to give space to the archer inside.

ARTILLERY

Various engines used to hurl, shoot or fire missiles. Medieval artillery consisted of a range of engines, including balistas, catapults, mangonels, trebuchets and cannons. Artillery could be used in battle and sieges, for attack and defence. The two main medieval developments were the invention of trebuchets using counterweights and cannons using gunpowder.

ASHLAR

Prepared stone for building – usually cut, squared or shaped, and smoothed. Ashlar is a sign of more carefully constructed buildings. It is thought the term meant being like a prepared timber or beam.

BAILEY

A castle enclosure, courtyard or ward. In a motte and bailey castle the bailey was the larger and lower enclosure. Castles often had two enclosures. Some had a motte with two baileys, some had inner and outer baileys, some had more than two, perhaps inner, central and outer.

BALEARIC SLING
A weapon noted for its speed. Richard the Lionheart was said to move more swiftly than one. The nature of it is uncertain, and it is not clear whether the speed refers to quickness in use or speed of missile through the air. It was presumably operated by a sling, probably an engine rather than a simple sling. Since the trebuchet worked by a sling it is possible that these were early trebuchets. It is thought they originated in the Balearic islands, and the term was certainly used with this sense, but this is possibly a mistake with the term originating from Greek *ballo* via Latin *baleare* (to throw). 'Balearic' in the Middle Ages was also used to mean satanic.

BALISTA (BALLISTA)
A shooting or throwing engine, otherwise a catapult. The name came from Greek *ballo*, Latin *baleare* – to throw. The Latin term *balista* could be either a crossbow or a catapult. The catapult operated like a crossbow, with a mechanism to wind back a string that, when released, shot a missile placed in its groove. Medieval chroniclers were often imprecise over names for engines. They often used this term for stone-throwing engines in general.

BARBICAN
Outwork of a castle or town defences, usually protecting the gate or sometimes a bridge over a moat. Its main purpose was to make entrance more difficult. It was often a carefully fortified walled passage to the entrance, commonly open to the air to allow defenders to attack from above those entering. *Barbicana* was a medieval Latin word, its origin unknown.

BASTIDE
In origin a new town, but mostly seen as a small, strongly fortified settlement. The medieval Latin term was *bastida*, our form being from French (from which *bastille* also derives). In modern French *bastide* means a country house or shooting lodge. The medieval *bastide* was a concept from 13th-century France. Edward I built over 50 *bastides* in English-held Gascony. *Bastides* were usually rectangular with a central square.

BASTION
A projecting mural tower, earthwork or structure from which the curtain wall can be defended. In early modern forts the bastion was commonly angled. The term is from Latin *bastire*, to build.

BELFRY
A siege tower on wheels used against town or castle walls, constructed to the height of the wall or greater. It was pushed close to the wall so men on it could use weapons against the defenders. A bridge could be lowered from the belfry to the wall so that the castle or town could be entered. The belfry could protect men mining the foot of a wall. Belfries were usually made from wood in several storeys. Wet matting or skins might cover the wood against fire. Belfries date from ancient times and were common in medieval sieges, as at Lisbon, Mallorca or against Constantinople.

BERGFRIED
A high slender tower, like a keep, found in some German castles. It translates as 'peace tower' but probably derives from the same base as belfry. It probably originated with the Roman watchtower and stood in isolation. Later it was often incorporated into a castle.

BERM
The space at the foot of the castle wall, a platform in front of the ditch or moat. It could offer a space for attackers to use for mining. Late castles used it as a gun platform for defence. The term probably means brim.

BORE
A device for demolishing walls, similar to a battering ram but with a pointed end

(usually of metal) to pierce gaps between stones.

BRATTICE (*BRETÈCHE*)
The same as hoarding, work in wood overhanging the top of a wall – a breastwork or gallery – allowing defenders to deal with attackers below. Machicolation was stonework with the same function. 'Brattice' was sometimes applied to any wooden work in the defences.

BRIGOLA (BRIGOLE)
A Saracen engine mentioned by Jaime I of Aragón. It had a beam, cords and a box and was probably a trebuchet.

CANNON
A medieval invention that revolutionised warfare. Cannons appeared in the west in the 14th century though gunpowder was known in the previous century. The 1326 *Milemete Manuscript* shows a cannon shaped like a vase, shooting a bolt rather than a ball. Cannons became more efficient and by the late Middle Ages were essential in battle and siege. The Bureau brothers in France improved cannons during the Hundred Years' War. They were produced in a variety of types and sizes, for example, bombards, serpentines, crapaudins, mortars and ribaudequins. By the end of the Middle Ages large cannons were produced, as by the Turks at Constantinople. The word comes from Greek *kanun* via Latin *canna*, meaning a tube.

CASTELLAN
The holder of a castle, generally holding it on behalf of a king or prince. In the 10th and 11th centuries central authority was less dominant and some castellans were virtually independent.

CASTLE-GUARD
A feudal obligation to defend a castle for a specified period as service to a lord – a means by which lords could garrison their own castles. The service was often performed on a rota system.

CAT (WELSH CAT)
A covered roof on wheels to shelter men so they could approach walls, as for mining. It was sometimes attached to the wall by iron nails. Other names for the same device were mouse, sow and tortoise. One at Lisbon in the Second Crusade had a roof of osiers; a group of youths from Ipswich moved it in the wake of a siege tower. One at Toulouse in 1218 had an interior platform and housed 400 knights plus 150 archers.

CATAPULT
An engine used from ancient times, shooting missiles by a string drawn by mechanical means, otherwise a balista. The missile was normally a large bolt placed in the groove of the machine.

COMBUSTIBLES
Fire was much used in siege warfare, especially against wooden structures. Hurling fire in one form or another was common practice, whether as fire-arrows, Greek Fire in jars, or bundles of flaming material such as tow. Fire-wheels were used in the Baltic crusade and in Malta against the Turks: a wheel or hoop covered with pitch or other combustible material and bowled against the enemy.

CONCENTRIC CASTLES
Castles with more than one surrounding curtain wall. The development towards this was gradual through the 12th century in France, England and the Holy Land. The concept reached its height with Master James of St George for Edward I on his Welsh castles, such as Beaumaris. The inner walls were higher than the outer so that attackers gaining the intervening ward could be dealt with from above.

COUNTER CASTLES (SIEGE CASTLES)
Structures to shelter besiegers against sorties and relief attempts, including temporary castles. Sometimes two or more were built against one target. William the Conqueror built counter castles against Brionne in the mid-11th century – William

of Poitiers calls them *castella*. The counter castle at Faringdon in 1145 had a rampart and stockade. That from the same period excavated at Bentley in Hampshire was similar to a motte and bailey castle.

CRAKKIS
Probably cannons, used by Edward III against the Scots in the 14th century, referred to as 'crakkis of war'.

CRENELLATION
The parapet on top of a castle or town wall, the battlements. The term comes from the French for embrasure. The familiar shape is of rectangular stone pieces (merlons) alternating with rectangular gaps (embrasures or crenels), thus giving a toothed effect. Defenders could shelter behind the stone pieces and shoot through the gaps. In England crenellation became the symbol of fortification, and a royal licence was required to crenellate a building.

CURTAIN
It has two senses, either the outer enclosing wall of a castle, or the wall joining two towers. The curtain was often strengthened with corner and mural towers.

DONJON
The stronghold of a castle, in England usually called the keep. Its meaning is the tower of a lord. It is the origin of the term dungeon but did not originally mean a prison.

DRAWBRIDGE
A bridge crossing a ditch or moat that could be lowered or raised. Its function was to make entrance difficult by rapidly raising it against undesired entrants. Drawbridges were usually of wood and commonly used.

EN BEC
A beak or projection of a rounded tower. It was a method of strengthening the base of a tower, especially against mining.

FONEVOL
A throwing engine. The name was used of engines used by Raymond of Toulouse in 1190 and by Jaime I of Aragón in the 13th century. The word probably derives from *funda* meaning sling and was probably a trebuchet.

FOREBUILDING
A structure before the entrance of a keep making the entrance more secure. It acted as a guardhouse. Attackers could not enter the keep without forcing the forebuilding. Entrance to the keep was often at first floor level by external steps enclosed within the forebuilding.

FUNDA
Latin for a siege engine, meaning 'sling', suggesting a trebuchet. The term was however used in 800 at Barcelona and 885 at Paris. Either a type of trebuchet appeared earlier than is thought, or the early term meant a hand sling or another engine.

GREEK FIRE
A combustible material. It could not easily be removed and, on impact, exploded into flames. It was invented for the Byzantines by Kallinikos in the 7th century and used at sea, especially in defence of Constantinople, as in 941 against the Rus. The Greeks shot it from a siphon or from catapults. Later its use was extended to land warfare and to other peoples. The Turks used it during the Crusades. Its first recorded use in western Europe was by Geoffrey V of Anjou at Montreuil-Bellay in 1151. He placed it in jars and hurled it from throwing engines. The recipe for Greek Fire was a secret and there were variant formulae in its manu-facture, some of which have been preserved. The major constituent was naphtha.

HOARDING
Wooden defences attached to a defended wall, the same as brattice-work. Hoarding made a gallery projecting over the wall with gaps through its floor. It protected defenders on top of the wall and allowed

missiles, oil etc to be dropped on attackers. Machicolation produced the same effect in stone. It was also a way to heighten walls against belfries.

KEEP
The stronghold of a castle, otherwise the donjon, normally a free-standing tower. Early castles usually had a keep on the motte or mound, surrounded by ditch and palisade. It might be wooden but there were early stone keeps. It was normally the residence of the lord of the castle. Early keeps were usually rectangular and on several storeys, with residential quarters and storage space. It was often built over a well to guarantee water supply. The top might have battlements. The entrance was often at first floor level, protected by a forebuilding. Later keeps were round or polygonal and sometimes were incorporated into the castle wall. Keep is an English term first used in the 16th century.

MACHICOLATION
Stone defence for the top of a wall, with the same function as wooden hoarding. It provided a gallery at the top of the wall, projecting over it and with gaps through the floor for defenders to hurl missiles or drop stones, oil etc. It became common in the later Middle Ages. It derives from French *machicoulis*, referring to the gaps in the floor.

MANGONEL
A type of throwing engine, from *manga* or *mangana*, meaning such an engine, probably from Greek *mangano* meaning crush or squeeze, i.e. 'a crusher'. Mangonels were usually relatively small. They worked by torsion from twisted ropes, with a spoon-like arm that revolved on release. The arm hit a cross bar causing the stone or object in the cup of the arm to be released. Mangonels date from ancient times and were used throughout the Middle Ages. Medieval chroniclers used terms in a confusing manner and could call any type of engine a mangonel.

MANTLET
A roofed protection for besiegers. The cat was a type of mantlet. The mantlet could be on wheels or it could be a portable roof. It protected those under it performing operations like mining. A mantlet could cover a smaller weapon, like a ram or bore, while it operated. (A mantlet wall was a defensive wall, generally low, around a tower.)

MERLON
Merlons were the stone teeth in battlements or crenellation. The term comes from *merlo* meaning battlement.

MEUTRIÈRES
'Murder holes', gaps in the floor of a chamber over a gatehouse or passage through which missiles or oil etc. could be dropped on attackers.

MINING
A common way to attack a wall or tower, usually by tunnelling under it, using wooden posts to replace the material removed. The posts would be fired and hopefully the structure would collapse. Counter mines might be built by defenders, allowing an attack on the miners *in situ*. Bores were useful for picking the initial hole in the wall to be mined. It was common to begin a tunnel at a distance to hide the intention. If the base of the wall was mined directly the operation could be covered, perhaps by a mantlet. At Caen in 1417 bowls of water were placed on the walls so that mining activity would disturb the water and warn the defenders.

MOAT
Defensive ditch around a tower, enclosure or castle, either wet or dry, though we normally mean a ditch filled with water. A moat made it more difficult to attack or climb the castle wall. In the late Middle Ages moats were made broader to keep cannons at a distance.

MOTTE

The main defensive mound of an earthwork castle, as in a motte and bailey castle, from French for a mound. Often a natural hill or height was used, sometimes shaped. Otherwise the motte could be constructed by hand, as at Hastings by William the Conqueror, illustrated on the *Bayeux Tapestry*. A keep of wood or stone was often built on the motte. Sometimes the motte was built around a tower. The origin of mottes is obscure. Possibly they were developed in the wars between Franks and Vikings, combining the existing fortification techniques of both sides.

PARAPET

A low wall at breast height, a breastwork. In the Middle Ages it was used for the top section added to a defensive wall. It usually projected outside the wall and protected a wall-walk. Crenellation could form a parapet.

PATERELL

A small throwing engine. Henry of Livonia refers to their use in the Baltic crusade. The probable derivation is from *patera*, meaning dish or cup, suggesting a form of mangonel.

PAVISE

A cover, shelter or screen for soldiers, especially archers. Pavises were often made of interwoven branches. A pavise could be like a shield set up on the ground before the man, supported by a prop. One chronicle describes pavises like doors that could be folded up with loopholes to shoot through.

PELE (PEEL)

A defensive and residential stone tower, sometimes with additional buildings, on the Scottish border. They compare to small keeps and were usually rectangular.

PETRARY (*PETRARIA*)

Literal general term for a stone-throwing engine, *petraria* in Latin. One hears of cords used for them but this would be true of almost any type of engine.

PORTCULLIS

Movable gate to block an entrance, from French, meaning 'sliding gate', commonly a grille of wood or metal lowered by chains or ropes in a groove. The lower struts were often pointed. Usually a chamber over the gate held winches to raise and lower it. It allowed a castle entrance to be shut rapidly against attack and was difficult to break through. Some gatehouses had two portcullises to trap those who entered first.

POSTERN

A lesser entrance or exit, rather like a back door. It might escape observation and allow secret or unexpected movement in and out.

RAM

A siege weapon for demolishing walls or gates, generally a log with a reinforced metal end. It was carried on a wheeled platform and swung from a beam on ropes or chains. It might have a protective roof. The ram was used in ancient times. During the Crusades ships' masts were used as rams.

RAMPART

Defensive earthwork wall, normally dug with a ditch before it and possibly topped by a stockade or stone wall.

RAVELIN

Forward construction, an outwork, triangular in shape with the point facing outwards, a common feature in early modern forts.

RENDABILITY

The duty to surrender one's castle to the feudal lord, an outcome of lords seeking to control castles in their region. They demanded that the castle should be rendered to them on request. It became a part of feudal agreements.

RIBAUDEQUIN (RIBAULD)

An early cannon, sometimes meaning simply 'gun'. They were tube-shaped with touch-holes. Ribaudequins were sometimes fixed together in a line and fired as one. The word appears often in the 14th century. At Bruges there were 'new engines called *ribaulde*'.

SCALING

The most common way to enter a castle or town, by climbing over the wall. All the obvious means were used, including ladders and ropes. Folding ladders and ladders of wood and leather were used. Ladders sometimes had hooks to grip on the wall. In 1453 the Turks brought 2,000 long ladders against Constantinople.

SCORPION

A small throwing engine, known from ancient times, *scorpio* in Latin, meaning a stinging insect, normally a form of balista to shoot bolts.

SOW (SCROPHA/PORCUS)

Term for a cat, a shelter for siege operations such as mining, apparently deriving from comparing men under the shelter to piglets suckling under their mother.

SPUR

Stone extension at the base of a tower, pointing outwards, to strengthen the tower against attack.

TALUS

A sloping extension at the foot of a tower or wall, otherwise a batter. The term originates from Latin for 'ankle'.

TESTUDO

Device to protect attackers, from Latin for tortoise, referring to its protective shell. The Romans used the term for a group of men covering their backs with shields. In the Middle Ages a *testudo* was a roof to protect men under it, with a similar function to a mantlet or cat.

TREBUCHET

Counterweight throwing engine, a major medieval invention. A container for heavy materials was placed on one end of a whippy pole, a sling to hold the stone or other missile at the other end. The pole was on a pivot. The loaded end was winched down and released. The weight made the loaded end rise rapidly and eject its contents, the sling whipping over at the last minute to give added impetus. The trebuchet had considerable range and impact. The date of origin is unclear. An engine called a traction trebuchet confuses the picture but was not a trebuchet proper, lacking a counterweight and operating by traction. The counterweight trebuchet probably first appeared in the 12th century, became important in the 13th century and remained the major siege engine until the development of effective cannons. The word may mean a three-legged stool and derive from the usual appearance of trebuchets on triangular frames. Another explanation is that it means three-armed, a reference to the common practice of making the counterweight arm in three sections to strengthen it.

WARD

Walled enclosure within a castle, a bailey, meaning a guarded place.

A cog, Luttrel Psalter

18 | Medieval naval warfare

NAVAL BATTLES

These have been dealt with in Part II in their national, political and geographical context. The following list covers some major battles found in Part II, with the relevant section in brackets after the name. Alexandretta 1294 [12], Curzola 1298 [12], Demetrias 1275 [7], Hafrsfjord 890 [3], Hals 980 [3], Hjörungavágr c.980 [3], Holy River 1026 [3], La Rochelle 1372 [9], Messina 1283 [12], Naples 1284 [12], Nissa 1062 [3], Phoenicus 655 [7], Pola 1379 [12], Sandwich 1217 [10], Sapienza 1354 [12], Sluys 1340 [9], Spetsai 1263 [7], Stilo 982 [7], Trapani 1264 [12].

A–Z OF TERMS

Carrack, carvel, clinker, cog, Greek Fire [17], hulk, keel, lateen, mizzen.

OUTLINE HISTORY

The two main scenes of action for medieval European naval warfare were the Mediterranean and the North Sea/English Channel. Conflicts between fleets were relatively few. Such as did occur were usually over transporting troops and supplies for war, or the domination of trade routes. Much medieval naval conflict had to do with illicit action by pirates – a plague to all sides though states often encouraged privateering. In the Mediterranean, the focus was on islands and ports on major routes. Attempts to clear out pirate bases, as at Rhodes, Sapienza or the Barbary Coast, were another type of conflict. Channel warfare was mostly over trade, as when England fought Flanders over wool and cloth, and France over wine. The wars between Venice and Genoa were about control of trade to the Middle and Far East. Fishing grounds also caused conflict.

State fleets were rare and usually small, supplemented in war by mercantile shipping. Ships involved in naval warfare were hardly different from those used for trade.
In the later Middle Ages naval powers built more ships as the expense of large war-
ships became too great for private enterprise. We do find some large fleets. In 1347
Edward III crossed the Channel with 738 ships carrying 32,000 men to Calais.

We know about ships from three main sources: from verbal description in narrative
sources, from manuscript illustration and works of art, and, increasingly important,
from archaeology. Ships buried on land were the first to provide evidence, as at Sutton
Hoo, but underwater work offers most for the future, especially on construction
methods.

Early Mediterranean ships were on the Roman model, galleys propelled partly by
oars. The Romans and others produced ships designed for war, a tradition continued
by the Byzantines. They had underwater rams to hit below water level and sink ships.
This was not a major feature in medieval warfare, where the projecting bow became
higher from at least the 10th century, making a beak rather than a ram, with the aim of
boarding rather than sinking. Outside the Mediterranean early ships were usually
clinker built, that is with overlapping planks nailed together. They were also partly
propelled by oars. Viking ships were clinker built and normally had a single sail. Early
northern ships were usually built upwards from the keel.

A major medieval contribution to naval warfare was the Byzantine invention of
Greek Fire, generally shot from a siphon. The exact ingredients remain unknown but
its effect was to ignite on impact – clearly effective against the hulls and sails of medieval ships. It was perhaps the chief reason that Constantinople remained free of
capture for so long. Eventually the west and the Turks learned how to use Greek Fire.

The main medieval developments were in shipbuilding and navigational knowledge. Ships became larger, useful for carrying larger cargoes but also for war. Larger
ships, known as cogs, were made through working on a frame, with straight stem and
stern posts. The frames were filled in with flush planks rather than overlapping. They
had rounder hulls. The mast (now larger) was stepped, making it firmer, and was generally placed more forward. From the 13th century one finds fixed decking. Caulking
material and varnish have been found in underwater excavation. There was a move
from a side to a rear rudder, though this did not necessarily improve manoeuvrability.
One development largely concerned with conflict was the heightening of structures at
prow and/or stern to make castles. At first these were added to an existing hull, but by
the 14th century they were part of the original structure. In conflict this favoured the
use of missile weapons especially by archers. Fighting tops were also built on the
masts.

In the later Middle Ages the larger ships, found in the Mediterranean and the North
Sea, were called carracks. They usually had two and later three masts. In 1420 the English royal fleet had 13 ships with two masts. By the end of the century three masts
were normal with a mainsail, foresail and lateen mizzen. By this time spritsails and
topsails were also common. The larger vessels could carry larger crews and more guns,
giving further advantage in conflict. The added sails made for greater manoeuvrability
than galleys.

Galleys remained important in the Mediterranean throughout the Middle Ages.
Oarsmen had the advantage of being able to manoeuvre and move quickly. The prob-

lem was a low draft that could mean flooding of the ship in bad weather and was impractical in the North Sea. In the later Middle Ages larger great galleys appeared with higher hulls, relying more on sails than oars – though having both. In the Mediterranean the advantage was mostly with the Christian powers. As Pryor has argued, this was because of weather conditions, winds and currents, giving advantage to those sailing from the north, allowing northern powers to control major ports and routes. The Italian sea powers took the lead in shipbuilding from the 11th century. Control of the sea prolonged the existence of the crusading states. Western domination was only threatened when the Arabs controlled the major islands in the early Middle Ages, and when the Ottomans controlled much of eastern Europe in the 15th century. Christian domination did not necessarily mean peace, and one of the most enduring naval conflicts of the Middle Ages was the struggle between the trade rivals from Italy – Venice and Genoa.

North Sea warfare was dominated by the Vikings in the early Middle Ages though their domination was such that warfare was rare and gave them the opportunity to raid and settle. Opposition came mainly on land. The Normans, under rulers descended from the Vikings, also utilised naval power to invade England and Sicily. In the Hundred Years' War England had the advantage over France in the Channel through much of the war following the early victory at Sluys.

At the end of the Middle Ages, navigational development made longer voyages easier. It is true that the Vikings had made remarkable voyages to Iceland, Greenland and North America but they did so with considerable danger. By the later Middle Ages, there were larger ships, better able to cope with oceanic conditions. Compasses, quadrants, astrolabes, globes and better knowledge of the heavens and the earth were available. There were capstans, pumps, bigger anchors and equipment for deep sounding. Iberia in particular took early advantage to make longer voyages and begin a new history of colonisation. Spain and Portugal were ideally placed to learn from Mediterranean and Channel developments and pioneered large ocean-going ships in the 15th century, often called caravels. They won control of much of the Mediterranean and pushed ahead with long-distance voyages round Africa and across the Atlantic.

A–Z OF TERMS

CARRACK
Larger type of ship in the late Middle Ages. It appeared in the 15th century with three masts plus spritsail and rear lateen sail, improving sailing qualities. It emerged in the Mediterranean but owed much to northern cogs.

CARVEL
Method of building a ship from a frame with a keel, adding flush planks to it, normally applied to late medieval ships. Such ships are sometimes called carvels or caravels.

CLINKER
Method of constructing a ship, usually from the keel upwards, by fixing together overlapping planks – as in Viking ships.

COG
The rounder type of ship that replaced clinker-built ships in the north. The hull was constructed with flush laid planks and the stem and stern posts were straight. The sides could still, however, be clinker-built.

GREEK FIRE
See Part III, Section 17.

HULK

Used technically of a later medieval ship with the rounded hull of a cog but planks that ended at the upper edge of the hull rather than on the stem and stern posts. The term probably originally meant a cargo ship. It came to apply to any large and slow ship.

KEEL

The great central bottom timber of the hull, usually attached at either end to stem and stern posts. A keel was also a type of medieval ship whose construction began from the keel, building upwards with clinker-built planks.

LATEEN

Triangular sail attached to a yard at an angle to the sea, rather than to an upright mast. It probably appeared first in the Mediterranean. Its function was for manoeuvrability. The term comes from French and means 'Latin', that is a Mediterranean sail.

MIZZEN

Both the sternmost mast of three, and the fore and aft sail on it. Italian *mezzana* and French *mizaine* have a common origin but both mean a foremast! Even more curiously all three terms seem to mean centre or middle! The only explanation that occurs is that the term was originally applied to the mast being between the two sails on it.

Templar knights leaving a crusader fortification in the Holy Land

19 | The medieval military orders

A–Z OF THE LEADING MEDIEVAL MILITARY ORDERS

Alcántara, Calatrava, Hospitallers, Santiago, Sword Brothers, Templars, Teutonic Knights.

OUTLINE HISTORY

The medieval military orders originated in the Holy Land with the establishment of the kingdom of Jerusalem. There were two main inspirations, firstly the need to protect Christian pilgrims in a hostile environment, and secondly the desire of many Christian knights to live a monastic existence. The orders were given their distinctive form through the efforts of St Bernard, who encouraged them, wrote a rule for the Templars and persuaded the papacy to grant the rule. The other orders followed a similar pattern thereafter, a monastic communal life with military duties in the outside world. The Templars began by protecting pilgrims wishing to bathe in the Jordan. The Hospitallers started by offering hospital and medical services to pilgrims. They were then organised as orders, which soon won respect and support from the west. They were granted lands and castles and garrisoned some of the most significant crusader castles. Through the history of the crusading kingdom they became something like a regular army always on call. They also developed houses in the west.

The end of the kingdom of Jerusalem, with the taking of Acre, led to the orders needing a new *raison d'être*, which they did not always succeed in finding. The Templars became guardians of royal treasure in their temples in France but attracted the acquisitive interest of Philip IV. He levelled grossly distorted charges against them, persuading his people and the papacy to support him. The Templars were dissolved.

The Hospitallers fared better. They made gains from the fall of the Templars. Their medical role stood them in good stead. They moved to new bases, in Crete and then more permanently in Rhodes. Here they withstood two major sieges by Muslims and held on until 1522 when they were forced out to Malta.

The third major order, the Teutonic Knights, though claiming early origins, became an order at the end of the 12th century. They had castles in the Holy Land but their major significance was elsewhere. With the fall of Acre they moved their headquarters to Venice and then to Marienburg. They received support from the Holy Roman Emperor and the King of Hungary. They spearheaded the Baltic crusade against pagans. The Sword Brothers were founded in the Baltic area using the Templar rule. After defeat in 1237 the remnants of the order were absorbed by the Teutonic Knights. The Knights came into conflict with neighbouring powers. At first they attracted wide western interest but after the conversion of the pagan peoples received less support. After defeat at Tannenberg in 1410 the order went into decline. Protestant and Russian opposition led to the break-up of the order in the 16th century.

Iberia was another major centre for military orders. As the home of the Christian *Reconquista* it attracted members from the main orders. It also saw the development of home-grown orders, those of Santiago, Alcántara and Calatrava in particular. The Knights at first protected Christians rather as in the Holy Land, including pilgrims going to St James (Santiago) de Compostela. They were more committed to religious war than some of their secular counterparts, were opposed to treating with Muslims and carried out raids and even atrocities, such as decapitating Muslim prisoners. As in the Holy Land they provided a permanent and useful army. The privileges and independence of the orders were apt to be resented by secular rulers. In the Holy Land they had often acted independently of royal wishes, and they did much the same in Spain. Once the *Reconquista* had been achieved the Christian monarchs were unwilling to allow them the same freedoms and their power declined.

A–Z OF THE LEADING MEDIEVAL MILITARY ORDERS

ALCÁNTARA, ORDER OF
The Knights of San Julián de Pereiro (the Sanjulianistas), as they began, established a base on the León border by 1170. They were granted lands and recognised as an order in 1176. They were connected to the Order of Calatrava. They wore a white habit. Like all the other Iberian orders, they gained through the *Reconquista*, taking over half of Extremadura. At the completion of the conquest the order was subjected to royal control, its property seized in 1523.

CALATRAVA, ORDER OF
Calatrava or Qalat Rawaah (the castle of war) was on the banks of the River Guadiana, captured by Alfonso VII in 1147. It was handed to the Templars. When they planned to abandon it, a group of Cistercian monks took over, intent on

defending it. They were recognised as an order in 1164. They wore a hooded white or grey tunic. The order expanded with the *Reconquista*. The order was reformed in the 14th century.

HOSPITALLERS
Otherwise the Knights of St John of the Hospital. Their origins are in the founding of a hospital in Jerusalem for pilgrims. There is mention of a hospital of St John the Almoner even before the First Crusade. In c.1150 the Knights of St John were founded as an order to tend the sick. It took on military aspects similar to the Templars. By 1187 it held 20 castles in the Holy Land, including Krak des Chevaliers, and spread in Europe. The monks wore a black mantle with a white cross. One of their officers was a Turcopolier who commanded native

troops. Grand master Garnier de Nablus, against orders, led the charge at Arsuf that led to victory. After the fall of Acre, the Hospitallers found a new base in Rhodes from 1306. They built houses for the various member nations in Rhodes Town, which may still be seen. They became a Mediterranean naval power. Rhodes held off Muslim sieges in 1444–6 and 1480. The Knights were forced out in 1522, going to Malta, where they survived until the time of Napoleon.

SANTIAGO, ORDER OF

The order of Santiago, or St James of the Sword, emulated in Spain the activities of the Templars in the Holy Land. They began by protecting pilgrims going to St James of Compostela (Santiago de Compostela). St James was said to have miraculously returned to lead Christians against the Muslims. They received a rule in 1171 from the papal legate, recognised by Pope Alexander III in 1175. It was based on the Augustinian rule. It allowed the acceptance of married knights. They wore a white habit with a red cross. They became defenders of the Christian frontier in the *Reconquista*. They gained land in Portugal, Spain and elsewhere in Europe including Hungary. Alfonso IX el Baboso (the slobberer) granted them a tenth of the value of all money coined in León. After the completion of the conquest they declined. Their property was taken over by Charles V in 1523, though this was not the end of the order.

SWORD BROTHERS (SCHWERTBRÜDER)

Riga was founded by bishop Albrecht in 1201 and he established the Sword Brothers there shortly afterwards, using the Templar rule. They wore a white habit with a red sword and a red cross on the shoulder. They learned military techniques, including how to operate siege engines. The grand master was based at Riga. They built other castles, including Wenden. They invaded Estonia against pagans to establish Marienland.

When invading Lithuania, they were defeated in 1237 at Siauliai by the Kurs in alliance with Mindaugas prince of Lithuania. The order dissolved and the survivors joined the Teutonic Knights.

TEMPLARS

The Poor Knights of the Temple of Solomon in Jerusalem, originally a group of monks to protect pilgrims wishing to bathe in the River Jordan. They attracted the interest of St Bernard in the European age of new monastic orders. He provided them with a rule and gained approval for it from the papacy. There is mention of a master of Knights of the Temple in 1123. The papacy recognised the rule in 1128. It became the model for further military orders. Templars spread through the Holy Land and Europe with their houses – preceptories or commanderies. They wore a hooded white mantle. Grand master Gerard de Ridefort persuaded King Guy to go to Tiberias, leading to the disaster at Hattin, after which the captured Knights were executed. The loss of the Holy Land was a blow to the Templars. They still had much property in the west but never really established a new justification for existence. Philip IV of France decided to destroy them. He arrested the French Templars in 1307. Charges were laid against them, including heretical and pagan practices, mostly distorted or even invented. Their grand master, Jacques de Molay, was burned at the stake in 1314. The papacy agreed to the dissolution of the order, whose possessions and wealth went to other orders and to the king.

TEUTONIC KNIGHTS

Founded in 1198 as the Teutonic Knights of St Mary. They originated in the Holy Land with a base at Acre. They had a white habit with a black and gold cross. They gained land and castles, including Montfort. The order became exclusively German. It was given European lands by Frederick II and Andrew II of Hungary with commanderies in Germany, Prussia and the Baltic region where they led the crusades against pagans.

In 1237 they absorbed the remnants of the order of the Sword Brothers. They suffered defeat against the Mongols at Liegnitz in 1241 when nine sacks of severed Knights' ears were hauled before Khān Batu, and in 1242 at Lake Peipus by Alexander Nevsky. The loss of the Holy Land was followed by the Knights moving their headquarters to Venice and then to Marienburg, now Malbork in Poland. It became the main base for the northern crusades, visited by among others Henry Bolingbroke. They built a hospital for elderly knights. Tannenberg in 1410 was a major disaster for the Knights at the hands of Poles and Lithuanians, when their grand master Von Juningen was killed and mutilated. They lost territories to Poland and Lithuania. After further defeats in the 15th century the order divided. Under Protestant criticism and Russian pressure the order disintegrated in the early 16th century.

PART IV

Further information

20 | Primary sources for the study of medieval warfare

Primary sources on medieval warfare are relatively few. One must include finds from archaeological excavations, including underwater examples for naval warfare. We only include works that for the most part are relatively easily available to the general reader, in short, works that have been translated and printed.

Most records and chronicles may have some bearing on the subject but again we exclude the broad run of such works and include only a few examples. We have also attempted to find sources broadly covering our sections and to include a select few. The general reader may well not wish to study primary sources but curious readers and budding historians perhaps will. No secondary opinion can ever be considered perfect and final, and the best way of reconsidering views is to return to the original evidence.

Roman writers on warfare had some effect on medieval warfare. They influenced medieval chroniclers, who were among the few then able to obtain copies of their work and read them. They influenced leaders who had education or had educated advisers. The most telling example is provided by John of Marmoutier about his hero Geoffrey le Bel of Anjou. At the siege of Montreuil-Bellay John tells us that, as the siege became bogged down, Geoffrey took to reading the Latin work *De Re Militari* by Vegetius. In it he found inspiration for how to proceed with the siege and eventually take the castle. A few works on military subjects were written during the Middle Ages. Two outstanding examples are mentioned. The first was amazingly by a woman, Christine de Pisan, who wrote on chivalry and knighthood. The second, also unique in its way, was by a medieval king, Jaime I of Aragón (1208–76). Jaime played an important part in the *Reconquista* and recovered the Balearic islands. He wrote about his own campaigns in telling detail.

For the modern student the best approach is often through especially selected sources, as in collections that exist for various wars and battles, reigns or periods, and some of these are included.

SELECT BIBLIOGRAPHY

Ailes, Adrian, 'Heraldry in Twelfth-century England: The Evidence', *England in the Twelfth Century: Proceedings of the 1988 Harlaxton Symposium*, Woodbridge, 1990, pp. 1–16

Alexander, Michael, ed., *The Earliest English Poems*, Harmondsworth, 1966

Anglo-Saxon Chronicle, The, ed. D. Whitelock, D.C. Douglas and S.I. Tucker, London, 1961

Asser, *Life of Alfred the Great* with other sources, ed. S. Keynes and M. Lapidge, Harmondsworth, 1983

Barbaro, Nicolo, *Diary of the Siege of Constantinople, 1453*, ed. J.R. Jones, New York, 1969

Bayeux Tapestry, The, ed. D.M. Wilson, London, 1985

Bertran de Born, The Poems of the Troubadour, ed. W.D. Paden Jr, T. Sankovitch and P.H. Stäblein, London, 1986

Bonet, Honoré, *The Tree of Battles*, ed. G.W. Coopland, Liverpool, 1949

Brown, R. Allen, ed., *The Norman Conquest*, London, 1984

Chronicle of the Morea: Crusaders as Conquerors, ed. H.E. Lurier, New York, 1964

Commynes, Philippe de, *Memoirs*, trans. M. Jones, Harmondsworth, 1972

Comnena, Anna, *The Alexiad*, trans. E.R.A. Sewter, Harmondsworth, 1969

De Expugnatione Lyxbonensi, ed. C.W. David, New York, 1976

Doukas, *The Decline and Fall of Byzantium to the Ottoman Turks*, ed. H.J. Magoulias, Detroit, 1975

Einhard, *The Life of Charlemagne*, ed. L. Thorpe (English translation), London, 1970

English Historical Documents, ed. D.C. Douglas, i, 2nd edition London 1979; ii, 2nd edition 1981; iii, 1975; iv, 1969

Fantosme, Jordan, *Chronicle*, ed. R.C. Johnston, Oxford, 1981

Freising, Otto of, and Rahewin, *The Deeds of Frederick Barbarossa*, ed. C.C. Mierow and R. Emery, New York, 1953

Froissart, Jean, *Chronicles*, ed. G. Brereton, 2nd edition, Harmondsworth, 1978

Froissart, Jean, *Chronicles*, ed. J. Jolliffe, London, 1967

Gabrieli, Francesco, *Arab Historians of the Crusades*, London, 1969

Gregory of Tours, *The History of the Franks*, ed. L. Thorpe, Harmondsworth, 1974

Hallam, Elizabeth, ed., *Chronicles of the Crusades*, London, 1989

Hill, Boyd H., *Medieval Monarchy in Action: The German Empire from Henry I to Henry IV*, Oxford, 1972

Hutchinson, Gillian, *Medieval Ships and Shipping*, London, 1994

James I King of Aragón, *Chronicle*, ed. J. Forster, 2 vols, London, 1883

Joinville and Hardouin, *Chronicles of the Crusades*, trans. M.R.B. Shaw, Harmondsworth, 1963

Jones, J.R.M., *The Siege of Constantinople, 1453: The Contemporary Accounts*, Amsterdam, 1972

King, P.D., ed, *Charlemagne: Translated Sources*, Kendal, 1987

Livonia, Henry of, *Chronicle*, ed. J.A. Brundage, New York, 1961

Morillo, Stephen, ed., *The Battle of Hastings*, Woodbridge, 1996

Nicolas, Sir Harris, *The History of the Battle of Agincourt*, London, 1970

Nicolle, David, *Medieval Warfare Source Book: Warfare in Western Christendom*, London, 1995

Nicolle, David, *Medieval Warfare Source Book, vol. II: Christian Europe and its Neighbours*, London, 1996

Oakeshott, E., *The Archaeology of Weapons*, London, 1960

Pisan, Christine de, *The Book of Faytes of Arms and Chyvalrye*, trans. W. Caxton, London, 1932

Procopius, *The Secret History*, trans. G.A. Williamson, London, 1990

Psellus, Michael, *Fourteen Byzantine Rulers (Chronographia)*, trans. E.R.A. Sewter, Harmondsworth, 1966

Riley-Smith, Louise and Jonathan, *The Crusades: Idea and Reality 1095–1274*, London, 1981

Sagas of Icelanders, The, Preface J. Smiley, Introduction R. Kellogg, London, 1997

Siege of Caerlaverock, The, ed. N.H. Nicolas, London, 1828

Simpson, L.B., trans., *The Poem of the Cid*, Berkeley, 1957

Smith, Colin, ed., *Christians and Moors in Spain*, i, *711–1150*, Warminster, 2nd edition, 1993

Smith, Colin, ed., *Christians and Moors in Spain*, ii, *1195–1614*, Warminster, 1989

Suger, *The Deeds of Louis the Fat*, ed. R.C. Cusimano and J. Moorhead, Washington, 1992

Thordemann, B., *Armour from the Battle of Visby*, Stockholm, 1939

Three Chronicles of the Reign of Edward IV, ed. K. Dockray, Gloucester, 1988

Upton-Ward, J.M., ed., *The Rule of the Templars*, Woodbridge, 1992

Usāmah Ibn-Munqidh, *Memoirs: An Arab-Syrian Gentleman and Warrior in the Period of the Crusades*, trans. P.K. Hitti, London, 1987

Van Houts, Elisabeth, ed., *The Normans in Europe*, Manchester, 2000

Vegetius, *Epitome of Military Science*, trans. N.P. Milner, Liverpool, 1993

William of Tyre, *A History of Deeds Done Beyond the Sea*, ed. R.B.C. Huygens, 2 vols, Brepols, 1986

Wrottesley, G., *Crecy and Calais from the Public Records*, London, 1898

21 | Historians of medieval warfare and recommendations for further reading

We have mentioned in our comments on primary sources that some medieval writers did comment on warfare as a subject, such as Christine de Pisan and Honoré de Bonet. Here we need to look at some of the main contributors to the discussion in modern times. We shall only include printed books, mainly in English. Journal articles have often made important contributions but we have restricted ourselves to books. The details of these works may be found in Section 22.

It is probably fair to suggest that the modern history of medieval warfare took off in Germany and France from the late 19th century. E.E. Viollet-le-Duc investigated military architecture. Delbrück, Köhler and Delpech devoted weighty tomes to the subject of general war. Delpech's major work on tactics was published in 1886 after 11 years' work. It was soon followed by Köhler's work. He was a Prussian general and was convinced that western war owed most to the Byzantines. Neither of these early historians was critical of his sources in a way that modern historians would expect.

Hans Delbrück (1848–1929) edited *Prussian Annals* and was Professor of History at Berlin. He is perhaps the earliest historian of medieval warfare whose work still commands respect, and is still available in English translation. Like many historians of that age however he tended to get others to do his dirty work, reading sources and so on.

In England Sir Charles Oman is the early parallel, and he indeed owed a good deal to Delbrück. His first slim volume was published in 1885, written while still an undergraduate, but his heftier two-volume *History of the Art of War* followed, published in a revised edition in 1924, filled out with extra sections that he wrote in 'the long parliamentary recess of 1923'. Another important early contribution from England came in the field of castle studies from Mrs Ella S. Armitage, whose seminal work on early Norman castles was published in 1912.

A new generation of historians provided more professional work, based on solid research. This does not mean of course that we need agree with all their conclusions. The scope of study also widened. F.M. Stenton made a fundamental study of feudalism, first elaborated in the Ford Lectures at Oxford, delivered in 1929 and published in 1932. American historians became increasingly important in this field. Sidney Painter published his work on French chivalry in 1940.

Post-war historical work has probably had more influence than anything earlier on current historians, as war history has become increasingly academic in one direction but also popular in terms of interest – perhaps a consequence of the war. Ferdinand Lot produced his work on the military art in two volumes in 1946, the fruit of earlier work. It contains much detail but seems rather obsessed by the size of armies, trusting too much in figures that cannot be reliable. J.F. Verbruggen's work on the art of warfare was first published in Dutch in 1954 and later in two editions in English. He too had published much work in advance of this his masterpiece. It concentrated on the details of battles. In that same year R.C. Smail published his history of crusading warfare, a pioneering effort that has since led to almost an industry in its own right. More recent basic information for all students of medieval warfare is found in the volume by Philippe Contamine. These works demonstrate the move from narrative in the earlier period to analysis which has largely dominated the academic contribution to the subject ever since.

More recent work has tended to specialise more – on individual wars, campaigns, periods or topics within the subject. One can only mention a few works that seem particularly important and be aware that one is omitting more than one is including. On castles the work of R. Allen Brown, both architectural and historical, has been important, as has that of Arnold Taylor, J.-F. Finó, M.W. Thompson and N.J.G. Pounds. Maurice Keen has written widely but perhaps his two most influential works have been on the laws of war and on chivalry – another growth industry, in which the names of G. Cohen, J. Flori, Malcolm Vale and W.H. Jackson also deserve mention. In terms of period Bernard S. Bachrach has added much to our knowledge of early medieval warfare. On the Anglo-Saxon and Norman Conquest period the analytical work of Warren Hollister has been invaluable. Subsequent contributions have been made by Richard Abels. Other recent important work on fiefs and vassals is that of F.L. Ganshof, I.J. Sanders, B.D. Lyon and Susan Reynolds. Many historians have worked on the military aspects of the Hundred Years' War, including Edouard Perroy, Kenneth Fowler, Ann Curry and Christopher Allmand. John Beeler produced volumes on warfare in England and Europe. There are many good books on the Wars of the Roses, including those by Anthony Goodman and Andrew W. Boardman. Among the most important military works on the Crusades have been those by Randy Rogers, John France and Christopher Marshall. On Byzantium the work of Mark C. Bartusis and John Haldon is valuable.

Works on individuals and individual battles are far too numerous to mention but one or two examples will suffice, where the military aspect looms large. Excellent examples are John Gillingham on Richard the Lionheart and Georges Duby on Bouvines. Among works on what one might call warfare topics, high on the list must come Frederick H. Russell's on the just war. Both J.O. Prestwich and M. Prestwich have added important work on the financing of war. The technological side of warfare has found several students, including Lynn White Junior and more recently Kelly DeVries.

On mercenaries we should include the work of Jean Boussard and Michael Mallett. Another topic to attract interest has been warhorses, with work by R.H.C. Davis and Ann Hyland. Oakeshott has pioneered work on the sword and weapons.

Yet one should not ignore the more popular works of history that focus on warfare and help to keep awake a wider interest. Among these one should mention the work of Alfred H. Burne on battlefields and on the Hundred Years' War. Works on topics include Geoffrey Trease on the *condottieri*. Richard Barber is not only a popularist but his contribution to English history and chivalry has had wide readership. The collections of chronicles and other material edited by Elizabeth Hallam are also useful for anyone starting out on historical study. Robert Hardy's work on the longbow has brought to history many who knew him first as an actor. This last paragraph could be expanded even more than all the others. I cannot name all those concerned in helping to make history popular and of course there is no absolute line that excludes all academics from the process. I express my own thanks to all those who have written books I have enjoyed and hope their works will do the same for you.

22 | Bibliography of secondary sources and further reading

Works that are particularly recommended for new students and make good introductions are starred *.

GENERAL WORKS

Barber, Richard, *The Reign of Chivalry*, New York, 1980 *
Cantor, Norman F., ed., *The Pimlico Encyclopedia of the Middle Ages*, London, 1999
Chambers Dictionary of World History, ed. B.P. Lenman, Edinburgh, 1993
Chronology of the Medieval World 800–1491, ed. R.L. Storey, Oxford, 1973
Cohen, G., *Histoire de la chevalerie en France au moyen âge*, Paris, 1949
Contamine, P., *War in the Middle Ages*, trans. M. Jones, Oxford, 1984
Delbrück, Hans, *History of the Art of War, iii, The Middle Ages*, trans. W.J. Renfroe Jr, Westport, 1982
Delpech, H., *La Tactique au XIIIe siècle*, 2 vols, Paris, 1886
DeVries, Kelly, *Medieval Military Technology*, Ontario, 1992
Dictionary of Ancient and Medieval Warfare, ed. M. Bennett, Oxford, 1998
Dupuy, R. Ernest and Trevor N. Dupuy, *The Collins Encyclopedia of Military History*, 4th edition, London, 1993
Encyclopedia of World History, ed. F. Alexander, Oxford, 1998
Gardiner, Juliet and Neil Wenborn, *The History Today Companion to British History*, London, 1995
Hallam, Elizabeth, ed., *Chronicles of the Age of Chivalry*, London, 1987 *
Hooper, N. and M. Bennett, *The Cambridge Illustrated Atlas of Warfare, The Middle Ages, 768–1487*, Cambridge, 1996
Keen, Maurice, *Chivalry*, London, 1984
Keen, Maurice, *The Laws of War in the Late Middle Ages*, London, 1965
Keen, Maurice, ed., *Medieval Warfare: A History*, Oxford, 1999

Koch, H.W., *Medieval Warfare*, London, 1978

Köhler, G., *Die Entwickelung des Kriegswesens und der Kriegführung in der Ritterzeit*, 5 vols, Breslau, 1886–9

Natkiel, R. and J. Pimlott, *Atlas of Warfare*, London, 1988

Nicolle, David, *Medieval Warfare Source Book: Warfare in Western Christendom*, London, 1995

Nicolle, David, *Medieval Warfare Source Book, vol. II: Christian Europe and its Neighbours*, London, 1996

Oman, C., *A History of the Art of War in the Middle Ages*, 2 vols, London 1991 (first published 1924)

Oman, C., *The Art of War in the Middle Ages*, ed. J.H. Beeler, Ithaca, 1953

Painter, Sidney, *French Chivalry*, Baltimore, 1940

Prestwich, M., *War, Politics and Finance under Edward I*, London, 1972

Russell, F.H., *The Just War in the Middle Ages*, Cambridge, 1975

Stenton, F.M., *The First Century of English Feudalism*, 2nd edition, Oxford, 1961

Vale, Malcolm, *War and Chivalry*, London, 1981

Verbruggen, J.F., *The Art of Warfare in Western Europe during the Middle Ages*, 2nd edition, Woodbridge, 1997

White, Lynn, Jr, *Medieval Technology and Social Change*, Oxford, 1962

SECONDARY WORKS RELATING TO SECTIONS IN THE BOOK

1 ROMANS AND BARBARIANS, 400–750

Bachrach, B.S., *Merovingian Military Organization, 481–751*, Minneapolis, 1972

Collins, R., *Early Medieval Europe 300–1000*, 2nd edition, London, 1999 *

James, E., *The Origins of France*, London, 1982

Randers-Pehrson, J.D., *Barbarians and Romans*, Norman, 1983

Wallace-Hadrill, J.M., *The Barbarian West 400–1000*, London, 1952 *

Wood, I., *The Merovingian Kingdoms 450–751*, Harlow, 1994

2 CHARLEMAGNE AND THE CAROLINGIANS, 750–850

Beeler, J., *Warfare in Feudal Europe, 730–1200*, London, 1972 *

Boussard, J., trans. F. Partridge, *The Civilisation of Charlemagne*, London, 1968

Bullough, D., *The Age of Charlemagne*, London, 1980

Collins, R., *Charlemagne*, London, 1998

Halphen, L., trans. G. De Nie, *Charlemagne and the Carolingian Empire*, Oxford, 1977

James, E., *The Origins of France from Clovis to the Capetians, 500–1000*, London, 1982 *

McKitterick, R., *The Frankish Kingdoms under the Carolingians, 751–987*, Harlow, 1983

Munz, P., *Life in the Age of Charlemagne*, London, 1969

Nelson, J.L., *Charles the Bald*, Harlow, 1992

Riché, P., trans. M.I. Allen, *The Carolingians, a Family who Forged Europe*, Philadelphia, 1993

Winston, R., *Charlemagne, from the Hammer to the Cross*, London, 1956 *

3 THE VIKINGS, SCANDINAVIA AND NORTHERN EUROPE, 850–1050

Arbman, Holger, *The Vikings*, London, 1961 *

Christiansen, E., *The Northern Crusades*, London, 1980

Foote, P.G. and D.M. Wilson, *The Viking Achievement*, London, 1970

Haywood, John, *Encyclopaedia of the Viking Age*, London, 2000
Jones, Gwyn, *A History of the Vikings*, Oxford, 1973
Logan, F. Donald, *The Vikings in History*, London, 1983
Magnusson, Magnus, *Vikings!*, London, 1980 *
Oxenstierna, Eric Graf, *The World of the Norsemen*, trans. J. Sondheimer, London, 1967
Poertner, Peter, *The Vikings*, trans. S. Wilkins, London, 1975
Roesdahl, Else, *The Vikings*, trans. S.M. Margeson and K. Williams, London, 1991
Sawyer, Peter, ed., *The Oxford Illustrated History of the Vikings*, Oxford, 1997
Wilson, David, *The Vikings and their Origins*, London, 1970

4 THE ANGLO-SAXON INVASIONS AND ENGLAND, 450–1066

Abels, Richard P., *Lordship and Military Obligation in Anglo-Saxon England*, London, 1988
Brandon, Peter, ed., *The South Saxons*, Chichester, 1978
Campbell, James, ed., *The Anglo-Saxons*, London, 1982 *
Henson, Donald, *A Guide to Late Anglo-Saxon England, from Aelfred to Eadgar II*,
    Hockwold-cum-Wilton, 1997
Holmes, Michael, *King Arthur, a Military History*, London, 1996
Kirby, D.P., *The Earliest English Kings*, 2nd edition, London, 2000
Loyn, H.R., *The Making of the English Nation*, London, 1991 *
Morris, John, *The Age of Arthur*, London, 1973
Pollingston, Stephen, *The English Warrior*, Hockwold-cum-Wilton, 1996
Stenton, F.M., *Anglo-Saxon England*, 2nd edition, Oxford, 1947
Sturdy, David, *Alfred the Great*, London, 1995
Whittock, Martyn J., *The Origins of England, 410–600*, London, 1986
Williams, Ann, *The English and the Norman Conquest*, Woodbridge, 1995
Wilson, D.M., *The Anglo-Saxons*, London, 1960 *

5 THE NORMAN CONQUESTS IN BRITAIN AND EUROPE, 911–1154

Bates, David, *Normandy before 1066*, Harlow, 1982
Bates, David, *William the Conqueror*, London, 1989 *
Beeler, John, *Warfare in England 1066–1189*, New York, 1966 *
Bradbury, Jim, *Stephen and Matilda*, Stroud, 1996
Bradbury, Jim, *The Battle of Hastings*, Stroud, 1998
Brown, R.A., *The Normans*, Woodbridge, 1984
Brown, R.A., *The Normans and the Norman Conquest*, 2nd edition, Woodbridge, 1985
Chibnall, Marjorie, *The Empress Matilda*, Oxford, 1991
Cronne, H.A., *The Reign of Stephen*, London, 1970
Curtis, Edmund, *Roger the Great*, London, 1912
Davis, R.H.C., *King Stephen*, 3rd edition, Harlow, 1990
Douglas, David C., *The Norman Achievement*, London, 1969
Douglas, David C., *The Norman Fate*, Berkeley and Los Angeles, 1976
Douglas, David C., *William the Conqueror*, London, 1964
Kapelle, William E., *The Norman Conquest of the North*, London, 1979
Le Patourel, John, *The Norman Empire*, Oxford, 1976
Loyn, H.R., *The Norman Conquest*, 3rd edition, London, 1982
Matthew, Donald, *The Norman Kingdom of Sicily*, Cambridge, 1992
Morillo, Stephen, *Warfare under the Anglo-Norman Kings*, Woodbridge, 1994
Norwich, John Julius, *The Kingdom in the Sun*, London, 1970 *
Norwich, John Julius, *The Normans in the South*, London, 1967 *
Williams, Ann, *The English and the Norman Conquest*, Woodbridge, 1995

6 THE HOLY ROMAN EMPIRE AND CENTRAL EUROPE, 850–1500

Abulafia, David, *Frederick II*, London, 1988

Arnold, Benjamin, *Medieval Germany, 500–1300*, London, 1997 *

Barraclough, Geoffrey, *Medieval Germany, 911–1250*, 2 vols, Oxford, 1938

Du Boulay, F.R.H., *Germany in the Later Middle Ages*, London, 1983

Hampe, Karl, *Germany under the Salian and Hohenstaufen Emperors*, trans. R. Bennett, Oxford, 1973

Leyser, K.J., *Medieval Germany and its Neighbours, 900–1250*, London, 1982

Lukowski, Jerzy and Hubert Zawadzki, *A Concise History of Poland*, Cambridge, 2001

Munz, Peter, *Frederick Barbarossa*, London, 1969 *

Reuter, Timothy, *Germany in the Early Middle Ages, 800–1056*, Harlow, 1991 *

7 THE BYZANTINE EMPIRE AND EASTERN EUROPE, 400–1453

Bartusis, Mark C., *The Late Byzantine Army*, Philadelphia, 1992

Baynes, Norman H. and H. St. L.B. Moss, eds., *Byzantium*, Oxford, 1948

Browning, R., *Byzantium and Bulgaria*, London, 1975

Fine, John V.A., *The Early Medieval Balkans*, Michigan, 1983

Fine, John V.A. Jr, *The Late Medieval Balkans*, Michigan, 1987

Freely, John, *Istanbul*, London, 1996 *

Haldon, John, *Warfare, State and Society in the Byzantine World, 565–1204*, London, 1999

Hoetzsch, Otto, *The Evolution of Russia*, London, 1966 *

Macartney, C.A., *Hungary, a Short History*, Edinburgh, 1962

Morgan, David, *The Mongols*, Oxford, 1986 *

Norwich, John Julius, *Byzantium*, 3 vols, London, 1988–95 *

Obolensky, Dimitri, *The Byzantine Commonwealth*, London, 1971

Runciman, Steven, *The Fall of Constantinople 1453*, Cambridge, 1965 *

Shaw, Stanford J., *History of the Ottoman Empire and Modern Turkey*, vol. I, Cambridge, 1976

Stiles, Andrina, *The Ottoman Empire 1450–1700*, London, 1989

Treadgold, Warren, *A Concise History of Byzantium*, Houndmills, 2001

Vryonis, Speros, *Byzantium and Europe*, London, 1967

Whitting, Philip, ed., *Byzantium, an Introduction*, Oxford, 1972

8 THE CRUSADES, 1095–1500

Billings, Malcolm, *The Cross and the Crescent*, London, 1987 *

France, John, *Western Warfare in the Age of the Crusades 1000–1300*, New York, 1999

Housley, Norman, *The Later Crusades*, Oxford, 1992

Godfrey, John, *1204, The Unholy Crusade*, Oxford, 1980 *

Maalouf, Amin, *The Crusades through Arab Eyes*, trans. Jon Rothschild, London, 1984

Madaule, Jacques, *The Albigensian Crusade*, trans. B. Wall, London, 1967

Marshall, Christopher, *Warfare in the Latin East 1192–1291*, Cambridge, 1992

Mayer, Hans Eberhard, *The Crusades*, Oxford, 1972

Riley-Smith, Jonathan, *The Crusades, a Short History*, London, 1987 *

Riley-Smith, Jonathan, ed., *The Atlas of the Crusades*, London, 1991

Riley-Smith, Jonathan, ed., *The Oxford Illustrated History of the Crusades*, Oxford, 1995

Rogers, R., *Latin Siege Warfare in the Twelfth Century*, Oxford, 1992

Runciman, Steven, *A History of the Crusades*, 3 vols, Cambridge, 1951–4

Smail, R.C., *Crusading Warfare 1097–1193*, Cambridge, 1956

Smail, R.C., *The Crusaders*, London, 1973

Strayer, Joseph R., *The Albigensian Crusades*, Michigan, 1971

Sumption, Jonathan, *The Albigensian Crusade*, London, 1978

9 THE CAPETIANS AND THE VALOIS, FRANCE 987–1500

Bradbury, Jim, *Philip Augustus*, London, 1988

Burne, Alfred H., *The Agincourt War*, London, 1956

Burne, Alfred H., *The Crecy War*, London, 1955

Curry, Anne and M. Hughes, eds., *Arms, Armies and Fortifications in the Hundred Years War*, Woodbridge, 1994

Duby, Georges, *France in the Middle Ages 987–1460*, trans. J. Vale, Oxford, 1991

Dunbabin, Jean, *France in the Making 843–1180*, Oxford, 1985 *

Fawtier, Robert, *The Capetian Kings of France*, trans. L. Butler and R.J. Adam, London, 1964

Fowler, Kenneth, *The Age of Plantagenet and Valois*, London, 1980

Funck-Brentano, Fr., *The National History of France: The Middle Ages*, trans. E. O'Neill, London, 1922

Hallam, Elizabeth M. and J. Everard, *Capetian France*, 2nd edition, London, 2001

Jones, Colin, *The Cambridge Illustrated History of France*, Cambridge, 1994

Nicholas, David, *Medieval Flanders*, Harlow, 1992

Perroy, Edouard, *The Hundred Years War*, trans. W.B. Wells, London, 1965

Seward, Desmond, *The Hundred Years War*, London, 1978 *

Sumption, Jonathan, *Trial by Battle: The Hundred Years War*, 2 vols, London, 1990–9

Tuchman, Barbara W., *A Distant Mirror: The Calamitous 14th Century*, London, 1979 *

Vaughan, Richard, *Valois Burgundy*, London, 1975

10 THE ANGEVINS TO THE TUDORS, BRITAIN 1154–1485

Boardman, A.W., *The Medieval Soldier in the Wars of the Roses*, Stroud, 1998

Burne, Alfred H., *The Battlefields of England*, 2nd edition, London, 1951

Burne, Alfred H., *More Battlefields of England*, London, 1952

Clanchy, M.T., *England and its Rulers, 1066–1272*, Oxford, 1983

Gillingham, J., *The Wars of the Roses*, London, 1981 *

Goodman, A., *A History of England from Edward II to James I*, London, 1977

Goodman, A., *The Wars of the Roses*, London, 1981

Greene, Howard, *The Battlefields of Britain and Ireland*, London, 1973

Mortimer, Richard, *Angevin England, 1154–1258*, Oxford, 1994

Seymour, William, *Battles in Britain*, vol. I, London, 1975

11 IBERIA AND THE *RECONQUISTA*, 850–1492

Bisson, T.N., *The Medieval Crown of Aragon*, Oxford, 1986

Burns, Robert I., ed., *The Worlds of Alfonso the Learned and James the Conqueror*, Princeton, 1985

Fernández-Armesto, Felipe, *Ferdinand and Isabella*, London, 1975 *

Jackson, Gabriel, *The Making of Medieval Spain*, London, 1972 *

Kennedy, Hugh, *Muslim Spain and Portugal*, Harlow, 1996

Mackay, A., *Spain in the Middle Ages*, London, 1977

Reilly, Bernard F., *The Medieval Spains*, Cambridge, 1993 *

Trevelyan, Raleigh, *Shades of the Alhambra*, London, 1984 *

12 RENAISSANCE ITALY, 1250–1525

Chamberlin, E.R., *The World of the Italian Renaissance*, London, 1982

Hale, J.R., ed., *A Concise Encyclopaedia of the Italian Renaissance*, London, 1981

Hay, Denys, *The Italian Renaissance*, 2nd edition, Cambridge, 1977 *
Laven, Peter, *Renaissance Italy*, London, 1966
Runciman, Steven, *The Sicilian Vespers*, Cambridge, 1958 *
Ryder, Alan, *The Kingdom of Naples under Alfonso the Magnanimous*, Oxford, 1976
Trease, Geoffrey, *The Condottieri*, London, 1970 *
Waley, Daniel, *The Italian City-Republics*, 3rd edition, Harlow, 1988

13 ARMS OF THE WARRIOR
Ashdown, C.H., *British and Continental Arms and Armour*, London, 1970
Boutell, C., *Arms and Armour in Antiquity and the Middle Ages*, trans. from M.P. Lacombe
    and ed., London, 1907
De Vries, K., *Medieval Military Technology*, Ontario, 1992 *
Hardy, Robert, *Longbow*, Portsmouth, 1986 *
Hawkes, S.C., ed., *Weapons and Warfare in Anglo-Saxon England*, Oxford, 1989
Hewitt, J., *Ancient Armour and Weapons in Europe*, 3 vols, London, 1855–60
Norman, V., *Arms and Armour*, London, 1969 *
Oakeshott, E., *The Archaeology of Weapons*, London, 1960
Oakeshott, E., *The Sword in the Age of Chivalry*, 2nd edition, Woodbridge, 1994
Peirce, Ian, *Swords of the Viking Age*, Woodbridge, 2002
Pollington, S., *The English Warrior*, Hockwold-cum-Wilton, 1996

14 ARMOUR
See also Section 13 books on arms and armour
Blair, C., *European Armour circa 1066 to circa 1700*, London, 1958
ffoulkes, C.J., *The Armourer and his Craft from the 11th to the 15th Century*, London,
    1912
Houston, M.G., *Medieval Costume in England and France*, London, 1939
Thordemann, B., *Armour from the Battle of Visby*, Stockholm, 1939
Waterer, J.W., *Leather and the Warrior*, Northampton, 1981

15 HERALDRY
Ailes, Adrian, 'Heraldry in Twelfth-century England: The Evidence', England in the Twelfth
    Century, *Proceedings of the 1988 Harlaxton Symposium*, Woodbridge, 1990, pp. 1–16
Brault, Gerard J., *Early Blazon*, Oxford, 1972
Franklyn, Julian, *Shield and Crest*, London, 1960
Neubecker, Ottfried, *Heraldry: Sources, Symbols and Meaning*, London, 1977
Pastoureau, Michel, *Heraldry, its Origins and Meaning*, trans. F. Garvie, London, 1997
Pine, L.G., *The Story of Heraldry*, London, 1952 *
Rothery, Guy Cadogan, *Concise Encyclopedia of Heraldry*, London, 1994
Wagner, Anthony, *Heralds and Ancestors*, London, 1978
Wagner, Anthony, *Historic Heraldry of Britain*, Oxford, 1939

16 MEDIEVAL ARMIES
See also general books on warfare
Davis, R.H.C., *The Medieval Warhorse*, London, 1989 *
Fowler, Kenneth, *Medieval Mercenaries, vol. I: The Great Companies*, Oxford, 2001
Hyland, Ann, *The Medieval Warhorse*, Stroud, 1994
Mallet, Michael E., *Mercenaries and their Masters*, London, 1974
Reynolds, Susan, *Fiefs and Vassals*, Oxford, 1994

17 CASTLES AND SIEGE WARFARE

Andersen, William, *Castles of Europe*, London, 1980
Armitage, Ella S., *The Early Norman Castles of the British Isles*, London, 1912
Bradbury, Jim, *The Medieval Siege*, Woodbridge, 1992
Brown, R. Allen, *English Castles*, 3rd edition, London, 1976
Brown, R. Allen, ed., *Castles: A History and Guide*, Poole, 1980 *
Corfis, Ivy A. and M. Wolfe, eds, *The Medieval City under Siege*, Woodbridge, 1995
Fedden, Robin and John Thomson, *Crusader Castles*, London, 1950
Finó, J.-F., *Forteresses de la France médiévale*, Paris, 1967
Kennedy, Hugh, *Crusader Castles*, Cambridge, 1994
King, D.J. Cathcart, *The Castle in England and Wales*, London, 1988
Love, Dane, *Scottish Castles*, Edinburgh, 1998
McNeill, Tom, *Castles in Ireland*, London, 1997
Pettifer, Adrian, *English Castles*, Woodbridge, 1995
Pounds, N.J.G., *The Medieval Castle in England and Wales*, Cambridge, 1990
Reid, Alan, *The Castles of Wales*, London, 1973
Renn, Derek, *Norman Castles*, 2nd edition, London, 1973
Rogers, R., *Latin Siege Warfare in the Twelfth Century*, Oxford, 1992
Taylor, Arnold, *Studies in Castles and Castle-building*, London, 1985
Taylor, Arnold, *The Welsh Castles of Edward I*, London, 1986
Thompson, A. Hamilton, *Military Architecture*, Wakefield, 1975
Thompson, M.W., *The Decline of the Castle*, Cambridge, 1987
Viollet-le-Duc, E.E., *Military Architecture*, 2nd edition, London, 1990
Wilson, David, *Moated Sites*, Princes Risborough, 1985

18 NAVAL WARFARE

Brooks, F.W., *The English Naval Forces 1199–1272*, London, 1933
Fernández-Armesto, Felipe, *Before Columbus*, London, 1987 *
Hutchinson, Gillian, *Medieval Ships and Shipping*, London, 1994 *
Pryor, John H., *Geography, Technology, and War: Studies in the Maritime History of the Mediterranean, 649–1571*, Cambridge, 1988
Rodgers, W.L., *Naval Warfare under Oars*, Annapolis, 1939

19 THE MILITARY ORDERS

Barber, Malcolm, *The New Knighthood: A History of the Order of the Temple*, Cambridge, 1994
Barber, Malcolm, *The Trial of the Templars*, Cambridge, 1978 *
Christiansen, E., *The Northern Crusades*, London, 1980
Forey, A.J., *The Military Orders*, London, 1992
Riley-Smith, Jonathan, *The Knights of St John in Jerusalem and Cyprus*, London, 1967
Seward, Desmond, *The Monks of War*, 3rd edition, London, 2000 *

23 | Aids to study

This section takes a brief look at various useful aids to the study of medieval warfare. The main topics listed or covered are the maps that appear in the book; a bibliography of atlases on medieval warfare; family trees of major medieval dynasties; a list of illustrations used; a chronology of major military events between 400 and 1500.

MAPS

 1 Barbarian kingdoms c.534
 2 The empire of Charlemagne, 768–814
 3 Viking Scandinavia and the Viking expansion
 4 England 899–924
 5 Norman Europe
 6 Frederick Barbarossa and Germany
 7 The empire of the Comneni (1081–1185)
 8 The Crusader States
 9 France in the reign of Philip the Fair
10 The Wars of the Roses, 1455–85
11 Christians, Jews and *conversos* in late medieval Iberia
12 The Italian peninsula at the Peace of Lodi, 1454

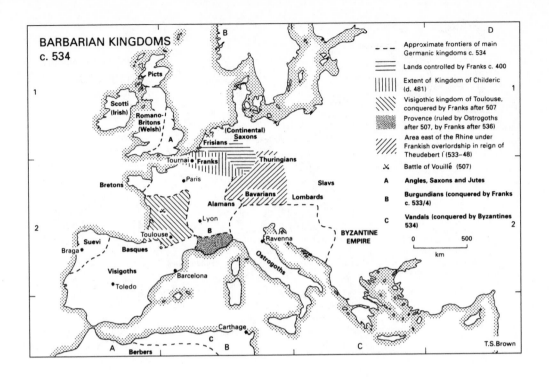

BARBARIAN KINGDOMS c. 534

- - - - Approximate frontiers of main Germanic kingdoms c. 534

Lands controlled by Franks c. 400

Extent of Kingdom of Childeric (d. 481)

Visigothic kingdom of Toulouse, conquered by Franks after 507

Provence (ruled by Ostrogoths after 507, by Franks after 536)

Area east of the Rhine under Frankish overlordship in reign of Theudebert I (533–48)

✕ Battle of Vouillé (507)

A Angles, Saxons and Jutes

B Burgundians (conquered by Franks c. 533/4)

C Vandals (conquered by Byzantines 534)

0   500
km

Picts
Scotti (Irish)
Romano-Britons (Welsh)
(Continental) Saxons
Frisians
Tournai • Franks
Thuringians
• Paris
Bretons
Slavs
Bavarians
Alamans   Lombards
• Lyon
Suevi
Braga •   Basques
Toulouse
BYZANTINE EMPIRE
• Ravenna
Visigoths
Barcelona
Ostrogoths
• Toledo
Carthage
A   C   B   C
Berbers

T.S.Brown

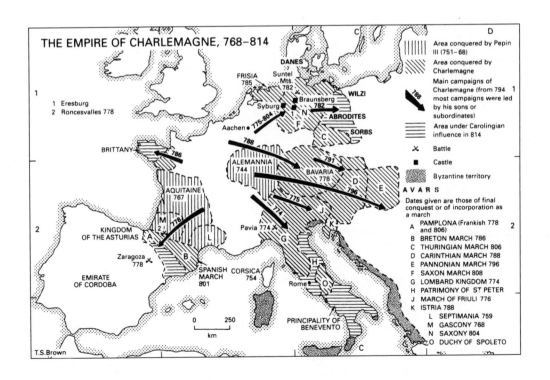

THE EMPIRE OF CHARLEMAGNE, 768–814

Area conquered by Pepin III (751–68)

Area conquered by Charlemagne

Main campaigns of Charlemagne (from 794 most campaigns were led by his sons or subordinates)

Area under Carolingian influence in 814

✕ Battle

■ Castle

Byzantine territory

A V A R S

Dates given are those of final conquest or of incorporation as a march

A PAMPLONA (Frankish 778 and 806)
B BRETON MARCH 786
C THURINGIAN MARCH 806
D CARINTHIAN MARCH 788
E PANNONIAN MARCH 796
F SAXON MARCH 808
G LOMBARD KINGDOM 774
H PATRIMONY OF ST PETER
J MARCH OF FRIULI 776
K ISTRIA 788
L SEPTIMANIA 759
M GASCONY 768
N SAXONY 804
O DUCHY OF SPOLETO

1 Eresburg
2 Roncesvalles 778

DANES
FRISIA 785
Suntel Mts. 782
WILZI
Syburg • Braunsberg 782
Aachen • 775-804
ABRODITES
SORBS
788
BRITTANY
786
ALEMANNIA 744
791
BAVARIA 778
AQUITAINE 767
775
774
796
KINGDOM OF THE ASTURIAS
778
Pavia 774
Zaragoza 778
SPANISH MARCH 801
CORSICA 754
Rome •
EMIRATE OF CORDOBA
0   250
km
PRINCIPALITY OF BENEVENTO

T.S.Brown

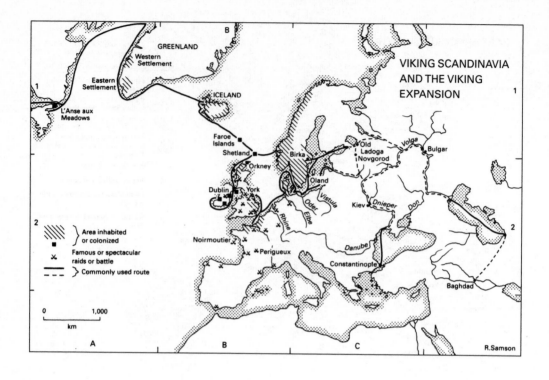

VIKING SCANDINAVIA
AND THE VIKING
EXPANSION

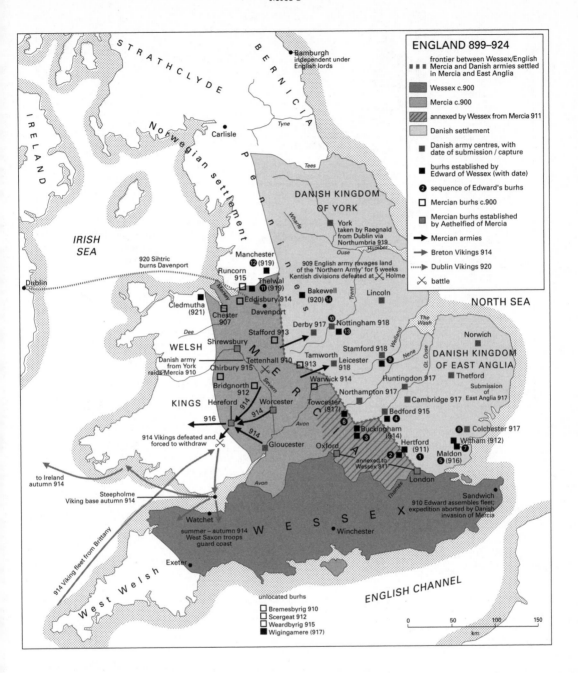

ENGLAND 899–924

■ ■ ■ frontier between Wessex/English Mercia and Danish armies settled in Mercia and East Anglia

▓ Wessex c.900

▒ Mercia c.900

▨ annexed by Wessex from Mercia 911

░ Danish settlement

■ Danish army centres, with date of submission / capture

■ burhs established by Edward of Wessex (with date)

❷ sequence of Edward's burhs

□ Mercian burhs c.900

▪ Mercian burhs established by Aethelfled of Mercia

➤ Mercian armies

→ Breton Vikings 914

⋯> Dublin Vikings 920

✕ battle

STRATHCLYDE

IRELAND

BERNICIA

Bamburgh
independent under
English lords

Tyne

Carlisle

Norwegian settlement

IRISH SEA

Tees

DANISH KINGDOM OF YORK

Wharfe

York
taken by Raegnald
from Dublin via
Northumbria 919

Ouse

Humber

Lincoln

NORTH SEA

920 Sihtric
burns Davenport

Dublin

Manchester
❶❷ (919)

Runcorn
915

Thelwal
❶❶ (919)

Eddisbury 914

Cledmutha
(921)

Chester
907

Davenport

Dee

WELSH

Shrewsbury

Bakewell
(920) ❶❹

909 English army ravages land
of the 'Northern Army' for 5 weeks
Kentish divisions defeated at Holme

Derby 917 ❶❿

Nottingham 918

❶❸

Stafford 913

MERCIA

Tamworth
913

Leicester
918

Stamford 918

❾

Welland

Norwich

DANISH KINGDOM OF EAST ANGLIA

Thetford

Trent

Nene

Gt. Ouse

The Wash

Danish army
from York
raids Mercia 910

Tettenhall 910

Chirbury 915

Bridgnorth
912

KINGS

Hereford

914

914

Worcester

Warwick 914

Northampton 917

Towcester
(917)

❻

Buckingham
(914)

❸

Huntingdon 917

Cambridge 917

Submission
of
East Anglia 917

Bedford 915

❹

Colchester 917

914 Vikings defeated and
forced to withdraw

Gloucester

Avon

916

Oxford

annexed to
Wessex 911

❷

Hertford
(911)

❶

❽

Witham (912)

❼

Maldon
(916)

❺

to Ireland
autumn 914

Steepholme
Viking base autumn 914

Watchet

summer – autumn 914
West Saxon troops
guard coast

Avon

W   E   S   S   E   X

Winchester

London

Thames

910 Edward assembles fleet;
expedition aborted by Danish
invasion of Mercia

Sandwich

914 Viking fleet from Brittany

West Welsh

Exeter

ENGLISH CHANNEL

unlocated burhs

□ Bremesbyrig 910
□ Scergeat 912
□ Weardbyrig 915
■ Wigingamere (917)

0   50   100   150
km

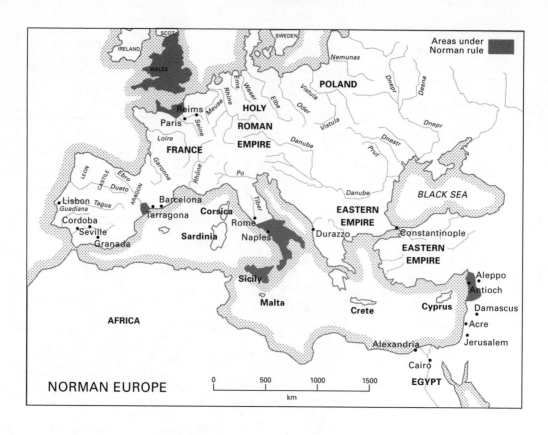

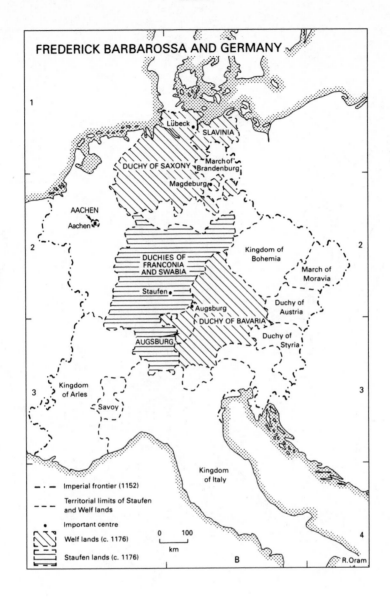

FREDERICK BARBAROSSA AND GERMANY

1

Lübeck
SLAVINIA

DUCHY OF SAXONY
March of
Brandenburg

Magdeburg

AACHEN
Aachen

2
Kingdom of
Bohemia
2

March of
Moravia

DUCHIES OF
FRANCONIA
AND SWABIA

Staufen

Duchy of
Austria

Augsburg
DUCHY OF BAVARIA

AUGSBURG
Duchy of
Styria

3
Kingdom
of Arles
3

Savoy

Kingdom
of Italy

— · — Imperial frontier (1152)

— — — Territorial limits of Staufen
and Welf lands

• Important centre

Welf lands (c. 1176)

Staufen lands (c. 1176)

0   100
km

B

R. Oram

4

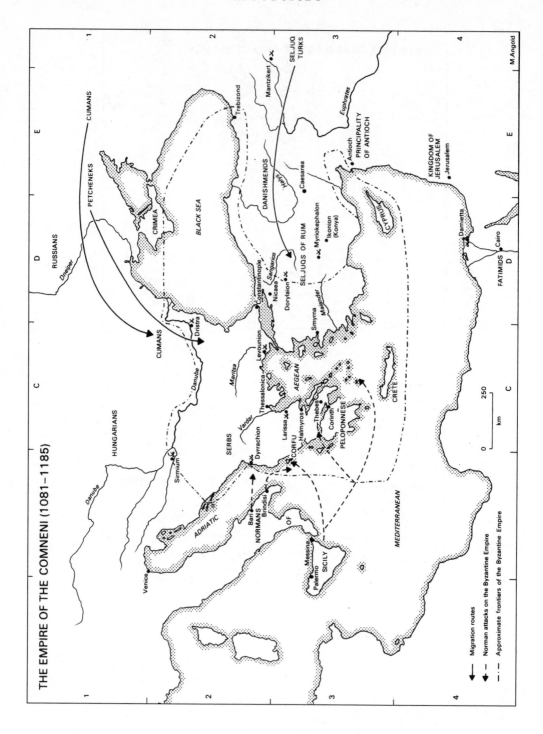

THE EMPIRE OF THE COMNENI (1081–1185)

M.Angold

RUSSIANS

CUMANS

PETCHENEKS

HUNGARIANS

SERBS

Dnjeper

CRIMEA

BLACK SEA

Trebizond

Mantzikert

SELJUQ TURKS

DANISHMENDS

Euphrates

Halys

Caesarea

PRINCIPALITY OF ANTIOCH

Antioch

KINGDOM OF JERUSALEM

Jerusalem

CYPRUS

Damietta

Cairo

FATIMIDS

Danube

Dristra

Constantinople

Sangarios

Nicaea

Dorylaion

SELJUQS OF RUM

Myriokephalon

Ikonion (Konya)

Smyrna

Maiander

CRETE

Sirmium

Maritsa

Vardar

Levounion

Thessalonica

AEGEAN

Larissa

Halmyros

Thebes

Corinth

PELOPONNESE

Dyrrachion

CORFU

Venice

ADRIATIC

Bari

Brindisi

NORMANS

OF

Messina

Palermo

SICILY

MEDITERRANEAN

250

0

km

Migration routes

Norman attacks on the Byzantine Empire

Approximate frontiers of the Byzantine Empire

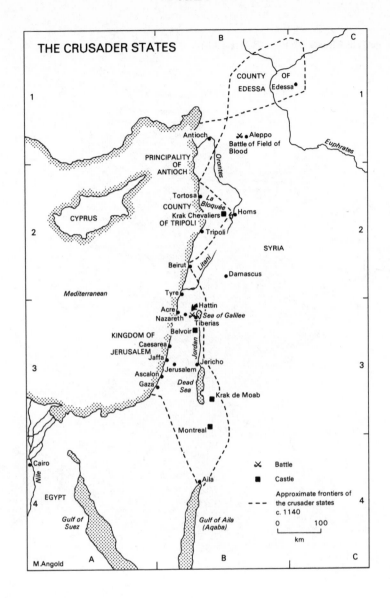

THE CRUSADER STATES

COUNTY OF EDESSA
Edessa

Antioch
Aleppo
Battle of Field of Blood

PRINCIPALITY OF ANTIOCH

Orontes

Euphrates

Tortosa
La Bloquée
COUNTY
Krak Chevaliers
OF TRIPOLI
Homs

CYPRUS

Tripoli

SYRIA

Beirut

Litani

Damascus

Mediterranean

Tyre

Hattin
Acre
Sea of Galilee
Nazareth
Tiberias
Belvoir

KINGDOM OF
Caesarea
JERUSALEM
Jaffa

Jordan

Jericho

Ascalon
Jerusalem
Gaza
Dead Sea
Krak de Moab

Montreal

Cairo

Nile

Battle
Castle
Approximate frontiers of the crusader states c. 1140
0   100
km

EGYPT

Gulf of Suez

Aila

Gulf of Aila (Aqaba)

M.Angold

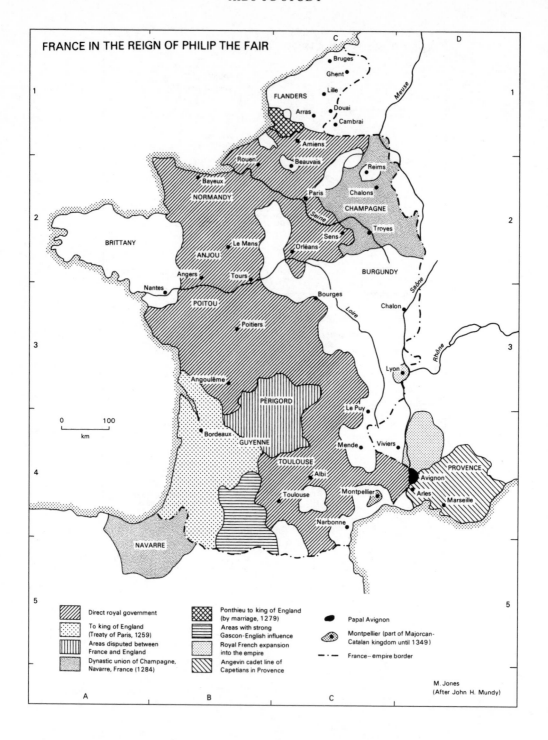

FRANCE IN THE REIGN OF PHILIP THE FAIR

Bruges
Ghent
Lille
FLANDERS
Arras
Douai
Cambrai

Amiens
Rouen
Beauvais
Reims
Bayeux
NORMANDY
Paris
Chalons
CHAMPAGNE
Sens
Troyes
Le Mans
Orléans
ANJOU
BURGUNDY
Angers
Tours
Bourges
Nantes
Chalon
POITOU
Poitiers
Lyon
Angoulême
PÉRIGORD
Le Puy
Bordeaux
Mende
Viviers
GUYENNE
PROVENCE
TOULOUSE
Avignon
Albi
Arles
Toulouse
Montpellier
Marseille
Narbonne
NAVARRE

BRITTANY

Meuse
Seine
Saône
Loire
Rhône

C   D
1   1
2   2
3   3
4   4
5   5

A   B   C

0   100
km

Direct royal government

To king of England
(Treaty of Paris, 1259)

Areas disputed between
France and England

Dynastic union of Champagne,
Navarre, France (1284)

Ponthieu to king of England
(by marriage, 1279)

Areas with strong
Gascon-English influence

Royal French expansion
into the empire

Angevin cadet line of
Capetians in Provence

Papal Avignon

Montpellier (part of Majorcan-
Catalan kingdom until 1349)

France–empire border

M. Jones
(After John H. Mundy)

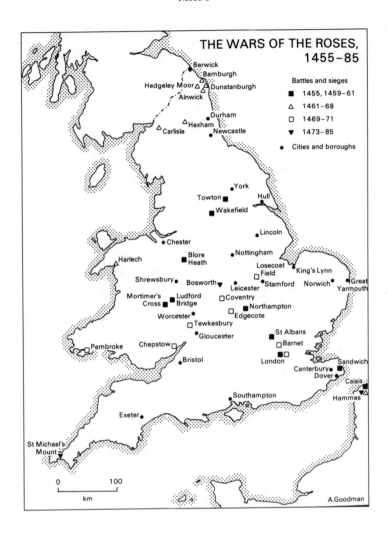

THE WARS OF THE ROSES,
1455-85

Battles and sieges

■ 1455, 1459-61

△ 1461-68

□ 1469-71

▼ 1473-85

● Cities and boroughs

Berwick
Bamburgh
Hedgeley Moor △ △ Dunstanburgh
Alnwick
Durham
△ Hexham
Carlisle ● Newcastle

York
Towton ■ Hull
● Wakefield

Lincoln

● Chester
Blore ● Nottingham
Harlech Heath
Losecoat
Field
Shrewsbury ● Bosworth ▼ King's Lynn
Leicester ● Stamford Norwich ● Great
Mortimer's Ludford □ Coventry Yarmouth
Cross ■ Bridge Northampton
Worcester ● Edgecote
□ Tewkesbury
● Gloucester St Albans
Pembroke □ Chepstow □ Barnet
● Bristol ■ □
London Sandwich
Canterbury ●
Dover ● Calais
Southampton Hammes

Exeter ●

St Michael's
Mount ▼

0   100
km

A.Goodman

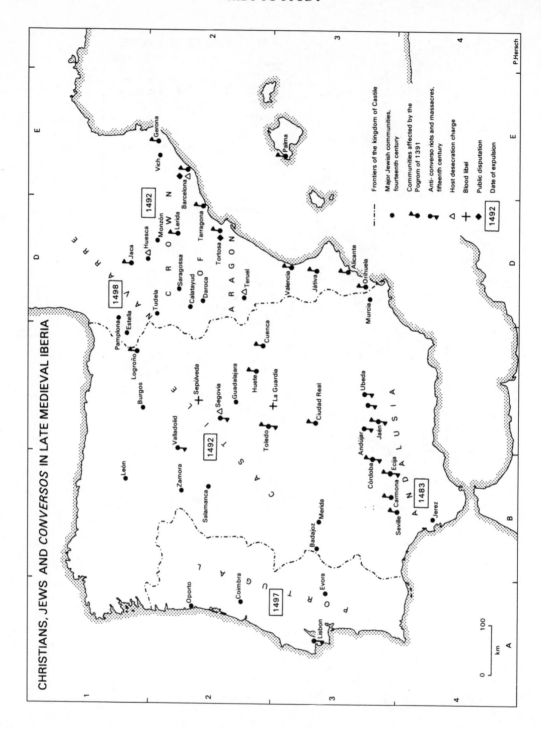

CHRISTIANS, JEWS AND *CONVERSOS* IN LATE MEDIEVAL IBERIA

P.Hersch

Frontiers of the kingdom of Castile

Major Jewish communities, fourteenth century

Communities affected by the Pogrom of 1391

Anti-*converso* riots and massacres, fifteenth century

Host desecration charge

Blood libel

Public disputation

1492 Date of expulsion

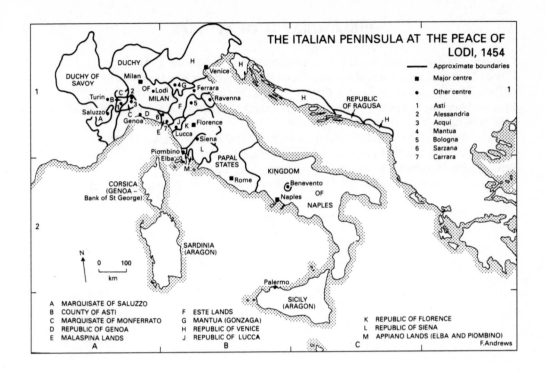

THE ITALIAN PENINSULA AT THE PEACE OF LODI, 1454

—— Approximate boundaries
■ Major centre
• Other centre

1 Asti
2 Alessandria
3 Acqui
4 Mantua
5 Bologna
6 Sarzana
7 Carrara

DUCHY OF SAVOY
DUCHY OF MILAN
Milan
Turin
Saluzzo
Genoa
Lodi
Ferrara
Ravenna
Venice
REPUBLIC OF RAGUSA
Florence
Lucca
Siena
Piombino
Elba
PAPAL STATES
CORSICA (GENOA – Bank of St George)
KINGDOM OF NAPLES
Rome
Benevento
Naples
SARDINIA (ARAGON)

N
0   100
km

Palermo
SICILY (ARAGON)

A MARQUISATE OF SALUZZO
B COUNTY OF ASTI
C MARQUISATE OF MONFERRATO
D REPUBLIC OF GENOA
E MALASPINA LANDS

F ESTE LANDS
G MANTUA (GONZAGA)
H REPUBLIC OF VENICE
J REPUBLIC OF LUCCA

K REPUBLIC OF FLORENCE
L REPUBLIC OF SIENA
M APPIANO LANDS (ELBA AND PIOMBINO)

F.Andrews

A   B   C

BIBLIOGRAPHY OF ATLASES

Cussons, Thomas and others, *The Times Atlas of History*, London, 1994

Falkus, Malcolm and John Gillingham, *Historical Atlas of Britain*, London, 1981

Gilbert, Martin, *The Dent Atlas of British History*, 2nd edition, London, 1993

Hooper, Nicholas and Matthew Bennett, *The Cambridge Illustrated Atlas of Warfare: The Middle Ages, 768–1487*, Cambridge, 1996

Mackay, Angus with David Ditchburn, *Atlas of Medieval Europe*, London, 1997

Natkiel, Richard and John Pimlott, *Atlas of Warfare*, London, 1988

Riley-Smith, Jonathan, ed., *The Atlas of the Crusades*, London, 1991

Treharne, R.F. and Harold Fullard, *Muir's Historical Atlas*, 6th edition, London, 1973

PEDIGREES OF MAJOR DYNASTIES

1 The Merovingians

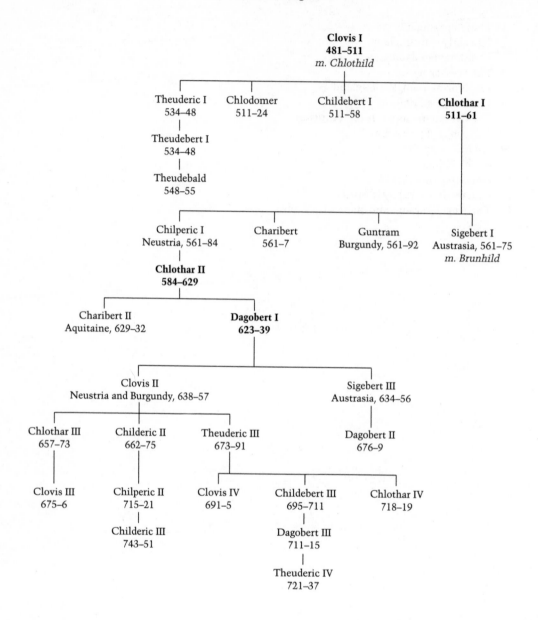

2 The early Carolingians

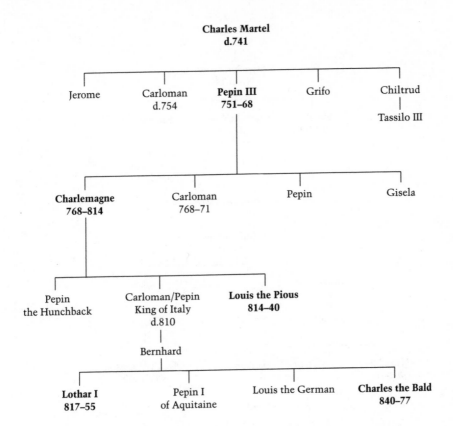

3 Scandinavian dynasties

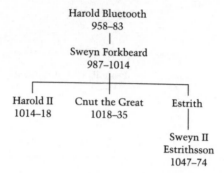

Harold Bluetooth
958–83

Sweyn Forkbeard
987–1014

Harold II	Cnut the Great	Estrith
1014–18	1018–35	

Sweyn II
Estrithsson
1047–74

Kings of Denmark

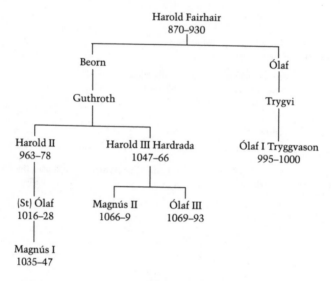

Harold Fairhair
870–930

Beorn

Ólaf

Guthroth

Trygvi

Harold II	Harold III Hardrada	Ólaf I Tryggvason
963–78	1047–66	995–1000

(St) Ólaf
1016–28

Magnús II
1066–9

Ólaf III
1069–93

Magnús I
1035–47

Kings of Norway

4 The Wessex dynasty

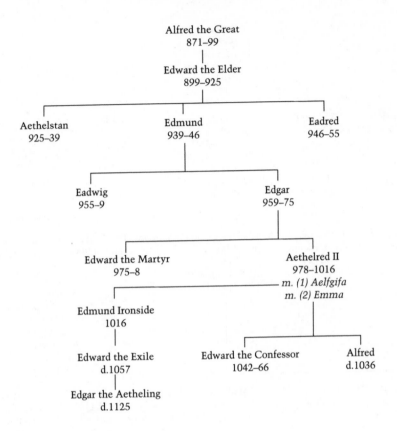

5 The Norman kings of England

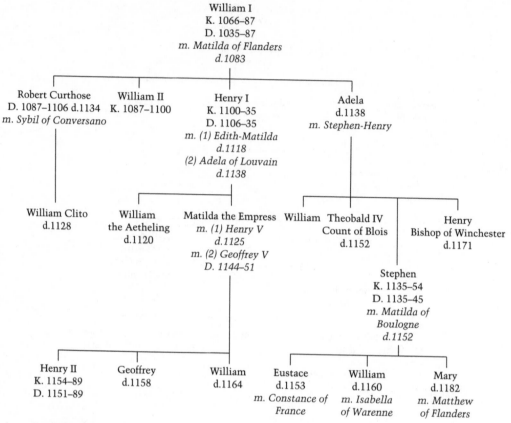

William I
K. 1066–87
D. 1035–87
m. Matilda of Flanders
d.1083

Robert Curthose
D. 1087–1106 d.1134
m. Sybil of Conversano

William II
K. 1087–1100

Henry I
K. 1100–35
D. 1106–35
m. (1) Edith-Matilda
d.1118
(2) Adela of Louvain
d.1138

Adela
d.1138
m. Stephen-Henry

William Clito
d.1128

William
the Aetheling
d.1120

Matilda the Empress
m. (1) Henry V
d.1125
m. (2) Geoffrey V
D. 1144–51

William

Theobald IV
Count of Blois
d.1152

Henry
Bishop of Winchester
d.1171

Stephen
K. 1135–54
D. 1135–45
m. Matilda of
Boulogne
d.1152

Henry II
K. 1154–89
D. 1151–89

Geoffrey
d.1158

William
d.1164

Eustace
d.1153
m. Constance of
France

William
d.1160
m. Isabella
of Warenne

Mary
d.1182
m. Matthew
of Flanders

D = Duke of Normandy
K = King of England

6 The Hohenstaufen

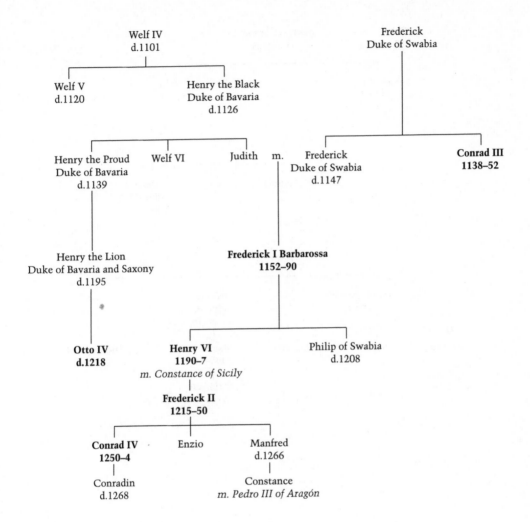

7 The Comneni emperors of Byzantium

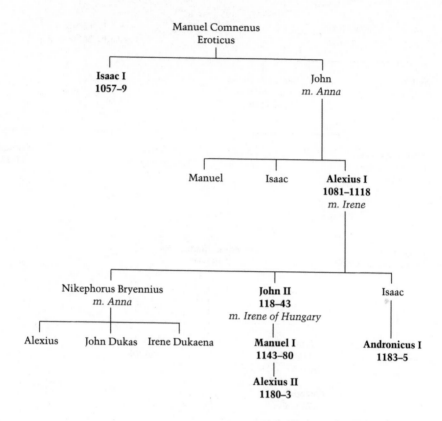

8 The kings of Jerusalem

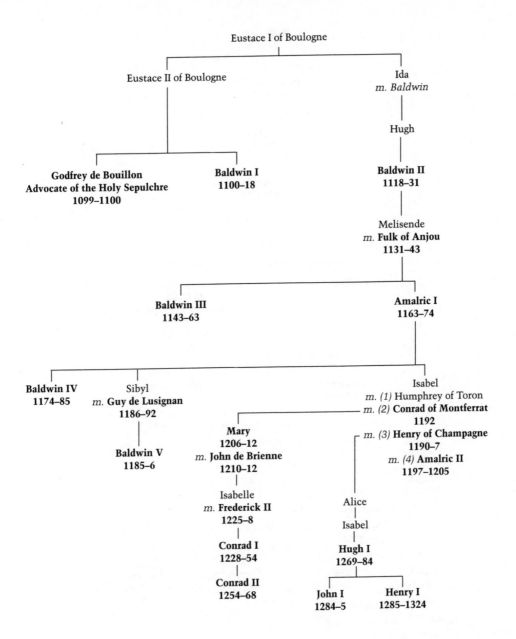

9 a) The Capetians

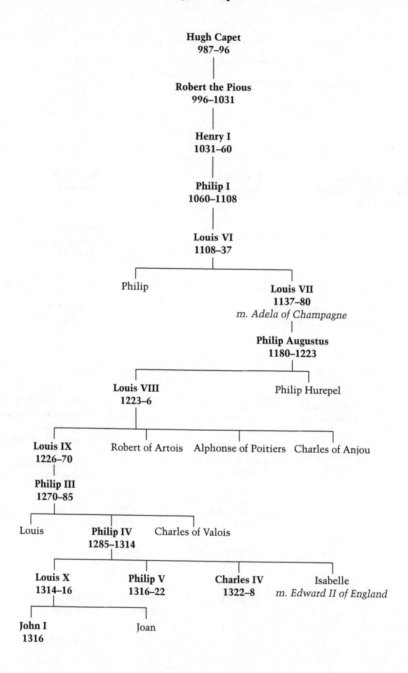

Hugh Capet
987–96

Robert the Pious
996–1031

Henry I
1031–60

Philip I
1060–1108

Louis VI
1108–37

Philip   **Louis VII**
              1137–80
              m. Adela of Champagne

              Philip Augustus
              1180–1223

Louis VIII   Philip Hurepel
1223–6

Louis IX   Robert of Artois   Alphonse of Poitiers   Charles of Anjou
1226–70

Philip III
1270–85

Louis   **Philip IV**   Charles of Valois
         1285–1314

Louis X   **Philip V**   **Charles IV**   Isabelle
1314–16   **1316–22**   **1322–8**   *m. Edward II of England*

John I   Joan
1316

9 b) The Valois

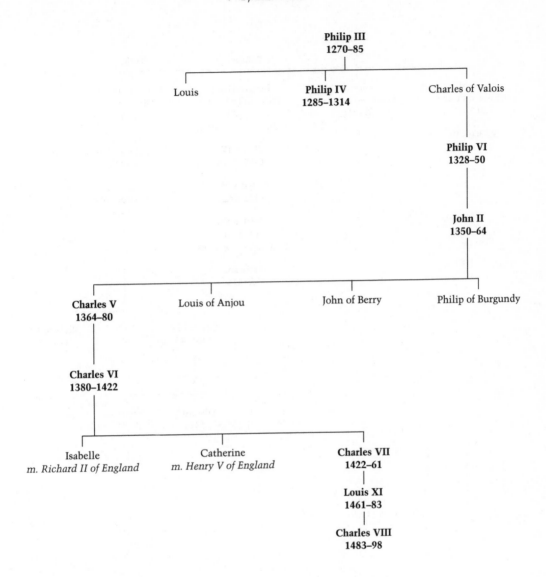

10 Lancaster and York

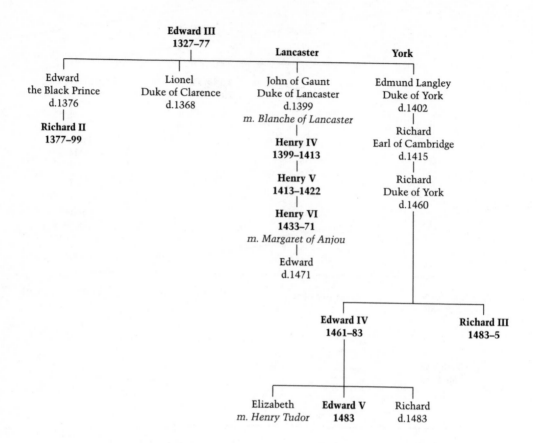

Edward III
1327–77

Lancaster   York

Edward
the Black Prince
d.1376

Lionel
Duke of Clarence
d.1368

John of Gaunt
Duke of Lancaster
d.1399
m. Blanche of Lancaster

Edmund Langley
Duke of York
d.1402

Richard II
1377–99

Henry IV
1399–1413

Richard
Earl of Cambridge
d.1415

Henry V
1413–1422

Richard
Duke of York
d.1460

Henry VI
1433–71
m. Margaret of Anjou

Edward
d.1471

Edward IV
1461–83

Richard III
1483–5

Elizabeth
m. Henry Tudor

Edward V
1483

Richard
d.1483

11 Late medieval rulers of Spain

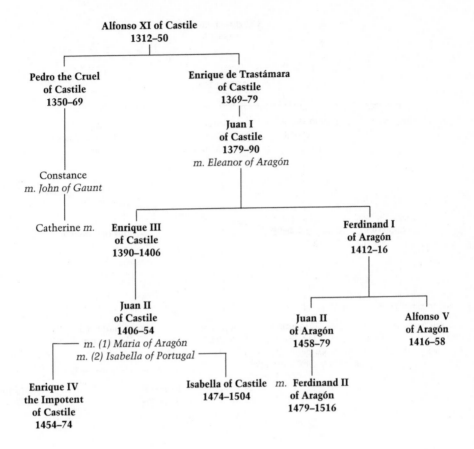

12 The Angevin kings and queens of Naples

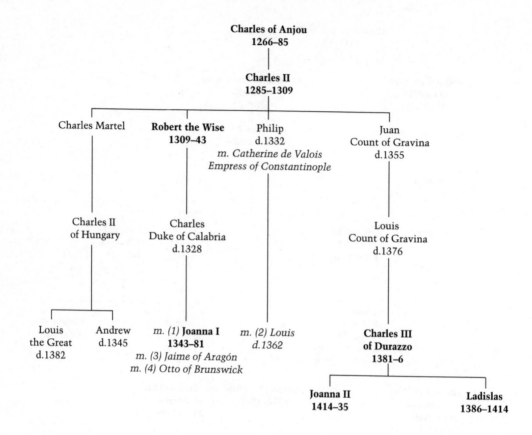

Charles of Anjou
1266–85

Charles II
1285–1309

Charles Martel

Robert the Wise
1309–43

Philip
d.1332
m. Catherine de Valois
Empress of Constantinople

Juan
Count of Gravina
d.1355

Charles II
of Hungary

Charles
Duke of Calabria
d.1328

Louis
Count of Gravina
d.1376

Louis
the Great
d.1382

Andrew
d.1345

m. (1) **Joanna I**
1343–81
m. (3) Jaime of Aragón
m. (4) Otto of Brunswick

m. (2) Louis
d.1362

Charles III
of Durazzo
1381–6

Joanna II
1414–35

Ladislas
1386–1414

A CHRONOLOGY OF MILITARY EVENTS, 400–1500

This chronology includes major battles and sieges and a few political markers such as the accession of important rulers. For brevity rulers of Germany are noted as HRE (Holy Roman Emperors), whether crowned only as King of the Romans or not. Byzantine Emperor is abbreviated as Byz., France as Fr., England as Eng., Spain as Sp. With long-lasting events, generally just the beginning is noted. * represents a battle; # a siege. The number in brackets shows the section in which details of the event can be found.

Date	Western Europe	Central and eastern Europe	Elsewhere
410	Alaric [1] sacks Rome		
415	Visigoths reach Sp.		
439	*Toulouse [1]		
451	*Châlons [1]		
452	*Aquileia [1]		
453		d. Attila [1]	
455	Sack of Rome		
471		Theoderic king of Ostrogoths [1]	
476	Odoacer [1] deposes Romulus Augustulus		
481	Clovis [1] king of Franks		
486	*Soissons [1]		
490	*Adda [1]		
496	*Tolbiac [1]		
527		Justinian I Byz. [7]	
531			Chosroes I Persia [7]
532		Nika Revolt [7]	
541		Totila king of Ostrogoths [1]	
552	*Busta Gallorum [1]		
577	*Deorham [4]		
582		Maurice Byz. [7]	
610		Heraclius Byz. [7]	
632			d. Mohammed
634	*Heavenfield [4]		
636			*Yarmuk [7]
638			Muslims take Jerusalem
695	#Dorestad		
710	Rodrigo I king of Visigoths [1]		
711	Tāriq invades Sp. [1]		
732	*Tours [1]		
737	Charles Martel takes power [1]		
751	Pepin king of Franks [2]		
757	Offa king of Mercia [4] Desiderius king of Lombards [2]		
771	Charlemagne sole king [2]		
772		Charlemagne invades Saxony [2]	

Date	Western Europe	Central and eastern Europe	Elsewhere
773	Charlemagne invades Lombardy [2]		
778	*Roncesvalles; #Zaragoza [2]		
782	Verden slaughter	*Süntel Mountains [2]	
786			Haroun al-Rashid
795		Charlemagne defeats the Avars	
800	Charlemagne crowned HRE *Barcelona [2]; Godfred king Denmark [3]		
808	Danewirk built	Krum khagan [7]	
811	*Tortosa [2]		
813		Leo V Byz. [7]	
814	d. Charlemagne Louis the Pious HRE [2]		
834	#Dorestad [7]		
841	*Fontenoy [7]		
843	Charles the Bald king [7]		
852	#Jeufosse [3]		
858	#Oissel [3]		
860		Rus attack Constantinople [7]	
865		Rus attack Constantinople [7]	
867		Basil I Byz. [7]	
870	Harold Finehair king Norway [3]		
871	*Ashdown; Alfred the Great king Wessex [4]		
876	*Andernach [2]		
878	Athelney; *Edington [4] Peace of Wedmore		
885	#Paris [3]		
886		Leo VI Byz. [7]	
891	*Dyle [3]		
893		First Bulgar empire	
900	*Hafrsfjord [3]		
911	Treaty of St-Clair-sur-Epte	Conrad I HRE [6]	
912	Abd er Rahman caliph [11]		
919		Henry the Fowler HRE [6]	
924	Aethelstan king Eng. [4]		
927		Symeon khan [7]	
932	#Toledo [11]		
933		*Riade [6]	
936	Louis IV king Fr.	Otto I HRE [6]	
937	*Brunanburh [4]		
955		*Lechfeld [6]	
958	Harold Bluetooth king Denmark [3]		
968			Fatimids invade Egypt
973		Otto II HRE [6]	

Date	Western Europe	Central and eastern Europe	Elsewhere
974	*Hals [3]		
976		Basil II Byz. [7]	
978	Aethelred II king Eng. [4]		
980	*Tara [3]		
983		Otto III HRE [6]	
987	Hugh Capet king Fr. [9]		
989	Sigtrygg Silkbeard king Dublin [3]		
991	*Maldon [4]		
992	*Conquereux [2]		
993		Otto III crowned Emperor [6]	
1000		Stephen king Hungary [6]	
1014	*Clontarf [3]		
1016	*Ashdown [4] Cnut king Eng. [4]		
1024		Conrad II HRE [6]	
1025	St Ólaf king Norway [3]		
1026	*Holy River [3]		
1030	*Stiklestad [3]		
1031	Henry I king Fr. [9]		
1035	William II duke Normandy [5] Magnús the Good king Norway [3]		
1038	George Maniakes invades Italy [7]		
1040	Macbeth king Scots		
1042	Edward the Confessor king Eng.		
1045	Harold Hardrada king Norway [3]		
1053	*Civitate [5]		
1056		Henry IV HRE [6]	
1060	Philip I king Fr. [9]		
1061	Normans invade Sicily		
1063		Alp Arslan sultan [7]	
1066	*Stamford Bridge [5] *Hastings [5]		
1071	*Cassel [9]	*Manzikert [7]	Seljuks over Anatolia
1072	Alfonso VI king León [11]		
1075			Seljuks take Jerusalem
1077	Meeting at Canossa		
1080	*Flarcheim [6]	*Durazzo [5] Alexius I Comnenus Byz. [7]	
1086	*Zalaka [11]		Kilij Arslan sultan [8]
1087	William Rufus king Eng. [5]		
1094	El Cid takes Valencia [11]		
1096			First Crusade
1097	#Huesca [11]	#Antioch [8]	

Date	Western Europe	Central and eastern Europe	Elsewhere
1099			#Jerusalem *Ascalon [8]
1100	Henry I king Eng. [5]		
1106	*Tinchebrai [5]		
1108	Louis VI king Fr. [9]		
1109	Alfonso I king Aragón [11]		
1111	Henry V HRE [6]		
1119	*Brémule [5]		
1127	Charles the Good killed		
1130	Roger II king Sicily [5]		
1135	Stephen king Eng. [5]		
1137	Louis VII king Fr. [9]	Conrad III HRE [6]	
1138	*Standard [5]		
1141	*Lincoln [5]		
1143		Manuel I Byz. [7]	
1144			#Edessa [8]
1147			Second Crusade
1148			#Damascus [8]
1152		Frederick Barbarossa HRE [6]	
1154	Henry II king Eng. [10]		
1155		Barbarossa crowned HRE [6]	
1165	William the Lion king Scots [10]		
1166	Alfonso VI king Castile [11]		
1169	Strongbow to Ireland [10]		
1170	d. Becket		
1175			Saladin rules Egypt and Syria
1176	*Legnano [6]		
1180	Philip Augustus king Fr. [9]		
1187		*Hattin #Jerusalem [8]	
1189	Richard the Lionheart king Eng. [10]		
1190			Third Crusade
1191			#Acre *Arsuf [8]
1196	*Alarcos [11]		
1197		Otto IV HRE [6]	
1199	John king Eng. [10]		
1202		#Zara, Fourth Crusade [8]	
1203	#Château-Gaillard [9]		
1204		#Constantinople [8] Baldwin I Byz. [7]	Emergence Genghis Khan
1208	Albigensian Crusade	Otto IV HRE [6]	
1212	*Las Navas de Tolosa [11]		
1213	*Muret [9]		
1214	*Bouvines [9]		
1215	Magna Carta	Frederick II HRE [6]	

Date	Western Europe	Central and eastern Europe	Elsewhere
1217	*Lincoln *Sandwich [10] Jaime I king Aragón [11]	Fifth Crusade	
1224	#Bedford [10]		
1226	St Louis king Fr. [9]		
1227			d. Genghis Khan
1228			Frederick II's Crusade
1229	Jaime I invades Mallorca		
1232	Jaime I attacks Valencia [11]		
1236	#Córdoba [11]		Mongols attack Hungary
1237	*Cortenuova [6]		
1241		*Leignitz [6] Mongols to Vienna	
1242	*Taillebourg [9]	*Lake Peipus [6]	
1243			#Jerusalem
1244	Montségur [9]		*La Forbie [8] Fall of Jerusalem
1247			Alexander Nevsky prince of Kiev [6]
1248			St Louis' Crusade
1250			*Mansurah [8]
1258	Treaties of Corbeil and Paris		Mongols take Baghdad
1260			*Ayn Jalut [8]
1261		Michael VIII enters Constantinople [7]	
			Emergence of Kublai Khān
1263	*Largs [10]		
1264	*Lewes [10]		
1265	*Evesham [10]		
1266	Charles of Anjou takes Sicily [12]		
	*Benevento [12]		
1268	*Tagliacozzo [12]		
1270			St Louis' Tunis Crusade
1271			d. St Louis [9]
1272	Edward I king Eng. [10]		Marco Polo goes east
1273		Rudolf I HRE [6]	
1279			Qalawun sultan [8]
1280			Othman sultan [7]
1282	Sicilian Vespers [12]		
1285	Philip IV king Fr. [9]		
1290			al-Ashraf sultan [8]
1291			Fall of Acre [8]
1296	*Dunbar [10]		
1297	*Stirling [10]		
1298	*Falkirk [10]		

Date	Western Europe	Central and eastern Europe	Elsewhere
1302	*Courtrai [9]		
1304	*Mons-en-Pévèle [9]		
1306	*Methven [10]		
1308		Henry VII HRE [6]	
1314	*Bannockburn [10]		
1315		*Morgarten [6]	
1322	*Boroughbridge [10]		
1324			Orhan sultan [7]
1327	Edward III king Eng. [10]		
1328	Philip VI king Fr. [9]		
	*Cassel [9]		
1333	*Halidon Hill [10]		
1336		Stephen Dušan king Serbia [7]	
1337	Opening of Hundred Years' War		
1340	*Sluys [9] *Salado [11]		
1346	*Neville's Cross [10]	Charles IV HRE [6]	
	*Crécy [9]		
1347	#Calais [9]		
	Black Death through Europe		
1356	*Poitiers [9]		
1358	Jacquerie [9]		
1359			Murad I sultan [7]
1360	Treaty of Brétigny		
1364	Charles V king Fr. [9]		
1366	Enrique de Trastámara king Castile [11]		
1367	*Nájera [11]		
1369			Tamberlane khan [7]
1370	#Limoges [9]		
1371		*Maritsa [6]	
1372	*La Rochelle [9]		
1376	War of the Eight Saints [12]	Wenceslas IV HRE [6]	
1378	Gian Galeazzo Visconti over Milan [12]		
1380	Charles VI king Fr. [9]	*Chioggia [12]	
1381	Peasants' Revolt [10]		
1382	*Roosebeke [9]		
1385	*Aljubarrota [11]		
1386	Louis of Anjou king Naples [12]		*Sempach [6]
1387	*Radcot Bridge [10]		
1388	*Otterburn [10]		
1389		*Kosovo [7]	Bayezit I sultan [7]
1391		Manuel II Byz. [7]	
1396		*Nicopolis [7]	
1399	Henry IV king Eng. [10]		

Date	Western Europe	Central and eastern Europe	Elsewhere
1402	*Homildon Hill [10]		*Ankara [7]
1403	*Shrewsbury [10]		
1407	Murder of Louis of Orléans		
1408	*Bramham Moor [10]		
1410		Sigismund HRE	*Tannenberg [6]
1412	Filippo Maria Visconti over Milan [12]		
1413	Henry V king Eng. [10]		
1415	*Agincourt [9]		
1419		Opening of Hussite Wars	
1420	Treaty of Troyes		
1421	*Baugé [9]		Murad II sultan [7]
1422	Henry VI king Eng. [10]		
1423	*Cravant [9]		
1429	Orléans relieved [9]		
1431	d. Joan of Arc [9]		
1434	Cosimo Medici over Florence [12]		
1435	Treaty of Arras		
1438		Albert II of Habsburg HRE	
1440		Frederick III HRE [6]	
1442	Alfonso I of Aragón king Naples [12]		#Rhodes [8]
1444		*Varna [8]	
1448		*2nd Kosovo [7]	
1450	Cade's Rebellion [10]		
	*Formigny [9]		
	Francesco Sforza over Milan [12]		
1451			Mehmet II sultan [7]
1453	*Castillon [9]	Fall of Constantinople [7]	
1455	*1st St Albans [10]		
1460	*Wakefield [10]		Ottomans over Peloponnese
1461	*2nd St Albans *Towton [10]		
	Louis XI king Fr. [9]		
1465	*Montlhéry [9]		
1469	Lorenzo the Magnificent over Florence [12]		
1471	*Barnet *Tewkesbury [10]		
1474	Ferdinand and Isabella over Castile [11]		
1476	*Grandson *Morat [6]		
1477	*Nancy [6]		
1479	*Guinegate		
1480		#Rhodes [8]	
1481			Bayezit II sultan [7]
1485	*Bosworth [10] Henry VII king Eng.		
1486		Maximilian I HRE [6]	
1487	*Stoke [10]		

Date	Western Europe	Central and eastern Europe	Elsewhere
1492	Taking of Granada [11]		Voyage of Columbus
1494	Charles VIII invades Italy [12]		
	Ludovico il Moro over Milan [12]		

LIST OF ILLUSTRATIONS

1 Gallic warrior fleeing, temple frieze, terracotta, 2nd century BC Celtic, from Civitalba, Italy
2 Carolingian sieges
3 The death of St Ólaf at the Battle of Stiklestad, Flateyjarbok
4 The English shield wall on the Bayeux Tapestry
5 Coronation of King Roger II, Palermo, Church of the Martorana
6 The Battle of Morat, 1476, from Diebold Schilling's *Chronicle*
7 Gentile Bellini, *Sultan Mehmet II*, 1480
8 *St Louis at Damietta*
9 Joan of Arc directing operations
10 A soldier's skull from the Battle of Towton, 1461
11 11th-century ivory carving from Cuenca (Spain) of a mounted warrior and an archer with a shortbow
12 Statue of Bartolomeo Colleoni, Venice, by Verrocchio
13 A crossbow with a steel bow
14 A complete suit of late medieval plate armour
15 Jean Courtois, Sicily Herald for the King of Aragón, c.1420
16 14th-century Flemish infantry on the Courtrai Chest
17 Krak des Chevaliers seen from the north-west of the castle
18 A cog, Luttrel Psalter
19 Templar knights leaving a crusader fortification in the Holy Land

PERMISSIONS AND CREDITS

Maps 1, 2, 3, 6, 7, 8, 9, 10, 11, 12 have been reproduced from *Atlas of Medieval Europe,* edited by Angus Mackay and David Ditchburn, Routledge, 1997.

Map 4 has been redrawn from an original in Nicholas Hooper and Matthew Bennett, *Cambridge Illustrated Atlas, Warfare, the Middle Ages*, Cambridge, 1996, CUP, p. 27.

Map 5 has been redrawn from an original in John Julius Norwich, *The Normans in the South*, London, 1967, Longman, p. 335, improved by Elisabeth van Houts trans. & ed.,*The Normans in Europe*, Manchester, 2000, Manchester University Press, p. 300.

Illustrations
1 The Art Archive/Archaeological Museum Ancona Italy/Dagli Orti
2 Stiftsbibliothek St. Gallen
3 GKS 1005 fol © Stofnun Arna Magnussonar
4 Copyright Reading Borough Council (Reading Museum Service). All rights reserved
5 © 1990 Photo SCALA, Florence
6 Courtesy of Burgerbibliothek Bern Mss.hist.helv.I.3, s. 757: Die Schlacht bei Murten
7 Oil on canvas. 70 × 52 cm. National Gallery, London, UK
8 Bibliothèque nationale de France
9 Bibliothèque nationale de France
10 Cranium of Towton 18 courtesy of the Biological Anthropology Research Centre (BARC), Department of Archaeological Sciences, University of Bradford

11 Museo Arqueologico, Madrid
12 © Bettmann/CORBIS
13 Jim Bradbury
14 From Norman Vesey, *Arms and Armour*, London, 1964, Weidenfeld and Nicolson, p. 8. Drawn by Russell Robinson
15 © The Bridgeman Art Library
16 © Simmons Aerofilms Ltd
17 © The British Library 1008635 220s
18 The Art Archive/Templar Chapel Cressac/Dagli Orti

Index

Figures for illustrations are in italics. Abbreviations: Aragón (Ar.), Byzantium (Byz.), England (Eng.), France (Fr.), Holy Roman Empire (HRE), Jerusalem (Jeru.) and Scotland (Scot.).